Characteristics of Teachers

COMMITTEE ON TEACHER CHARACTERISTICS STUDY

Appointed by the American Council on Education

Herold C. Hunt, General Superintendent of Schools, Chicago; subsequently Charles William Eliot Professor of Education, Harvard University, *Chairman*, 1950–

Robert C. Challman, Menninger Foundation (resigned 1951)

G. Frederic Kuder, Professor of Psychology, Duke University

Lester W. Nelson, Principal, Scarsdale (N.Y.) High School; subsequently with the Ford Foundation

Willard B. Spalding, Dean, College of Education, University of Illinois; subsequently, Director, General Extension Division, Oregon State System of Higher Education

L. L. Thurstone, Professor of Psychology, University of Chicago (died September 29, 1955)

Roscoe L. West, President Emeritus, New Jersey State Teachers College, Trenton, New Jersey

------

DIRECTOR OF THE STUDY

David G. Ryans, Professor of Educational Psychology and Research, University of California, Los Angeles (now Chairman, Department of Educational Psychology, University of Texas)

CHARACTERISTICS OF TEACHERS

Their Description, Comparison, and Appraisal

A RESEARCH STUDY

DAVID G. RYANS

● ● ●

CHAIRMAN, DEPARTMENT OF EDUCATIONAL PSYCHOLOGY
UNIVERSITY OF TEXAS

AMERICAN COUNCIL ON EDUCATION, Washington, D.C.

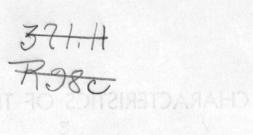

© 1960 BY AMERICAN COUNCIL ON EDUCATION
1785 MASSACHUSETTS AVENUE, N.W., WASHINGTON, D.C.

LIBRARY OF CONGRESS CATALOG CARD NO. 60-7727

PRINTED IN THE UNITED STATES OF AMERICA
BY GEORGE BANTA COMPANY, INC., MENASHA, WISCONSIN

Foreword

THIS IS A research study in every sense of the phrase. Neither time nor expense has been spared to make it as valid in method as such a study can be, and the conclusions are stated with careful accuracy.

Consequently the volume will be disappointing to those who seek a quick, superficial answer to one of the most difficult and complicated questions in education: What makes a good teacher? That disappointment merely emphasizes the rigorous scholarship of Dr. Ryans and his associates.

The American Council on Education is grateful to The Grant Foundation for the financial support which made possible both the long and painstaking investigation and the publication of the report. We consider this book a major contribution to educational research.

ARTHUR S. ADAMS, *President*
American Council on Education

Prefatory Note

ASSOCIATION WITH Dr. Ryans before as well as after the inception and completion of this massive study of teacher characteristics makes it a pleasant privilege to have this opportunity of recording my admiration for a study carried out in a rigorously scientific method and reported in a manner that may well be called a model of strict adherence to the facts and relations revealed by careful analysis of experimental data.

Despite the great progress that has been made in the measurement of human traits during the past half century, the appraisal of personal qualities has proved to be an elusive quarry. Good teachers, no less than successful persons in other professions, have always been more readily recognized than objectively described.

Through the efforts of Dr. Ryans, his colleagues, and his sponsors, and with the cooperation of numerous school administrators and teachers throughout the nation, an impressive amount of talent and skill has been brought to bear on this problem of defining and appraising the characteristics of good teachers. A judicious combination of refined observational techniques, statistical analysis, and standardized testing procedures has yielded findings that are likely to be highly significant for the teaching profession.

Dr. Ryans' proclivity for scientific methodology and for cautious interpretation of research findings has led him to prepare this report as a scholarly document. He has carefully refrained from going beyond his data or making unwarranted generalizations from his results. Other research workers in this field will doubtless appreciate his thorough, yet prudent, logging of the course of the Teacher Characteristics Study.

Those who are looking for a quick and easy method for selecting youngsters who will make good teachers, or who want a simple device for screening teachers at the point of employment or promotions, will not find the answer to their quest in this report. For, as the author vigorously stresses, the qualities of good teachers are not absolutes; they are, instead, interacting traits that vary in their merits, depending upon educational philosophy, pupil characteristics, course level and content, and other factors.

Dr. Ryans has succeeded, however, in identifying certain types of teacher traits that are significantly related to teacher success in a wide variety of situations, and he has developed pencil-and-paper inventories for experimental use in appraising these traits. He has paved the way for

CHARACTERISTICS OF TEACHERS

further validation studies that may well lead to improved selection, training, and evaluative procedures for personnel in the teaching profession.

It is to be hoped that in subsequent publications the results of this study will be interpreted for the school administrator and others who work with teacher personnel but who are not research specialists. Maximum benefits will be derived from the study if the findings are implemented by further research and applications at the local level.

Dr. Ryans and his colleagues are to be congratulated for having taken on a difficult assignment and having carried it through to a stage of promising fruition.

BEN D. WOOD

November 10, 1959

Acknowledgments

THE RESEARCH AND the conceptualizing of problems relating to teacher personality reported in this volume obviously do not represent the accomplishments of the author alone. Many persons, too numerous to name—teachers, friends, and professional acquaintances of the author, members of the Teacher Characteristics Study staff, and others doing research on problems of individual and social behavior—have been involved in the thinking behind the Study. The author wishes to mention a few sources of direct aid to which he feels deeply indebted.

It is a privilege to make acknowledgment to The Grant Foundation for the generous subsidy and interest which made the Teacher Characteristics Study possible. Mr. William T. Grant, founder and chairman of the Board of Trustees of The Grant Foundation, has done much to advance the cause of measurement and the study of human behavior through his interest and aid in numerous research studies, such as the Harvard University Grant Study of Human Behavior, the University of Michigan Study of the Role of the Family in Social Relations, the Teachers College Study of the Prediction of Occupational Success, and service projects such as the American Council on Education's Measurement Book Project,[1] the University of Maryland Child Study Program, and many others. Mr. Perrin C. Galpin, executive director of The Grant Foundation from 1947 to 1955, and Miss Adele W. Morrison, presently associate director and secretary, deserve special mention; the writer feels a personal sense of gratitude toward both for their understanding, counsel, and encouragement.

The author takes particular pleasure in acknowledging the assistance of Dr. Ben D. Wood. Without the aid of Dr. Wood, to whom such other measurement projects as the Cooperative Test Service and the National Teacher Examinations of the American Council on Education owe their existence, the Teacher Characteristics Study never would have been possible. It was he who first gave tangible hope for the study when, as director of the National Teacher Examinations in 1941, he first conferred with Mr. William T. Grant concerning the possibility of undertaking an investigation of certain traits of successful teachers. Throughout the Study he has advised the writer frequently, has given unfailing support to the view that measurement of teacher behavior is possible,

[1] This project produced the volume entitled *Educational Measurement*, edited by E. F. Lindquist, with chapters by authorities in testing, published by the American Council on Education, 1951.

and has come to the aid of the project each time called upon, giving most generously of his time and sage advice. The successful completion of the project is in no small part due to Dr. Wood.

The Advisory Committee to the Teacher Characteristics Study, appointed by the American Council on Education, has been helpful in conducting the research, both as a group and as individual members. Special recognition is due the chairman, Dr. Herold C. Hunt, who was general superintendent of schools in Chicago during much of the Study, for his most willing support at all times and assistance in gaining access to school systems throughout the country. To another committee member, the late Professor L. L. Thurstone, of the University of Chicago and the University of North Carolina, the Study was particularly indebted for the ideas he suggested for possible correlates or predictors of teacher behavior, many of which were employed in experimental forms of the Teacher Characteristics Study instruments.

The staff of the Teacher Characteristics Study, a changing one over the six-year period of research, has been characterized by both quality and faithfulness. In particular, the aid of Dr. Edwin Wandt, Mr. James Ziegler, Dr. Glen Fulkerson, and Dr. Alfred Jensen is acknowledged.

To the administration of the University of California, appreciation is appropriately acknowledged for the provision of various facilities and the opportunity permitted the author to direct the Teacher Characteristics Study in conjunction with his teaching and research.

As director of the Teacher Characteristics Study, the writer would achieve satisfaction from feeling he had more properly acknowledged a great debt if it were possible to name the school systems and their administrators, the schools and their principals, and, most of all, the teachers who cooperated in various phases of the Study. Unfortunately this is not possible, since throughout the investigation it appeared necessary for the complete cooperation required by such research to guarantee that the data would be employed exclusively for research purposes and that complete anonymity of participants would be preserved. To these unnamed contributors the Teacher Characteristics Study is deeply indebted.

Lastly, appreciation is expressed to the following journals for the privilege of reproducing substantial portions of certain materials originally submitted to them for publication: *Educational and Psychological Measurement, The Educational Record, The Journal of Educational Psychology, The Journal of Educational Research, The Journal of Experimental Education, The California Journal of Educational Research,* and *The Journal of Genetic Psychology.*

D. G. R.

Contents

Contents

List of Tables

List of Figures

1. The Investigation of Teacher Characteristics

"A TEACHER AFFECTS eternity; he can never tell where his influence stops." So observed the historian-philosopher, Henry Adams.

For many teachers this is earnestly to be hoped; with regard to others it is a despairing thought. It seems reasonable to assume that good teachers—those who are skillful in developing understanding of the world in which man lives, insightful with respect to the ways and means of stimulating intellectual appetites, and capable of patience, understanding, and sincere feelings for others—may pave the way for an enlightened and productive society. Poor teaching, contrariwise, would seem to be a significant contributor of its unfortunate share to the perpetuation of ignorance, misunderstanding, and intellectual and cultural stagnation.

Both the lay public and professional educators generally agree that the "goodness" of an education program is determined to a large extent by the teaching. The identification of qualified and able teaching personnel, therefore, constitutes one of the most important of all educational concerns. Obtaining capable teachers is an intrinsic interest and obligation of education. If competent teachers can be obtained, the likelihood of attaining desirable educational outcomes is substantial. On the other hand, although schools may have excellent material resources in the form of equipment, buildings, and textbooks, and although curricula may be appropriately adapted to community requirements, if the teachers are misfits or are indifferent to their responsibilities, the whole program is likely to be ineffective and largely wasted.

The focal importance of the teacher is not new to educational thinking. But in spite of the recognition and lip service accorded good teaching, relatively little reliable information is available regarding its nature and the teacher characteristics which contribute to it. A number of conditions share responsibility for this situation, not the least of which is the lack of any clear understanding of the various patterns of behavior that characterize teachers in general. It seems probable that, without losing sight of the important need for developing means of recognizing good teachers, the attention of research might first more properly (and more profitably) be directed toward the identification and estimation of some of the major patterns of teacher characteristics underlying

1

teacher behavior. This essentially represents the point of view of the research undertaken by the Teacher Characteristics Study as reported in this volume.

Teacher Effectiveness—An Ambiguous Concept

"What constitutes effective teaching?" and "What are the distinguishing characteristics of competent teachers?" are provocative and recurring questions. Unfortunately, no universally acceptable definitive answers can be given to these complex queries.

True, it may be said that teaching is effective to the extent that the teacher acts in ways that are favorable to the development of basic skills, understanding, work habits, desirable attitudes, value judgments, and adequate personal adjustment of the pupil. But even such an operational-appearing definition really is very general and abstract and is not easily translatable into terms relating to specific teacher behaviors.

Embarrassing as it may be for professional educators to recognize, relatively little progress has been made in supplementing this definition with the details that are necessary for describing competent teaching or the characteristics of effective teachers for a specific situation or cultural setting.

Undoubtedly there have been both good and poor teachers since the beginnings of man's social life. Some of the really notable teachers have been memorialized by history, and the number of competent teachers in the schools today probably is sizable. But, since usually very little is known about such teachers or what makes them effective, professional education has not been able to take advantage of an understanding of their characteristics and modes of performance to the end of improving teacher training and teacher selection procedures.

Granted, most educators and most parents do have some idea of what constitutes effective teaching. These conceptualizations, however, usually are vague and far removed from specific observable behaviors of teachers. Frequently the ideas are highly individualized, with very little agreement existing among different persons, even with regard to such hazy abstractions. One is reminded of the old familiar fable of the blind men who perceived an elephant in widely varying manners depending on the part of the elephant's body that each one touched.

Educators seem to be similarly in disagreement with respect to the specific contributors to effective teaching. Those associated with licensing groups (e.g., state departments of education) believe good teaching to be a result of the teacher's training in certain college or university courses. Some believe it to be a matter of the teacher's "dynamic personality," which is diversely defined. And some are convinced it is revealed in the discipline the teacher is able to maintain in the classroom.

Disagreement and ambiguity with respect to the description of teacher effectiveness are to be expected, and cannot be entirely avoided, because competent teaching undoubtedly is a relative matter. A person's concept of a "good" teacher depends, first, on his acculturation, his past experience, and the value attitudes he has come to accept, and, second, on the aspect of teaching which may be foremost in his consideration at any given time. Pupil F, therefore, may differ widely from Pupil G in his assessment of the essential attributes of an effective teacher. If Pupil F is relatively bright, academically minded, well adjusted, and independent, he may value most the teacher who is serious, rigorously academic, and perhaps even relatively impersonal. If Pupil G, on the other hand, is more sensitive and requires considerable succor, he may find the teacher just described not at all to his liking and literally "impossible." In the mind of Pupil G, the better teacher may very well be one who is somewhat less exacting from an academic standpoint but who is characteristically sympathetic, understanding, and the like.

Similarly, Principal X and Principal Y, or Parent M and Parent N, or College Professor Q and College Professor R may consider quite different attributes in conceptualizing the competent teacher.

Answers to the question, "What is an effective teacher like?" also may vary to a degree with the particular kind of teacher one chooses to consider. One might hypothesize that, even if it were possible to agree upon a generalized definition of effective teaching which would be acceptable to a number of different cultures, and if our thinking might be objectified to the point where effective teaching could be described on a factual basis, "good" teachers of different grades and different subject matters still might vary considerably in personal and social characteristics and in various domains of classroom behavior. The National Teacher Examinations results of teachers of different grades and subject matters, for example, consistently have shown dissimilar profiles with respect to amount of knowledge of various areas of professional educational information, levels of certain mental abilities and basic language skills, and the degree of understanding of general cultural materials. Similarly, data assembled by the Teacher Characteristics Study suggest that the combination of personal and social characteristics is not identical for elementary and secondary school teachers and, furthermore, that in the secondary school the pattern of characteristics is not the same for teachers of different subject matter. The interests, attitudes, and viewpoints of teachers appear to vary with the teaching areas.

The concept of competent teaching must, therefore, be considered to be relative to at least two major sets of conditions: (1) the social or cultural group in which the teacher operates, involving social values which frequently differ from person to person, community to community, culture to culture, and time to time, and (2) the grade level and subject matter taught.

It is not surprising, then, to note the difficulties that have confronted those seeking to establish *criteria* of teaching effectiveness, the dearth of testable hypotheses produced in such research as has been undertaken, and the general lack of understanding of the problem of the characteristics of effective teachers. One very important reason why effective or ineffective teachers cannot be described with any assurance is the wide variation that exists in tasks performed by teachers and in value concepts of what constitutes desirable teaching objectives.

Lack of Understanding of Teacher Characteristics

Still another condition contributes to the existing confusion in the understanding and description of teacher competence. The validity of various assumptions and opinions regarding teaching cannot be readily studied because there is so little understanding, and no adequate descriptions or measures, of the general classes of behaviors and personal and social qualities which characterize teachers. Adequate descriptions of major teacher characteristics, which might provide a basis for studying the relationships of teacher behavior to the varying objectives of teaching and concepts of teaching competence, have not been developed.

Unfortunate as this situation is, it really is understandable, for teaching is complex and many-sided, demanding a variety of human traits and abilities. In general, these may be grouped into two major categories: (1) those involving the teacher's mental abilities and skills, his understanding of psychological and educational principles, and his knowledge of general and special subject matter to be taught; and (2) those qualities stemming from the teacher's personality, his interests, attitudes, and beliefs, his behavior in working relationships with pupils and other individuals, and the like.

The intellectual characteristics of teachers can be measured with a considerable degree of success. However, relatively little information is available about the second group of characteristics—those commonly classified in the composite as the "personality" of the teacher. Reliable and valid methods for identifying and measuring behavior variables in this important area are scarce.

In this connection, it may be noted that the personal and social characteristics of teachers have sometimes been regarded as educational intangibles, not amenable to objective study. The results of attempts to measure interests and personality and behavioral traits in other occupational and professional fields, however, suggest the feasibility of such an approach in the teaching area.

It does not seem unreasonable to hypothesize that: (1) teachers may be described in terms of their observable behaviors and self-expressed opinions, viewpoints, and typical responses in defined situations, and (2) devices utilizing *correlates* of behavioral dimensions may be developed for the prediction of such characteristics.

Perhaps the first step toward a better understanding of problems relating to teacher competency may be the intensive and extensive study of teacher characteristics. If certain patterns of teacher behavior and characteristics could be mapped out, it should be possible to ascertain the extent of relation between such patterns and specified criteria deduced from whatever definition or concept of teacher effectiveness one might choose. It should also be possible to judge how well specified patterns of teacher characteristics conform with a selected set of educational objectives. In addition, it should not be too difficult to identify teachers who demonstrate these characteristics to a considerable degree. Certainly teachers who were found to rank high—say, in the top 20 percent—on a number of sets of teacher characteristics generally agreed to be important in a particular culture could be regarded as being effective teachers. It should also be possible to study the relation of such patterns to various conditions of teaching, teacher training, home background, and the like.[1]

The Teacher Characteristics Study

It is with problems relating to the description of teacher characteristics that the research reported in this volume was primarily concerned. In much of the research of the Teacher Characteristics Study, consideration of the effectiveness or ineffectiveness of particular behaviors of teachers was intentionally set aside. Instead, attention was focused on the study of possible teacher behavior dimensions, these dimensions being conceptualized as generalizations which define teacher behavior variables in terms of clusters of relatively homogeneous behaviors.

Implied in this approach was the assumption that a teacher may be

---

[1] Such matters as the designation of criteria and their components, the development of criterion measures, and the adequacy of various criterion measures in the study of teacher behavior will be considered in chap. 2.

described in terms of a position on each of a number of specified behavior dimensions, such descriptions relating to observable behavior and being of an essentially factual nature rather than involving value judgments (judgments of relative effectiveness).

In keeping with this approach, an effort was made to describe a teacher as objectively as possible with regard to various dimensions of teacher behavior without directly attempting to make value judgments of the merits or deficiencies of that behavior. Thus, a teacher who entered freely into pupil activities, who exchanged ideas with pupils, who encouraged pupil decision, and who tended to "put pupils on their own" might be described by a position near the "democratic" pole of an "autocratic-democratic" dimension. But, in so describing the teacher, no judgment of effectiveness or ineffectiveness of autocratic or democratic teaching need be implied.

This project of the American Council on Education and The Grant Foundation, the Teacher Characteristics Study, represents one of the most extensive research programs that has been directed at the objective study of teachers. During the six years of the major study, approximately 100 separate research projects were carried out, and more than 6,000 teachers in 1,700 schools and about 450 school systems participated in various phases of the research. Many of the basic studies involved extensive classroom observation, by trained observers, of teachers in public schools for the purpose of discovering significant patterns of teacher behavior and of pupil behavior reflecting teacher behavior. A number of paper-and-pencil inventories were developed and analyzed in an effort to identify individuals characterized by particular patterns of classroom behavior and specified clusters of attitudes and viewpoints. Still other investigations were concerned with the survey of teacher activities, preferences, attitudes, and viewpoints and the comparison of various defined groups of teachers (elementary teachers vs. secondary teachers, married teachers vs. unmarried teachers, teachers in progressive school systems vs. teachers in traditional school systems, etc.)

Lest it appear that the question of teacher effectiveness was begged entirely, it may be noted that several phases of the research may be considered explorations in this area. For example, a final chapter of the report deals with certain characteristics of groups of teachers who were classifiable as high, average, or low with respect to the major patterns of teacher classroom behavior considered in the Study. Probably it is not too far amiss to think of such groups, each comprising roughly 2 percent of the basic study population, as representing good, average, and poor teachers in present-day American culture. In another study, reported in chapter 6, principals' nominations of outstandingly superior and outstandingly poor teachers were obtained, and certain comparisons were made of the teachers so identified. Still another phase of the research involved premeasurement and postmeasurement of the third- and fourth-grade pupils of a number of teachers and a study of the relation between observed teacher behaviors and changes that took place in the pupils.

BACKGROUND OF THE TEACHER CHARACTERISTICS STUDY

The Teacher Characteristics Study was, in part, an outgrowth of certain aspects of the interests and research of the staff of another American Council on Education project, the National Teacher Examinations.[2] In 1939 the Council's National Committee on Teacher Examinations was appointed and a staff was assigned the task of making available to school systems and colleges an examining service which would provide for the comparable measurement of certain abilities and knowledges of prospective teachers.

The whole problem of teacher competency was considered at length in planning that project. In the light of the experience of the Council's Cooperative Test Service[3] and the demand for measures of achievement and cultural knowledge to be employed for selection purposes in large city school systems, the development of a battery of tests to measure the intellectual backgrounds and professional knowledge of teachers seemed feasible and appropriate. During early discussions, attention also was given to the personal and social characteristics of teachers, but the relative absence of reliable research relating to the understanding of teacher personality suggested the need for caution in extending activities of the Committee on Teacher Examinations in that direction. As a result, activities in connection with the National Teacher Examinations were channeled toward the provision of aptitude tests relating to nonverbal and verbal abilities, tests measuring information in four different professional education areas, achievement tests concerned with basic English skills and general cultural knowledge, and tests of subject matter to be taught.

It was a hope of the author and certain other members of the staff of the National Teacher Examinations project that once the program was

---

[2] The National Teacher Examinations project was operated from 1939 to 1948 by the American Council on Education. The project was assigned to the Educational Testing Service in 1948 and it subsequently has been conducted by that organization.

[3] The Cooperative Test Service was established in 1930 and was operated until 1948 by the American Council on Education, when it was merged with the Educational Testing Service. The National Teacher Examinations program was developed in 1939 as an outgrowth of the Cooperative Test Service's activities.

under way, attention might be devoted to research in the areas of personal and social characteristics of teachers. However, because of the
lack of financial means to conduct research and also because of the stabi-
lization of the purposes of the National Teacher Examinations program
and its concentration upon the intellectual background and professional
knowledge of teachers, such coordinate goals were not realized. Furthermore, during the war years, 1942–45, the lack of personnel offered still
another obstacle to research in the area of teacher behaviors.

Following the war, during 1946 and 1947, discussions of the problem
were revived and preliminary studies were conducted in connection
with the Teacher Examinations program to determine the feasibility of
a major research project. Interest in such a project was expressed by
The Grant Foundation, and the American Council on Education's
Committee on Measurement and Guidance agreed that such a study
might properly be conducted under the sponsorship of the Council.
Subsequently, plans for a project directed toward a better understanding of teacher characteristics were drawn up, approved by the Council,
and forwarded as a formal proposal to The Grant Foundation. In May
1948 the trustees of The Grant Foundation appropriated funds for a
project staff of the Council to conduct what originally was intended to
be a three-year research program.

An advisory committee for the Teacher Characteristics Study was
appointed by the Council in the summer of 1948, consisting of Dr. L.
L. Thurstone, Dr. Frederic Kuder, Dr. Willard D. Spalding, Dr. Lester
Nelson, Dr. Roscoe West, and Dr. Robert C. Challman. Dr. Herold C.
Hunt was appointed chairman of the committee in 1950.

Project offices were established at the University of California, Los
Angeles, in October 1948, and preliminary work on the Teacher Characteristics Study was begun during the same month.

The Teacher Characteristics Study, throughout its program of research, enjoyed the sponsorship of the Council and assistance from the
advisory committee appointed by the Council. Financial support, as
well as frequent good counsel, were generously provided by The Grant
Foundation. An initial subsidy of $60,000 appropriated by the trustees
of The Grant Foundation in May 1948 was followed by additional grants
of $8,900 in 1950, $90,160 in 1951, $15,000 in 1954, and $20,000 in 1957.
As might be expected, the staff associated with the activities of the
Study varied in size from year to year and was characterized by frequent
changes in personnel. The names of the staff members are listed in
Appendix B. Seventy-five individuals are listed, of whom fifty-one provided services to the central office and twenty-four served on the field

staff of observers. In addition, a number of unlisted persons were employed by the Study as test administrators or as assistants in minor projects.

OBJECTIVES

As has been indicated, a major drawback to the improvement of teaching has been the lack of understanding of teacher characteristics and of ways of estimating them. It was this need for research on the personality patterns of teachers that motivated the planning of the Study. More specifically, the needs that prompted the research were:

1. The need for the accumulation of evidence permitting extension of understanding of the personal, social, and intellectual attributes of persons who teach in the schools, and perhaps contributing to the development of teacher behavior theory and to the improvement of teacher education.
2. The need for procedures for appraising certain characteristics of prospective teachers before or during preservice training and at the time of employment by school systems to help improve teacher selection and assignment.

The major objectives of the Study, growing out of these needs, may be described as follows:

Objective I: The identification and analysis of some of the patterns of classroom behavior, attitudes, viewpoints, and intellectual and emotional qualities which may characterize teachers.—With the intention of improving understanding of the personal-social behavior of teachers, answers to such questions as the following were sought: Do overt teacher behaviors and teachers' reports of their preferences, viewpoints, and activities fall into discernible patterns? If so, what is the nature of such patterns?

Objective II: The development of paper-and-pencil instruments suitable for the estimation of certain patterns of classroom behavior and personal qualities of teachers.—Assuming that characteristic patterns of teacher behavior and personality might be identifiable, a second intention of the Study was to develop self-report materials which might aid in predicting such patterns.

In the development of psychometric instruments for the prediction of teacher behavior, it was assumed that such behaviors are determined, in part, by substrata of related attitudinal response "sets" (social, intellectual, emotional, etc.) to numerous specific situations, which become stable and integrated over the life period of the individual and which predispose him to behave in a relatively reliable and predictable manner. The further assumption was made that it is possible to detect these underlying predispositions through the use of paper-and-pencil instruments which permit the expression of preferences, beliefs, and typical behaviors.

Objective III: The comparison of characteristics of various groups of teachers.—A third intent of the Teacher Characteristics Study was the comparison of certain characteristics of teachers classified according to various individual and situational factors such as age, experience, sex, size of school, and cultural climate of the community.

It was recognized that certain teacher characteristics might be associated with both individual and situational conditions. That is, patterns of teacher characteristics might be (*a*) functions of characteristics of the individual such as age, extent of experience, and sex, and (*b*) either resultants of experiences of a teacher in certain kinds of educational and social situations, or contributors which predisposed a teacher to seek such types of situations.

GENERAL PROCEDURE OF STUDY

The research undertaken consisted of four major phases, which may be described broadly as follows: (1) the development of instruments for use in recording assessments of teacher behavior in the classroom, and the refinement of observational methods to increase the reliability of assessments; (2) the determination of some major patterns of teacher behavior, as observed in the classroom; (3) the development of paper-and-pencil instruments consisting of items hypothetically related to teacher classroom behavior and other personal characteristics of teachers, and the empirical derivation of scoring keys for such instruments; and (4) the comparison of certain groups of teachers from the standpoint of their major patterns of characteristics.

The first of these phases involved intensive review of the literature and employment of the "critical incidents" approach in the study of teacher behaviors. After a number of tryouts and revisions, this led to the production of the Classroom Observation Record and Glossary, and to standardized observational procedures employing selected observers who were trained to make analytical, factual assessments of teacher behavior.

The determination of major patterns of observed teacher behavior in the second phase of the study was accomplished through factor analyses of the intercorrelations of the various assessments of observed teacher behavior at both the elementary and secondary levels of teaching.

In the third phase, a number of specially developed instruments prepared by the staff of the Teacher Characteristics Study, as well as several existing personality schedules and inventories, were administered to teachers who previously had been observed. An effort was made to discover among the responses of teachers (*a*) correlates capable of predicting the major factors of teacher classroom behavior and (*b*) predictors of such traits of teachers as their attitudes toward pupils and others, their "traditional" *vs.* "permissive" educational viewpoints, their verbal ability, and their emotional adjustment.

After the first three steps had been completed, it was possible in the fourth phase to survey teachers throughout the United States and to make comparisons of teachers who were classified in many different ways with respect to some ten characteristics.

USE OF THE RESULTS OF THE TEACHER CHARACTERISTICS STUDY

The Teacher Characteristics Study was conducted with two possible uses of the results in mind: first, by school systems as an aid in identifying teachers who, at the time of selection for employment or perhaps in connection with promotion, have characteristics similar to those deemed important and desirable by the particular school system and the culture it represents; and, second, by teacher education institutions as an aid to a better understanding of teacher characteristics and associated conditions, which would contribute to improved procedures for selecting teacher candidates and to the improvement of professional courses and curricula.

In the application of the results and conclusions reported in the following chapters, it is important to realize that one is dealing with inductive inferences from empirical data and, therefore, that: first, generalizations are appropriate only when made to populations which are essentially similar to the populations employed in the Study;[4] second, all conclusions necessarily are approximate rather than exact (as are all inferences based on empirical data, which, by their very nature, are characterized by some degree of unreliability) and are probability estimates rather than statements of certainties; and, third, as is true of all predictions of human behavior, greater confidence can be placed in the conclusions when they are applied to groups of teachers than when they are applied to individual cases.

Similar limitations, of course, apply generally to inductive inferences and particularly to inferences relating to human behavior, but they are

---

[4] See chap. 3 for further discussion.

so frequently overlooked in practice that frequent repetition is warranted. Lest the reader allow such a statement of restrictions to induce an unduly pessimistic attitude toward the identification and estimation of teacher characteristics, it must be recalled that a prcoedure need not be evaluated in terms of whether perfection is achieved. If it represents an improvement over other procedures, it is of some value. It is the writer's belief that the activities of the Study have extended substantially the understanding of teacher behavior, and that both school systems and teacher education institutions may find the results to be of considerable value in carrying out their responsibilities.

2. Theoretical Framework and Some Persistent Problems

ALTHOUGH TEACHER behavior is a focal concern of teacher education institutions and school systems and also of the society at large that depends principally upon teachers for the propagation of accumulated knowledge and cultural values, relatively little is known about teacher characteristics, the behavior patterns these characteristics form, the description and measurement of such behavior patterns, or their genesis and cultivation.

Furthermore, most of what *is* known about teacher characteristics has been accumulated in a haphazard fashion with relatively little attention to the organization or systematization of facts about teacher behavior or to the assumptions and definitions upon which a study of teacher behavior may be based.

Advantages of a Theoretical Framework

Strong arguments have been presented by social and behavioral scientists to show that theoretical formulations in an area of knowledge have considerable utility, and that systematic theories and theoretical models are highly desirable, particularly for research guidance, if maximum productivity and progress are to be attained. Proponents of this viewpoint point out that advanced understanding and usable knowledge frequently have increased markedly as the study of problems in an area has progressed from exploratory, "catch-as-catch-can" investigations to selective observation guided by hypotheses derived from systematic theory and employing empirical tests to determine the place, if any, of such hypotheses in the basis theory.

Essentially, this procedure represents a *rapprochement* between formal (deductive) logic and modern science with its demands for the inclusion of pragmatic considerations (empirical evidence) in judging the admissibility of conclusions to a body of knowledge. Such axiomatic, or hypothetico-deductive, theory has been popular during recent years.

Another sort of "theorizing" (which some supporters would emphatically deny to be theorizing) attempts to be rigorously inductive and culminates in an organized body of facts or empirically derived conclusions. This kind of theory employs operational definitions ex-

13

tensively and seeks to limit itself to reasoning which proceeds from the observed characteristics of sample data to generalizations applicable to larger homogeneous classes of phenomena. Conclusions are admissible to such a theory if they (1) are based on fair (representative) samples, (2) satisfy pragmatic criteria, and (3) fit into a pattern with other empirically obtained data in the same area. Hypotheses may be derived from the resulting pattern of accumulated facts, and to this extent the approach is also deductive. Inductively generated theories, or systemizations, purport to be descriptions only and to make no pretense of explanation.

Educational researchers and practitioners seem to have found little need for either kind of theory development in approaching the problem of teacher behavior. A recent statement attributes the lack of productive research on teacher effectiveness, in part, to neglect of theory:

> The present condition of research on teacher effectiveness holds little promise of yielding results commensurate with the needs of American education. This condition has two significant characteristics: disorganization, and lack of orientation to other behavioral sciences. By disorganization, we mean the condition in which, at present, research too often proceeds without explicit theoretical framework, in intellectual disarray, to the testing of myriads of arbitrary, unrationalized hypotheses. The studies too often interact little with each other, do not fall into place within any scheme, and hence add little to the understanding of the teaching process. [2, p. 657.]

Some Characteristics of Theories

All systemizations, whether of the axiomatic, hypothetico-deductive type or of an empirical, inductive sort, must begin with certain assumptions and definitions. In the case of inductively slanted theory, assumptions are very largely expressions of faith in the inductive method (faith in the consistency and observability of nature), and definitions are predominantly of the operational kind. In axiomatic theory, assumptions are likely to be the working premises, or general propositions, from which the theory proceeds to noncontradictory hypotheses (postulates and the theorems derived from the assumptions or general propositions), which in turn (in deference to the pragmatic character of science) may be tested to determine their probable validity. Inductive systemization plunges at once into observation, stressing classification and cross-classification of facts,[1] on the one hand, and the experimental testing of sporadic hypotheses, on the other. The resulting specific de-

---

[1] A fact may be considered to be simply a hypothesis for which there is considerable evidence or support; it fits other facts well enough to justify its acceptance with a high degree of confidence.

scriptions of properties and of functional relationships lead, with confirming replications, to generalizations in the form of inductive principles and laws, which then may be systematized and organized into a coherent body of knowledge. The ultimate goal of theory, either axiomatic or operationist, is the prediction of phenomena from their antecedents.

The assumptions of any theory are simply judgments or propositions which are accepted or taken for granted. Thus, depending on the kind of theorizing we are attempting, the assumptions may be based on propositions held to be axiomatic; or, they may be propositions deductively *derived* from either axiomatic or empirically confirmed premises; or, they may be based *directly* on previously admitted empirical evidence (evidence accepted as valid, or admissible, because it already has passed tests which satisfy experts in the area); or, again, the assumptions may even be concepts or propositions that are not capable of immediate confirmation in any manner, but are accepted because they are necessary for the investigation of phenomena in the area of the theory.

Hypotheses, in the case of hypothetico-deductive theory, are derivable from the assumptions or basic propositions that grow out of the questions, problems, or needs suggested by the basic assumptions of the theory. In inductively oriented theory, hypotheses are cued by experience, which arises from sources such as previous observation or empirically obtained evidence. In either case, hypotheses are essentially creations of their originators' imagination—educated guesses that suggest specific answers to specific questions.

Steps Toward a Theory of Teacher Behavior

What progress can be made toward a theory of teacher behavior? What might be some of the assumptions and definitions? Those to be suggested in this chapter do not constitute a complete inventory of all assumptions required for a theory of teacher behavior. Nor is any particular claim made at this point for theoretical rigor. But if in the area of teacher behavior there are advantages in resolving and systematizing our thinking, a starting point is necessary regardless of how tentative it may be. Trial and error, criticism, and research should provide the necessary clarification, revision, and extension which will lead to a more generally acceptable theory of teacher behavior.

It is suggested that for our purposes *teacher behavior may be defined simply as the behavior, or activities, of persons as they go about doing whatever is required of teachers, particularly those activities which are concerned with the guidance or direction of the learning of others.*

There are at least two important postulates implied by this straight-forward operational definition:

Postulate A: Teacher behavior is social behavior.—One implication of the definition stated above is that teacher behavior is social behavior; that, in addition to the teacher, there must be learners, or pupils, who are in communication with the teacher and with each other, and who presumably are influenced by the behavior of the teacher. It also should be noted that the relation between teacher behavior and pupil behavior may be of a reciprocal nature: not only do teachers affect pupil behavior, but pupils may influence teacher behavior as well. This raises a whole series of questions—questions that researchers have had relatively little success in answering—relative to what aspects of teacher behavior actually do influence the behaviors of learners and how they operate to produce their effects.

Postulate B: Teacher behavior is relative.—Another implication of our definition of teacher behavior is that what a teacher does is a product of social conditioning and is relative to the cultural setting in which the teacher teaches. It follows that there is nothing inherently good or bad in any given teacher behavior or set of behaviors. Instead, teacher behavior is good or bad, right or wrong, effective or ineffective, only to the extent that such behavior conforms or fails to conform to a particular culture's value system or set of objectives relating to (1) the activities expected of a teacher and (2) the kinds of pupil learning (attainment) desired and the methods of teaching to be employed to bring about this learning [17, 26].

SOME BASIC ASSUMPTIONS OF A THEORY OF TEACHER BEHAVIOR

At least two major assumptions appear to be necessary for a theory of teacher behavior: (I) Teacher behavior is a function of situational factors and characteristics of the individual teacher. (II) Teacher behavior is observable.

Assumption I: Teacher behavior is a function of situational factors and characteristics of the individual teacher.—In setting out to formulate some theory of teacher behavior, the basic assumption might well be expected to bear resemblance to formulations made for similar purposes in connection with learning theory and personality theory. Indeed, in behavior theory, some expression of faith in the reliability, or consistency, of behavior is required. In the present case the basic assumption may be summarized in the proposition that teacher behavior is a resultant of (*a*) certain situational factors and (*b*) certain organismic conditions, and their interaction—or, simply, that teacher behavior is a function of certain environmental influences and the learned and unlearned characteristics of the individual teacher.

Figure 1 suggests a verbal model reminiscent of Cattell's "source" and "surface" trait description of human personality. It starts at the bottom with the most general features of (a) the individual teacher and (b) the social situation or environment in which we function, and proceeds through different levels of generality—from specific conditions (at the bottom of the figure) to the unique behavior of a teacher in a particular situation (at the top of the figure). It is important to take into account at each level, and in relation to preceding levels, both (a) the conditions and characteristics of the teacher and (b) those of the *situation*, and also the *interaction* and interdependence of teacher characteristics and situational conditions.

Just how these various situational and organismic conditions interact and what takes place in the teacher's nervous system as they interact (how, as some theorists would put it, the energy input-output transfer takes place) certainly is not known, and we are completely incapable of describing the process except in terms of inferences based upon observable[2] inputs and observable responses of the teacher. The fact that little is known about such processes does not mean that persons interested in behavior theory have not been actively concerned with the problem. Certain groups of theorists have been both active and ingenious. One such group, which is interested in speculating upon the generality of behavior theory—whether the systems involved are atoms, viruses, cells, individual persons, society, solar systems, or what not—views the organism, or the teacher in our case, as an "open system" (a bounded region in space-time), with negative feedback which distributes information to subsystems to keep them in orderly balance. Miller [12] has described in some detail the intriguing explorations of the "general systems theory" group, with its behavior model homologous to electronic systems, and has offered a number of presumably testable theorems or propositions.

Other theorists have been particularly concerned with how individuals in a social environment interact and condition one another's behavior, not only in an immediate situation but also in future situations, as a result of the integration of response-produced stimuli into the total stimulus pattern. Sears [28] has suggested, for example, a necessary expansion of the basic monadic unit of behavior, which various learning theories have employed, into a dyadic one which describes

---

[2] Observable, as here used, refers to that which may be perceived either by another person or by the experiencing individual, or which may be recorded by some instrument.

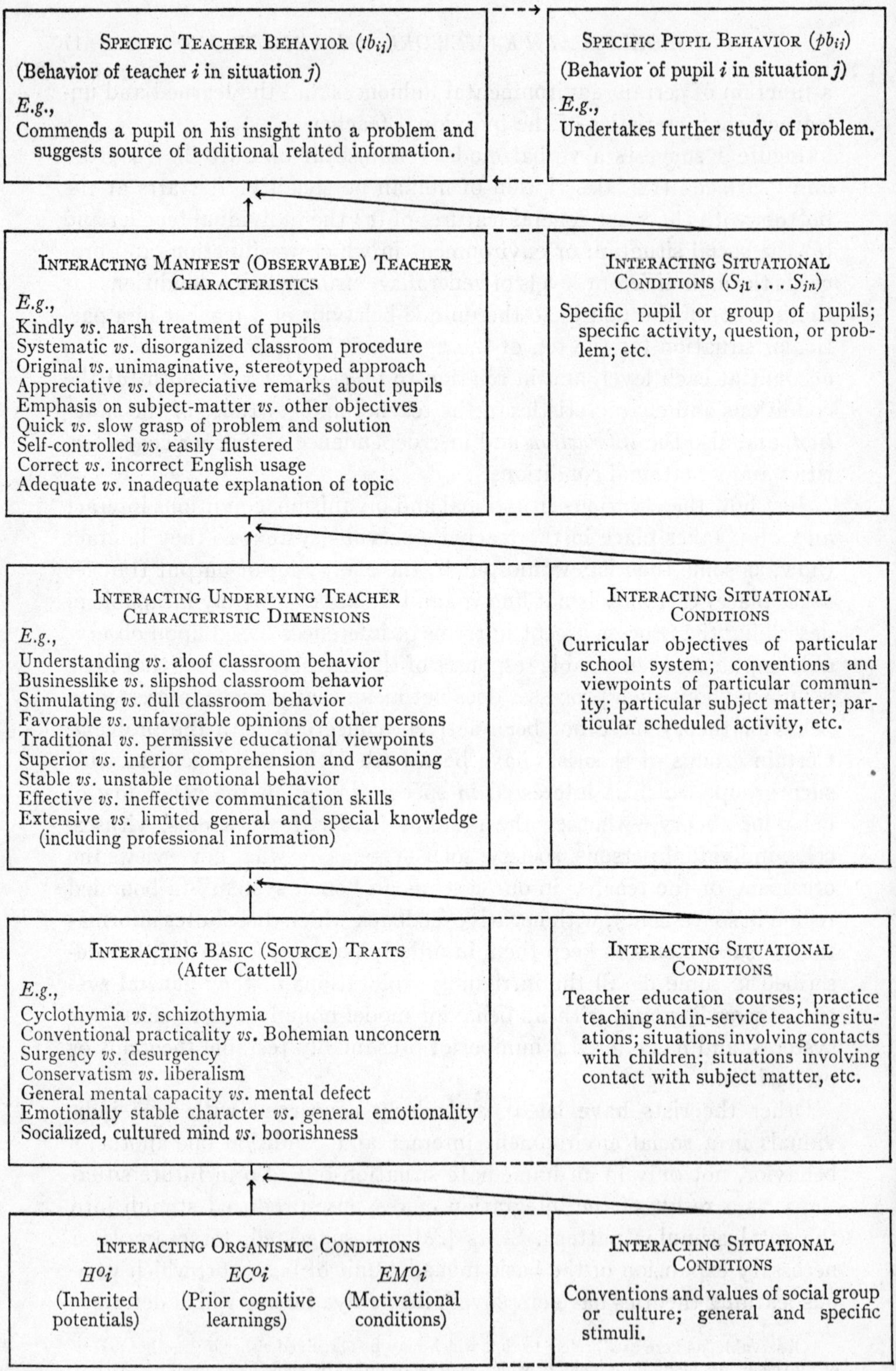

SPECIFIC TEACHER BEHAVIOR (tb_{ij})
(Behavior of teacher i in situation j)

E.g.,

Commends a pupil on his insight into a problem and suggests source of additional related information.

SPECIFIC PUPIL BEHAVIOR (pb_{ij})
(Behavior of pupil i in situation j)

E.g.,

Undertakes further study of problem.

INTERACTING MANIFEST (OBSERVABLE) TEACHER CHARACTERISTICS

E.g.,

Kindly *vs.* harsh treatment of pupils
Systematic *vs.* disorganized classroom procedure
Original *vs.* unimaginative, stereotyped approach
Appreciative *vs.* depreciative remarks about pupils
Emphasis on subject-matter *vs.* other objectives
Quick *vs.* slow grasp of problem and solution
Self-controlled *vs.* easily flustered
Correct *vs.* incorrect English usage
Adequate *vs.* inadequate explanation of topic

INTERACTING SITUATIONAL CONDITIONS ($S_{j1} \ldots S_{jn}$)

Specific pupil or group of pupils; specific activity, question, or problem; etc.

INTERACTING UNDERLYING TEACHER CHARACTERISTIC DIMENSIONS

E.g.,

Understanding *vs.* aloof classroom behavior
Businesslike *vs.* slipshod classroom behavior
Stimulating *vs.* dull classroom behavior
Favorable *vs.* unfavorable opinions of other persons
Traditional *vs.* permissive educational viewpoints
Superior *vs.* inferior comprehension and reasoning
Stable *vs.* unstable emotional behavior
Effective *vs.* ineffective communication skills
Extensive *vs.* limited general and special knowledge
    (including professional information)

INTERACTING SITUATIONAL CONDITIONS

Curricular objectives of particular school system; conventions and viewpoints of particular community; particular subject matter; particular scheduled activity, etc.

INTERACTING BASIC (SOURCE) TRAITS
(After Cattell)

E.g.,

Cyclothymia *vs.* schizothymia
Conventional practicality *vs.* Bohemian unconcern
Surgency *vs.* desurgency
Conservatism *vs.* liberalism
General mental capacity *vs.* mental defect
Emotionally stable character *vs.* general emotionality
Socialized, cultured mind *vs.* boorishness

INTERACTING SITUATIONAL CONDITIONS

Teacher education courses; practice teaching and in-service teaching situations; situations involving contacts with children; situations involving contact with subject matter, etc.

INTERACTING ORGANISMIC CONDITIONS

$H^o i$ (Inherited potentials)
$EC^o i$ (Prior cognitive learnings)
$EM^o i$ (Motivational conditions)

INTERACTING SITUATIONAL CONDITIONS

Conventions and values of social group or culture; general and specific stimuli.

FIG. 1.—Paradigm illustrating the integration of teacher behavior.

the combined actions of two or more individuals. The proposition that a dyadic unit is essential if the relationships between people are to be taken into account in theory should impress the teacher-behavior theorist as being entirely reasonable.

The dyadic approach strikes at the heart of the teacher-pupil relationship problem. The models which follow, (Figures 2 and 3) conceptualize teacher behavior first in terms of the monadic, and then the dyadic, behavior sequence. Alpha may be presumed to be the teacher, and Beta the pupil.

It is proposed, then, that the basic assumption of teacher behavior theory (that teacher behavior is a function of interaction of (a) situational factors, including the teacher's pupils, and (b) characteristics of the teacher) may be summarized by equations and symbolic expressions of the same sort employed by learning and personality theorists and by Sears-type models. (One kind of equation which was intended to generalize teacher behavior was presented in one of the writer's earlier reports of the Teacher Characteristics Study and appeared in the *Journal of Educational Psychology* under the title, "Theory Development and the Study of Teacher Behavior" [27, p. 468].)

Growing out of the basic assumption that teacher behavior is a function of the conditions under which it occurs are a number of implications or subassumptions, which follow.

Postulate I-A: Teacher behavior is characterized by some degree of consistency.—One implication of the basic assumption is that teacher behavior (and social behavior, with which education deals) is characterized by some degree of uniformity; that, as Mill put it: ". . . there are such things in nature as parallel cases, that what happens once will, under sufficient degree of similarity of circumstances, happen again." [11, p. 223.] We are stating simply that teacher behavior (a particular kind of behavior of a particular teacher) is not haphazard or fortuitous, but instead is consistent, or reliable, and therefore is capable of being predicted.

Postulate I-B: Teacher behavior is characterized by a limited number of responses.—Another implication of the basic assumption (and perhaps it is so fundamental to scientific theory that it is unnecessary to state it explicitly with respect to teacher behavior) is expressed by Keynes' Postulate of Limited Independent Qualities, which states that: ". . . objects in a field over which our generalizations extend, do not have an infinite number of independent qualities; . . . their characteristics, however numerous, cohere together in groups of invariable connections, which are finite in number." [9, p. 256.] Accordingly, the number of responses the individual teacher is capable of making, and the number

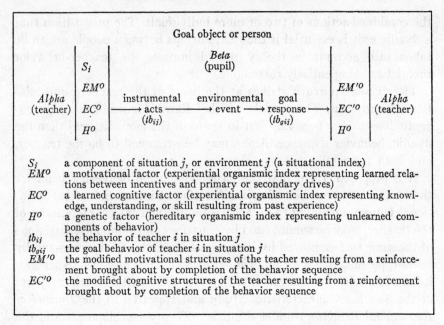

FIG. 2.—The monadic instigation, action sequence. (After Sears [*28*, p. 479].)

of stimulus situations and organismic variables that may affect a teacher's behavior, are limited. This assumption is important if we hope to predict teacher behavior. It presents the researcher with a "tolerable" problem.

Postulate I-C: Teacher behavior is always probable rather than certain.—All human behavior, characterized as it is by variability rather than

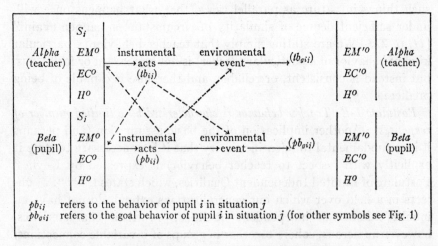

FIG. 3.—The dyadic sequence. (After Sears [*28*, p. 479].)

by *complete* uniformity or consistency, must always be considered in the light of probability instead of from the standpoint of invariable cause-effect relationships. The error[3] component resulting from such variability will inevitably be present in any assessment that is attempted of either (a) situational or stimulus conditions, (b) organismic conditions (genetic bases, past experience, motivation), or (c) teacher behavior (the dependent variable, or criterion). Behavior can be predicted only with varying degrees of probability.

Postulate I-D: Teacher behavior is a function of personal characteristics of the individual teacher.—Teacher behavior is determined in part by the teacher's personal and social characteristics (e.g., in the intellectual, emotional, temperamental, attitudinal, and interest domains), which have their sources in both the genetic (unlearned) and experiential (learned) backgrounds of the individual. Knowledge of such characteristics contributes to prediction, within limits, of teacher behavior.

Postulate I-E: Teacher behavior is a function of general features of the situation in which it takes place.—Teacher behavior is determined, in part, by general features of the situation in which it has its setting—features which may be observed to be common to situations of a general class and which, therefore, may be distinguished from the unique features of specific teaching situations. Information about such relevant features assists in the prediction, within limits, of teacher behavior.

Postulate I-F: Teacher behavior is a function of the specific situation in which it takes place.—Finally, teacher behavior is determined, in part, by unique features of the particular situation in which it has its setting at a particular time. These features vary from situation to situation and contribute to the aspect of teacher behavior which is, to an extent, unique to the particular situation.

Assumption II: Teacher behavior is observable.—When we attempt to study teacher behavior, we also make the assumption that teacher behavior may be identified objectively, either by direct observation or by indirect approaches that provide correlative indices of teacher behaviors. Examples of the indirect approaches are the assessment of pupil behavior, the use of tests of teacher abilities and knowledge, and

---

[3] *Error* here is used in its broad sense and therefore subsumes such sources of variability as: (1) observation errors, e.g., variability attributable to inaccuracies of perception, measurement, and recording; (2) sampling variability due to either intentional or unintentional bias; and (3) random sampling variability growing out of (a) variation from individual to individual, (b) variation from one group to another, (c) variation within the individual from one time to another, (d) variation within the individual from one behavior to another behavior, and (e) variation within the individual from one measurement (measuring device) to another.

the use of interviews or inventories to elicit expression of teacher preferences, interests, beliefs, and attitudes.

Several implications of this assumption may be noted here in the
form of the following postulates.

Postulate II-A: Teacher behaviors are distinguishable.—If teacher behaviors are observable, it follows that those with certain features must
be capable of being identified and described so as to be distinguished
from other teacher behaviors. Some behaviors have certain characteristics in common, which constitute generic or core components that may
be abstracted to facilitate (a) communication of generalized descriptions of those behaviors, and (b) the identification of such behaviors in
individual teachers. Teacher behaviors can be distinguished under observation.

*Postulate II-B: Teacher behaviors are classifiable qualitatively and
quantitatively.*—A second aspect of the assumption of the observability
of teacher behavior is that teacher behaviors are classifiable, both qualitatively and quantitatively. A class, or category, of teacher behaviors is
simply a grouping of specific behaviors which have many resemblances
to one another and relatively few *important* differences. When we find
such behavioral analogues, we take them as an indication that still other
resemblances may exist, since resemblances in nature tend to go together
in fairly large groups (Postulate of Limited Independent Qualities).
When behaviors have been grouped together in the light of their resemblances, it becomes possible to abstract the general class description
from the descriptions of specific manifestations and thereby provide
the basis for a "concept" of teacher behavior of a certain kind and permit greater common understanding of the behavior.

Teacher behaviors that are similar, that have certain resemblances or
common elements, may be classified in the same qualitative category.
Within any given category, these behaviors may be further assigned to
subclasses which may be treated quantitatively. This is to say that
teacher behaviors are subjectable to measurement—albeit approximate
measurement. These quantitative subclasses may be of either of two
types: (1) those permitting enumeration, or counting, only, or (2) those
characterized by continuity and varying as a metric (exemplified at the
lowest level of refinement by ordinal subclasses and at successively more
refined levels by equal-interval and equal-ratio subclasses).

It is pertinent to recall at this point that the measurement of teacher
behavior always must be approximate rather than exact—this being not
only a theoretical consideration growing out of the assumption of continuity but also an empirical fact as a consequence of (a) the complexity

of organism-situation patterns and the resulting variability of behavior and the (*b*) imperfection of behavior descriptions and of devices employed to obtain measurements of described behaviors. As a result, the existence of error must always be assumed.

Various qualitative classifications of teacher behaviors are possible. For example, we might choose to group teacher behaviors broadly into such general categories as: those involving instruction and relationships with pupils; those involving relationships with the school, its organization, and its administration; and those involving relationships with the community. Or, we might classify teacher behaviors more specifically in establishing the framework, employing such categories as verbal aptitude, emotional stability, favorable attitude toward pupils, friendly-understanding behavior in dealing with pupils, responsible-businesslike behavior, and stimulating-original behavior.

For any defined category we might conceivably assign quantitative subclasses.

Postulate II-C: Teacher behaviors are revealed through overt behavior and also by symptoms or correlates of behavior.—Teacher behaviors may be revealed, or may be observed, either (1) by the representative *sampling* of specific teacher acts or behaviors, or (2) by specific signs, or indicators, or *correlates*, of the behavior under consideration.

In sampling behavior, we assume that the performance of the individual during the behavior sample is approximately (and at some level of probability) representative of the larger aspects, or universe, of his behavior. In judging behavior from signs or correlates, it is assumed that a behavior can be inferred or estimated approximately, in probability terms, from observed correlates of that behavior—from phenomena that are known to have been associated with that behavior in the past.

SOME PROPOSITIONS AND HYPOTHESES

From the standpoint of the Teacher Characteristics Study, the foregoing definition and basic assumptions, together with their implications, provide a theoretical framework and starting point from which the researcher might reasonably proceed to propositions regarding teacher behavior—propositions that may be employed as hypotheses and tested against empirical data.

The number of descriptive classifications and specific propositions which might be generated with regard to teacher behavior is almost limitless, although we probably would not be interested in all such hypotheses even if it were possible to assemble them. Some classifications and some hypotheses seem more relevant than others. No doubt many of them could be incorporated in existing research designs and tested to determine their probable acceptability.

At this point, it might be well to recall that there are various approaches to the testing of hypotheses. Ideally, to test any hypothesis, the researcher would prefer to devise and manipulate the experimental situation at will, employing a basic design involving (1) premeasurement of equivalent experimental and control groups, (2) introduction of an experimental variable or treatment (the hypothesized influence) with the experimental group, while withholding it from the control group, and (3) postmeasurement and judgment of the probable validity of the hypothesis by comparing the two groups (against the background of a probability model) with respect to the dependent variable or criterion behavior. This, of course, is the typical application of Mill's joint method of agreement and difference. The procedure may be modified to permit simultaneous comparison of a number of main effects, analysis of interaction effects, and such.

Such an approach frequently is not feasible in the study of teacher behavior, however. Instead, teacher behavior often must be investigated in the "natural" or "field" situation, where antecedent conditions are difficult or impossible to assess and where only postevaluation can be employed. Under such conditions the researcher resorts to ex post facto experiments, selected comparisons of characteristics of defined groups of teachers, or intercorrelational and factor analytic studies. Much of the research on teacher behavior may have to be of this *status quo* or pseudo-experimental type.

Tests of a number of hypotheses about teacher classroom behaviors and other teacher characteristics were attempted by the Teacher Characteristics Study, and a major portion of this volume is given to reporting the data that were collected for these tests. It is not appropriate to list in this chapter—which deals with general theory of teacher behavior and problems related thereto—all the propositions or hypotheses which guided the research of the project. However, to illustrate the kind of propositions which may grow out of the basic assumptions and postulates stated earlier, a few of those to which the staff of the Teacher Characteristics Study gave attention are listed below.[4]

---

[4] The propositions presented here are stated in very general terms and *not* with sufficient specificity to permit their ready conversion into exact and testable null-hypothesis form. In fact, a proposition may, and often does, subsume a family of more specific subhypotheses which become the immediate interest of the researcher.

It also should be noted that the inclusion of a proposition does not imply that the specific hypotheses which may be derived from it received support from the empirical data assembled by the Teacher Characteristics Study; these are simply a few propositions illustrative of those that guided the research.

Proposition: General classes of teacher classroom behaviors fall into relatively homogeneous clusters characterized by substantial inter-correlation of behaviors within a cluster. Teacher behavior *in toto* may be described in terms of a limited number of such major clusters of behaviors.

Proposition: The major clusters or families formed by teacher behaviors have the characteristics of *dimensions*. Individual teachers, in their manifestations of a particular behavior pattern, vary along a continuum between two behaviorally describable poles.

Proposition: Reliable estimates of teacher behavior constituting a major cluster (positions along a major dimension) may be obtained through assessments derived from the observations of trained observers.

Proposition: The classroom behavior of a teacher with respect to a major dimension, as represented by assessments made by trained observers, is characterized by substantial stability over considerable periods of time.

Proposition: The extent of intercorrelation among major dimensions of teacher behavior varies for different subpopulations of teachers, such as elementary teachers and secondary teachers.

Proposition: Correlates scales may be developed, using paper-and-pencil responses of teachers as indicators which will permit the indirect estimation of various kinds of teacher characteristics such as social attitudes, educational viewpoints, verbal ability, and emotionality.

Proposition: Teacher characteristics of the type described in the preceding proposition, as revealed by *correlates* in the form of paper-and-pencil responses of teachers to questions about their preferences, activities, and the like, are consistent and stable over substantial periods of time.

Proposition: Different subpopulations of teachers, classified according to grade level and subject matter taught, differ significantly in teacher characteristics.

Proposition: Certain teacher characteristics vary with the age of the teacher.

Proposition: Certain teacher characteristics are correlated with grades or marks earned by the teacher when in college.

Proposition: Certain teacher characteristics are related to the earlier youth activities of the teacher.

For some of these propositions there is considerable evidential support. For others considered by the Teacher Characteristics Study, lack of statistical corroboration or, equally often, absence of adequate controls, indicates that rejection, or at least suspended judgment, is in order. These findings are discussed in later chapters.

The Criterion Problem in the Study of Teacher Characteristics

Conceptually, and chronologically as well, the first problem that arose when the research for the Study was being planned was concerned with the criterion, or criteria, which might be employed in the study of teacher behavior. Questions very basic to the pursuance of the Study, such as the following, were raised and given extended consideration.

1. How shall judgments and decisions be reached, in as rational and objective a manner as possible, regarding the nature of major criteria of teacher behavior? In the development of procedures for the description and estimation of teacher characteristics, what means shall be employed in determining the important behavior domains (criteria) involved?

2. After decisions have been reached regarding the important areas of teacher behavior and their general description, how shall the components of a particular criterion be determined? What specific behavior dimensions make up a particular criterion, and how may such components be operationally defined?

3. How are the constituent behaviors making up a criterion dimension interrelated? How are the criterion components patterned? How much importance, or weight, should be assigned each constituent in the combination forming a criterion dimension?

4. How generalizable are the criterion dimensions of teacher behavior?

5. How, and to what extent, are the major criterion dimensions of teacher behavior interrelated?

6. How shall measures of the criterion behavior be obtained? What approaches to the measurement of criterion data may be employed, and what are the advantages and disadvantages associated with the different approaches? To what extent do different measures of the same criterion agree with one another?

THE CRITERION IN BEHAVIORAL RESEARCH

A criterion is a standard description, or definition, which is accepted in undertaking research and is used to provide a frame of reference for judging whether or not some phenomenon occurs (and often the degree to which it occurs). It is a base, often of a rather arbitrary nature and ultimately *involving value judgments*, against which comparisons may be made.

The criterion problem demands consideration in every research undertaking. In many educational and social research studies, the criteria have been arbitrary standards derived from presumed expert opinion. In experimental research, the dependent variable represents behavior which has been accepted as a criterion. In prediction research, the criterion is the behavior the researcher attempts to predict and against which the relevance and usefulness of his predictors may be judged.

A criterion frequently is complex, consisting of a number of component dimensions.[5] Usually the complexity of a criterion is in direct proportion to the breadth of the behavior with which the researcher is concerned. If the criterion behavior is readily definable and is not complicated, determination of its major relevant features and derivation of suitable criterion measures may be no great problem. Job-sample performance tests are fairly easily developed for tasks requiring a restricted set of operations. Even in dealing with behavior that is relatively complex, but where the end-product (the "pay-off" feature) is readily discernible, criterion measures may be fairly easily found. Thus, however varied and numerous are the activities of the insurance salesman or the baseball player, policy sales of the insurance man and hits, runs, errors, and the like for the baseball player provide convenient and valid criterion data. But determination of the criterion behavior of the physician, the lawyer, the clergyman, or the teacher may be quite a different matter. In such cases we seldom attempt use of the singular *criterion*, but often correctly assume the plural, *criteria*, recognizing from the outset the multidimensionality and complexity of the criterion behavior. Research in the area of teacher effectiveness has been sterile, largely because of difficulties inherent in defining criteria adequately and obtaining criterion measures of teacher competence.

ARMCHAIR, RATIONAL-ANALYTIC, AND EMPIRICAL APPROACHES TO THE CRITERION PROBLEM

In spite of the importance of the criterion problem, it frequently has been neglected or at best treated in a common-sense manner with little apparent attention to possible biasing conditions. Thus, hundreds of "criteria" for teacher effectiveness, school housing, textbooks, teacher load, salary schedules, vocational success, and the like, have been arbitrarily set up and employed by professional educators. Typically, such criteria are based on an *armchair approach* to the criterion. This approach is highly subject to intentional and unintentional selection, or bias, in that it utilizes unanalyzed retrospective impressions, based upon nonsystematic observation and often characterized by free association. As a result, it is likely to result in incomplete and unsatisfactory descriptions of criteria. Furthermore, as Brogden and Taylor warn,

---

[5] To communicate more precisely, the following definitions of terms are used:

Specific behavior and *specific teacher behavior* mean an act or action at a specific time (tb_{ij}).

First-order behavior dimensions, elemental behavior, and *criterion component* mean a class of behavior which includes a number of specific behaviors or acts; a trait name abstracted from specific behaviors which have features in common.

Teacher behavior criterion, criterion dimension, and *major criterion dimension* mean a behavior cluster or family formed by first-order behavior dimension which are intercorrelated; a factor identified through factor analysis; a general class of behavior.

many unsophisticated (armchair) concepts of criteria take their descriptions from readily available and apparently "obvious" criterion measures. Brogden and Taylor state:

From reports of validation studies found in the literature, it may be judged that the usual first step in criterion development is the search for available criterion measures. . . . The discovery of several already available or readily obtained measures that are *apparently* suitable is inclined to lead to neglect of the systematic observation and analysis necessary to insure that all important aspects of on-the-job productivity have been identified." [*4*, p. 162.]

The gap between armchair approaches and a rational, or logical, approach (which may appear to be superficially similar to the armchair technique) is a large one. The *rational-analytic approach* plays an important part in every serious investigation involving a criterion and is centered in systematic observation and the logical analysis of the criterion behavior and its products, leading to an inclusive and exclusive designation of the components of the standard to be employed in making comparisons. Rational analysis is systematic and comprehensive. It aims to result in a description based on the relevancy of possible criterion components, judged from the standpoint of belongingness and representative sampling. It frequently employs content analysis, using the critical incidents approach to teacher behavior.

The *empirical approach* to the criterion is a pragmatic one which both follows and proceeds beyond rational-analytic efforts. It consists essentially of trying out hypothesized descriptions of the criterion, or dimensions composing the criterion, and accepting, modifying, or rejecting the criterion framework in the light of experience. In the study of teacher classroom behavior, one empirical approach to the designation and refinement of criteria might involve factor analysis of the intercorrelations among observers' estimates of a number of definable teacher behaviors (first-order teacher behavior dimensions) with the intent of discovering families of component behaviors which contribute criterion dimensions. This was one of the approaches followed in the Teacher Characteristics Study.

Serious attention to the criterion problem demands not only that decisions be reached regarding the working model, or description, of the criterion to be adopted and the criterion measure (or measures) to be employed, but also that such decisions be based insofar as possible upon empirically supported considerations.

Such decisions often are difficult to reach. For example, a type of decision that frequently confronts the researcher involves the selection of a criterion behavior representative of some particular segment, or time sample, from the life history of a specific person. Thorndike [*29*] has called attention to this problem, noting the distinction between immediate, intermediate, and ultimate criteria and emphasizing the need for specifying which kind of criterion one attempts to predict. Another discussion of criteria of teacher behavior [*26*] presented a generalized classification of *pupil behavior* (the hypothesized product of teacher behavior) which included immediate criterion data such as "manifestations of pupil interest in on-going class activities," intermediate criterion data, such as "manifestations of accomplishment upon completion of pupil's exposure to a particular teacher," and ultimate criterion data, such as "manifestations of occupational and social adjustment and accomplishment in the after-school life of the pupil." Each of these segments of criterion behavior has importance; and each poses different problems.

The choice of a *criterion measure* also rests upon the judgment of the researcher, and often a number of criterion measures may seem to be employable interchangeably. Such appearances of interchangeability may be deceptive, however. The intercorrelations between hypothesized criterion measures frequently have been found to range from low to high, and occasionally even to be negative [*14, 19*]. Nevertheless, alternative methods of obtaining criterion data usually are available to the researcher, and decisions must be made in the light of both technical considerations and practical convenience. One such decision, for example, may involve a choice between direct and indirect measures of criterion data. The use of data derived from observations of ongoing criterion behavior, *behavior in process*, exemplifies a direct approach. Obtaining data relative to the outcomes of criterion behavior, the *product* of the behavior (e.g., pupil accomplishment or pupil adjustment), illustrates an indirect approach. Both provide significant data. One method may be preferred over the other in view of the objective of a particular research. But both kinds may be obtained, and they may lead to quite different kinds of conclusions. In fact, as Brogden and Taylor aptly note,

One factor frequently making for criterion deficiency is the inclination of investigators to employ only one type of criterion measure. . . . If an adequate analysis of the job situation were accomplished and a decision as to criterion content were made before consideration is given to the most desirable measuring techniques for each job element, it would seem that production records would often be found most desirable for some of the criterion elements and ratings or job samples most desirable for other elements. [*4*, p. 166.]

Assuming a multiplicity of approaches to a criterion, it is incumbent upon the researcher to conduct preliminary investigation of the criterion and criterion measures in order to be reasonably assured of their relevance and usability.

Characteristics of a Criterion

The first set of problems requiring the researcher's decisions involves: (1) *the composition of the criterion* in terms of the functional integrals[6] of behavior which comprise it, and the related problem of the sampling adequacy of the working model or description of the criterion; (2) *the interrelations of the major criteria, or criterion dimensions;* and (3) *the generalizability of criterion descriptions* to other samples of the same population or to other populations.

It is apparent that if such decisions are to have the advantage of empirical evidence as well as rational support, data must be obtained through the use of selected criterion measures. Thus, a circularity is introduced: criterion measures cannot be chosen until certain decisions have been made regarding the nature of the criterion; and some of the judgments relative to the criterion must remain tentative until reliable estimates of the hypothesized dimensions have been made. This is characteristic of all research, however, in that hypotheses are rationally derived, empirically tested, and then altered as a result of empirical evidence and further rational analysis.

So, criterion definition and criterion measurement interact and, in a sense, all conclusions about a criterion are relative to the type of measurement or observation approach employed. Therefore, in discussing the composition of the criterion, particularly from the standpoints of dimensionality, weighting, and generalizability, we must recognize that the terms "criterion" and "criterion measure" cannot be entirely independent.

---

[6] The term *integral* is used for convenience to distinguish between (*a*) aspects or elements of behavior that by themselves bear no apparent relationship to the criterion and (*b*) integrals of behavior, which may be either simple behaviors such as a particular motor or verbal response or combinations of behaviors of varying degrees of complexity, which have *functional integrity* in the sense that they represent significant or salient components of the criterion. For example, smiling may be a trait, or element, of the teacher's behavior repertoire, but one which by itself might not form an *integral* of behavior in the sense that it designated a major pattern of teacher behavior. Smiling, alone, might be too fragmentary and specific to be of importance. But smiling, together with other related behaviors, might form a pattern of "friendly, understanding" teacher behavior which appeared to have enough wholeness, or integrity, to be useful in describing teacher behavior.

Frequently, the researcher gives too little thought to this matter of identification of the functional integrals of behavior. The criterion he accepts, or attempts to predict, sometimes is too specific and fragmentary to be of importance—or, at the other extreme, it may be too broad and abstract to permit estimation and prediction.

COMPOSITION OF A CRITERION

In considering the composition of a criterion, it is appropriate to take into account (*a*) the first-order behavior dimensions making up the criterion dimension and the relative importance of each component, and (*b*) the adequacy or representativeness of the resulting analytical description of the criterion.

DIMENSIONABILITY OF THE CRITERION

Few criteria of practical importance for the student of behavior consist of simple, highly specific, unitary performances. A smile, a gesture, a particular spoken word or phrase, or a single correct answer often bears little relationship to significant aspects of behavior that the researcher is attempting to describe or predict. More frequently, a criterion is complex rather than simple, multidimensional rather than unidimensional.

A major concern of the investigator, therefore, is the structure of the over-all criterion and its first-order component dimensions. Here the researcher seeks to identify the variables which contribute appreciably to the criterion, and to determine how the constituent behavioral elements may be organized into meaningful patterns. Furthermore, he is interested in formulating the most parsimonious description of the dimensionality of the universe of behavior under consideration and of the structure of each major criterion dimension. Thus, one set of questions subsumed under "dimensionality of the criterion" is concerned with determining the behavior integrals comprising the criteria. Logical classification and intercorrelational study, including factor analysis, have been found to be useful approaches to dealing with such problems.

A related set of questions deals with how the behavioral components comprising a criterion should be weighted when combined. If the criterion dimension consists of elemental behaviors $X_1, X_2, X_3, \ldots, X_n$, what weights should be assigned to each of these elements so that the summation will best represent the hypothetical true-criterion dimension? The researcher is concerned, therefore, not only with the identification of criterion dimensions, but also with the assignment of the proper relative weight to each. General discussions of this problem have been provided by Brogden and Taylor [4], Toops [30], Thorndike [29], and others. In a paper reporting one phase of the research of the Teacher Characteristics Study, certain techniques of weighting criterion data in the investigation of teacher behaviors were compared [20].

SAMPLING THE ADEQUACY OF THE CRITERION

In studying the composition of a criterion, the goal is, of course, to establish a working model, or operational definition, which is characterized by both inclusiveness and exclusiveness. The criterion description should include all important behavior integrals which contribute to the criterion behavior and should exclude all variables that are unrelated to the criterion.

Thus, inseparably linked with the identification of criterion dimensions and their components is the problem of the representativeness or sampling adequacy of the resulting descriptions. Brogden and Taylor [4], Bellows [3], and others have called attention to sources of criterion bias and the need for careful job analysis and systematic study of criterion behavior as a means of guarding against bias. In their excellent discussion of "The Theory and Classification of Criterion Bias," Brogden and Taylor define a biasing factor as "any variable, except errors of measurement and sampling error, producing a deviation of obtained criterion scores from a hypothetical 'true' criterion score." [4, p. 161.] They go on to classify the major sources of criterion imperfection: (1) *criterion deficiency*—omission of pertinent elements from the criterion; (2) *criterion contamination*—introducing extraneous elements into the criterion; (3) *criterion scale-unit bias*—inequality of scale units in the criterion; and (4) *criterion distortion*—improper weighting in combining criterion elements. A review of the literature relating to teacher effectiveness suggests numerous examples of each of these criterion weaknesses. The vulnerability to criterion bias of certain approaches to criterion designation and measurement will be noted in subsequent paragraphs.

INTERRELATIONSHIPS OF CRITERION DIMENSIONS

The relative extent of overlapping or interdependence of the defined criterion dimensions is of practical as well as theoretical concern to the researcher. More often than not, criteria may be expected to be positively correlated, to show overlapping rather than independence. If the intercorrelations between estimates of criterion dimensions are substantial, differential identification and prediction becomes difficult and often lacks feasibility even though the dimensions appear to have rational integrity. For example, even though the dimensions of height, width, and depth of a container each may have logical integrity, it may be difficult to find a predictor of one dimension which does not also predict the others because the dimensions of physical objects are often highly intercorrelated.

The interrelationships among many criterion dimensions may vary with the population studied. For example, research findings reported in chapter 4 show higher intercorrelations among certain dimensions of teacher classroom behavior for elementary school teachers than for teachers at the secondary school level.

GENERALIZABILITY OF CRITERION DIMENSIONS

Still another closely related problem concerns the generalizability of criterion dimensions. This problem has two parts: (*a*) the generalizability of a particular sample of criterion behavior to other samples in the same behavior domain or universe, and (*b*) the generalizability of the criterion to additional samples of the same population and to samples of other populations.

With regard to *a* above, teacher behavior could be highly specific and situational (e.g., the extent of "friendly, understanding" teacher behavior demonstrated by a given teacher might vary with the pupil, the time of day, the mood of the teacher, the subject matter, and other conditions) or, on the other hand, within the limits of definable variability, the "friendly, understanding" behavior of a teacher might have considerable generality (and therefore predictability) for different children, at different times of day, in different situations, etc. Only to the extent that the behavior is generalizable, of course, is prediction of any sort possible.

One aspect of the problem noted in *b* above relates to whether defined criterion dimensions are specific to given samples within populations of teachers (teachers of a given school or school system) or, on the other hand, if criterion *generalization* is possible. It may be assumed that this is basically a sampling problem, and that care in the drawing of a random sample or a stratified random sample may ensure a certain amount of generality, provided reliable criterion integrals or dimensions have been specified. The other aspect of *b* above refers to the possibility of criterion *extension*—whether or not the criterion dimensions are generalizable from one population to another (e.g., are dimensions of teacher behavior that apply to elementary teachers equally applicable to high school teachers, or to college teachers?).[7] It seems reasonable to hypothesize that although the magnitude of the interrelationships among criterion dimensions may vary from one teacher population to another, the dimensions themselves have a considerable degree of generaliza-

---

[7] It should be noted that even when considerable generalizability of criterion dimensions may be assumed, there is no implication of similar generalizability of correlates and predictors of the criterion dimensions.

bility. Several factor-analytic studies, for example, have yielded generally similar dimensions of teacher behavior in the elementary school, the secondary school, and the college.

The Designation and Measurement of Criteria

The derivation of the working model of a broad area of behavior, including the designation of the criterion dimensions and the components of each, ideally is a function of the interaction of both rationally and empirically obtained evidence, but the final decisions of the process must be a set of judgments. The researcher thus is obligated to acquire a degree of "expertness" with respect to the criterion he is using, and his judgment presumably will be reached after an extensive review of others researchers' findings and also, perhaps, empirical study on his own part.

Often the researcher feels more secure in his selection of criterion dimensions if the decisions are based on judgments of other qualified persons in addition to himself. Needless to say, assurance will tend to be greater, the larger the number of authorities involved and the more representative such individuals may be of the totality of persons considered expert in the area.

Since expert judgment inevitably involves opinion (value judgments), the researcher must be assured he is not employing a nonrandom or nonrepresentative sample of authorities (e.g., a sample made up of individuals with whom he happens to be acquainted, or persons he or his immediate associates assume to be authorities, or judges who merely happen to be readily available). Criterion inadequacy and criterion contamination frequently are reflections of the employment of biased judges at the point of the designation of criterion dimensions.

Essentially, the process of defining the criterion consists of (a) selecting the authorities who will contribute to the necessary decisions, (b) specifying the procedure to be employed by the judges, and (c) assembling and analyzing the responses of the judges to determine the consensus. Various ways of selecting judges and various approaches which may be employed in obtaining the required judgments (free response, description of critical incidents, observation and time sampling, paired comparisons of hypothesized components, etc.) have been considered in some detail elsewhere [22].

Suffice it to say that only after systematic and comprehensive consideration has been given to teacher behavior criteria and their composition may attention be turned to the selection and development of measures suitable for obtaining working criterion data.

As noted earlier, the description of a criterion and the development of criterion measures are related and often interacting aspects of the same problem. Brogden and Taylor [4] comment on this relationship, observing that the systematic investigation of a situation in which criterion behavior occurs often supplies the investigator with cues regarding means of subsequently measuring the components of the criterion. And there is also a feedback from the preliminary tryout and analysis of potential or hypothesized criterion measures which contributes to the more complete definition and designation of criterion dimensions. Thus, interaction, rather than a sequential relationship, characterizes these two steps in the consideration of the criterion problem.

The development of a criterion measure involves judging the relevance of various measurement approaches, attempting to attenuate problems of controls and sources of bias associated with the use of available approaches, evaluating reliability and intercorrelational data, establishing units of measurement, weighting, etc. Again, as in the description of a criterion, both rational and empirical procedures are employed.

REQUIREMENTS OF AN ADEQUATE CRITERION MEASURE

What are some of the standards against which the adequacy of a particular criterion measure or approach may be judged? Basically, there are three characteristics of criterion measures with which the researcher is concerned: validity (or relevance), reliability, and feasibility.

VALIDITY OR RELEVANCE OF A CRITERION MEASURE

The relevance of a criterion measure is, of course, the really basic consideration. Casual inspection of any matrix of intercorrelations of presumed criterion measures shows far-from-perfect relationships between measurements which, on an a priori basis, may have been presumed to be comparable or alternative estimates of the same criterion dimension. In factor analysis it is frequently found that there is little common variance among criterion measures, which indicates they are not generally interchangeable, and it also raises the question of their possible lack of validity relative to the criterion they are assumed to measure.

How may the researcher evaluate the validity of measures of a criterion? What are some of the conditions that cause invalidity which should be recognized? These problems will now be considered.

Construct validity:—*The basic approach to judgment of relevance of criterion measures.* Several kinds of validity[8] have been discussed by persons dealing with the measurement of behavior. One of these kinds

---

[8] Logical validity, face validity, content validity, construct validity, congruent validity, concurrent validity, predictive validity, etc.

recently has been called "construct validity." It is construct validity with which the researcher is concerned in evaluating the adequacy of a criterion measure. Construct validity is rational, or logical, validity. It is closely related to the concept of "face validity" (apparent validity), but goes beyond it.

Mosier [15] calls attention to various aspects of *face validity*, including validity by appearance, validity by assumption, validity by hypothesis, and validity by sampling. Certainly the uncritical acceptance of a criterion measure in the light of either appearance of validity or assumed validity is dangerous. Yet, these often provide the starting point for consideration of criterion measures, and when such measurement approaches are suggested by either systematic study of the criterion or extended experience, or both, their hypothesization may have considerable support.

Although the concepts are not greatly different and they tend to merge, a distinction should be made between face validity and construct validity. The term *construct validity* refers to validity or relevance that is inferred from indirect, though logically related, evidence—validity which may *reasonably* be assumed, but which is implied rather than directly indicated. Construct validity with respect to a criterion measure might be regarded as including Mosier's validity by hypothesis and also, perhaps, validity by sampling.[9] Thus, in the study of teacher characteristics, critical analysis might lead the researcher to hypothesize that achievement tests of English expression, or of knowledge of subject matter to be taught, or of understanding of child development, provide relevant criterion measures of those dimensions of teacher behavior that are involved in the communication of subject matter and the motivation of learners. Or, the employment of observers' assessments based on time samples of teacher behavior obtained under varying conditions might be said to have construct validity (*validity by sampling*—valid because a fair sample of the universe, or totality, of the behavior of individual teachers had been obtained) for the measurement of a criterion of teacher classroom behavior. Again, the discovery through factor analysis of a general factor, or of a group factor common to several criterion measures, and the choice of criterion measures on the basis of their loadings on such a factor would be an example of the use of construct validity. Such merging of rational and empirical evi-

---

[9] Sampling validity sometimes is considered a subtopic under content validity, but it also has characteristics of construct validity. In the study of teacher behavior, it may be more appropriate to consider sampling validity as an area of overlapping of construct and content validity.

dence, for the most part relatively indirectly, provides an important and useful source of information for judging the relevance of criterion measures.

Sampling adequacy of criterion measures.—As in the establishment of criterion dimensions, in the development of criterion measures the researcher must be constantly on guard against bias. It is important that a criterion measure be both comprehensive, or inclusive, and also that it *not* measure behaviors extraneous to the criterion dimension under consideration.

Again, attention is called to the thorough discussion by Brogden and Taylor of sources of criterion bias and the need for assurance that criterion measures are as bias-free as possible. As those writers point out, the chief reason for avoiding criterion bias in prediction and diagnostic research is to obviate the possibility that obtained measurements will be estimates of behaviors or characteristics other than those embraced by the criterion description. Thus, the research worker must be especially alert to the problem of *measure-correlated bias* in the criterion. Brogden and Taylor are quoted as follows:

Biasing factors correlating with the predictors will obviously distort the validities and the partial regression weights of the various predictors. They may even result in the inclusion of tests in the battery that predict only bias and have no relationship to the "true" criterion. The introduction of bias having no relation to the predictors is . . . equivalent . . . to an increase in the error of measurement of the criterion. . . . In spite of . . . adverse effects of test-free bias, it is believed that, effectively, it is the presence or absence of test-correlated bias that "makes" or "breaks" the criterion. [4, pp. 163–64.]

The imminence of criterion measure-correlated bias and the need to be on the lookout particularly for measure-related contaminating characteristics of criterion measures is especially acute at the time of selection and development of criterion measures.

Of the sources of error they describe, Brogden and Taylor observe that *contamination* and *scale-unit bias* are the classes of bias most apt to be introduced in the development and application of measures of a criterion. Among the sources of criterion contamination frequently associated with criterion measurement are: (1) *opportunity bias*—bias resulting from differences in opportunity for production, or behavior, among different individuals (e.g., during a given time sample no situation may occur which might provide Teacher A with an opportunity to demonstrate certain characteristics she actually possesses, whereas Teacher B, in a similar time sample, may be presented with ample opportunity to reveal behavior in the domain under observation); (2) *experience bias*—bias resulting from varying amounts of experience of different individuals relative to a given performance (e.g., a student teacher or practice teacher may exhibit characteristics of classroom behavior differing qualitatively and quantitatively from those of a more experienced inservice teacher); and (3) various *rating biases*, such as those associated with halo effects and with inferences based on assumed symptom-criterion relationships [4].

In addition, it may be noted that when ratings or assessments are employed, criterion *distortion* frequently is introduced through duplication, or inclusion of highly similar components, in the criterion measure. (This should not be confused with replication of measurement, which is generally desirable.) Such duplication, for example, may be present when several generally similar behaviors are included in a rating scale, thus giving unintended disproportionate weight to the duplicated aspect of the criterion. Still other rating errors such as the so-called "central tendency" error and "leniency" error (resulting, respectively, in leptokurtic and skewed distributions of assessments) contribute to criterion scale-unit bias.

RELIABILITY OF A CRITERION MEASURE

A second standard by which the adequacy of criterion measures is judged is that of consistency, or reliability. Consideration of this characteristic of a criterion measure follows the same general rationale that is applied to the problem of test reliability, and the same approaches (e.g., equivalence, stability, and internal consistency) may be employed.

Strictly speaking, reliability of criterion measures might properly be considered a subtopic of validity. Certainly a criterion measure can be valid only when it is relatively stable, and the development of a predictor becomes possible only when the criterion measure presents some degree of consistency.

A criterion measure yields reliable data to the extent that the measurements it provides are free from fluctuations, or variable error. A product of performance, taken as a criterion measure, is reliable if it may be replicated and if such replications show a high degree of similarity or consistency. Ratings of behavior-in-process are reliable if those made by different observers at different times are similar or consistent.

The generalizability of a criterion measure to other samples of the same or different populations is also a reliability consideration. Unless a measure maintains its relevance when it is applied to the criterion behavior of similar samples of the same population, it has no value for the researcher. If the measure continues to be relevant when its application is extended to other populations, its potential usefulness is still greater.

Other things being equal, the reliability of criterion data may be expected to be greater under the following conditions: (1) the more extensive the replication of the criterion measurement (including extension of the time sample); (2) the more objective the recording of observations of behavior or evaluations of a product (which implies the employment of comparable units of measurement); (3) the fewer the conditions leading to varied interpretations of the behavior or product; (4) the less the variation in the situation in which the behavior takes place from time to time; (5) the more homogeneous and operationally describable the criterion dimension.

The reliability of criterion measures may be estimated by obtaining correlations between (1) products, (2) repeated measures of production, (3) assessments of different observers, or (4) repeated assessments by the same observer over varying periods of time. As in test analysis, the problem of reliability may be approached either from the standpoint of correlation and covariance or from that of the error of measurement.

It also may be noted that where replication of criterion measures is employed, the Spearman-Brown formula may be used to estimate the reliability of the combined measures.

FEASIBILITY

A third, and obvious, requirement of a criterion measure is that it be relatively convenient to use. There is no denying the importance of practical considerations and the frequent need for compromise, resulting in the use of measurement procedures that are somewhat more subject to error than would be desired in an optimal measure. Probably in most situations involving natural behavior, or field behavior, it is necessary to employ criterion measures which have technical shortcomings. It is important that the researcher recognize such shortcomings and their possible (though usually unknown) effects upon the resulting data. Thus, while argument can be mustered for "pupil change" as a criterion measure in the study of certain dimensions of teacher behavior, practical (and also technical) difficulties are likely to preclude its use. Classroom observations by trained observers may provide a more feasible method of obtaining the criterion data.

SOME APPROACHES TO OBTAINING CRITERION DATA

Various approaches to obtaining criterion data in the study of teacher characteristics and related problems have been suggested in the reports of the American Educational Research Association's Committee on Criteria of Teacher Effectiveness [1, 2], by the writer in various publications [19, 25, 26], and by others. The present comments call attention to certain classes of criterion measurement which may be employed, such as (1) direct measurement of ongoing behavior through systematic observation and assessment, (2) indirect measurement based upon records of ongoing behavior, (3) indirect measurement by nontrained observers and based upon recall of the behavior assessed, (4) measurement of a product (pupil behavior) of teacher behavior, and (5) measurement of concomitants of criterion behavior.

DIRECT MEASUREMENT OF THE ONGOING CRITERION BEHAVIOR

Direct measurement of the criterion requires the assessment of behavior-in-process—the actual performance of a task. The assessment by trained observers of the behavior of a teacher while conducting a class is an example of the direct measurement of criterion behavior.

Direct measurement of criterion dimensions may involve either the assessment of criterion behavior in its natural setting, or assessment in artificially structured situations approximating, or simulating, the natural behavior. The observation and assessment of teacher behavior in the teacher's own classroom illustrates the first case; observation and ratings under situational test conditions (exemplified by the procedures developed by the OSS during World War II, by teaching tests employed in some school systems, and by performance tests sometimes used by industry) are illustrations of the second. There are certain advantages in the employment of artificially structured situations, and such situations often have a degree of face validity. Nevertheless, experience suggests that particular attention should be given to considerations of *sampling* adequacy (e.g., vulnerability to various kinds of criterion bias) and *generalizability* when criterion measurement is attempted under artificial conditions.

The actual observation and assessment involved in direct measurement of a criterion of teacher behavior may involve either (*a*) time sampling, with replicated systematic observation and assessment, by trained observers, or (*b*) nonsystematic observation and assessment by untrained observers.

Time sampling involving replicated systematic observation and immediate assessment of the criterion behavior by trained observers.—Probably the most satisfactory approach to the direct measurement of criterion behavior is through the use of observers who are trained to observe specified criterion elements or components and to record assessments thereof immediately. Such systematic observation implies prior analysis of the criterion behavior, designation of the component criterion elements and major dimensions, development (including tryout and subsequent analysis) of the observation record or assessment scale, investigation of the relevance and reliability of the assessment procedure with additional samples of teachers, and intensive training of the observers both in making systematic observations and in the use of the assessment record. Only when such steps are followed can the influence of criterion bias be minimized.

Various considerations involved in obtaining criterion data through systematic observation and assessment, including methods of obtaining representative samples of the criterion behavior, conditions affecting the validity and reliability of assessments, the observation procedure and training of observers, and devices for recording assessments, as well as the experience and results of the employment of trained observers in the Study, are discussed in some detail in chapter 4. Suffice it to note here that when direct measurement of criterion dimensions of teacher behavior is undertaken, the obtained data are more likely to be relevant to the extent that:

1. The dimensions of the criterion behavior have been specified and unequivocally defined in operational terms;
2. The observer recognizes the relevant behaviors and assesses those, and *only those*, characteristics;
3. The observer focuses his attention on specific actions and carefully avoids contamination of assessment by general impressions, reactions to behaviors that stand out prominently or unusual behaviors that obscure typical behavior, inferences about the meaning of behaviors, and inferences about what the behavior might be like in unobserved situations;
4. The observations are conducted with proper attention to time sampling—the observations are not too limited to provide for opportunity for occurrence of the criterion behavior;
5. The observer makes his assessments during or immediately following observation;
6. The observer makes separate assessments of each specified component of the criterion dimension considered independently;
7. The naturalness of the situation in which the criterion behavior occurs is preserved;
8. The observer is capable of recognizing and avoiding the influence of personal biases relative to individuals or behaviors under observation;

9. The observer conscientiously seeks to avoid various rating biases, such as the central-tendency error, the leniency error, and others;
10. Provisions are made for replication of observation and assessment by independent, similarly trained observers.

A word of caution is offered here, which applies to any situation in which direct measurement is employed. This has to do with the control of conditions introduced by the influence of the observer upon the behavior of individuals whose criterion behavior is being observed and assessed. Procedures for reducing the effects of such a contaminant frequently have been discussed and employed by social researchers.

Nonsystematized observation and immediate assessment by nontrained observers.—The measurement of behavioral criteria sometimes is undertaken with the use of nontrained observers who make ratings on the basis of directly observed segments of behavior. Observers who have had little or no instruction relative to the definition and description of the behavior dimensions to be assessed and who have had no supervised training in behavioral observation and assessment are likely to be at considerable variance with one another in their judgments and in the ratings they produce. Their assessments are likely to be heavily influenced by the casual nature of the observation and by biases resulting from criterion deficiency and contamination. Usually, therefore, they are of little value as criterion measurements.

INDIRECT MEASUREMENT: ASSESSMENT BASED ON A PRESERVED
RECORD OF THE BEHAVIOR-IN-PROCESS

Under certain conditions, bias resulting from difficulties of control in direct observation may be reduced through the recording of behavior-in-process and its preservation for later analysis and assessment. Thus, through the use of motion pictures, sound tracks, tape recordings, and the like, it may be possible to circumvent one set of difficulties encountered in the direct observation and immediate assessment of behavior —namely, the problem of adequate analysis and assessment of behavior which is momentary or transitory. With a preserved record, a behavior may be reviewed any number of times, analyzed in detail, and assessed by many more judges or observers than usually can be employed in direct observation. There are obvious advantages to such a procedure if it may be adapted to the criterion behavior with which the researcher is concerned. But often, as in a teacher-classroom situation, many practical difficulties are encountered. For instance, sound motion pictures, taken with a hidden camera and with adequate distribution of microphones, of samples of teacher-class behavior appear to provide a very desirable means of obtaining certain kinds of criterion data. But the problems of lighting, photography, obtaining the films and records without knowledge of the participants, etc., ordinarily rule out such an approach. The principal control problem, therefore, is centered on the use of the recording equipment and its possible distorting effect on the natural behavior of subjects whose criterion behaviors are being photographed or recorded.

Needless to say, if such an approach is applicable, recording errors are reduced to a minimum and subsequent systematic observation and assessment by trained judges should be expected to yield highly reliable criterion data.

INDIRECT MEASUREMENT: ASSESSMENT BY NONTRAINED OBSERVERS AND BASED ON RECALL OF PAST BEHAVIOR

The most frequently employed (and also the most hazardous and most poorly controlled) behavior measurement procedure utilizes untrained observers who base their assessment upon the recall of past behavior of the individuals being rated—behavior in situations varying widely in kind and number.

Assessment of criterion behavior by untrained observers may be either analytical (separate evaluations of each of several designated criterion components) or global (over-all ratings of broad, general features of the criterion behavior). Although analytical assessments appear to be superior when observers have been trained to make systematic observations, there is some evidence that such an advantage does not hold for nonsystematized observation by untrained observers. Nonanalytical or global ratings are at least as satisfactory as analytical assessments when the numerous uncontrolled conditions operating in informal evaluation are involved.

Ratings or assessments based upon nonsystematized observation may be contributed by observers, or raters, associated in various relationships with the individual being judged. In the literature relating to teacher behavior and teacher effectiveness, assessments made by school principals and supervisors are reported very frequently. Assessments made by the teacher's pupils or peers have also been used in research studies.

Criterion data based upon the self-ratings of individuals are sometimes employed. It seems debatable that self-ratings of criterion behavior can be of value for other than very specialized purposes, however. They are likely to provide usable criterion data only when (1) the criterion behavior involved is not very complex, (2) the respondent is good at introspection and retrospection and is able to make objective self-judgments, (3) the self-ratings are based upon behavior that has been clearly and operationally defined, and which takes place under relatively rigidly defined conditions, (4) replication is employed to obtain self-ratings covering an adequate number of situations in which the criterion behavior may occur, and (5) the respondent is willing to reveal his self-judgments. For the investigation of complex personal behavior, such as teacher classroom behavior, self-ratings do not seem likely to be useful as criterion measures.

The use of any of these rater groups (administrator, peer, pupil, or self) presents unique problems relative to bias and control, and all are subject in common to serious limitations with respect to sampling adequacy. Assessment by untrained observers, based upon nonsystematized observation, is vulnerable to all the classes of bias listed by Brogden and Taylor—deficiency, contamination, distortion, and scale-unit bias.

MEASUREMENT OF A PRODUCT OF THE CRITERION BEHAVIOR

An opinion held by many in the field of prediction research is that the most satisfactory measure of a criterion is one derived from the product of performance—that judgments and assessments based upon the observation of behavior-in-process merely are incidental and are of little value as compared with measurements of the product.

In employing products for the measurement of criterion dimensions, details of the actual performance-in-process usually are ignored; interest is centered not in the behavior per se that contributes to production, but rather in the final outcome in the form of *effects of behaviors*. Thus, in research on learning, the most reasonable criterion of learning behavior is usually held to be achievement resulting from the difficult-to-observe learning process. Similarly, the behavior of pupils (their accomplishments) may be considered to be the *product* of a teacher's efforts, and as such is a suitable criterion measure of teacher behavior.

The chief disadvantage in the use of products as criterion measures is the difficulty of adequately controlling external factors in order to provide reasonable assurance that the hypothesized product is truly a product of the criterion behavior rather than that of a wide range of uncontrolled conditions occurring before and during the criterion behavior.

If the situation is such that conditions can be carefully controlled (as in laboratory learning studies), the behavior product probably will be accepted as the most desirable criterion measure. As situations become more complex and control becomes less possible, however, the value of the product as a criterion measure diminishes.

In situations where the criterion behavior-product relationship may be assumed to be direct and uncontaminated, use of the product for the measurement of the criterion is of unquestionable value. In such cases, the product is affected solely, or almost so, by the criterion behavior; other conditions that may influence the product can be effectively controlled. Such control is difficult to achieve, but it is possible in certain kinds of relatively straightforward studies, particularly those amenable to laboratory investigation.

In the study of teacher behavior, the employment of pupil change for criterion measurement probably can be defended best for narrowly defined experimental situations, such as one in which (*a*) the teachers being judged carry out their teaching with groups of children who have been matched with respect to a number of relevant factors (including similarity of earlier teacher influences and learning experiences) and (*b*) the measured product (learning) is related to a relatively simple task which can be completed in a single sitting or experimental session. Such controls, difficult as they may seem to be to execute, still are far from complete. They illustrate the exactitude required of experimental designs in which it could be reasonably assumed that pupil change was really a product of teacher behavior.

In the employment of behavior products for criterion measurement, the more usual situation is one in which the product under consideration may be assumed to be a product not only of the criterion performance, but of various uncontrolled factors as well. Thus, at the opposite extreme from the rigidly controlled example cited above might be the estimation of teacher behavior from its presumed product, consisting of pupil achievement in some specified subject matter, measured at the end of a semester's exposure to the teacher. Factors in addition to the teacher that might contribute to pupil achievement (textbooks, prior learning, previous teachers, home influence, influence of peers, ability, study habits, emotional make-up, etc.) and their differential effects on different pupils are not taken into account in such a research design.

Examples illustrating an intermediate position, involving pretesting and posttesting of pupils and the control of certain factors, occasionally are found in the literature. The efficacy of such an approach to criterion measurement may be judged to be intermediate between the two extremes, depending upon the extent to which control is possible.

An additional consideration in the use of products for the purpose of criterion measurement involves the *proximity in time* of the product evaluation to the occurrence of the behavior which is hypothesized to be the producer. Frequently the passage of time and the consequent introduction of additional influences have considerable effect upon a product. Thus, product measurements might show significant differences, depending upon whether they are obtained (1) concurrently with the producing behavior (e.g., direct observation and assessment of pupil behavior while the teacher is teaching), (2) immediately following the producing behavior (e.g., testing of pupil knowledge, skills, attitudes, etc., following exposure to the teacher), or (3) with a time interval separating exposure to the teacher and evaluation of attainment (e.g., judgment of success of pupils in later adult life). In each case, many biasing conditions may be influencing the product and reducing the validity of the criterion measure. What really is being measured in each case is a product once removed from its hypothesized producer (a *product* of *pupil behavior* is measured and taken as a measure of a product of teacher behavior).

The measurement of a product has attained considerable recognition in attempts to study teacher competence. When measurement of the product is accomplished by obtaining estimates of pupil change, the problem of variable potential gain (pupils who score high on the initial measurement being closer to their "ceilings" than pupils who originally score low are to theirs) is particularly plaguing to the researcher. However, if the rationale of the product (pupil performance) criterion is accepted, and if the complex control problem presented by a multiplicity of producers and the multidimensionality of the criterion can be satisfactorily handled, pupil change becomes an intriguing approach to the measurement of teacher behavior criteria. Mitzel and Gross [13] have dealt critically with the development and use of the pupil-change criterion in the study of teacher effectiveness. The excellent review of Morsh and Wilder [14] covers the literature to 1952 and presents the case for and against the employment of measurements of pupil change, and of observation and assessment, as well.

MEASUREMENT OF CONCOMITANTS OF CRITERION BEHAVIOR

Judging from studies reported in the literature, it is not uncommon to employ measurements of concomitants of a criterion as substitutes for basic criterion data. The use of substitute data of this sort is defended frequently on the grounds of assumed "obvious" relationship, as in the case of the use of an "educational principles and methods" test to provide measurements of teaching ability, and sometimes because of the unavailability or impracticality of more direct measurement of a criterion.

Such concomitants sometimes have been empirically validated and are known to be related to the basic criterion data, but often they are merely assumed to be related to the criterion.

Measurement of behaviors, or products known to be related to the criterion.—Obviously the most defensible use of correlates or concomitants for the measurement of a criterion dimension is in the case where the correlate is a behavior or a product of behavior that is *known* to be related (for which there is considerable evidence of relationship) to the criterion behavior. Knowledge of such relationship implies prior study which has been sufficiently extensive to permit generalization. For example, certain data from the Teacher Characteristics Study strongly suggest that such teen-age activities as reading to other children, caring for children outside the home, and taking charge of a class for a teacher are positively and significantly correlated with direct measurements of certain dimensions of later-life teacher behavior as assessed by trained observers. Under certain circumstances the use of indirect data provided by such known concomitants of a criterion dimension would seem to be acceptable. It should be recognized, nevertheless, that existing biases in both the original criterion measure and the correlate may thus be compounded. But *if reliable correlates of a criterion dimension can be ascertained, and if such correlates are fairly numerous, the measurement of concomitants may provide an acceptable substitute* for more direct criterion data. In fact, in some instances where the original criterion measurements are unreliable, it is conceivable that a battery of concomitants might even provide measurements superior to the original data that were obtained more directly.

The inventory developed by the Teacher Characteristics Study (the Teacher Characteristics Schedule) is made up of items selected for inclusion because responses to them correlated with more direct criterion data reflecting several dimensions. Scores on teacher characteristics scales, thus empirically derived, may be employed as secondary criterion data.

Measurement of behavior or products assumed to be related to the criterion.—More frequent than where the concomitant-criterion relationship is known is the case where some concomitant is assumed to be associated with a criterion. The acceptability of measurements of assumed concomitants usually is not as great as in the section above. Nevertheless, indirect evidence sometimes tends to support the use of assumed concomitants of teacher behavior such as attainment in a child development course or in practice teaching. Certainly the teacher-training curricula, of which such courses are a part, are predicated on the assumption that understanding of course content and apprenticeship behavior are related to teacher classroom behavior. Concomitants of this nature, involving validity by assumption, by inference, and perhaps by hypothesis, frequently are employed in obtaining criterion measurements. In this connection, Thorndike's discussion [29] of immediate, intermediate, and ultimate criteria should be recalled.

The measurement of criterion behavior in terms of concomitants assumed to be related to that behavior has been undertaken in several manners, some of which are described below.

Measurement of concomitants of a criterion, based upon systematic observation.—A single example will be cited. Such characteristics as good health, freedom from physical disability, and the like, often are assumed to be concomitants of the satisfactory performance of teaching responsibilities. Provided the assumption of such a relationship is acceptable, criterion data may be obtained through systematic observation (physical examination) and the assessment of aspects of health and physical well-being by a qualified medical examiner.

Measurement of concomitants of a criterion through nonsystematic observation.—Such characteristics as "being anxious to please," "causing no trouble," and other similar abstract qualities sometimes are assumed to be related to dimensions of a criterion (e.g., teacher behavior) and measurement of presumed criterion behavior are derived from assessments of such qualities by an individual's associates (ratings submitted by a teacher's principal, his students, his fellow teachers). The assumption of a relationship between such characteristics and a criterion dimension of teacher behavior should be viewed with extreme caution. Furthermore, the general impressions upon which such ratings are based are subject to many sources of bias. So-called criterion data of this sort usually can be of little value.

Measurement of concomitants of a criterion through self-reports.—Occasionally, in studies of teacher behavior, self-reports of the teacher's liking for his work, satisfaction with working conditions, recognition of his shortcomings, etc., are assumed to be reliable correlates of important criteria of teacher behavior. Similarly, estimates of the success of a counseling procedure, or the value of a conference program, are sometimes obtained through self-reports of the client, or the participant, who indicates on a rating scale the extent to which he believes that he has profited from the experience. Aside from the unknown relationship between an assumed concomitant and salient aspects of a criterion, such self-reports seldom can be expected to be free from the deficiency and contamination biases which characterize so many criterion measures.

Measurement of behavior products assumed to be concomitants of the criterion.—Scores derived from tests, inventories, questionnaires, and the like, frequently are employed as criterion measures without any evidence that such *products* are related to the criterion behavior. The argument for the usability of such substitute measures of criterion behavior is largely from the standpoint of construct validity—general agreement of authorities that certain knowledge, abilities, skills, and personal characteristics are closely associated with performances constituting the designated criterion behavior. It could be argued, for example, that measurements derived from suitable achievement tests in English expression and communication skills yield data suggestive of teacher performance on certain criterion dimensions. However, for many types of presumed criterion data derived from tests and inventories (numerous examples of which may be noted in the literature), the case is not well supported, and the use of such substitute measures often contributes materially to criterion contamination.

Generally speaking, the employment of any kind of assumed concomitants of criterion behavior to obtain criterion data is highly open to error and should be undertaken only when the rationale is particularly sound—and then with extreme caution.

A SUMMARY OF METHODS OF CRITERION MEASUREMENT

The rather extended discussion of approaches to the measurement of dimensions of the criterion is summarized below to provide a more compact view of this important problem. The following methods of obtaining criterion data have been discussed:

1. Direct measurement of *ongoing* teacher behavior.
   a) Time sampling involving replicated systematic observation and immediate assessment by trained observers.
   b) Nonsystematized observation and immediate assessment by nontrained observers.
2. Indirect measurement based on preserved records of ongoing teacher behavior, using devices such as tape recordings or motion pictures.
   a) Assessment by trained observers.
   b) Assessment by nontrained observers.
3. Indirect measurement by nontrained observers, based on recall of teacher behavior and assessment thereof.
   a) Rating by administrative personnel.
   b) Rating by students or pupils of teacher.
   c) Rating by peers or colleagues of teachers.
   d) Teacher self-rating.

4. Measurement of a *product* of teacher behavior.
   a) Direct observation and assessment of ongoing student behavior involving participation in class activities, acceptance of responsibilities, understanding of principles studied, learning of skills, etc., or of a preserved record thereof, simultaneous with exposure to the hypothesized producer (teacher behavior).
   1) Time sampling involving replicated systematic observation and immediate assessment by trained observers.
   2) Nonsystematized observation and assessment by nontrained observers.
   b) Measurement of a product of student behavior which, in turn, is assumed to be a product of teacher behavior, immediately following exposure to the hypothesized producer (teacher behavior).
   1) Testing of knowledge, skills, understanding, etc.
   2) Inventorying of attitudes, interests, preferences, etc.
   c) Delayed measurement of a product of student behavior with time intervals intervening between exposure to the hypothesized producer (teacher behavior) and evaluation of the product.
   1) Measurement of skills, understanding, attitudes, participation, etc., during succeeding phases of the student's education.
   2) Measurement of success in occupational and civic affairs during later life of student.
   d) Measurement of a product in terms of changes in student behavior.
   1) Pre- and post-testing of knowledge, skills, understanding, etc., and determination of gains or losses.
   2) Pre- and post-inventorying of attitudes, interests, preferences, etc., and determination of changes.
5. Measurement of concomitants of the criterion of teacher effectiveness.
   a) Concomitants *known* to be reliably related to the criterion (e.g., biographical data or inventory scores which have been demonstrated to be empirically correlated with some accepted criterion).
   b) Concomitants *assumed* to be related to the criterion (e.g., courses required for teaching credentials or appearance as revealed by photographs which are believed to be associated with an accepted criterion).

These several approaches to measurement vary in rationale, and they yield criterion data that differ with respect to reliability and correlations with predictors. Measurement of ongoing behavior of the teacher is the most direct approach. Measurement of products and concomitants are more indirect and more subject to the effects of confounding conditions.

Concomitants are not used for criterion measurement when behavior or the products of behavior can be conveniently measured. However, in investigations involving extensive sampling, where other measurement approaches are impractical, the use of known concomitants as substitutes for process or product data is defensible.

Of the measurement approaches employing observation and assessment, only *time sampling involving replicated systematic observation by trained observers* produces sufficiently reliable data to justify its use in fundamental research. Less well controlled variations may be employed, however, when only coarse discrimination (e.g., "best" and "poorest" teachers with respect to some criterion or criterion component) is required, and when the larger expected error is recognized and accepted. Various assessment techniques have been developed, and the more reliable and promising of these appear to be (1) graphic scales with operationally defined poles or units, (2) observation check lists and (3) forced-choice scales. The chief shortcoming of observation and assessment techniques has been lack of reliability, but recent research has indicated that reliability can be improved by defining terms carefully, developing more precise scales, and training the observers or judges.

Product measurements have been acclaimed as desirable criterion data, but have been used relatively infrequently. The most defensible of the product measurement techniques are (1) the direct observation and assessment of the behavior of the teacher's students while they are in his charge and (2) measurement of student change from before to after exposure to the teacher.

The Validity of Predictors

A second important set of problems encountered in the Study involved judging the probable validity of inventory items and scores as predictors of teacher characteristics. It should be recalled that the development of paper-and-pencil correlates of certain defined criteria of teacher-classroom behavior was one of the major objectives of the Study.

In approaching the tasks of selecting item responses as predictors and determining the validity of empirically derived scoring keys, a number of questions had to be considered. Some of these questions[10] were:

---

[10] Additional questions and related data are presented in chap. 4.

Shall the criterion groups employed for response selection be homogeneous or heterogeneous with respect to variables such as sex, subject area, and grade level?

Shall the criterion groups for response selection be random samples of teachers, or should they be samples of intact groups of teachers in certain schools or school systems?

Shall the selection of responses that are to be used as predictors of the criterion be based upon experience with a single sample, or will replication be employed with at least two samples? (The latter method inevitably is accompanied by shrinkage of validity coefficients, but it has the advantage of justifying greater confidence in the predictors which survive.) If response selection is based on replication, shall the ultimate scoring key be based on responses that correlate with the criterion at or beyond a specified significance level (*a*) in either sample, (*b*) in both samples, or (*c*) on the basis of the compound probabilities in the two samples?

Will a scoring key derived from one sample of teachers from a particular group (population) continue to be effective when applied to another sample of teachers of the same kind drawn from the same population?

Will a scoring key derived from a sample of one group of teachers maintain its effectiveness when applied to a different group? For example, will responses that are correlated with Criterion X in a group of third- and fourth-grade teachers be useful for predicting Criterion X in a group of high school mathematics teachers?

Will a scoring key derived from random samples of teachers maintain its effectiveness when used with intact groups of teachers who have certain relevant characteristics in common (e.g., will a key derived from random samples of teachers in the United States be effective in predicting teacher behavior in School System A which is known to cultivate a particular educational philosophy or viewpoint)?

Will a scoring key derived with regard to a particular criterion measure maintain its effectiveness when tested against a similar, but somewhat differently obtained, criterion measure (e.g., will item responses that correlate with a criterion of teacher behavior based upon assessments of trained observers maintain their effectiveness with a criterion based upon principals' ratings of teachers)?

Shall the item-response selection be based on concurrently obtained criterion data, or on criterion data that are obtained at a later time?

Will a scoring key that is derived from the responses of a group of in-service teachers maintain its effectiveness when it is used to predict the *future* classroom behavior of students who lack teaching experience at the time they fill out the inventory?

Will a scoring key that is effective in situations characterized by neutral motivation (where ego involvement of respondent is at a minimum) maintain its effectiveness in situations characterized by strong incentive conditions (where respondent is ego-involved and there is an advantage in making a good impression)?

Will prediction be attempted for selected criterion dimensions singly or for a composite such as over-all teaching behavior, which involves a number of heterogeneous components or dimensions?

In 1948–49, when this Study was just getting under way, answers to some of these questions seemed very remote, particularly in view of the sequential nature of many of the operations involved. The sequence envisaged was: job analysis, development of criterion-producing procedures, analysis of criterion data, development of rationales for inventory materials, the preparation and preliminary tryout of verbal and nonverbal items, observation of large samples of teachers, completion of final forms of the inventory materials and administration of them to the teachers who had been observed, item-counting and item selection, and, finally, validation studies of the derived scoring keys. Nevertheless, plans for obtaining answers were made, and the necessary data were eventually obtained for at least limited answers to each type of question.

Formulation of the problems relating to predictor validation as presented here reflects various influences, but it is most directly an outgrowth of (*a*) staff discussions of methods of ascertaining the validity of scoring keys of the Teacher Characteristics Schedule and (*b*) Mosier's excellent discussion, "Problems and Designs of Cross-Validation" [*16*]. Indeed, the present treatment, adopting Mosier's terms "validity generalization" and "validity extension," leans heavily on certain features of Mosier's conceptualization of the validity problem.

All of the problems recognized by Mosier, and certain additional ones, faced the staff in its efforts to discover correlates of teacher behavior. It was in the light of this need for a clearly conceptualized picture of the validation problem, as a necessary prior step, that the formulation took place.

The following classification of research designs summarizes a number of approaches which may be employed to obtain the evidence required to judge the probable usefulness of correlates of criterion behavior for predicting such behavior. *It should be noted that the following possible variations apply to each of the methods indicated:*

a) Item responses and criterion data concurrently obtained;
b) Item responses obtained prior to experience upon which criterion data are based; obtaining of criterion data delayed:
   (1) Item responses obtained under strong incentive conditions.
   (2) Item responses obtained under conditions of neutral motivation.

I. DESIGNS FOR ITEM VALIDATION AND SELECTION

A. *Designs involving criterion group, or groups, derived from a single homogeneous population*
   1. Item selection based on a single criterion group, randomly selected from population.

2. Item selection based upon multiple (replicated) criterion groups randomly drawn from population; ultimate selection of items based on some combination of probability values yielded by the several samples.

B. *Designs involving criterion groups derived from multiple populations (populations differing in some identifiable, hypothetically relevant characteristic)*
   1. Item selection based upon one criterion sample from each population; ultimate selection of items based on some combination of probability values yielded by the samples.
   2. Item selection based upon multiple criterion samples from each population; ultimate selection of items based on some combination of probability values yielded by the samples.

II. Designs for Estimating Validity of Item Combinations (Scoring Keys)

A. *Random sampling validity designs*
   1. Cross-validation (combination of item responses selected from one random sample of the population applied to a second similarly drawn sample to test the effectiveness of the scoring key).
   2. Double cross-validation (item responses selected separately for two samples randomly drawn from the population; set of responses selected for each sample applied to the *other* sample to test the effectiveness of the respective scoring keys).
   3. Hold-out sample validation (item responses selected, presumably from replicated random criterion samples, and applied to still another random sample of the population that was "held out" of the item studies for testing the effectiveness of the scoring key.

B. *Validity generalization designs* (item responses selected for samples from one population, presumably cross-validated at that stage, and then applied to another sample drawn from a *differently defined population*, but utilizing the same kind of criterion, to estimate the generalizability of the scoring key to the second population).
   1. Validation with populations of individual respondents (sample unit is the individual respondent).
   2. Validation with population of intact groups (sampling unit is the composite of some group of respondents, hypothesized to have relevant characteristics in common).

C. *Validity extension designs* (item responses selected for samples from one population, presumably cross-validated at that stage, and applied to another sample drawn from a different population, utilizing a different criterion measure, to estimate the generalizability of the scoring key to the second population and to the second criterion measure).
   1. Validation with populations of individual respondents.
   2. Validation with populations of intact groups.

The designs outlined fall into two general classes: (1) those concerned with the validation of responses or items for the purpose of selecting test or inventory *items*, and (2) those involving the validation of *"scores."*

In relation to validation for response selection, attention has been called to variations in design involving (*a*) a single sample of subjects, (*b*) multiple samples of subjects, (*c*) samples from a single homogeneous population, and (*d*) samples from multiple populations.

With regard to the validation of scores or scoring keys, the different approaches described involve (*a*) additional random samples of the same population, (*b*) samples of additional populations, but employing the same criterion measure, (*c*) samples of additional populations, employing a measure of the criterion different from that used in response selection, (*d*) cross-validation, (*e*) double cross-validation, (*f*) hold-out sample validation, (*g*) the individual as the sampling unit, and (*h*) intact groups as the sampling unit.

Regardless of whether the designs apply to responses, items, or scores, the variations may include either concurrent or predictive validation, and either strong or neutral incentive conditions.

Procedure of the Study in the Light of Certain Criterion and Prediction Problems

Obviously, attainment of the major objectives of the Study—namely, the description of the major dimensions of teacher behavior and the development of paper-and-pencil instruments for use in predicting such dimensions of behavior and other teacher characteristics—was intimately dependent upon the solution of the problems concerning the criteria and the validity of their prediction. Therefore a major portion of this volume is given to a detailed description of the procedures that were used in trying to satisfy as many of the necessary conditions as possible.

Following is a brief outline of some of the important phases of the Study: (1) the designation of dimensions of teacher behavior was approached both rationally and empirically through (*a*) the development of observation procedures based on review of personality descriptions and critical incidents reports relative to teacher behaviors, (*b*) systematic observations, by trained observers, of teachers in their classrooms, and (*c*) factorial analyses of the assessments made by the observers; (2) after the major dimensions of teacher behavior and the components of such dimensions had been identified, relatively large samples of teachers of different grades and subjects were observed and assessed; (3) forced-choice typical behavior items, requiring responses which were hypothesized to be correlated with the major dimensions of teacher behavior and other teacher traits, were (*a*) prepared and administered to the teachers who had been observed, (*b*) subsequently subjected to item analyses to determine the value of each response as a predictor of the observer-assessed teacher behavior, and (*c*) cast into scoring keys through the procedure described in the previous section dealing with item validation and selection; and (4) further research was carried out, involving cross-validation, hold-out sample validation, validity generalization study, and validity extension study, to determine the probable usefulness of the scoring keys in the light of such questions as those listed in the foregoing discussion of the validity of predictors.

Bibliography

1. AMERICAN EDUCATIONAL RESEARCH ASSOCIATION. "Report of the Committee on the Criteria of Teacher Effectiveness," *Review of Educational Research*, **22**: 238–53, 1952.
2. ———. "Second Report of the Committee on Criteria of Teacher Effectiveness," *Journal of Educational Research*, **46**: 641–58, 1953.
3. BELLOWS, R. M. "Procedures for Evaluating Vocational Criteria," *Journal of Applied Psychology*, **25**: 499–513, 1941.
4. BROGDEN, H. E., and TAYLOR, E. K. "The Theory and Classification of Criterion Bias," *Educational and Psychological Measurement*, **10**: 159–86, 1950.
5. CASTETTER, D. D., *et al.* "Teacher Effectiveness: An Annotated Bibliography," *Bulletin of the Institute of Educational Research*, **1**, No. 1. Bloomington, Ind.: Indiana University School of Education, 1954.
6. CHARTERS, W. W., and WAPLES, D. *The Commonwealth Teacher-Training Study.* Chicago: University of Chicago Press, 1929.
7. CURETON, E. E. "Validity," *Educational Measurement*, ed. E. F. LINDQUIST. Washington: American Council on Education, 1951. Pp. 621–94.
8. DOMAS, S. J., and TIEDEMAN, D. V. "Teacher Competence: An Annotated Bibliography," *Journal of Experimental Education*, **19**: 101–18, 1950.
9. KEYNES, J. M. *A Treatise on Probability.* New York: Macmillan Co., 1921.
10. McCALL, W. A. *Measurement of Teacher Merit.* Raleigh, N.C.: State Department of Public Instruction, 1952.
11. MILL, J. S. *A System of Logic.* New York: Longmans, Green & Co., 1872.
12. MILLER, J. G. "Toward a General Theory for the Behavioral Sciences," *American Psychologist*, **10**: 513–31, 1955.
13. MITZEL, H. E., and GROSS, C. F. *A Critical Review of the Development of Pupil Growth Criteria in Studies of Teacher Effectiveness.* New York: Office of Research and Evaluation, Division of Teacher Education, Board of Higher Education of the City of New York, 1956.
14. MORSH, J. E., and WILDER, E. W. *Identifying the Effective Instructor: A Review of the Quantitative Studies, 1900–1952.* San Antonio, Texas: Air Force Personnel and Training Research Center, 1954.
15. MOSIER, C. I. "A Critical Examination of the Concepts of Face Validity," *Educational and Psychological Measurement*, **7**: 191–205, 1947.
16. ———. "Problems and Designs of Cross-Validation," *Educational and Psychological Measurement*, **11**: 5–12, 1951.

17. RABINOWITZ, W., and TRAVERS, R. M. W. "Problems of Defining and Assessing Teacher Effectiveness," *Educational Theory*, 3: 212–19, 1953.
18. RYANS, D. G. "A Note on Methods of Test Validation," *Journal of Educational Psychology*, 30: 315–20, 1939.
19. ———. "A Study of Criterion Data (A Factor Analysis of Teacher Behaviors in the Elementary School)," *Educational and Psychological Measurement*, 12: 333–44, 1952.
20. ———. "An Analysis and Comparison of Certain Techniques for Weighting Criterion Data," *Educational and Psychological Measurement*, 14: 449–58, 1954.
21. ———. "Appraising Teacher Personnel," *Journal of Experimental Education*, 16: 1–30, 1947.
22. ———. "Notes on the Criterion Problem in Research, with Special Reference to the Study of Teacher Characteristics," *Journal of Genetic Psychology*, 91: 33–61, 1957.
23. ———. "Prediction of Teacher Effectiveness," *Encyclopedia of Educational Research* (3rd ed.). New York: Macmillan Co., 1960. (*In press.*)
24. ———. "Research Designs for the Empirical Validation of Tests and Inventories," *Educational and Psychological Measurement*, 17: 175–84, 1957.
25. ———. "The Criteria of Teaching Effectiveness," *Journal of Educational Research*, 42: 690–99, 1949.
26. ———. "The Investigation of Teacher Characteristics," *Educational Record*, 34: 370–96, 1953.
27. ———. "Theory Development and the Study of Teacher Behavior," *Journal of Educational Psychology*, 47: 462–75, 1956.
28. SEARS, R. R. "A Theoretical Framework for Personality and Social Behavior," *American Psychologist*, 6: 476–83, 1951.
29. THORNDIKE, R. L. *Personnel Selection*. New York: John Wiley & Sons, 1949.
30. TOOPS, H. A. "The Criterion," *Educational and Psychological Measurement*, 4: 271–97, 1944.

3. The Samples Employed in the Study

TEACHER CHARACTERISTICS research, like all empirical study, is inductive in its approach and is necessarily dependent upon samples for the data employed to test its hypotheses. Throughout such research, and in the use of the results, it is implicitly assumed that the sample provides a replica of the characteristics of the parent population (although, at best, this may only be approximated in behavioral studies), or, if knowledge of the representativeness of the sample is lacking, it is assumed that the only differences between the sample and the population are those which may be attributed to random sampling. Attention must therefore be given to various aspects of sampling design, including choice and definition of the population, nature of the sampling unit, size of the sample, and sampling method to be used. The first three aspects involve no insurmountable difficulties. The last, that of sampling method, presents no insoluble problems from the standpoint of theory, but in practice it confronts teacher characteristics research with a predicament offering little hope of adequate solution.

The random sampling model is one which permits the selection of r teachers out of the population of n teachers, in a manner such that any of the $_nC_r$ samples has the same chance of being selected as any other. It follows that each teacher in the population under consideration should have an equal chance of being included in a sample. Obviously, the educational system in this country does not permit the use of a random sampling design or even a modification thereof for which adjustments for systematic error may be made with any great assurance. The cooperation of a school system, a school, or a teacher in a research project must remain voluntary in any decentralized system of education. Furthermore, adequate population control data relative to teachers, which would be necessary for making adjustments for systematic errors in sampling, are for the most part unavailable.

In the light of the sampling obstacles confronted in the Study, it is not possible to state with conclusiveness that the samples employed were either representative or random samples of the totality of teachers in the United States. Perhaps the most reasonable position to take regarding the data reported in this volume is a strictly operational one similar to that suggested by Cochran, Mosteller, and Tukey in connection with their discussion of statistical problems of the Kinsey Report, when they state:

If the physicist is aware of systematic errors of serious magnitude and has no basis for adjustment, his practice is to name the measured quantity something, like Brinnell hardness, Charpy impact strength, or if he is a chemist—iodine value, heavy metals as Pb, etc. By analogy, those who feel that the combination of recall and interview technique make Kinsey's results subject to great systematic error might well define "KPM sexual behavior" as a standard term, and work with this. [*1*, p. 34.]

Perhaps we should similarly, and properly, describe the teacher behavior and teacher characteristics dimensions investigated in the Study operationally in such standard terms as "TCS understanding friendly behavior," "TCS businesslike-responsible behavior," "TCS stimulating-original behavior," "TCS attitude toward pupils," "TCS traditional educational viewpoint," and "TCS verbal ability."

This is tantamount to saying that the characteristics of teachers identified in this study, and the related research findings, apply most exactly to a hypothetical population of which the teachers who voluntarily cooperated comprise a random sample. The extent to which the results may be generalized to teachers-in-general, or to any particular group of teachers, is a function of the similarity between the teachers studied and the group in question.[1]

With this consideration in mind, it becomes a responsibility to describe in some detail the groups of teachers who participated in the Study and the known characteristics of the samples employed in the various analyses and comparisons that are reported in the following chapters.

Participation in the Teacher Characteristics Study

The activities of the Teacher Characteristics Study, with respect to both teacher participation and the nature of the problems investigated, may be classified as those having to do with: (1) the observation of teacher classroom behavior and the selection of paper-and-pencil materials for the prediction of classroom behavior dimensions and other sets of teacher characteristics; (2) a national survey of teacher characteristics, as estimated from the Teacher Characteristics Schedule; and (3) special studies growing out of the basic investigations of teacher behaviors and their prediction, including studies of validity generalization and extension, statistical and case studies of teachers who were indicated by observers to be extreme deviates with respect to patterns

---

[1] This position may be more cautious than is necessary. Other research studies, such as those of Coffman, Gibb, Creager, and others cited in chap. 4, employing different approaches, have, for example, suggested teacher behavior dimensions similar to those reported by the Teacher Characteristics Study.

of teacher behavior, etc. For convenience, the first group of activities will be designated as the *Basic Analysis Study*, and the teachers involved as the Basic Analysis Sample, the second as the *Survey Study*, and the teachers as the Survey Sample, and the third as *Special Studies*.

Participation in the various phases of the Study involved over six thousand teachers from more than seventeen hundred schools. The participation data are shown in Tables 1, 2, and 3. It may be noted from Table 1, for example, that 3,883 teachers from 274 elementary and 103 secondary schools in 33 school systems took part in the Basic Analysis Study and in the training observations which preceded it. Participation in the Survey Study and Special Studies is shown similarly. Table 2 presents a breakdown indicating in detail the nature of the services pro-

TABLE I

Participation of Schools and of School Systems in the Teacher Characteristics Study

STUDY	NO. OF SCHOOLS			NO. OF SCHOOL SYSTEMS	NO. OF TEACHERS
	Elementary	Secondary	Total		
Basic Analysis Study (and training)...	274	103	377	33	3,883
Survey Study....................	408	554	962	271	1,638
Special Studies.................	155	253	408	142	658
Total.....................	837	910	1,747	446	6,179

vided by cooperating teachers, and Table 3 summarizes the same data.

Participation in the Study extended from 1948 through 1954. The first two years were devoted chiefly to preliminary and exploratory study of the methods and devices to be used. The school year 1952–53 marked the peak of teacher participation in the Basic Analysis Study and in the Special Studies. Approximately 7 percent of all teachers participating (other than in the Survey Study) contributed their services in the years 1948–50, 16 percent in 1950–51, 26 percent in 1951–52, 45 percent in 1952–53, and 6 percent in 1953–54. The Survey Study was conducted during the spring of 1954.

How the Samples Were Obtained

It is important that the two principal samples of teachers participating in the Teacher Characteristics Study, and the procedures employed in assembling them, be described in some detail. This is attempted both in this section and in the succeeding section, entitled "Some Comparisons of the Samples."

TABLE 2

Analysis of Teacher Participation in the Study

KIND OF PARTICIPATION	TRAINING OBSERVATIONS		BASIC ANALYSIS STUDY		SURVEY STUDY	SPECIAL STUDIES		TOTAL	
	No. of Teachers	No. of Observations	No. of Teachers	No. of Observations	No. of Teachers	No. of Teachers	No. of Observations	No. of Teachers	No. of Observations
Elementary teachers									
Observed by TCS staff; Schedule not completed..	120	149	293	633	......	......	......	413	782
Observed by TCS staff; Schedule completed.....	......	......	1,225	2,646	......	176	350	1,401	2,996
No observation; Schedule completed.....	......	......	......	......	670	206	......	876	......
Special ratings; Schedule completed.....	......	......	......	......	......	315	......	315	......
Secondary teachers									
Observed by TCS staff; Schedule not completed..	158	182	381	823	......	......	......	539	1,005
Observed by TCS staff; Schedule completed.....	......	......	1,530	3,304	......	......	......	1,530	3,304
No observations; Schedule completed.....	......	......	......	......	970	......	......	970	......
Special ratings; Schedule completed.....	......	......	......	......	......	343	......	343	......

TABLE 3

Summary of Teacher Participation in the Study

KIND OF PARTICIPATION	ELEMENTARY TEACHERS		SECONDARY TEACHERS		TOTAL	
	No. of Teachers	No. of Observations	No. of Teachers	No. of Observations	No. of Teachers	No. of Observations
Observed by TCS staff..................	1,814	3,778	2,069	4,309	3,883	8,087
Observed by TCS staff; Schedule completed	1,401	2,996	1,530	3,304	2,931	6,300
No observations; Schedule completed....	876	.....	970	.....	1,846	.....
Special ratings; Schedule completed......	315	.....	343	.....	658	.....
Total completing Schedule............	2,592	.....	2,843	.....	5,435	.....
Total number participating...........	3,005	.....	3,382	.....	6,387	.....

BASIC ANALYSIS STUDY

When plans for the Study were being formulated, it was hoped that, although it might be necessary to utilize conveniently available teachers for preliminary or pilot studies, the major analyses involving the observation of teachers and the use of inventory materials could be conducted with teachers who had been selected in such a way as to provide approximate probability samples.

In the planning, it appeared desirable to give particular attention to three general factors which might reasonably be assumed to influence the characteristic responses of teachers and therefore should be taken into account in obtaining the samples. These were: (1) the size of the community or school system in which the teacher was employed; (2) the section of the United States in which the school system was located; and (3) the salary level of the school system in which the teacher was employed. Available data suggested that the interrelationships among these variables probably were significant, although considerable unique variance might be associated with community size and section of the country in which the school was located.

An effort was made to design a sample which would allow these factors to be controlled to some extent. As might have been anticipated, however, it was not possible to obtain the cooperation of a number of school systems in which teachers were selected for study. Thus, the teachers who did take part comprised groups, or samples, representing (a) a population of school systems (or school superintendents) who were willing to have their teachers participate and (b) a population of teachers who were willing to participate by being observed and by giving the time required to complete the inventory materials.

The desired random sample of United States school systems and teachers, stratified with respect to the variables noted, was not attainable.

Still another condition that affected the sampling was the extremely high cost of visiting and observing sufficiently large numbers of teachers in one-room schools and small school systems. This led to restricting the Study, to a very great extent, to larger city school systems.

At least three other factors appeared to be of sufficient relevance to merit consideration with the view to control: grade or subject matter taught; extent of teaching experience; and sex of the teacher.

With respect to the first of these, it seemed reasonable to undertake separate studies or analyses of the groups of teachers most numerous in the schools. Certainly the argument for considering elementary teachers apart from secondary teachers appeared sound. At the secondary school level, it seemed reasonable to give chief attention to teachers of the basic subjects—English, social studies, science, and mathematics. Accordingly, steps were taken to carry out the Basic Analysis Study with samples of elementary teachers, English–social studies teachers, and mathematics-science teachers.

It was recognized that teachers of Grade 1 and Grade 6, who deal with children so different in developmental level, might conceivably be characterized by quite different classroom behaviors, interests, and other traits. At the beginning, it did not seem feasible to undertake investigation of the entire range of elementary teachers. The extreme grades were therefore omitted, and teachers of Grades 3 and 4 were first selected for observation and study. Later, as the study progressed, it became possible to extend the research to a fair-sized sample of Grades 1 and 2 teachers and a somewhat smaller group of Grades 5 and 6 teachers.

The analyses of secondary teachers were conducted with two major samples—one from the English–social studies area, and the other from the mathematics-science area. Since many of the teachers of English and of social studies (or of mathematics and science) had majored in one of these somewhat related areas and minored in the other when in college, and since assignment of teaching responsibilities frequently cuts across the English–social studies area or the mathematics-science area, the original plan was to consider each of these combinations as a single sample for the Study. As in the case of the elementary sample, it later became possible to expand the research, and separate samples of mathematics, science, English, and social studies teachers were obtained. Additional samples consisting of foreign language teachers and business education teachers were also included.

Although data on the extent of teaching experience were obtained for each participating teacher, no effort was made in the basic studies to stratify the samples by experience or to select the participants so as to regulate the distribution of experience among the teachers in the samples. It appeared to be more realistic to sample teachers as they are found in the school systems and to let the distribution of experience be governed by the existing situation.

How to deal with the sex of the teacher in the sampling presented something of a dilemma. Rather extensive preliminary research conducted by the Study, particularly in the domains of interests and activities of teachers, indicated some significant differences between the traits of male and female teachers which, if not taken into account in the analyses, might bias the data in the direction of the more numerous female teachers. On the other hand, two very practical considerations argued against the continuation of separate investigations of men and women teachers: First, it seemed reasonable to assume that the description and analysis of teacher characteristics, and the development of instruments for predicting these characteristics, should be related as closely as possible to the actual school situation, which is characterized by a disproportionate number of women teachers. Second, regardless of possible group differences in interests, activities, and such, which may be attributed to sex, the schools must generally think in terms of a single standard for the sexes in matters of selection and promotion, which suggests that any descriptions or instruments should be applicable to both men and women and should be based upon samples consisting of men and women in approximately the same proportions as they are found in the schools.

The sex of each teacher participating in the Study was, of course, recorded. In some phases of the research, separate sets of predictors were isolated for men and for women. For the most part, however, except for the analyses of observation data and of scores on keys of the Teacher Characteristics Schedule reported in chapter 7, the data for men and for women were not separately considered.

Cooperation in the Basic Analysis Study, indicated by willingness to have observations conducted and to complete the inventory materials following observations, varied from school to school. In the elementary schools, the returns ranged from 73 percent to 100 percent for the teachers observed in a particular school building, and in the secondary schools the percentage returns ranged from 65 percent to 97 percent. Throughout the entire period of the Study the percentage of usable returns of all teachers observed was approximately 81 percent for elementary teachers and 80 percent for secondary school teachers. A larger percentage of men in the elementary schools returned inventory materials than did women—87 percent, as compared with 80 percent. Among secondary school teachers, 77 percent of the men returned the Schedules, as against 83 percent of the women. Both men and women teachers of mathematics and science returned the materials more frequently than did teachers of social studies and English (mathematics-science: men—79 percent, women—83 percent; social studies–English: men—76 percent, women—82 percent). There was some indication, based upon the comparison of returns with observers' impressions of morale in a school, that participation was a function not only of the individual teacher but also of the social climate in a particular school.

SURVEY STUDY

In the interest of obtaining a national sample of teachers which might supplement the Basic Analysis Study group and provide a somewhat more adequate basis for the description of teachers in terms of characteristics revealed by the Schedule, a mail administration of this inventory was undertaken. For the purposes of this national survey, five different groups of teachers were considered: (1) elementary urban, (2) secondary urban, (3) secondary private, (4) elementary and secondary parochial, and (5) elementary rural.

Essentially, the procedure followed in the Survey Study was to write to school principals or headmasters, county superintendents (for rural schools), and diocese or district superintendents (for Catholic and Lutheran parochial schools respectively), requesting that packets containing the Schedule, a covering letter, and other materials be passed along to randomly selected teachers in the school unit. The mailing to some 2,800 principals or superintendents, identified through the directory numbers of the *National Association of Secondary-School Principals Bulletin* and the *National Elementary Principal* (National Education Association), in the *Education Directory: Part 2, Counties and Cities* (U. S. Office of Education), the *Directory of Secondary Day Schools in the United States*, and *Patterson's American Educational Directory*, was completed between April 1 and April 6, 1954.

To obtain a sample of elementary teachers of urban schools, two teacher packets (containing the Schedule, a covering letter, an answer sheet and special pencil for marking the answer sheet, and a stamped envelope for return of the materials) were sent to each of 900 elementary school principals selected to represent the schools of the United States proportionately from the standpoints of size of community and state location.

For the sampling of secondary teachers of urban schools, two teacher packets were mailed to each of 1,200 secondary school principals.

To obtain responses of secondary private school teachers, two teacher packets were sent to each of 150 headmasters or headmistresses, selected to provide geographical proportional representation of private secondary schools and also to ensure inclusion of (*a*) boys' nonmilitary, non-church-related schools, (*b*) military schools, (*c*) girls' non-church-related schools, (*d*) coeducational non-church-related schools, and (*e*) church-related, but nonparochial schools.

The method of obtaining the parochial teacher samples was less direct. In this case, covering letters and teacher packets were sent to the superintendents of the several Catholic dioceses and archdioceses and to the superintendents of Lutheran school districts. Four elementary teacher packets were sent to each of 102 diocese superintendents for distribution, and seven secondary teacher packets were mailed to each of 52 archdiocese superintendents and chairmen of Lutheran district boards of education.

In obtaining the elementary rural teacher samples, 400 county superintendents of schools were contacted, two teacher packets going to each superintendent to be passed along to teachers of one-room or small rural schools.

A total of 1,640 usable returns of the Schedule (all items of the Schedule being responded to, and the answer sheet being free of multiple responses to single-response items and other peculiarities of marking which might make for ambiguity) were obtained prior to the deadline required for scoring and tabulation. The returns represented responses from each of the forty-eight states for each of the major teaching fields. Of the total returns, 670 usable responses were obtained from elementary teachers and 970 from secondary teachers.

Some Comparisons of the Samples

Tables 4 through 7 provide comparative data relative to the composition of the Basic Analysis and the Survey Samples.

From Table 4 it is apparent that the Basic Analysis Sample is significantly different in geographic distribution from the teacher population of the United States. The basic analyses were conducted to a disproportionate extent with teachers from the Central and Western parts of the country. However, quite a different picture is presented by the Survey Sample of teachers. The geographic distribution of the Survey Sample fairly closely approximates that of all teachers employed in the United States, that of the population of the country as a whole, and that of the teachers who returned questionnaires in a 1956 survey of

TABLE 4

Geographic Composition of Basic Analysis Sample* and Survey Sample

Region of U.S.	Percent of Basic Analysis Sample*	Percent of Survey Sample (1954)	Percent of All Teachers Employed in U.S.† (1950)	Percent of Total U.S. Population† (1950)	Percent of Teachers in NEA Study [2] (1956)
East.................	4	28	25	27	27
South-Southwest......	3	27	32	30	28
Central..............	34	32	31	30	27
West................	59	13	12	13	18
Total.............	100	100	100	100	100

* Teachers for whom observers' assessments and Schedule results were complete.
† Compiled from Bureau of the Census data.

American public school teachers conducted by the Research Division of the National Education Association [2].[2]

A further breakdown of the Survey teacher group by geographic divisions, as shown in Table 5, indicates the striking similarity between the Survey Sample and the teacher population of the United States. This does not imply, however, that the Survey Sample constitutes a representative sample of the teachers in the nation with respect to all important characteristics.

Table 6 provides comparisons of the Basic Analysis Sample and the Survey Sample from the standpoint of size of community in which the teachers were employed. As pointed out earlier, much of the Basic Analysis Study was conducted in school systems of fairly large-sized cities. In contrast, a relatively large percentage of teachers employed in the United States are located in communities of less than 2,500 population. Even the Survey Sample differs from the other national distributions of teachers at the two lowest intervals of the distributions—communities of populations less than 2,500 and between 2,500 and 49,999. However, if these two categories are combined, we find them represented by 71 percent of the Survey Sample as against 68 percent of the total teacher population of the country and 75 percent of the NEA study.

Further comparisons of the Basic Analysis and Survey Samples are presented in Table 7, where the distributions for these groups and for

[2] The NEA survey, published under the title *The Status of the American Public School Teacher*, employed a stratified random sample derived from a sampling frame consisting of teachers listed in several thousand state and local school directories. Data reported were based on 5,602 usable replies, representing a 46.3 percent return. Some slight bias appeared likely, but in general the sample was judged to be typical of the teacher population with respect to such conditions as salary and size of classes taught. The reporting teachers, as might be expected, did include more NEA members (61.9 percent) than does the national teacher population (53 percent). Separate tabulation of the results of the original wave and two follow-ups showed few consistent differences when compared from the standpoint of preparation, experience, marital status, NEA membership, and willingness to teach again.

TABLE 5

Geographic Composition of Survey Sample

DIVISION OF U.S.	SURVEY SAMPLE (1954)		PERCENT OF ALL TEACHERS EMPLOYED IN U.S.* (1950)	PERCENT OF TOTAL U.S. POPULATION* (1950)
	No.	Percent		
New England....	116	7	6	6
Middle Atlantic..	335	21	19	21
East Southern....	92	6	6	6
Southern........	212	13	16	15
Central.........	449	27	27	27
Midwestern......	83	5	4	3
Southwestern....	125	8	10	9
Mountain.......	56	3	3	3
West Coast......	168	10	9	10
Total.........	1,636†	100	100	100

* Compiled from Bureau of the Census data.
† Information not given by 4 of the 1,640 participants.

the National Education Association's 1956 sample are given by age, sex, marital status, and type of college attended.

With respect to sex, the proportionate representations in the Basic Analysis, Survey, and NEA samples are very similar. When the samples are considered from the standpoints of age, marital status, and type of college attended, larger differences between the two TCS groups become apparent. The differences between the Basic Analysis and Survey Samples are most notable when the total samples are broken down into subgroups of elementary and secondary teachers. When the elementary and secondary teacher groups are combined, differences in the age distributions become relatively small, but those for marital status and type of college attended remain substantial. A somewhat larger proportion of

TABLE 6

Composition of Basic Analysis and Survey Samples, by Size of Community

Population of Community	Percent of Basic Analysis Sample*	Percent of Survey Sample (1954)	Percent of All Teachers Employed in U.S.† (1950)	Percent of Total U.S. Population† (1950)	Percent of Teachers in NEA Study [2] (1956)
500,000 or more...	46	9	11	17	11
100,000–499,999..	9	12	14	12	14
50,000– 99,999..	8	8	7	6⎱	32
2,500– 49,999..	36	51	26	22⎰	
Less than 2,500...	1	20	42	43	43
Total..........	100	100	100	100	100

* Teachers for whom observers' assessments and Schedule results were complete.
† Compiled from Bureau of the Census data.

TABLE 7

Comparisons of the Basic Analysis and Survey Samples, by Age, Sex, Marital Status, and Type of College Attended

CLASSIFICATION	PERCENT OF BASIC ANALYSIS SAMPLE		PERCENT OF SURVEY SAMPLE		Percent of All Teachers in NEA Study [2]
	Elementary Teachers	Secondary Teachers	Elementary Teachers	Secondary Teachers	
Age					
Under 30...................	38	10	24	21	23
30–39........................	23	23	23	26	22
40–54........................	33	45	43	41	43
Over 55......................	6	22	10	12	12
Total.....................	100	100	100	100	100

				Elementary	Secondary
Sex					
Male.........................	14	46	11	48	14	49
Female......................	86	54	89	52	86	51
Total.....................	100	100	100	100	100	100
Marital status						
Single.......................	29	29	43	37	28	31
Married......................	59	62	48	58	61	62
Separated (divorced—widowed)..	12	9	9	5	11	7
Total.....................	100	100	100	100	100	100
Type of college attended						
Teachers college or state college..	38	13	55	29	56	29
Liberal arts or women's college..	27	31	28	44⎱	44	71
Large university..............	35	56	17	27⎰		
Total.....................	100	100	100	100	100	100

the Basic Analysis Sample, particularly in the elementary teacher group, are married. Of the several characteristics considered in Table 7, the Basic Analysis and the Survey Samples are least similar with regard to type of college attended. Greater proportions of the Survey Sample attended teachers colleges, state colleges, liberal arts colleges, or women's colleges, whereas substantially more of the Basic Analysis Sample acquired their teacher education at large universities.

The proportions of different ages in the Survey and NEA samples are similar, but the Basic Analysis Sample shows some deviations. With regard to marital status, the NEA sample and the Basic Analysis Sample are much alike, but they differ from the Survey Sample. The Survey Sample and the NEA sample show little difference in kind of teacher education institution attended, but the Basic Analysis Sample differs from both the others.

It seems that the teachers participating in the Survey Study constitute a sample which is not very different from the population of teachers in the United States. Certainly, members of the Survey Sample fall into categories in about the same proportions as teachers-in-general with respect to such seemingly important characteristics as section of the country and size of community in which employed, sex, age, and kind of teacher education institution attended. Teachers participating in the Basic Analysis Study appear to be less representative of the national population, except with regard to marital status. Recalling the ways in which the Basic Analysis Sample and Survey Sample were obtained, the apparently greater representativeness of the latter group was not unexpected—in fact, it was to provide a more typical sample for the collection of various teacher data that the Survey Study was conducted.

However, the results pertaining to the Basic Analysis Sample also may be generalizable to a considerable extent. Comparisons of characteristics of teachers, as presented in chapter 7, indicate that the findings obtained with the Basic Analysis Sample in many instances show the same trends as those of the more representative Survey Sample. Such agreement was encouraging to the effort to describe teachers and to study conditions related to major teacher characteristics.

Bibliography

1. COCHRAN, W. G.; MOSTELLER, F.; and TUKEY, J. W. "Principles of Sampling," *Journal of the American Statistical Association*, 49: 13–35, 1953.
2. NATIONAL EDUCATION ASSOCIATION. *The Status of the American Public School Teacher*. (NEA Research Bulletin, Vol. 35, No. 1.) Washington: The Association, 1957.

4. Patterns of Teacher Classroom Behavior and Their Assessment

THIS CHAPTER reports the experiences and procedures of the Teacher Characteristics Study with respect to (1) the designation of major dimensions or criteria of teacher classroom behavior and components of those criteria, and (2) the collection of criterion data for elementary and secondary school teachers comprising the Basic Analysis Sample.

In attacking the first of these problems, the interaction of the rational and empirical approaches will be noted. Intensive study was made of the literature covering the function of the teacher as seen from various educational viewpoints, and of previous research undertaken in the areas of human personality and particularly teacher personnel. Reports of critical incidents of teacher behavior were accumulated and analyzed. Assessments of teacher behavior on a number of first-order dimensions (hypothesized in the light of teacher traits suggested by the literature and by reported critical incidents) were obtained and factor-analyzed. And, finally, the patterns of teacher classroom behavior, in the light of which much of the Study was conducted, were described.

In obtaining estimates of teacher classroom behavior, systematic observation and immediate assessment of ongoing teacher behavior by trained observers were employed. This approach was adopted in view of the fact that it appeared to be less subject to biasing conditions and lack of control than were other methods (see chapter 2). It also was more practicable. With all the attractiveness of judgment of teacher behavior from its products (e.g., pupil change) and perhaps of the collection of pupil opinions about their teachers' behavior, the disadvantages of such approaches seemed to outweigh their advantages. Furthermore, it was reasoned that systematic observation by trained observers also could be employed to obtain estimates of pupil behavior—the immediate product of teacher behavior. Thus, data on teacher performance could be obtained from the standpoint of both behavior in process and the immediate products of teacher behavior, utilizing the procedure which seemed to suffer least from potential biasing conditions and impracticability.

The Observer and the Observation Process

The success of direct observation and assessment for the identification and estimation of behavior characteristics depends to a very great extent upon the ability of the observer to perceive accurately, upon the degree to which the procedures employed in observing and assessing behavior may be objectified and standardized, and upon the extent to which significant aspects of the situation or behavior under study may be identified and sampled. How to select potentially competent observers, how to achieve standardized observer performance, what assessment procedures to employ, and how to sample behavior in a natural social situation were important questions for the Teacher Characteristics Study.

QUALITIES ASSOCIATED WITH EFFICIENT OBSERVATION

In the literature [3, 26, 27, among others] attention frequently has been called to the variability of individuals in their efficiency as observers[1] or judges of behavior characteristics of other persons, and consequently to the need for careful selection of observers in the light of personal traits conducive to competent observation. For satisfactory observation, such characteristics of the observer as the following might reasonably be assumed to be essential: (a) sensory acuity; (b) perceptual speed; (c) general mental alertness; (d) the ability to observe and recall details (perhaps involving good imagery); (e) understanding and acceptance of the definitions of behaviors to be observed; (f) ability to maintain attention—not easily distracted by nonessentials; (g) familiarity with the behaviors to be observed; and, certainly, (h) ability to set aside personal predispositions and biases which might influence perception of the behaviors to be observed.

NEED FOR OBSERVER TRAINING

Much of the ambiguity of the data based upon direct observation and assessment appears to arise from the lack of common understanding and procedure on the part of different observers. Recognizing the varying experiential backgrounds of different persons which predispose them to perceive the same behavior in different ways, and also considering the semantic difficulties that militate against common agreement on the operational or behavioral meaning of a trait name, it would seem that any substantial agreement among untrained observers seldom could be expected except by chance.

Therefore, in addition to the needs for careful selection of observers and operational definitions of the criterion components, the requirement that observers be carefully trained is inescapable for competent observation and assessment of behavior. Furthermore, once the observer has

---

[1] Usually judged by interrater agreement.

undergone a program of training, it cannot be assumed that his observational procedures will remain uniform over a period of time without occasional check-ups and retraining; rather, it is necessary to reinstitute training at regular intervals to ensure that there has been no shift in the definition and perception of the behaviors being observed.

Observer training involves, first, the provision of information, and its understanding by the observer, regarding the behaviors to be observed and assessed, and second, practice in observing, followed by discussion and comparison of procedures and assessments of a particular observer with those of other observers. During the training period it is necessary to repeat this procedure a number of times and to continue the training until approximate agreement among the observers is obtained.

The first stage of training consists primarily of study and discussion of the operational definitions of the behaviors under consideration. Practice in observing (involving observation, assessment, comparison, and discussion) is directed at the development of the ability to perceive and to record perceptions accurately in a specific situation, and has as its goal consistency of assessment.

In the training process, observations first were made of the same teacher simultaneously (although independently) by two or more observers-in-training, with subsequent comparison and discussion of various aspects of the observing and assessment processes and with particular attention being given to discrepancies in assessments made by different observers. In later phases of the training, observations of the same teacher were made at different times by different observers-in-training, the observations again being followed by comparison of assessment data and discussion of observer variance.

THE ASSESSMENT PROCESS

The observation of behavior always has as its goal either verbal or quantitative behavior descriptions. Both kinds of descriptions may be regarded as assessments. But the quantitative estimates are more useful to the researcher, since they permit comparisons to be made with known probability distributions. In reporting the research of this study, the term "assessment" is used to refer to quantitative descriptions.

The processes of observation and assessment are interdependent, and the relative success or failure of the method of direct observation can be judged only in terms of the resulting assessments. In turn, the success of the assessments depends upon the appropriateness, efficiency, and practicability of the assessment devices employed and the skill with which they are used by observers.

Various kinds of assessment recording devices have been utilized in behavioral studies (graphic rating scales, behavior check lists, multiple-choice questionnaires, man-to-man rating scales, and paired-comparison scales, etc.), ranging from those intended to provide only global, non-analytical evaluations of very complex behavior patterns to others at the opposite extreme which seek to analyze and dissect behavior into specific acts and to provide frequency counts of such acts.

The question of the type of assessment recording device which is most effective has been discussed at considerable length in the literature. There is little evidence of the superiority of a particular type of instrument, but apparently advantages can be gained by making an analytical approach to assessment, instead of trying to evaluate very broad areas of behavior. It is interesting to note that one well-designed research study [3] directed at a number of problems relating to the methodology of ratings recently reported little differences in validity resulting from the use of several different rating techniques, and showed that the *rater* seemed to be of substantially more importance than the particular *rating technique* used.

Obviously, the adoption of an assessment device is closely related to the designation of significant criterion components. Regardless of the particular device employed, its effectiveness will depend to a very large extent on how clearly the behaviors involved are defined—how well general and abstract trait names are explained in terms of observable behaviors requiring a minimum of inference. To this end, a carefully compiled glossary is a primary requirement.

Other considerations relative to the assessment device employed bear upon the measurement "scale" it incorporates. Questions involved here are: (1) the scope or range of the scale and (2) the psychological equivalence of the intervals. Scales utilizing a moderate number of categories (four to eleven) seem to show some superiority over those having either very many or only two or three intervals. While certain advantages theoretically may be gained by the use of a device which has been precisely psychophysically scaled (which meets, or approximates, the requirements of the definition of a measurement *scale*), reports of experiences comparing such instruments with more statistically crude and arbitrary ones leave room for considerable doubt regarding the value which is added.

Still another aspect of assessment concerns the number of observations required to obtain composite assessments of behavior of sufficiently high reliability, and the related problem of the method of combining independent assessments to form a composite.

The rationale for the replication of observations and assessments is clear. Observations and assessments, at their best, are subject to observer bias; also, the behavior observed cannot be expected to be completely consistent from one situation or one observation period to another. One way of taking these factors into account is by averaging them out—by replicating the observations and assessments and combining the several independently obtained sets of data into a composite assessment.

The combination of assessments into a composite theoretically poses a problem. Appropriate means of combining ratings, taking into account the reliability and validity of the judges, have been suggested [*13*, for example]. However, there is no conclusive evidence to show that taking into account whether an observer is a hard or easy rater, or a reliable or unreliable rater, adds appreciably to the usefulness of the composite assessment. This appeared to be borne out by the experience of this Study, and the position is supported by other reports in the literature. Lawshe and Nagle [*17*] write that they are " . . . forced to conclude that much of the time and effort spent in determining the reliabilities of raters and combining their ratings into differential weights is for naught." Lawshe and Nagle observed that even where large differences in the reliability of raters existed, the elimination of the very low rater did not seem to improve the composite reliability [*17*, p. 273]. Perhaps it is not amiss to convert the raw assessment data of different observers to comparable standard deviation units before combination, but additional attention to the differential weighting of observers' assessments seems to provide little gain.

In summary, it may be noted that the reliability and validity of assessments made from direct observations of behavior are enhanced by: (1) attention to the selection of a limited number of relevant behavior dimensions for observation and assessment; (2) the provision of specific and unequivocal operational definitions of the behaviors to be assessed; (3) the observer being well acquainted with the behaviors to be assessed and with the situations in which the behaviors frequently are manifest; (4) the observer focusing his attention on the specified behaviors and carefully avoiding the influence of general impressions, unusual or dramatic behaviors, and inferences about what behaviors might occur in unobserved situations; (5) the immediate assessment of the behavior, during or shortly following observations; (6) the independent assessment of each specified behavior; (7) the recognition and suppression by the observer of personal biases relative to individuals or behaviors; (8) care on the part of the observer to avoid such rating biases as the central tendency error, the leniency error, etc.; and (9) the replication of observations and assessments by independent, though similarly trained, observers.

THE SITUATION OBSERVED

Direct observation may have as its object the behavior of (1) an isolated individual in a controlled, nonsocial situation, (2) an isolated individual in a natural, or nonlaboratory, nonsocial situation, (3) a particular individual in a controlled social situation, (4) a particular individual in a natural social situation, (5) a group of individuals in a controlled situation, or (6) a group of individuals in a natural, nonlaboratory, situation.

So far as the study of teacher behavior is concerned, we are, as noted in chapter 2, primarily concerned with item 4 above, a particular individual in a natural social situation, and also, insofar as teacher behavior may be considered to be reflected by pupil behavior, with item 6, a group of individuals in a natural situation.

In the observational situation, the problem of the sampling of behavior is important. The use of direct observation and assessment assumes that during the course of observation the behaviors observed will constitute a representative or a random sample of the universe of behaviors for the individuals or groups in question. The extent to which this assumption may be valid will depend upon a number of conditions, such as, (1) the normal frequency of occurrence of a particular behavior, (2) the amount of time devoted to observation and the number of observation periods conducted, (3) the extent to which the behavior observed may be influenced by the presence of the observer, and (4) the reliability or consistency of the behavior under consideration.

In the observation and assessment of teacher behavior it is necessary to keep in mind that teacher behaviors occur in relation to pupil behavior and therefore may be expected to vary to some extent from one group of pupils to another, and also that teacher behavior is a function of the content or subject matter taught—e.g., behaviors manifested by an elementary teacher while engaged in arithmetic instruction may differ from those demonstrated during a class in music or rhythms. Although such conditions have an attenuating effect on assessments of teacher behavior, they are integral parts of the teaching situation, and, in the interest of preserving the naturalness of the behavior under study, it would seem desirable not to attempt to eliminate or control such conditions, but rather to replicate the observations and observational situations in order to provide as broad and comprehensive an assessment basis as possible.

The Study Approach: An Overview

Through (1) a review of the literature on the organization of human personality and on traits hypothesized to be desirable for teachers, (2) assembly of reports of "critical incidents" observed in the classroom performance of teachers and subsequent determination of relevant first-order teacher behavior dimensions, (3) the assessment, with respect to such dimensions, of the classroom behavior of large numbers of elementary and secondary school teachers, and (4) statistical analysis of the teacher behavior assessments, the Teacher Characteristics Study identified three major clusters of observable teacher behaviors which were accorded primary attention throughout the research and which served as criteria in the efforts of the Study to determine correlates of teacher behavior in the classroom. These three principal dimensions, or criteria, of teacher classroom behavior were:

TCS Pattern X_o: understanding, friendly vs. aloof, egocentric, restricted teacher behavior

TCS Pattern Y_o: responsible, businesslike, systematic vs. evading, unplanned, slipshod teacher behavior

TCS Pattern Z_o: stimulating, imaginative, surgent or enthusiastic vs. dull, routine teacher behavior

The steps leading to the designation and description of these patterns will be recounted in the following paragraphs.

Original Selection of Specific Teacher Behaviors

A first consideration in research directed at the description and understanding of behavior is concerned with the question, "What specific data are relevant to the area of behavior under investigation?" In seeking a framework or context which might provide a starting point for the research of the Study, two general approaches were employed. First, extensive and intensive review of the literature was undertaken with particular attention to (a) research reports, and also statements of opinion, which sought to define the essential characteristics of teaching or to list qualities believed to be desirable in teachers and contributive to good teaching, and (b) studies which attempted to describe and analyze human personality. Second, clues were sought to critical teacher behaviors in the reports of specific classroom incidents which, in the view of the reporters, described teacher acts that had contributed to outstandingly good or poor teaching performance.

SELECTION OF BEHAVIORS FROM THOSE MENTIONED IN THE LITERATURE

All available teacher rating scales were studied with attention to the teacher traits and characteristics incorporated in them, and common or frequently appearing elements of the various devices were noted. The findings of the Commonwealth Teacher Training Study [5] were examined with care. Similarly, the fairly numerous, but unfortunately generally inadequate, investigations of teacher competency,[2] or teacher effectiveness, were analyzed, and suggestions of desirable teacher behaviors were sought. Reports of factor analyses of personality traits were reviewed and particular consideration was given to Cattell's attempt to describe the structure of personality [4]. (Although published subsequent to the design of the Teacher Characteristics Study, French's summary of factor analyses of personality measurements [11] was examined with interest when it appeared, and it served as a backdrop against which the results of the Study's research could be viewed.)

Analysis of these reports, made in as objective and eclectic a manner as possible and with attention to the similarity and frequency of mention of various teacher characteristics, revealed some forty-six seemingly relevant characteristics which might reasonably be hypothesized to contribute to a description of the classroom behavior of teachers with particular emphasis upon teacher-pupil relationships.

In selecting relevant teacher behaviors to be included in this preliminary list, a number of criteria were employed by the Study. The limiting conditions, or criteria, for inclusion of a behavior in this preliminary list were: (1) the behavior should be within the *personal-social* domain; (2) the behavior should be one for which there is considerable evidence, preferably both logical and empirical, of its *relation to teaching;* (3) the behavior should be one that can be conceptualized in *dimensional* form— describable in terms of the extremes or poles of a behavior dimension (e.g., stimulating . . . dull); (4) the behavior should be describable in *unambiguous* terms; (5) the behavior should be *observable* (either observable teacher acts, or possibly observable pupil acts in response to teacher acts); (6) the behavior should be capable of description, and of observation and assessment, in terms of *specific acts or performances* (as contrasted with general or abstract behavior descriptions); (7) the behavior, insofar as it is possible to judge, should be relatively *independent* of other behaviors included in the list (obviously overlapping behaviors should be avoided); (8) insofar as possible, the behavior should be equally applicable to teachers in *different kinds of school situations*

---

[2] Several summaries of the research on teacher effectiveness are available. One of the most adequate is that of Morsh and Wilder [19].

(group activities, individual activities, social studies instruction, arithmetic instruction, etc.); and (9) selection of a behavior should be *independent of a particular philosophy* or theory of education (there should be no intentional selection of behaviors to conform to a particular educational philosophy).

CRITICAL BEHAVIORS IN TEACHING

In determining the teacher classroom behaviors to be considered in observation and assessment, a second line of attack employed by the Study consisted of collecting "critical incidents" of teaching, or critical behaviors of teachers [9, 15], reports of such incidents being submitted by persons closely associated with teaching, and being based upon first-hand knowledge of acts of teachers in specific situations.

A "critical incident" was defined as any observable teacher behavior or act which might make the difference between success or failure in some specified teaching situation. The approach intentionally excluded those aspects of teaching which seem to show relatively small variance among teachers so far as acceptability or inacceptability is concerned. It sought to note only those behaviors which seem to differentiate between extreme teacher groups.

Thus, the procedure followed in investigating critical behaviors of teachers involved collecting analytical reports of what the respondents considered to be especially effective or ineffective classroom behaviors of unnamed teachers. The reports were provided by teacher supervisors, training teachers, school principals, teachers, student teachers, and students in education methods courses in a teacher-training institution.

Critical incidents of teaching may be formally collected or they may be assembled on the basis of informal interview. The latter process is most useful in exploratory stages of a study. Early in this research study, for example, personal inquiries were made of selected persons, largely older adults of considerable educational experience, during which each was asked to attempt to recall the "very best" and "very poorest" teachers he had had when in school and, further, to describe some incident or something outstanding that was remembered over the years about that teacher. Although such a procedure is useful in providing clues, its usefulness is likely to be limited by restricted sampling and the lack of readily comparable data. Therefore, in order to formalize and systematize the critical teacher behavior study, the use of a TCS Critical Incidents Blank was introduced. Suggestions from the reports of Flanagan and his co-workers at the American Institute for Research [9], who have made extensive use of the critical incidents technique and have explored many of its possibilities, provided the basis for the development of such a blank upon which critical incidents relative to teaching might be recorded.

Prior to the writing of the descriptions of critical teacher behaviors by participants in this preliminary phase of the Study, the characteristics of usable critical incidents were pointed out and illustrated by example. Participants were specifically cautioned that a critical incident description was *not* usable if it (*a*) merely named or listed traits or behavior categories believed to characterize the teacher in question, or (*b*) reported a behavior which impressed the reporter primarily because it was personally acceptable or personally irritating or annoying to him, or (*c*) simply reflected general stereotyped ideas of what is considered effective or ineffective in teaching, rather than describing specific behavior in relation to a situation in which it occurred, or (*d*) reported a behavior which had impressed the reporter primarily because of its dramatic qualities.

Rather, it was pointed out that a critical incident description to be usable for the Study *must* (*a*) describe teacher behavior actually observed in a specific situation, (*b*) provide an accurate, detailed description of specific acts, (*c*) be an objective, unbiased report of the behavior, and (*d*) relate to a behavior believed by the reporter to be either clearly effective or clearly ineffective. It was emphasized that a critical incident should describe *what some teacher did in a specific situation at a specific time.*

The participants were asked to respond to six situations or questions, each printed on a separate page of the TCS Critical Incidents Blank. The six sets of directions read as follows:

1. Think of the elementary or high school teachers with whom you have been closely associated recently. Of those teachers, think of the one teacher you consider most *ineffective.* The teacher you are thinking of probably did a lot of things which caused you to feel that he or she was ineffective, but what was the particular incident that stands out in your mind as a clearcut example of ineffectiveness? Describe the situation and just what the teacher did that convinced you of his ineffectiveness on the job. What specific act demonstrated the teacher's ineffectiveness?

2. Think of the most *effective* elementary or high school teacher with whom you have been closely associated recently. The person you have in mind probably did many things that convinced you that he or she was effective, but what was some outstanding act which made you consider him especially effective? Describe some specific thing that he did that makes him stand out in your mind as being particularly effective on the job.

3. Think over the past month or two and recall the last time you observed a teacher in elementary or high school do something especially *ineffective*

(it need not have been done by a generally ineffective person). Just what was done on this particular occasion? What was the act? What did the teacher do?

4. Think over the last month or two and recall the last time you observed any teacher do something especially *effective*. Just what was done on this particular occasion? What was the act? What did the teacher do?

5. Think back about the teachers you had when in elementary and high school. Try to think of the most *ineffective* teacher you ever had. Now try to recall some specific incident that stands out in your memory as an illustration of the ineffectiveness of this teacher. What was the situation? What did the teacher do?

6. Think back about the teachers you had when in elementary and high school. Try to think of the most *effective* teacher you had. Now try to recall a specific incident that stands out in your memory as an illustration of the effectiveness of this teacher. What was the situation? What did the teacher do?

Following the preparation and submission of the reports, they were reviewed in the light of a set of criteria developed to provide assurance that each behavior surviving the review was clearly described, that it seemed to be an individual response of the teacher (rather than one directly attributable to professional training, requirements of the school system, etc.), and that it was something a teacher did in a specific classroom situation. Following the review, each objective description of a specific teacher behavior was transcribed to a separate record card which carried certain identification information, a summary statement of the specific teacher behavior reported, a summary description of the situation in which the behavior occurred, and identification of the behavior as effective or ineffective.

The final phase of the critical behaviors study, involving sorting the record cards and classifying the reported incidents into appropriate categories, was carried out in the following five steps: (1) identification of the salient features in each incident of teacher behavior reported; (2) derivation of a rough classification scheme for the reported incidents to facilitate ordering of the data; (3) classification of each critical behavior into one of these categories; (4) derivation of a generalized descriptive statement covering each category; and (5) final refinement of the classification scheme and preparation of generalized descriptions of the principal classes of teacher behaviors.

The more than 500 critical incidents submitted by participants in this study were reduced to the following list of generalized behaviors, which seemed to summarize adequately the original specific behavior descriptions.

GENERALIZED DESCRIPTIONS OF CRITICAL BEHAVIORS OF TEACHERS

Effective Behaviors	*Ineffective Behaviors*
1. Alert, appears enthusiastic.	1. Is apathetic, dull, appears bored.
2. Appears interested in pupils and classroom activities.	2. Appears uninterested in pupils and classroom activities.
3. Cheerful, optimistic.	3. Is depressed, pessimistic; appears unhappy.
4. Self-controlled, not easily upset.	4. Looses temper, is easily upset.
5. Likes fun, has a sense of humor.	5. Is overly serious, too occupied for humor.
6. Recognizes and admits own mistakes.	6. Is unaware of, or fails to admit, own mistakes.
7. Is fair, impartial, and objective in treatment of pupils.	7. Is unfair or partial in dealing with pupils.
8. Is patient.	8. Is impatient.
9. Shows understanding and sympathy in working with pupils.	9. Is short with pupils, uses sarcastic remarks, or in other ways shows lack of sympathy with pupils.
10. Is friendly and courteous in relations with pupils.	10. Is aloof and removed in relations with pupils.
11. Helps pupils with personal as well as educational problems.	11. Seems unaware of pupils' personal needs and problems.
12. Commends effort and gives praise for work well done.	12. Does not commend pupils, is disapproving, hypercritical.
13. Accepts pupils' efforts as sincere.	13. Is suspicious of pupil motives.
14. Anticipates reactions of others in social situations.	14. Does not anticipate reactions of others in social situations.
15. Encourages pupils to try to do their best.	15. Makes no effort to encourage pupils to try to do their best.
16. Classroom procedure is planned and well organized.	16. Procedure is without plan, disorganized.
17. Classroom procedure is flexible within over-all plan.	17. Shows extreme rigidity of procedure, inability to depart from plan.
18. Anticipates individual needs.	18. Fails to provide for individual differences and needs of pupils.
19. Stimulates pupils through interesting and original materials and techniques.	19. Uninteresting materials and teaching techniques used.
20. Conducts clear, practical demonstrations and explanations.	20. Demonstrations and explanations are not clear and are poorly conducted.
21. Is clear and thorough in giving directions.	21. Directions are incomplete, vague.
22. Encourages pupils to work through their own problems and evaluate their accomplishments.	22. Fails to give pupils opportunity to work out own problems or evaluate their own work.
23. Disciplines in quiet, dignified, and positive manner.	23. Reprimands at length, ridicules, resorts to cruel or meaningless forms of correction.
24. Gives help willingly.	24. Fails to give help or gives it grudgingly.
25. Foresees and attempts to resolve potential difficulties.	25. Is unable to foresee and resolve potential difficulties.

In attempting to determine relevant and important areas of teacher behavior that might be studied empirically, considerable emphasis was placed by the Study on the foregoing list of behaviors derived from the collection of critical teaching incidents. It was felt that this approach to the identification and description of significant teacher behaviors was basically more sound than the frequently employed procedure of asking educators or others to name the traits or qualities they believe to be desirable for teachers. Needless to say, employment of this approach, with its emphasis upon actual behavior, neither circumvents nor denies the importance of value judgments in designating important aspects of teacher behavior. However, the critical incidents technique does represent an effort to determine the bases of value judgments, to objectify descriptions of teacher behavior, and to provide an operational frame of references for the assessment of teacher behavior.

Development of an Assessment Procedure and Record

Having developed preliminary lists of (*a*) teacher behaviors frequently cited in the literature and (*b*) significant behaviors of teachers generalized from reports of critical incidents, the problem faced by the Study was that of selecting the best method for collecting data relating to these behaviors. As already noted, it had previously been decided that criterion data would be obtained through direct observation and assessment, since such an approach seemed to be more feasible and less susceptible to biasing conditions than others that might be employed. The immediate task, therefore, was to devise an *assessment record* and an appropriate glossary describing behaviorally and operationally the dimensions listed on the assessment blank.

After reviewing the different kinds of rating devices that might be employed, a form was adopted that was similar to the one used by The Grant Study (Harvard University Department of Hygiene, "Studies in the Relation of Personality to Field of Work") in the investigation of means of selecting candidates for Army and Navy officer training [*28*].

The assessment procedure assumed that many personal-social traits of teachers may be hypothesized to constitute dimensions, the opposite extreme poles of which can be described operationally with considerable precision.

The dimensions that were chosen for use in this Study were derived from the previously described lists of significant teacher behaviors. In selecting the behavior dimensions to be included on the assessment record, each potential dimension was reviewed in the light of the criteria referred to on pages 78–79. The resulting assessment blank came to be known as the Classroom Observation Record.

As noted earlier, effective employment of direct observation and assessment requires thorough training of observers in understanding and identifying the behaviors under consideration. The guide for such training, and for observation and assessment in practice, was provided by a Glossary that listed specific teacher behaviors exemplifying the various first-order dimensions included in the Classroom Observation Record.

The Classroom Observation Record underwent a number of revisions in the process of its development. The first form to be tried out covered forty dimensions of teacher behavior and six dimensions of pupil behavior. It was found to be unwieldy, to include some closely overlapping dimensions, and to refer to certain behaviors that in practice observers had little or no opportunity to assess. Successive revisions represented modifications made in light of the experiences of the staff of observers and statistical analyses of resulting assessments of teacher behavior during the procedures-development stage of the Teacher Characteristics Study.

At one stage in the development of the Record an effort was made to reduce the assessment procedure to the tabulation of the frequency with which each of the specific behaviors (such as those included in the Glossary) was observed for a particular teacher. Tabulation by the observer was followed by the assignment of scale values in accordance with a prearranged scoring system which took into account the relative frequency of behaviors representing the opposite poles of a particular dimension. A number of scoring systems for such a check-list approach were derived and tried out, but the technique proved cumbersome and less reliable, as judged by interobserver correlations, than the earlier-used estimation procedure. The apparent objectivity of a check-list approach makes it particularly attractive, and the results obtained in this type of attempt to assess teacher behavior was disappointing to the staff of the Study.[3] Use of check lists, therefore, was discarded in favor of the more intuitive procedure, standardized and controlled through use of the Glossary and by training of the observers, but nevertheless

---

[3] It is encouraging that studies recently conducted with Air Force instructional personnel have been successful in developing relatively short check lists, which can be objectively scored, relating to instructor behavior and student behavior. Validation of the check-list data against criteria such as student ratings, supervisor ratings, and student gains suggests their practicability, at least in the kind of situations involved in the particular Air Force courses under consideration. Generally, check-list items concerned with instructor behaviors tended to be related to criterion data provided by supervisors' ratings, and check-list items referring to student behaviors, especially inattentive behavior, tended to be correlated with the "student gains" criterion.

relying upon a less objective summing-up of specific behaviors in arriving at an assessment.

Early forms of the Record required assessments to be made relative to a particular behavior dimension on a bipolar scale consisting of four intervals, or categories, plus a fifth "no opportunity for observation" category. Intervals 1 and 4 were used to indicate marked occurrence of behaviors exemplifying one of the two poles of the dimension; intervals 2 and 3 were used to indicate noteworthy but less marked occurrence of the behaviors.

The form of the Record employed during the major portion of the research utilized a seven-point, or seven-interval, scale. Observers were found to be quite capable of making the discriminations required by a seven-category scale, and the increased spread of scale values appeared to increase slightly the reliability of the assessments.

Separate elementary teacher and secondary teacher Classroom Observation Records, covering respectively twenty-six (twenty teacher and six pupil behaviors) and twenty-five (twenty-one teacher behaviors and four pupil behaviors) similar but not identical dimensions, were used for the observation of more than 600 teachers during the early stages of the Study. Experience indicated, however, that while teacher behaviors at the elementary and secondary levels differ in setting, they do not appear to differ greatly in kind, and that it was not only feasible but also desirable to employ a single assessment form for both groups.

During the fall of 1951, the forms of the Record in use at that time were extensively studied and the final revision was accomplished, resulting in what was believed to be a superior instrument for the purposes of the Study. The dimensions of teacher behavior covered by the final form represented only minor revisions of those of the separate elementary and secondary forms of the assessment instrument, and comparability with the immediately preceding forms was readily achieved. The Glossary of teacher behaviors was slightly extended and revised in an effort to make it more explicit and useful to the observer. The final form of the Classroom Observation Record, incorporating eighteen teacher behavior dimensions and four pupil behavior dimensions, is shown in Figure 4. The complete Glossary, providing examples of the specific behaviors contributing to the polar descriptions of the first-order dimensions, is shown in the list that follows Figure 4.

CLASSROOM OBSERVATION RECORD
9-22-51
TEACHER CHARACTERISTICS STUDY

Teacher................................ No.......... Sex.......... Class or Subject.............. Date..........

City.................................. School.............. Time.......... Observer..........

PUPIL BEHAVIOR   REMARKS:

1. Apathetic	1	2	3	4	5	6	7	N	Alert
2. Obstructive	1	2	3	4	5	6	7	N	Responsible
3. Uncertain	1	2	3	4	5	6	7	N	Confident
4. Dependent	1	2	3	4	5	6	7	N	Initiating

TEACHER BEHAVIOR

5. Partial	1	2	3	4	5	6	7	N	Fair
6. Autocratic	1	2	3	4	5	6	7	N	Democratic
7. Aloof	1	2	3	4	5	6	7	N	Responsive
8. Restricted	1	2	3	4	5	6	7	N	Understanding
9. Harsh	1	2	3	4	5	6	7	N	Kindly
10. Dull	1	2	3	4	5	6	7	N	Stimulating
11. Stereotyped	1	2	3	4	5	6	7	N	Original
12. Apathetic	1	2	3	4	5	6	7	N	Alert
13. Unimpressive	1	2	3	4	5	6	7	N	Attractive
14. Evading	1	2	3	4	5	6	7	N	Responsible
15. Erratic	1	2	3	4	5	6	7	N	Steady
16. Excitable	1	2	3	4	5	6	7	N	Poised
17. Uncertain	1	2	3	4	5	6	7	N	Confident
18. Disorganized	1	2	3	4	5	6	7	N	Systematic
19. Inflexible	1	2	3	4	5	6	7	N	Adaptable
20. Pessimistic	1	2	3	4	5	6	7	N	Optimistic
21. Immature	1	2	3	4	5	6	7	N	Integrated
22. Narrow	1	2	3	4	5	6	7	N	Broad

FIG. 4.—Assessment blank employed by observers.

GLOSSARY

(*To be used with Classroom Observation Record*)

PUPIL BEHAVIORS

1. Apathetic-Alert Pupil Behavior

Apathetic	*Alert*
1. Listless.	1. Appeared anxious to recite and participate.
2. Bored-acting.	
3. Entered into activities half-heartedly.	2. Watched teacher attentively.
4. Restless.	3. Worked concentratedly.
5. Attention wandered.	4. Seemed to respond eagerly.
6. Slow in getting under way.	5. Prompt and ready to take part in activities when they begin.

2. Obstructive-Responsible Pupil Behavior

Obstructive

1. Rude to one another and/or to teacher.
2. Interrupting; demanding attention; disturbing.
3. Obstinate; sullen.
4. Refusal to participate.
5. Quarrelsome; irritable.
6. Engaged in name-calling and/or tattling.
7. Unprepared.

Responsible

1. Courteous, cooperative, friendly with each other and with teacher.
2. Completed assignments without complaining or unhappiness.
3. Controlled voices.
4. Received help and criticism attentively.
5. Asked for help when needed.
6. Orderly without specific directions from teacher.
7. Prepared.

3. Uncertain-Confident Pupil Behavior

Uncertain

1. Seemed afraid to try; unsure.
2. Hesitant; restrained.
3. Appeared embarrassed.
4. Frequent display of nervous habits, nail-biting, etc.
5. Appeared shy and timid.
6. Hesitant and/or stammering speech.

Confident

1. Seemed anxious to try new problems or activities.
2. Undisturbed by mistakes.
3. Volunteered to recite.
4. Entered freely into activities.
5. Appeared relaxed.
6. Spoke with assurance.

4. Dependent-Initiating Pupil Behavior

Dependent

1. Relied on teacher for explicit directions.
2. Showed little ability to work things out for selves.
3. Unable to proceed when initiative called for.
4. Appeared reluctant to take lead or to accept responsibility.

Initiating

1. Volunteered ideas and suggestions.
2. Showed resourcefulness.
3. Took lead willingly.
4. Assumed responsibilities without evasion.

TEACHER BEHAVIORS

5. Partial-Fair Teacher Behavior

Partial

1. Repeatedly slighted a pupil.
2. Corrected or criticized certain pupils repeatedly.
3. Repeatedly gave a pupil special advantages.
4. Gave most attention to one or a few pupils.
5. Showed prejudice (favorable or unfavorable) toward some social, racial, or religious groups.
6. Expressed suspicion of motives of a pupil.

Fair

1. Treated all pupils approximately equally.
2. In case of controversy pupil allowed to explain his side.
3. Distributed attention to many pupils.
4. Rotated leadership impartially.
5. Based criticism or praise on factual evidence, not hearsay.

6. Autocratic-Democratic Teacher Behavior

Autocratic

1. Told pupils each step to take.
2. Intolerant of pupils' ideas.
3. Mandatory in giving directions; orders to be obeyed at once.
4. Interrupted pupils although their discussion was relevant.
5. Always directed rather than participated.

Democratic

1. Guided pupils without being mandatory.
2. Exchanged ideas with pupils.
3. Encouraged (asked for) pupil opinion.
4. Encouraged pupils to make own decisions.
5. Entered into activities without domination.

7. Aloof-Responsive Teacher Behavior

Aloof

1. Stiff and formal in relations with pupils.
2. Apart; removed from class activity.
3. Condescending to pupils.
4. Routine and subject matter only concern; pupils as persons ignored.
5. Referred to pupil as "this child" or "that child."

Responsive

1. Approachable to all pupils.
2. Participated in class activity.
3. Responded to reasonable requests and/or questions.
4. Spoke to pupils as equals.
5. Commended effort.
6. Gave encouragement.
7. Recognized individual differences.

8. Restricted-Understanding Teacher Behavior

Restricted

1. Recognized only academic accomplishments of pupils; no concern for personal problems.
2. Completely unsympathetic with a pupil's failure at a task.
3. Called attention only to very good or very poor work.
4. Was impatient with a pupil.

Understanding

1. Showed awareness of a pupil's personal emotional problems and needs.
2. Was tolerant of error on part of pupil.
3. Patient with a pupil beyond ordinary limits of patience.
4. Showed what appeared to be sincere sympathy with a pupil's viewpoint.

9. Harsh-Kindly Teacher Behavior

Harsh

1. Hypercritical; fault-finding.
2. Cross; curt.
3. Depreciated pupil's efforts; was sarcastic.
4. Scolded a great deal.
5. Lost temper.
6. Used threats.
7. Permitted pupils to laugh at mistakes of others.

Kindly

1. Went out of way to be pleasant and/or to help pupils; friendly.
2. Gave a pupil a deserved compliment.
3. Found good things in pupils to call attention to.
4. Seemed to show sincere concern for a pupil's personal problem.
5. Showed affection without being demonstrative.
6. Disengaged self from a pupil without bluntness.

10. Dull-Stimulating Teacher Behavior

Dull

1. Uninteresting, monotonous explanations.
2. Assignments provided little or no motivation.
3. Failed to provide challenge.
4. Lacked animation.
5. Failed to capitalize on pupil interests.
6. Pedantic, boring.
7. Lacked enthusiasm; bored-acting.

Stimulating

1. Highly interesting presentation; got and held attention without being flashy.
2. Clever and witty, though not smart-alecky or wisecracking.
3. Enthusiastic; animated.
4. Assignments challenging.
5. Took advantage of pupil interests.
6. Brought lesson successfully to a climax.
7. Seemed to provoke thinking.

11. Stereotyped-Original Teacher Behavior

Stereotyped

1. Used routine procedures without variation.
2. Would not depart from procedure to take advantage of a relevant question or situation.
3. Presentation seemed unimaginative.
4. Not resourceful in answering questions or providing explanations.

Original

1. Used what seemed to be original and relatively unique devices to aid instruction.
2. Tried new materials or methods.
3. Seemed imaginative and able to develop presentation around a question or situation.
4. Resourceful in answering questions; had many pertinent illustrations available.

12. Apathetic-Alert Teacher Behavior

Apathetic

1. Seemed listless; languid; lacked enthusiasm.
2. Seemed bored by pupils.
3. Passive in response to pupils.
4. Seemed preoccupied.
5. Attention seemed to wander.
6. Sat in chair most of time; took no active part in class activities.

Alert

1. Appeared buoyant; wide-awake; enthusiastic about activity of the moment.
2. Kept constructively busy.
3. Gave attention to, and seemed interested in, what was going on in class.
4. Prompt to "pick up" class when pupils' attention showed signs of lagging.

13. Unimpressive-Attractive Teacher Behavior

Unimpressive

1. Untidy or sloppily dressed.
2. Inappropriately dressed.
3. Drab, colorless.
4. Posture and bearing unattractive.
5. Possessed distracting personal habits.
6. Mumbled; inaudible speech; limited expression; disagreeable voice tone; poor inflection.

Attractive

1. Clean and neat.
2. Well-groomed; dress showed good taste.
3. Posture and bearing attractive.
4. Free from distracting personal habits.
5. Plainly audible speech; good expression; agreeable voice tone; good inflection.

14. *Evading-Responsible Teacher Behavior*

Evading

1. Avoided responsibility; disinclined to make decisions.
2. "Passed the buck" to class, to other teachers, etc.
3. Left learning to pupil, failing to give adequate help.
4. Let a difficult situation get out of control.
5. Assignments and directions indefinite.
6. No insistence on either individual or group standards.
7. Inattentive with pupils.
8. Cursory.

Responsible

1. Assumed responsibility; made decisions as required.
2. Conscientious.
3. Punctual.
4. Painstaking; careful.
5. Suggested aids to learning.
6. Controlled a difficult situation.
7. Gave definite directions.
8. Called attention to standards of quality.
9. Attentive to class.
10. Thorough.

15. *Erratic-Steady Teacher Behavior*

Erratic

1. Impulsive; uncontrolled; temperamental; unsteady.
2. Course of action easily swayed by circumstances of the moment.
3. Inconsistent.

Steady

1. Calm; controlled.
2. Maintained progress toward objective.
3. Stable, consistent, predictable.

16. *Excitable-Poised Teacher Behavior*

Excitable

1. Easily disturbed and upset; flustered by classroom situation.
2. Hurried in class activities; spoke rapidly using many words and gestures.
3. Was "jumpy"; nervous.

Poised

1. Seemed at ease at all times.
2. Unruffled by situation that developed in classroom; dignified without being stiff or formal.
3. Unhurried in class activities; spoke quietly and slowly.
4. Successfully diverted attention from a stress situation in classroom.

17. *Uncertain-Confident Teacher Behavior*

Uncertain

1. Seemed unsure of self; faltering, hesitant.
2. Appeared timid and shy.
3. Appeared artificial.
4. Disturbed and embarrassed by mistakes and/or criticism.

Confident

1. Seemed sure of self; self-confident in relations with pupils.
2. Undisturbed and unembarrassed by mistakes and/or criticism.

18. Disorganized-Systematic Teacher Behavior

Disorganized

1. No plan for classwork.
2. Unprepared.
3. Objectives not apparent; undecided as to next step.
4. Wasted time.
5. Explanations not to the point.
6. Easily distracted from matter at hand.

Systematic

1. Evidence of a planned though flexible procedure.
2. Well prepared.
3. Careful in planning with pupils.
4. Systematic about procedure of class.
5. Had anticipated needs.
6. Provided reasonable explanations.
7. Held discussion together; objectives apparent.

19. Inflexible-Adaptable Teacher Behavior

Inflexible

1. Rigid in conforming to routine.
2. Made no attempt to adapt materials to individual pupils.
3. Appeared incapable of modifying explanation or activities to meet particular classroom situations.
4. Impatient with interruptions and digressions.

Adaptable

1. Flexible in adapting explanations.
2. Individualized materials for pupils as required; adapted activities to pupils.
3. Took advantage of pupils' questions to further clarify ideas.
4. Met an unusual classroom situation competently.

20. Pessimistic-Optimistic Teacher Behavior

Pessimistic

1. Depressed; unhappy.
2. Skeptical.
3. Called attention to potential "bad."
4. Expressed hopelessness of "education today," the school system, or fellow educators.
5. Noted mistakes; ignored good points.
6. Frowned a great deal; had unpleasant facial expression.

Optimistic

1. Cheerful; good-natured.
2. Genial.
3. Joked with pupils on occasion.
4. Emphasized potential "good."
5. Looked on bright side; spoke optimistically of the future.
6. Called attention to good points; emphasized the positive.

21. Immature-Integrated Teacher Behavior

Immature

1. Appeared naïve in approach to classroom situations.
2. Self-pitying; complaining; demanding.
3. Boastful; conceited.

Integrated

1. Maintained class as center of activity; kept self out of spotlight; referred to class's activities, not own.
2. Emotionally well controlled.

22. Narrow-Broad Teacher Behavior

Narrow	*Broad*
1. Presentation strongly suggested limited background in subject or material; lack of scholarship.	1. Presentation suggested good background in subject; good scholarship suggested.
2. Did not depart from text.	2. Drew examples and explanations from various sources and related fields.
3. Failed to enrich discussions with illustrations from related areas.	3. Showed evidence of broad cultural background in science, art, literature, history, etc.
4. Showed little evidence of breadth of cultural background in such areas as science, arts, literature, and history.	4. Gave satisfying, complete, and accurate answers to questions.
5. Answers to pupils' questions incomplete or inaccurate.	5. Was constructively critical in approach to subject matter.
6. Noncritical approach to subject.	

In using the Record, the observer made notes regarding specific behaviors and events transpiring during an observation and attempted to relate specific behaviors of a teacher (or her pupils) to those behaviors listed in the Glossary. Immediately following an observation, the observer summarized the teacher behaviors relative to a particular dimension of the Record by estimating the extent to which one or the other pole of the dimension was approximated by the behavior of the teacher in question. On the seven-point scale, marked occurrence of behaviors described by one or the other of the poles of a dimension were assigned assessments of 1 or 7, an assessment of four representing an average, or neutral, assessment on the dimension.

The Observers and Their Training

In preparing for the observation and assessment of teacher behavior, serious attention was given to the selection and training of observers. An effort was made to employ observers who met, insofar as possible, such qualifications as those described at the beginning of the chapter.

All observers employed were, first of all, persons with previous experience in teaching, preferably at both the elementary and secondary school levels. The majority were former teachers who were enrolled for graduate study in such areas as educational psychology, educational supervision, and educational administration. Both sexes were represented. Special attention was given to the selection of observers who, on the basis of interviews, and usually preliminary tryouts, appeared to be (1) above average with respect to the ability to attend and to perceive, (2) not only familiar with teacher behavior, but also interested in its analysis and assessment, (3) able and willing to set aside personal biases and to employ an objective approach to the dimensions of teacher behavior selected for study, (4) capable of making a good impression upon the teachers participating in the Study and able to put them at ease (which required considerable social skill), (5) above average in general ability, and (6) emotionally well adjusted.

Twenty-four observers were employed throughout the course of the Study. Only four of the observers served for more than one academic year. The observing crews varied in size from year to year, ranging from as few as two to as many as twelve.

With the frequently changing observer personnel, continuity was maintained largely through the employment of two senior observers, each of whom served through approximately one-half the period of the Study. The senior observers served, in a sense, as anchors. They were responsible not only for making local arrangements for observations and for conducting observations on their own part, but, particularly, for observer training.

Observers were trained both individually and in groups, the latter being the more frequent practice. The training procedure consisted of several phases, which may be summarized as follows: (1) the observer trainee met with the senior observer for briefing, review of the Record and Glossary, and discussion of the problems involved in direct observation and assessment; (2) the observer trainee studied the Record and Glossary at length; (3) the trainee and senior observer simultaneously observed a teacher for one class period and made independent assessments on copies of the Record; (4) the trainee met with the senior observer to discuss the observation just completed, to compare assessments, and to clarify the bases for assessments as given in the Glossary; (5) additional simultaneous observations and assessments were made by the trainee and senior observer, followed by further consultation; (6) in the final phase of training, the trainee and the senior observer made forty-five minute observations of the same teachers, but *at different times*, and subsequently conferred to compare and discuss the assessments made.

During the process of training, correlations between the assessments of the trainee and those of the senior observer were computed as a check upon the training. By the completion of training, observer reliability as measured by correlations of the trainee–senior observer assessments usually were between .8 and .9,[4] which signified substantial agreement.

Subsequent to training, the observers were given regular assignments

---

[4] This level of agreement was not usually maintained over an extended series of observations and assessments. Refresher training often was required.

for teacher observations. After a teacher had been rated by more than one observer, the assessments of pairs of observers were plotted on a scattergraph. These bivariate distributions were used for continuous observer-checking.

Observation and Assessment in Practice

Although the training and supervision of the observers by a senior observer and the use of the Glossary were intended to make the observation and assessment processes uniform and consistent, and although a considerable degree of equivalence actually was attained, it obviously would be unrealistic to assume that the concepts employed by the different observers in making assessments were invariant, or that the concepts did not shift from time to time with a particular observer. Several precautions were taken in the attempt to reduce such variance.

In the first place, the desirability of replicating observations and assessments was recognized. Through replication it was possible to take into account, in the aggregate at least, such sources of variability as sampling error (with respect to both the behavior universe of a particular teacher and the universe of classroom situations), systematic differences between types of classroom situations observed and teacher behavior in such situations, and systematic differences between observer sets and procedures.

As many as eight independent observations and assessments were made on one small group of teachers, but usually two, and occasionally three, observations and assessments were made of each teacher. In general, the literature and the experience of the Study indicated that the accuracy of assessments of behavior increases as the number of independent assessments is increased, but with successively diminishing returns, and, furthermore, that very high reliability appears to be unattainable even with a very large number of assessments.

The standard procedure finally adopted, therefore, called for two one-class period[5] observations of each teacher, the observations to be made at different times by different observers. The two independent assessments of a teacher's classroom behavior became the complete record for a teacher *provided* the two assessments did not show substantial discrepancy. If the assessments showed considerable divergence on any

[5] Observations were scheduled to permit an observer to be present in a teacher's classroom throughout one class period. This length of observation was adopted in light of the staff's experience during preliminary studies of the optimum observation period and because of administrative convenience—lack of interference with the school program. In a limited number of cases, thirty-minute observations were conducted; most observations consumed approximately forty-five minutes.

teacher behavior pattern,[6] a third observation and assessment was made by a different observer.

To facilitate this sequential assessment process, separate scatterplots for each of the teacher behavior patterns were maintained in the central office for each possible pairing of observers. (These scattergraphs were *not* available to the observers.) The assessments recorded on the Records were scored daily by the central office staff, and each teacher was represented on the appropriate scatterplot as soon as he had been observed twice. A third observation was made as a follow-up whenever the two assessments placed a teacher in one of the negative quadrants of the scatterplot for a particular teacher behavior pattern. Table 8 indicates, for one group of ten observers employed during the fall of 1953, the extent to which each of the observers was involved in a discrepancy of assessments which required a third observation.

TABLE 8

Comparison of Ten Observers from the Standpoint of the Number and Percent of Third Observations Required

Observer No.	No. of Original Observations	Third Observations Required	
		No.	Percent
1.....	217	36	17
2.....	73	9	12
3.....	269	48	18
4.....	91	20	22
5.....	103	17	17
6.....	92	13	14
7.....	66	9	14
8.....	167	21	13
9.....	46	6	13
10.....	212	31	15

Attention already has been called to the second procedure that was used to stabilize the assessments over a period of time. Records of the individual observers indicated that as the interval following training became greater, the assessments of a given observer frequently began to show an increasing number of discrepancies when compared with the assessments of other observers. Ideally, an observer would be retrained as soon as major discrepancies began to appear. This was not always practicable when the observers were working at some distance from the senior observer, but insofar as possible arrangements were made for additional common observations and renewed discussion of the assessment procedure with a senior observer.

[6] TCS patterns X_o, Y_o, and Z_o, as described on p. 107, in Table 13, and elsewhere in this report.

Major Clusters of Teacher Classroom Behavior

Having designated the component first-order dimensions of teacher behavior to be considered and having developed the observation and assessment procedure for obtaining information about teachers relative to such behaviors, the staff was prepared to proceed toward the first of its major objectives—to study data provided by observers' assessments, with particular attention to the manner in which teacher classroom behaviors may be organized.

The literature pertaining to the characteristics of teachers and teaching suggests that until recently little recognition was shown the problem of the organization of behaviors that comprise teaching. Individual traits or qualities of teachers frequently were chosen for study without apparent rhyme or reason and usually with minimum attention to definition and reliability of estimation. Sometimes the acceptance of one of two extreme views seems to have been implied (one assuming that teacher behavior is completely general, and perhaps unanalyzable, and the other that it is extremely fragmentary and situational), but researchers seldom have bothered to investigate the evidence with regard to the position assumed.

Actually, the problem of how the personal and social characteristics manifested in the classroom behavior of the teacher are organized is important from both the theoretical and practical viewpoints. If education is going to be at all concerned with the components of teacher behavior, it is imperative that something be learned of how these components are organized; or, if there is no discernible organization among them, this should be known. The problem cannot be ignored or begged.

It would be possible, of course, for specific teacher behaviors to be completely unrelated to one another and for teaching to consist of a very large number of independent performances or responses. However, this does not seem very reasonable, particularly since general aspects of the classroom to which teachers respond are relatively stable from situation to situation and from time to time. If, on the other hand, there is some tendency for teacher behaviors to "go together," or to be correlated, questions arise as to whether the correlation and overlapping are typical of all possible teacher behaviors, or if they apply only to certain groups, or clusters, of behaviors. There also is the question of whether clusters or patterns of teacher behaviors, if they exist, tend to have low or high correlations with other patterns or clusters.

It seemed reasonable to hypothesize, in the light of studies of the organization of personality which have appeared during the past twenty years, that some of the designated teacher behaviors might be more closely intercorrelated than others and that the correlation matrix might indicate the possibility of a substantial reduction in the number of major dimensions required for the description of teacher behavior. To the end of better understanding the organization of teacher classroom behaviors, two independent factor analyses were undertaken— one on the intercorrelations of assessments of elementary school teachers, and the other on the intercorrelations of assessments of secondary teachers. Subsequently, similarities between the elementary teacher factor matrix and the secondary teacher factor matrix were taken into account, the major patterns were selected and further studied statistically, and, finally, the composition of TCS Patterns X_o, Y_o, and Z_o was determined. These patterns were given primary attention in the Study and paper-and-pencil predictors subsequently were sought for them.

PRELIMINARY SELECTION OF TCS PATTERNS X_o, Y_o, AND Z_o

The factor analysis of assessments of elementary teacher behavior [22] was carried out with a sample consisting of third- and fourth-grade teachers from four different communities of 50,000 to 100,000 population. The number of teachers (and classrooms of pupils) observed was 275. All the teachers were women. They varied widely with regard to age, extent of teaching experience, amount and kind of training, socioeconomic area in which they taught, and other factors. Each of the teachers was independently observed on different occasions by three, and in one community, four, observers who previously had undergone five weeks' training. Immediately following an observation, each teacher was assessed by the observer on each dimension of the elementary form (twenty-six first-order dimensions) of the Classroom Observation Record. Upon completion of all observations, the data of the several observers were combined to provide a composite assessment for each teacher on each dimension.

Product-moment correlation coefficients [22] were computed among twenty-four of the dimensions.[7] The resulting table of intercorrelations was factor-analyzed by the centroid method and both orthogonal and oblique rotations were attempted. Five centroid factors were extracted. Orthogonal rotation of these factors did not yield an acceptable solution. The oblique factors shown in Table 9, however, provided a solution that more satisfactorily met the customary criteria of simple structure.

Factor I is related to both pupil behavior and teacher behavior and appears to be associated with the teacher's ability to encourage pupil

---

[7] Two dimensions, narrow-broad and unreflective-thoughtful, were not included because of the frequency with which "no opportunity for observation" had been noted by the observers.

participation and initiative. The teacher who is assessed high on Factor I is characterized by descriptions such as original, resourceful, imaginative, adaptable, flexible, democratic, "puts pupils on their own," and "encourages pupil initiative." From the standpoint of observable teacher behaviors, Factor I appears to be defined in terms of originality and adaptability.

TABLE 9

Oblique Factor Matrix Based on Centroid Factors Extracted from the Intercorrelations of Composite Observer Assessments of Elementary Teacher and Pupil Behaviors

DIMENSION	FACTOR				
	I	II	III	IV	V
Pupil behavior					
Disinterested-alert............	.30	.50	.11	.08	.00
Obstructive-constructive.....	.16	.63	−.07	.07	.04
Restrained-participating......	.40	.10	.04	.00	.18
Rude–self-controlled.........	−.01	.66	.10	.16	−.05
Apathetic-initiating..........	.60	.29	.05	−.08	.02
Dependent-responsible.......	.46	.49	.19	−.03	−.10
Teacher behavior					
Partial-fair.................	.11	.06	.39	.30	.00
Autocratic-democratic........	.42	−.11	.35	.13	−.01
Aloof (G)-responsive*........	.00	−.09	.03	.59	−.02
Restricted-understanding.....	.27	−.06	.44	.24	.03
Unattractive-attractive......	.00	.02	.02	.03	.35
Disorganized-systematic......	−.01	.56	.12	−.15	.28
Inarticulate-fluent...........	.00	.33	−.04	.02	.36
Inflexible-adaptable..........	.36	.02	.26	.21	−.04
Harsh-kindly................	.25	.08	.37	.43	−.30
Apathetic-alert..............	.05	.08	−.40	.23	.36
Aloof (I)-responsive†........	−.02	−.10	.05	.62	−.01
Stereotyped-original.........	.52	.14	−.05	−.03	.09
Changeable-constant.........	−.04	.54	.43	−.10	.17
Excitable-calm..............	.00	.36	.58	.05	.01
Uncertain-confident.........	−.02	.44	.08	.04	.28
Irresponsible-responsible......	.04	.60	−.06	.03	.14
Pessimistic-optimistic........	.05	.04	−.02	.53	.03
Infantile-mature.............	.21	.44	.04	.14	−.04

* To group.
† To individuals.

Factor II is also derived from both pupil and teacher behaviors. Pupil traits which have high loadings on this factor seem to relate to constructive, responsible, cooperative, controlled pupil activity. With regard to observable teacher behaviors, Factor II seems to refer to responsible, systematic, businesslike *vs.* unplanned, slipshod classroom procedure. The teacher who is assessed high on Factor II frequently is described as systematic, well prepared, definite, consistent, thorough, responsible, and self-controlled.

Rationally interpreted, Factor III seems really to involve two clusters of teacher behaviors, one having to do with an understanding, kindly, warm classroom manner and the other with a tendency for the teacher to be composed, calm, and perhaps easygoing. The teacher who is assessed high on Factor III probably is liked by others for such human traits as kindliness, patience, and understanding.

Factor IV appears to relate to sociability. The teacher who is high on Factor IV probably likes people and enjoys contacts with them (the social environment consisting of eight- to ten-year-old children in this case). Such a teacher is described as approachable, friendly, tactful, gregarious, cooperative, genial, good-natured, and "looks on the bright side."

Factor V evidently stems from such qualities as animation and buoyancy, a pleasing voice, expressive speech, personal charm, and grooming. This factor may be interpreted perhaps as having to do with dramatic qualities, or the "stage appearance" of the teacher—with the more obvious characteristics of a person, such as his physique, voice, and expressive movements.

It is of interest to note that the pupil behavior traits contribute significantly to Factors I and II, but these traits have only slight loadings on Factors III, IV, and V. This might suggest that, in the elementary schools, pupil behavior in class may be to a considerable extent a function of the teacher's ability (*a*) to stimulate the pupils and (*b*) to maintain situations in which the pupils are alert and responsible and are participating in constructive activities.

A table of the intercorrelations of the factors is given in the original report of this Study [22]. It will be noted here only that Factors I, IV, and V are fairly highly correlated with one another and Factors I, II, and III have relatively low intercorrelations.

For the factor analysis of assessments of secondary school teacher behaviors [23], observations were conducted in the classrooms of 249 teachers of mathematics, science, English, and social studies. There were 115 men and 134 women teachers involved. The teachers were drawn from three communities of varying size, one of approximately 40,000 population, the second with a population of approximately 80,000, and a third of a population of roughly 300,000. Two of the communities were in the same geographic area, while the third was some four hundred miles away. Ten different high schools were represented, the student populations of which were drawn from neighborhoods covering a wide range with regard to socioeconomic status.

Each subject was observed on different occasions by at least two, and frequently three, trained observers. Each observation covered approximately fifty minutes. Following the submission of assessments, the data of the several observers were combined to provide a composite assessment for each teacher (and class of students). Product-moment correlation coefficients [23] were computed among the twenty-five dimensions of the high school form of the Classroom Observation Record.

TABLE 10

Oblique Factor Matrix Based on Centroid Factors Extracted from the Intercorrelations of Composite Observer Assessments of Secondary Teacher and Pupil Behaviors

DIMENSION	FACTOR					
	I	II	III	IV	V	VI
Pupil behavior						
Apathetic-alert............	.07	.01	.53	.21	.05	−.05
Obstructive-responsible.....	−.02	.03	.46	.04	−.06	.10
Uncertain-confident........	.17	.02	.43	−.01	.17	−.03
Dependent-initiating.......	.00	−.05	.55	.04	.21	−.02
Teacher behavior						
Partial-fair................	.42	.26	−.04	.10	−.11	.05
Autocratic-democratic.....	.54	−.05	−.02	.01	.47	−.04
Aloof (G)-responsive*......	.36	−.08	.25	.34	.03	.12
Aloof (I)-responsive†.......	.54	.05	−.02	.35	.06	.03
Restricted-understanding...	.44	.17	.08	.26	.10	.03
Harsh-kindly..............	.52	.07	−.02	−.05	.12	.15
Dull-stimulating...........	−.08	.06	.32	.14	.28	.17
Stereotyped-original.......	.01	.05	.17	.01	.40	.13
Apathetic-alert............	.04	.08	.12	.41	−.01	.02
Unimpressive-attractive....	.02	.00	.01	−.04	.07	.39
Monotonous-pleasant (voice)	.05	−.06	−.01	.05	−.07	.46
Inarticulate-articulate......	−.14	.17	−.04	.08	−.05	.35
Evading-responsible.......	.14	.52	−.08	.20	.03	−.07
Erratic-steady.............	.07	.43	.08	−.25	.08	.17
Excitable-poised...........	.04	.20	.06	−.39	.16	.36
Uncertain-confident........	−.01	.20	.20	−.11	.12	.27
Disorganized-systematic....	−.02	.50	.02	.02	.02	.03
Inflexible-adaptable........	.48	.09	.00	.09	.35	.00
Pessimistic-optimistic......	.34	−.08	.19	.14	.09	.17
Immature-integrated.......	.14	.16	.20	−.06	.09	.30
Narrow-broad..............	.05	.34	−.06	−.03	.30	.03

* To group.
† To individuals.

Centroid analysis of the intercorrelations of the twenty-five variables resulted in the extraction of six factors. An orthogonal rotation was attempted, but the plot suggested that an oblique solution would better satisfy the requirements for simple structure. The rotated oblique factor matrix is shown in Table 10.

Factor I appears to reflect the tendencies of a teacher to be understanding and democratic *vs.* aloof, harsh, and autocratic in dealings with pupils. The teacher who is assessed high on Factor I is characterized by such descriptions as friendly, understanding, tactful, good-natured, sympathetic, kindly, democratic, and fair.

Factor II seems to reflect the extent to which a teacher is business-like, systematic, and responsible *vs.* unorganized and slipshod in conducting class. Factor II may be described as representing systematic, consistent, definite, thorough, self-controlled, well-prepared, and responsible behavior.

Factor III is related to the several pupil behaviors observed and involves principally pupil participation and controlled pupil activity *vs.* apathy, dependence, and lack of control in pupils. The teacher whose class ranks high on this factor apparently is one who is challenging to the pupil, is interesting, is helpful and encouraging, and who holds the respect of the class.

Factor IV appears to be a factor reflecting the extent to which a teacher is reactive rather than calm and composed. Apparently it relates to such traits as alertness, enthusiasm, buoyancy, and, also, impulsiveness and excitability.

Factor V appears to refer to originality, adaptability, ability to stimulate, and perhaps democratic-openmindedness *vs.* dullness, inflexibility, and stereotyped behavior on the part of the teacher. The teacher who is assessed high on this factor is characterized as original, resourceful, imaginative, adaptable, democratic, and stimulating.

Factor VI has contributions from such qualities as pleasing voice, fluency, good choice of words, personal charm, grooming, self-possession, and personal dignity. This factor seems to relate to the "stage appearance" or dramatic qualities manifested by the teacher.

As in the case of the elementary teacher factor analysis, it should again be noted that the factors that emerged from the analysis were not, for the most part, orthogonal. The intercorrelations among the primary factors are shown in the original report [23]. Principal exceptions to the tendency for the factors to overlap is noted in the case of Factors I and II, which are correlated $-.01$. Factors I and III also approach independence ($r=.11$). The remainder of the intercorrelations range from .18 to .63. The only significant negative correlation is one of $-.38$ between Factors I and IV. From the standpoint of intercorrelation with other factors, Factor I appears to be the most clearly distinct, its only sizable correlation being that of $-.38$ with Factor IV, as noted above. Factor III has relatively low correlations with most of the factors, but is significantly correlated with Factor II ($r=.60$). Factors II, IV, V, and VI are all rather highly intercorrelated.

The findings of these two factor analyses suggest that the personal and interpersonal behavior of teachers in the classroom probably may best be described in terms of a limited number of major dimensions, or families of behaviors. However, it is important to note that these major dimensions, as identified by the factors which emerged, tend to overlap and to be positively correlated. From the practical standpoint of teacher recruitment and selection, this fact that teachers who are high, or low, with respect to one dimension of observable teacher behavior tend to be relatively high, or low, with regard to other dimensions of observable classroom behavior may be significant. The principal exception to this generalization is the independence of the friendly-understanding factor and the businesslike-responsible factor among secondary school teachers (a finding which seems to have considerable support, as will be noted later).

In interpreting the findings of these factor analyses, it should be kept in mind that the basic data for the Study were assessments provided by trained observers. Where such assessments are involved, there always is a possibility that the resulting descriptions may be descriptions of characteristics of the observers, or judges, as much as they are descriptions of the behavior of the individuals assessed. However, it is believed that the careful and extensive training of the observers employed by the Study gives some assurance that the assessments provide estimates of the behaviors of the teacher observed.

Although the results of the factor analyses of the assessments of elementary and secondary teachers do not duplicate one another, there are readily discernible similarities, suggesting that at least three correlated factors, or sets of behaviors, stand out from the rest and that these may be common to both elementary and secondary teachers.[8] These primary teacher classroom behavior patterns were designated as follows: TCS Pattern X_o, reflecting understanding, friendliness, and responsiveness vs. aloofness and egocentrism on the part of the teacher; TCS Pattern Y_o, reflecting responsible, businesslike, systematic vs. evading, unplanned, slipshod teacher behavior; and TCS Pattern Z_o, reflecting stimulating, imaginative, original vs. dull, routine teacher behavior. Pattern X_o cuts across Factors II and IV of the elementary teacher behavior factor analysis and is Factor I of the secondary teacher analysis. Pattern Y_o is Factor II of the elementary teacher analysis

[8] It may be noted that the elementary and secondary factor analyses yielded a fourth factor, relating to the "stage appearance" or dramatic qualities of the teacher. This factor is very definitely identified in both analyses. Perhaps it would have been proper to have selected this pattern of characteristics along with the three which were given principal attention.

and also Factor II of the secondary teacher analysis. Pattern Z_o is Factor I of the elementary teacher analysis and Factor V of the secondary teacher analysis.

Obviously all teacher behavior does not fall into one of these three patterns suggested by the factor analyses. On the other hand, practical experience as well as the empirical data indicate that these are three of the principal areas involved in interpersonal relations, and that they might well be given basic consideration in the theory of teacher behavior and also in teacher personnel procedures. It was these three factors, or patterns, therefore, that the Study chose to concentrate upon in its investigations of teacher behavior in the classroom. It was felt that an adequate theory of teacher behavior must take such patterns into account.

FURTHER STUDY OF THE COMPOSITION OF TCS PATTERNS X_o, Y_o, AND Z_o

With the completion of the factor analyses of assessments of elementary and secondary teachers on the dimensions of the Classroom Observation Record, a significant preliminary step was made in the direction of the first major objective of the Study, namely, the identification of possible criterion dimensions of teacher classroom behavior.

However, before employing these patterns, or criteria, in proceeding to further analyses of teacher behavior and to the development of paper-and-pencil predictors of such criteria, additional assurance was sought regarding the adequacy of the dimensions suggested by factor analysis. The approach to obtaining such confirmation followed two lines, one concerned with the generality or reliability of the Patterns X_o, Y_o, and Z_o (the extent to which these patterns appear to be generalizable to new samples of teachers observed later in the course of the Study and assessed by different observers), and the other having to do with the definitiveness and distinctness of the patterns (the most defensible combinations of components of each pattern, considered in the light of the first-order dimensions of the Record behaviors, which yielded (*a*) the highest possible reliability for each pattern and (*b*) the lowest intercorrelations between patterns).

To these ends a series of studies was instituted. The investigations were necessarily fragmentary at first as observation and assessment data were being accumulated. They culminated, however, in three principal analyses, all of which seemed to confirm the existence of the three major dimensions within the framework of the behaviors incorporated in the Record. Furthermore, additional confirmation appeared from time to time in reports of research other than those of the Teacher Characteristics Study. The accumulating evidence, therefore, appeared to lend considerable support for TCS Patterns X_o, Y_o, and Z_o.

The first of the studies undertaken to probe further into the description of teacher classroom behavior involved computing correlations between each of the composite X_o, Y_o, and Z_o assessments and the assessments on component behavior dimensions which were indicated by the elementary teacher factor analysis to make up Patterns X_o, Y_o, and Z_o.

A new randomly selected sample of 150 elementary teachers, involving 300 observations, was employed. Product-moment correlations coefficients were computed for (1) observer assessments of the component first-order dimensions suggested by the elementary factor analysis with the composite factor scores[9] and (2) observer assessments on the component dimensions suggested by the factor analysis with pattern scores consisting of the composite *less* the dimension with which it was being correlated.

The findings of this correlational analysis showed a very high degree of agreement with the original elementary teacher factor analysis. All of the previously identified components correlated significantly with the composites that they were hypothesized to comprise. The highest correlations between component dimensions and the composite *less* the dimension in question were between .72 and .77 (aloof-responsive, harsh-kindly, and restricted-understanding with Pattern X_o; evading-responsible with Pattern Y_o; and dull-stimulating with Pattern Z_o). The lowest correlation was .52 between excitable-poised and Pattern X_o.

While the study just mentioned indicated that the first-order dimensions suggested by the elementary factor analysis did seem to hold up with an additional sample of teachers so far as their contribution to a particular criterion dimension was concerned, it was felt that additional studies of the composition of the teacher behavior patterns should be undertaken before final decisions were reached. The remainder of the research would rest heavily on these decisions.

Further investigation of the reliabilities of the patterns and the intercorrelations among the patterns seemed to be in order. A second analysis was therefore made, involving different combinations of behaviors contributing to the Patterns X_o, Y_o, and Z_o, with attention being di-

[9] The dimensions partial-fair, autocratic-democratic, aloof-responsive, restricted-understanding, harsh-kindly, excitable-poised, and pessimistic-optimistic tentatively were selected to comprise Pattern X_o; the dimensions obstructive-responsible (pupil behavior), evading-responsible, erratic-steady, uncertain-confident, disorganized-systematic, and immature-integrated, Pattern Y_o; and apathetic-alert (pupil behavior), dependent-initiating (pupil behavior), dull-stimulating (a new dimension of teaching behavior that had been added to the final form of the Record), stereotyped-original, and inflexible-adaptable, Pattern Z_o.

rected at the pattern reliabilities and pattern intercorrelations resulting from use of these different combinations.

Three random samples of 150 elementary teachers each were studied, employing three different combinations of dimensions composing Patterns X_o, Y_o, and Z_o. In general, relatively little variation was found from sample to sample or from one combination of component behaviors (for a particular pattern) to another. The original combinations of dimensions and the reconstituted combinations correlated between .93 and .96, suggesting that relatively little variance was accounted for by shifting the elements of the patterns. The reliabilities varied from sample to sample and from pattern to pattern, but differed little from one combination of dimensions to another for a given pattern within a given sample (range .51 to .88). Pattern X_o and Sample 1 consistently yielded the highest reliabilities, and Pattern Z_o and Sample 3, the lowest. The intercorrelations among patterns ranged from .47 to .79, the median intercorrelation being approximately .6 when all samples and all combinations of dimensions were considered.

In the light of the high intercorrelations between Patterns X_o, Y_o, and Z_o and the fact that the pattern reliabilities hardly exceeded the intercorrelations, considerable attention was given to the possibility of employing a *single composite estimate* of teacher behavior (rather than separate estimates for the three patterns), at least so far as *elementary* teacher classroom behaviors were concerned. Certainly the statistical analyses just described provided little defense for considering the patterns separately. However, studies were concurrently under way to provide paper-and-pencil predictors of teacher classroom behavior, and efforts to obtain adequately cross-validated scoring keys for these predictors gave little promise of success when a *single composite* of behaviors was used as the criterion in the response analysis. On the other hand, when the Patterns X_o, Y_o, and Z_o were considered separately as criteria for the response analysis and cross-validation, encouraging results were obtained. In view of repeated empirical findings of this nature, it was deemed advisable not to adopt a single composite, or general pattern of teacher classroom behavior, but rather to proceed with consideration of the three patterns, X_o, Y_o, and Z_o.

The ultimate decisions on the composition of the TCS Patterns X_o, Y_o, and Z_o were reached after considering a number of sources of evidence, such as the factor analyses and the studies cited in the immediately preceding paragraphs, but with particular attention being given to the data in Tables 11 and 12. These tables show (*a*) the correlations between *individual* observer assessments of each of the first-

TABLE 11

Correlations between Observer Assessments of First-Order Dimensions of Teacher Behavior and Composite Observer Assessments of Teacher Behavior Patterns X_o, Y_o, and Z_o

DIMENSION	ELEMENTARY TEACHERS (3,026 Observations of 1,513 Teachers) Teacher Behavior Pattern			SECONDARY TEACHERS (3,814 Observations of 1,907 Teachers) Teacher Behavior Pattern		
	X_o	Y_o	Z_o	X_o	Y_o	Z_o
Pupil behavior						
Apathetic-alert............	.51	.70	.79	.39	.40	.77
Obstructive-responsible.....	.44	.79*	.62	.40	.49	.50
Uncertain-confident........	.48	.47	.60	.38	.23	.58
Dependent-initiating.......	.51	.46	.73	.40	.24	.71
Teacher behavior						
Partial-fair...............	.61	.49	.44	.51	.31	.31
Autocratic-democratic......	.70*	.35	.52	.63*	.18	.37
Aloof-responsive...........	.89*	.47	.59	.85*	.28	.50
Restricted-understanding...	.86*	.56	.61	.82*	.34	.46
Harsh-kindly..............	.87*	.49	.52	.82*	.28	.37
Dull-stimulating..........	.55	.60	.83*	.48	.42	.82*
Stereotyped-original.......	.44	.50	.80*	.44	.43	.80*
Apathetic-alert............	.45	.56	.58	.40	.47	.59
Unimpressive-attractive....	.46	.41	.40	.40	.32	.33
Evading-responsible.......	.40	.79*	.55	.31	.81*	.49
Erratic-steady............	.53	.77*	.48	.38	.69	.27
Excitable-poised...........	.54	.72*	.48	.37	.57	.27
Uncertain-confident........	.45	.80	.55	.37	.53	.48
Disorganized-systematic....	.35	.79*	.52	.24	.84*	.41
Inflexible-adaptable........	.63	.48	.73	.56	.31	.54
Pessimistic-optimistic......	.81*	.52	.59	.77*	.33	.52
Immature-integrated.......	.62	.73	.59	.57	.50	.48
Narrow-broad.............	.46	.56	.58	.39	.50	.55

* The dimension was a component of the particular teacher behavior pattern; the resulting part-whole correlation is spuriously high.

order dimensions in the Record and *composite* observer assessments on Patterns X_o, Y_o, and Z_o, and (b) observer reliabilities (correlations between the first and second assessments) for the twenty-two first-order dimensions listed on the Record. The data in these two tables are based upon observations made on more than 1,500 elementary teachers and 1,900 secondary teachers.

In selecting the component first-order dimensions to represent a particular pattern, preference was given to behaviors (a) most highly correlated with the particular pattern, (b) least highly correlated with patterns that they are not hypothesized to represent, and (c) yielding relatively high reliabilities.

Review of all relevant data led to the determination of the components of TCS Patterns X_o, Y_o, and Z_o as shown in Table 13 (on page 108). Throughout the remainder of this report the major dimensions or

TABLE 12

Reliabilities of Assessments of 22 Teacher and Pupil Behavior
Dimensions, Based on Correlations of Assessments of
First and Second Observers without Regard to
Individual Identity of the Observers

DIMENSION	RELIABILITY COEFFICIENT*	
	Elementary Teachers ($N=1,513$)	Secondary Teachers ($N=1,907$)
Pupil behavior		
Apathetic-alert..............	.58	.55
Obstructive-responsible.......	.65	.63
Uncertain-confident..........	.43	.43
Dependent-initiating.........	.44	.50
Teacher behavior		
Partial-fair.................	.43	.43
Autocratic-democratic........	.61	.64
Aloof-responsive.............	.55	.59
Restricted-understanding.....	.52	.58
Harsh-kindly................	.58	.63
Dull-stimulating.............	.58	.67
Stereotyped-original.........	.54	.65
Apathetic-alert..............	.53	.62
Unimpressive-attractive......	.58	.63
Evading-responsible.........	.52	.63
Erratic-steady..............	.54	.56
Excitable-poised.............	.54	.47
Uncertain-confident..........	.45	.57
Disorganized-systematic......	.51	.62
Inflexible-adaptable..........	.52	.55
Pessimistic-optimistic........	.53	.58
Immature-integrated.........	.54	.58
Narrow-broad...............	.51	.65

* Spearman-Brown estimate of the reliability of the composite assessment.

clusters of teacher classroom behavior specified are Patterns X_o, Y_o, and Z_o composed of the dimensions listed in this table.

TCS Pattern X_o may be considered a major bipolar family of teacher classroom behaviors defined by understanding, friendly behavior at one pole and by aloof, egocentric, restricted behavior at the other. Similarly TCS Pattern Y_o appears to be definable as a continuum extending between the extremes of responsible, businesslike, systematic classroom behavior and evading, unplanned, slipshod classroom behavior. The poles of TCS Pattern Z_o may be described as stimulating, imaginative, surgent teacher classroom behavior and dull, routine teacher classroom behavior. Attention is called again to Table 11, which indicates in terms of product-moment correlation coefficients the relative contribution of each of the dimensions of the Classroom Observation Record to each of the Patterns X_o, Y_o, and Z_o.

TABLE 13

First-Order Dimensions Comprising TCS Teacher Classroom Behavior Patterns X_o, Y_o, and Z_o

TEACHER	TCS PATTERN X_o (Kindly, understanding, friendly vs. aloof, egocentric, restricted teacher behavior)	TCS PATTERN Y_o (Responsible, systematic, businesslike vs. evading, unplanned, slipshod teacher behavior)	TCS PATTERN Z_o (Stimulating, imaginative, surgent vs. dull, routine teacher behavior)
Elementary teachers	Autocratic-democratic Aloof-responsive Restricted-understanding Harsh-kindly Pessimistic-optimistic	Obstructive-responsible (PB*) Evading-responsible Erratic-steady Excitable-poised Disorganized-systematic	Dull-stimulating Stereotyped-original
Secondary teachers	Autocratic-democratic Aloof-responsive Restricted-understanding Harsh-kindly Pessimistic-optimistic	Evading-responsible Disorganized-systematic	Dull-stimulating Stereotyped-original

* Obstructive-responsible refers to pupil behavior in teacher's class, assumed to be partially a product of teacher behavior.

108

It is of interest to observe that the TCS Patterns X_o, Y_o, and Z_o are not unique to the Teacher Characteristics Study—that they are supported not only by rational analysis of the teaching process but also by reports of other factor analyses and investigations concerned with the exploration of personal behavior, particularly teacher behavior. Coffman [6], for example, asked college students to assess their instructors on some nineteen defined traits, using graphic rating scales, and he subsequently derived the correlation matrix and completed a factor analysis. Among the factors yielded by this analysis was one which Coffman referred to as *empathy* (involving such traits as feeling between instructor and student, ability to arouse student interest, sense of humor, and tolerance) which seems to correspond to certain features of TCS Pattern X_o and perhaps to overlap with TCS Pattern Z_o. Coffman's analysis also yielded a factor relating to *organization* (preparation for class meetings, organization of course, scholarship) which appears to resemble TCS Pattern Y_o, a factor concerned with *appearance* (personal appearance, punctuality, lack of peculiarities), and another factor which seemed to be describable as *verbal fluency*, or expressiveness.

A study conducted by French [10] under Horst's direction, involving the derivation of college students' concepts of effective teaching based on student ratings of college instructors suggested that, at the university level, teacher characteristics such as those comprising TCS Pattern X_o may tend to become less important, while characteristics such as those making up TCS Patterns Y_o and Z_o may tend to take on greater significance. French found that the college students were concerned with their instructor's ability to interpret abstract ideas clearly, get students interested in the subject, increase skills of thinking, broaden interests, make good use of examples and illustrations, motivate the student to do his best work, and the like, and less concerned with the instructor's sense of humor, appearance, willingness to give individual attention, avoidance of embarrassment of the student, friendliness of manner, and such. These findings are generally consistent with those of Coffman.

It appears quite possible, as suggested by these data and by the results of the TCS elementary and secondary teacher factor analyses, that as the picture shifts from elementary school teacher performance through high school and into university teaching, the Pattern X_o may take on progressively less importance, and that characteristics similar to those comprising Patterns Y_o and Z_o attain greater significance.

Gibb [12] recently submitted a 165-item Teacher Behavior Description Questionnaire, covering nine dimensions of teacher behavior, to college students to obtain ratings of their instructors. Factor analysis of the intercorrelations of the ratings yielded five oblique factors: *friendly, democratic* behavior; *communicative* behavior; *businesslike* behavior; *academic emphasis* behavior; and a residual factor. The first and third of Gibb's factors appear to bear close resemblance to TCS Patterns X_o and Y_o.[10]

Earlier studies by Creager [8] and by Smalzried and Remmers [25] involved factor analyses of college students' assessments of their instructors, employing the Purdue Rating Scale. While showing some variation, these studies resulted in approximately similar factor patterns emphasizing *rapport* (Creager) or *empathy* (Smalzried and Remmers), defined in terms of sympathy, fairness, and related traits, as one principal factor, and another which was defined as *professional impression* (Creager) or *professional maturity* (Smalzried and Remmers). The empathy-rapport factor appears to be very similar to TCS Pattern X_o.

In areas other than teaching, Comrey, High, and Goldberg [7, 14] have reported a series of investigations of the factorial dimensions of organizational behavior. In one study, for example, the field service employees of the United States Forestry Service filled out multiple-choice questionnaires covering fourteen behavior dimensions to provide ratings of their supervisors. Factor analysis of the intercorrelations yielded four oblique factors: *efficient management* (similar to TCS Pattern Y_o); *consultative supervision; familiarity with subordinates* (similar to TCS Pattern X_o); and *forceful supervision*. In another investigation in which aircraft workers similarly rated their supervisors, factor analysis again suggested patterns relating to *efficient management, consultative supervision*, and *familiarity with subordinates*, and also a *group cohesion* factor.

In his extensive investigation of personality, Cattell [4, and more recent work] has described such behavior traits as (1) *cyclothymia* (warm, trustful, cooperative) and (2) *schizothymia* (impersonal, aloof,

---

[10] A presently unpublished study, reported at the 1959 American Psychological Association meetings by T. F. Hodgson and Paul Horst, described a factor analysis of the responses of several thousand students who judged 133 university professors on 41 items. The analysis resulted in eight primary factors and one general ("halo effect") factor, the primary factors appearing to relate to: I, organization of subject matter; II, personal and academic acceptance; III, sensitivity, sincerity, and tolerance; IV, stimulation of intellectual interest; V, motivation of student achievement; VI, professional satisfaction; VII, fair grading practices; and VIII, a non-interpretable factor. According to the descriptions provided by Hodgson and Horst, their Factor III seems to be very similar to the TCS Pattern X_o; their Factor I similar to TCS Pattern Y_o; their Factors IV and V similar to TCS Pattern Z_o; and their Factor II similar to the "appearance" factor emerging from the Study's elementary and secondary factor analyses.

uncooperative) and (3) *paranoid cyclothymia* (suspicious, jealous) which seems to be related to TCS Pattern X_o (kindly, understanding, democratic *vs.* aloof, restricted, egocentric teacher behavior). Also, Cattell's *conventional practicality* (conventional, dependable, practical) and *Bohemian unconcern* (undependable, unconcerned about practicality, unconventional) seem to be not unrelated to TCS Pattern Y_o (responsible, systematic *vs.* evading, unplanned teacher behavior) and his *surgency* (resourceful, original, energetic) and *desurgency* (stereotyped, languid) appear to involve the same behavior as TCS Pattern Z_o (stimulating, imaginative *vs.* dull, routine teacher behavior).

Consideration, then, of the observation data provided by the Teacher Characteristics Study, together with suggestions from other sources, give considerable support to the hypothesis that the Patterns X_o, Y_o, and Z_o are related to significant aspects of personal-social behavior and indicate the desirability of studying such patterns in the description of teacher behavior and in the extension of teacher behavior theory.

A Pupil Classroom Behavior Pattern

As will be recalled, the final form of the Classroom Observation Record provided for assessment not only of teacher behaviors but also of certain personal-social behaviors of the pupils in a teacher's class, namely, the four dimensions: apathetic-alert pupil behavior; obstructive-responsible pupil behavior; uncertain-confident pupil behavior; and dependent-initiating pupil behavior. Obviously these dimensions do not provide a complete inventory of pupil behaviors or their products; they do not, for example, yield estimates of pupil achievement in academic subject matter. It could perhaps be argued, however, that with individual pupil ability and study habits held constant, such dimensions as these four might reasonably be expected to reflect academic achievement. And since academic achievement cannot be reliably assessed through limited direct observation (or by observation of groups of pupils rather than individuals), experience with early forms of the Record led the TCS staff to center its attention on the assessment of the above-named characteristics of pupils in a teacher's classroom.

The correlation pattern of the pupil behavior dimensions, as suggested by the factor analyses, is fairly clear in the case of secondary school teachers—the pupil dimensions being substantially intercorrelated and contributing to a factor which may be designated as *pupil behavior*. For elementary teachers, however, such a pattern is by no means distinct, and pupil behaviors appear to be very closely related to teacher behavior Patterns X_o and Z_o and to only a slightly lesser extent to Pattern Y_o.

With these two differing sets of findings in mind, and after considerable deliberation, it was arbitrarily decided to obtain for the class of each teacher observed a pupil behavior pattern score, TCS Pattern P_o. The availability of such a composite score made possible various comparisons of teacher characteristics with the aspects of pupil behavior embodied in the Record. The P_o score for a teacher's class was an unweighted sum of an observer's assessments of the class with respect to the four dimensions of pupil behavior. The composite P_o assessment was an unweighted average of the standard score equivalents of the several observers' P_o scores.

Weighting vs. Nonweighting of Components of Patterns

After the components of the major dimensions of teacher classroom behavior to be considered by the Study had been determined, there remained the important consideration of the proper weights to assign each of the several dimensions comprising a pattern. Up to this point in the research, equal weight had been assigned to each element contributing to a pattern; the pattern score was simply the sum of the assessments on the component dimensions.

The problem of weighting is basic for research which deals with either description or prediction. It becomes particularly important where the research is directed toward the validation of predictors. In prediction research, the correlates of some *hypothetical true criteria* are sought. To the extent that obtained criteria measures are representative of the true criterion (that they represent the criterion behavior both inclusively and exclusively), it is possible to estimate the validity of correlates. If the obtained criterion measures differ systematically from the true criterion and represent biased estimates of the true criterion behavior, the validity of correlates must necessarily be in doubt.

Various aspects of criterion bias were discussed in chapter 2. One such variety of criterion bias is *criterion distortion*, and it is principally in relation to this possible biasing condition that the problem of assigning weights to different elements of the criterion becomes the focus of attention. The problem is stated specifically by the question: "If the criterion consists of elements $x_1, x_2, x_3 \ldots, x_n$, what weight should be assigned to each of these elements so that the hypothetical true criterion will be best represented?"

The decision with regard to weighting often depends upon logical considerations; it will rest to a large extent upon the judgments of concerned and competent persons about the relative importance of the elements making up the criterion. On the other hand, the problem also may be approached empirically and statistically. Such a statistical analysis of a number of weighting devices applied to components of a pattern of teacher classroom behavior was undertaken in this study.

One pattern of elementary teacher classroom behavior (Pattern X_o—friendly, understanding *vs.* aloof, restricted teacher behavior) was selected for detailed statistical investigation. The seven first-order dimensions having the highest factor loadings on Factors III and IV of the elementary teacher behavior factor analysis were considered.[11]

Two independent, randomly selected samples, each consisting of 150 Grades 3–4 female teachers, were employed. The same procedures were carried out with each sample, the two independent samples being used simply to provide replication.

The following ten methods of assigning weights to observers' assessments of the component dimensions contributing to the composite X_o pattern score were studied:

Criterion Score I was obtained by simply adding the seven assessments of an observer (made on the original seven-point scale) for the first-order dimensions making up the composite criterion.

Criterion Score II was obtained by reducing assessments of 1 or 2 to 0, assessments of 3, 4, or 5 to 1, and assessments of 6 or 7 to 2. The assessments on the dimensions, with these new weights of 0, 1, or 2, were then added to obtain the criterion score.

Criterion Score III was obtained by computing the biserial correlation between *each assessment* (1, 2, 3, 4, 5, 6, or 7) *on each* first-order *dimension* with Criterion Score I (above), using the weights provided by the correlation coefficients, and adding the products to obtain the composite score.

Criterion Score IV was obtained by computing the biserial correlation between *each assessment* (1, 2, 3, 4, 5, 6, or 7) *on each first-order dimension* with *Criterion Score I minus the contribution of that particular dimension*, using the weights provided by the correlation coefficients, and adding these products.

Criterion Score V was obtained by computing the correlation between each first-order dimension composite observer assessment and Criterion Score I, using these weights as multiplying factors, and adding the resultant products to obtain the composite.

Criterion Score VI was obtained by computing the correlations between each first-order dimension composite observer assessment and *Criterion Score I minus the contribution of that particular dimension*, using these weights as multiplying factors, and adding the resulting products.

[11] The dimensions were: partial-fair, autocratic-democratic, aloof-responsive, restricted-understanding, harsh-kindly, excitable-poised, and pessimistic-optimistic.

Criterion Score VII was obtained by computing the coefficients of predictive efficiency corresponding to the correlations between each first-order dimension and Criterion Score I, using these weights as multiplying factors, and adding the products.

Criterion Score VIII was obtained by computing the coefficients of predictive efficiency corresponding to the correlations between each first-order dimension and *Criterion Score I minus the contribution of that particular dimension*, using these as the weights, and adding the products.

Criterion Score IX was obtained by using the factor loadings of each first-order dimension on the "friendly, understanding" factor (Factor III of the earlier reported multiple factor analysis) as the multiplying weights, and adding these products.

Criterion Score X was obtained by computing the reciprocals of the standard deviations of each first-order dimension, using these as multiplying factors for obtaining the weights, and adding the products.

The composite Pattern X_o scores obtained by each of these ten methods were analyzed with regard to mean, standard deviation, ratio of standard deviation to range, skewness (g_1) and kurtosis (g_2), correlation with the arbitrarily weighted Criterion Score I, and reliability for each of the two samples of elementary teachers. The reliability data were considered to be the most crucial test of the value of a weighting technique. If one technique showed substantially higher reliability than another, it seemed reasonable to believe that this might be acceptable evidence of greater usefulness.

Tables summarizing the statistics were presented in the original report of this study [20] and are omitted here. Generally speaking, there was no clear indication of superiority of any of the weighting techniques over the unweighted composite represented by Criterion Score I. The correlations of the Pattern X_o scores based on the unweighted composite with derived scores provided by the various weighting schemes all were high. One coefficient (between Criterion Score I and Criterion Score II) was as low as .79; the remainder were .95 or above, six of the weighting methods yielding, for each sample, correlations of .99.

The reliabilities of the pattern scores based on the various weighting techniques all were in the middle seventies with the exception of that for Criterion Score II (.66). The highest reliability coefficient obtained (.76) was for Criterion Score I, the unweighted composite.

It was concluded that the considerable amount of labor involved in assigning empirically derived weights to components of the pattern of teacher classroom behavior studied, Pattern X_o, appeared to be of little practical value. No evidence was found for the greater satisfactoriness of any of the weighting systems over the use of the arbitrary values (one to seven) employed by the observers in making the original assessments. In the light of similar findings frequently reported by studies of methods of weighting attitude scale and test items, it was concluded that extension of the analysis to teacher classroom behavior Patterns Y_0 and Z_0 likely would result in comparable findings, and therefore was not necessary. The research subsequently undertaken by the Study employed unitary weights for each of the components comprising a pattern of teacher classroom behavior.

Reliability of Assessments of the Teacher Classroom Behavior Patterns

As was noted earlier, the efficiency of direct observation and assessment as a method for obtaining criterion data on human behavior is a function, first of all, of the unambiguous operational definition of the behavioral components to be observed and, second, of the observers' skill in identifying and assessing the component behaviors. The attention given to the designation of the components of teacher behavior, to the development of the Classroom Observation Record, and to the training of observers has been described. To provide still further assurance that the assessment data reliably reflected teacher behavior in the classroom, the observations and assessments were replicated, independent observations of the same teacher being conducted by different observers at different times.

While these precautionary steps had been taken, the need for evidence of the extent of their success remained. The efficacy of the methods employed could be determined only by the accumulation of empirical data and their analysis. The Study necessarily was concerned, therefore, with questions concerning the extent to which the several observers employed tended to agree in their assessments of teacher behavior, and the extent of agreement of different assessments of the same observer when observations were repeated over a period of time.

It should be noted that insofar as empirical analysis is concerned, no independent approach to the validity of the assessment data was possible. The problem of the validity and the reliability of observers' assessments, therefore, were treated as one and the same. The relevance of the component first-order dimensions of teacher classroom behavior having been determined as described in earlier sections of the chapter, the basic problem became that of determining how consistent and reliable were the assessments of such components, and the patterns of teacher behavior they comprise.

Before considering the evidence obtained on observer reliability, attention should be called to at least two difficulties inherent in the assessment data which impose limitations upon conclusions: (1) In comparing assessments based upon observations made at different times, it must be recognized that, in addition to variance contributed by the observer, there also may be systematic variations in the teacher-class situation from one time to another which tend to reduce obtained interobserver correlations.[12] (2) In analyses involving the comparison of repeated observations conducted by the same observer, obtained correlations may be spuriously high due to the carry-over of the same observer biases from one observation to the other and also, possibly, as a result of recall by the observer of aspects of the earlier observation.

One other point may be noted before proceeding to the observer reliability data. This has to do with the fact that it was the practice to employ for criterion purposes a composite assessment based upon the combined assessments of two or more independent observers. The resulting reliability of the combined assessments obviously is greater than either assessment taken singly and it is appropriate to employ as an index of reliability an estimate obtained by application of the Spearman-Brown formula which in the case of two observations reduces to $r = \dfrac{2r_{12}}{1+r_{12}}$ where r_{12} is the correlation between the assessments of the observers. In the tables of data which will be presented, the equivalence estimates of reliability, based upon interobserver correlations, have been corrected by application of the formula. Estimates of the stability of observation data, based upon repeated observations by the same observers, of course, have *not* been so corrected.

ESTIMATES OF RELIABILITY BASED ON EQUIVALENCE OF OBSERVERS' ASSESSMENTS

Data relative to the reliability of assessments as indicated by interobserver correlations are shown in Tables 12, 14, and 15. In Table 12 (on page 107) the reliability of each first-order dimension appearing on the Record is considered separately. With respect to elementary teachers, the teacher behavior dimensions yielding the highest reliability appear to be autocratic-democratic, harsh-kindly, dull-stimulating, and unimpressive-attractive, whereas the lowest reliabilities are for dimensions partial-fair and uncertain-confident. Among the secondary teachers the highest teacher behavior reliabilities were obtained for such dimensions as dull-stimulating, stereotyped-original, and narrow-

[12] For example, teacher-pupil relationships and resulting teacher behaviors may be quite different in an elementary school class during a period devoted to spelling from those in a social studies period where group participation may receive greater emphasis.

TABLE 14

Reliability Coefficients, Derived from Independent Observations Made by Given Pairs of Observers, for Assessments of Teacher Behavior Patterns X_o, Y_o, and Z_o

TEACHERS OBSERVED	NO. OF OBSERVERS	NO. OF TEACHER SAMPLES	RANGE OF SIZE OF SAMPLES	RELIABILITY COEFFICIENT*					
				X_o†		Y_o‡		Z_o§	
				Range for the Several Samples	Median	Range for the Several Samples	Median	Range for the Several Samples	Median
Elementary	4	5	43–173	.64–.85	.77	.77–.84	.81	.67–.79	.75
Elementary	4	3	22–96	.64–.88	.85	.61–.89	.84	.28–.88	.81
Elementary	10	34	7–83	.21–.90	.60	−.12–.99	.51	.06–.85	.54
Secondary	3	3	50	.67–.81	.72	.77–.82	.81	.52–.80	.70
Secondary	6	14	10–71	.04–.89	.73	.46–.88	.82		
Secondary	3	6	30–79	.66–.90	.81	.77–.87	.83	.60–.89	.77
Secondary, math-science	3	3	30–47	.79–.90	.86	.80–.87	.86	.60–.87	.69
Secondary, English-social studies	3	3	68–79	.66–.82	.68	.77–.84	.82	.64–.89	.84

* Spearman-Brown estimate of the reliability of the composite assessment.
† Understanding, friendly vs. aloof, restricted teacher behavior.
‡ Responsible, businesslike vs. unplanned, slipshod teacher behavior.
§ Stimulating, imaginative vs. dull, routine teacher behavior.

TABLE 15

Reliabilities of Assessments of Teacher Behaviors X_o, Y_o, and Z_o, Based on Correlation of Assessments of First Observer and Second Observer without Regard to Individual Identity of the Observers

TEACHERS OBSERVED	No. OF OBSERVERS INVOLVED	No. OF TEACHERS OBSERVED	RELIABILITY COEFFICIENT*		
			X_o	Y_o	Z_o
Elementary Sample 1...	5	150	.84	.82	.82
Elementary Sample 2...	23	150	.62	.61	.66
Elementary Sample 3...	23	150	.51	.39	.56
Elementary composite....	*23*	*450*	*.69*	*.64*	*.70*
Secondary Sample 1....	7	404	.81	.77	.77
Secondary Sample 2....	17	1,503	.69	.63	.69
Secondary composite.....	*17*	*1,907*	*.71*	*.66*	*.70*

* Spearman-Brown estimate of the reliability of the composite assessment.

broad, with the lowest reliabilities for partial-fair and excitable-poised. Among the pupil behavior dimensions, obstructive-responsible and apathetic-alert yielded the highest reliabilities, and uncertain-confident yielded the lowest for classes of both elementary and secondary teachers.

Table 14 summarizes a number of reliability studies conducted by the Study with different groups of teachers. The study to which the first line of the table refers, for example, involved the intercorrelations of assessments of four observers (each observer with every other observer) with five different samples of elementary teachers, the smallest sample consisting of 43 teachers and the largest of 173. The ranges and medians of the interobserver correlations are given for TCS Patterns X_o, Y_o, and Z_o.

It may be noted from Table 14 that some of the interobserver reliabilities appear to be much too low to be of value in providing estimates of criterion behaviors. Occasionally it was found that an observer, regardless of care and amount of training, consistently submitted assessments which were at variance with those of other observers. Such observers were eliminated from the Study as soon as such inconsistency was detected. It also was found that even with reliable observers two assessments of a teacher might be markedly different, and in such cases, as was noted earlier, an independent observation by a different observer was obtained before the assessment data were combined to form the composite pattern score. The reliabilities reported in Table 14, therefore, probably underestimate the composite assessment reliabilities.

Table 15 shows the reliability coefficients obtained by another approach that was used to determine the equivalence of observer assessments. The data in this table are based upon the correlation between the first observation assessment made of a teacher and the second observation assessment, regardless of the identity of the observers involved. Thus, the observations of one particular teacher in one of the samples here described may have been conducted by Observers 2 and 10, on another teacher they may have been conducted by Observers 5 and 9, and on still another by Observers 2 and 3. The correlations are those between the first and second assessments on each of the Patterns X_o, Y_o, and Z_o.

A matter of some concern was whether or not the amount of time elasping between observations had a significant effect upon the degree of agreement shown by the assessments of different observers. Table 16 shows the comparison of assessments of the same teachers made by two different observers when the observations were conducted with varying amounts of time between observations. The number of cases in each of the four samples is small. For each of the teacher behavior Patterns X_o, Y_o, and Z_o, and for pupil behavior, P_o, the mean observer difference is shown for each of the samples under consideration. The standard error of the mean observer difference and the interobserver correlations also are shown. For these samples and these observers, at least, the observers showed considerable agreement in their assessments and, furthermore, the interval between observations appears to have little effect upon the extent of agreement.

ESTIMATES OF RELIABILITY BASED ON STABILITY OF OBSERVERS' ASSESSMENTS

Two studies were made of the stability of observers' assessments of teacher and pupil classroom behavior.

In the first of these analyses, each of forty-eight elementary teachers was observed *twice by each* of four observers, the second observation following the first by fourteen days. Correlations between the first and second assessments made by a particular observer are shown in Table 17. The initial-repeat assessment correlations for the different observers range from .59 to .67 for Pattern X_o, .71 to .76 for Pattern Y_o, and .46 to .66 for Pattern Z_o. (The median interobserver correlations, rather than intraobserver correlations, were .56 for X_o, .69 for Y_o, and .57 for Z_o.)

The second study of the stability of assessments involved a single observer, one of the senior observers, who reobserved a sample of 99 secondary teachers between twenty and twenty-three months following

TABLE 16

Comparison of Assessments of the Same Teachers Made by Observers 1 and 19 with Varying Amounts of Time between Observations

OBSERVATIONS	N	X_o			Y_o			Z_o			P_o		
		Mean Diff.	σ Diff.	$r_{1\,19}$	Mean Diff.	σ Diff.	$r_{1\,19}$	Mean Diff.	σ Diff.	$r_{1\,19}$	Mean Diff.	σ Diff.	$r_{1\,19}$
Same half-day, interval of 30 min. or less..........	31	4.8	(4.8)	.85	9.3	(6.4)	.62	7.0	(5.7)	.52	6.5	(4.1)	.62
Same half-day, interval of more than 30 min........	31	5.8	(4.2)	.85	7.6	(6.4)	.63	6.3	(4.3)	.78	4.7	(5.5)	.84
Same day, different half-day..........	10	6.0	(3.6)	.85	8.0	(5.5)	.85	6.9	(4.3)	.82	5.9	(3.4)	.72
Same school year, interval of more than 1 month.....	26	5.5	(4.9)	.75	8.5	(8.0)	.52	4.6	(2.7)	.78	7.0	(5.9)	.64

TABLE 17

Stability of Assessments of TCS Teacher Classroom
Behavior Patterns X_o, Y_o, and Z_o, Based on
Two Observations Made Fourteen Days
Apart by Each of Four Observers

($N=48$ elementary teachers)

OBSERVER	CORRELATION BETWEEN FIRST AND SECOND ASSESSMENTS		
	X_o	Y_o	Z_o
11.....	.59	.76	.64
23.....	.67	.72	.56
22.....	.65	.76	.66
21.....	.63	.71	.46

the original observation. The complete table of intercorrelations for the first and second assessments of teacher behavior Patterns X_o, Y_o, and Z_o and pupil behavior Pattern P_o are shown in Table 18. Means and standard deviations of the assessments are given in Table 19. The stability coefficients of .54 for X_o, .65 for Y_o, and .60 for Z_o suggest substantial consistency of the assessment data over the period of almost two years. Since classes change, it is not surprising that the P_o correlation is relatively lower—a coefficient of .35. The mean assessments of the observer increased for Patterns X_o and Z_o and decreased for Y_o over the twenty-month period. The variabilities for Patterns X_o and Z_o decreased while that of Pattern Y_o increased.

TABLE 18

Stability over a Period of Twenty Months of One Observer's
Assessments of Teacher and Pupil Behavior,
Based on Repeated Observations*

($N=99$ secondary teachers)

	Y_{o1}	Z_{o1}	P_{o1}	X_{o2}	Y_{o2}	Z_{o2}	P_{o2}
Intercorrelations between First and Second Assessments of X_o, Y_o, Z_o, and P_o							
X_{o1}.....	−.13	.18	.00	.54	.09	.18	−.07
Y_{o1}.....		.19	.17	−.07	.65	.09	.08
Z_{o1}......			−.21	.13	.21	.60	.23
P_{o1}.....				.25	.21	.24	.35
X_{o2}.....					−.03	.06	.14
Y_{o2}.....						.15	.15
Z_{o2}......							.21

* X_{o1} refers to the X_o assessment resulting from the original observation; X_{o2} refers to the X_o assessment based on the repeated observation; etc.

TABLE 19

Means and Standard Deviations of First and Second Assessments of X_o, Y_o, and Z_o, Made Twenty Months Apart

(N = 99 secondary teachers)

OBSERVATION	X_o		Y_o		Z_o	
	M	σ	M	σ	M	σ
Original observation						
Composite assessment of Observer 1, and other observers......	50.1	7.9	51.5	7.0	48.9	8.3
Assessment of Observer 1.......	49.3	9.7	51.1	7.9	47.5	10.5
Second observation						
Assessment of Observer 1.......	51.6	8.1	49.4	9.5	49.7	8.6

Obtaining Composite Assessments Relative to TCS Patterns X_o, Y_o, and Z_o

As has been noted, replication of observation and assessment became a standard procedure in the effort to obtain acceptable estimates of the teacher classroom behavior Patterns X_o, Y_o, and Z_o of a particular teacher. Once the independent assessments of a teacher had been obtained, the problem faced was how to combine the assessment data provided by each of the several different observers to provide a composite index or score for each teacher on each of the teacher behavior patterns. Such considerations seemed important both for theoretical and for practical reasons. From a theoretical standpoint, there was the question of how to combine the assessment data in order to obtain the most accurate descriptions of a major dimension of teacher behavior. And in the light of a very practical purpose for which the assessment data were later to be employed (to comprise criterion groups against which inventory responses might be validated in an effort to isolate predictors of teacher behavior), it was necessary to consider the appropriateness of different methods of combining the assessments to provide the most accurate criterion data.

The variations in the distributions of the raw assessment data of different observers, as shown in Table 20, and the fact that a four-category assessment scale had been used earlier for some assessments, and a seven-category scale for others, dictated the employment of some kind of transformation, such as standard scores, into which the assessments of each observer could be converted. The assessments of the different observers could then be combined.

A standard score scale with a mean of 50 and a standard deviation of 10 was adopted, and standard scores were derived for each observer for each teacher behavior pattern and separately for the four-category and

TABLE 20

Central Tendency and Variability of Raw Assessments of Each Observer on Teacher Behaviors X_o, Y_o, and Z_o

Observer No.	No. of Teachers Observed	X_o			Y_o			Z_o		
		M	σ	Range	M	σ	Range	M	σ	Range
ELEMENTARY TEACHERS										
Seven-Category Assessment Scale										
1...	293	22.1	3.2	13–31	22.3	3.3	10–31	7.5	1.6	3–13
2...	111	21.9	4.3	12–31	23.3	3.7	12–32	7.5	1.7	4–13
3...	291	22.3	3.9	12–33	21.6	3.7	11–30	7.6	1.7	3–13
4...	126	21.3	3.3	11–30	22.6	3.2	10–30	7.8	1.4	5–12
5...	144	23.0	3.0	13–29	24.5	2.8	16–31	7.9	1.5	5–12
6...	157	22.8	3.6	11–30	23.2	4.3	10–33	7.5	1.7	4–11
7...	100	22.1	4.8	9–32	22.4	3.8	13–31	8.2	1.7	4–14
8...	231	20.5	4.5	8–31	21.2	4.0	10–30	7.5	1.4	2–11
9...	76	21.0	3.9	14–29	22.3	3.0	13–30	8.4	1.5	6–12
10...	310	21.3	3.8	7–32	22.0	3.3	10–30	8.4	1.4	4–12
11...	110	22.9	3.8	13–32	23.2	4.3	8–33	7.9	2.2	3–13
12...	154	22.5	4.3	9–32	22.3	5.6	13–34	7.5	1.9	4–13
13...	15	21.3	5.0	14–28	22.7	3.9	16–30	8.5	1.7	4–11
14...	10	19.0	4.0	13–25	20.7	3.0	17–27	7.4	1.4	6–11
15...	45	22.1	3.5	15–32	22.9	5.5	15–30	7.2	1.5	4–11
17...	68	20.0	6.5	5–35	23.6	5.9	9–34	7.9	2.6	3–14
18...	66	20.1	6.3	7–32	23.1	5.9	10–32	8.2	2.7	3–14
19...	162	21.6	3.0	13–28	21.3	2.9	13–27	7.7	1.6	4–11
Four-Category Assessment Scale										
11...	374	15.5	1.9	10–20	16.1	2.2	8–20	6.2	.9	4–8
20...	72	15.6	2.1	10–20	16.1	1.8	12–20	6.0	1.2	4–8
21...	266	14.8	2.4	6–20	16.6	2.3	7–20	6.0	1.1	3–8
22...	192	16.1	2.2	10–20	16.2	2.1	10–20	6.3	1.1	3–8
23...	194	14.7	2.2	8–20	17.5	2.1	12–20	6.1	.8	3–8
24...	75	15.6	2.8	9–20	16.9	2.8	9–20	6.6	.8	4–8
SECONDARY TEACHERS										
Seven-Category Assessment Scale										
1...	649	21.7	3.0	13–30	8.9	1.4	4–12	7.0	1.7	3–12
2...	21	21.4	3.7	12–29	9.1	1.2	6–11	7.2	1.7	4–10
3...	258	22.4	3.5	12–33	9.6	1.7	4–13	7.7	1.8	4–14
4...	74	21.5	2.9	14–28	9.1	1.4	3–12	7.8	1.7	3–12
5...	111	22.9	3.0	13–29	9.7	1.4	5–13	7.9	1.9	3–14
6...	126	21.8	3.4	13–29	9.7	1.5	5–12	7.5	1.7	4–11
7...	42	21.9	5.3	7–32	9.0	2.3	2–13	8.1	2.2	2–12
8...	270	21.2	3.6	8–28	8.7	1.6	4–12	7.5	1.5	4–12
9...	36	21.3	3.3	16–28	8.9	1.8	6–12	7.8	1.7	5–11
10...	233	22.3	3.9	12–34	9.3	1.5	4–12	8.6	1.7	4–13
11...	398	23.2	3.4	9–33	9.0	1.8	2–14	8.3	2.0	2–14
12...	428	23.0	3.4	12–31	9.1	1.6	4–12	7.7	1.8	4–14
13...	86	23.4	3.8	11–32	9.8	1.8	5–14	8.5	2.2	3–13
14...	68	22.3	6.5	11–30	9.3	1.8	5–13	8.7	2.0	4–13
15...	171	22.2	2.6	13–28	8.4	1.6	4–12	6.3	1.2	4–11
16...	257	20.8	3.6	9–28	8.3	2.0	3–12	7.0	1.9	4–13
Four-Category Assessment Scale										
3...	192	16.1	2.2	9–20	6.6	1.2	3–8	5.8	.9	4–8
11...	314	16.0	2.8	10–20	6.2	1.0	3–8	5.9	1.0	3–8
20...	233	16.0	2.3	9–20	6.4	1.3	2–8	5.8	1.3	2–8

the seven-category forms of the Record. It became possible in this manner to (*a*) approach comparability of the four- and seven-category scales and (*b*) adjust for systematic tendencies of observers to be high or low in their assessments of teacher behaviors and either to spread out their assessments or cluster them more closely about a central value. In all the analyses and studies subsequently to be reported, estimates of teacher behavior Patterns X_o, Y_o, and Z_o (and also of P_o) are based upon composites obtained by combining and averaging these standard scores of the assessments of the observers conducting observations of a particular teacher.

In the absence of acceptable evidence of the desirability of differentially weighting the pattern scores of different observers, each observer's assessment of a teacher behavior pattern (in standard score form) was given an equal weight of unity in forming a composite assessment.

Interrelationships among the Patterns of Teacher Behavior

In the discussion of the derivation of Patterns X_o, Y_o, and Z_o, attention was called to the fact that in general the patterns were positively correlated and that there was some variation in the magnitude of the correlations for elementary teacher groups as compared with groups of secondary teachers. The data presented in Table 21 summarize intercorrelation data, based upon composite observer assessments, for teacher behavior Patterns X_o, Y_o, and Z_o and for pupil behavior, P_o. Data for three samples of elementary teachers and for five variously comprised secondary teacher groups are shown.

For the elementary teacher group, teacher behavior Patterns X_o, Y_o, and Z_o are substantially intercorrelated and each is also highly correlated with pupil behavior Pattern P_o. Intercorrelations for these samples of elementary teachers are almost as high as the reliability coefficients for the patterns. From these data one might reasonably conclude that in the elementary classroom the patterns of teacher behavior have considerable common variance and that there is substantial interdependence and interaction among teacher behavior Patterns X_o, Y_o, and Z_o and pupil behavior P_o.

For secondary teachers the picture is somewhat different. Teacher behavior Patterns X_o and Z_o and also Y_o and Z_o are markedly correlated, while, in general, the correlations between Patterns X_o and Y_o are distinctly lower. It is interesting to find that assessments of pupil behavior, as revealed by Pattern P_o, have positive, but *low*, correlations with the teacher behavior Patterns X_o, Y_o, and Z_o for teachers in the major

TABLE 21

Intercorrelations between Composite Observer Assessments for Teacher Behavior Patterns X_o, Y_o, and Z_o and for Pupil Behavior P_o

Subsample	N	Pattern	r Y_o	Z_o	P_o
Elementary teachers					
Grades 1–6 teachers	978	X_o	.61	.67	.82
		Y_o		.67	.80
		Z_o			.75
Grades 1–6 teachers	144	X_o	.60	.78	.83
		Y_o		.56	.78
		Z_o			.80
Grades 1–8 teachers	97	X_o	.36	.61	.57
		Y_o		.56	.50
		Z_o			.66
Secondary teachers					
Mathematics, science, English, and social studies teachers	114	X_o	.11	.50	.07
		Y_o		.41	.11
		Z_o			.14
Mathematics and science teachers	497	X_o	.34	.48	.20
		Y_o		.57	.18
		Z_o			.21
English and social studies teachers	568	X_o	.19	.48	.18
		Y_o		.48	.21
		Z_o			.26
Business education teachers	125	X_o	.34	.60	.63
		Y_o		.52	.53
		Z_o			.57
Foreign language teachers	116	X_o	.55	.69	.60
		Y_o		.62	.49
		Z_o			.58
Combined elementary and secondary teachers	2,043	X_o	.44	.57	.34
		Y_o		.60	.34
		Z_o			.35

secondary groups studied (i.e., mathematics, science, English, and social studies). The correlations for small samples of business education and foreign language teachers do not, however, follow this pattern, the magnitude of the relationship between pupil behavior and teacher behavior being more like that obtained for elementary teachers.

Generalizing, it seems that the patterns of teacher behavior X_o, Y_o, and Z_o are somewhat more distinctly discernible, or more independent, among secondary teachers than among elementary teachers and that pupil behavior also is more independent of teacher behavior in the secondary school than in the elementary school. As will be shown in the following chapter, data obtained from inventory responses of teachers also tend to bear out this conclusion.

Comparisons of Teachers Relative to Teacher Behavior Patterns X_o, Y_o, and Z_o and Pupil Behavior Pattern P_o

It is of interest to note at this point certain comparisons of groups of teachers classified with regard to behavior Patterns X_o, Y_o, and Z_o and the teachers' classes assessed with regard to pupil behavior P_o.

Several comments and notes are in order and should be kept in mind as these comparisons are described. First, all comparisons refer to *group data*, to group means and measures of variability. The data may, therefore, suggest certain generalizations, but such generalizations by no means apply to all members of a group. As in the case of actuarial data upon which the operations of life insurance companies are based, the generalizations drawn from these data must be interpreted in the light of probability. Second, the position of a teacher near one of the poles of a teacher behavior pattern is intended to provide a *factual description* of certain aspects of that teacher's behavior and does not necessarily identify a teacher as "effective" or "ineffective." Describing a teacher as friendly and understanding does not per se mean that the teacher is a competent teacher—that friendliness and understanding necessarily denote effectiveness. Third, in reviewing comparisons of teacher behaviors and pupil behavior, it is necessary to remember that the observation data pertaining to pupils and teachers are mutually contaminated, since the assessments of pupils and of teachers were made by the same observer at the same time. In spite of this, however, it is worthwhile to note group variations on an index made up of a composite of the pupil behavior dimensions.

The means and standard deviations shown in the tables that follow are based on composite observer assessments of the individual teachers —the average of the combined standard score assessments of the different observers who observed a particular teacher.

It will be seen that the mean composite observer assessments for Patterns X_o, Y_o, and Z_o for the *total elementary* group and *total secondary* group generally exceed 50 (the mean of the standard score scale to which the individual assessments originally were converted) and that the standard deviations are smaller than 10 (the standard deviation of the scale to which the assessments originally were converted). These variations are a result of the fact that the data presented in these tables are not based upon the complete set of observations, but rather upon the observations of those teachers who returned all materials they were requested to submit, and furthermore, those who participated in the Study subsequent to the standardization and reduction of the inventory materials to a single booklet. A number of teachers who were observed, and who were included in the distributions from which the standard scores were derived for each of the observers, did not fill out the inventory materials as required. In tabulating the data, observation records were excluded for those teachers whose Study data were incomplete, and also for those teachers who were observed prior to the fall of 1951. Teachers comprising the samples here compared, therefore, appear to be more highly selected with respect to Patterns X_o, Y_o, and Z_o than the total group of teachers observed during the entire course of the Study.

One further comment is in order regarding the comparisons to be presented. In chapter 7 similar comparisons are made on the basis of teachers' responses to a paper-and-pencil inventory (the Teacher Characteristics Schedule). As will be noted in the later chapter, the comparisons based on Teacher Characteristics Schedule scores X_{co}, Y_{co}, and Z_{co} generally correspond with the comparisons presented here for X_o, Y_o, and Z_o. There are, however, minor variations between the two sets of data, one being based on direct observation and assessment and the other on correlates of observed behavior in the form of inventory responses. Also, it will be evident that some of the differences between groups yielded by observers' assessments are accentuated when the comparisons are based on the Schedule responses. This is not unreasonable. It may well be that the measurements yielded by the inventory responses are better indicators of the hypothesized underlying behavior patterns than are the criterion measurements (assessments of observed behavior) employed in the research. The inventory responses may be less influenced by contaminating extraneous variance than are the criteria themselves.

COMPARISONS OF ASSESSMENTS WITH RESPECT TO SEX OF TEACHER AND TO GRADE AND SUBJECT MATTER TAUGHT

Table 22 shows the means and standard deviations of composite observer assessments on Patterns X_o, Y_o, Z_o, and P_o for teachers classified according to grade and subject taught and sex. In general, there are no great differences between the teacher groups with respect to mean assessments on Pattern X_o (friendly-understanding teacher behavior).

The groups that were assessed highest on Pattern X_o are those made up of men social studies teachers, women English teachers, women Grades 5–6 teachers, and women social studies teachers, and the most homogeneous groups on Pattern X_o are the Grades 5–6 women and the men science teachers. Women science teachers comprised the lowest assessed group on Pattern X_o. The F ratio is not significant at the .05 level for Pattern X_o.

With regard to Pattern Y_o (businesslike, responsible teacher behavior) the highest mean assessments were received by Grades 5–6 women teachers, mathematics women teachers, and social studies women teachers, with the means of English men and social studies men teachers dis-

TABLE 22

Comparison of Composite Observer Assessments X_o, Y_o, Z_o, and P_o of Teachers in Basic Analysis Sample Classified According to Grade or Subject Taught and Sex

Grade or Subject Taught and Sex	N	X_o		Y_o		Z_o		P_o	
		M	σ	M	σ	M	σ	M	σ
Elementary teachers									
Grades 1–2; female........	190	50.7	8.7	49.5	8.5	50.6	7.2	50.0	8.9
Grades 3–4; female........	431	50.9	9.9	50.4	9.5	51.1	8.9	50.5	9.0
Grades 5–6; female........	97	51.5	7.2	53.7	9.7	52.5	8.7	52.4	6.5
Grades 3–6; male..........	116	50.6	7.6	50.4	7.4	49.5	8.8	50.3	8.1
Secondary teachers									
Mathematics; female.......	104	50.1	9.3	53.1	6.6	50.1	6.7	53.0	10.1
Mathematics; male........	105	49.6	8.1	50.0	7.6	49.5	6.9	47.7	9.7
Science; female............	90	49.3	7.5	50.8	8.1	51.5	7.5	50.6	9.5
Science; male.............	148	49.8	7.3	49.3	8.0	50.8	8.4	48.4	9.5
English; female...........	195	51.5	8.2	49.9	7.1	49.0	7.5	48.0	10.2
English; male.............	86	50.7	9.6	47.4	6.9	50.1	8.7	46.8	9.3
Social studies; female......	121	51.4	7.9	52.5	8.1	51.7	8.1	52.2	9.8
Social studies; male........	102	51.6	7.7	47.2	7.6	50.5	8.7	50.4	9.0
Elementary "hold-out" validation sample.................	144	49.3	8.5	49.9	7.5	49.5	7.3	49.1	8.4
Secondary "hold-out" validation sample...................	114	50.7	8.3	50.3	7.9	50.5	8.0	49.4	9.9
Elementary teachers, total group	978	50.7	9.0	50.5	8.9	50.7	8.4	50.4	8.6
Secondary teachers, total group.	1,065	50.7	8.3	50.3	7.9	50.5	8.0	49.4	9.9

tinctly lower. The women mathematics teachers were the most homogeneous group on Y_o.

Again on teacher behavior Pattern Z_o the Grades 5–6 women teachers received the highest mean assessment, followed by women teachers of social studies and of science. Women English teachers were assessed lowest.

With respect to pupil behavior the classes of women mathematics teachers and women Grades 5–6 teachers received the higher mean assessments, with men English teachers and men mathematics teachers among the lowest of the groups. Variability was lowest for the classes of Grades 5–6 women teachers.

Differences between means of teachers classified according to grade and subject taught and sex as noted above were statistically significant at the .05 level (F tests) for Patterns Y_o, Z_o, and P_o, but not for Pattern X_o. It also seems that the mean assessments of women teachers tend to be higher than those of men. There are no significant differences between elementary and secondary teachers taken as total groups.

COMPARISON OF ASSESSMENTS WITH REGARD TO AGE, EXPERIENCE, AND MARITAL STATUS OF THE TEACHER

Table 23 shows the means and standard deviations of composite observer assessments on Patterns X_o, Y_o, Z_o, and P_o for teachers classified according to age.

TABLE 23

Comparison of Composite Observer Assessments X_o, Y_o, Z_o, and P_o of Teachers in Basic Analysis Sample Classified According to Age

AGE	N	X_o		Y_o		Z_o		P_o	
		M	σ	M	σ	M	σ	M	σ
Elementary teachers									
29 years or younger...	374	51.1	9.5	49.8	9.4	50.5	8.7	50.1	9.1
30–39 years..........	226	51.4	8.1	50.7	7.9	51.2	7.9	51.1	8.3
40–54 years..........	322	50.9	9.1	51.7	9.4	51.4	8.8	51.2	8.1
55 years or older.....	56	48.1	9.0	49.5	9.2	50.1	8.0	48.7	8.9
Mathematics-science teachers									
29 years or younger...	51	50.1	7.9	50.4	6.6	50.5	6.8	46.3	8.9
30–39 years..........	104	52.0	7.4	50.4	8.4	51.7	7.8	49.1	10.5
40–54 years..........	226	50.3	8.5	51.5	7.9	51.4	8.0	51.4	9.8
55 years or older.....	116	48.0	7.7	50.7	7.8	48.8	6.9	48.2	9.5
English–social studies teachers									
29 years or younger...	54	50.6	8.2	48.4	6.2	49.6	7.7	45.6	8.9
30–39 years..........	136	52.2	8.4	47.6	7.2	50.6	8.6	48.1	10.4
40–54 years..........	259	51.8	8.4	50.2	8.2	50.6	8.1	50.2	9.6
55 years or older.....	119	49.0	8.0	51.1	7.5	49.2	8.0	49.8	9.8

With respect to teacher behavior Pattern X_o, there appears to be a a tendency for teachers between the ages of 30 and 39 years to receive somewhat higher assessments than do the older or younger teachers, and for teachers over 55 years of age to receive the lowest assessments. F ratios were significant at the .05 level for the secondary teacher sample, but not for the elementary teacher sample.

With respect to Pattern Y_o elementary teachers and mathematics-science teachers of the 40–54 years age group attain the highest assessments. Among English–social studies teachers, those over 40 years of age were observed to be distinctly more systematic and responsible than the younger teachers. F ratios were significant at the .05 level for the elementary and English–social studies samples, but not for the mathematics-science teachers.

From the standpoint of stimulating teacher behavior Pattern Z_o, the teachers of age groups 30–39 and 40–54 appear to be similar and to receive somewhat higher mean assessments than the other age groups. The F ratio was significant (.05 level) only for the mathematics-science teachers.

Pupil behaviors appear to be assessed lower in classes of the youngest group of teachers (less than 30 years of age) than in those of the middle age ranges, this being particularly true for secondary school teachers. Classes of the older teacher group (more than 55 years of age) also receive lower mean ratings than those of teachers of the middle age ranges in most instances. F tests yielded significant ratios (.05 level) for the mathematics-science and English–social studies samples.

The means and standard deviations of assessments of the teacher and pupil behavior patterns of teachers classified according to the amount of teaching experience are shown in Tables 24 and 25. Some of the experience groups to which these tables apply represent fairly small numbers of teachers, and it is difficult to observe trends. However, among the elementary teachers, the 5–9 year and 15–19 year experience groups receive higher mean assessments on all of the teacher behavior patterns. There is a slight but inconsistent tendency for teachers with less experience to be more lowly assessed and those with greater amounts of experience more highly assessed on Pattern Y_o. The relationships between extent of experience and classroom behavior patterns of elementary teachers appear to be curvilinear, according to the data in Table 25. Teacher groups with less than five years of experience and those with ten or more years of experience receive lower average assessments on all three patterns than does the 5–9 year experience group.

Marital status of the teacher seems to bear little relation to observed teacher classroom behavior. The means and standard deviations on Patterns X_o, Y_o, Z_o, and P_o shown in Table 26 vary slightly and, for the most part, insignificantly. For elementary teachers the means of married teachers are slightly higher than those of the single teachers. For mathematics-science teachers the mean assessments of single teachers exceed those of married teachers on each of the teacher behavior patterns. The mean assessment of pupil behavior, P_o, in classes of single mathematics-science teachers is significantly greater (at the .01 level) than that of classes of married teachers. There is no consistent trend to be found in the differences between mean assessments of single and

TABLE 24

Comparison of Composite Observer Assessments X_o, Y_o, Z_o, and P_o of Teachers in Basic Analysis Sample Classified According to Amount of Teaching Experience

EXTENT OF EXPERIENCE	N	X_o		Y_o		Z_o		P_o	
		M	σ	M	σ	M	σ	M	σ
Elementary teachers									
Less than 1 year.....	99	49.8	8.9	48.4	8.9	49.4	7.8	48.8	9.8
1–2 years............	196	50.9	9.7	49.6	10.2	49.9	9.6	49.8	9.2
3 years..............	84	50.7	7.9	50.0	7.9	51.1	7.5	50.6	8.3
4 years..............	55	49.8	8.5	49.9	7.5	49.7	7.1	49.5	8.4
5–9 years............	160	51.7	8.8	51.5	8.1	52.0	7.3	51.9	8.3
10–14 years.........	117	50.1	8.0	49.6	7.6	50.0	7.6	49.5	7.6
15–19 years.........	105	51.9	9.5	53.5	10.3	53.0	9.7	52.3	7.2
20 or more years.....	162	49.6	9.0	51.0	7.8	50.4	8.1	50.1	8.5
Mathematics-science teachers									
Less than 1 year.....	14	50.2	4.7	49.1	5.5	47.8	6.5	47.4	5.4
1–2 years............	23	47.4	8.0	50.8	7.4	52.8	9.3	49.1	9.6
3 years..............	28	52.5	6.0	49.1	8.6	50.2	4.9	48.0	9.7
4 years..............	24	52.3	7.0	51.7	8.1	52.7	9.0	53.3	12.7
5–9 years............	65	50.2	8.3	50.6	8.0	51.0	7.7	49.6	8.7
10–14 years.........	60	50.5	7.1	51.0	6.7	51.1	7.5	49.2	9.8
15–19 years.........	64	50.6	7.9	51.6	8.0	51.9	8.0	50.9	9.0
20 or more years.....	219	49.6	8.9	51.3	8.1	50.1	7.6	50.5	10.1
English–social studies teachers									
Less than 1 year.....	14	51.8	8.2	48.4	8.0	49.8	6.4	47.9	8.7
1–2 years............	33	51.2	8.3	46.0	6.3	46.8	8.1	45.2	9.6
3 years..............	25	50.9	7.7	47.5	6.6	51.0	8.5	46.9	8.4
4 years..............	24	50.9	7.6	48.4	6.4	50.6	7.9	50.6	8.4
5–9 years............	86	51.8	8.9	48.6	7.9	51.5	8.0	48.1	10.4
10–14 years.........	78	51.4	9.0	48.3	6.5	49.3	8.8	48.8	9.5
15–19 years.........	91	52.1	7.5	49.8	7.9	50.0	8.3	49.8	9.4
20 or more years.....	217	50.6	8.4	51.4	8.0	50.4	7.9	50.9	9.7

married English–social studies teachers, the differences that do occur being slightly in favor of married teachers for Patterns X_o and Z_o and slightly in favor of the single teachers for Patterns Y_o and P_o. The numbers of widowed and of separated or divorced teachers are too small to permit conclusions to be drawn, although the relatively lower pupil behavior indices in classes of widowed teachers may be noteworthy. It

TABLE 25

Comparison of Composite Observer Assessments of an Independent Sample of Elementary Teachers Classified by Extent of Teaching Experience

EXTENT OF EXPERIENCE	N	X_o		Y_o		Z_o		P_o	
		M	σ	M	σ	M	σ	M	σ
1–4 years..............	60	49.4	8.4	47.2	8.7	50.2	7.7	48.2	8.2
5–9 years..............	32	54.5	9.3	52.9	8.4	54.6	9.9	52.6	9.8
10 or more years.......	111	49.6	7.5	51.7	7.4	49.0	8.3	50.5	7.3

TABLE 26

Comparison of Composite Observer Assessments X_o, Y_o, Z_o, and P_o of Teachers in Basic Analysis Sample Classified According to Marital Status

MARITAL STATUS	N	X_o		Y_o		Z_o		P_o	
		M	σ	M	σ	M	σ	M	σ
Elementary teachers									
Single...............	283	50.4	10.4	50.4	10.6	50.3	10.0	49.7	9.0
Married.............	575	50.9	8.3	50.8	8.1	50.9	7.7	50.8	8.4
Separated-divorced ...	69	51.3	8.3	49.2	8.8	51.8	7.7	50.5	8.4
Widowed...........	51	48.2	9.0	49.5	7.4	50.0	7.5	48.9	8.1
Mathematics-science teachers									
Single...............	114	50.7	8.9	51.8	8.1	51.7	7.4	52.0	10.3
Married.............	339	50.1	7.9	50.9	7.8	50.6	7.9	49.1	9.7
Separated-divorced ...	21	49.8	7.8	48.4	8.3	50.4	5.1	51.0	9.7
Widowed...........	23	46.9	7.8	51.0	7.7	48.7	8.0	46.9	10.5
English–social studies teachers									
Single...............	199	50.4	8.0	51.0	7.3	50.2	7.7	50.0	9.3
Married.............	318	51.9	8.6	48.9	8.1	50.5	8.4	49.1	10.3
Separated-divorced ...	26	50.4	7.4	47.9	8.2	47.7	7.9	47.2	8.5
Widowed...........	25	50.9	7.6	51.0	5.8	49.9	8.3	46.8	10.4

also is of interest to note that among elementary teachers the highest means on Patterns X_o and Z_o were obtained by the separated-divorced group.

ADDITIONAL COMPARISONS OF ASSESSMENTS OF ELEMENTARY TEACHERS DERIVED FROM AN INDEPENDENT SAMPLE

During early phases of the Study, a number of comparisons were made of observers' assessments in relation to the teachers' personal characteristics and employment conditions. The comparisons reported in this section involve an independent sample of women teachers of Grades 3 and 4, employed in four different municipalities that ranged in population size from fifty thousand to approximately one hundred thousand and were located in the same geographic area. In spite of the fact that four different school systems supplied the teachers, the sample apparently was quite homogeneous. At least there were no significant differences between the means of the teachers in the four communities with respect to X_o, Y_o, Z_o, and P_o assessment scores. Obviously, this does not imply that community differences in teacher behavior patterns do not exist elsewhere.

COMPARISON OF TEACHERS ACCORDING TO AMOUNT OF COLLEGE TRAINING

Table 27 shows the mean X_o, Y_o, Z_o, and P_o assessments of teachers in this sample when they are classified into three "amount of college training" groups. None of the differences approached significance, indi-

TABLE 27

Comparison of Composite Observer Assessments of Elementary Teachers Classified by Amount of College Training

Amount of College Training	N	X_o		Y_o		Z_o		P_o	
		M	σ	M	σ	M	σ	M	σ
Less than 4 years.......	75	50.2	8.1	50.5	8.1	50.5	7.8	50.0	7.7
4–5 years..............	107	49.8	8.8	50.1	9.0	49.7	9.3	49.9	8.9
6 or more years........	9	50.0	5.2	50.1	5.0	50.4	5.7	50.0	5.9

cating that, at least for the particular samples, categories, and teacher behavior patterns employed, there was little relationship between extent of college study and classroom behavior.

COMPARISON OF TEACHERS ACCORDING TO SOCIOECONOMIC STATUS OF COMMUNITY IN WHICH TEACHING IS PERFORMED

When the teachers were classified by socioeconomic status of the neighborhood in which their school was located, the differences obtained were small, and none of the F tests indicated significance approaching the 5 percent level. For these particular communities, it appears that the kind of neighborhood from which the pupils were drawn did not have discernible effects on either teacher or pupil behavior at the third- and fourth-grade levels. The data are shown in Table 28.

TABLE 28

Comparison of Composite Observer Assessments of Elementary Teachers Classified by Socioeconomic Status of Community in Which Teaching Is Performed

Socioeconomic* Status	N	X_o		Y_o		Z_o		P_o	
		M	σ	M	σ	M	σ	M	σ
Above average.........	40	48.7	7.7	50.6	6.7	49.9	7.5	50.0	6.1
Average...............	212	50.0	8.3	49.9	8.6	50.0	8.4	49.8	8.4
Below average.........	23	51.2	7.0	50.3	6.9	49.3	7.5	49.8	7.6

* A seven-category scale for the rating of socioeconomic status of communities was developed by a modified paired-comparison technique. For the comparisons of teachers presented here, the seven-point scale was condensed to provide three groupings of school communities, with ratings of 3, 4, and 5 constituting the "average" category.

COMPARISON OF TEACHERS ACCORDING TO TEACHER-PRINCIPAL AGREEMENT OF EDUCATIONAL VIEWPOINTS

To test the hypothesis that teacher performance may be related to "school performance," as indicated by agreement in viewpoint of teachers and principal relative to educational questions, an Educational Viewpoint Inquiry[13] was administered both to teachers and to the principals

[13] The Educational Viewpoint Inquiry is described in chap. 5.

of their schools. An index was employed to indicate the extent of agreement between the Inquiry responses of the teachers and their principals. In Table 29, extreme groups, made up of the 27 percent of the teachers in greatest agreement with their principals and the 27 percent in least agreement with their principals, are compared with regard to mean X_o, Y_o, Z_o, and P_o assessments. The groups do not differ significantly on any of these behavior patterns.

TABLE 29

Comparison of Composite Observer Assessments of Elementary Teachers Comprising High 27 Percent and Low 27 Percent Groups on Extent of Agreement of Teacher's Responses with Her Principal's Responses to the Educational Viewpoints Inquiry

Group	N	X_o		Y_o		Z_o		P_o	
		M	σ	M	σ	M	σ	M	σ
Teachers high in agreement with principals...	41	50.9	8.0	49.9	7.8	50.8	8.0	50.0	8.0
Teachers low in agreement with principals...	41	49.1	8.9	50.0	8.7	50.0	9.3	49.3	8.9

COMPARISONS OF TEACHER GROUPS RELATIVE TO PERSONAL TRAITS

In another investigation conducted with this independent elementary teacher sample, the teachers were divided into high and low criterion groups (upper 27 percent and lower 27 percent) with respect to each of the teacher behavior Patterns X_o, Y_o, Z_o, and P_o, and means were computed for the four high criterion groups and the four low criterion groups for the dimensions measured by (a) the Thurstone Temperament Schedule (active, vigorous, impulsive, dominant, stable, sociable, and reflective scales), (b) the Minnesota Multiphasic Personality Inventory (hypochondriasis, depression, hysteria, psychopathic deviate, masculine interests, paranoia, psychasthenia, schizophrenia, hypomania, responsibility, and social status scales), and (c) the Allport-Vernon Study of Values (theoretical, economic, esthetic, social, political, and religious scales).

Among sixty-eight different comparisons of the high and low group means involving the eleven scales of the Minnesota Multiphasic Personality Inventory and the six scales of the Allport-Vernon Study of Values, only one difference was found to be significant at the 5 percent level. For these teachers, at least, it appears that personal traits measured by the scales of these two inventories are unrelated to the classroom behavior Patterns X_o, Y_o, Z_o, and P_o.

The Thurstone Temperament Schedule, even though it is generally regarded as a somewhat unreliable instrument, presumably is made up of scales which may be related to Patterns X_o, Y_o, Z_o, and P_o. The high criterion group with respect to Pattern X_o differed significantly from the low criterion group, attaining higher mean scores on the impulsive, dominant, and sociable scales. The high Z_o group made higher scores than the low group on the vigorous, impulsive, dominant, and sociable scales. The high P_o criterion group achieved higher mean scores than the low group on the dominant and sociable scales. No significant differences, however, were obtained with respect to the Pattern Y_o.[14]

Bibliography

1. BARR, A. S., *et al.* "The Measurement and Prediction of Teaching Efficiency: A Summary of Investigations," *Journal of Experimental Education,* **16**: 203–83, 1948.
2. BAXTER, B. *Teacher-Pupil Relationships.* New York: Macmillan Co., 1941.
3. BAYROFF, A. G.; HAGGERTY, H. R.; and RUNDQUIST, E. A. "Validity of Ratings as Related to Rating Techniques and Conditions," *Personal Psychology,* **7**: 93–113, 1954.
4. CATTELL, R. B. *Description and Measurement of Personality.* Yonkers, N.Y.: World Book Co., 1946.
5. CHARTERS, W. W., and WAPLES, D. *The Commonwealth Teacher Training Study.* Chicago: University of Chicago Press, 1929.
6. COFFMAN, W. E. "Determining Students' Concepts of Effective Teaching from Their Ratings of Instructors," *Journal of Educational Psychology,* **45**: 277–86, 1954.
7. COMREY, A. L.; HIGH, W. S.; and GOLDBERG, L. L. "Factorial Dimensions of Organizational Behavior, I: Field Service Workers," *Educational and Psychological Measurement,* **15**: 225–35, 1955.
8. CREAGER, J. A. "A Multiple Factor Analysis of the Purdue Rating Scale for Instructors," *Studies in Higher Education, LXX.* Lafayette, Ind.: Purdue University, **70**: 75–96, 1950.
9. FLANAGAN, J. C. "The Critical Incident Technique," *Psychological Bulletin,* **51**: 327–58, 1954.
10. FRENCH, G. M. *College Students' Concepts of Effective Teaching Determined by an Analysis of Teacher Ratings.* Mimeographed. Seattle, Wash.: University of Washington, February 1957.
11. FRENCH, J. W. *The Description of Personality Measurements in Terms of Rotated Factors.* Princeton, N.J.: Educational Testing Service, 1953.

---

[14] It should be noted that some of the definitions of the Thurstone traits differ from what the layman might assume from the trait names. Thus, *impulsive* is defined as " . . . makes decisions quickly, enjoys competition, and changes easily from one task to another . . . person who doggedly 'hangs on' when acting or thinking is typically low in this area." With respect to *dominance,* those who score high " . . . enjoy public speaking, organizing social activities, promoting new projects, and persuading others . . . they are not domineering, even though they have leadership ability." Persons with high scores on the *sociable* scale " . . . enjoy the company of others, make friends easily, and are sympathetic, cooperative, and agreeable in their relations with people. Strangers readily tell them about personal troubles."

12. GIBB, C. A. "Classroom Behavior of the College Teacher," *Educational and Psychological Measurement*, **15**: 254–63, 1955.
13. GUILFORD, J. P. *Psychometric Methods*. New York: McGraw-Hill Book Co., 1955.
14. HIGH, W. S.; GOLDBERG, L. L.; and COMREY, A. L. "Factorial Dimensions of Organizational Behavior, II: Aircraft Workers," *Educational and Psychological Measurement*, **15**: 371–82, 1955.
15. JENSEN, A. C. "Determining Critical Requirements for Teachers," *Journal of Experimental Education*, **20**: 79–86, 1951.
16. KELLEY, T. L. *Fundamentals of Statistics*. Cambridge, Mass.: Harvard University Press, 1947.
17. LAWSHE, C. H., and NAGLE, B. F. "A Note on the Combination of Ratings on the Basis of Reliability," *Psychological Bulletin*, **49**: 270–73, 1952.
18. MORSH, J. E. *Systematic Observation of Instructor Behavior*. (Development Report AFPTRC-TN-56-52.) Lackland Air Force Base, Texas: Air Force Personnel and Training Research Center, 1956.
19. MORSH, J. E., and WILDER, E. W. *Identifying the Effective Instructor: A Review of the Quantitative Studies, 1900–1952*. San Antonio, Texas: Air Force Personnel and Training Research Center, 1954.
20. RYANS, D. G. "An Analysis and Comparison of Certain Techniques for Weighting Criterion Data," *Educational and Psychological Measurement*, **14**: 449–58, 1954.
21. ———. "The Investigation of Teacher Characteristics," *Educational Record*, **34**: 370–96, 1953.
22. ———. "A Study of Criterion Data (A Factor Analysis of Teacher Behaviors in the Elementary School)," *Educational and Psychological Measurement*, **12**: 333–44, 1952.
23. RYANS, D. G., and WANDT, E. "A Factor Analysis of Observed Teacher Behavior in the Secondary School: A Study of Criterion Data," *Educational and Psychological Measurement*, **12**: 574–86, 1952.
24. SHEN, E. "The Reliability Coefficient of Personal Ratings," *Journal of Educational Psychology*, **16**: 232–36, 1925.
25. SMALZRIED, N. T., and REMMERS, H. H. "A Factor Analysis of the Purdue Rating Scale for Instructors," *Journal of Educational Psychology*, **34**: 363–67, 1943.
26. SYMONDS, P. M. *Diagnosing Personality and Conduct*. New York: Appleton-Century Co., 1931.
27. TAFT, R. "The Ability To Judge People," *Psychological Bulletin*, **51**: 1–23, 1955.
28. WOODS, W. L.; BROUHA, L.; and SELTZER, C. C. *Selection of Officer Candidates*. Cambridge, Mass.: Harvard University Press, 1943.

5. Estimation of Teacher Attitudes, Educational Viewpoints, Verbal Understanding, and Adjustment from Responses to Direct Questions

ALTHOUGH ONE of the major interests of the Teacher Characteristics Study was the classroom behaviors of teachers, it was recognized from the beginning of the project that various other teacher characteristic domains also must be considered in any attempt to describe teacher personality. What the teacher does in the classroom—the actual performance—naturally is of prime concern. Certain conative and cognitive characteristics of the teacher, however, also may be important. Such questions as the following seemed to merit attention in the Study:

1. How may *teachers' attitudes* toward children, toward other persons with whom teachers frequently come in contact, and toward "democratic classroom practices" be described, identified, and estimated?

2. How may *teachers' educational viewpoints* be identified and estimated? What are the teachers' beliefs about the relative importance of providing instruction in the fundamentals and traditional subject matter, as compared with other objectives espoused by schools; about the emphasis to be placed on academic achievement and high standards of accomplishments; about teacher participation in other than strictly instructional responsibilities?

3. How are teacher attitudes and viewpoints related to teacher performance in the classroom, and to other characteristics of the teacher, such as age and experience? How are (a) general verbal comprehension and (b) emotional stability, or adjustment, of the teacher related to his classroom behavior, and to other personal and professional characteristics?

To investigate such problems, a considerable amount of time was devoted to the analysis of teachers' attitudes, educational viewpoints, verbal understanding, and emotional adjustment, and to the development of questionnaires for providing estimates of such characteristics of teachers. A word about the general approach employed to obtain the basic data regarding these characteristics is in order.

Up to the present time no one has been able to devise a more reliable or more valid method of obtaining data in the conative and cognitive domains of human behavior than that involving estimation based upon the direct questioning of the individual. The basic assumptions (and the possible weaknesses) of direct-inquiry methods are that the responding individual is (1) able to understand the questions put to him and to provide the required judgments or information, and (2) willing to reveal the responses which, in his own case, seem to be either the correct or the best answers to the questions.

In the instance of a question calling for knowledge, understanding, or problem-solving (e.g., vocabulary items, verbal analogies), there is a unique response which represents the best answer or correct solution for all persons, and it is assumed that the respondent will try to give the required answers to the best of his ability.

For questions concerned with past, present, or future *personal behavior* of the individual, no unique answers are equally applicable for all respondents. The use of direct questioning here assumes, in addition, certain capabilities on the part of the respondent to (*a*) recognize his preferences, likes, dislikes, etc., (*b*) analyze his own behavior and its motivation, (*c*) recall his past behavior and generalize to probable behavior in similar future situations, (*d*) maintain a certain amount of objectivity in making judgments about himself, and (*e*) demonstrate willingness to record his honest judgments, avoiding the temptation to give other responses that may appear to be more socially acceptable or individually advantageous.

In spite of these demanding conditions upon which validity of response is dependent, there probably is no better way of obtaining information (criterion data) about certain personal characteristics than by direct questioning [*8*]. The physician must rely upon this method to a very great extent in arriving at diagnostic judgments; legal procedure recognizes verbal examination as basic to the accumulation of evidence leading to judgment of guilt or absence of guilt; the psychologist, regardless of his devotion to overt behavior manifestations, would be blocked repeatedly in his progress toward an understanding of human behavior if he were not able to communicate with his subjects and to assume the usability of their responses to his questions.

It seemed reasonable to the staff, therefore, to proceed on the assumption that within the normal range of many characteristics of human behavior, self-appraisal of personal and social responses can be used effectively to provide criterion data. It appeared proper to assemble questions having a sound rationale for the purposes employed and, after empirical testing, to employ them for identifying individuals with respect to designated characteristics. The shortcomings of the method were, of course, recognized, and study was devoted to the avoidance of possible sources of invalidity and unreliability in question-writing, to methods of item analysis, and also to the development of means of detecting tendency to fake or give other than the individually valid response.

The direct inquiry method was then used to obtain criterion data relative to attitudes, educational viewpoints, verbal intelligence, emotional adjustment, and tendency to give valid responses of individual teachers participating in the research. This chapter will consider the research conducted and procedures employed in the development of direct-question materials for obtaining estimates of such conative and cognitive characteristics of teachers.

Investigating the Social Attitudes of Teachers

To anyone concerned with teaching, the desirability of attempting to understand motivational backgrounds as revealed in teachers' opinions about school-related matters is self-evident. While the extent of relationship between verbally expressed attitudes, or opinions, and pupil-influencing teacher practices is generally unknown, the case for studying social attitudes has been ably argued (e.g., Murphy [5], and others), and opinion measurement as a guide to the understanding and prediction of human behavior has been extensively employed.

Studies of *teacher* attitudes, interestingly enough, have not been as numerous as might be expected. Perhaps the best-known investigations have been those growing out of Leeds' work and the subsequent development of the Minnesota Teacher Attitude Inventory [2], a questionnaire concerned with teachers' opinions on teacher-pupil relationships.

Early efforts of the Teacher Characteristics Study in the investigation of teacher attitudes were directed toward the development of two scales utilizing Thurstone's equal-appearing intervals method [10]: Inventory T, a sixteen-item scale relating to opinions about teachers and teaching as a profession; and Inventory P, a ten-item scale concerned with opinions about pupils and ways of dealing with children. These typically Thurstone-type opinionnaires were employed for preliminary studies during the first three years of the project.

Concurrently, however, the problem of teacher attitudes was undergoing intensive systematic study by the staff under the supervision of Dr. Edwin Wandt, and, as the findings became available, the newly developed and more clearly defined materials of the Inventory of Teacher Opinion were incorporated into the program.

TEACHERS' ATTITUDES TOWARD GROUPS OF PERSONS ENCOUNTERED IN THE SCHOOLS[1]

The basic research of the Study dealing with teacher attitudes were directed toward (1) the construction of scales for estimating teachers' attitudes toward specified groups of persons encountered in the school

[1] More detailed description of the Study's basic investigations of teachers' attitudes may be found in bibliographical references 11, 12, and 13 (see p. 160).

and toward school practices employed in dealing with such persons, (2) exploration of the interrelationships of attitudes revealed by such scales by means of multiple-factor analyses, (3) investigation of relationships between teacher attitudes and certain teacher conditions such as grade or subject taught, amount of teaching experience, sex, age, and observed teacher classroom behaviors, and (4) study of the feasibility of measuring teachers' attitudes by means of disguised-structured items. In the course of the research, the influence of positive or negative form of opinion statements also was studied as a matter of methodological interest.

CONSTRUCTION OF THE ATTITUDE SCALES

Sixteen scales were constructed at the beginning of the major research on teacher attitudes, each consisting of twelve statements or items. Two scales were developed in each of eight areas, one consisting of statements which indicated a favorable opinion (positively worded statements), and the other being made up of statements which indicated an unfavorable opinion (negatively worded statements). The scales were hypothesized to estimate teachers' attitudes toward each of the following types of persons or procedures:

> Administrators
> Supervisors
> Pupils
> Parents
> Teachers
> Nonteaching employees
> Democratic classroom procedures
> Democratic administrative procedures

In preparing the statements for these scales, a form was devised for obtaining (with a minimum amount of cueing) teachers' reactions to the various groups with whom they are associated in carrying out their functions. This form was made up of two parts. Part I consisted of open-end, or completion, items (e.g., "Teaching can be very pleasant with pupils _____."). Part II provided space for any statement the respondent wished to make—free expressions by the teacher about pupils, parents, principals, supervisors, teachers, and nonteaching employees. The forms were mailed to a random sample of female teachers in Los Angeles County with the request that they be returned to the Study upon completion. Analysis of the completed forms, together with study of other attitude scales which had been employed in the area of investigation, provided the background for the actual writing of the "attitude" items or statements. The resulting statements, intended to represent value judgments expressed in the form of opinions, are exemplified by:

"Pupils usually can be trusted" (favorable opinion).

"Most administrators feel very superior to teachers" (negative opinion).

As is customary with such research, a much larger number of statements was prepared for each of the scales than was ultimately used. From this reservoir, a total of 192 items (twelve items in each of the sixteen scales) was selected and assembled into an instrument known as the Inventory of Teacher Opinion.

The several sets of statements (relating to administrators, pupils, etc.) were not classified nor identified with respect to category of reference in the Inventory. The individual statements simply were numbered consecutively from 1 to 192 and were arranged to permit alternation of scales and also of acceptable (positively worded) and unacceptable (negatively worded) statements. The required response to each statement consisted of indication of agreement or disagreement on a scale consisting of five categories (1—strongly disagree; 2—disagree; 3—uncertain or indifferent; 4—agree; 5—strongly agree).

The Inventory of Teacher Opinion and a specially devised answer sheet were mailed to random samples of teachers on a state-wide population basis. An item analysis sample of 240 teachers, stratified by years of teaching experience and grade level taught, was selected for the purpose of determining the internal consistency of the scales. The Likert method [3] of estimating the reliability, or belonging, of a statement in a scale was employed. That this technique may not result in a "true," or homogeneous, scale is granted. However, homogeneous scaling with respect to highly specific aspects of teachers' attitudes seemed neither feasible nor desirable. Each of the sixteen scales was scored by summing the responses to the items for that particular hypothesized scale. After scores were assigned, internal consistency of the scales was examined through item analysis, employing the upper and lower 27 percents of the total scores on each scale as criterion groups. The significance level of the difference between the means of the upper and lower criterion groups for each item response was computed. It had been intended that items showing low significance ratios would be discarded, but the discrimination indices proved to be uniformly high and only one item was dropped at this stage of the research.

FACTOR ANALYSES OF TEACHERS' ATTITUDES

As has been noted, one interest of the Study was the analysis of the interrelationships and patterning of teachers' attitudes. To this end, product-moment intercorrelation coefficients, based on the stratified sample of 240 teachers, were computed among scores on the sixteen attitude scales. Three separate factor analyses were carried out:[2] (1) an analysis of the eight positive statement scales, (2) an analysis of the eight negative statement scales, and (3) an analysis of all sixteen scales, followed, in turn, by a second-order analysis of the primary factors. Thurstone's centroid method was employed in all of the factor analyses, with rotation to oblique simple structure.

TABLE 30

Oblique Factor Matrices Resulting from Three Factor Analyses of Teachers' Attitudes toward Groups Encountered in the Schools

ATTITUDE SCALE	FACTOR ANALYSES OF POSITIVE STATEMENT SCALES			FACTOR ANALYSES OF NEGATIVE STATEMENT SCALES			SECOND-ORDER FACTOR ANALYSES		
	I	II	III	I	II	III	I	II	III
Administrators..........	.07	.53	.04	−.01	.49	.11	.02	.45	.11
Supervisors..............	−.04	.66	−.09	−.03	.54	.02	.04	.62	−.09
Pupils..................	.64	.02	.09	.48	.04	.15	.57	−.02	.27
Parents.................	.36	.11	.19	.34	−.05	.34	.34	.00	.37
Teachers...............	−.02	.02	.52	−.05	.08	.43	−.09	.12	.40
Nonteaching school employees..............	.04	.03	.41	.06	−.03	.50	.03	−.09	.52
Democratic classroom procedures..............	.65	−.02	−.09	.66	.06	−.14	.75	.06	.00
Democratic administrative procedures............	−.05	−.45	.50	.37	−.40	.10	.07	−.61	.48

The results of the factor analyses are shown in Table 30. Both of the eight-variable analyses yielded three oblique factors which were identifiable as: I—attitude toward pupils (Factor R), II—attitude toward administrative-supervisory personnel (Factor A), and III—attitude toward teachers and other nonadministrative personnel (Factor N). Factor analysis of the sixteen scales yielded eight oblique (doublet) factors, one in each of the eight areas of teacher attitudes for which scales had been developed. A second-order analysis of the correlation matrix of the eight primary factors yielded three oblique factors which were interpreted in the same manner as those resulting from the eight-variable analyses.

The correlations among the three factors were very high in all three analyses and also in additional studies utilizing factor scores. The correlation between Factors A and N (attitude toward administrators and attitude toward teachers and nonadministrative personnel) indicated a particularly high degree of overlapping and, consequently, in later re-

[2] See bibliographical item 12 (p. 160) for the source of the correlation matrices and complete tables of data.

search these two factors were combined. This combined scale is designated later in this report as Characteristic Q. Similarly, attitude toward pupils came to be designated as Characteristic R. (It also should be noted that in data reported in the following chapters, Teacher Characteristics Schedule results are shown with separate scores for Characteristic R [favorable opinions of pupils] and Characteristic R_1 [favorable opinions of democratic pupil practices].) This arbitrary division of Factor R has no empirical justification, as the very great amount of common variance between R and R_1 found in all comparisons indicate.

The split-half reliabilities of the attitude factor scores, based upon administration of the scales to additional samples of teachers, were all .89 or higher.

RELATIONSHIPS BETWEEN TEACHER ATTITUDE FACTOR SCORES AND CERTAIN CHARACTERISTICS OF TEACHERS

Utilizing teacher scores on the attitude factors yielded by the factor analyses (Factors R, A, and N), a number of relationships between attitudes and other teacher characteristics were investigated [12, 13].

Elementary teachers, as a group, generally showed more favorable attitudes than did secondary teachers, the differences being significant for all three factors and most pronounced with respect to teachers' attitude toward pupils and democratic pupil practices, Factor R. Within the elementary school and secondary school samples no significant differences were found among teachers of different grades.

When teachers were classified with respect to amount of teaching experience, few clear-cut differences emerged among the groups on Factors R, A, and N. Among elementary school teachers, those with less teaching experience tended to be more favorable toward democratic classroom procedures than did those with more experience. At the secondary school level, there also was a slight tendency for teachers with more than twenty years of experience to be lower on the scale measuring attitude toward pupils and higher on the scale measuring attitude toward administrators than were the other experience groups.

Age does not appear to be associated with the attitudes of the teachers studied. No significant trends were found at either the elementary or secondary levels.

Studies of the relationship between teacher classroom behavior and attitudes showed that teachers who were high on Characteristic X_o (sympathetic, understanding classroom behavior) expressed more favorable attitudes toward pupils and democratic classroom procedures (Factor R) than did teachers who received lower assessments on Pattern X_o.

MEASUREMENT OF ATTITUDES BY MEANS OF
DISGUISED-STRUCTURED ITEMS

As was noted in the introductory paragraphs of this chapter, when attitude scales of the direct-question type are used in situations where the respondent is identified and where there is an advantage in his making a favorable impression, it is possible that true attitudes may be concealed. With this in mind, studies were conducted to determine the extent to which *disguised-structured* items [1] might be used to estimate the same attitudes measured by the direct-question nondisguised opinion scales which had been developed.

A number of indirect, or disguised, items in the forms of multiple-choice questions with four possible responses were constructed and administered to teachers who also had completed the Inventory of Teacher Opinion. Scores on the original attitude scales were employed to select external criterion groups consisting of the upper 27 percent and the lower 27 percent of respondents on each scale. The significance of the differences between the responses of the high and low groups were computed for all choices of the disguised-structured items, using each of the sixteen original scales in turn as the criterion. The method employed is illustrated by the following sample item.

What percent of teachers say their principals do a good job?

a. 20%
b. 40%
c. 60%
d. 80%

RESPONSE	TEACHERS IN HIGH CRITERION GROUP		TEACHERS IN LOW CRITERION GROUP		PERCENT DIFFERENCE BETWEEN GROUPS	P
	N	%	N	N		
a.........	1	2	11	17	15	.01
b.........	2	3	19	29	26	.001
c.........	20	31	31	48	17	.05
d.........	42	65	4	6	59	.001

There appears to be little doubt that a teacher's reply to the question "What percent of teachers say their principals do a good job?" reflects that teacher's own attitude toward administrators even though an estimate of group opinion was requested. Many of the indirect, or disguised, items (of which the illustrative item represents only one of several types employed) distinguished sharply between the criterion groups, indicating that such materials might be successfully used in identifying teacher attitudes, while probably avoiding some of the pitfalls of the direct-inquiry approach. Chapter 6 deals with the development of a number of indirect scales employed to estimate various teacher characteristics.

COMPARISONS OF THE ATTITUDES OF CONTRASTED GROUPS OF TEACHERS

In an attempt to further the understanding of the relationship between teacher motivation, as revealed in the teachers' attitudes, and ongoing teacher behavior in the school, a study [11] was undertaken of the attitudes of teachers judged by their principals to be outstandingly superior or notably poor. In order to enhance the validity of this investigation, the data were obtained by a unique mail technique which maintained complete anonymity of the teacher.

Six hundred school principals selected to be representative of those throughout the United States were requested by mail to nominate teachers who were believed to be "outstanding" in that they were judged to deviate significantly either above or below the typical average teacher. The sample of principals consisted of three subgroups, the first group being 200 elementary principals, each of whom was asked to nominate one high and one low teacher from his school. The second group consisted of 200 high school principals who nominated one high and one low teacher in the fields of mathematics and/or science, and the third group included 200 high school principals who nominated one high and one low teacher in the fields of English and/or social studies.

Each principal received two copies of the Inventory of Teacher Opinion (in sealed packets) to pass along, without comment or reference to the nominating phase of the research, to the two teachers nominated (one as a "superior" teacher and one as a "poor" teacher) from his school.

Upon completing the attitude scales, the teachers mailed them, unsigned, directly to the office of the Study. The names of the teachers were never known, the principals' nominations and the returns of the high and low teacher groups being distinguishable by color coding and numbering. Elementary teacher returns were received from thirty states; English–social studies returns from thirty-two states, and mathematics-science returns from thirty-eight states.

To determine whether the contrasted samples of teachers differed significantly in their attitudes toward groups of persons encountered in the schools, the mean scores on the three factor scales were computed for the "outstandingly superior" and "notably poor" groups of teachers in each of the three subject-matter areas. The null hypothesis was tested in each case by computing the significance of the difference between the means. Table 31 summarizes the results of this study.

The data with respect to the three subject-matter areas are strikingly similar. The superior teachers were significantly (beyond .01 level) more favorable in their opinions of pupils than were the low teachers. This was true among elementary teachers, English–social studies teachers, and mathematics-science teachers alike. The superior teachers also expressed more favorable attitudes toward administrators in the case of each group, these differences all being significant at the .05 level. *None* of the differences on Scale N, however, was statistically significant. Correlations between the attitudes of matched secondary teacher groups were not significantly different from zero for any of the three attitude scales, and matching with respect to geographical location, size of school, etc., in addition to grade or subject, had no effect upon the obtained results.

It is interesting to note that although the attitudes revealed by Scales A and N repeatedly have been observed to overlap to a very great extent ($r_{AN} = .82$), Scale A, measuring attitude toward administrators, consistently discriminated between teachers judged to be "superior" and "poor" while Scale N, measuring attitude toward certain adult nonadministrative groups, did not discriminate between any of the contrasted samples.

The significant finding of this particular research lies in the strong indication that teaching behavior (based upon principals' judgments of outstandingly superior and notably poor teaching) and teachers' attitudes toward pupils and also toward administrators, tend to be significantly related. These data support the previously noted relationship between certain teacher behaviors, as assessed by trained observers, and teachers' attitudes.

Investigating Teachers' Educational Viewpoints[3]

Educational viewpoints quite reasonably are presumed to be important factors in determining *what* shall be taught in the schools of a particular community and *how* it shall be taught. The composite of educational viewpoints, or the "educational philosophy," accepted by an administrator and his supervisory and teaching staffs (presumably with approval of the school board and, in turn, the community), defines the objectives of teaching to which a school system is committed. The school

---

[3] Adapted, in part, from the publication cited in bibliographical reference 7 (see p. 160).

TABLE 31

Comparison of Attitude Scores of Teachers Judged by Their Principals To Be Outstandingly Superior or Notably Poor

Teacher Group	N	Scale R, Attitude toward Pupils			Scale A, Attitude toward Administrative-Supervisory Personnel			Scale N, Attitude toward Teachers, Nonteaching Personnel, and Parents		
		M	σ	r*	M	σ	r*	M	σ	r*
Elementary teachers:										
Superior...........	41	*91.3*	12.0		*94.9*	11.0		86.6	12.4	
Poor...............	26	*83.4*	11.2		*89.0*	12.4		88.6	10.7	
Secondary mathematics-science teachers:										
Superior...........	58	*83.3*	8.9	.03	*89.4*	9.4	.01	84.8	7.2	.05
Poor...............	58	*79.0*	8.7		*85.4*	10.0		85.2	10.1	
Secondary English-social studies teachers:										
Superior...........	59	*86.9*	10.0	.01	*87.8*	12.3	−.01	85.1	9.8	−.13
Poor...............	59	*78.1*	11.9		*82.9*	14.9		84.6	10.1	

* Correlations between attitudes of teachers matched by school. (Elementary teachers not matched.)
NOTE: Italicized means of superior and poor groups are significantly different at or beyond the .05 level.

147

system expects individual teachers to conduct their classes in keeping with such defined objectives.

In practice, however, the educational viewpoints of an individual teacher may or may not conform to the objectives of the school system in which he is employed. Furthermore, because of lack of real understanding of the implications of viewpoints held, or inability to translate the viewpoints into classroom behavior (or perhaps because of external pressures), a teacher may not actually conduct his classes in keeping with the viewpoints *he* professes about educational matters. Nevertheless, one might expect a teacher committed to a particular set of educational viewpoints to behave differently in specified school situations from a teacher committed to some different educational viewpoint. Or, to put it briefly, it seems reasonable to assume that teacher behavior is influenced by the educational values held by the individual teacher.

With the assumption that beliefs in particular educational goals and practices serve as motivating conditions which help to determine teacher behavior, the Study undertook research aimed at clarifying understanding of the organization of teachers' educational viewpoints and the relationships between these viewpoints and other personal, social, and professional characteristics.

FACTOR ANALYSES OF EDUCATIONAL VIEWPOINTS OF TEACHERS[4]

In the thinking of the staff, it seemed reasonable to hypothesize that the educational viewpoints of teachers might be organized into several clusters with respect to such matters as curricular organization, academic achievement standards, pupil participation in class planning, and the like. To test this hypothesis the following steps were taken: (*a*) two forms of an Educational Viewpoints Inquiry were developed and administered to elementary and secondary teachers enrolled in summer session classes in geographically scattered colleges of teacher education, (*b*) tetrachoric intercorrelation coefficients among the Inquiry items of each form were computed, and (*c*) each of the two resulting correlation matrices was factor-analyzed.

The Educational Viewpoints Inquiry was a direct-question type instrument made up of twenty items, each item forcing a choice between contrasting viewpoints regarding educational purposes or practices. The following item illustrates those incorporated in the Inquiry.

  3. In planning units of classwork, do you believe that
       ( ) this should be largely the responsibility of the teacher?
       ( ) the suggestions should come principally from the children in the class?

---

[4] Reference 7 gives complete tables of intercorrelations, centroid and rotated factor loadings, etc.

The items included in the Inquiry were devised to sample viewpoints with respect to (*a*) curricular organization and scope; (*b*) course planning and classroom procedure (including pupil participation in these activities); (*c*) academic achievement standards; (*d*) division of teaching and administrative responsibilities; and (*e*) parent participation in the educational program. A number of item rationales were developed in each major category, and materials were selected for apparent representativeness and probable significance. Each item in the elementary form of the Inquiry had its approximate counterpart in the form used with teachers in secondary schools, although the specific content of the questions necessarily differed.

The Inquiry underwent four revisions, based upon the experiences of respondents in pilot studies, in the interest of employing content coverage and phrasing which might be expected to yield valid data.

In the opinion of the Study staff members, the Inquiry had satisfactory logical, or construct, validity. No means were available to test the validity of the instrument against external criteria of "educational philosophy," but it was believed that the teacher's anonymous expression of a viewpoint, when that expression was subject to no external pressure, probably was as valid an indicator of what the teacher believed as could be obtained.

The Inquiry was completed by samples consisting of 213 elementary school teachers and 338 secondary school teachers during the summer of 1950. The respondents were enrolled in summer sessions at ten teacher education institutions in nine states ranging from California to Pennsylvania and Michigan to Florida. Eight of the institutions were public universities, one was a state college, and one was a private university. The respondents represented both experienced teachers and teachers-in-training, the ratio of experienced to inexperienced teachers in the samples being approximately two to one.

Following administration of the Inquiry, tetrachoric correlation coefficients were computed between each item and every other item, the procedure being duplicated for the elementary and the secondary teacher samples. Before carrying out the factor analyses, the items and intercorrelations were reviewed and some items were eliminated in the light of disproportionate acceptance of one response over the alternative response. For example, 330 of the 338 secondary school teachers answered "yes" to the question: "Do you believe a high school instructor should have considerable freedom to modify courses of study or units of work from class to class?" With such a split of responses, no meaningful relationship between this item and other items could be established. Fifteen of the original twenty items were included in the correlation matrices upon which the factor analyses were based.

The intercorrelations of the responses of teachers to the Inquiry covered a wide range, from .01 to .56 for the elementary teacher sample, and from .02 to .68 for the secondary teacher sample. Factor analyses, accomplished by Thurstone's centroid method, resulted in the extraction of six centroid factors in each of the two analyses. In each of the analyses the factors subsequently were rotated to oblique simple structure.

The results of the separate factor analyses of the responses of elementary and secondary teachers were generally similar. The individual items of the Inquiry appeared to be relatively independent (substantial amounts of item variance not being accounted for by group factors extracted), a finding which suggests that the educational viewpoints of teachers may be rather highly specific. In each of the analyses, only three of the factors extracted seemed to be significant enough to warrant further study. Descriptions assigned to these factors and the items contributing significant loadings to each factor are indicated in the following listing.

ITEMS HAVING SIGNIFICANT LOADINGS ON THE THREE MOST PROMINENT
OBLIQUE FACTORS RESULTING FROM FACTOR ANALYSES ON THE
EDUCATIONAL VIEWPOINTS OF ELEMENTARY AND SECONDARY
TEACHERS: FAVORED PRACTICE OR VIEWPOINT

Elementary Teacher Analysis

Factor I: Academic-centered school program (vs. *school program stressing other objectives*)

17. Importance of pupils' academic achievement (*vs.* importance of other objectives).
18. Separation (*vs.* overlapping) of instructional and administrative responsibilities in the school.
19. Desirability (*vs.* undesirability) of pupil home study.
20. Requirement of high (*vs.* minimum) standards of academic achievement for pupil promotion.

Factor II: Rigid school program (vs. *flexible school program, involving pupil and parent participation*)

2. Nonparticipation (*vs.* participation) of parents in planning the school program.
7. Inability (*vs.* ability) of pupils to exercise adultlike self-control.
13. Closed (*vs.* open) parent visitation during regular class hours.
16. Nonfreedom (*vs.* freedom) of teacher to modify courses of study or units of work.

Factor III: Teacher-directed learning in traditional subject-matter fields (vs. *learning directed by pupil interests and abilities*)

3. Teacher responsibility (*vs.* pupil responsibility) for planning units of classwork.
5. One class activity (*vs.* several activities) in progress at a given time.
8. Separation (*vs.* integration) of different subject matters or courses.
9. Development of classwork around subject-matter content (*vs.* development around out-of-school activities).

Secondary Teacher Analysis

Factor I: Academic-centered school program (vs. *school program stressing other objectives*)

11. Separate teachers for specialized subjects (*vs.* same teacher for several subjects).
17. Importance of pupils' academic achievement (*vs.* importance of other objectives).
18. Separation (*vs.* overlapping) of instructional and administrative responsibilities in the school.
20. Requirement of high (*vs.* minimum) standards of academic achievement for pupil promotion.

Factor II: Rigid school program (vs. *flexible school program, involving pupil and parent participation*)

2. Nonparticipation (*vs.* participation) of parents in planning the school program.
9. Development of classwork around subject-matter content (*vs.* development around out-of-school activities.)
14. Impracticality (*vs.* practicality) of *class* assuming responsibility for pupil control.

Factor III: Teacher-directed learning in traditional subject-matter fields (vs. *learning directed by pupil interests and abilities*)

3. Teacher responsibility (*vs.* pupil responsibility) for planning units of classwork.
5. One class activity (*vs.* several activities) in progress at a given time.
10. Effectiveness for learning of a single, unified pupil group (*vs.* several subgroups).

Review of the factor analysis data led to the conclusions that: (1) such patterning of teachers' educational viewpoints as does exist, while varying in certain details, seems to be of a very similar nature for elementary and secondary teachers, and suggests three possible dimensions (I— belief in an academic-centered school program *vs.* a program stressing other objectives; II—belief in a rigid school program *vs.* a flexible program involving pupil and parent participation; III—belief in teacher-directed learning in traditional subject-matter fields *vs.* learning directed by pupil interests and activities); and (2) in view of the obvious overlapping of the three most prominent factors (both from the standpoint of content and in the light of relatively high factor intercorrelations) it would be unwise to attempt to identify teachers with respect to each of the several different sets of educational viewpoints. An alternative was to think of the teacher's educational philosophy in terms of a not-too-homogeneous composite, the opposite poles of which might be roughly described by the familiar and overused rubrics "traditional" and "progressive" or, perhaps, "traditional" and "permissive."

Thus, with the somewhat inconclusive results of the factorial analyses in mind, it was decided that the Study would deal with a single continuum of educational viewpoints, Characteristic *B*. The teacher whose viewpoints lie at one end of this continuum appears to believe in strong emphasis upon academic subject matter and academic achievement and in the teacher's responsibility for determining what shall be learned and how it shall be learned. At the other end of the continuum is the teacher who appears to believe that other educational objectives are equally or more important than those of an academic nature, that pupils and parents should participate actively in planning and conducting the class and school program, and that subject matters should be integrated among themselves and also with out-of-school activities. The educational viewpoints of teachers on this continuum constitute the characteristic referred to as Characteristic *B* in the following section and in later chapters.

RELATIONSHIPS BETWEEN TEACHERS' EDUCATIONAL VIEWPOINTS AND CERTAIN OTHER CHARACTERISTICS

Secondary teachers as a group tended to express educational viewpoints more toward the traditional, academic end of the scale and elementary teachers more toward the child-centered, permissive pole. This trend toward greater academic emphasis in the higher grades was observable even within the elementary school, Grade 7–8 teachers having the most traditional educational viewpoints and Grade 2 teachers having the most permissive viewpoints. In the secondary school, business education, mathematics, and physical science teachers tended to be more traditional in educational beliefs and values, while English and social studies teachers leaned toward liberal, permissive viewpoints.

There appeared to be no significant sex differences among teachers within the elementary school, men and women indicating viewpoints about equally inclined toward the permissive end of the continuum. At the secondary level, men teachers manifested more traditional educational viewpoints than did women teachers.

Considered from the standpoint of age, teachers under 30 years of age, in both the elementary and secondary schools, appeared to be more liberal in their educational beliefs, and teachers over 45 years of age, at all levels, seemed to be the most traditional.

Elementary teachers with smaller amounts of teaching experience (up to four or five years) tended to express more permissive educational viewpoints, and those with ten years or more of teaching experiences more traditional. On the secondary school level there was a definite tendency for teachers with experience beyond fifteen years to be more traditional in educational viewpoints.

Sympathetic, understanding teacher classroom behavior (Characteristic X_o) was positively, though slightly, correlated with the expression of more permissive, child-centered educational viewpoints; businesslike, systematic classroom behavior (Characteristic Y_o) was slightly positively associated with traditional educational viewpoints; and stimulating teacher behavior (Characteristic Z_o), as well as observed pupil behavior (P_o) were slightly positively correlated with educational viewpoints toward the liberal, permissive end of the scale.

Estimating Verbal Ability, Emotional Adjustment, and Validity of Response

A considerable portion of the time and efforts of the Study was spent in (a) the description of major dimensions of teacher classroom behavior and development of predictors of such patterns and (b) the estimation of hypothesized teacher-motivating conditions as manifested in the expressed attitudes and educational viewpoints of teachers. Much of the research was directed at the investigation of characteristics of teachers in the area of interpersonal relations.

At least two other aspects of teacher personality, namely, status with respect to (a) verbal intelligence and (b) emotional stability or adjustment, inevitably must be considered in relation to other teacher characteristics. Although recognized, these traits were accorded only cursory attention during the earlier stages of the Study,[5] and systematic investigation was not undertaken until 1952–53. At that time, attention was turned to the development of short samples of items for estimating verbal intelligence, or verbal understanding (subsequently referred to as Characteristic I), and emotional adjustment (referred to as Characteristic S). Concurrently, an attempt also was made to develop materials which might be useful in identifying individuals who tended to make excessive use of socially acceptable and self-enhancing responses to direct-inquiry inventory materials. This trait, relating to the tendency to use socially desirable responses, or perhaps to try to make a good impression (and sometimes to "fake"), subsequently is referred to as Characteristic V, or "validity of response."

Certainly such characteristics as verbal intelligence and emotional stability could have been estimated by administration of available tests and inventories. To follow such a procedure, however, would have required that all participants fill out several separate test forms (as was done during the first years of the project) and would have materially increased administration time. Both of these conditions would have tended to discourage responses. Since experience had indicated the possibility of obtaining relatively reliable estimates of verbal ability and

[5] The Minnesota Multiphasic Personality Inventory and the Thurstone Temperament Schedule were completed by participants during the first three years. Some of the obtained data were reported in chap. 4.

emotional adjustment from fairly small numbers of carefully selected items, it seemed desirable to give attention to the development of special materials in these areas. By assembling such items with those developed for the estimation of other teacher characteristics, indices of verbal intelligence and emotional adjustment, and also of validity of response, could be obtained simultaneously with other data.

DEVELOPMENT OF SCALES

In developing materials for estimating verbal understanding, emotional adjustment, and "validity of response," items hypothesized to reflect those behaviors were prepared and assembled in a booklet which was known during the development phase as Inventory ISV.

General objectives which guided the planning and subsequent analyses of these materials included the following: (1) Each scale should be made up of a small number of highly reliable items requiring a minimum amount of time for administration. (2) The items should be similar in general form and appearance to those employed for the paper-and-pencil estimation of teacher classroom behavior (e.g., items requiring responses indicating preferences, judgments, behavior appraisals, and descriptions, etc.). (3) The items should be so constructed as to disguise, insofar as possible, the characteristics they actually were intended to measure. (4) The materials should be capable of administration in uncontrolled situations, *i.e.*, they should be essentially self-administering. With these purposes in mind, a pool of items was developed.

Items hypothesized to contribute to Characteristic *I* consisted of vocabulary and verbal analogy items, cast in a form slightly different from that which is usually used in tests. The two items which follow are typical of those intended to estimate verbal understanding.

Illustrative verbal understanding items:

Which of the following responses most frequently comes to your mind when you see the word *placate?*

1 Chemical.
2 Sign.
*3 Appease.
4 Scold.
5 Never heard of the word.

Which of the following words do you associate with *beginning* in the same way you associate *birth* with *death?*

1 Certain.
2 Joy.
*3 End.

4 Sadness.

5 Old age.

* Indicates the response which when marked contributed to the respondent's Characteristic *I* score.

Items hypothesized to contribute to Characteristic *S* were of a forced-choice, two-response type similar to those shown below.

Illustrative emotional adjustment items:

Which of the following is more true of you?

1 I tend to worry.

*2 I tend to be easygoing.

Which of the following is more true of you?

1 I can't concentrate in a noisy place.

*2 I can study or concentrate on something else even when the television or radio *is* on loud.

* Indicates the response which when marked contributed to the respondent's Characteristic *S* score.

Items hypothesized to contribute to Characteristic *V* were similar in appearance to those employed for estimating verbal understanding and emotional stability, but actually were constructed to give the respondent an opportunity to mark a response (*a*) which was known by the TCS staff to be either typical (in terms of the way most individuals behave) or correct (as the starred fifth response in the second item of those which follow) or (*b*) one which seemed to be socially acceptable and enhancing to the respondent's status from either a personal or intellectual standpoint, although the TCS staff knew that such a response was atypical, or even necessarily false.

Illustrative validity-of-response items:

Which of the following is more true of you?

*1 I sometimes pretend to know more than I really do.

2 I like everyone I know.

Which of the following responses comes to your mind when you see the word *tamber?*

1 Condiment.

2 Ingenuity.

3 Cudged.

4 Collusion.

*5 Never heard of the word.

* Indicates the response which when marked contributed to the respondent's Characteristic *V* score.

The original sets of items intended to estimate the three characteristics were administered to a sample of college students, scored,[6] and item-analyzed, employing upper and lower 27 percent criterion groups (based on total score on a given characteristic). A revised form of the Inventory ISV was prepared from items which survived.

The revised materials were, in turn, widely administered to new samples of adults and subsequently subjected to additional item analyses. These item analyses for Characteristics I and S were conducted with criterion groups representing the extreme tails of the distributions —the upper 10 percent and the lower 10 percent of the total group on a given characteristic. Each response to an item was tabulated and both frequency-of-acceptance indices and approximations of biserial r's were read from appropriate tables.

Three separate item analyses were conducted with respect to Characteristic V at this phase of study, one involving upper and lower 10 percent criterion groups, a second employing upper and lower 27 percent criterion groups, and a third in which the lower criterion group consisted of the lowest 10 percent while the upper criterion group was made up of a random sample of 100 cases drawn from the upper 60 percent of the total distribution. This latter constitution of criterion groups was employed experimentally in the light of the nature of the validity-of-response trait being analyzed and the somewhat negatively skewed form of the score distribution. While discrimination indices based on the three methods did vary slightly, the agreement was actually very close, and it was evident that any one of the methods employed would have served the purpose of the item analysis.

Following the analyses of items comprising the second form of Inventory ISV, the third form of the instrument was assembled from the selected items. This revision consisted of three sets of items—fourteen relating to Characteristic I, seventeen to Characteristic S, and seventeen to Characteristic V. The Kuder-Richardson reliabilities of these short scales were found to be between .70 and .80, these values probably representing underestimations of the true reliabilities.

The third form of Inventory ISV was mailed to elementary teachers and secondary teachers who previously had completed other paper-and-pencil instruments developed for the prediction of teacher classroom behavior, teacher attitudes, and teacher educational viewpoints. Returns available for over 700 elementary teachers and 900 secondary teachers were utilized in additional analyses directed at the identification of indirect and disguised items which showed significant correlations with I, S, and V scores, as described in chapter 6.

[6] High scores on the scales were assumed to indicate superior verbal intelligence, superior emotional adjustment, and tendency to give valid responses to direct questions.

Intercorrelations between Characteristics *I*, *S*, and *V* were of a low order, the matrices differing slightly for elementary teachers and secondary teachers. The product-moment correlation between verbal intelligence and emotional stability was approximately .20 for elementary teachers and .05 for secondary teachers. The correlation between verbal intelligence and validity of response was .06 for elementary teachers and .13 for secondary teachers. Emotional adjustment and validity of response correlated negatively in both elementary and secondary teacher groups, typical coefficients being −.08 for elementary and −.16 for secondary teachers. Although the correlation estimates vary slightly in magnitude, the direction of the relationship between given characteristics is consistent for elementary and high school teachers.

RELATIONSHIPS OF VERBAL UNDERSTANDING, EMOTIONAL ADJUSTMENT, AND VALIDITY OF RESPONSE TO CERTAIN OTHER CHARACTERISTICS

The relationship of verbal understanding, emotional adjustment, and validity of response of teachers to conditions such as grade or subject taught and teaching experience, and personal characteristics such as assessed classroom behaviors X_o, Y_o, and Z_o, are noted in the following paragraphs.

VERBAL UNDERSTANDING RELATIONSHIPS

The mean verbal intelligence scores of secondary teachers were significantly higher (.01 level) than those of elementary teachers. Within the elementary school, average verbal intelligence scores of teachers classified according to grade taught increased from Grades 1–2 to Grades 7–8. Within the secondary teacher group studied, the highest verbal understanding scores were attained by English teachers.

From the standpoint of amount of teaching experience, little, if any, trend with respect to verbal understanding scores could be observed. At the elementary level there was a slight tendency for teachers with lesser experience to score higher than did teachers with greater amounts of experience. This tendency was not very pronounced and was not similarly characteristic of secondary teachers.

There appeared to be a slight trend for older teachers to receive higher verbal intelligence scores than did younger teachers. When a cutting point was set at age thirty, teachers who were less than thirty years of age scored significantly lower than did those who were over thirty years of age.

Women teachers attained higher verbal intelligence scores than did men teachers. This trend was in evidence at both the elementary and secondary level, although it was more pronounced in the latter group.

Sympathetic, understanding teacher classroom behavior (Characteristic X_o) and stimulating teacher behavior (Characteristic Z_o) had low, but positive, correlations with verbal understanding scores. Businesslike, systematic classroom behavior (Y_o) was unrelated, or very slightly positively related, to verbal intelligence. Observed pupil behavior (P_o) appeared to have no relationship to the verbal understanding scores of the pupils' teachers.

EMOTIONAL ADJUSTMENT RELATIONSHIPS

Elementary and secondary teachers appeared to be generally similar with respect to emotional stability as measured by Inventory ISV. Within the elementary school there was a tendency for teachers of the lower grades to have adjustment scores that were somewhat higher than those of the teachers of upper grade levels. At the secondary school level, science teachers attained somewhat higher emotional adjustment scores and women teachers of English had somewhat lower scores in comparison with the other groups.

There was a tendency for elementary teachers with lesser amounts of teaching experience to be slightly more emotionally stable than the more experienced teachers. At the secondary level, little trend of any kind was in evidence.

In general, older teachers appeared to be slightly less emotionally stable than the younger ones.

Male teachers scored higher on emotional adjustment items than did female teachers at both the elementary and the secondary levels, the difference between sexes being significant at the .01 level in the secondary school.

There appeared to be a low positive relationship between emotional stability and Characteristic X_o (understanding, sympathetic classroom behavior), the association being somewhat closer in the elementary school than in the secondary. The correlation with Characteristic Z_o (stimulating teacher behavior) also was consistently positive, but slight. Businesslike, systematic teacher classroom behavior (Y_o) was slightly negatively correlated with emotional stability scores. Observed pupil behavior (P_o) appeared to be unrelated to the emotional adjustment of the teacher.

VALIDITY-OF-RESPONSE RELATIONSHIPS

There appeared to be no consistent significant relationships between teachers' validity-of-response scores on Inventory ISV and grade or subject taught, amount of teaching experience, age, sex, or teacher classroom behavior.

Subsequent Utilization of the Direct-Inquiry Materials

As has been noted, the development of materials to measure such characteristics of teachers as their attitudes, educational viewpoints, verbal ability, and emotional adjustment involved a number of independent projects and culminated in several separate instruments. These were the Inventory of Teacher Opinion, the Educational Viewpoints Inquiry, and Inventory ISV. A number of other independent sets of materials were prepared in separate booklets during the early phase of the Study in an effort to discover paper-and-pencil correlates of observed teacher classroom behavior. During the first years of the research program, participating teachers received various separate booklets of items to complete, which involved inconvenience and inefficiency for both the Study staff and the participants.

The desirability of assembling into a single booklet the items which survived the various response analyses was apparent. The first form of a single booklet, Teacher Characteristics Schedule, Form X, appeared in 1951 and consisted of 600 items involving over 2,000 responses. Additional forms of the Schedule appeared in 1952 and in 1954, the latter form being similar to the 1952 form except for the addition of items selected from Inventory ISV.

Direct-inquiry "criterion items," relating to the teacher characteristics discussed in this chapter, were incorporated into the Schedule as indicated below.

TEACHER CHARACTERISTICS	ITEMS APPEARING IN THE TEACHER CHARACTERISTICS SCHEDULE		
	Form X (1951)	Form '52	Form '54
Attitude:			
Toward administrators..................	12		
Toward supervisors.....................	12		
Toward parents........................	12	10	10
Toward teachers.......................	12		
Toward nonteaching personnel...........	12		
Toward democratic classroom procedures...	12	4	4
Toward pupils.........................	12	8	8
Educational viewpoints....................	12	10	10
Verbal understanding......................			11
Emotional stability.......................			10
Validity of response......................			12

In anticipation of the discussion to follow in Chapter 6, it may be noted that in the studies seeking to identify *correlates* of teacher characteristics, all responses to all of the items in the Schedule were correlated against criteria based upon observed teacher behaviors (Patterns X_o, Y_o, and Z_o) and also against criteria comprised of the direct-inquiry items extracted from the Inventory of Teacher Opinion, the Educational Viewpoints Inquiry, and Inventory ISV. The end result was a number of "correlates" keys, the chief values of which were expected to be (a) economy of time and effort, particularly in the use of paper-and-pencil correlates for the prediction of observed teacher classroom behavior, and (b) alleviation, through the use of disguised items, of invalidity attributable to the respondent's tendency to try to make a good impression when expressing attitudes, viewpoints, and the like.

Bibliography

1. CAMPBELL, D. T. "The Indirect Assessment of Social Attitudes," *Psychological Bulletin*, **47**: 15–38, 1950.
2. LEEDS, C. H., and COOK, W. W. "The Construction and Differential Value of a Scale for Determining Teacher-Pupil Attitudes," *Journal of Experimental Education*, **16**: 149–59, 1947.
3. LIKERT, R. A. "A Technique for the Measurement of Attitudes," *Archives of Psychology*, **22**: No. 140, 1–55, 1932.
4. McNEMAR, Q. "Opinion-Attitude Methodology," *Psychological Bulletin*, **43**: 289–374, 1946.
5. MURPHY, G., *et al. Experimental Social Psychology*. New York: Harper & Bros., 1937.
6. RYANS, D. G. "A Statistical Analysis of Certain Educational Viewpoints Held by Teachers," *Journal of Experimental Education*, **22**: 119–31, 1953.
7. ———. *The Development of a Short Inventory for Estimating Certain Traits of Teachers*. Dittoed. Los Angeles: Teacher Characteristics Study, 1953.
8. THURSTONE, L. L. *Experimental Tests of Temperament*. Chicago: University of Chicago Psychometric Laboratory, 1951.
9. ———. "Theory of Attitude Measurement," *Psychological Review*, **36**: 222–41, 1929.
10. THURSTONE, L. L., and CHAVE, E. J. *The Measurement of Attitude*. Chicago: University of Chicago Press, 1929.
11. WANDT, E. "A Comparison of the Attitudes of Contrasting Groups of Teachers," *Educational and Psychological Measurement*, **14**: 418–22, 1954.
12. ———. "The Measurement and Analysis of Teachers' Attitudes." Unpublished doctoral dissertation, University of California, Los Angeles, 1951.
13. ———. "The Measurement of Teachers' Attitudes toward Groups Contacted in the Schools," *Journal of Educational Research*, **46**: 113–22, 1952.

6. The Indirect Estimation of Teacher Class-room Behaviors and Other Characteristics from Correlated Inventory Responses

THIS CHAPTER describes the efforts of the Teacher Characteristics Study to derive scales for estimating the classroom behaviors, attitudes, educational viewpoints, verbal intelligence, and emotional adjustment of teachers from their responses to multiple-choice and check-list items relating to preferences, judgments, activities, family and home backgrounds, and the like. The inventory employed, the Teacher Characteristics Schedule, was made up of materials originally incorporated in a number of experimental instruments which had been constructed and subjected to analysis by the Study. The objective of this phase of the research was the prediction of classroom behaviors and relevant personal and social characteristics of teachers (described in chapters 4 and 5) from correlates, or symptomatic responses to questionnaire materials.

The Use of Correlates for Measurement and Prediction

The goals of both scientific research in education and educational operations and services are, generally speaking, the prediction and control of human behavior.

Only very occasionally is present individual or group performance, or the description of such performance, the ultimate objective of either the researcher or the practitioner. Teaching in a fourth-grade schoolroom at a given time obviously must be concerned with immediate achievement, but actually the interest of the teacher and school in present accomplishment exists only because of the transfer value of the learning in question to future life situations, and Johnny's score on an arithmetic test or his course mark has real importance only as it serves as a predictor of how Johnny may be expected to perform in future situations involving similar or related subject matter. If a test score or a mark possesses no generality—if it is specific to the particular problems on which Johnny was tested and bears no relation to his future behavior—it is of little conceivable value or use, and the measurement procedure from which such a score or mark is derived is difficult to justify.

The description of teacher behavior, similarly, is undertaken for the purpose of predicting the probable future behavior of teachers and teacher groups. An understanding of the personal and social characteristics of teachers is sought in order to provide more complete information and to predict probable future manifestations of such characteristics in teachers.

Chapter 4 described those endeavors of the Study that were concerned with the *direct* estimation of overt teacher behavior in the classroom, based upon records provided by trained observers, and chapter 5 reported research concerned with the *direct* estimation of teacher attitudes and viewpoints, verbal ability, and emotional adjustment from expressed opinions and beliefs, responses to vocabulary and verbal reasoning test items, and self-judgments.

In the direct estimation of teacher characteristics, emphasis was placed upon obtaining representative samples of either (*a*) classroom behaviors or (*b*) manifestations of psychological traits, and generalizing or inferring from those samples the probable classroom performances or personal-social characteristics of the teacher in the broader universes of behavior represented by the samples. Where direct estimation is involved, the adequacy of the sampling is basic to successful measurement and prediction.

But the actual sampling of a teacher's classroom behaviors usually is inconvenient and frequently is impossible in practice. Furthermore, the employment of direct-inquiry methods to obtain a sample of responses in a particular trait domain may result in extremely distorted estimates if an incentive situation, conducive to either intentional or unintentional falsification of responses, is involved.

To circumvent some of these difficulties, an alternative approach to the estimation of teacher classroom behaviors and certain teaching-related personal and social traits of teachers was undertaken: that of attempting to identify teacher traits and behaviors indirectly from *correlates*, or "symptoms," of those behaviors and traits.

Such a procedure is less satisfying than that which is based upon actual samples of the behavior in question, but it is useful and is widely employed in science and the applications of science. The chemist or physicist or biologist often is faced with the unavailability of direct evidence, and must resort to the identification of a phenomenon from assembled signs or indicators. Medical diagnosis is more certain when a disease-producing bacillus can be identified in a sample of the patient's blood under the microscope, but the diagnosis often can proceed quite successfully by the observation and analysis of accumulated symptoms —that is, the identification and classification of conditions and behaviors known to be correlated with the presence of the disease-producing bacillus.

The two approaches to the measurement of human behavior—the use of samples and the use of correlates—are summarized in the paradigm which follows. In both approaches, the goal is the prediction of some criterion behavior. And the success or failure of either procedure rests upon the criterion-predictor relationship—the degree of confidence with which the criterion may be estimated from the predictor.

SOME APPROACHES TO THE MEASUREMENT AND PREDICTION OF BEHAVIOR

Criterion Behavior	*Predictor*
(*Goal of prediction*)	(*Approach employed to provide estimates or predictions of the criterion behavior*)

I. Future manifestations, or performances of patterns of *overt behavior in concrete situations* (such as TCS Patterns X_o, Y_o, and Z_o described in chapter 4)

    A. *Direct estimation* of respondents' overt behavior sampled in concrete situations of the same kind as those eliciting the criterion behavior.

    B. *Indirect estimation* of respondents' overt behavior from correlates—conditions or responses known to be associated with direct estimates of overt behavior samples in concrete situations of the same kind as those eliciting the criterion behavior.

        E.g.: biographical data; responses to personal reaction questionnaires (preferences, estimates of behavior of other persons, free associations, statements of past, present, and anticipated future responses, etc.); perceptual responses; responses to performance and psychomotor tests; responses to paper-and-pencil tests.

II. Future manifestations of abstract traits (psychological constructs) hypothesized to affect potentiality for overt behavior in concrete situations (such as TCS Characteristics R, B, I, and S, relating to attitudes, viewpoints, ability, and adjustment, described in chapter 5)

    A. *Direct estimation* of respondents' psychological traits from samples of trait manifestations based on (1) reports of other persons, or (2) the respondents' self-reports in the form of expressed opinions and beliefs, answers to knowledge- and reasoning-type questions, or statements of past, present, and probable future conative behavior.

    B. *Indirect estimation* of respondents' psychological traits from correlates—conditions or responses known to be associated with direct estimates of those traits.

        E.g.: As above.

Ordinarily, indirect estimation through the use of correlates would not be undertaken if direct estimation were feasible. The chief, and very obvious, disadvantage of estimation from correlates lies in the fact that it is a step removed from direct estimation. The amount of variance common to a reliable estimate of a behavior obtained by direct methods and any single correlate seldom exceeds 25 percent and often is no more than 5 percent. Therefore, the accumulation of a reasonably large number of such correlates is necessary to ensure acceptably reliable indirect estimation. The advantages of the use of correlates for measurement and prediction are, however, substantial. The employment of correlates makes measurement possible in areas of behavior which otherwise would be practically inaccessible. It also provides more economical measurement in many instances than does direct measurement. It *helps* to avoid (but does not entirely escape) the distortion of measurement of personal characteristics which frequently occurs when "tendency to give a socially acceptable response" is involved, as in direct questioning. And the use of correlates may permit the tapping of subtle aspects of a criterion behavior which ordinarily elude description and are not immediately apparent from direct estimates.

A major portion of the research of the Study was devoted to problems concerned with the determination of correlates (signs, symptoms, or indicators) of the major teacher classroom behavior dimensions described in chapter 4 and of such teacher traits as those referred to in chapter 5.

Discovering and Selecting Correlates for the Prediction of Teacher Characteristics: General Procedure

The employment of correlates of behavior for prediction purposes implies an empirical approach requiring (*a*) the designation of criterion groups of individuals with regard to the trait or behavior under study, (*b*) the hypothesizing of conditions and responses which may predict the criterion behavior, and (*c*) the determination of those hypothesized conditions or responses which experience shows actually to distinguish between the criterion groups. In conforming to this pattern of empirical analysis, the various investigations of the Study that were directed toward the discovery and selection of correlates of teacher behaviors and traits involved, as a general approach, the following steps:

1. Designation and operational definition of the teacher behavior or trait to be predicted (e.g., X, Y, Z, R, B, I, S).
2. Development of hypotheses with respect to kinds of paper-and-pencil situations and responses that might be correlated with the behavior or trait under study.
3. The preparation of test and inventory situations and responses in conformance with the hypotheses which have been developed.
4. Administration of the prepared materials to an item analysis population (e.g., elementary teachers in general; Grades 3–4 women teachers; secondary teachers in general; mathematics-science teachers).
5. Random splitting of each item-analysis population into item-analysis samples.
6. Classification of the members of each item-analysis sample, followed by selection, in each sample, of criterion groups ranking high and low with respect to the designated behavior or trait for which correlates are to be determined.

7. Determination in each item-analysis sample of the extent to which each response, or unit, of the hypothesized predictor materials is correlated with, or predicts, the behavior or trait under study.

8. Selection of the most efficient predictor units, or responses, in each sample.

9. Double cross-validation involving the scoring of the responses of each sample with a "scoring key" derived from the item analysis of the other sample, followed by determining the correlation, in each sample, between the summated correlates score and the criterion measure.

10. Selection and assembly of situations and responses which survive the double cross-validation analyses to form correlates scoring keys for the prediction of the given behavior or trait in a given population.

11. Administration of the selected correlates materials for (a) further validation involving determination of the effectiveness of the correlates scores in predicting the criterion behavior or trait in additional validation samples, and (b) normative and comparative purposes.

This was essentially the order of procedure followed in developing the materials which culminated in the Teacher Characteristics Schedule. In the case of the teacher behavior dimensions X, Y, and Z, the criterion groups of teachers were constituted on the basis of the composite observer assessments previously described. Scores derived from the direct-inquiry materials described in chapter 5 provided the basis for the composition of criterion groups with respect to teacher attitudes, educational viewpoints, verbal comprehension, and emotional stability or adjustment.

Preparation of Materials Hypothesized To Be Correlates of Teacher Behaviors

Several separate instruments or sets of hypothesized predictor materials were developed and employed at various stages of the research. Each of these instruments went through two to five revisions, based upon review and a sequence of item analyses. The end product of the inventory and test development program was the Teacher Characteristics Schedule, first produced in a 600-item, all-teacher form, and later revised with separate forms consisting of 300 items each, specifically designed respectively for elementary teachers, English–social studies teachers, and mathematics-science teachers.[1]

[1] The Thurstone Temperament Schedule, the Minnesota Multiphasic Personality Inventory, the Allport-Vernon-Lindzey Study of Values, the Kuder Preference Record—Personal, and the Rosenzweig Picture Frustration Study also were administered to samples (but not all) of the participants during the first few years of the project. These inventories were scored with the scoring keys provided by the test publishers. Scores on each of the scales were studied in relation to composite assessments of the teachers relative to the several aspects, or factors, of teacher classroom behavior. These instruments were not, however, item-analyzed against the criteria. A number of the items comprising these instruments undoubtedly would have been found to be associated with the teacher behaviors and traits under investigation.

TYPES OF MATERIAL DEVELOPED

The plan followed in the development of each of the separate sets of predictor materials was essentially the same. First, there was the important matter of establishing the rationales, or formulating the hypotheses, with respect to kinds of materials that might be expected to predict a behavior or trait. Considerable assistance, particularly in developing hypotheses relative to teacher classroom behavior, was provided at this stage by the fertile mind of the late L. L. Thurstone, a member of the Advisory Committee. Following the setting-up of rationales, the literature was searched for suggestions as to specific types of materials which might be applicable. A third step consisted of the development of questions and alternative responses in accordance with the agreed-upon rationales, and the compilation from such items of tentative or preliminary forms of the instruments to be used. Finally, the developed materials were subjected to review and criticism and to a series of experimental tryouts with typical teacher groups.

Some of the measuring devices constructed were never actually subjected to extended item analysis or further development, either because preliminary tryout and study cast doubt upon their usefulness and the extent to which they were measuring the qualities they had been hypothesized to measure, or because of difficulties presented by administration or scoring. Examples of the latter were Exercise SC, consisting of open-end, incomplete sentences, and Picture Situations, Form X, described below, which appeared to have possible value in predicting teacher behavior. The use of these was discontinued after tryout and preliminary investigation because they could not be scored objectively.

Brief descriptions of the instruments developed and used in connection with the Teacher Characteristics Study, together with sample items illustrating the kinds of materials involved, are presented below.

Inventory P, 4th Revision, 1948–49

A set of statements, scaled by the equal-appearing intervals method, expressing opinions about pupils. The respondent indicated agreement or disagreement with each statement.

	Agree	Disagree
4. There is too much leniency today in the handling of children.*		
10. A teacher can always find time to listen to a child's problem.*		

* The scale values for these items were 4.1 and 1.2, respectively.

Inventory T, 4th Revision, 1948–49

A set of statements, scaled by the equal-appearing intervals method, expressing opinions about teachers and teaching. The respondent indicated agreement or disagreement with each statement.

	Agree	Disagree
9. Teaching is one of the best methods of serving humanity.*...............................	_____	_____
12. Teaching develops a cynical attitude toward life.*..................................	_____	_____

* The scale values for these items were 1.0 and 4.4, respectively.

Exercise SC, 2nd Revision, 1948–49

A set of open-end statements to be completed by the respondent. Content of the responses was hypothesized to be classifiable into general categories related to the set predisposing a teacher to identifiable behavior or trait patterns.

10. Teaching develops . . .
26. It is fun to . . .

Picture Situations, X, Revision, 1948–49

Twenty-four incompletely structured line drawings portraying teacher-teacher and teacher-pupil situations. In each frame, the remarks of some person appearing in the drawing were omitted and were provided by the respondent. Content of the responses was hypothesized to be classifiable into general categories related to the set predisposing a teacher to identifiable behavior or trait patterns.

Fig. 5.—Typical line drawings from the Picture Situations test.

Exercise H, Revision, 1948–49

A set of 92 homonyms, read to the respondents by the examiner, with the respondent being required to write the word (the first word occurring to him) which he perceived the examiner to have read. The respondent's choice of words was hypothesized to indicate acquaintance with, and depth of interest in, children, teaching, personal and social behavior of persons, etc.

10. Attendance—attendants   41. No—know
17. Cruise—crews   69. Role—roll

Exercise CA, 2nd and 3rd Revisions, 1948–49

This exercise was used in both (1) a 150-item free-response form (the respondent writing the first word that occurred to him after reading a stimulus word) and (2) a 45-item multiple-choice form (in which each stimulus word was followed by four responses, one of which was to be selected by the respondent as the word which would first occur to him after hearing the stimulus word). It was hypothesized that choice of synonyms of words reflecting positive feeling tone, acceptance, friendliness, etc., and antonyms of words reflecting negative feeling tone, aggression, etc., might be related to teacher behaviors and traits.

9. *Cooperative*   12. *Easygoing*
   a. helpful   a. happy-go-lucky
   b. willing   b. good-natured
   c. obstructive   c. strained
   d. disinclined   d. rigorous

Exercise J, 2nd and 3rd Revisions, 1948–49

Exercise J (first used as a 56-item free-response test, and later produced in two 30-item multiple-choice forms, J-1 and J-2) was made up of items which required the respondent to utilize judgment and reasoning in making estimates in situations where an accurate answer was presumed not to be available. It was hypothesized that the estimates of teachers in situations posed by the test might distinguish between criterion groups of teachers.

9. Approximately how many books might you expect to find in a public library in a typical city of 100,000 population?

   9-1   5,000
   9-2   10,000
   9-3   25,000
   9-4   125,000
   9-5   600,000

20. Approximately how many boys under fifteen years of age in a city of 25,000 population own (or have owned) bicycles?

   20-1   300
   20-2   800
   20-3   1,300
   20-4   1,800
   20-5   2,300

Exercises Y and Z, Revisions, 1948–49, 1949–50

Exercise Y.—Exercise Y was a set of reproductions of paintings. It was individually administered, with the respondent being required to indicate his preference for one or the other of pictures presented in pairs. The picture pairs represented contrasts of people and objects, strong and weak color, action and inaction, children and adults, individuals and groups, etc. It was hypothesized that choice of pictures

FIG. 6.—Typical line drawings from Exercise Z.

with specified characteristics might be related to identifiable teacher behaviors and traits.

Exercise Z.—Exercise Z consisted of 100 black-and-white line drawings, some structured and others consisting of geometric patterns. (See Figure 6.) The drawings were presented in pairs, each of the 50 pairs being developed around a hypothesis, e.g., choice of formal planting over free growth of plants hypothesized to relate to systematic, disciplined behavior; choice of rounded, curved designs over angular design hypothesized to reflect poise and emotional balance. The respondent followed three separate sets of directions: (1) indication of "like" or "dislike" for each drawing; (2) indication of preference of one picture in each pair; and (3) indication of preference (in each pair) that would be expressed by a school child. (In an additional approach which subsequently was abandoned, each respondent was asked to indicate with a single word the most appropriate title, or name, for each of the one hundred drawings.)

Exercise W, 2nd Revision, 1948–49

Exercise W was designed to obtain samples of the respondent's handwriting as an indicator of "expressive movements." The exercise was disguised as a spelling test in order to provide control of the characters written by the respondents. The exercise was used to test the hypothesis that differences in certain teacher behaviors and traits might be related to the products of expressive movements of the individual.

Exercise FA, 2nd Revision, 1948–49

A free-association test requiring the respondent to write the words suggested to him by a stimulus word. Two hypotheses were involved: (1) that *fluency* might be associated with teacher traits and behaviors and (2) that word *content* might be classifiable into categories related to teacher behaviors and traits (e.g., words having to do with classroom situations, children, people, etc.).

Case History Inquiry, C, 3rd Revision, 1948–49

A free-response questionnaire used to obtain information about status, home, and family conditions which might be hypothesized to influence teacher behaviors or traits. Education, vocational experience, marital status, parental information, frequently engaged-in activities, personal problems, and the like, often were revealed by the respondents.

Case History Check List, D, 3rd Revision, 1948–49

A 54-item check list (multiple-choice form) covering the same areas as Case History Inquiry C, but adapted to more convenient scoring and recording.

3. During most of his life what was the general nature of your father's occupation?
   a. Professional
   b. Farming
   c. Skilled (machinist, printer, etc.)
   d. Unskilled labor
   e. Business

17. As a child, how often were you punished?
    a. Very frequently
    b. More than average child
    c. Occasionally
    d. Rarely
    e. Never

Autobiography, E

The autobiography was an attempt to obtain additional information about the personal and family backgrounds of the teacher. There was no structuring except for the suggestion that the autobiographical sketch include personal incidents and their relation to childhood, home and family activities, family relationships, emotional peaks in the individual's experience, skills and training, and present status relative to health, social life, emotional problems, etc.

Inquiry L, 2nd Revision, 1948–49

Inquiry L was an activity log intended to provide a record of the teacher's classroom activities over a specified period of time. The respondent was instructed to record his remembered activities each day from the time of arrival until leaving school, including parent interviews, clerical duties, yard duty, clubs, and other such activities in addition to those of the classroom.

Exercise DU, 2nd Revision, 1948–49

The respondent was presented with a list of words often used in describing persons and was directed to indicate whether the word referred to a trait that was *desirable* or *undesirable* in an adult. The stimulus words were ambiguous, and it was hypothesized that a respondent's choice of a word as "desirable" or "undesirable" might be related to certain criterion behaviors or traits.

	Desirable Trait	Undesirable Trait
Easy going...............................	_____	_____
Strong-willed............................	_____	_____
Reserved................................	_____	_____

Exercise K

A free-response exercise in which the respondent was directed to write as many words as he might think of which could be used to describe a person. It was hypothesized that the words written by an individual might be classified according to *content* or *reference,* and that given categories might be related to identifiable teacher behaviors or traits.

Inquiries A and B, 3rd Revision, 1949–50

Inquiry A and Inquiry B were early forms of the Educational Viewpoints Inquiry described in chapter 5. Forms of the Inquiry were prepared for elementary teachers, secondary teachers, elementary principals, and secondary principals.

5. If it were necessary to follow a minimum school day for your class, do you believe it would be better to keep approximately the regularly allotted time for reading and number work, limiting somewhat the time for social studies?........................ Yes _____
No _____

13. Do you find that children make real contributions to
    the planning of their own units of work?............ Yes _____
    No _____

Preference Inventory, Form 49-A, 1949–50

A set of 150 multiple-choice items covering a wide variety of situations, the respondent being required to make a choice from the responses given to each item.

If you could choose an achievement for your son, which of the following would you prefer?

1. Perfection of a cure for tuberculosis.
2. Success as an artist.
3. Invention of a new industrial process.
4. Election to Congress.
5. Selection for a professorship in a college or university.

When you plan your future activities, which of the following is *most* attractive to you?

1. Owning a home of my own.
2. Rearing my children.
3. Spending a year in travel.
4. Developing skill in an avocation.
5. Getting ahead in my profession.

Inventory of Teacher Opinion

The Inventory of Teacher Opinion, described in chapter 5, consisted of Likert-type scales with eight positive statements and eight negative statements relating to the respondent's opinions toward (1) pupils, (2) other teachers, (3) parents, (4) supervisors, (5) administrators, (6) nonteaching personnel in the school, (7) democratic classroom procedures, and (8) democratic administrative procedures. The respondent indicated degree of agreement or disagreement (strongly agree, agree, uncertain or indifferent, disagree, strongly disagree) to each statement.

1. Most administrators try to help their teachers as best they can.
2. Most supervisors spend too much of their time finding fault.
3. Pupils make teaching a very enjoyable job.
4. Parents only come to school when they have a complaint to make.

Inventory Form 49-B, 1949–50

Inventory Form 49-B consisted of 117 multiple-choice items relating to personal preferences, self-judgments, typical behavior reports (of self), interpretations of the behavior of others, and factual information.

1. If a pertinent question occurs to you when attending a public lecture, which of the following are you likely to do?
   1-1 Ask the question in the discussion period after the lecture.
   1-2 See the speaker later to ask the question.
   1-3 Not ask the question at all.

10. How many hours per week does the average teacher spend in outside preparation for classes?
    10-1 Less than 3 hours.
    10-2 8 hours.
    10-3 14 hours.
    10-4 20 hours or more.

Inventory Form 49-N, 1949–50

A set of 113 multiple-choice items similar to those in Preference Inventory 49-A, except that the respondent was instructed to indicate the "least-preferred" or "least-applicable" response to each item.

9. Which of the following would you *least* like to do?
    9-1 Take a young cousin to the circus.
    9-2 Select a book of fairy tales to give a young cousin as a Christmas present.
    9-3 Select a sweater to give a young cousin.
    9-4 Repair a broken toy for a young cousin.

Biographical and Activity Check List

This instrument was a comprehensive check list (involving 457 possible responses) providing biographical data and information relative to the activities of the respondent. The materials included fell into the general categories: (1) essential factual data, e.g., age, amount of teaching experience, other occupations engaged in; (2) principal activities during the recent past, e.g., hobbies, sports, reading, music; (3) childhood and adolescent activities, e.g., care of younger children, membership in clubs; (4) parental data, e.g., occupations of parents, schooling of parents, parents' economic status; and (5) factors influencing the respondent's choice of teaching as a career.

8. Are you
    8-1 Single?
    8-2 Married?
    8-3 Separated or divorced?
    8-4 Widowed?

52. How would you rate the economic status of your family?
    52-1 Independently wealthy.
    52-2 Well-to-do.
    52-3 Comfortable.
    52-4 Poor.
    52-5 Poverty-stricken.

PRELIMINARY TESTING OF THE HYPOTHESIZED MATERIALS

The various types of items described in the preceding section were subjected to several successive phases of study and selection, which culminated in a single omnibus instrument embracing materials from a number of the previously developed exercises and inventories. The

analysis and review upon which selection of items for further consideration was based consisted essentially of (*a*) determination of criterion-
discrimination and frequency-of-choice values for each response, and
(*b*) attention to the practicality and convenience of administration and
scoring of materials of a particular type.

Estimation of the extent to which responses distinguished between
groups of teachers selected to represent high and low criterion classifications presented difficulties (and necessarily was tentative during the
early stages of the Study) due to the fact that attack upon several
major problems was proceeding simultaneously. Attention was being
given to (1) analyses leading to the definition and designation of criterion behaviors and traits, (2) the accumulation of relevant teacher
data by observer assessments of teacher classroom behavior and direct-
inquiry data pertaining to teacher attitudes and beliefs, and (3) the
development of indirect-estimation materials hypothesized to predict
the evolving descriptions of teacher behaviors and traits. Obviously, in
the relatively limited time available for the research, it was not possible to set aside the correlates-development phase to await completion
of teacher observing and assessment and the basic analyses of teacher
behaviors and traits. As a result, an attempt was made to conduct preliminary investigations of the probable usefulness of the correlates materials at the same time the first sets of criterion data were being accumulated.

Thus, simultaneously with the observation and assessment of the
first 600 elementary and secondary teachers, and long before the factor
analyses and correlational studies leading to the selection of teacher behaviors X_o, Y_o, and Z_o were conducted, tentative forms of the hypothesized predictor materials were being administered to teachers observed, and preliminary item analyses were being conducted, and replicated, on samples of teachers as they became available. The criteria employed were necessarily tentative and incomplete during the preliminary
analyses.

The teacher samples that were used for the preliminary item analyses
were independent of the Basic Analysis groups of elementary and secondary teachers used for the response analyses conducted in deriving
final forms of the Teacher Characteristics Study scoring keys (described
in a following portion of this chapter).

During the early stages of the research, the teachers who had been
observed were assembled on a Saturday, when they were free from
school responsibilities (they were given remuneration for testing time
and travel expense), for administration of the various instruments.

Materials which depended upon the presence of an examiner were administered during this testing session; others which were largely self-administering were filled out by the participants subsequent to the testing session and were returned by mail or picked up by the examiner at the teachers' schools. Since the instruments were not all developed at once, but appeared in their various revisions over a number of months, *not* all exercises and inventories were administered to all teachers. The responses to each instrument, however, were tabulated and analyzed in relation to the relative frequency of acceptance among high and low criterion groups of three to five samples each of elementary and secondary teachers.

A number of investigations of item-selection techniques were undertaken in 1949–50 and 1950–51 in an effort to determine their relative effectiveness from the standpoint of revealing the relationships between correlates scores (summed scorable responses) and criterion indices in independent "hold-out" validation samples. For example, responses selected on the basis of discrimination at various levels of significance (e.g., .10 level, .05 level, and .01 level) were compared for subsamples made up of intact teacher groups (i.e., all members of a group from the same school system) and for combined samples of teachers of a particular grade level or subject matter (e.g., Grades 3–4 elementary teachers, mathematics-science teachers, and English–social studies teachers). Responses selected on the basis of their discrimination at a given level of significance in *each* sample, in replicated subsamples, and in the composite samples (e.g., responses discriminating in two of four available intact samples, and in a single composite sample obtained by pooling or combining the intact subsample groups) also were compared. The results of such research suggested that, when attempting to select correlates of an external criterion (such as observer assessments of teacher behavior) with relatively small samples available, there may be some advantage (judged by hold-out groups validation indices) in employing the .05 level of significance and requiring that a correlate (response) distinguish between the high and low criterion groups of three out of four replicates, or subsamples. While such studies were, in a sense, incidental to the main stream of the Study, answers to the questions which instigated them seemed essential to the proper progress of the research directed at the determination of correlates of teacher behavior. A considerable portion of time was devoted to such methodological studies.

During the course of the preliminary investigation of correlates materials, it became apparent that large-scale investigation of the obtained correlates of teacher behaviors would necessitate the use, exclusively, of materials which were self-administering and of multiple-choice or check-list response types. Useful as free response might be, the difficulties of scoring and tabulation were so great as to render such an approach in-feasible. A major consideration in the selection of materials for further use, therefore, was the extent to which they could be adapted to a mul-tiple-choice response form. A number of items which originally were used in free-response form were recast with a listing of possible re-sponses; for many others, however, such revision was not possible and consequently they were dropped from further study.

Following preliminary investigation of the hypothesized correlates materials, those which appeared to offer the greatest promise were selected for further study, such selections being based on (1) extent to which a response distinguished between criterion groups of teachers, (2) frequency of choice of a response by the combined samples of teach-ers of a given level or grade, (3) capability of self-administration, and (4) amenability to objective scoring. Upper and lower 30 percents of the teacher distributions were used to constitute the criterion groups in these second-phase item-analysis studies. An item was retained for still further consideration whenever (*a*) one of its responses discriminated at the .05 level of significance in at least three samples of teachers of a particular grade or subject matter and (*b*) the discriminating response was selected by at least 5 percent of the total sample employed in the particular analysis. Independent analyses were conducted for elemen-tary, mathematics-science, and English–social studies teachers.

Principal attention during the preliminary and second-phase analyses and collection of correlates was given to the prediction of the major teacher classroom behavior dimensions, i.e., to the discovery of re-sponses which discriminated between criterion groups with respect to composite observer assessments of X_o (understanding, friendly teacher classroom behavior), Y_o (responsible, businesslike teacher classroom be-havior), and Z_o (stimulating, surgent teacher classroom behavior). There seemed reason to believe that correlates of these actual class-room behaviors might be more elusive than correlates of other teacher traits involving criterion data derived from verbal (direct-inquiry) ma-terials, and that chief attention, therefore, should be given to the *be-havior* correlates problem.

In connection with the selection of discriminating responses, it is im-portant to note that responses frequently were found to interact with the classification of teachers as elementary, mathematics-science, or English–social studies—that responses often were found to be differ-entially discriminating depending upon the teacher group considered.

Thus, a response which reliably distinguished between criterion groups of Grades 3–4 elementary teachers might have no discriminating ability for mathematics-science criterion groups. True, some responses seemed to show considerable generality in that they appeared to discriminate among criterion groups regardless of the classification of the teachers. But the samples of discriminating items differed considerably as elementary, mathematics-science, and English–social studies teachers were considered, and occasionally a response which distinguished in favor of the high or low criterion group for elementary teachers was found to discriminate in favor of the opposite criterion group for, say, mathematics-science or English–social studies teachers.

ASSEMBLY OF MATERIALS IN A SINGLE BOOKLET INVENTORY: THE TEACHER CHARACTERISTICS SCHEDULE

Following the selection of the more promising correlates items for the separate exercises and inventories described in the preceding section, the materials which survived were incorporated during the winter of 1950–51 into a single, omnibus instrument which, in its first form, was known as Teacher Characteristics Schedule, Form X.

Form X consisted of 600 multiple-choice and check-list type items, involving over two thousand possible responses. It was made up of items embracing responses which discriminated among *any* of the teacher groups studied. In other words, the items that seemed to hold the most promise were included in Form X, without regard to the particular teacher group (elementary, mathematics-science, English–social studies) in which they discriminated. Form X, then, was intended for use with all teachers, irrespective of grade or subject taught.

Form X was given to all teachers observed in connection with the Study during the spring and fall of 1951 and the spring of 1952. It also was completed by a large number of teachers participating in special studies or projects undertaken by the Study during this period.

Experience with Form X showed that it required from three to five hours for completion and that failure of observed teachers to complete the Schedule frequently could be attributed to the length of time demanded. The staff was of the opinion that the number of items making up the Schedule could be substantially reduced in two ways: first, by further response analysis and the elimination of items for which the responses did not appear to be holding up as correlates of teacher behavior, and second, by including in the printed booklet submitted to a teacher only those items which seemed to be discriminating for the teacher group of which the participant was a member.

Accordingly, a third stage of item analyses was undertaken, during which the available responses of the three major groups of teachers on Form X were analyzed against (*a*) the teacher classroom behavior criteria (TCS Patterns X_o, Y_o, and Z_o), and (*b*) three teacher trait criteria —attitude toward pupils (Characteristic *R*); attitude toward administrative and nonadministrative personnel in the schools (Characteristic *Q*); and educational viewpoints (Characteristic *B*). Each of these response analyses was accomplished separately for Grades 3–4 elementary teachers, mathematics-science secondary teachers, and English–social studies secondary teachers.

Similar analyses were conducted to find responses which discriminated significantly between male and female teachers, irrespective of the particular teacher behaviors or traits under consideration.

Following these analyses and evaluation of the results, three revised forms of the Schedule were produced. Appearing in the fall of 1952, these forms were known as Form E '52 (for elementary teachers), Form SE '52 (for English and social studies teachers), and Form MS '52 (for mathematics and science teachers). Each of the three revised forms of the Schedule was a 300-item booklet. Of the 300 items, 194 were common to the English–social studies and the mathematics-science booklets, 174 were common to the elementary and the mathematics-science booklets, 174 were common to the elementary and English–social studies booklets, and 118 were common to all three of the Form '52 booklets. The item overlapping among the booklets was approximately 58 percent for elementary and mathematics-science, 58 percent for elementary and English–social studies, 65 percent for English–social studies and mathematics-science, and 39 percent for elementary and secondary.

Examples of items typical of those appearing in the Teacher Characteristics Schedule, Form E '52, follow.

Preference Items

7. Which of the following would you prefer to do?
   7-1 Plan a Christmas campaign for help for the needy.
   7-2 Buy food and supplies for needy families.
   7-3 Canvass for contributions to needy families.
   7-4 Take Christmas baskets to needy families.
   7-5 Compile statistics on the progress of a campaign for charity funds.

19. Which of the following would you prefer to do?
    19-1 Build a dog kennel.
    19-2 Write an article about dogs.
    19-3 Teach tricks to a dog.

Typical Behavior Item

10. If you are to present a paper to your club, which of the following would you do?

    10-1 Ask competent criticism of the paper, but make only the changes you think necessary.

    10-2 Ask competent criticism of the paper, making any changes suggested.

    10-3 Show the paper only to your close friends.

    10-4 Feel your own judgment is good enough and not ask for criticism.

Disguised Typical Behavior Item

56. How many hours per week does the average teacher spend in outside preparation for classes?

    56-1 Less than 3 hours

    56-2 8 hours

    56-3 14 hours

    56-4 20 hours or more

Association Items

53. Which of the following do you associate with the word *comment?*

    53-1 Crass

    53-2 Frequency

    53-3 Taste

    53-4 Mutual

60. Which of the following words do you think *most people* give as their response to the word *bad?*

    60-1 Good

    60-2 Mischief

    60-3 Sad

    60-4 Terrible

Self-Judgment Item

34. Which of the following is the strongest trait in your make-up?

    34-1 Accuracy

    34-2 Ambition

    34-3 Cheerfulness

    34-4 Decisiveness

Estimation Item

112. A party has been announced for 8:00 P.M. About what time do you think most of the guests would be likely to arrive?

    112-1 Before 8:00 P.M.

    112-2 8:00–8:05 P.M.

    112-3 8:15–8:20 P.M.

    112-4 8:30–8:35 P.M.

    112-5 8:45–8:50 P.M.

Graphic Preference Item

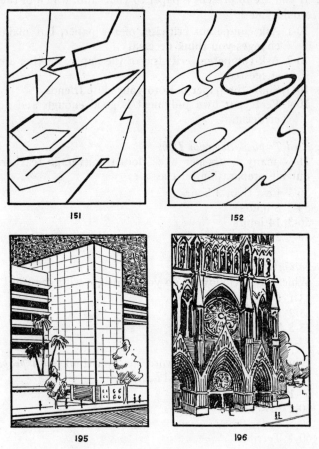

FIG. 7.—Graphic Preference items.

Attitudes Item

218. In light of your experience with children, what do you think of the following statement?

"Most pupils try to do their work to the best of their ability."

218-1 Strongly disagree
218-2 Disagree
218-3 Indifferent
218-4 Agree
218-5 Strongly agree

Educational Viewpoints Item

247. How do you feel about the following statement?

"It is possible to develop most school classwork around 'out-of-school' activities."

247-1 Strongly disagree
247-2 Disagree
247-3 Indifferent
247-4 Agree
247-5 Strongly agree

Biographical Item
How old are you?

249-1 Under 20   250-1 40 to 44
249-2 20 to 24   250-2 45 to 49
249-3 25 to 29   250-3 50 to 54
249-4 30 to 34   250-4 55 to 59
249-5 35 to 39   250-5 60 or older

Indicate which of the following organizations you have belonged to or now belong to:

289-1 High school or college sorority or fraternity
289-2 Hobby club
289-3 Honor society (scholastic, scientific, or professional)
289-4 Debating society or club
289-5 Community social organization (bridge club, country club, etc.)

Activity Items
Which of the following did you do during the past year?

271-1 Visited an art gallery or museum.
271-2 Did some redecorating in my home or office to make it more attractive.
271-3 Read one or more books about art, artists, or art history.
271-4 Attended an art lecture.
271-5 Bought some painting or other art work.

Check any of the following activities in which you have spent an average of three hours or more per week during the past three weeks (or the most recent three-week period when such activities were in season):

281-1 Gardening
281-2 Indoor games (cards, chess, etc.)
281-3 Indoor exercise (handball, gymnastics, etc.)
281-4 Painting, sculpture, etc.
281-5 Attending concerts, exhibits, etc.

The Teacher Characteristics Schedule Forms E '52, SE '52, and MS '52 were completed by teachers participating in the Basic Analysis studies and also in various special studies during the fall of 1952, the spring and fall of 1953, and the first three months of 1954.

In anticipation of the national survey of teachers to be conducted during the spring of 1954, still another revision of the Schedule was prepared, consisting essentially of a reprinting and extension of the 1952 forms. The first 300 items in each of the new forms (Revised Form E '54; Revised Form MS '54; and Revised Form SE '54) were identical to those in the 1952 forms. An additional 50 items (the same items for all three forms) were added to the original 300. These items were of two general types—(1) direct-inquiry items relating to the teacher traits of verbal understanding (*I*), emotional adjustment (*S*), and validity of response (*V*) as described in chapter 5, and (2) information, or control items, to be used for purposes of comparison and classification of teachers participating in the national survey project. Eleven verbal understanding items, ten emotional items, twelve validity items, and eleven control items (plus six nonscored orientation items) comprised the newly added materials. Examples of such items follow.

Verbal Understanding Item
337. Which of the following responses *first* comes to your mind when you see the word *phlegmatic?*
   337-1 Happy
   337-2 Nervous
   337-3 Spasmodic
   337-4 Sluggish
   337-5 Never heard of the word

Emotional Stability Item
327. Which of the following is more true of you?
   327-1 I wish I weren't so nervous.
   327-2 I wish I had more responsibility.

Validity-of-Response Item
334. Which of the following is more true of you?
   334-1 I have never to my knowledge told a lie.
   334-2 I sometimes exaggerate or stretch stories a little in retelling them.

Control Items
In what state are you now teaching?
301-1 Either Maine, New Hampshire, Vermont, Massachusetts, Rhode Island, or Connecticut
301-2 Either New York, New Jersey, Pennsylvania, Delaware, Maryland, or District of Columbia
301-3 Either Virginia, West Virginia, or North Carolina
301-4 Either South Carolina, Georgia, Alabama, Mississippi, Louisiana, Florida, Kentucky, or Tennessee
301-5 Either Ohio, Indiana, Michigan, Illinois, Wisconsin, Minnesota, Iowa, or Missouri
302-1 Either Kansas, Nebraska, North Dakota, or South Dakota
302-2 Either Oklahoma, Texas, Arkansas, Arizona, or New Mexico

302-3 Either Montana, Idaho, Wyoming, Utah, Colorado, or Nevada
302-4 Either California, Washington, or Oregon

In which of the following kinds of schools are you now teaching?

306-1 One-room, one-teacher school
306-2 School of 2 to 5 teachers
306-3 School of 6 to 16 teachers
306-4 School of 17 to 50 teachers
306-5 School of more than 50 teachers

Derivation of Teacher Characteristics Schedule Scoring Keys

As has been noted, the items incorporated in the Schedule originated in various separate instruments and owed their selection to a succession of analyses and evaluations. Serious attention to the derivation of final correlates scoring keys for the several teacher behaviors and traits under consideration was postponed, however, until a substantial number of teachers of various grades and subjects had been observed in their classrooms and also had completed one of the forms of the Schedule. By the fall of 1953, the necessary data were available for over two thousand teachers and it then seemed feasible to proceed with the item analyses required for the derivation of scoring keys which might permit the estimation of X_o, Y_o, Z_o, R, R_1, Q, B, I, S, and V, as described in chapters 4 and 5, from responses to the Schedule.

It should be noted at this point that the extensive response analyses and other statistical studies conducted by the Study, beginning in 1953, were made possible by the availability of facilities provided by the Institute of Numerical Analysis (a branch of the National Bureau of Standards, located on the campus of the University of California, Los Angeles), later designated as Numerical Analysis Research, with sponsorship, successively, of the University of California, Los Angeles, and the Bureau of Naval Research. Chief among the facilities offered by the Institute of Numerical Analysis (and Numerical Analysis Research) was an electronic computer, SWAC (Standard's Western Automatic Computer), which was ideally suited for large-scale item analysis and other tabulating and statistical operations involved in test construction research.

The computer, SWAC, was employed for a number of different kinds of analyses of Study data (e.g., computation of biserial r's and frequency-of-choice indices for response analysis purposes, computation of product-moment correlation coefficients, scoring of the Schedule responses of individual teachers with the various keys which were derived from response analysis, computation of means and standard deviations summarizing the Schedule scores of teachers classified in various ways), but one of its principal contributions was in the response analyses basic to the derivation of correlates scoring keys. The combination of utilization of the binary number systems with a large-capacity, high-speed electromagnetic memory made possible the rapid counting of the responses of criterion groups and the scoring of values for the computation of correlation coefficients.

The Schedule responses of each participating teacher were punched into IBM cards. In the response analyses, the IBM cards of sorted criterion groups were fed into SWAC and summary cards were periodically punched out, these cards showing for each item response the percent frequency of choice of that response by members of the high, middle, and low criterion groups, and of the sample as a whole. An adaptation of Flanagan's table for estimating product-moment coefficients from data at the tails of a distribution[2] was stored in the electromagnetic memory, the summary cards were fed into SWAC, and the required item-analysis data were automatically punched out on IBM cards for subsequent listing by the IBM Tabulator to provide a printed record. Thus, for each of the responses to the Schedule items, it was possible to obtain for any specified criterion for a designated sample (1) the percent of each criterion group (high, middle, and low) selecting that response; (2) the percent of the entire sample (high, low, and middle groups combined) selecting the response; and (3) the estimated biserial correlation of the response with the criterion. Mr. James Ziegler was responsible for the extensive computations required, utilizing SWAC, both for this phase of the research and later statistical analyses undertaken.

SOME STUDIES OF ITEM ANALYSIS TECHNIQUES

As was noted in a preceding section, a set of problems arose concerning the response analysis procedures that would be most appropriate for selecting items for the several revisions of the Schedule and for deriving Schedule correlates scoring keys. Answers to some of the questions were not immediately available, and it seemed desirable to give attention to them before proceeding with the application of response analysis to the derivation of scoring keys.

---

[2] The tables provided by Flanagan permit estimation of r's from the responses of the upper and lower 27 percent criterion groups, the column and row headings representing percentages from 1 to 99 of the upper and lower criterion groups. An adaptation of this table was made in view of the binary system utilized by SWAC. Column and row headings, representing fractions of the upper and lower criterion groups were divided to provide 128 entries for any one row or column. Linearity between any two adjacent entries in the original Flanagan table was assumed in making the adaptation.

For example, the criterion data on teacher classroom behavior (X_o, Y_o, and Z_o) consisted of teacher behavior assessments that were contributed by trained observers. Such criterion data had certain characteristics which are not common to criterion data frequently employed in tests and inventory item analysis, particularly in internal consistency approaches where the criterion often is a collection of items representing relatively homogeneous replications. Thus, one problem concerned methods of *combining assessments* of observers in composing the criterion groups of teachers for item-analysis purposes. For example, should the cutting scores employed in making up the criterion groups be (*a*) values representing an average of the assessments made by the several observers of a particular teacher (regression approach) or (*b*) based on the multiple cutoff principle, requiring that the assessment made by *each* observer of a particular teacher be above or below a designated value?

A related problem involved the *position of the designated cutoff points* used to define the criterion groups of a particular behavior. That is, should the criterion data be represented by (*a*) high and low groups of teachers falling near the extremes of the distribution of the external criterion, where the reliability of the judgments is likely to be fairly high, but where the number of cases contributing to the analysis is relatively small, or by (*b*) high and low groups representing greater portions of the total range of the distribution?[3]

Still other considerations relating to item-analysis procedures involved standards (criteria) to be employed in the selection of responses to comprise scoring keys, including attention to the most effective compromise of risks of Type I and Type II error in the actual selection of responses which, collectively, would serve as a correlates score to predict a teacher trait. This set of problems concerning response selection standards was approached empirically, and various methods of item selection were compared in light of their relative validity, based upon cross-validation indices.

Special note should, perhaps, be made of the basis for evaluating the various procedures which were compared. Comparisons of test analysis

---

[3] Kelley [*3*] presented arguments some time ago favoring upper, middle, and lower criterion groups consisting of 27 percent, 46 percent, and 27 percent, respectively, and Flanagan [*2*], in a systematic empirical study, found that the estimation of biserial *r*'s from upper and lower 27 percent criterion groups seemed to be a quite satisfactory method for approximating product-moment correlation coefficients, judged by the comparison of indices obtained from random samples with known population values. It seemed desirable for the Study also to conduct studies in the area, seeking evidence regarding the appropriateness of using upper and lower 27 percents, or other proportions of the criterion distribution, in designating the criterion groups.

techniques sometimes have been made in light of the sampling error. It seems reasonable, however, to assume the ultimate basis for judgment to be the validity of scores yielded by a technique. With this as the guiding principle, comparisons of the procedures investigated by the Study were made in light of cross-validation coefficients.

Other investigations of response analysis techniques also were carried out during various phases of the Study. For example, one involving the composition of criterion groups in a special case of a skewed distribution was noted in chapter 5 in connection with the analyses and selection of validity-of-response materials for Inventory ISV. Others, relating to criteria for the selection of items, were mentioned earlier in this chapter in discussing preliminary item analyses of the original materials. The more systematic and extensive investigations are very briefly summarized in the following paragraphs and tables.

Methods of Selecting Criterion Groups in Inventory Response Analysis on the Basis of Cross-Validity Indices

In these studies, the twofold concern was to study the relative effectiveness of (a) multiple cutoff as compared with regression approaches in combining observer assessments of teachers to form criterion groups, and (b) criterion groups composed of more and less extreme portions of the distribution of teachers on a criterion. The basis for comparison of the results was the relative validity of the derived Schedule scoring keys (X_{co}) when the various procedures were employed for predicting the criterion behavior (X_o) in randomly selected cross-validation samples.

TCS Pattern X_o was employed as the criterion to be predicted, and two different levels of significance were applied in selecting responses for the scoring keys. These levels were: (a) minimum compound probability of .01 for each response, based upon combination of the probability estimates yielded by the independent samples; and (b) minimum compound probability of .17, based upon combination of the probability estimates yielded by the independent samples. For convenience, only positively discriminating responses (those discriminating in favor of the high criterion groups) were used in the analyses.

The subjects consisted of 595 third- and fourth-grade teachers employed in urban communities of the Central and West Coast regions. The total sample was randomly split into two subsamples, one of 297 teachers and the other of 298 teachers, for item analysis and subsequent cross-validity study. Each teacher had been independently observed and assessed relative to classroom behavior by a minimum of two trained observers, and each also had completed the Schedule.

In each of the two subsamples, the subjects were assigned to high and low item-analysis groups, on the basis of their ratings on "understanding, friendly" teacher behavior, by eight different methods. Four of these were multiple cutoff methods, with the cutoff points being set at .1, .2, .3, or .6 standard deviation units from the mean assessment of each observer. The other four were regression methods, in which the observers' assessments were averaged in standard score form, and the criterion groups were composed of the extreme 10, 15, 27, or 45 percents at each end of the distributions.

Response-criterion correlations and frequency-of-choice indices were computed for each response for each method of criterion group composition within each subsample. Responses meeting the prescribed standards—(a) compound probability of .01, and choice of response by between 5 and 95 percent of the total subsample; and (b) compound probability of .17 with choice of response by between 5 and 95 percent of the total subsample—were incorporated in correlates scoring keys (X_{co}) derived by each of the experimental methods for each of the subsamples.

The Schedule responses of each subsample of teachers then were scored with the scoring key (X_{co}) derived from the other independent subsamples, and cross-validity correlations were computed between the scores and the criterion indices based upon observers' assessments of X_o. The results are summarized in Table 32.

It will be noted that the several methods of composing the criterion groups yielded cross-validity coefficients of approximately the same magnitude, ranging from .28 to .45. The differences between the validity coefficients were too small to suggest significance. The regression approach, at least for methods E, F, and G, appeared to be slightly superior to the multiple cutoff approaches. Within the two major approaches, the differences, again, were small, and there appeared little choice regarding portions of the item-analysis sample which should be included in the criterion groups.

The frequently employed upper and lower 27 percents, based upon the averages of replicated assessments in standard score form, probably is as useful as any composition of the criterion groups. With large samples, the use of extremes represented by upper and lower 10 percent criterion groups may have some slight advantage. Even with fairly small criterion groups, when those groups constituted extremes of the criterion distribution, the obtained cross-validity coefficients were comparable with those obtained with groups several times as large.

As would be expected, fewer operating (discriminating) responses were obtained when (a) more demanding levels of significance were re-

TABLE 32

Cross-Validity Coefficients Obtained for Schedule Scores X_{co} with Scoring Keys Resulting from Various Methods of Composing Elementary Teacher Criterion Groups for Item Analysis

($N_{53}=297$, $N_{54}=298$, Grades 3–4 Teachers)

METHOD OF COMPOSING HIGH AND LOW CRITERION GROUPS ON X_o	SUBSAMPLE USED FOR DERIVING SCORING KEY	N_H	N_L	VALIDATION SUBSAMPLE	NO. OF DISCRIMINATING RESPONSES IN KEY		CROSS-VALIDITY COEFFICIENT $r_{X_A X_{co}}$	
					Significance Level I*	Significance Level II†	Significance Level I*	Significance Level II†
Multiple Cutoff								
A. *Each* observer's assessment ≥ .6σ... or ≤ −.6σ...	(54) (53)	62 59	59 51	(53) (54)	74 77	127 157	.41 .39	.38 .39
B. *Each* observer's assessment ≥ .3σ... or ≤ −.3σ...	(54) (53)	86 77	86 75	(53) (54)	43 47	95 111	.39 .39	.38 .39
C. *Each* observer's assessment ≥ .2σ... or ≤ −.2σ...	(54) (53)	92 92	98 83	(53) (54)	42 36	85 94	.39 .38	.37 .37
D. *Each* observer's assessment ≥ .1σ... or ≤ −.1σ...	(54) (53)	104 104	104 89	(53) (54)	26 33	71 86	.38 .37	.37 .36
Regression								
E. Mean assessment in high 10%... or low 10%...	(54) (53)	30 30	30 30	(53) (54)	101 101	153 149	.44 .44	.40 .42
F. Mean assessment in high 15%... or low 15%...	(54) (53)	45 45	45 45	(53) (54)	73 81	127 149	.45 .40	.43 .40
G. Mean assessment in high 27%... or low 27%...	(54) (53)	80 80	80 80	(53) (54)	41 35	94 94	.42 .38	.43 .39
H. Mean assessment in high 45%... or low 45%...	(54) (53)	134 134	134 134	(53) (54)	9 7	48 50	.28 .37	.29 .37

* Minimum compound probability of .01 required of each response.
† Minimum compound probability of .17 required of each response.

quired for selection and (*b*) the groups comprised larger portions of the total distribution. The obtained validity coefficients were slightly higher the more rigorous the significance level required, the more the criterion groups represented extremes of the distribution, the larger the number of discriminating responses contributing to a score, and when the regression approach was employed.

Methods of Inventory Response Selection in Terms of Cross-Validity Indices

In these researches the Study was concerned with the comparison of standards of significance and frequency of response to be met by Schedule responses for inclusion in a correlates scoring key. The criterion employed was teacher trait R_{ci}, based upon teachers' responses to direct-inquiry type items, as described in chapter 5, relating to favorable *vs.* unfavorable teacher attitudes toward pupils. The teacher population was the same as that used in the studies of the composition of criterion groups (Grades 3–4 teachers) reported in the immediately preceding section. Cross-validity coefficients were employed as indices of the relative effectiveness of the methods being compared.

For each teacher, a criterion score relative to his opinions of pupils, R_{ci}, and his responses to the Schedule were available. In each subsample, teachers were assigned to high or low criterion groups, respectively, if their R_{ci} scores placed them in the upper or the lower 27 percent of the distribution. Scores on the criterion R_{ci} ranged from 15 to 60 with means of 44.26 and 43.20 and standard deviations of 5.50 and 5.78 in subsamples 53 and 54, respectively. Criterion scores of 46 or above in subsample 53 and 47 or above in subsample 54 placed a teacher in the high criterion group, and scores of 40 or below in subsample 53 and 37 or below in subsample 54 placed a teacher in the low criterion group. The distributions relative to favorable opinions of pupils thus were slightly negatively skewed. The high criterion group and the low criterion group in each subsample, 53 and 54, were made up of 80 teachers.

Fourteen separate response analyses (ten principal methods, with modifications of four as shown below) were conducted with each of the two subsamples, each analysis involving a variation in standards required for selecting a response as a contributor to the scoring key. These fourteen variations of selection standards are noted below.

Method 1: For selection, a response was required to
a) yield a minimum compound probability (significance level of discrimination), based upon combination of the probability estimates yielded by independent samples, of .01;

b) be chosen by at least 5 percent and not more than 95 percent of the total subsample.

Method 2.1: For selection, a response was required to
a) yield a minimum compound probability (significance level of discrimination), based upon combination of the probability estimates yielded by independent samples, of .05;
b) be chosen by at least 5 percent and not more than 95 percent of the total subsample.

Method 2.2: For selection, a response was required to
a) yield a minimum compound probability (significance level of discrimination), based upon combination of the probability estimates yielded by independent samples, .05;
b) be chosen by at least 10 percent and not more than 90 percent of the total subsample.

Method 3: For selection, a response was required to
a) yield a minimum compound probability (significance level of discrimination), based upon combination of the probability estimates yielded by independent samples, of .05;
b) manifest *linearity*, as indicated by successive increase, or successive decrease, in frequency of choice in the high, middle, and low criterion groups;
c) be chosen by at least 5 percent and not more than 95 percent of the total subsample.

Method 4.1: For selection, a response was required to
a) yield a minimum compound probability (significance level of discrimination), based upon combination of the probability estimates yielded by independent samples, of .10;
b) be chosen by at least 5 percent and not more than 95 percent of the total subsample.

Method 4.2: For selection, a response was required to
a) yield a minimum compound probability (significance level of discrimination), based upon combination of the probability estimates yielded by independent samples, of .10;
b) be chosen by at least 10 percent and not more than 90 percent of the total subsample.

Method 5: For selection, a response was required to
a) yield a biserial r of $\geq.30$ in one sample and $\geq.10$ in a second sample;
b) be chosen by at least 5 percent and not more than 95 percent of the total subsample.

Method 6: For selection, a response was required to
a) yield a biserial r of $\geq.15$ in one sample and $\geq.04$ in a second sample;
b) be chosen by at least 5 percent and not more than 95 percent of the total subsample.

Method 7: For selection, a response was required to
a) yield a biserial r of $\geq.10$ in one sample and $\geq.04$ in a second sample;

b) be chosen by at least 5 percent and not more than 95 percent of the total subsample.

Method 8.1: For selection, a response was required to
a) yield a biserial *r* of $\geq.10$ and $\leq.20$ in one sample and $\geq.04$ in a second sample;
b) be chosen by at least 5 percent and not more than 95 percent of the total subsample.

Method 8.2: For selection, a response was required to
a) yield a biserial *r* of $\geq.10$ and $\leq.20$ in one sample and $\geq.04$ in a second sample;
b) be chosen by at least 10 percent and not more than 90 percent of the total subsample.

Method 9: For selection, a response was required to
a) yield a biserial *r* of $\geq.10$ and $\leq.20$ in one sample and $\geq.04$ in a second sample;
b) manifest *linearity*, as indicated by successive increase, or successive decrease, in frequency of choice, in the high, middle, and low criterion groups;
c) be chosen by at least 5 percent and not more than 95 percent of the total subsample.

Method 10.1: For selection, a response was required to
a) yield a biserial *r* of $\geq.01$ in one sample and $\geq.04$ in a second sample, with scoring weights assigned responses in proportion to magnitude of the biserial *r* in the first sample (e.g., $r \geq.60$, weight 15; $r = .50-.59$, weight 14; etc.);
b) be chosen by at least 5 percent and not more than 95 percent of the total subsample.

Method 10.2: For selection, a response was required to
a) yield a biserial *r* of $\geq.01$ in one sample and $\geq.04$ in a second sample, with scoring weights assigned responses in proportion to magnitude of the biserial *r* in the first sample (e.g., $r \geq.60$, weight 15; $r = .50-.59$, weight 14; etc.);
b) be chosen by at least 10 percent and not more than 90 percent of the total subsample.

Response-criterion correlations were computed for each response, and scoring keys made up of responses meeting the prescribed standards were developed. The Schedule responses of each subsample of teachers were then scored with the key derived from the other subsample, and cross-validity correlations were computed between the scores and the criterion R_{ci}. The results are shown in Table 33, the significant data being the cross-validity coefficients in the last two columns.

The several variations in standards of response selection produce correlates scoring keys which are substantially alike in their prediction of the criterion. The range in magnitude of the obtained coefficients is relatively small, and most of the differences may be attributed to chance.

It almost seems that as long as responses are relatively reliably correlated with a criterion and, of course, replicated to the extent of, say, one hundred responses, the magnitude of the response-criterion correlations need not be of great concern. True, more rigorous response selection standards and differential weighting may result in small increases in validity, but the improvement is far from substantial.

TABLE 33

Cross-Validity Coefficients Obtained for Schedule Scores R_{ci} with Scoring Keys Derived by Various Methods of Selecting Scorable Responses

($N_{53} = 297$, $N_{54} = 298$, Grades 3–4 Teachers)

METHOD* OF SELECTING RESPONSES FOR KEY	SUBSAMPLE 53 USED FOR DERIVING SCORING KEY, SUBSAMPLE 54 USED FOR CROSS-VALIDATION		SUBSAMPLE 54 USED FOR DERIVING SCORING KEY, SUBSAMPLE 53 USED FOR CROSS-VALIDATION	
	No. of Discriminating Responses in Key	Cross-Validity Coefficient r_{RciRco}	No. of Discriminating Responses in Key	Cross-Validity Coefficient r_{RciRco}
1.	100	.63	98	.63
2.1....	155	.61	156	.59
2.2....	131	.61	126	.58
3.	145	.60	143	.63
4.1....	152	.62	156	.60
4.2....	133	.61	136	.58
5.	18	.51	16	.55
6.	101	.62	99	.59
7.	140	.61	150	.60
8.1....	91	.54	110	.54
8.2....	102	.52	87	.53
9.	58	.50	74	.49
10.1....	208	.63	210	.64
10.2....	186	.61	193	.64

* See description of methods on pp. 189–91.

In the studies just reported, attention was given only to those responses which correlated positively with the criterion, or discriminated in favor of the high group. Obviously, negatively correlated responses, discriminating in favor of the low criterion group, are equally useful for scoring purposes. In order to evaluate the contributions of the positively and negatively discriminating responses, separate positive and negative correlates keys were derived for Characteristic R by the first of the methods described above. (A third score, based upon the number of nondiscriminating responses which were marked, also was obtained for each teacher in the subsamples 53 and 54.) Subsample 53 was then scored with the scoring keys derived from subsample 54, and subsample 54 with the scoring keys derived from subsample 53. Both the positive and the negative keys seem to function as would have been anticipated and to approximately the same degree. Combining the positively and negatively contributing response to form a single key improved the criterion prediction, but only slightly. The correlation between positive and negative response scoring keys (an estimate of reliability) was .81 and .76, respectively, in the two subsamples. The obtained correlations are shown in Table 34.

In order to study further the influence of different methods of response selection, methods 1 and 7, as described on pages 189–90 and 190–91, were applied to data relative to TCS patterns X and Y of

TABLE 34

Correlation Coefficients between Various Scores Relative to Characteristic R

VARIABLES CORRELATED		PRODUCT-MOMENT CORRELATION COEFFICIENT	
		Subsample 53	Subsample 54
Criterion R_{ci} based on subsample 53 or 54	Positively discriminating responses *plus* negatively discriminating responses derived from other subsample......	.66	.66
Criterion R_{ci} based on subsample 53 or 54	Positively discriminating responses derived from other subsample........	.63	.63
Criterion R_{ci} based on subsample 53 or 54	Negatively discriminating responses derived from other subsample........	−.62	−.59
Criterion R_{ci} based on subsample 53 or 54	Nondiscriminating responses derived from other subsample.............	.04	.12
Positively discriminating responses derived from subsample 53 or 54	Negatively discriminating responses derived from *same* subsample.........	−.81	−.76

teacher classroom behavior. Additional teacher samples were constituted (samples 57 and 58, each consisting of 65 Grades 3–6 men teachers; samples 59 and 60, rerandomized samples of Grades 3–4 women teachers, each consisting of 295 teachers; and samples 61 and 62, each consisting of 50 elementary teachers drawn from a restricted homogeneous area). Schedule correlates scoring keys were derived by both methods 1 and 7 for the dimensions X_o (friendly, understanding teacher behavior) and Y_o (systematic, businesslike teacher classroom behavior). It should be recalled that the studies of response selection standards reported in Table 33 were conducted with regard to the teacher trait R_{ci} (attitude toward pupils), where the criterion consisted of verbally expressed opinions in the form of responses to direct-inquiry items. It seemed desirable now to employ the same procedures with criteria involving data based upon observers' assessments of teacher classroom behavior.

Following derivation of the appropriate scoring keys, the Schedule responses of the subsamples of teachers were scored (in each pair, a particular subsample was scored with the key derived from the other subsample of that pair) and, subsequently, correlations were computed between the correlates scores for a particular behavior (X or Y) and observers' assessments of that behavior. The obtained cross-validity coefficients relative to teacher behaviors X_o and Y_o were of a lower order than those for teacher trait R (as would be expected from the greater complexity of the criteria, and as were the coefficients reported in Table 32). They also were lower for the samples involving men teachers than they were for women. But the two selection methods yielded similar results, as they did in the studies with Characteristic R. These supplementary studies support in general the conclusions of the other comparisons of selection techniques. Criterion-response correlations significant at either the .05 or .01 levels appeared to be useful for inclusion in correlates scoring keys employed for the prediction of teacher behaviors X_o and Y_o.

Additional investigations, involving over one hundred response analyses of Schedule materials, were conducted at this stage of the Study. There is no need to report these results in detail, since the chief purpose was to confirm, with different teacher groups and data, conclusions already noted. For the most part, these investigations involved: (1) the application of a selected combination of response selection standards and criterion group composition to a variety of teacher samples (e.g., Grades 1–2 women teachers, Grades 5–6 men teachers, Grades 5–6 men combined with Grades 3–6 women teachers) for derivation of X_{co}, Y_{co}, and Z_{co} Scoring Keys; (2) scoring of the teachers' Schedules with the resulting keys; and (3) computation and evaluation of predictor-criterion correlations in an effort to determine (a) the combinations of response analysis techniques which would provide scoring keys yielding the maximum correlations with criterion data and (b) the extent to which the techniques interacted with such conditions as size of sample and heterogeneity of the teachers comprising a sample.

Another kind of problem with which the Study was concerned at this stage of its investigation related to the possibility of (1) predicting total, or over-all, teacher behavior (T_o), and (2) employing a composite (C_{co}) of scorable responses common to X_{co}, Y_{co}, and Z_{co} to predict either X_o, Y_o, or Z_o separately or the combination of T_o. It was anticipated that X_o, Y_o, and Z_o would be more predictable as separate dimensions than would be T_o, and that the individual Scoring Keys X_{co}, Y_{co}, and Z_{co} would predict more successfully than a composite based on all three. Several studies of this general type were carried out, one of which will be reported very briefly.

In this instance, a sample of elementary teachers of various grades was split randomly into two groups, one consisting of 533 and the other of 534 teachers. For each sample separately, the Schedule responses were subjected to item analysis against observers' assessments of (1) friendly, understanding teacher behavior (X_o), (2) systematic, businesslike teacher classroom behavior (Y_o), (3) stimulating teacher behavior (Z_o), and (4) over-all teacher behavior (T_o), as estimated from the sum of assessments of X_o, Y_o, and Z_o. Responses were selected for inclusion in the scoring keys when the response-criterion correlation reached or exceeded .10 in one sample and .04 in the other, and when the response was chosen by between 5 and 95 percent of the teachers in each subsample.

Two principal scoring keys were derived and subsequently applied to selected subsamples of elementary teachers: (1) a T_{co} Scoring Key, made up of all responses for which the response-criterion T_o correlation (and frequency of choice) met the standards noted above; and (2) a C_{co} Scoring Key made up of all responses which were *common* to the separately derived Scoring Keys X_o, Y_o, and Z_o.

Table 35 shows the correlations (*not* validity coefficients) of the scores yielded by the T_{co} and C_{co} Scoring Keys with teacher behaviors X_o, Y_o, Z_o, and T_o for different subgroups of elementary teachers. For the most part, the obtained correlations are substantially lower than those between scores resulting from the application of separate X_{co}, Y_{co}, and Z_{co} Keys and assessments of X_o, Y_o, and Z_o separately. It is

TABLE 35

Correlations for Selected Subsamples between Teacher Characteristics Schedule Scores Intended To Estimate Over-All Teacher Behavior and Observers' Assessments of Teacher Classroom Behavior

ELEMENTARY TEACHER SUBSAMPLE	N	CORRELATION BETWEEN C_{co} SCORES AND				CORRELATION BETWEEN T_{co} SCORES AND			
		X_o	Y_o	Z_o	T_o	X_o	Y_o	Z_o	T_o
Female..................	933	.27	.09	.20	.21	.22	.12	.19	.20
Male.....................	134	.16	.06	.02	.05	.19	−.03	.11	.10
20–30 years of age........	389	.24	.07	.17	.16	.19	.08	.13	.14
40 or more years of age....	434	.28	.14	.23	.27	.20	.12	.16	.21
Community M, 1949 Sample	49	.26	.08	.36	.23	.37	.31	.45	.41
Community M, 1951 Sample	77	.37	.05	.29	.28	.31	.03	.24	.24
Community N, 1951 Sample	143	.22	.01	.17	.11	.09	.04	.08	.04
Grades 1–2..............	247	.06	.06	.02	.01	.26	.18	.21	.23
Grades 3–4..............	608	.34	.12	.24	.26	.22	.07	.17	.18
Grades 5–6..............	212	.25	.08	.11	.18	.15	.04	.16	.13

interesting to note that in most cases teacher behavior X_o was predicted by the T_{co} and C_{co} Scoring Keys slightly more successfully than was over-all teacher behavior T_o.

It also may be noted here that no serious effort was made in later phases of the Study to predict over-all teacher behavior.[4]

DERIVATION OF CORRELATES SCORING KEYS RELATIVE TO TEACHER CLASSROOM BEHAVIORS X_o, Y_o, AND Z_o

The research reported in the immediately preceding paragraphs was preliminary to the derivation of the correlates scoring keys, in which the interests of the Study were focused in this phase of its program. Attention now was turned to the application of the response selection techniques to the development of Schedule scoring keys which might be used for subsequent comparisons of teacher groups and other research. A number of different keys for estimating X_o, Y_o, and Z_o from Schedule responses were assembled and evaluated in the light of their appropriateness for use with specified teacher populations. The present section will describe the various X_{co}, Y_{co}, and Z_{co} Scoring Keys which were derived.

From the outset of the Study, the heterogeneity of teacher groups representing different grade levels and subject matters was recognized. It seemed likely that some characteristics might be common to teachers in general, distinguishing them from other occupational populations, but it also appeared probable that certain other characteristics might apply to one kind of teacher and yet be atypical for another teacher group. Such considerations were prominent in the thinking of the Study staff when the matter of developing Schedule keys was approached. Whether a scoring key would be equally applicable for different groups of teachers or whether multiple keys might be required was a problem of practical as well as theoretical interest. From the standpoint of everyday use, it would be convenient to employ a scoring key which would serve equally well for any group of teachers to which it was applied. A number of clues growing out of the Study, however, suggested that different groups of teachers did vary—not only in degree to which different behavior patterns found expression, but also in their characteristic preferences and activities—and that such variations were pronounced enough to suggest that scores derived from keys for different teacher groups might show considerable unique variance. In approach-

---

[4] Chap. 8 is given to the description, in terms of Schedule responses, of teachers who were uniformly high, average, or low with respect to observers' assessments on all three of the TCS Patterns X_o, Y_o, and Z_o, but no attempt is made to predict a composite criterion.

TABLE 36

Samples and Response Selection Standards Employed in Deriving X_{co}, Y_{co}, and Z_{co} Scoring Keys

SAMPLE No.	COMPOSITION OF SAMPLE	SAMPLE SIZE (N) Randomly Split Cross-validation Subsamples		MINIMUM RESPONSE-CRITERION BISERIAL r's REQUIRED FOR SELECTION OF A RESPONSE FOR FINAL SCORING KEY	
		1	2	First Subsample	Second Subsample
71	Grades 1–2 women.............	95	95	.20	.10
72	Grades 3–4 women.............	216	215	.15	.07
73	Grades 5–6 women.............	48	49	.28	.14
74	Grades 3–6 women.............	264	264	.13	.06
75	Grades 1–6 women.............	359	359	.11	.05
76	Grades 5–6 men.................	44	43	.30	.15
77	Grades 3–6 men.................	58	58	.25	.13
78	Grades 5–6 men and women......	92	92	.20	.10
79	Grades 3–6 men and women......	322	322	.11	.06
111	Grades 1–6 men and women (All Elementary)..................	417	417	.15	.06
81	Mathematics, men...............	52	53	.26	.13
82	Mathematics, women............	52	52	.26	.13
83	Science, men....................	74	74	.20	.10
84	Science, women.................	45	45	.28	.14
85	English, men....................	43	43	.28	.14
86	English, women.................	98	97	.16	.08
87	Social studies, men.............	51	51	.26	.13
88	Social studies, women...........	61	60	.26	.13
89	Mathematics-science, men........	126	127	.16	.08
90	Mathematics-science, women......	97	97	.18	.09
91	English, social studies, men.......	94	94	.18	.09
92	English, social studies, women.....	158	158	.15	.08
93	Mathematics, men and women....	104	105	.18	.09
94	Science, men and women.........	119	119	.16	.08
95	English, men and women.........	140	141	.16	.08
96	Social studies, men and women....	111	112	.16	.08
97	Mathematics-science, men and women	224	223	.12	.09
98	English, social studies, men and women.....................	252	252	.12	.09
100	Mathematics, science, English, social studies, men and women (All Secondary)....................	476	475	.13	.05
99	Elementary and secondary, men women (All Teacher).........	893	892	.10	.04

ing this problem empirically, some thirty basic scoring keys were developed (those noted in Table 36), and several "combination keys" also were attempted.

The probable usefulness of a key was evaluated in the light of the correlation between scores obtained through the use of that particular key and appropriate criterion data. With the basic keys noted in Table 36, the first interest was in the extent to which the randomly drawn samples from a single defined population of teachers would yield similar correlates-criterion correlations. Also of interest, however, was the extent to which a scoring key derived from one population of teachers would yield scores predictive of criterion data when applied to a differently defined teacher population.

The problems of cross-validation and validity generalization, with the presentation of representative data, are treated in a following section of this chapter. The present discussion will be confined to descriptions of the procedures followed in deriving the scoring keys and the operational definition of the keys as revealed by the contents of discriminating responses.

In the second column of Table 36 are descriptions of the various subgroups of teachers with respect to which scoring keys were derived. In the other columns are shown the number of teachers comprising the two cross-validation subsamples into which each teacher group was split and the minimum biserial correlation required between a response and a criterion for that response to be selected for inclusion in a scoring key.

The procedure followed in selecting responses to comprise a scoring key was (a) to determine for each response the frequency of its acceptance by the total sample under consideration and the estimated biserial correlation between the criterion (X_o, Y_o, or Z_o) under study and acceptance of the response, and then (b) to identify those responses which were accepted by between 2 and 97 percent of each sample and which also yielded a correlation equaling or exceeding the value noted opposite the teacher group in the last two columns of Table 36.

With scoring keys thus derived, it was possible to obtain Schedule correlates scores for any defined group of teachers and to determine the relative effectiveness of a scoring key for predicting the criterion in question.

Although intercorrelations of the scoring keys and also the correlates score–criterion correlations (presented later) suggest considerable unique variance associated with many of the keys and, therefore, limited generalizability to teacher groups other than ones made up of teachers of the same type as those from which the key was derived, it obviously is not practical in most teacher personnel operations to employ different bases for appraising teachers, depending upon the level or subject taught by a teacher and perhaps also the teacher's sex. Such a procedure would complicate the teacher evaluation process greatly. This practical consideration was constantly in the minds of the staff during this stage of the investigation. The *principal* scoring keys considered, therefore, and those with which most of the data reported in subsequent sections of this report are concerned are those described as:

All-Elementary Teacher Scoring Keys (111)
(Based on elementary teachers of Grades 1–6)

All-Secondary Teacher Scoring Keys (100)
    (Based on secondary teachers of the most frequently taught sub-
    jects—English, social studies, mathematics, and science)

All-Teacher Scoring Keys (99)
    (Based on elementary teachers of Grades 1–6 and secondary
    teachers of English, social studies, mathematics, and science)

Two additional elementary scoring keys, combination keys for which
the code numbers 143 and 150 were employed, also seemed likely to have
considerable usefulness when dealing with special groups of elementary
teachers. Elementary Teacher Scoring Keys 143 were combination keys
for Characteristics X, Y, and Z, made up of responses constituting
Keys 71 and 72. They were thus applicable to Grades 1–4 elementary
teachers. Elementary Teacher Scoring Keys 150 were combination keys
for X, Y, and Z, made up of responses constituting Keys 73 and 77.
They were intended for use with special groups consisting of men elementary teachers and Grades 5–6 women teachers.

At the secondary level, Keys 97 for mathematics and science teachers
and Keys 98 for English and social studies teachers also seemed to be
potentially useful, particularly for research purposes and when attention might be limited to the specific groups of teachers for which they
had been developed.

An obvious disadvantage of multiple scoring keys is, of course, the
impossibility of direct comparability of the scores of individuals identified or described by different keys. Thus, elementary and secondary
teachers can be directly compared only when the All-Teacher (99) Keys
are used, and different groups of secondary teachers can be compared
only when the All-Secondary Keys (100) are employed. In using the
more general keys, a certain amount of validity and accuracy of description appears to be sacrificed. But there is no way out of the dilemma,
and determination of the scoring key to be employed inevitably must
be a function of the purpose of the user. For many *research* and *comparative* purposes, the appropriate keys probably should be those which
are the most specific of those which embrace all the groups under study.
For *operational* studies and surveys of teacher personnel in school systems, elementary and secondary teachers probably should be considered
separately, using Scoring Keys 111 and 100, respectively, but greater
specificity probably would be impractical. In such investigations, it
may, in fact, be more appropriate to employ the most general of all the
scoring keys developed, the All-Teacher (99) Keys.

Table 37 provides some comparisons (*not validity data*) of the application of various scoring keys, the basis for comparison being correlation
coefficients between Schedule scores resulting from the use of the vari-

TABLE 37

Correlations between Scores Yielded by the Various Scoring Keys and Composite Observer Assessments for Component Subsamples of the Basic Analysis Population

TEACHER SUBSAMPLE	SCORING KEYS	CORRELATIONS		
		$X_{co}X_o$	$Y_{co}Y_o$	$Z_{co}Z_o$
Elementary teachers				
Grades 1–2 women ($N=190$)................	99	.27	.29	.26
	111	.37	.41	.24
	143	.39	.39	.39
	150	.06	.12	.12
Grades 3–4 women ($N=431$).................	99	.36	.22	.29
	111	.42	.34	.38
	143	.38	.38	.38
	150	.12	.03	.13
Grades 5–6 women ($N=97$).................	99	.32	.15	.34
	111	.43	.17	.28
	143	.33	−.03	.22
	150	.56	.31	.44
Grades 3–6 men ($N=116$)...................	99	.26	.11	.22
	111	.34	.22	.33
	143	.20	.18	.06
	150	.43	.33	.47
Secondary teachers				
Mathematics men ($N=105$).................	99	.27	.28	.20
	100	.28	.30	.26
Mathematics women ($N=104$)...............	99	.28	.05	.26
	100	.39	.37	.45
Science men ($N=148$)......................	99	.26	.09	.16
	100	.33	.19	.35
Science women ($N=90$).....................	99	.38	.20	.22
	100	.49	.39	.44
English men ($N=86$).......................	99	.53	.21	.27
	100	.60	.42	.54
English women ($N=195$).....................	99	.47	.17	.43
	100	.44	.34	.47
Social studies men ($N=102$).................	99	.28	.13	.36
	100	.35	.33	.41
Social studies women ($N=121$)...............	99	.28	.36	.14
	100	.38	.45	.42
Mathematics-science men and women ($N=447$).	99	.28	.23	.21
	100	.35	.35	.37
English–social studies men and women ($N=504$).	99	.21	.41	.28
	100	.42	.46	.40

ous scoring keys and composite observer assessments of X_o, Y_o, and Z_o for specified subgroups of the Basic Analysis population. In general, the data reported in Table 37 support the recommendations of the preceding paragraphs.

A word concerning "what is measured by the correlates keys" probably is in order. In view of the manner in which the correlates keys were derived (i.e., in the light of the correlation between acceptance of a response by a teacher and observer assessment of that teacher's classroom behavior relative to X_o, Y_o, and Z_o), certainly they may be thought of as reflecting friendly, understanding classroom behavior (X_{co}), responsible, businesslike classroom behavior (Y_{co}), and stimulating, surgent classroom behavior (Z_{co}) on the part of the teacher. Still another way of regarding what may be measured by the correlates scoring keys, however, might be to look to the *content* of the responses which correlate significantly with the criteria. Such content study may, at the same time, provide a more directly operational definition of the correlates scoring keys and also throw additional light on the meaning of the criteria themselves. Samples of positively and negatively correlated responses contributing to the major scoring keys (Elementary Teacher Scoring Keys 111 and Secondary Teacher Scoring Keys 100), for each of the teacher classroom behavior dimensions X, Y, and Z, are given in the list which follows.

SCHEDULE RESPONSES ILLUSTRATING THOSE COMPRISING CORRELATES
SCORING KEY X_{co} (UNDERSTANDING, FRIENDLY TEACHER
CLASSROOM BEHAVIOR)

Elementary Teacher Scoring Key, 111 X_{co}

Positively Correlated Responses	*Negatively Correlated Responses*
Would prefer to sell stamps at a post office (rather than to sort or collect mail).	Would prefer playing solitaire (to tennis or softball).
Would prefer to administer a typing test to applicants for a position as typist (rather than compute typing test scores or maintain typewriters used for typing tests).	Would prefer taking children to a movie (rather than taking children on a picnic or showing them through a newspaper office).
In self, believes cheerfulness a stronger trait than accuracy, ambition, or decisiveness.	In self, believes common sense a stronger trait than enthusiasm, leadership, or refinement.
Tends to be suspicious of people who are aloof.	At an amusement park, prefers the penny arcade to the roller coaster.
Prefers frequently changing activities to methodical work.	Thinks a majority of persons (80 percent) are influenced in their opinions and attitudes toward others by feelings of jealousy.
Believes it is better to have several activities going on at once in a class (rather than only one activity in progress at a time).	At a party announced for 8 P.M., thinks most of the guests would be likely to arrive before 8 o'clock.
Strongly agrees with statement, "Most teachers take a sincere interest in their students."	As a child, parents were very insistent upon high standards of performance and conduct.
Went hunting, fishing, or camping during this past year.	At the third- or fourth-grade levels, believes it is important to set and require relatively high standards of pupil achievement in the subjects taught.
Interest in social problems influenced choice of teaching as a career.	
Belonged to a high school or college sorority or fraternity.	

Secondary Teacher Scoring Key, 100 X$_{oo}$

Positively Correlated Responses	Negatively Correlated Responses

Considers a severe and aloof manner a more serious failing in a teacher than inadequate mastery of subject matter or inability to maintain a systematic and orderly approach to work.

Prefers frequently changing activities to methodical work.

If in disagreement with a friend on politics, usually will explain views and allow friend to explain his, but will *not* try to change friend's views (rather than trying to persuade friend to accept own views, or refusing to discuss the matter further).

Believes very few high school students (less than 1 percent) intentionally try to tax the patience of the teacher.

Thinks it more important that a teacher possess "good taste" (compared with conscientiousness, consistency of action and policy, or self-possession and dignity).

Thinks students who are listless or conforming dully are more indicative of a poor class than disorderliness and noise, hesitancy, and unsureness on the part of the students, or dependency of the students.

Is married (rather than single, separated or divorced, or widowed).

Desire to help people contributed toward choice of teaching as a career.

Has belonged to an honor society or debating society.

Finds thinking about plans for "rearing own children" more attractive than plans for owning a home, spending a year in travel, developing skills in an avocation, or getting ahead in profession.

If among people waiting at a grocery store, when a late comer pushes ahead and gets served, is more likely to inform clerk of priority and insist upon being waited on at once, rather than following some other course of action.

Would rather read a book on explorations than one on "The Hows and the Whys of Human Behavior" or one dealing with new styles in clothing.

In self, considers weakest trait to be enthusiasm (compared with common sense, leadership, and refinement).

Considers a severe and aloof manner to be a less important failing in a teacher than inadequate mastery of subject matter or inability to maintain a systematic and orderly approach.

At the tenth-grade level, believes it is important that relatively high standards of academic achievement be set up and required in the subjects offered.

Disagrees with the statement, "Most pupils are obedient."

Disagrees with statement, "Pupils can behave themselves without constant supervision."

Is 55 years of age or older.

Would not like activity which involved advising people regarding personality improvement.

Schedule Responses Illustrating Those Comprising Correlates Scoring Key Y_{co} (Responsible, Businesslike Teacher Classroom Behavior)

Elementary Teacher Scoring Key 111 Y_{co}

Positively Correlated Responses

Would prefer to compile statistics on the progress of a campaign for charity funds (rather than planning the campaign, buying food and supplies, canvassing for contributions, or taking baskets to needy families).

Believes there is more truth in the statement, "Most teachers are ineffective in maintaining discipline" than in statements that most teachers tend to talk over the heads of their students or that most teachers are narrow-minded.

In self, thinks thoroughness is a stronger trait than resourcefulness, self-confidence, or truthfulness.

In self, thinks leadership is a stronger trait than enthusiasm, common sense, or refinement.

Is bothered more by noise and confusion than by continued silence.

Strongly agrees with the statement, "Any class is capable of governing itself sensibly if the teacher will allow it to do so."

Has had fifteen or more years of teaching experience in the elementary grades.

Bought or sold stocks, bonds, or property (or made similar financial investments) during past year.

Most of childhood spent in a small town of under 5,000 population.

Spent several hours a week at gardening when in season.

Negatively Correlated Responses

Believes there is more truth in the proverb "Better late than never" (as compared with "Birds of a feather flock together," "One shouldn't cry over spilt milk," "One man's meat is another man's poison," or "The early bird catches the worm").

Thinks it more characteristic of the average person that he accepts too much abuse without complaint (rather than that he complains too much).

Estimates the average teacher spends about eight hours a week in outside preparation for classes. (Other available responses: less than three hours; fourteen hours; twenty hours or more.)

Would *least* like to be considered by friends as industrious (as compared with systematic, goodhearted, or cultured).

Believes that classroom responsibilities and administrative responsibilities are fairly distinct and should be clearly defined and separated in the most effective school program.

Strongly disagrees with statement, "Most pupils take their responsibilities seriously."

Strongly disagrees with statement, "Most teachers are broadly educated."

As a child, had fewer assigned chores or duties at home than had most children.

Secondary Teacher Scoring Key 100 Y_{co}

Positively Correlated Responses

In self, believes decisiveness is a stronger trait than accuracy, ambition, or cheerfulness.

Believes that no high school classes are "almost impossible to control."

Negatively Correlated Responses

Prefers having no definite course of study, but planning work from day to day in light of what seems appropriate (compared with: following a prescribed course of study, using a prescribed outline with modifications to suit particular

Secondary Teacher Scoring Key 100 Y_{co} *(Continued)*

Positively Correlated Responses	*Negatively Correlated Responses*

Would rather read a book about new styles in clothing (compared with books about exploration or on "The Hows and Whys of Human Behavior."

Believes graduation from high school should be based primarily on meeting prescribed academic standards (rather than on the attainment of other educational objectives).

Strongly agrees with statement, "Pupils are usually quite competent to select their own topics for themes and speeches."

Has had twenty or more years experience teaching in the secondary grades.

As a child or adolescent, "played school" or took charge of a class when teacher was absent.

Taught a Sunday school class.

During past year, wrote a letter or sent a telegram to a public official.

During past three weeks, spent an average of three or more hours a week at indoor games such as cards or chess.

Frequently reads books on travel and adventure during leisure time.

class, or developing own course of study).

Would prefer to invent new toys for children (rather than tell stories to children or draw illustrations for children's books).

Would prefer to teach a class of children of widely varying ability (to classes of exceptionally bright, slow or retarded, or average children).

Thinks relatively few teachers (about 10 percent) feel they should not have to spend any time on yard duty or similar duties.

In high school classes, believes it is best to have English closely related to the social studies unit.

Disagrees with statement, "Most supervisors are fair-minded."

When in college, was an average student.

Is a male.

SCHEDULE RESPONSES ILLUSTRATING THOSE COMPRISING CORRELATES SCORING KEY Z_{co} (STIMULATING, IMAGINATIVE TEACHER CLASSROOM BEHAVIOR)

Elementary Teacher Scoring Key 111 Z_{co}

Positively Correlated Responses	*Negatively Correlated Responses*

Would prefer to be president of a club (rather than secretary, treasurer, or committee chairman).

In self, believes initiative a stronger trait than adaptability, alertness, or foresight.

In self, believes resourcefulness a stronger trait than self-confidence, thoroughness, or truthfulness,

Applied to self, feels, "I enjoy the tired feeling that comes after strenuous exercise" is more true than, "I don't believe in exercising too strenuously."

Prefers Charles Dickens to such other novelists as Thomas Hardy, Sinclair Lewis, Jane Austen, or Emily Brontë.

Would rather be secretary or treasurer of a group than president or chairman of the membership or program committee.

Would get more satisfaction from finding a particularly good bargain than from making a successful after-dinner speech or making a sale to a particularly difficult customer.

Believes a substantial number (about 65 percent) of high school classes are dis-

Elementary Teacher Scoring Key 111 Z_{co} (Continued)

Positively Correlated Responses

Believes the average teacher spends about fourteen hours a week in outside preparation for classes. (Other available responses: less than three hours; eight hours; twenty hours or more.)

Believes students learn more effectively in several small groups than in a single unified group.

Strongly agrees with statement, "The teacher should sometimes allow a class to do as it wishes, even if it conflicts with previously made plans."

During the past year, read one or more books about music.

During the past year, listened to lectures about science or visited a science museum or exhibition of scientific inventions.

During the past year, engaged in some form of handwork.

Negatively Correlated Responses

ruptive in that students frequently "get off the subject," either intentionally or unintentionally.

Would like a job preparing customers' bills, rather than being a sales clerk or handling customers' complaints.

Strongly disagrees with statement, "Pupils should be allowed to speak with each other without first getting the teacher's permission."

Disagrees with statement, "Pupils are usually quite competent to select their own topics for themes and speeches."

Secondary Teacher Scoring Key 100 Z_{co}

Positively Correlated Responses

Of self, believes originality is more characteristic than good judgment, sympathy, or conscientiousness.

Would prefer to plan a Christmas campaign for help of the needy (rather than buy supplies, canvass for contributions, compile statistics on the progress of the campaign, or take baskets to the needy families).

Would prefer own course of study for classes (rather than follow a prescribed course of study, use prescribed course of study as point of departure, or have no definite course of study and develop classwork from day to day).

Would prefer to make salable articles for a church bazaar (rather than soliciting contributions for a church fund or keeping records of contributions made to a church fund).

Feels own best work has resulted from inspiration (rather than from long, hard work).

In preparing a paper for a study club, would prefer to write on "Will Science

Negatively Correlated Responses

If a substantial sum of money was unexpectedly inherited, would buy a nice home (rather than invest it in bonds, buy luxuries, invest in a friend's business, or give it to charity).

Would prefer using a prescribed course of study, with modification to suit particular class (rather than exactly following prescribed course of study, developing own course of study, or having no definite course of study for class).

In self, considers common sense and refinement to be stronger traits than enthusiasm or leadership.

Prefers methodical work to frequently changing activities.

Strongly disagrees with statement, "Most teachers are tactful."

Strongly disagrees with statement, "Students will usually select good students for their class officers."

Is 55 years of age or older.

Would prefer to teach ninth grade (rather than senior high school, junior

Secondary Teacher Scoring Key 100 Z$_{co}$ (Continued)

Positively Correlated Responses   *Negatively Correlated Responses*

Ever Be Able To Create Life?" (rather than "Do Comic Books Contribute to Juvenile Delinquency?" or "Does Australia Offer Greater Economic Opportunity than the United States?").

college, or college or university).

Favorable prospect of professional advancement contributed toward choice of teaching as a career.

Would prefer to teach a class of exceptionally bright children (rather than slow and retarded children, average children, or children of widely varying ability).

Strongly agrees with statement, "Pupils should be allowed to speak with each other without first getting the teacher's permission."

Claims to have been an outstanding student when in college.

As a child or adolescent, was a class officer.

During the past year, has read books on art, attended art lectures, or bought paintings or other art works.

DERIVATION OF CORRELATES SCORING KEYS FOR THE INDIRECT ESTIMATION OF TEACHER ATTITUDES R, R$_1$, Q, AND EDUCATIONAL VIEWPOINTS, B

Among the dimensions of teacher characteristics given primary consideration in the descriptions and comparisons of teachers which appear in following sections of this report are the three sets of teacher attitudes, Characteristics R, R_1, and Q, and the dimension relating to the educational viewpoints of teachers, Characteristic B, previously described in chapter 5. These characteristics have been defined as:

Characteristic R—teachers' favorable *vs.* unfavorable opinions of pupils.
Characteristic R_1—teachers' favorable *vs.* unfavorable opinions regarding democratic pupil practices.
Characteristic Q—teachers' favorable *vs.* unfavorable opinions of school personnel, particularly fellow teachers.
Characteristic B—teachers' traditional, subject-matter-centered viewpoints *vs.* social-personal-oriented, child-centered-permissive viewpoints.

These characteristics, particularly R, R_1, and B seem to have much in common.

In chapter 5 it was pointed out that consideration of the attitudes-toward-pupils dimension (R) and the attitudes-toward-school-staff-personnel dimension (Q) appeared to be justified in light of statistical analyses. It was noted, however, that the employment of separate attitude-toward-pupils (R) and attitude-toward-pupil-practices (R_1) indices was completely arbitrary, having no statistical support (the correlations between R and R_1 scores were very high), and was done solely because of the current concern in many school circles over pupil participation and permissive teacher-pupil relationships. It also will be recalled that teacher response data to direct-inquiry items concerned with traditional *vs.* permissive educational viewpoints (B) were found to possess considerable variance in common with the teacher attitudes studied, particularly attitude toward pupils (R) and attitude toward democratic pupil practices (R_1). There is, therefore, substantial duplication among the direct-inquiry scales R, R_1, and B. Similarly, with regard to the correlates scoring keys derived from responses to the Teacher Characteristics Schedule, overlapping is extensive and the intercorrelations are pronounced. It is necessary that this be kept in mind in considering both the criterion data and the correlates scoring keys for teacher attitudes and viewpoints.

In deriving correlates scoring keys for Characteristics R, R_1, Q, and B, the procedures followed were relatively straightforward and consumed considerably less time than did the derivation of correlates keys for X_o, Y_o, and Z_o.

Studies of response analysis techniques, involving the selection of responses correlated with Characteristic R, and the comparison of various selection standards and approaches to criterion group composition in the light of cross-validation data were mentioned in an earlier section of this chapter. It will be recalled that the cross-validity data were highly uniform and that the validity coefficients were satisfactorily significant for most of the response analysis approaches investigated. In addition, comparisons undertaken of Schedule correlates of teacher attitudes and viewpoints which had been derived from different random samples were found to show marked similarity of validity and consistency from one sample of teachers to another. With these considerations in mind, it seemed reasonable to assume greater generalizability of the derived scoring keys than was the case with the correlates of teacher classroom behaviors.

The general procedure followed in deriving correlates scoring keys for Characteristics R, R_1, Q, and B consisted essentially of: (1) obtaining teachers' responses to direct-inquiry items relative to a particular area of teacher opinion or viewpoints; (2) arranging the resulting direct-inquiry scores in order of magnitude and segregating the upper 27 percent, middle 46 percent, and lower 27 percent to form criterion groups for the analysis; (3) determining, for each response to the items of the Schedule, (*a*) the frequency of acceptance of the response, and (*b*) the correlation between acceptance of the response and membership in the high and low criterion groups; and (4) selecting those responses which met minimum frequency-of-response and response-criterion correlation standards, these responses being retained for inclusion in the scoring key.

For the derivation of correlates scoring keys for teacher attitudes and viewpoints, the criterion data consisted of responses to the direct-inquiry materials described in chapter 5. The items which follow are typical of those which made up the criterion data for Characteristics R, R_1, Q, and B.

Characteristic R_{ei} Items (Attitude toward Pupils)

218. In light of your experience with children, what do you think of the following statement?

    "Most pupils try to do their work to the best of their ability."

    218-1 Strongly disagree
    218-2 Disagree
    218-3 Indifferent
    218-4 Agree
    218-5 Strongly agree

230. In light of your experience with teen-age youth, what do you think of the following statement?

    "Pupils can behave themselves without constant supervision."

    230-1 Strongly disagree
    230-2 Disagree
    230-3 Indifferent
    230-4 Agree
    230-5 Strongly agree

Typical Characteristic R_{1ei} Items (Attitude toward Democratic Pupil Practices)

216. How do you feel about the following statement?

    "A teacher should occasionally leave a class to its own management."

    216-1 Strongly disagree
    216-2 Disagree
    216-3 Indifferent
    216-4 Agree
    216-5 Strongly agree

225. How do you feel about the following statement?

    "Democracy can be successfully practiced in the average classroom."

225-1 Strongly disagree
225-2 Disagree
225-3 Indifferent
225-4 Agree
225-5 Strongly agree

Typical Characteristic Q_{ci} *Items* (*Attitude toward School Staff Personnel*)
220. In light of your experience, do you think the following observation is valid?

"Most supervisors are fair-minded."
220-1 Strongly disagree
220-2 Disagree
220-3 Indifferent
220-4 Agree
220-5 Strongly agree

232. In light of your acquaintance with teachers, what do you think of the following statement?

"Most teachers are willing to assume their share of the unpleasant tasks associated with teaching."
232-1 Strongly disagree
232-2 Disagree
232-3 Indifferent
232-4 Agree
232-5 Strongly agree

Typical Characteristic B_{ci} *Items* (*Traditional vs. "Permissive" Educational Viewpoints*)
209. In an elementary school class do you think it is better to have
209-1 the number work and the social studies work set up in relatively distinct units?
209-2 the number work closely related to the social studies unit?

214. At the tenth-grade level do you believe
214-1 it is important that relatively high standards of academic achievement be set up and required in the subjects offered?
214-2 academic achievement is relatively unimportant as compared with other objectives?

In view of the considerable homogeneity of attitudes and viewpoints expressed by teachers of different grades and subject matters, only two major samples of teachers were employed in conducting the response analyses for characteristics in these areas. An elementary teacher sample was made up of both women and men teachers of Grades 1–6, and a secondary sample was comprised of both men and women teachers of the four major subject-matter groups—mathematics, science, English, and social studies.

The elementary response analysis sample consisted of 871 teachers, and the secondary analysis sample was made up of 961 teachers.

For the elementary response analyses, a minimum response-criterion correlation of .15, together with 5 to 95 percent acceptance by the total elementary analysis group, was required for inclusion of a response in a correlates scoring key for a particular characteristic.

In conducting the secondary response analyses, the secondary sample was divided into two randomly split subsamples, and for inclusion of a response in a particular attitudes or viewpoints scoring key it was required that the response-criterion correlation be at least .15 in one subsample and at least .05 in the other and also that the response be accepted by 5 to 95 percent of each sample. All-Teacher Scoring Keys were prepared simply by combining the scorable responses of the previously derived elementary and secondary scoring keys for all items which were common to the elementary, mathematics-science, and social studies–English forms of the Schedule.

Employing these procedures, correlates scoring keys for Characteristic R, Characteristic R_1, Characteristic Q, and Characteristic B were developed for All-Elementary Teachers, All-Secondary Teachers, and All-Teachers (elementary and secondary teachers combined). These were identified by the code numbers 111 R_{co}, 111 R_{1co}, 111 Q_{co}, 111 B_{co} for elementary teachers, 100 R_{co}, 100 R_{1co}, 100 Q_{co}, and 100 B_{co} for secondary teachers, and 99 R_{co}, 99 R_{1co}, 99 Q_{co}, and 99 B_{co} for elementary and secondary teachers together.

Generally speaking, the only possible approach to validity with respect to the attitudes and viewpoints correlates scoring keys was of a rational, rather than empirical, nature. Thus, the argument might run, if the direct-inquiry materials which provided the criterion data had construct validity, similar construct validity (a step removed perhaps) would also hold for the correlates scoring keys. One bit of evidence of congruent validity also was available with respect to teachers' educational viewpoints, Characteristic B. Teachers who were members of the Survey Sample had been asked to classify themselves as "traditional" or "progressive" with regard to methodological emphasis in teaching. The difference in mean score on the 99 B_{co} items of groups of self-judged traditional and progressive teachers was over twelve times its standard error, indicating that the 99 B_{co} scores did reliably reflect the teachers' viewpoints in this area, as judged from the teacher's own expressed acceptance of a particular set of educational principles.

As already has been noted, the similarity between Characteristics R, R_1, Q, and B is substantial, and these characteristics have a considerable amount of variance in common. This fact is further supported by the intercorrelations between correlates scores of the Keys R_{co}, R_{1co}, Q_{co}, and B_{co}, shown in Table 38. It is evident that these keys measure a great deal in common, and that, in most instances, one might be substituted for any other without greater loss than that incurred in the use of alternate forms of tests. From the standpoint of unique contribution to the description of teachers, there probably is little justification for the employment of all four scores. Teachers' favorable attitudes

TABLE 38
Intercorrelations between Scores Yielded by Scoring Keys R_{co}, R_{1co}, Q_{co}, and B_{co}

ELEMENTARY TEACHER SCORING KEYS (111)

	ELEMENTARY BASIC ANALYSIS SAMPLE ($N=978$)				ELEMENTARY SURVEY SAMPLE ($N=670$)		
	R_{1co}	Q_{co}	B_{co}		R_{1co}	Q_{co}	B_{co}
R_{co}	.88	.76	−.69	R_{co}	.87	.73	−.66
R_{1co}		.80	−.65	R_{1co}		.78	−.66
Q_{co}			−.41	Q_{co}			−.46

SECONDARY TEACHER SCORING KEYS (100)

	SECONDARY BASIC ANALYSIS SAMPLE ($N=1,065$)				SECONDARY SURVEY SAMPLE ($N=970$)		
	R_{1co}	Q_{co}	B_{co}		R_{1co}	Q_{co}	B_{co}
R_{co}	.79	.76	−.72	R_{co}	.72	.77	−.53
R_{1co}		.53	−.89	R_{1co}		.40	−.81
Q_{co}			−.34	Q_{co}			−.14

ALL-TEACHER SCORING KEYS (99)

	ELEMENTARY-SECONDARY BASIC ANALYSIS SAMPLE ($N=2,043$)				ELEMENTARY-SECONDARY SURVEY SAMPLE ($N=1,640$)		
	R_{1co}	Q_{co}	B_{co}		R_{1co}	Q_{co}	B_{co}
R_{co}	.85	.82	−.68	R_{co}	.81	.73	−.34
R_{1co}		.61	−.81	R_{1co}		.59	−.45
Q_{co}			−.38	Q_{co}			−.21

toward pupils, toward democratic pupil practices, and toward other school personnel, together with their child-centered, permissive, educational viewpoints appear to fit together to form a teacher model with respect to such characteristics. In spite of this striking similarity, separate scores for these characteristics were computed, and they appear in comparisons of teachers made in chapter 7. Regardless of the obvious overlapping of the teacher attitudes and viewpoints, some notable differences in their manifestation by different groups of teachers frequently were found.

The R_{co}, R_{1co}, Q_{co}, and B_{co} Scoring Keys which were derived to estimate indirectly teacher attitudes and educational viewpoints may be operationally described in terms of typical responses which the analyses showed to be significantly correlated with the respective direct-inquiry scores of teachers. Samples of the responses contributing to the several keys are shown, separately for elementary and secondary teachers, in the list which follows.

SCHEDULE RESPONSES ILLUSTRATING THOSE COMPRISING CORRELATES SCORING KEY R_{co} (FAVORABLE ATTITUDE TOWARD PUPILS)

Elementary Teacher Scoring Key 111 R_{co}

Positively Correlated Responses

Considers a severe and aloof manner a more serious failing in a teacher than inadequate mastery of subject matter or inability to maintain a systematic and orderly approach.

Finds continued silence more bothersome than noise and confusion.

Would prefer to teach a class of children of widely varying ability (rather than average, exceptionally bright, or slow and retarded children).

Thinks very few (less than 1 percent) students try to tax the patience of their teacher.

Thinks very few students (less than 1 percent) possess irritating nervous mannerisms.

Feels most people (about 90 percent) stop to think about the consequences of their acts as they affect their associates.

Feels most people (about 90 percent) are generally able to keep their emotions under good control.

Estimates the typical nine-year-old child can swim one hundred fifty feet or more.

Strongly agrees with statement, "Most parents make an effort to teach their children good manners."

Past activities have included working on a playground.

During the past year, attended an art lecture or bought some painting or other art work.

Belongs to, or has belonged to, a hobby club.

Negatively Correlated Responses

If giving a children's party, would prefer to send out the invitations (rather than prepare refreshments, serve refreshments, or direct the games).

Is inclined to be suspicious of people who are overfriendly.

Prefers to teach a class of average children, rather than children of widely varying ability or bright or retarded children.

When teacher sends students to the principal's office, believes it seldom (about 10 percent of the time) is the fault of the teacher rather than the student.

Would *least* like to take children on a picnic (compared with taking children to a movie or on a trip through a newspaper office).

Believes that parents should not be permitted to visit classrooms during regular class hours.

Spent most of childhood in a very large metropolitan area.

Disagrees with statement, "Most teachers have an unusual ability for leadership."

Disagrees with statement, "Most parents make an effort to be pals to their children."

Secondary Teacher Scoring Key 100 R$_{\infty}$

Positively Correlated Responses

In giving a children's party, would prefer to direct the games (compared with preparing refreshments, serving refreshments, or sending invitations).

Prefers spending a free Saturday taking a Girl or Boy Scout troop on a hike (compared with taking a drive with a group of fellow teachers, playing tennis or golf, or tinkering with a radio set).

Thinks very few (less than 1 percent) high school students are not respectful toward their teachers.

Thinks few people (about 10 percent) are influenced in their opinions and attitudes towards others by feelings of jealousy.

Agrees with statement, "Most teachers have an unusual ability for leadership."

Agrees with statement, "It is possible to develop most school classwork around out-of-school activities."

As a child or adolescent cared for younger children, either in own family or outside immediate family.

During past year, attended meetings of some local civic group.

During past year, visited an art gallery or museum.

Interest in community activity was contributing factor toward choice of teaching as a career.

Enjoyment of school environment was contributing factor toward choice of teaching as a career.

Negatively Correlated Responses

Would prefer taking children to a movie, rather than on a picnic or showing them through a newspaper office.

Admires Katharine Cornell more than other women, such as Dorothy Thompson, Jane Addams, or Susan B. Anthony.

In an average class of thirty pupils, thinks there may be as many as four students who are difficult behavior problems. (Other choices: one, two, three students.)

Believes very few (about 10 percent) teachers really take a personal interest in individual students in their classes.

Thinks disorderliness and noise is more indicative of a poor class than dependency of students, hesitancy and unsureness of students, or students who are listless or conforming dully.

Disagrees with statement, "Pupils are usually quite competent to select their own topics for themes and speeches."

Is a boys' physical education teacher.

SCHEDULE RESPONSES ILLUSTRATING THOSE COMPRISING
CORRELATES SCORING KEYS R_{1co} (FAVORABLE ATTITUDE
TOWARD DEMOCRATIC PUPIL PRACTICES)

Elementary Teacher Scoring Key 111 R_{1co}

Positively Correlated Responses

Would prefer to have a job as a receptionist (rather than addressing envelopes or keeping correspondence files).

Thinks it is more important for the teacher to help pupils develop a sense of responsibility (compared with helping them master subject matter or conform to classroom rules).

Thinks a majority of teachers (about 70 percent) feel effective control in classroom can be achieved by making each class itself completely responsible for such control.

Would like most to read a story having its setting in a coal field (compared to one set in a fashionable summer resort or in a film studio).

Believes most teachers (about 95 percent) feel they should have some voice in making administrative decisions.

In self, thinks weakest trait is accuracy (compared with ambition, cheerfulness, or decisiveness).

Feels an artist should be free to choose his own mode of expression without considering the preferences of others.

Strongly agrees with the statement, "Most teachers are sincere in their actions."

Negatively Correlated Responses

In self, believes accuracy is strongest trait (compared with ambition, cheerfulness, or decisiveness).

Believes reason for a teacher's leaving the profession to engage in some other activity lies in the fact that dealing with active children requires the expenditure of a great deal of energy.

In self, thinks weakest trait is resourcefulness (compared with self-confidence, thoroughness, and truthfulness).

Looks forward to owning home of own (more than rearing children, traveling, developing skill in an avocation, or getting ahead in profession).

In class, believes it is better generally to have one activity in progress at a time.

Disagrees with statement, "Parents usually realize that children are not perfect."

Disagrees with statement, "Most teachers are willing to assume their share of the unpleasant tasks associated with teaching."

Secondary Teacher Scoring Key 100 R_{1co}

Positively Correlated Responses

Would prefer to tell stories to children (rather than draw illustrations for children's books or invent toys for children).

In self, believes strongest trait is enthusiasm (compared with common sense, leadership, and refinement).

In self, thinks common sense is weakest trait (rather than enthusiasm, leadership, or refinement).

Negatively Correlated Responses

Believes the proverb, "Birds of a feather flock together" contains the most truth (compared with "One shouldn't cry over spilt milk," "One man's meat is another man's poison," "The early bird catches the worm," "Better late than never").

Likes to "play it safe" rather than take a chance.

Thinks it is most important that a teach-

Secondary Teacher Scoring Key 100 R$_{1co}$ (Continued)

Positively Correlated Responses

Strongly agrees with statement, "The teacher should sometimes allow a class to do as it wishes, even if it conflicts with previously made plans."

Is an English, foreign language, or social studies teacher.

During past year, read one or more books about politics.

Interest in social problems was a factor contributing toward choice of teaching as a career.

Had a room of own when a child.

Negatively Correlated Responses

er show self-possession and dignity (compared with good taste, conscientiousness, and consistency of action and policy).

Thinks attentiveness of the students is most indicative of a good class (compared with courtesy of the students to the teacher and each other, willingness of the students to try, and students being well-prepared).

Disagrees with statement, "A teacher should occasionally leave the class to its own management."

Disagrees with statement, "Parents are usually considerate of the teacher's feelings."

Strongly disagrees with statement, "At the high school level, planning units of classwork should be a responsibility of the students of the class who, in turn, make recommendations to the teacher."

Is a teacher of mathematics, biologica science, or physical science.

SCHEDULE RESPONSES ILLUSTRATING THOSE COMPRISING CORRELATES SCORING KEY Q$_{co}$ (FAVORABLE ATTITUDE TOWARD SCHOOL STAFF PERSONNEL)

Elementary Teacher Scoring Key 111 Q$_{co}$

Positively Correlated Responses

Would prefer spending a free afternoon entertaining friends at a small home party (rather than in setting out new plants in garden, attending recital or concert, or going to a baseball game).

Thinks most teachers prefer to help pupils establish friendly realtionships with classmates (rather than helping them learn school regulations).

Would prefer a job as a sales clerk (rather than one which involved handling complaints or preparing customers' bills).

Strongly agrees with statement, "Pupils will usually select good students for their class officers."

Negatively Correlated Responses

If giving a children's party, would prefer to prepare the refreshments (rather than serve refreshments, send out invitations, or direct games).

Thinks the average person complains too much (rather than accepting too much abuse without complaint).

Thinks many high school students (about 60 percent) have difficulty in conforming to the requirements for systematic study.

Thinks relatively few high school teachers (about 10 percent) develop original ways of presenting course materials.

Thinks few people (about 10 percent) stop to think about the consequences of

(*Continued on next page.*)

Elementary Teacher Scoring Key 111 Q∞ (Continued)

Positively Correlated Responses

Strongly agrees with statement, "Parents usually try to meet the teacher halfway."

Satisfying experience in school work was factor contributing to choice of teaching as a career.

As a child, parents agreed.

Thinks very few teachers (about 10 percent) feel that they should not have to spend any time on yard duty or similar duties.

Negatively Correlated Responses

their acts as they affect their associates.

Thinks relatively few teachers willingly assume their full share of extra duties in the school.

Secondary Teacher Scoring Key 100 Q∞

Positively Correlated Responses

Would prefer to solicit contributions to a church fund (rather than make salable articles for a church bazaar or keep records of contributions made to a church fund).

Thinks most teachers (about 90 percent) take a personal interest in the individual students in their classes.

Thinks relatively few people (about 10 percent) are inclined to worry more than they should.

Thinks most people (about 90 percent) stop to think about the consequences of their acts as they affect their associates.

Agrees with statement, "Most teachers are tactful."

Agrees with statement, "Parents are usually considerate of the teacher's feelings."

During past year, contributed money to some political cause or group.

Negatively Correlated Responses

Thinks very few people (about 10 percent) stop to think about the consequences of their acts as they affect their associates.

Strongly disagrees with statement, "Pupils should be allowed to speak with each other without first getting the teacher's permission."

Strongly disagrees with statement, "Most teachers are broadly educated."

Disagrees with statement, "Parents usually can see the teacher's side of the problem when something happens in school."

Disagrees with statement, "Nonteaching employees are usually quiet and unassuming."

Has completed less than four years of college work.

Major part of undergraduate study completed at a women's college.

Memories of childhood are rather unhappy.

Schedule Responses Illustrating Those Comprising Correlates Scoring Key B_{co} (Traditional *vs.* Permissive Educational Viewpoints)

Elementary Teacher Scoring Key 111 B_{co}

Positively Correlated Responses (Traditional, Subject-Matter-Centered Viewpoints)

Positively Correlated Responses (Social-Personal-Oriented, Permissive Viewpoints)

If preparing a paper for presentation to a club, would feel own judgment good enough and not ask for criticism.

Likes methodical work better than frequently changing activities.

Would *least* like to read about peculiarities of human behavior (compared with reading about explorations, or styles in clothing).

Disagrees with statement, "Most pupils take their responsibilities seriously."

Disagrees with statement, "Pupils can behave themselves without constant supervision."

Strongly agrees with statement, "Most teachers have a good understanding of child psychology."

Strongly disagrees with statement, "Pupils are usually quite competent to select their own topics for themes and speeches."

Disagrees with statement, "It is possible to develop most school classwork around out-of-school activities."

Agrees with statement, "Third-grade children should be required to meet prescribed academic standards before beginning the work of the fourth grade."

Has not taken a college course for five years or more.

If giving a children's party, would prefer to direct the games (rather than prepare or serve the refreshments or send out the invitations).

In self, believes enthusiasm is strongest trait (as compared with common sense, leadership, and refinement).

Thinks it is *less* important for a teacher to help pupils master subject matter (compared with helping pupils conform to classroom procedure and helping them develop a sense of responsibility).

Thinks inadequate mastery of subject matter is a *less* important failing in a teacher than a severe and aloof manner or inability to maintain a systematic and orderly approach.

Strongly agrees with statement, "Most pupils take their responsibilities seriously."

Has had from five to nine years teaching experience in the elementary grades.

Has read one or more books about art during past year.

Has engaged in hobbies and handicrafts three hours or more a week during the past three weeks.

During past year has followed art as a hobby.

Secondary Teacher Scoring Key 100 B$_{oo}$

| Positively Correlated Responses (Traditional, Subject-Matter-Centered Viewpoints) | Positively Correlated Responses (Social-Personal-Oriented, Permissive Viewpoints) |

Positively Correlated Responses
(Traditional, Subject-Matter-
Centered Viewpoints)

Prefers the *American Magazine* to *Harper's Magazine* or *Popular Mechanics*.

Believes there is more truth in the proverb, "The early bird catches the worm" (compared with such proverbs as "Birds of a feather flock together," "One shouldn't cry over spilt milk," "One man's meat is another man's poison," or "Better late than never").

Thinks inadequate mastery of subject matter is a more serious failing in a teacher than a severe and aloof manner or inability to maintain a systematic and orderly approach.

In self, feels self-confidence is stronger trait than resourcefulness, thoroughness, or truthfulness.

Believes own best work has resulted from long, hard work (rather than from inspiration).

Believes it is more important for a teacher to extend subject-matter knowledge by summer courses and reading (compared with taking part in community activities or keeping up to date on educational theories and trends).

Thinks students being well-prepared for the class meeting is more indicative of a good class than courtesy of the students, attentiveness of the students, or willingness of the students to try and volunteer.

Has had twenty or more years experience teaching secondary grades.

Has not been enrolled in a college course for three or more years.

Positively Correlated Responses
(Social-Personal-Oriented,
Permissive Viewpoints)

Would prefer going on a cruise to South America (rather than going to Europe, to Hawaii, or touring the United States).

In self, feels leadership is a stronger trait than enthusiasm, common sense, or refinement.

Prefers frequently changing activities to methodical work.

Thinks learning more successfully accomplished through class or group discussion than by reading a book or article dealing with the topic.

Believes when teachers send students to the principal's office, the *teacher*, rather than the student, is usually at fault (about 80 percent of the time).

Thinks hesitancy and unsureness on the part of the student is more indicative of a poor class than listless student performance, disorderliness and noise, or student dependency.

Would least like to teach a class of exceptionally bright children (compared with classes of slow children, average children, or children of widely varying ability).

Strongly agrees with statement, "Most teachers are willing to assume their share of the unpleasant tasks associated with teaching."

During past three weeks, has spent at least three hours a week attending concerts, exhibits, etc.

DERIVATION OF CORRELATES SCORING KEYS FOR THE INDIRECT ESTIMATION OF VERBAL UNDERSTANDING, EMOTIONAL ADJUSTMENT, AND VALIDITY OF RESPONSE

The procedures followed in the derivation of Schedule correlates scoring keys for the indirect estimation of verbal comprehension, emotional adjustment, and validity of response (Characteristics *I*, *S*, and *V*) of teachers were essentially the same as those employed in developing the teacher attitudes and viewpoints correlates scoring keys. Perhaps the chief difference was that for Characteristics *I*, *S*, and *V* the final response analyses (on which the scoring keys were based) were accomplished with teachers comprising the Study's Survey Sample.

In seeking correlates of emotional stability, and even of validity of response, the psychologist is on fairly familiar ground, since prediction and diagnosis of typical personal behaviors frequently have involved the use of signs and symptoms. However, to attempt to estimate a cognitive ability, such as verbal comprehension (Characteristic *I*), from correlates is another matter—the very nature of the behavior under consideration suggests obtaining samples of that behavior under maximum performance ("do your best") directions. The literature yields few reports of the attempt to measure intellectual abilities indirectly through the employment of reports of individual preferences, self-judgments, activities, and the like. Nevertheless, the idea that responses of these kinds might be employed to estimate mental abilities was intriguing, and it seemed reasonable to hypothesize that correlates scoring keys derived from the Schedule might be employed to estimate verbal comprehension. An obvious advantage to be gained, if this were possible, was obviation of the need to administer a different type of measuring instrument along with the inventories of major dimensions of teacher performance. A preliminary study in this area will be mentioned briefly before continuing with a description of the derivation of the final *I*, *S*, and *V* Scoring Keys.

As early as 1951, the Study considered the question of the extent to which responses to the Schedule might be correlated with the kinds of data yielded by mental ability tests. A preliminary response analysis of the Schedule was designed, employing as criteria for the analyses the scores derived from the American Council on Education Psychological Examination. This is a typical maximum performance test, providing estimates of both verbal and quantitative ability. In this study, a sample of 220 students enrolled at the University of California at Los Angeles filled out the Schedule and took the ACE Psychological Examination. Separate analyses were made of the Schedule responses with respect to the *Q* scores (quantitative abilities), *L* scores (verbal or linguistic abilities), and Total scores yielded by the ACE Psychological Examination.

Results of the three independent response analyses were interesting and encouraging from the standpoint of estimation of general intellectual abilities from correlates, or signs, taking the form of self-reports of typical personal behavior. Significant responses far exceeding the number to be expected if chance alone were operating suggested the feasibility of further study of this approach. While it was recognized that the obtained data were derived from a single, relatively small sample of students of education, who possibly responded differently to the Schedule than would experienced teachers in a school, the results were promising and further study seemed in order.

Partially as an outgrowth of this preliminary study of the use of Schedule responses to predict scores yielded by the ACE Psychological Examination, and (as noted in chapter 5) in part as a step in the purification of the direct-inquiry type of material, Inventory ISV was mailed with a request for its completion to teachers who previously had filled out the Schedule. It thus became possible to conduct investigations of the Schedule correlates of Characteristics I_{ci}, S_{ci}, and V_{ci}. Such response analyses were undertaken, and the results gave still further support to the idea of employing indirect estimates derived from responses to the Schedule.

The final correlates scoring keys for Characteristics I, S, and V were derived independently of the exploratory studies just reviewed. For these response analyses, the Survey Sample of teachers was employed, the teachers having completed the 1954 forms of the Schedule, which included among a supplementary set of 50 items the I_{ci}, S_{ci}, and V_{ci} direct-inquiry items.

The items which follow are illustrative of the direct-inquiry materials employed for criterion purposes in deriving the I_{co}, S_{co}, and V_{co} scoring keys.

Typical Characteristic I_{ci} Items

315. Which of the following responses *first* comes to your mind when you see the word "orison"?

    315-1 Song
    315-2 Constellation
    315-3 East
    315-4 Prayer
    315-5 Never heard of the word

317. Which of the following words do you associate with "hill" in the same way you associate "roof" with "pitch"?

    317-1 Catch
    317-2 Mountain
    317-3 Tar
    317-4 Grade
    317-5 Altitude

Typical Characteristic S_{oi} *Items*

324. Which of the following is more true of you?

    324-1 I take things as they come and they don't bother me.

    324-2 I have always been somewhat uneasy about things.

340. Which of the following is more true of you?

    340-1 I wish I could be as happy as other people seem to be.

    340-2 I wish there were more emphasis on practical things.

Typical Characteristic V_{oi} *Items*

320. Which of the following is more true of you?

    320-1 Occasionally I put off until tomorrow what I should do today.

    320-2 I never get discouraged.

330. Which of the following is more true of you?

    330-1 I seldom act on the spur of the moment without stopping to think.

    330-2 I sometimes get angry.

Three sets of scoring keys were developed: 111 I_{co}, 111 S_{co}, and 111 V_{co}, for use with elementary teachers; 100 I_{co}, 100 S_{co}, and 100 V_{co} for secondary teachers; and 99 I_{co}, 99 S_{co}, and 99 V_{co} for teachers without designation of grade or subject taught.

For the All-Elementary Teacher (111) Scoring Keys, the analysis sample consisted of 650 elementary teachers. The secondary analysis sample, employed for deriving the All-Secondary (100) Scoring Keys, was made up of 951 teachers.

To be included in a scoring key, a response had to be correlated with the core items (direct-inquiry items) making up the criterion to the extent of .15 or greater, and it also had to be accepted by 5 to 95 percent of the teachers in the sample under consideration. The All-Teacher Scoring Keys (99 I_{co}, 99 S_{co}, and 99 V_{co}) consisted of all responses which met the criteria for either the 111 or the 100 Keys and which also were among the 118 items common to the elementary, mathematics-science, and English–social studies booklets.

Samples of the responses which correlated either positively or negatively with the criteria are shown below. The content of the criterion items and of the correlated responses define the dimensions estimated by the I_{co}, S_{co}, and V_{co} Scoring Keys.

SCHEDULE RESPONSES ILLUSTRATING THOSE COMPRISING
CORRELATES SCORING KEY I_{co} (VERBAL UNDERSTANDING)

Elementary Teacher Scoring Key 111 I_{co}

Positively Correlated Responses

Prefers *Harper's Magazine* to the *American Magazine* or *Popular Mechanics*.

Would get most satisfaction from making a successful after-dinner speech (compared with finding a particularly good bargain or making a sale to a particularly difficult customer).

Would find developing skill in an avocation more attractive than owning home of own, rearing children, or getting ahead in profession.

Thinks willingness of students to "try" and to volunteer is more indicative of a good class than courtesy of students, attentiveness of students, or preparedness of students.

During past year, read book reviews once a month or more.

During past year, read books and magazines regularly.

During leisure time, frequently reads books dealing with travel and adventure.

During leisure time, frequently reads books of biography.

Major portion of expenses of college education were defrayed by scholarship or fellowship.

When in college, was either an "outstanding student" or a "good student."

In self, feels strongest trait is decisiveness(compared with accuracy, ambition, and cheerfulness).

Negatively Correlated Responses

If preparing a paper for presentation to a group, would ask competent criticism, making changes suggested (rather than feeling own judgment good enough, showing paper only to close friends, or asking criticism but making only changes which seemed most appropriate).

As a hobby, finds more appeal in making model airplanes than in amateur dramatics, flower arrangement, or collecting.

In self, feels strongest trait is ambition (compared with accuracy, cheerfulness, or decisiveness).

As a child, preferred straightening up room to taking care of pets or working in garden.

Would get more satisfaction from finding a particularly good bargain than from making a difficult sale or making a successful after-dinner speech.

Would prefer to teach a class of slow and retarded children (rather than a class of exceptionally bright children, one of average children, or one of children of widely varying ability).

Thinks an experienced teacher should expect to devote four or more hours a day to preparing and planning classwork.

Would like being a scientist *less* than being president of a large industrial concern.

Is strongly in agreement with statement, "Cleanliness is a more valuable human trait than curiosity."

Secondary Teacher Scoring Key 100 I_{co}

Positively Correlated Responses

Prefers *Harper's Magazine* to the *American Magazine* or *Popular Mechanics*.

Would prefer to select and arrange books for children's room in a library (rather than to supervise a summer playground

Negatively Correlated Responses

Thinks there is more truth in the proverb, "Better late than never" (compared with "Birds of a feather flock together," "One shouldn't cry over spilt milk," "One man's meat is another man's poi-

Secondary Teacher Scoring Key 100 I_{co} (Continued)

Positively Correlated Responses

for children or to design children's clothing).

In self, feels strongest trait is resourcefulness (compared with self-confidence, thoroughness, or truthfulness).

In a free-association test, thinks most people would give the response "sorrow" as their response to the word "joy" (rather than grand, happiness, or sad).

Thinks learning is accomplished more successfully by reading a book or article dealing with a topic than through class or group discussion.

When in college, was an outstanding student.

As a child or adolescent, tutored or coached a student in some subject.

During past year has read book reviews regularly.

During past year has attended a lecture to hear some author.

Interest in books was a factor contributing to choice of teaching as a career.

During leisure time, frequently reads collections of poems, essays, stories, etc.

There were at least fifty books in childhood home.

Negatively Correlated Responses

son," "The early bird catches the worm").

In self, thinks ambition is strongest trait (compared with accuracy, cheerfulness, and decisiveness).

Would prefer to teach a class of average children (rather than exceptionally bright children, slow and retarded children, or children of widely varying abilities).

Thinks a majority of high school classes (about 65 percent) are disruptive in that the students frequently "get off the subject" either intentionally or unintentionally.

Thinks few people (19–30 percent) are generally able to keep their emotions under good control.

Thinks disorderliness and noise is more indicative of a poor class than listless student performance, hesitancy on part of student, or dependency of students.

Strongly disagrees with statement, "A teacher should occasionally leave a class to its own management."

Strongly disagrees with statement, "Most teachers are willing to assume their share of the unpleasant tasks associated with teaching."

When in college, was "an average student."

SCHEDULE RESPONSES ILLUSTRATING THOSE COMPRISING CORRELATES SCORING KEY S_{co} (EMOTIONAL ADJUSTMENT)

Elementary Teacher Scoring Key 111 S_{co}

Positively Correlated Responses

At a carnival or amusement park, enjoys the shooting gallery (more than the ferris wheel, roller coaster, merry-go-round, or wheel of fortune).

In self, thinks self-confidence is strongest trait (compared with resourcefulness, thoroughness, and truthfulness).

Thinks most people (about 90 percent) are able to keep their emotions under good control.

Negatively Correlated Responses

When in school, was influenced most in dislike for a teacher by lack of patience (rather than lack of sense of humor, excessive preciseness, or insistence on too high standards).

Would prefer a job addressing envelopes or keeping files to one as a receptionist in an office.

In self, considers thoroughness a stronger trait than resourcefulness, self-confi-

(Continued on next page.)

Elementary Teacher Scoring Key 111 S$_{co}$ *(Continued)*

Positively Correlated Responses

Thinks few teachers (about 5 percent) suffer from stomach trouble brought on by unusual tensions related to their work.

Thinks few people (about 10 percent) are inclined to worry more than they should.

Dreams typically involve bright colors and motion (rather than familiar scenes, new places, dramatic situations, or often-repeated situations).

Feels most fit during evening (compared with morning or afternoon).

Strongly agrees with statement, "A teacher should occasionally leave a class to its own management."

Frequently engages in social dancing.

In his childhood, parents "never" or "not often" scolded or berated him.

Negatively Correlated Responses

dence, or truthfulness.

Is bothered more by noise and confusion than by continued silence.

Thinks a majority of high school students (about 60 percent) intentionally try to tax the patience of the teacher.

Thinks very few people (about 10 percent) are generally able to keep their emotions under good control.

Thinks many teachers (about 60 percent) suffer from stomach trouble brought on by unusual tensions related to their work.

Disagrees with statement, "Parents usually try to meet the teacher halfway."

Memories of childhood are either "rather unhappy" or "decidedly unhappy."

Secondary Teacher Scoring Key 100 S$_{co}$

Positively Correlated Responses

Believes good judgment better applies to self as a dominant trait than sympathy, originality, or conscientiousness.

Prefers supervising a summer playground for children (rather than selecting and arranging books for children or designing children's clothing).

In self, considers cheerfulness a stronger trait than accuracy, ambition, or decisiveness.

Considers it more important that a teacher possess consistency of action and policy (than good taste, conscientiousness, or self-possession and dignity).

Strongly agrees with statement, "Most parents are reasonable in their attitudes toward teachers."

Is a teacher of physical science.

Has been engaged in vocations other than teaching for three or more years.

Is married.

Memories of childhood are more happy than the average.

Is a male.

Negatively Correlated Responses

In self, considers leadership a *weaker* trait than enthusiasm, common sense, or refinement.

Strongly disagrees with statement, "Parents usually respect the teacher's opinion."

Strongly disagrees with statement, "Pupils are usually quite competent to select their own topics for themes and speeches."

Memories of childhood are unhappy.

During past year attended a lecture to hear some author.

During past year attended meetings of a writers' or literary group.

Is interested in literature as a hobby.

Would prefer sending out the invitations for a party (rather than preparing refreshments, serving refreshments, or directing games).

Schedule Responses Illustrating Those Comprising Correlates Scoring Key V_{co} (Avoidance of Excessive Use of Self-Enhancing and Socially Acceptable Responses)

Elementary Teacher Scoring Key 111 V_{co}

Positively Correlated Responses

Likes carefree people better than thrifty people.

As a child, liked to care for pets better than working in garden or straightening room.

In a free-association test, thinks most people would give the response "gentle" to the word "kind" (rather than bad, gracious, or mean).

Thinks most people (90 percent) are inclined to worry more than they should.

Thinks an experienced teacher should expect to devote about one hour a day to preparation or planning for classwork.

Would rather be an actor than a judge or musician.

If someone was bereaved, would prefer sending flowers and a brief note (rather than making a personal call or writing a letter).

Disagrees with statement, "Most teachers are willing to assume their share of the unpleasant tasks associated with teaching."

Own parents were not insistent upon high standards of performance and conduct, but permitted extensive freedom of activity.

In his childhood, parents frequently scolded him.

Negatively Correlated Responses

Would prefer showing children through a newspaper office to taking them to a movie or to a picnic.

Would prefer teaching in a tenement district of a large industrial city to teaching in other types of communities.

Likes thrifty people better than carefree people.

Would get more satisfaction from making a sale to a particularly difficult customer than from making a successful after-dinner speech or finding a good bargain.

Considers "getting ahead in my profession" more attractive than owning a home, rearing children, traveling, or developing skill in an avocation.

During past year, wrote an essay, story, poem, or play.

In his childhood, parents never scolded or berated him.

Secondary Teacher Scoring Key 100 V_{co}

Positively Correlated Responses

Admires Katharine Cornell more than such women as Dorothy Thompson, Jane Addams, Susan B. Anthony.

In high school classes, believes it is better to have English and social studies activities set up as relatively distinct units.

Negatively Correlated Responses

Thinks most teachers (90 percent) really like to take a personal interest in the individual students in their classes.

Thinks disorderliness and noise are more indicative of a poor class than are listless, hesitant, or dependent students.

Reports extremely happy memories of

(Continued on next page.)

Secondary Teacher Scoring Key 100 V_{co} *(Continued)*

Positively Correlated Responses	Negatively Correlated Responses
Does not believe it is possible to develop the course content of most high school classes around "real life" situations.	childhood.
	Reports having read stories to children as a child or adolescent.
Would prefer to make salable articles for a church bazaar (rather than solicit contributions or keep records of contributions for a church fund).	Reports having taken charge of a class when a child or adolescent when a teacher was absent.
During leisure time, frequently reads fiction.	During past year, frequently listened to religious programs on the radio.
When a child, was assigned fewer chores or duties at home than most children.	Desire to help people was contributing factor to choice of teaching as a career.

A word perhaps should be added concerning the validity of response or "tendency to avoid excessive use of socially acceptable responses" (V_{co}) scoring key. It will be recalled that this dimension of teacher behavior was considered entirely from the standpoint of the probability of detecting individuals whose scores might make their underlying characteristics and behaviors appear different from what they really were. There was no interest in validity of response in and of itself. As will be noted later, whatever is measured by the V_{co} scale is not particularly reliable. Neither is it easily definable in terms of the responses which contribute to a V_{co} score.

The staff was of the opinion that only lower extreme deviations in V_{co} scores should be accorded attention, and that the only interpretation to be given such scores should be that judgment probably should be suspended regarding other characteristics measured by the Schedule until additional supporting data might be obtained regarding the individual teacher in question.

Intercorrelations between the correlates scores I_{co}, S_{co}, and V_{co} are shown in Table 39. It is interesting to note that estimates of verbal understanding and of emotional stability are highly correlated among elementary teachers, but that the correlation is low and negative among secondary teachers. These, and other data to be reported later, suggest again that the organization of traits and behaviors of elementary teachers may be considerably different from that of secondary teachers. In this case, superior verbal intelligence and good emotional adjustment tend to go together among elementary teachers but seem to be largely independent among secondary teachers, with a slight tendency for verbal comprehension to be associated with poorer emotional adjustment. These findings considered in connection with a rather marked tendency (to be reported later) for secondary teachers to attain higher

TABLE 39

Intercorrelations between Scores Yielded by Keys I_{co}, S_{co}, and V_{co}*

ELEMENTARY TEACHER SCORING KEYS
(111)

ELEMENTARY BASIC ANALYSIS SAMPLE
($N=978$)

	S_{co}	V_{co}
I_{co}	.63	.08
S_{co}		−.09

SECONDARY TEACHER SCORING KEYS
(100)

SECONDARY BASIC ANALYSIS SAMPLE
($N=1,065$)

	S_{co}	V_{co}
I_{co}	−.25	.16
S_{co}		−.08

ALL-TEACHER SCORING KEYS (99)

ELEMENTARY-SECONDARY BASIC ANALYSIS SAMPLE
($N=2,043$)

	S_{co}	V_{co}
I_{co}	.25	.18
S_{co}		−.21

* Keys derived from Survey Samples.

I_{co} scores than elementary teachers, suggest a curvilinear over-all relationship between I_{co} and S_{co} in the All-Teacher sample.

MOST FREQUENTLY USED SCORING KEYS

The Teacher Characteristics Schedule scoring keys most frequently used for the comparisons of various teacher groups and in other research were the 111_{co} Keys, based upon elementary teachers of grades one through six, the 100_{co} Scoring Keys, derived from the responses of mathematics, science, English, and social studies secondary school teachers, and the 99_{co} Scoring Keys, derived from the responses of combined elementary and secondary teacher groups. Separate X_{co}, Y_{co}, Z_{co}, R_{co}, R_{1co}, Q_{co}, B_{co}, I_{co}, S_{co}, and V_{co} Scoring Keys were available for each of the three groupings of teachers.

The number of responses contributing to each of these scoring keys and certain others are shown in Table 40.

Means and standard deviations of the Schedule correlates scores for the Basic Analysis and Survey elementary teachers, secondary teachers,

TABLE 40

Number of Responses Comprising the Most Frequently Used Teacher Characteristics Schedule Correlates Scoring Keys

TEACHER CHARAC- TERISTIC	Elementary, Grades 1-6 (Keys 111_{co})			Elementary Women, Grades 1-4 (Keys 143_{co})			Secondary Math.-Science, Engl.-Soc. Studies (Keys 100_{co})			Secondary Math.-Science (Keys 97_{co})			Secondary Engl.-Soc. Studies (Keys 98_{co})			Elementary-Secondary, Grades 1-6, Math.- Science, Engl.-Soc. Studies (Keys 99_{co})		
	+ Scored Resp.	− Scored Resp.	Tot.	+ Scored Resp.	− Scored Resp.	Tot.	+ Scored Resp.	− Scored Resp.	Tot.	+ Scored Resp.	− Scored Resp.	Tot.	+ Scored Resp.	− Scored Resp.	Tot.	+ Scored Resp.	− Scored Resp.	Tot.
X....	107	97	204	121	37	158	55	49	104	43	35	78	59	63	122	48	33	81
Y....	78	89	167	112	33	145	54	40	94	57	45	102	55	59	114	27	24	51
Z....	121	78	199	95	28	123	52	44	96	45	47	92	48	57	105	34	25	59
R....	85	76	161				89	76	165							58	49	107
O....	61	56	117				90	75	165							48	32	80
Q....	55	52	107		—Same as 111_{co} Keys—		53	46	99		—Same as 100_{co} Keys—			—Same as 100_{co} Keys—		53	37	90
B....	46	43	89				72	109	181							38	55	93
I....	68	45	113				69	52	121							48	30	78
S....	80	52	132				36	48	84							44	24	68
V....	35	39	74				43	39	82							26	28	54

228

and elementary-secondary teachers combined are presented in Table 72, chapter 7. Table 72 gives the means and standard deviations for the 99, 111, and 100 Scoring Keys. Data for the Basic Analysis and Survey Samples combined, shown in the same table, provide the most complete norms for the several sets of scoring keys relative to the characteristics (X_{co}, Y_{co}, etc.) measured by the Schedule.

Scores on the various characteristics were obtained by summing the criterion correlated responses of a teacher—by merely counting the number of responses marked by the teacher which corresponded to those comprising the scoring key.

As has been noted (Table 40 and elsewhere), responses correlating with a criterion both positively and negatively were determined, thus providing what amounted to two scores—one made up of positively correlated responses and the other of negatively correlated responses—for each characteristic (X, Y, Z, etc.).

Actually the "plus scores" (positively correlated responses) and "minus scores" (negatively correlated responses) for a characteristic may be used more or less interchangeably. As indicated in Table 44, the correlations between scores derived from the positively correlated responses and negatively correlated responses are high. For most purposes, use of the plus keys alone should prove entirely satisfactory.

However, for comparisons of teacher groups and various other researches conducted by the Study, a total score based on both positively and negatively correlated responses was employed. In order to avoid total scores which were negative and thereby to facilitate computation, a constant of 40 was added to each positive correlates characteristic score, and then the sum of the negatively correlating responses was subtracted. In one case, Characteristic B for secondary teacher samples (100 B_{co}), it was necessary to add an additional constant of 25 to the positive correlates score, making the added constant in this instance 65.

Intercorrelations of Teacher Characteristics Schedule Correlates Scores

Intercorrelations among the scores yielded by the Schedule are given in Tables 41, 42, and 43 for elementary teachers, secondary teachers, and elementary-secondary teachers combined. In each table, the correlation matrix is presented for the Basic Analysis Sample and also for the Survey Sample.

The intercorrelation variables for the Basic Analysis and the Survey groups were similar except that in computing the correlations among I, S, and V in the case of the Survey Sample, the scores were based on the *criterion items* (I_{ci}, S_{ci}, and V_{ci}) rather than correlates.

In general, there is fairly close correspondence between the intercorrelations of the Basic Analysis and Survey samples of teachers with respect to the variables X_{co}, Y_{co}, Z_{co}, R_{co}, R_{1co}, Q_{co}, and B_{co}, which were directly comparable. Exceptions, however, do occur as illustrated by the substantially lower $Y_{co}Z_{co}$ correlation in the Basic Analysis Sample

TABLE 41

Intercorrelations among Scores Yielded by the Elementary Teacher Scoring Keys (111)

BASIC ANALYSIS SAMPLE ELEMENTARY TEACHERS ($N=978$)

	Y_{co}	Z_{co}	R_{co}	R_{1co}	Q_{co}	B_{co}	I_{co}	S_{co}	V_{co}
X_{co}	.48	.80	.79	.73	.59	−.70	.51	.77	−.11
Y_{co}		.48	.54	.62	.60	−.32	.30	.44	−.18
Z_{co}			.69	.62	.45	−.61	.45	.68	−.04
R_{co}				.88	.76	−.69	.49	.79	−.22
R_{1co}					.80	−.65	.51	.78	−.16
Q_{co}						−.41	.45	.62	−.18
B_{co}							−.36	−.60	.06
I_{co}								.63	.08
S_{co}									−.09

SURVEY SAMPLE ELEMENTARY TEACHERS ($N=670$)

	Y_{co}	Z_{co}	R_{co}	R_{1co}	Q_{co}	B_{co}	I_{ci}	S_{ci}	V_{ci}
X_{co}	.56	.81	.79	.78	.62	−.70	.19	.32	.02
Y_{co}		.51	.57	.62	.59	−.38	.15	.15	.00
Z_{co}			.68	.65	.45	−.63	.21	.25	.07
R_{co}				.87	.73	−.66	.13	.31	−.05
R_{1co}					.78	−.66	.20	.30	−.02
Q_{co}						−.46	.20	.25	−.05
B_{co}							−.04	−.15	.06
I_{ci}								.19	.06
S_{ci}									.08

of secondary teachers, as compared with the corresponding correlation for the Survey Sample.

Additional complete intercorrelation tables were computed for some thirty different groups of teachers, including the different subsamples of elementary and secondary teachers of the Basic Analysis Sample, subgroups of the Survey Sample, the elementary and secondary holdout validation samples, and various special study groups. These tables included intercorrelations not only for the Elementary (111), Secondary (100), and All-Teacher (99) Scoring Keys, but also for additional scoring keys, such as those for Grades 1–4 women (143 X_{co}, Y_{co}, and Z_{co}), elementary men teachers (150 X_{co}, Y_{co}, and Z_{co}), mathematics-science teachers (97 X_{co}, Y_{co}, and Z_{co}), and for social studies–English teachers (98 X_{co}, Y_{co}, and Z_{co}).

The intercorrelations in these various tables are of the same general order as those noted in Tables 41, 42, and 43. The additional tables, therefore, are omitted in this report.

The intercorrelations among scores of elementary teachers, as com-

TABLE 42
Intercorrelations among Scores Yielded by the Secondary Teacher Scoring Keys (100)

BASIC ANALYSIS SAMPLE SECONDARY TEACHERS ($N = 1,065$)

	Y_{co}	Z_{co}	R_{co}	R_{1co}	Q_{co}	B_{co}	I_{co}	S_{co}	V_{co}
X_{co}	$-.09$	.54	.74	.73	.41	$-.74$	.46	.26	$-.02$
Y_{co}		.12	$-.09$	.01	$-.01$	.14	.39	$-.46$	.05
Z_{co}			.38	.48	.13	$-.52$	.38	.21	.07
R_{co}				.79	.76	$-.72$	.37	.28	$-.27$
R_{1co}					.53	$-.89$	.57	.06	$-.07$
Q_{co}						$-.34$	.18	.24	$-.28$
B_{co}							$-.55$	$-.09$	.10
I_{co}								$-.25$	.16
S_{co}									$-.08$

SURVEY SAMPLE SECONDARY TEACHERS ($N = 970$)

	Y_{co}	Z_{co}	R_{co}	R_{1co}	Q_{co}	B_{co}	I_{ci}	S_{ci}	V_{ci}
X_{co}	.06	.45	.64	.67	.31	$-.63$	.22	.08	.02
Y_{co}		.44	.15	.18	.16	.08	.24	.05	.21
Z_{co}			.44	.40	.29	$-.31$	.18	.22	.18
R_{co}				.72	.77	$-.53$	.16	.22	.01
R_{1co}					.40	$-.81$	.22	.03	.02
Q_{co}						$-.14$	.12	.26	.04
B_{co}							$-.16$	.01	.08
I_{ci}								.07	.14
S_{ci}									$-.03$

pared with those of secondary teachers, bear out differences already noted between these two major teacher groups. For example, whereas X_{co}, Y_{co}, and Z_{co} are substantially intercorrelated among elementary teachers, among secondary teachers X_{co} and Z_{co}, and also Y_{co} and Z_{co}, are positively correlated, but X_{co} and Y_{co} are virtually independent of one another.

Attempts to discern families, or factors, of characteristics represented by their intercorrelations indicated, perhaps foremost, a pattern among both elementary and secondary teachers which involved principally Characteristics X and B (permissive viewpoints). The prominence of this pattern which seemed to have as its core warm, friendly, under-standing classroom behavior and permissive, child-centered educational viewpoints, is noteworthy.

The families formed by the intercorrelations vary slightly from one teacher sample to another. Among the Basic Analysis Sample of ele-mentary teachers, two oblique or correlated patterns may be noted—one made up of X_{co}, Z_{co}, and B_{co}, and the other of R_{co}, R_{1co}, Q_{co}, Y_{co}, S_{co},

TABLE 43

Intercorrelations among Scores Yielded by the All-Teacher Scoring Keys (99)

BASIC ANALYSIS SAMPLE ELEMENTARY-SECONDARY TEACHERS
($N = 2,043$)

	Y_{co}	Z_{co}	R_{co}	R_{1co}	Q_{co}	B_{co}	I_{co}	S_{co}	V_{co}
X_{co}	.30	.74	.78	.79	.57	−.75	.48	.59	−.10
Y_{co}		.32	.26	.23	.14	−.12	.19	−.10	−.01
Z_{co}			.67	.75	.43	−.72	.41	.47	−.01
R_{co}				.85	.82	−.68	.46	.59	−.23
R_{1co}					.61	−.81	.52	.55	−.07
Q_{co}						−.38	.25	.55	−.42
B_{co}							−.56	.51	−.03
I_{co}								.25	.18
S_{co}									−.21

SURVEY SAMPLE ELEMENTARY-SECONDARY TEACHERS ($N = 1,640$)

	Y_{co}	Z_{co}	R_{co}	R_{1co}	Q_{co}	B_{co}	I_{ci}	S_{ci}	V_{ci}
X_{co}	.31	.47	.70	.73	.59	−.41	.20	.18	.01
Y_{co}		.11	.20	.22	.14	−.19	.08	−.07	.06
Z_{co}			.56	.56	.23	−.31	.04	.04	−.02
R_{co}				.81	.73	−.34	.16	.17	−.05
R_{1co}					.59	−.45	.19	.15	.00
Q_{co}						−.21	.13	.19	−.08
B_{co}							−.04	−.05	.03
I_{ci}								.12	.12
S_{ci}									−.12

and I_{co}. The first factor seems to represent friendly and stimulating teacher classroom behavior combined with permissive, child-centered educational viewpoints, and the second seems to be definable in terms of favorable opinions of other persons, together with good emotional adjustment and above-average verbal understanding.

In the Basic Analysis elementary sample the correlations of X_{co} with Z_{co} and R_{co} with R_{1co} are the two highest. Characteristics scores S_{co} and I_{co} are positively correlated.

Turning to the Survey Sample of elementary teachers, two correlated patterns again are in evidence, one made up of X_{co}, Z_{co}, and B_{co} and the other of R_{co}, R_{1co}, Q_{co}, and Y_{co}. These may be interpreted, in general, in the same manner as were the factors in the Basic Analysis elementary sample, except that in this case, where the I_{ci}, S_{ci}, and V_{ci} scores were involved, both I_{ci} and S_{ci} appear to be distributed between the two major patterns (V_{ci} being relatively independent). The correlations between X_{co} and Z_{co}, on the one hand, and R_{co} and R_{1co}, on the other, are higher than others in the matrix. In addition, Q_{co} and Y_{co} (favorable attitudes toward school staff personnel and systematic, responsible, businesslike classroom behavior) are moderately correlated. The correlation between S_{ci} and I_{ci} is low, but positive, in this elementary Survey group.

The patterns of the secondary teacher group are similar in meaning to those of the elementary teachers, but are somewhat differently constituted. Among the Basic Analysis Sample of secondary teachers, two rather *lowly* correlated families of scores appear, one consisting of R_{1co}, B_{co}, R_{co}, X_{co}, Z_{co}, Q_{co}, and I_{co}, and the other Y_{co} and negative S_{co} (poor emotional adjustment). The first of these patterns apparently is quite general and is related to favorable attitudes toward persons, permissive educational viewpoints, above-average verbal understanding, friendly, sympathetic classroom behavior, and stimulating, original classroom behavior. The other has to do with responsible, businesslike classroom behavior combined, interestingly, with below-average emotional adjustment. R_{1co} and B_{co} are the most highly correlated variables. X_{co} and Z_{co} are moderately positively correlated, and X_{co} and Y_{co} are lowly correlated. S_{co} is relatively lowly correlated with other variables, and V_{co} appears to be almost independent.

With the Survey Sample of secondary teachers, two correlated patterns of variables emerge, one principally from R_{1co}, X_{co}, and B_{co}, and the other from Q_{co}, R_{co}, Z_{co}, and Y_{co}. The first family of characteristics seems to relate to permissive educational viewpoints, favorable attitudes toward democratic pupil practices, and friendly, understanding teacher classroom behavior. The second apparently involves favorable attitudes toward pupils and staff personnel, combined with stimulating classroom behavior and businesslike classroom behavior. R_{1co} and B_{co} are more highly intercorrelated than other variables. I_{ci} appears to be distributed between the two factors. I_{ci} and S_{ci} are relatively lowly correlated with one another. S_{ci} is lowly positively correlated with R_{co} and Z_{co}. V_{ci} appears to be relatively independent of the other variables. X_{co} and Y_{co} are independent and X_{co} and Z_{co} are positively correlated.

Evaluation of the Teacher Characteristics Schedule Scoring Keys

To this point the discussion has been directed entirely to the description of the correlates keys, and judgment of the effectiveness of the keys in indicating the behaviors or characteristics they purport to estimate has been postponed. Answers to questions growing out of this area of concern provide the bases for judgments of the relative usefulness of the correlates materials.

The more important characteristics of behavior estimates scores upon which their usefulness depends are (1) *reliability*, and (2) *validity*. Obviously, matters of precision of measurement in proportion to the precision required for a particular use, administrative and scoring convenience, acceptability to the consumer, adequacy of norms data, and the like, are also matters of importance to the test or inventory user. Questions of reliability and validity, however, must be answered, and upon them really stands or falls the usefulness of measuring instruments, regardless of other practical and theoretical considerations.

The reliability problem was approached from two standpoints—first, the *equivalence* of separate estimates yielded by the scoring keys (agreement of teachers' scores based on positively contributing responses with their scores based on negatively contributing responses), and, second, the *stability* of scores of the same teachers over varying periods of time.

In studying the validity of the scoring keys, the approaches described in chapter 2 were employed, and evidence was sought relative to concurrent double cross-validity, concurrent hold-out sample validity, predictive validity with neutral motivation, predictive validity with positive motivation, concurrent validity generalization, concurrent validity extension, and predictive validity extension.

RELIABILITY OF THE CORRELATES SCORING KEYS

Reliability coefficients in the form of equivalency indices for the scorings keys most frequently employed with the Schedule are shown in Table 44. It will be observed that these reliability coefficients, based upon the correlation of scores derived from negatively contributing response scores with scores derived from positively contributing response scores, were computed for the Basic Analysis Sample for all characteristics for which scoring keys had been derived. Similar coefficients were obtained also for X_{co}, Y_{co}, and Z_{co} for random samples drawn from the Survey Sample.

Reliability, as measured by the correlation between the positive response and negative response scoring keys, appears to be generally satisfactory. The Scoring Keys X_{co}, relating to understanding, friendly, teacher classroom behavior, seemed consistently to be among the most reliable of the keys based on correlates of teacher classroom behavior. The validity-of-response Key V_{co} almost uniformly yielded the lowest

TABLE 44

Reliability Coefficients* (Estimated from Plus-Minus Correlations) of Scores Yielded by Teacher Characteristics Schedule Scoring Keys

Teacher Characteristics Schedule Score	All-Elementary Teacher Scoring Keys (111)		All-Secondary Teacher Scoring Keys (100)		All-Teacher Scoring Keys (99)			
					Basic Analysis Group			Sample of Survey Group (Combined Elementary and Secondary) ($N=150$)
	Basic Analysis Group ($N=978$)	Sample of Survey Group ($N=100$)	Basic Analysis Group ($N=1,065$)	Sample of Survey Group ($N=100$)	Elementary ($N=978$)	Math.-Science ($N=497$)	Engl.-Soc. St. ($N=568$)	
X_{co}	.89	.88	.83	.72	.79	.78	.80	.82
Y_{co}	.78	.77	.76	.70	.58	.69	.62	.68
Z_{co}	.79	.77	.65	.52	.70	.64	.70	.62
R_{co}	.85		.88		.82	.79	.84	
R_{100}	.87		.83		.72	.67	.72	
Q_{co}	.82		.81		.73	.70	.76	
B_{co}	.86		.87		.86	.87	.87	
I_{co}	.72		.64		.71	.69	.72	
S_{co}	.78		.70		.73	.74	.72	
V_{co}	.64		.52		.64	.58	.58	

* Spearman-Brown.

235

reliability coefficients, but fortunately, this scale does not relate to one of the major variables with which the Study was concerned in identifying and comparing teachers.

Among the several sets of keys—those for elementary teachers (111_{co}), secondary teachers (100_{co}), and elementary-secondary teachers combined (99_{co})—the elementary teacher keys appeared to be slightly more reliable than the secondary keys, and the secondary keys, in turn, tended to be more reliable than the elementary-secondary combined keys.

The coefficients yielded by scores of teachers making up the Basic Analysis Sample and those of teachers in the subsamples randomly drawn from the Survey Sample are in substantial agreement, although the Survey group correlations are lower in most instances.

The second approach to the evaluation of the consistency of the scores was from the standpoint of stability, and it involved study of test-retest data covering varying periods of time. These studies were conducted with secondary teacher samples. The teachers participating in these investigations did not know, at the time they originally completed the Schedule, that they would be asked to perform the task a second time. Random samples of teachers who had (1) just completed the Schedule within the past three weeks, (2) completed the Schedule one year earlier, and (3) completed the Schedule two to three years earlier were selected and requested to further participate in the Study by completing the Schedule a second time.

Table 45 shows the test-retest results. In general, all the keys (with the exception of V_{co}) seemed to possess considerable stability over a three-week interval, but some, such as Z_{co} (stimulating teacher classroom behavior) and S_{co} (emotional stability) show rather marked differences when the interval between responses was either one year, or two to three years. The X_{co}, R_{co}, R_{1co}, and B_{co} Keys seemed to hold up relatively well regardless of the interval, although, as might be anticipated, the coefficients are lower for the longer intervals of time.

It should be recalled that in stability, or test-retest coefficients, there always is a confounding of conditions which make for unreliability (uncontrolled variance) in the measuring procedure, on the one hand, and conditions associated with systematic and more or less permanent changes taking place in the measured individual over a period of time. In the light of the high stability coefficients over short periods of time (three weeks), it does not seem unreasonable to interpret the lower correlations for measurements obtained with an intervening interval of several years as reflecting changes in the behaviors under consideration.

TABLE 45

Stability (Test-Retest Reliability) over Varying Periods of Time of Scores Yielded by Teacher Characteristics Schedule Secondary Teacher Scoring Keys

	TEST-RETEST CORRELATION COEFFICIENTS														
TEACHER CHARACTER- ISTICS SCHEDULE SCORE	All-Secondary Teacher Scoring Keys (100)									Math-Science Teacher Scoring Keys (97)*			Engl.-Social Studies Teacher Scoring Keys (98)*		
	3-Wk. Interval			1-Yr. Interval			2-3-Yr. Interval								
	Total (N=45)	M-S (N=25)	E-SS (N=20)	Total (N=112)	M-S (N=57)	E-SS (N=55)	Total (N=114)	M-S (N=56)	E-SS (N=58)	3-Wk. (N=25)	1-Yr. (N=57)	2-3-Yr. (N=56)	3-Wk. (N=20)	1-Yr. (N=55)	2-3-Yr. (N=58)
X_{co}	.83	.90	.70	.73	.70	.75	.70	.68	.69	.88	.57	.73	.68	.79	.56
Y_{co}	.78	.72	.84	.63	.61	.65	.51	.51	.55	.84	.58	.55	.94	.83	.75
Z_{co}	.85	.88	.83	.34	.16	.68	.48	.49	.50	.60	.10	.23	.83	.69	.35
R_{co}	.83	.85	.75	.77	.79	.75	.67	.67	.67	.85	.79	.67	.75	.75	.67
R_{1co}	.89	.90	.77	.70	.64	.74	.73	.70	.63	.90	.64	.70	.77	.74	.63
Q_{co}	.70	.75	.56	.68	.72	.65	.50	.51	.50	.75	.72	.51	.56	.65	.50
B_{co}	.90	.93	.79	.73	.68	.71	.70	.67	.56	.93	.68	.67	.79	.71	.56
L_{co}	.85	.89	.75	.78	.77	.76	.57	.54	.66	.89	.77	.54	.75	.76	.66
S_{co}	.90	.89	.91	.22	.45	.12	.28	.15	.46	.89	.45	.15	.91	.12	.46
V_{co}	.72	.83	.39	.22	.06	.37	.14	.07	.22	.83	.06	.07	.39	.37	.22

* Scoring keys 97 and 98 differ from the 100 keys only with respect to X_{co}, Y_{co}, and Z_{co}.

237

It will be recalled from chapter 4 that assessments of the same teachers over a period of twenty months correlated to the extent of .54, .65, and .60 for X_o, Y_o, and Z_o, respectively, these coefficients being somewhat lower than those obtained for interobserver assessments when observations were conducted within a few days of each other.

In summary, the correlates keys derived from the Schedule seem to possess adequate reliability for their use in further study of problems relating to teacher characteristics, the keys for elementary and secondary teachers yielding coefficients generally ranging between .65 and .90.

VALIDITY OF THE CORRELATES SCORING KEYS

Validity of evidence is the most important single concern, regardless of the particular area of man's thinking or behavior. Traditionally, it is the domain of logic, and it extends to all aspects of man's existence. In scientific research it is the principal goal of design. In the measurement of human behavior, it is the characteristic of the measuring instrument which ultimately determines its usefulness.

In introducing considerations of the validity of the Schedule scoring keys, it should be recalled that the validity of any measuring instrument is not general, in the sense that a device may be thought of as being valid for a wide range of situations in which it might conceivably be used. Properly viewed, validity is specific to particular situations in which it has been demonstrated, and only when an instrument has been studied under a variety of situations (replications) can the kinds of instances in which it may be expected to yield valid data be determined.

In attempts to ascertain the validity of a measuring device, several general classes of situations may be designated, as observed in chapter 2. Thus, an instrument may be considered from the standpoint of its validity for estimating criterion data which are obtained at approximately the same time as the estimates themselves (concurrent validity). On the other hand, it may be important to look for the validity of estimates for foretelling criterion behavior that will take place at some future time, i.e., criterion data obtained perhaps years following the obtaining of the estimates used for prediction. (This kind of validity sometimes is distinguished from concurrent validity by the term "predictive validity," although actually prediction is involved in all behavior estimation, a crucial consideration being the length of time intervening between the estimate and the behavior it purports to estimate.) An instrument which performs creditably in estimating contemporarily gathered criterion data might very possibly fall short of predicting criteria which represent substantially different behaviors from those which typified the individual at the time the estimates were obtained. Because of the changing behavior of persons with experience and time, predictive validity, particularly over substantial periods of time, is most difficult to establish.

It was with considerations such as these in mind and others discussed in chapter 2, that a variety of approaches to the validity of the Schedule scoring keys was undertaken.

CONCURRENT DOUBLE CROSS-VALIDITY (NEUTRAL MOTIVATION) OF THE X_{co}, Y_{co}, AND Z_{co} SCORING KEYS

As noted in earlier sections of this chapter, the general practice of the Study in the derivation of correlates scoring keys was to split a specified sample of teachers randomly into two subsamples, and select responses which met standards involving minimum response-criterion correlations in each subsample. Data derived from the scoring key of one randomly selected subsample with keys derived from response analysis of another random subsample provide information for the evaluation of one aspect of validity—concurrent validity—of the scoring keys.

In the results reported here, concurrent double cross-validity of the Elementary Teacher Scoring Keys (111_{co}), Secondary Teacher Scoring Keys (100_{co}), and All-Teacher Scoring Keys (99_{co}) for Patterns X, Y, and Z was the focal interest.

It is important to note that these studies involved "neutral motivation" in the sense that no incentive condition (such as prospective employment) was known to be operating which might induce the respondents to attempt to give answers that they thought would enhance their chances for favorable consideration. The data are based upon the Basic Analysis Sample of teachers, teachers who had been assured that their participation in the study was in the interest of research, and that the results were to be used for no supervisory or administrative purposes.

The data are presented in Table 46. Validity coefficients are given for each of the cross-validation samples in each of the teacher groups for the three patterns of teacher behavior. In general, the cross-validity coefficients are lowest for the All-Teacher Keys (elementary and secondary teachers combined). This seems reasonable, and it was anticipated in the light of the heterogeneity of behavior represented by teachers of a variety of levels and subject matters involving quite different objectives and content.

The validity coefficients for the Elementary Teacher Scoring Keys are of the greatest magnitude, and those of the Secondary Teacher Scoring Keys fall between the All-Teacher and the Elementary Keys. For

TABLE 46

Cross-Validity Coefficients for Scores Yielded by the X_{co}, Y_{co}, and Z_{co} Keys, Based on Randomly Split Halves of the Basic Analysis Samples

Schedule Score	Criterion	Validation Group	Group on Which Key was Based	r
\multicolumn{5}{c}{Elementary Teacher Scoring Keys (111)}				
\multicolumn{5}{c}{($N_{1111}=417$; $N_{1112}=417$)}				
111 X_{co}	X_o	1111	1112	.40
		1112	1111	.43
111 Y_{co}	Y_o	1111	1112	.34
		1112	1111	.36
111 Z_{co}	Z_o	1111	1112	.37
		1112	1111	.32
\multicolumn{5}{c}{Secondary Teacher Scoring Keys (100)}				
\multicolumn{5}{c}{($N_{1001}=476$; $N_{1002}=475$)}				
100 X_{co}	X_o	1001	1002	.36
		1002	1001	.34
100 Y_{co}	Y_o	1001	1002	.25
		1002	1001	.31
100 Z_{co}	Z_o	1001	1002	.31
		1002	1001	.30
\multicolumn{5}{c}{All-Teacher Scoring Keys (99)}				
\multicolumn{5}{c}{($N_{991}=893$; $N_{992}=893$)}				
99 X_{co}	X_o	991	992	.25
		992	991	.28
99 Y_{co}	Y_o	991	992	.15
		992	991	.15
99 Z_{co}	Z_o	991	992	.20
		992	991	.22

each group of teachers, the X_{co} Keys, measuring friendly, understanding teacher classroom behavior, appear to yield somewhat higher cross-validity coefficients than do the keys for the other patterns. The keys for Y_{co}, businesslike, systematic classroom behavior, generally yielded the lowest cross-validity coefficients.

Concurrent Hold-Out Sample Validity (Neutral Motivation) of the X_{co}, Y_{co}, and Z_{co} Scoring Keys

Another approach to the appraisal of the validity of the X_{co}, Y_{co}, and Z_{co} Scoring Keys was quite similar to that just described, and involved the employment of what were designated by the Study as "hold-out" samples. A hold-out sample consisted of what may be considered a random sample of teachers who, prior to the response analyses, were drawn from the total available group and excluded from the statistical analyses which were basic to the development of the scoring keys. These groups were literally held out for later investigation in connection with the validity of the scoring keys which had been derived with respect to their peers. The hold-out samples were not strictly random samples. In one case the sample consisted simply of teachers who had participated in the Study prior to the introduction of the first single booklet form of the Schedule in 1950–51. Other hold-out samples (e.g., Hold-Out Sample 1) consisted of teachers for whom the last digit of their identification number was a one or a two.[5]

It was believed that data on the hold-out samples would provide some of the more pertinent information on the usefulness of the correlates scoring keys for other groups of teachers similar to those participating in the basic studies. Four hold-out samples were drawn— two elementary samples consisting of 136 and 143 teachers, respectively, and two secondary samples consisting of 114 and 99 teachers.

Validity coefficients for the hold-out samples are shown in Table 47. Data are provided for the final Elementary, Secondary, and All-Teacher (elementary-secondary combined) Scoring Keys (111_{co}, 100_{co}, and 99_{co}) and also for the separate keys derived from each of the randomly split subsamples employed in response analysis.

In general, the picture is quite similar to that provided by the cross-validity coefficients. The elementary Scoring Keys appeared to yield the highest validity coefficients, the All-Teacher (elementary-secondary combined) Keys the lowest, and the Secondary Teacher Keys values intermediate between the other two. Again, this does not seem unreasonable in view of the fact that the classroom behaviors of elementary teachers are perhaps more homogeneous than are those of secondary teachers, and the behaviors represented by a group of elementary-secondary teachers are the most heterogeneous of all.

The X_{co} Keys, measuring friendly, understanding teacher classroom behavior generally appeared to perform more creditably than Y_{co} or Z_{co}, although the differences were not always pronounced.

It may be of interest to note the expectancy charts shown in Figures 8

---

[5] The teachers were assigned identification numbers at the time of arrangement for their observation. For a school system participating in the Study, the roster of teachers, by schools, was obtained. The numbering, therefore, was consecutive within a school and, generally speaking, although not always, within a school system.

TABLE 47

Hold-Out Sample Validity Coefficients for Scores Yielded by the X_{co}, Y_{co}, and Z_{co} Keys

VARIABLES	SCORING KEY	VALIDATION GROUP*	r
ELEMENTARY TEACHER SCORING KEYS (111)			
$X_o 111 X_{co}$	$1111 \, X_{co}$	El HO-1	.43
	$1112 \, X_{co}$	El HO-1	.41
	$111 \, X_{co}$	El HO-1	.43
	$111 \, X_{co}$	El HO-2	.45
$Y_o 111 Y_{co}$	$1111 \, Y_{co}$	El HO-1	.29
	$1112 \, Y_{co}$	El HO-1	.29
	$111 \, Y_{co}$	El HO-1	.32
	$111 \, Y_{co}$	El HO-2	.40
$Z_o 111 Z_{co}$	$1111 \, Z_{co}$	El HO-1	.33
	$1112 \, Z_{co}$	El HO-1	.32
	$111 \, Z_{co}$	El HO-1	.39
	$111 \, Z_{co}$	El HO-2	.61
SECONDARY TEACHER SCORING KEYS (100)			
$X_o 100 X_{co}$	$1001 \, X_{co}$	Sec HO-1	.27
	$1002 \, X_{co}$	Sec HO-1	.28
	$100 \, X_{co}$	Sec HO-1	.31
	$100 \, X_{co}$	Sec HO-2	.29
$Y_o 100 Y_{co}$	$1001 \, Y_{co}$	Sec HO-1	.31
	$1002 \, Y_{co}$	Sec HO-1	.31
	$100 \, Y_{co}$	Sec HO-1	.36
	$100 \, Y_{co}$	Sec HO-2	.32
$Z_o 100 Z_{co}$	$1001 \, Z_{co}$	Sec HO-1	.13
	$1002 \, Z_{co}$	Sec HO-1	.15
	$100 \, Z_{co}$	Sec HO-1	.16
	$100 \, Z_{co}$	Sec HO-2	.29
ALL-TEACHER SCORING KEYS (99)			
$X_o 99 X_{co}$	$991 \, X_{co}$	El-Sec HO-1	.27
	$992 \, X_{co}$	El-Sec HO-1	.26
	$99 \, X_{co}$	El-Sec HO-1	.28
	$99 \, X_{co}$	El HO-1	.33
	$99 \, X_{co}$	Sec HO-1	.25
$Y_o 99 Y_{co}$	$991 \, Y_{co}$	El-Sec HO-1	.05
	$992 \, Y_{co}$	El-Sec HO-1	.10
	$99 \, Y_{co}$	El-Sec HO-1	.10
	$99 \, Y_{co}$	El HO-1	.12
	$99 \, Y_{co}$	Sec HO-1	.10
$Z_o 99 Z_{co}$	$991 \, Z_{co}$	El-Sec HO-1	.14
	$992 \, Z_{co}$	El-Sec HO-1	.15
	$99 \, Z_{co}$	El-Sec HO-1	.15
	$99 \, Z_{co}$	El HO-1	.23
	$99 \, Z_{co}$	Sec HO-1	.09

* Numbers of teachers in validation groups: El HO-1 = 144; Sec HO-1 = 114; El-Sec HO-1 = 254; El HO-2 = 143; Sec HO-2 = 99.

through 13. The data portrayed graphically apply to the elementary hold-out sample and the secondary hold-out sample. For the patterns X_o, Y_o, and Z_o separately, the percentage of teachers attaining different Schedule score levels are shown in relation to placement in the highest 30 percent and lowest 30 percent of the criterion, i.e., composite observer assessments.

Comparable charts were prepared from the Basic Analysis data, such charts naturally showing extremely marked discrimination since they refer to the groups upon which the analyses were conducted. The present charts, representing the application of the keys to new samples, show much less clear-cut discrimination except for the highest and lowest categories of scores. This lesser discrimination at intermediate levels of the criterion scale is, of course, not discouraging, since less attention and concern usually is expressed regarding behaviors approaching the central tendency of a distribution, and both research and practical interests most often are focused on the relatively extreme deviates of behavior. And, further revision and refinement of the types of materials employed by the Study should result in scoring keys capable of even more precise discrimination.

The validity and reliability data pertaining to the hold-out samples are brought together in Table 48 (on page 248), following a method of presentation suggested in correspondence by Professor Donald T. Campbell of Northwestern University. The table shows multiple-method, multiple-trait matrices of correlation data provided by the elementary and secondary hold-out samples.

Table 48 is a key table of this report. It summarizes very meaningfully important reliability and validity data relative to the Teacher Characteristics Schedule correlates of teacher classroom behavior.

As Campbell points out, the *cross-method submatrix diagonal of validity coefficients* should be made up of values higher than the other cross-method coefficients which are off the diagonal. Also, in an ideal situation, the values in the cross-method submatrix would be symmetrical, with values above the diagonal being similar to those below the diagonal. (Ideally, also, the values in the cross-method submatrix should parallel, though at a lower level, those of the intramethod matrix corners.)

In general, the summary provided by Table 48 is promising and is suggestive of the usefulness of the Schedule scoring keys with such groups of teachers as those represented by the hold-out samples.

(*Text continued on page 249.*)

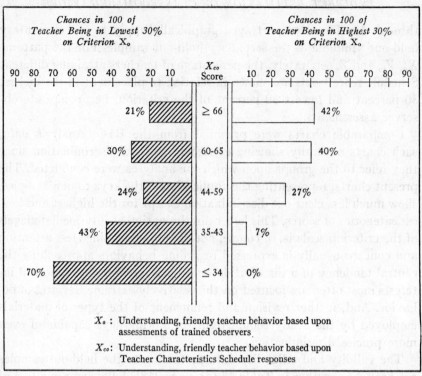

Chances in 100 of
Teacher Being in Lowest 30%
on Criterion X₀

Chances in 100 of
Teacher Being in Highest 30%
on Criterion X₀

X_{co} Score

| 90 80 70 60 50 40 30 20 10 | | 10 20 30 40 50 60 70 80 90 |

21%   ≥ 66   42%

30%   60-65   40%

24%   44-59   27%

43%   35-43   7%

70%   ≤ 34   0%

X_o : Understanding, friendly teacher behavior based upon
assessments of trained observers

X_{co}: Understanding, friendly teacher behavior based upon
Teacher Characteristics Schedule responses

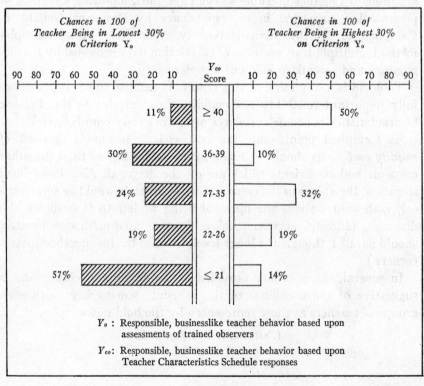

Chances in 100 of
Teacher Being in Lowest 30%
on Criterion Y₀

Chances in 100 of
Teacher Being in Highest 30%
on Criterion Y₀

Y_{co} Score

| 90 80 70 60 50 40 30 20 10 | | 10 20 30 40 50 60 70 80 90 |

11%   ≥ 40   50%

30%   36-39   10%

24%   27-35   32%

19%   22-26   19%

57%   ≤ 21   14%

Y_o : Responsible, businesslike teacher behavior based upon
assessments of trained observers

Y_{co}: Responsible, businesslike teacher behavior based upon
Teacher Characteristics Schedule responses

FIG. 8.—Graphic representation of the concurrent variability of Teacher Characteristics Schedule scores (111 X_{co}) and placement in the highest 30 percent and the lowest 30 percent of composite observer assessments (X_o) for teachers in the elementary hold-out sample ($N = 144$).

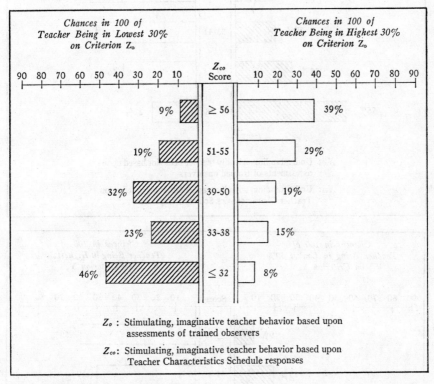

FIG. 10.—Graphic representation of the concurrent variability of Teacher Characteristics Schedule scores (111 Z_{co}) and placement in the highest 30 percent and the lowest 30 percent of composite observer assessments (Z_o) for teachers in the elementary hold-out sample ($N = 144$).

FIG. 9.—Graphic representation of the concurrent variability of Teacher Characteristics Schedule scores (111 Y_{co}) and placement in the highest 30 percent and the lowest 30 percent of composite observer assessments (Y_o) for teachers in the elementary hold-out sample ($N = 144$).

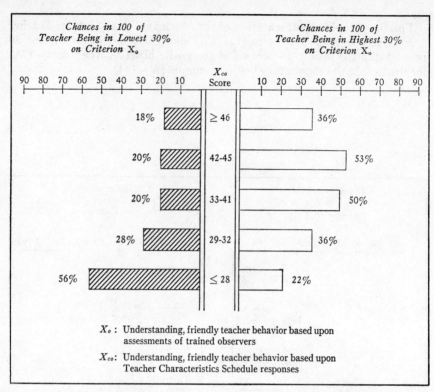

Chances in 100 of
Teacher Being in Lowest 30%
on Criterion X_o

Chances in 100 of
Teacher Being in Highest 30%
on Criterion X_o

	X_{co} Score	
18%	≥ 46	36%
20%	42-45	53%
20%	33-41	50%
28%	29-32	36%
56%	≤ 28	22%

X_o : Understanding, friendly teacher behavior based upon assessments of trained observers

X_{co} : Understanding, friendly teacher behavior based upon Teacher Characteristics Schedule responses

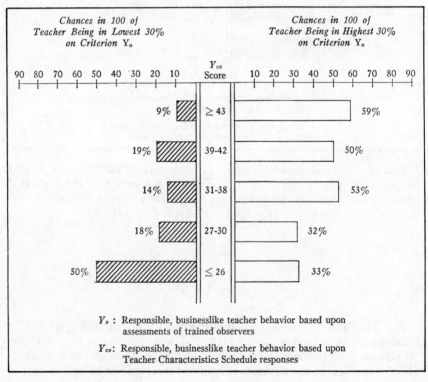

Chances in 100 of
Teacher Being in Lowest 30%
on Criterion Y_o

Chances in 100 of
Teacher Being in Highest 30%
on Criterion Y_o

	Y_{co} Score	
9%	≥ 43	59%
19%	39-42	50%
14%	31-38	53%
18%	27-30	32%
50%	≤ 26	33%

Y_o : Responsible, businesslike teacher behavior based upon assessments of trained observers

Y_{co}: Responsible, businesslike teacher behavior based upon Teacher Characteristics Schedule responses

Fig. 11.—Graphic representation of the concurrent variability of Teacher Characteristics Schedule scores (100 X_{co}) and placement in the highest 30 percent and the lowest 30 percent of composite observer assessments (X_o) for teachers in the secondary hold-out sample ($N = 114$).

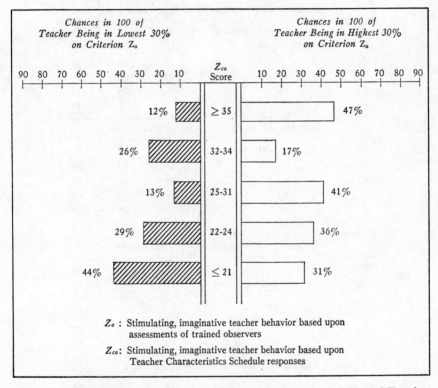

Fig. 13.—Graphic representation of the concurrent variability of Teacher Characteristics Schedule scores (100 Z_{co}) and placement in the highest 30 percent and the lowest 30 percent of composite observer assessments (Z_o) for teachers in the secondary hold-out sample ($N = 114$).

Fig. 12.—Graphic representation of the concurrent variability of Teacher Characteristics Schedule scores (100 Y_{co}) and placement in the highest 30 percent and the lowest 30 percent of composite observer assessments (Y_o) for teachers in the secondary hold-out sample ($N = 114$).

TABLE 48

Intercorrelation Coefficients among Composite Observer Assessments X_o, Y_o, and Z_o and Schedule Scores X_{co}, Y_{co}, and Z_{co} for the Hold-Out Samples

(Single underlined coefficients in the diagonals represent reliability estimates*; double underlined coefficients are validity estimates)

	X_o	Y_o	Z_o	X_{co}	Y_{co}	Z_{co}
ELEMENTARY TEACHER HOLD-OUT SAMPLE 1						
X_o	.72	.55	.65	.43	.28	.41
Y_o		.68	.58	.12	.32	.11
Z_o			.70	.34	.29	.39
X_{co}				.89	.47	.82
Y_{co}					.78	.43
Z_{co}						.79
ELEMENTARY TEACHER HOLD-OUT SAMPLE 2						
X_o	.72	.60	.78	.45	.20	.54
Y_o		.68	.56	.16	.40	.30
Z_o			.70	.52	.19	.61
X_{co}				.89	.10	.86
Y_{co}					.78	.29
Z_{co}						.79
SECONDARY TEACHER HOLD-OUT SAMPLE 1						
X_o	.73	.11	.50	.31	−.03	.10
Y_o		.73	.41	−.11	.36	−.12
Z_o			.71	.18	.07	.16
X_{co}				.83	−.14	.54
Y_{co}					.76	.06
Z_{co}						.65
SECONDARY TEACHER HOLD-OUT SAMPLE 2						
X_o	.73	−.15	.34	.29	−.05	.06
Y_o		.73	.28	−.09	.32	.04
Z_o			.71	.02	.08	.29
X_{co}				.83	−.10	.36
Y_{co}					.76	.19
Z_{co}						.65

* Reliability coefficients for X_o, Y_o, and Z_o are typical values estimated from replicated reliability studies reported in chap. 4. The coefficients for X_{co}, Y_{co}, and Z_{co} are those shown in Table 44 for the positive-negative response studies.

A STUDY OF LONG-TERM PREDICTIVE VALIDITY
WITH NEUTRAL MOTIVATION

In an investigation of the relationships between correlates of teacher classroom behavior and criterion data when the correlates had been obtained several years preceding the criterion observations, the Schedule was administered to a group of students at the beginning of their final year of college training, with collection of criterion information having been postponed until these individuals had become experienced teachers. Schedule data were available for a total of 132 students, all of whom had their training in the same educational institution. Three years later, observations were undertaken of those teachers who were employed in a public school system which normally drew a substantial portion of the teachers trained in the institution in question. It should be noted that a relatively rigorous selection system is followed in the particular school system, and only those graduates who successfully passed written and oral screening examinations became eligible for appointment. Of those teachers originally completing the Schedule while in college, only 56 were available for later observation. These teachers, conducting classes in Grades 1 through 6, were observed by trained observers employed by the Study, and analyses were made of scores attained on keys of the Schedule in relation to on-the-job assessment three years following their response to the Schedule.

Table 49 provides certain comparisons of the 56 teachers participating in this study with the student group of which they were originally a part, and also with the elementary Basic Analysis Sample. It will be noted that the experimental group was slightly higher in mean score on X_o, and significantly higher with respect to Y_o and Z_o as compared with the elementary Basic Analysis Sample, suggesting that from the standpoint of observed "businesslike" and "stimulating" classroom behaviors this group was somewhat more highly selected than might usually be the case.

The mean scores of the 56 teachers comprising the experimental group were quite similar to those of teachers in the larger student population ($N = 132$) originally tested except with respect to B_{co}, in which case the experimental group was more "child-centered and permissive" in educational viewpoints.

The Basic Analysis Sample was more "child-centered" in their educational viewpoints as compared with this particular group of individuals tested while college students. The X_{co} (friendly, understanding behavior) correlates scores of the teachers who completed the Schedule while in college were about the same as the scores of the experienced teachers in the Basic Analysis Sample, but the Y_{co} (businesslike, systematic classroom behavior) and Z_{co} (stimulating classroom behavior) correlates

TABLE 49

Composite Observer Assessments and Schedule Scores of 56 Elementary Teachers Employed in School System H, Compared with Data Based on (a) the Student Group to Which the Observed Teachers Originally Belonged and (b) Basic Analysis Sample Elementary Teachers

BEHAVIOR PATTERN OR CORRELATES SCORE	56 TEACHERS WHO COMPLETED THE SCHEDULE AS STUDENTS AND WERE OBSERVED FOLLOWING EMPLOYMENT		STUDENT GROUP TO WHICH OBSERVED TEACHERS ORIGINALLY BELONGED ($N=132$)		ELEMENTARY BASIC ANALYSIS SAMPLE ($N=978$)	
	Mean	σ	Mean	σ	Mean	σ
X_o........	51.2	8.6			50.7	9.0
Y_o........	53.6	13.0			50.5	8.9
Z_o........	53.9	8.3			50.7	8.4
111 X_{co}....	52.3	15.0	52.1	13.4	51.2	15.6
111 Y_{co}....	25.4	7.6	25.2	7.2	30.9	9.0
111 Z_{co}....	40.8	12.0	40.9	10.6	44.4	11.4
99 R_{co}....	35.9	13.0	34.4	10.8	36.6	9.4
99 B_{co}....	18.0	9.7	22.8	9.5	16.8	9.2
99 I_{co}....	36.2	7.7	35.8	6.5	35.9	7.1
99 S_{co}....	35.3	6.7	37.2	6.3	36.6	6.1

scores of the college students were significantly lower, reflecting perhaps the lack of experience at the time of responding to the inventory. It does not seem unreasonable to infer that teaching experience may be of considerable importance in influencing scores in these areas of classroom behavior. The groups compared in Table 49 do not differ greatly with respect to R_{co}, I_{co}, or S_{co}.

Table 50 presents the correlation coefficients between observer assessments and Schedule scores for the fifty-six elementary teachers who completed the Schedule when students and were observed following employment. Validity coefficients are presented for both the 111 X_{co}, 111 Y_{co}, 111 Z_{co}, and the 143 X_{co}, 143 Y_{co}, and 143 Z_{co} Scoring Keys. The predictive validity of the keys indicated by these coefficients is not high, the values for $X_o X_{co}$, $Y_o Y_{co}$, and $Z_o Z_{co}$ ranging from .01 to .22. It also is of interest to note that the Y_{co} Keys in this case predict Z_o to a greater extent than they do Y_o. In fact, it appears that in this study the Y_o Scoring Keys predicted Z_o as well as did the Z_o Scoring Keys.

The highest correlations of any of the scores with observer assessments was that of $-.34$ between B_{co} and X_o. Apparently the tendency of teachers in this group toward "child-centered" educational viewpoints when students predicted friendly, understanding classroom behavior three years later better than any other variable. Similarly, traditional, academically centered educational viewpoints seemed to be the most satisfactory predictor of later Y_o (businesslike, systematic classroom behavior) assessments, as indicated by a correlation coefficient of .25. Thus, "friendly" and "businesslike" teacher classroom behaviors were best predicted three years earlier by the student teachers' educational viewpoints. "Stimulating" behavior was best predicted by the 143 Y_{co} and 143 Z_{co} scores.

TABLE 50

Correlation Coefficients between Composite Observer Assessments X_o, Y_o, and Z_o and Schedule Scores for 56 Elementary Teachers Who Completed the Schedule When Students and Were Observed Three Years Later Following Employment

BEHAVIOR PATTERN OR CORRELATES SCORE	OBSERVER ASSESSMENTS		
	X_o	Y_o	Z_o
X_o..........		.07	.32
Y_o..........			.62
111 X_{co}......	.15	−.13	.01
111 Y_{co}......	.11	.05	.16
111 Z_{co}......	.18	−.11	.07
143 X_{co}......	.15	−.08	.01
143 Y_{co}......	−.09	.01	.21
143 Z_{co}......	.05	.08	.22
111 R_{co}......	.19	−.10	−.04
111 R_{1co}.....	.05	−.12	−.12
111 Q_{co}......	.10	.10	−.09
111 B_{co}......	−.34	.25	−.02
111 I_{co}......	.13	−.13	.05
111 S_{co}......	.10	.02	−.09

Practice teaching course marks also were made available to the Study for the student-teachers who had completed the Schedule. These marks, reflecting observation data obtained when the teachers-to-be were taking their apprentice teaching, correlated with the assessments of classroom behavior made by trained observers following employment of the teachers to the extent of .09 with X_o, .29 with Y_o, and .30 with Z_o. In view of the similarity of the basic data, this is an anticipated but nevertheless pertinent finding. Insofar as these data are concerned, practice teaching marks in the institution involved apparently did a fairly good job of describing the teacher's future behavior with respect to systematic and stimulating characteristics, but were less successful with regard to predicting understanding, friendly teacher relations with the pupils.

A STUDY OF LONG-TERM PREDICTIVE VALIDITY WITH POSITIVE MOTIVATION

A second study of elementary teachers was made with interests centered on predictive validity, in this case under conditions which were intended to simulate the employment situation.

The subjects in this study were applicants for positions in a public school system. All of them had survived an original screening consisting of a comprehensive written examination covering professional information as it related to the elementary school. At the time of submitting to oral examination, the teachers were provided with a copy of the Schedule and asked to complete it, sign it, and return it to the personnel office of the school system. The teacher-applicants were not told that their responses would be taken into consideration in the selection process, but neither were they given any indication to the contrary. It seems reasonable to assume that, under these conditions, the applicants would tend to approach the task of completing the Schedule with the same seriousness and purpose in mind as they would in approaching other aspects of the selection procedure.

Approximately 300 teachers completed the Schedule under these conditions, and of those who survived the oral selection examination and were employed by the school system, 97 teachers were available *two years later for observation*. Assessments were made of these teachers, following the procedure described in chapter 4, by trained observers of the Study, and the earlier-obtained scores were analyzed in relation to these observer assessments.

Table 51 provides a comparison of the 97 teachers who completed the Schedule at the time of the oral examination for employment and the teachers comprising the elementary Basic Analysis Sample. The two groups do not differ greatly with respect to assessments on patterns X_o, Y_o, and Z_o, although the mean scores of the experimental group are below those of the Basic Analysis Sample, particularly for X_o. Several significant differences are apparent when the Schedule scores of these 97 teachers are compared with those of the Basic Analysis group. The mean X_{co} score of the experimental group is substantially above that of the already-employed (Basic Analysis) teachers, while the Y_{co} mean score is lower for the experimental group. There is a suggestion that the Schedule items may be answered in such a way as to reflect the *response-*

set of the teacher, thus permitting teachers who felt, for example, that they should appear outgoing, permissive, and friendly, to answer the items so as to make themselves seem more like the model for pattern *X* than they really are. In reviewing the scores, it will be noted that the applicants-for-employment group does show higher means with respect to characteristics which related to "permissive" current emphases in elementary school teaching, including R_{co}, R_{1co}, and $-B_{co}$ as well as X_{co}. Whether the applicants really were this way or merely were trying to make themselves appear as such is not possible to determine. It also may be noted that these applicants showed significantly higher mean

TABLE 51

Composite Observer Assessments and Schedule Scores of a Group of 97 Elementary Teachers Who Completed the Schedule at Time of Selection for Employment Compared with Data for Basic Analysis Sample Elementary Teachers

Behavior Pattern or Correlates Score	97 Teachers Who Completed Inventory at Time of Screening for Employment		Elementary Basic Analysis Sample ($N = 978$)	
	Mean	σ	Mean	σ
X_o	48.6	10.8	50.7	9.0
Y_o	50.1	9.9	50.5	8.9
Z_o	49.6	88.6	50.7	8.4
111 X_{co}	59.5	13.4	51.2	15.6
111 Y_{co}	27.3	8.3	30.9	9.0
111 Z_{co}	46.8	10.1	44.4	11.4
111 R_{co}	43.2	14.6	40.6	15.2
111 R_{1co}	36.5	11.7	32.9	11.2
111 Q_{co}	33.4	10.8	32.6	9.8
111 B_{co}	17.6	7.4	22.7	9.4
111 I_{co}	44.5	7.2	42.0	7.5
111 S_{co}	47.7	10.7	43.0	9.8

scores on the scales which purport to estimate verbal comprehension (I_{co}) and emotional stability (S_{co}). This might be expected in light of the selection process in operation.

Table 52 shows the correlations between the Schedule scores of the 97 applicants and their assessments two years later in the classrooms. The obtained coefficients are low, although positive, ranging from .04 to .22 for X_oX_{co}, Y_oY_{co}, Z_oZ_{co}. Actually, the best single predictor of X_o over the two-year period was the Scoring Key I_{co}, measuring verbal understanding, the same being true for pattern Z_o. Scoring Key Y_{co} was the best single predictor of pattern Y_o.

Selection examination scores, both written and oral, also were available for the teachers comprising this group. The correlations with observer assessments of the various patterns of classroom behavior ranged

TABLE 52

Correlation Coefficients between Composite Observer
Assessments X_o, Y_o, and Z_o and Schedule Scores for
97 Teachers Who Completed the Schedule at
Time of Selection for Employment

BEHAVIOR PATTERN OR CORRELATES SCORE	OBSERVER ASSESSMENTS		
	X_o	Y_o	Z_o
X_o..........		.40	.54
Y_o..........			.47
111 X_{co}......	.04	−.01	.06
111 Y_{co}......	−.10	.22	.15
111 Z_{co}......	.06	.15	.10
143 X_{co}......	.07	.08	.02
143 Y_{co}......	.05	.21	.09
143 Z_{co}......	−.07	.17	.16
111 R_{co}......	−.09	−.04	−.02
111 R_{1co}.....	−.10	.02	.00
111 Q_{co}......	−.09	.02	−.06
111 B_{co}......	.01	.10	−.04
111 I_{co}......	.22	.12	.25
111 S_{co}......	−.16	−.09	−.06

from .07 to .21. In general, they seemed to be achieving approximately
the same goals as the Schedule, measured against the criterion of observer assessments of classroom behaviors.

In this study of administration of the Teacher Characteristics Schedule under incentive conditions and with criterion data obtained after a
long intervening period (two years), the obtained correlations, while
mostly positive, were substantially lower than those relative to concurrent validation. As in the previous study, it seems possible that the
correlations reported are underestimates of the relationships between
the several predictor variables and the observation data, as a result of
the exclusion of teachers who did not survive the selection process.

COMPARISON OF CONCURRENT AND PREDICTIVE VALIDITY OF SCORING
KEYS X_{co}, Y_{co}, AND Z_{co} FOR A GROUP OF SECONDARY TEACHERS

Data for a group of 99 secondary teachers made possible the comparison of correlation coefficients between Schedule scores and observer
assessments of X_o, Y_o, and Z_o obtained on two occasions twenty months
apart. The obtained correlations between Schedule scores and original
observations may be regarded as concurrent validity coefficients, and
those between the Schedule scores and assessments obtained roughly
two years later as predictive validity coefficients.

Table 53 provides a description of the experimental group of 99

TABLE 53

Means and Standard Deviations of Teacher
Characteristics Schedule Scores for 99
Secondary Teachers Who Were
Observed on Two Occasions
Twenty Months Apart

CORRELATES SCORE	99 TEACHERS IN GROUP OBSERVED TWICE		SECONDARY BASIC ANALYSIS SAMPLE	
	M	σ	M	σ
100 X_{co}.....	39.9	7.2	36.8	8.5
100 Y_{co}.....	32.9	7.8	34.2	7.6
100 Z_{co}.....	29.1	6.0	28.0	6.4
100 R_{co}.....	43.8	12.1	40.2	13.0
100 R_{1co}....	40.0	11.6	34.7	12.6
100 Q_{co}.....	34.2	8.6	31.4	8.0
100 B_{co}.....	40.2	17.6	51.9	15.4
100 I_{co}.....	40.3	9.2	40.1	9.1
100 S_{co}.....	27.1	4.8	27.3	4.9

teachers from the standpoint of the Schedule scores. Differences between the mean scores earned by this group and those of the secondary
Basic Analysis Sample are variable. The groups appeared to be approximately alike with respect to verbal understanding (I_{co}) and emotional
stability (S_{co}), but there is some indication of more favorable attitudes (toward pupils, school personnel, and democratic classroom procedures), more permissive educational viewpoints, and, in general,
more child-centered behavior on the part of the experimental group as
compared with the Basic Analysis Sample.

TABLE 54

Correlations of Teacher Characteristics Schedule Scores with Behavior
Assessments Obtained Concurrently and Twenty Months Later

(Secondary Teachers, $N=99$)

CORRELATES SCORE	OBSERVER ASSESSMENT OF TEACHER CLASSROOM BEHAVIOR					
	X_o		Y_o		Z_o	
	First Assessment	Second Assessment	First Assessment	Second Assessment	First Assessment	Second Assessment
100 X_{co}	.22	.11	−.08	−.07	.03	.05
100 Y_{co}	−.10	.01	.25	.21	−.05	−.05
100 Z_{co}	−.05	−.04	.07	.05	.26	.37
100 R_{co}	.03	−.06	−.18	−.12	.03	.03
100 R_{1co}	.02	−.10	−.14	−.10	.04	.07
100 Q_{co}	−.10	−.18	−.04	−.15	−.04	−.05
100 B_{co}	.02	.04	.06	.03	.07	.03
100 I_{co}	.09	.03	−.10	−.01	.05	.05
100 S_{co}	−.07	−.10	−.16	−.27	.04	.03

The obtained correlation coefficients appear in Table 54. The correlation between X_{co} and X_o scores falls off from .22 for the first assessment to .11 for the second assessment, but in the case of $Y_{co}Y_o$ and $Z_{co}Z_o$ the relationships are similar and, in fact, there is an increase from first to second assessment with respect to the correlation involving pattern Z.

In interpreting these data, a word of caution is appropriate. The same observer assessed these teachers on both occasions. Although this observer saw several hundred teachers in the twenty-month interim, it is impossible to say that there was no contamination of the second observation by the first. Nevertheless, it is worth noting that in this case, which is the only study of predictive validity that was conducted with secondary teachers, the correlations of the scores with the criteria are of approximately the same order on the two occasions. The situation may be considered one of neutral motivation.

STUDIES OF CONCURRENT VALIDITY GENERALIZATION OF X_{co}, Y_{co}, AND Z_{co} SCORING KEYS

Validity generalization was described in chapter 2 as involving the applicability of validity data drawn from a sample of one population to a sample of a different population, with the criterion measure remaining the same. In the investigation reported here, the Schedule scoring keys derived from certain samples of teacher groups were applied to samples of teachers representing other groups, and the X_oX_{co}, Y_oY_{co}, and Z_oZ_{co} correlations were computed.

With regard to validity generalization, one normally would expect scoring keys to maintain their validity best when they are applied either to samples of the same population from which they were derived or to samples of similar populations. Validity coefficients might be expected to generalize least to populations which differ markedly from the response analysis group. Data reported in earlier tables relative to concurrent cross validity and concurrent hold-out sample validity may be used as standards for evaluating the present results.

Table 55 shows the correlations obtained between assessments of teacher behavior and Schedule scores when the scoring keys were applied to samples of populations other than those from which the keys were derived.

While the range of the correlations is wide, it is of some interest to find that they are predominantly positive in spite of the differences in general character between some of the populations from which the keys were derived and those for which they were employed for predictive purposes in this set of studies.

TABLE 55

Correlations between Assessments of Teacher Behaviors X_o, Y_o, and Z_o and
Schedule Scores X_{co}, Y_{co}, and Z_{co} Yielded by Various Scoring Keys
Applied to Samples of Populations *Other* than Those
from Which the Keys Were Derived

TEACHER GROUP ON WHICH X_{co}, Y_{co}, Z_{co} SCORING KEYS BASED	TEACHER GROUP EMPLOYED IN COMPUTING OBSERVER ASSESSMENT-SCHEDULE SCORE CORRELATIONS	CORRELATED VARIABLES		
		X_oX_{co}	Y_oY_{co}	Z_oZ_{co}
Grades 1–4 women ($N=621$)	Grades 5–6 women ($N=97$)	.33	.03	.22
	Grades 3–6 men ($N=122$)	.20	.18	.06
Grades 1–2 women ($N=190$)	Grades 3–4 women ($N=537$)	.16	.01	.01
	Grades 3–6 men and women ($N=726$).	.16	.02	.06
Grades 5–6 women and 3–6 men ($N=203$)	Grades 1–2 women ($N=220$)	.06	.12	.12
	Grades 3–4 women ($N=537$)	.12	.03	.13
Grades 3–4 women ($N=431$)	Grades 1–2 women ($N=220$)	.15	.14	.06
	Grades 5–6 women ($N=97$)	.12	.08	.23
	Grades 5–6 men and women ($N=184$).	.10	.07	.19
Grades 5–6 women ($N=97$)	Grades 1–2 women ($N=220$)	.12	.08	.08
	Grades 3–4 women ($N=537$)	.12	.04	.06
	Grades 5–6 men ($N=87$)	.29	.06	.15
Grades 3–6 women ($N=528$)	Grades 1–2 women ($N=220$)	.13	.16	.04
	Grades 5–6 men ($N=87$)	.13	.12	.15
Grades 1–6 women ($N=718$)	Grades 5–6 men ($N=87$)	.26	.06	.16
Grades 5–6 men ($N=87$)	Grades 1–2 women ($N=220$)	.15	−.23	.00
	Grades 3–4 women ($N=537$)	.13	.03	.09
	Grades 5–6 women ($N=97$)	.22	.11	.11
Mathematics, science, English, social studies—men and women ($N=951$)	Business Education—men and women ($N=125$)	.18	−.02	.06
	Foreign Language—men and women ($N=116$)	.28	.07	.21
Mathematics—men and women ($N=209$)	Science—men and women ($N=268$)	.26	.32	.35
English—men and women ($N=281$)	Social Studies—men and women ($N=244$)	.48	.46	.23

The validity of a device usually is specific to the kind of population used in the original analyses. Nevertheless, many of the Schedule scoring keys seem to show a certain degree of generalizability.

STUDIES OF VALIDITY EXTENSION OF X_{co}, Y_{co}, AND Z_{co} SCORING KEYS

As explained in chapter 2, validity extension is involved when the scoring keys derived from a sample of one population are applied to another sample, drawn from a different population and *a different criterion measure is used*. In the studies reported in this section, principals' ratings of teachers—criterion data quite different from the assessments of trained observers which had been used in the derivation of the correlates keys—were employed.

The first investigation of validity extension involved a sample of teachers who had taken the National Teacher Examinations several years earlier and whose responses to professional educational information items had been analyzed by the writer in a comparison of item-analysis data with the employment of internal and external criteria [6]. Assessments of these teachers had been obtained from their school principals at the time of the earlier research, such assessments relating to "pupil behaviors in teacher's class," "teacher's personal-social behavior," "teacher's intellectual-educational background," and "over-all, or general, teaching performance."

Three years later, copies of the Schedule were sent to the same teachers with the request that they mark their responses to the items and return the Schedule to the offices of the Study. Returns were obtained from a total of 113 teachers, principally from the Eastern seaboard. Correlation coefficients were computed between various scores yielded by the Schedule and evaluations provided earlier by the teachers' principals. None of the obtained correlation coefficients was large enough to merit comment other than of its probable insignificance. Table 56 presents the coefficients obtained between certain variables and "general

TABLE 56

Correlations of Teacher Characteristics Schedule Scores and NTE Professional Education and Reading Comprehension Scores with Principals' Ratings of General Teaching Effectiveness for a Sample (Mail Sample I) of Public School Teachers

Schedule or Teacher Examination Score	Elementary Teachers ($N=49$)	Grades 7–8 Teachers ($N=26$)	Grades 9–12 Teachers ($N=38$)	Elementary and Secondary Teachers ($N=113$)
Schedule scores				
99 X_{co}	.03	.11	−.08	.01
99 Y_{co}	.07	.42	.14	.18
99 Z_{co}	.16	.10	−.04	.07
99 R_{co}	.01	.02	.07	.01
99 B_{co}	.02	.05	.01	.04
99 I_{co}	.03	−.06	.01	.01
99 S_{co}	−.03	.05	−.11	−.07
NTE test scores				
Professional information	.07	.10	−.16	−.01
Verbal comprehension	.08	−.24	−.09	−.06

teaching effectiveness" as judged by the principal. In the light of the nonsignificant correlations also obtained between the criterion (principals' ratings) and scores on well-established professional information and verbal comprehension tests, there is the strong suggestion that the *criterion data were so invalid and unreliable* (so affected by deficiency and contamination factors) as to render them useless, thus obviating any possibility of prediction.

A second study of validity extension was designed with special attention to obtaining *discriminating* assessments of teacher performance from school principals who were presumed to be untrained in observation and assessment techniques.

Six hundred school principals, from schools selected to be approximately representative of those throughout the United States,[6] were requested by mail to nominate (using a procedure that did not require actual naming of the teacher) teachers who were "outstandingly superior" and "notably poor" compared with the typical or average teacher. The 600 principals consisted of three groups: (1) 200 elementary school principals, each of whom was asked to nominate one superior and one poor teacher from his school; (2) 200 high school principals, each required to nominate one superior and one poor teacher in the fields of mathematics and/or science; and (3) 200 high school principals, each asked to nominate one superior and one poor teacher in the fields of English and/or social studies. The covering letter explained that if the principal did not feel there was a teacher in his school who qualified as outstanding in either direction, no nomination should be made.

After having identified in his own mind such superior and poor teachers, the principal was asked to perform two further services—(1) on special nomination cards which were provided (a white card for the superior teacher and a yellow card for the poor teacher), to rank the outstanding characteristics of each teacher and return the cards to the Study offices; and (2) to give a packet to each teacher who was nominated, taking care to see that the code number on the packet agreed with the code number on the card that was used for nominating and assessing the particular teacher.

The packets contained copies of a covering letter to the teacher, the Schedule and answer sheet, a special pencil for marking the answer sheet, and a stamped envelope for return of the answer sheet to the Study.

In the principal's ranking of the outstanding characteristics of the teachers, four categories of teacher behavior were employed: (*a*) understanding, kindly teacher behavior *vs.* aloof, harsh, intolerant teacher behavior; (*b*) systematic, responsible teacher behavior *vs.* unplanned, irresponsible teacher behavior; (*c*) ability to teach subject matter *vs.*

---

[6] Sampling of the principals was accomplished through the use of sampling frames consisting of the directories of members of the National Association of Elementary School Principals and the National Association of Secondary-School Principals.

lack of subject-matter teaching ability; and (*d*) outstandingly superior over-all teacher behavior *vs.* notably poor over-all teacher behavior. The first two of these classes of criteria bear at least verbal resemblance to Classroom Behavior Patterns X_o and Y_o, for which the X_{co} and Y_{co} Scoring Keys were originally developed. However, it should be noted that in this phase of the Study, school principals rather than trained observers made the assessments and that the assessment procedure was markedly different.

For purposes of analysis, the teachers were classified into "superior" and "poor" subgroups with respect to each of the four criteria named.

Teachers included in the superior group with respect to understanding, kindly teacher behavior were those nominated by their principals as superior and who were, in addition, those for whom the principals claimed that understanding and kindliness were the *most* outstanding of all their characteristics. Similarly, the poor group was made up of teachers who had been nominated as poor and for whom, in addition, it was claimed that such traits as aloofness, intolerance, and harshness were the most pronounced of all their characteristics. The superior and poor teacher groups for the criteria relating to "systematic, responsible behavior" and "ability to teach subject matter" were obtained through a similar procedure. The superior and poor groups of teachers with regard to the over-all teacher behavior criterion were formed simply by separating the white (superior) and yellow (poor) nomination cards.

The complete report of this study has been published elsewhere [7] and the data will be only summarized here, together with presentation of tables providing the basic comparisons. Tables 57, 58, and 59 show the scores of elementary, mathematics-science, and English–social studies teachers on the Schedule, classified according to principals' judgments of superiority or inferiority with regard to the areas of behavior referred to above. Table 60 provides a quick-glance summary of the differences between means which were significant at the .05 level and indicates the scoring keys that yielded significant differences.

It may be noted that a number of scoring keys appear to distinguish between the groups designated as superior and poor. Thirty-one significant differences (exclusive of those relating to the V_{co} Key) in mean score were found to be significant at or beyond the .05 level, whereas the expected number might be six. Sixteen of the significant differences were with respect to elementary teachers, seven to mathematics-science teachers, and eight to English–social studies teachers. The criteria within which superior and poor groups of teachers were most success-

(*Text continued on page 265.*)

TABLE 57

Means and Standard Deviations of Teacher Characteristics Schedule Scores (111_{co} Scoring Keys) of Elementary Teachers (Mail Sample 2) Judged by Their Principals To Be Outstandingly Superior or Notably Poor

CLASSIFICATION	N	Teacher Characteristics Schedule Score																				
		X_{co}		Y_{co}		Z_{co}		R_{co}		R_{1co}		Q_{co}		B_{co}		I_{co}		S_{co}		V_{co}	
		M	σ	M	σ	M	σ	M	σ	M	σ	M	σ	M	σ	M	σ	M	σ	M	σ
Understanding teacher behavior																					
Superior	25	52.4*	14.0	34.8*	9.2	45.0*	9.1	40.7*	13.9	33.4*	13.2	33.3	11.4	20.8*	8.1	42.1*	9.0	44.1*	10.4	23.9	3.0
Poor	8	30.6	11.0	29.2	5.9	30.2	8.1	24.0	13.9	23.7	12.7	29.4	9.0	32.7	5.1	35.0	4.7	30.5	10.4	24.0	4.1
Organized, responsible teacher behavior																					
Superior	13	49.5	11.0	34.4*	10.0	43.6	8.6	39.2	13.4	31.9	12.3	31.2	12.7	22.0	7.0	41.1	8.1	41.1	6.8	24.2	2.9
Poor	16	42.5	9.3	28.2	5.0	36.5	9.4	33.1	9.2	28.0	7.2	27.1	8.8	25.1	6.7	39.6	6.4	36.9	6.0	24.0	5.0
Subject-matter teaching																					
Superior	14	48.6	14.5	33.9	9.4	45.1	8.6	38.3	15.1	29.7	13.5	30.6	13.0	23.1	7.6	41.4	7.9	41.4	7.2	23.4	3.5
Poor	4	38.7	11.1	27.2	7.8	35.5	12.4	30.2	8.7	25.0	9.6	31.2	2.5	32.0	7.6	35.7	7.1	31.2	6.1	23.5	2.9
Over-all evaluation of teacher																					
Superior	35	50.1*	14.3	34.1*	8.5	44.6*	9.6	39.1*	13.9	31.9	13.2	31.8	11.7	21.9*	7.7	42.7*	8.6	43.8*	10.7	23.6	3.5
Poor	25	37.4	12.0	27.7	5.8	33.4	9.7	29.6	12.1	26.2	9.8	27.9	9.4	28.7	7.4	37.2	6.1	34.2	8.2	23.5	4.5
Total elementary sample	60	44.9	14.7	31.5	8.1	40.2	11.1	35.2	13.9	29.5	12.2	30.1	11.0	24.6	8.2	40.6	8.1	39.8	10.7	23.7	4.0

* Difference between means of superior and poor groups significant at .05 level.

TABLE 58

Means and Standard Deviations of Teacher Characteristics Schedule Scores (97$_{co}$ Scoring Keys) of Mathematics-Science Teachers (Mail Sample 2) Judged by Their Principals To Be Outstandingly Superior or Notably Poor

CLASSIFICATION	N	TEACHER CHARACTERISTICS SCHEDULE SCORE																		
		X_{co}		Y_{co}		Z_{co}		R_{co}		R_{1co}		Q_{co}		B_{co}		I_{co}		S_{eo}		V_{eo}	
		M	σ	M	σ	M	σ	M	σ	M	σ	M	σ	M	σ	M	σ	M	σ	M	σ
Understanding teacher behavior																					
Superior	31	32.3	4.6	38.1	7.6	32.5	5.7	38.9	10.8	29.4	8.9	30.7	7.4	59.1	9.4	38.1	7.7	27.6	4.3	21.9	4.4
Poor	21	31.8	4.3	35.3	5.7	29.5	4.5	35.1	9.1	25.8	7.1	29.0	8.4	60.3	7.8	36.4	8.6	27.1	4.5	19.6	5.7
Organized, responsible teacher behavior																					
Superior	29	32.3*	4.9	38.6*	6.3	31.9	4.6	35.8	10.4	26.2	9.7	29.4	6.1	61.4	12.3	38.8*	7.0	26.2	4.1	23.8*	5.0
Poor	20	30.4	4.5	34.4	6.3	28.7	6.6	35.6	9.6	28.0	9.2	28.7	7.0	56.4	12.5	31.4	9.4	28.1	3.5	18.8	6.1
Subject-matter teaching																					
Superior	47	33.1	5.2	38.4	6.4	32.5*	4.7	37.7	10.9	28.1	9.9	30.0	7.0	60.9	12.4	38.2	7.6	27.0	4.4	23.2*	4.6
Poor	12	30.5	5.2	34.7	4.0	28.6	6.3	37.5	8.7	25.7	10.9	31.7	5.7	61.2	13.8	34.2	8.5	26.7	3.9	19.6	4.5
Over-all evaluation of teacher																					
Superior	76	32.5*	5.1	38.1*	6.7	31.9*	5.1	36.8	11.4	27.2	9.8	29.5	7.1	60.8	11.8	37.6*	8.2	27.1	4.6	22.8*	4.5
Poor	62	30.6	4.6	35.6	5.8	29.1	6.0	34.7	9.5	27.0	9.6	29.4	7.5	59.8	11.6	34.2	9.0	26.7	4.4	20.1	5.6
Total mathematics-science sample	138	31.7	5.0	37.0	6.4	30.6	5.7	35.9	10.6	27.2	9.7	29.5	7.3	60.4	11.7	36.1	8.7	26.9	4.5	21.6	5.0

* Difference between means of superior and poor groups significant at .05 level.

TABLE 59

Means and Standard Deviations of the Teacher Characteristics Schedule Scores (98$_{co}$ Scoring Keys) of English–Social Studies Teachers (Mail Sample 2) Judged by Their Principals To Be Outstandingly Superior or Notably Poor

CLASSIFICATION	N	TEACHER CHARACTERISTICS SCHEDULE SCORE																		
		X_{co}		Y_{co}		Z_{co}		R_{co}		R_{Lco}		Q_{co}		B_{co}		I_{co}		S_{co}		V_{co}	
		M	σ	M	σ	M	σ	M	σ	M	σ	M	σ	M	σ	M	σ	M	σ	M	σ
Understanding teacher behavior																					
Superior	34	36.1	8.2	29.3	8.4	32.3	6.1	42.6	12.1	40.2	10.5	30.7	7.9	44.6	13.5	44.5	9.2	24.4	5.1	22.7	4.0
Poor	15	30.3	8.2	27.3	11.6	28.0	6.3	38.3	8.4	33.3	12.2	26.9	9.2	47.8	14.6	45.5	16.6	29.0	19.2	29.9	18.5
Organized, responsible teacher behavior																					
Superior	24	35.0	7.2	29.9	6.8	31.3	6.2	44.3*	13.0	40.5	10.8	32.7	9.1	47.5	12.8	42.5	9.8	23.0	4.9	22.0	4.6
Poor	19	32.5	8.1	27.2	10.7	30.7	4.7	35.7	12.5	35.8	12.0	29.6	7.4	48.7	15.3	40.5	8.6	25.3	4.6	22.6	5.9
Subject-matter teaching																					
Superior	33	34.7	7.6	31.4	8.7	32.3*	5.1	43.6	10.0	41.7	7.8	32.9	7.4	45.7	10.5	44.2	8.1	22.9	5.3	22.7	4.5
Poor	25	31.0	11.9	26.8	18.2	27.1	9.1	37.9	14.5	35.6	14.0	28.7	8.5	39.9	18.3	38.0	13.4	23.0	8.3	24.5	16.4
Over-all evaluation of teacher																					
Superior	76	36.3*	7.7	29.6	8.4	32.7*	5.6	43.4*	11.0	41.0*	9.2	31.0*	7.3	44.3	12.1	43.9*	8.1	23.9	4.9	22.5	4.4
Poor	65	29.1	11.2	29.5	16.1	26.7	9.4	35.4	14.3	32.5	14.2	28.0	10.2	46.3	19.2	39.4	16.2	25.0	14.8	24.7	17.5
Total English-social studies sample	141	33.0	10.1	29.6	12.6	30.0	8.1	39.7	13.3	37.1	12.5	29.6	8.9	45.2	15.8	41.8	12.7	24.4	10.7	23.5	12.4

* Difference between means of superior and poor groups significant at .05 level.

TABLE 60

Summary of Differences between Mean Teacher Characteristics Schedule Scores of Teachers Judged by Their Principals To Be Outstandingly Superior or Notably Poor

Criterion	Teacher Sample	Teacher Characteristics Schedule Keys Showing Difference between Superior and Poor Groups Significant at .05 Level
Understanding, friendly teacher behavior	(1) Elementary...............	$X_{co}, Y_{co}, Z_{co}, R_{co}, R_{1co}, B_{co}, I_{co}, S_{co}$
	(2) Mathematics-science.....	
	(3) English-social studies.....	
Organized, responsible teacher behavior	(1) Elementary...............	Y_{co}
	(2) Mathematics-science.....	Y_{co}, I_{co}, V_{co}
	(3) English-social studies.....	R_{co}
Subject-matter teaching ability	(1) Elementary...............	$Z_{co},$
	(2) Mathematics-science.....	Z_{co}, V_{co}
	(3) English-social studies.....	
Over-all teaching effectiveness	(1) Elementary...............	$X_{co}, Y_{co}, Z_{co}, R_{co}, B_{co}, I_{co}, S_{co}$
	(2) Mathematics-science.....	$X_{co}, Y_{co}, Z_{co}, I_{co}, V_{co}$
	(3) English-social studies.....	$X_{co}, Z_{co}, R_{40}, R_{1co}, Q_{co}, I_{co}$

fully identified by the scoring keys were "understanding teacher behavior" and "over-all evaluation" for elementary teachers, "organized, responsible teacher behaviors" and "over-all evaluation" for mathematics-science teachers, and "over-all evaluation" for the English–social studies teachers.

Significant differences were most frequently associated with Z_{co} (stimulating teacher behavior), Y_{co} (businesslike teacher behavior), I_{co} (verbal understanding), X_{co} (understanding, friendly teacher behavior), and R_{co} (favorable teacher opinions of pupils). For these groups of teachers at least, the keys seem to be rather successful in identifying subgroups judged by their principals to be outstandingly superior or notably poor.

An interesting by-product of the study of validity extension was insight gained regarding the teacher qualities that principals apparently associate with teaching superiority and poorness.

Of elementary teachers nominated by their principals as outstandingly superior, the outstanding characteristics of such teachers were most frequently said to be "understanding, kindly" classroom behavior. Approximately 70 percent of the superior teachers were said to have this as their best trait, suggesting that the principals' conceptualization of the superior elementary teacher may be heavily influenced by outgoing, friendly classroom behavior. Of the elementary teachers nominated as notably poor, the poorest traits of such teachers were most frequently said to be "lack of system, organization, and responsibility." Some 68 percent of the poor teachers were said to be most notably characterized by this lack, suggesting that the principals' conceptualization of the poor elementary teacher is heavily influenced by unplanned, slipshod, irresponsible classroom behavior.

Among the mathematics-science teachers, 61 percent of those nominated as superior were said to have as their outstanding characteristic "ability to teach subject matter." Regarding the poor mathematics-science teachers, 36 percent of the principals named "lack of system, organization, and responsibility" as the teacher's poorest characteristic. It is suggested, then, that the principals' idea of the superior mathematics-science teacher is heavily influenced by "subject-matter teaching ability" and the principals' concept of the poor mathematics-science teacher is most influenced by "lack of system and organization."

Among the superior English–social studies teachers, the principals named "understanding, kindly" teacher behavior and "subject-matter teaching ability" as their most pronounced characteristics, each set of characteristics being ascribed to 47 percent of the superior teachers. "Lack of subject-matter teaching ability" and "lack of system and organization" (36 percent and 34 percent, respectively) were the most frequently named traits of the English–social studies teachers nominated as being poor. Principals' concepts of superior English–social studies teachers seemed, thus, to be dominated by outgoing, friendly teacher behavior and subject-matter competence, and their ideas of poor English–social studies teachers seemed to be most influenced by lack of teaching ability and lack of organization and system.

Predictive Validity Extension of the X_{co}, Y_{co}, and Z_{co} Scoring Keys Employing the Criterion of Pupil Change

In chapter 2, notice was taken of "change in pupil behavior" as a criterion of teacher behavior, and some of the difficulties involved in its use were considered. Because of these difficulties, pupil-change measures were set aside in favor of trained observers' assessments of classroom behavior in the major portion of research undertaken by the Study.

The criterion of pupil change was not completely ignored, however, although certain obstacles prevented completion of this phase of the research and left the Study without results or conclusions to report for this criterion. The investigation which was begun, but not completed, was one of the several investigations of validity extension of the X_{co}, Y_{co}, and Z_{co} Scoring Keys of the Schedule. It was designed to analyze the relationships between changes in measurable pupil behaviors taking place during a child's experience with a teacher and teacher classroom behavior as estimated from assessments of trained observers and, in particular, estimates derived from correlates scores of the Schedule.

This study was undertaken in a large city school system with the classes of teachers who previously had been assessed by the Study's observers and who also had completed the Schedule. Essentially, the procedure consisted of administering the specially constructed Omnibus Pupil Inquiry to pupils in the classes of these third- and fourth-grade teachers during the first week of school in September 1953 and readministration of the same instrument to the same classes during the last week of the semester in January 1954. In view of the fact that it was not possible to match the pupils in the various classes at the beginning of the experiment with respect to relevant control variables, approximate statistical control of those conditions was sought through before-after measurement procedure and employment of analysis of covariance.

A number of unexpected difficulties, including administrative and personnel problems, prevented the pursuit of this research to the point of analysis of data. One major stumbling block was the inconclusive nature of pupils' test scores, due to lack of anticipated minimum reading ability and the confounding of this condition with responses to all sections of the instrument, including reading comprehension, mechanics of English expression, arithmetic skills, social studies knowledge, health and science knowledge, study habits, social attitudes and adjustment, and emotional adjustment. Apparently the tryout samples employed in item analyses during construction of the instrument had been more highly selected from the standpoint of reading level than the samples of pupils used for the actual research.

It is hoped that a validity extension study of the X_{co}, Y_{co}, and Z_{co} scores of the Schedule may be conducted in the near future.

SUSCEPTIBILITY OF TEACHER CHARACTERISTICS SCHEDULE CORRELATES SCORES TO FALSIFICATION

A danger in the use of inventory responses, as mentioned at several points in the preceding discussion, lies in their susceptibility to falsification or "faking." It should be explained that this type of falsification may not actually involve a dishonest response on the part of the respondent, but rather may be due to a personal tendency, apparently rather deeply imbedded in his response repertoire, to attempt to give a good impression of himself. Thus, falsification as here used may refer either to the intentional giving of false answers which are advantageous to the respondent or to a general *tendency*, perhaps unintentional, to *give socially acceptable answers*.

The susceptibility of the direct-inquiry type of materials to such a source of invalidity is obvious and already has been noted. Earlier discussion has indicated that the attempt to develop correlates scoring keys for such characteristics as teacher attitudes and teachers' educational viewpoints was undertaken primarily to alleviate this difficulty. The development of the V_{ei} and V_{co} Scoring Keys was intended to provide some indication of the respondent's tendency to give self-enhancing and socially acceptable responses.

Still another approach to the problem, undertaken by the Study, was research with a scoring key designated as a Faking-Adjusted Key. The elementary teacher Faking-Adjusted Key which was employed for this purpose was developed by *excluding* from the basic elementary teacher keys for X_{co}, Y_{co}, and Z_{co} those responses which (*a*) correlated significantly with V_{ei} (validity of response, as described in chapter 5) and/or (*b*) items involving responses judged by a panel of researchers well acquainted with personality inventories to be "desirable" or particularly socially acceptable.

The use of these adaptations of the 111_{co} Scoring Keys for reflecting Patterns X_o, Y_o, and Z_o led to somewhat reduced reliability (based upon positive-negative response correlations) and very slightly increased validity when applied to the hold-out and other validity samples. Reliability was reduced to the extent of .07 for X_{co}, .13 for Y_{co}, and .08 for Z_{co}. Use of the Faking-Adjusted Keys with other samples employed in validation studies (111_{fa} and 99_{fa} adaptations) resulted in slight but statistically insignificant increases in the validity coefficients. In a few instances, the Faking-Adjusted Z_{co} Scoring Keys showed improvements in validity coefficients up to .08, but for X_{co} and Y_{co} the amount of shift was very small.

A systematic study of certain items selected from the Schedule (and also involving other inventories purporting to estimate attitudes and personal traits) was recently undertaken by Dr. M. Steven Sheldon. In Sheldon's studies, subjects were administered the items on two occasions, once under so-called standard conditions, and once with the direction to falsify their responses. Among the several sets of directions employed in the over-all study were instructions to falsify answers to appear more "traditional" with respect to educational values, to appear more "progressive," and simply to fake responses to make the best possible impression (without indication of a specific direction). Random samples of subjects were employed under the various conditions of the investigation, and a number of analyses of variance were undertaken. Some results are presented in Table 61. Of principal interest was the finding that (employing items selected from the secondary teacher booklets of the Schedule and applying the 100 X_{co}, 100 Y_{co}, and 100 Z_{co} Scoring Keys) the X_{co} scores were capable of falsification when direction in which the faking should proceed was specified, but Y_{co} and Z_{co} scores apparently were not materially affected. When the subjects simply were instructed to falsify responses to give the best possible impression of themselves (without specific direction), there appeared to be no important changes in scores as compared with those obtained under standard conditions.

In summary, it seems probable that although the scores yielded by the Schedule keys are not immune to the effects of response sets toward falsification or giving socially acceptable responses, so long as the respondent is not given specific direction but is left to his own orientation, the effects will not be marked.

TABLE 61

Summary of Mean Differences in X_{co}, Y_{co}, and Z_{co} Teacher Characteristics Schedule Scores* of Secondary Teaching Candidates When Responding under (a) Standard Conditions and (b) Instructions To Falsify Their Responses†

RESPONDING SETS COMPARED	SUB-SAMPLE N	TEACHER CHARACTERISTICS SCHEDULE SCORES					
		X_{co}		Y_{co}		Z_{co}	
		Diff. in Means	σDiff.	Diff. in Means	σDiff.	Diff. in Means	σDiff.
"Progressive" and standard.........	24	5.17‡	1.44	.21	1.16	2.04	1.06
"Traditional" and standard.........	24	-4.25‡	1.44	1.75	1.16	-1.63	1.06
"Applying for job" and standard....	24	1.42	1.44	0.00	1.16	1.46	1.06

* Items employed in this study were the verbal items common to the MS and SE forms of the Schedule (picture items omitted) which contained responses employed in the 100 X_{co}, 100 Y_{co}, or 100 Z_{co} Scoring Keys. These items were reproduced in a separate booklet, changing somewhat the stimulus situation provided by use of the complete 300-item booklets.

† The subjects responded to the items twice, once under standard conditions ("Mark response which best applies") and once with instructions to falsify responses. One-third of the total sample was instructed to falsify responses to appear "progressive," one-third to falsify responses to appear "traditional," and one-third to falsify simply to give best possible impression to prospective employer.

‡ t ratio significant at .05 level.

In employing the scores, a desirable practice probably would be to scrutinize the V_{ci} (rather than the V_{co}) scores, and intensify the investigation of individuals whose scores with respect to validity of response are one or more standard deviations below the mean. No attempts have been made to employ the V scores as a suppressor variable. The V_{ci} scores, however, may be employed as a check or control in the manner just suggested, with the exercise of greater caution in interpreting the Schedule scores of individuals whose V_{ci} scores are particularly low.

Intercorrelations among Schedule Scores, Teacher Behavior Assessments, and Other Variables

Tables 62 through 71 summarize correlational data pertaining to the Teacher Characteristics Schedule scores as they are viewed from the standpoint of their association with (a) observers' assessments, (b) certain other evaluations of teacher performance, and (c) other Schedule scores of twenty-one different samples of teachers. The variables involved in the intercorrelations, and descriptions of the samples to which the correlations apply, are given in the legend preceding this set of tables.

Attempts at improving the prediction of Patterns X_o, Y_o, and Z_o by the introduction of other correlates scores in combination with X_{co}, Y_{co}, and Z_{co} met with little success. In elementary Hold-Out Sample 1, for example, by employing a combination of X_{co} and Z_{co} scores to predict observers' assessments of friendly, understanding classroom behavior, X_o, the multiple R was found to be only .02 higher (.45) than the zero order correlation $X_{co}X_o$.

Similarly, the multiple correlation coefficient involving both Y_{co} and Z_{co} scores was only slightly higher than the zero order $Z_{co}Z_o$ correlation in predicting stimulating classroom behavior, Z_o.

The contribution of scores other than Y_{co} to the prediction of Y_o was negligible. Characteristics R_{co}, R_{1co}, Q_{co}, B_{co}, I_{co}, and S_{co} added very little to the prediction of either X_o, Y_o, or Z_o in this sample. The data presented in Tables 62–71 suggest that combination of Schedule scores probably has slight effect on the prediction of classroom behaviors X_o, Y_o, and Z_o.

Study of the elementary and secondary Hold-Out Samples 1 and 2 reveals that, in general, X_{co} and Z_{co} provide the best predictions of friendly, understanding teacher classroom behavior (X_o); that Y_{co} best predicts responsible, businesslike classroom behavior (Y_o); and that Z_{co} yields the best prediction of stimulating, imaginative classroom be-

(Text continued on page 283.)

DESCRIPTIONS OF VARIABLES FOR TABLES 62–71

X_o* TCS understanding, friendly *vs.* aloof, egocentric, restricted teacher behavior (observers' assessment)

Y_o TCS responsible, businesslike, systematic *vs.* unplanned, slipshod, evading teacher behavior (observers' assessment)

Z_o TCS stimulating, imaginative, surgent *vs.* dull, routine teacher behavior (observers' assessment)

P_o TCS alert, initiating, responsible, confident *vs.* apathetic, dependent, obstructive, uncertain *pupil* behavior (observers' assessment)

X_{co}† Understanding, friendly *vs.* aloof teacher behavior (estimated from Schedule correlates)

Y_{co} Responsible *vs.* unplanned teacher behavior (estimated from Schedule correlates)

Z_{co} Stimulating *vs.* dull teacher behavior (estimated from Schedule correlates)

R_{co} Favorable *vs.* unfavorable opinions of pupils (estimated from Schedule correlates)

R_{1co} Favorable *vs.* unfavorable opinions regarding democratic classroom procedures (estimated from Schedule correlates)

Q_{co} Favorable *vs.* Unfavorable opinions of administrative and other school personnel (estimated from Schedule correlates)

B_{co} Academic-centered "traditional" *vs.* "permissive" educational viewpoints (estimated from Schedule correlates)

I_{ci} Verbal reasoning and word recognition (based on a homogeneous set of previously validated vocabulary and verbal analogy items)

I_{co} Verbal reasoning and word recognition (estimated from Schedule correlates)

S_{ci} Emotional adjustment (based on a homogeneous set of previously validated two-choice "typical response" emotionality items)

S_{co} Emotional adjustment (estimated from Schedule correlates)

V_{ci} Validity of Schedule responses (based on a homogeneous set of previously validated items permitting choice of a "common" response and a "socially approved" response)

V_{co} Validity of Schedule responses (estimated from Schedule correlates)

EExp English Expression Test (National Teacher Examinations)

CEx Tot Total of Common Examinations (National Teacher Examinations)

---

* The subscript *o* indicates that scores on this variable are derived from composite assessments of trained observers (individual assessments comprising the composite being based on independent, time-separated observations).

† The subscript *co* indicates that scores on this variable are based upon Schedule responses which are *correlated* with specified criterion scores.

Prof.Inf	Tests of Professional Information *re* Education (National Teacher Examinations)
EdElSch	Education in the Elementary School Test (National Teacher Examinations)
Written Ex	Written Professional Education Test (City Schools Teacher Selections Examination)
Oral Ex	Oral Interview (City Schools Teacher Selection Examination)
Pract. Teach. Mark	Course mark in practice teaching

DESCRIPTIONS OF SAMPLES FOR TABLES 62–71

1. Elementary teachers, Basic Analysis Sample; $N = 834$. (N's of cross-validation samples $= 417$ and 417.)
2. Elementary teachers, Survey Group; $N = 670$.
3. Elementary teachers, Hold-Out Sample 1 from Basic Analysis Study; $N = 144$.
4. Elementary teachers, Hold-Out Sample 2 from Basic Analysis Study; $N = 143$.
5. Elementary teachers, women, Grades 1–6, Special Study Group of individuals inventoried while college seniors and observed three years later following employment; $N = 56$.
6. Elementary teachers, women, Grades 1–6, Special Study Group of teaching candidates inventoried at time of examination and observed following employment; $N = 97$.
7. Elementary teachers, Special Study Group, Mail Sample 1; $N = 49$.
8. Secondary teachers, Basic Analysis Group; $N = 951$. (N's of cross-validation samples $= 476$ and 475.)
9. Secondary teachers, Survey Group; $N = 970$.
10. Secondary teachers, hold-out sample from Basic Analysis Study; $N = 114$.
11. Secondary teachers, hold-out sample from Basic Analysis Study; $N = 99$.
12. Secondary teachers of mathematics and science, Basic Analysis Group; $N = 447$.
13. Secondary teachers of mathematics and science, Survey Group; $N = 481$.
14. Secondary teachers of English and social studies, Basic Analysis Group; $N = 504$.
15. Secondary teachers of English and social studies, Survey Group; $N = 489$.
16. Secondary teachers of business education, Special Study Group; $N = 125$.
17. Secondary teachers of foreign language, Special Study Group, $N = 116$.
18. Secondary teachers, Special Study Group, Mail Sample 1; $N = 38$.
19. Elementary and secondary teachers combined, Basic Analysis Group, $N = 1,785$. (N's of cross-validation samples $= 893$ and 892.)
20. Elementary and secondary teachers combined, Survey Group; $N = 1,640$.
21. Elementary and secondary teachers combined, Special Study Group, Mail Sample 1; $N = 113$.

TABLE 62

Summary of Correlations between "Understanding, Friendly Teacher Behavior" Schedule Scores, X_{co}, and Other Indices of Teacher Characteristics

(See accompanying legend [on pages 271–72] for identification of samples 1–21 and of variables listed in Column 1)

Column groupings:
- **ELEMENTARY TEACHER SAMPLES** — Elem. (111) Scoring Keys: 1, 2*, 3, 4, 5†, 6†; All-T. (99) Scoring Keys: 1, 2*, 7
- **SECONDARY TEACHER SAMPLES** — Secondary (100) Scoring Keys: 8, 9*, 10, 11, 12, 13*, 14, 15*, 16, 17; All-T. (99) Scoring Keys: 15*, 13*, 18
- **EL. & SEC. SAMPLES** — All-T. (99) Scoring Keys: 19, 20*, 21

X_{co} SCORES CORRELATED WITH:	1	2*	3	4	5†	6†	1	2*	7	8	9*	10	11	12	13*	14	15*	16	17	15*	13*	18	19	20*	21
TCS X_{co}	.42‡									.35‡													.27‡		
TCS Y_{co}			.43	.45	.13	.07						.31	.29					.18	.28						
TCS Z_{co}			.12	.16	-.15	.08						-.11	-.09					-.03	.17						
TCS P_{co}			.34	.52	-.08	.02						.18	.02					.01	.05						
TCS V_{co}	.48	.56	.47	.10	.50	.38	.28	.39	.08	-.09	.06	-.14	-.10	-.09	.04	-.12	.10	-.04	-.01	.24	.29	.32	.30	.31	.26
TCS Z_{co}	.80	.81	.82	.86	.54	.28	.75	.42	.58	.54	.45	.54	.36	.54	.56	.53	.48	.56	.55	.73	.31	.66	.74	.47	.64
TCS K_{co}	.79	.79	.78	.76	.21	.64	.79	.79	.74	.74	.67	.74	.65	.69	.70	.75	.67	.70	.69	.76	.50	.57	.78	.70	.68
TCS R_{co}	.73	.78	.72	.72	.06	.59	.79	.80		.73	.67	.74	.64	.70	.68	.75	.67	.69	.66	.77	.61		.79	.73	
TCS Q_{co}	.59	.62	.59	.54	.64	.53	.59	.59		.41	.31	.47	.20	.37	.36	.43	.36	.34	.37	.62	.58		.57	.59	
TCS B_{co}	-.70	-.70	-.78	-.72	-.37	-.49	-.72	-.37	-.72	-.74	-.63	-.72	-.47	-.71	-.70	-.76	-.58	-.67	-.67	-.26	-.63	-.71	-.75	-.41	-.71
TCS I_{ci} or I_{co}	.51	.19	.56	.41	.63	.52	.51	.25	.52	.46	.22	.42	.33	.35	.26	.49	.18	.33	.41	.15	.23	.46	.48	.20	.46
TCS S_{ci} or S_{co}	.77	.32	.78	.75	.72	.71	.65	.26	.60	.26	.07	.41	.10	.32	.14	.34	.07	.16	.44	.09	.17	.54	.59	.18	.57
TCS V_{ci} or V_{co}	-.11	.02	-.11	-.01	-.02	-.29	.16	.04		-.02	.02	-.06	-.19	.00	-.04	-.05	.09	.06	-.14	.05	-.05		-.10	.01	
NTE EExp.					.11	.00			.29																
NTE CEx Tot.					.16				.42													.12	.17		
NTE Prof.Inf.					.12																	.05	.24		
NTE EdElSch.					.20																				
Select. Written Ex.						-.12																			
Select. Oral Ex.																									
Pract. Teach.Mark.					.07																				

* Original criterion items (I_{ci}, S_{ci}, V_{ci}) employed to obtain I, S, and V scores in this sample.

† Elementary 143 Scoring Keys (based on Grades 1–4 women teachers) employed for X_{co}, Y_{co}, and Z_{co} in this sample.

‡ This correlation is the median of correlations yielded by cross-validation samples.

273

TABLE 63

Summary of Correlations between "Responsible, Businesslike Teacher Behavior" Schedule Scores, Y_{co}, and Other Indices of Teacher Characteristics

(See accompanying legend for identification of samples 1–21 and of variables listed in Column 1)

Y_{co} Scores Correlated with:	ELEMENTARY TEACHER SAMPLES									SECONDARY TEACHER SAMPLES													EL. & SEC. SAMPLES		
	Elem. (111) Scoring Keys						All-T. (99) Scoring Keys			Secondary (100) Scoring Keys										All-T. (99) Scoring Keys			All-T. (99) Scoring Keys		
	1	2*	3	4	5†	6†	1	2*	7	8	9*	10	11	12	13*	14	15*	16	17	15*	13*	18	19	20*	21
TCS X_o		.35‡	.28	.20	−.07	.05	.28	.39	.08			−.03	−.05					−.10	.16	.24	.29	.32	.30	.31	.26
TCS Y_o		.56	.32	.40	.04	.21	.31	.07	.26	.28‡		.36	.32					−.02	.07	.28	−.03	.48	.15‡	.11	.44
TCS Z_o		.51	.29	.19	.21	.09	.23	.30	.11			.07	.08					−.08	.02	.19	.07	.13	.26	.20	.26
TCS P_o		.57	.31		−.02	.04	.19	.30				.00	.16					.07	.22	.21	.10		.23	.22	
TCS X_{co}	.48	.63	.47	.10	.50	.38	.12	.21		−.09	.06	−.14	−.10	−.09	.04	−.12	.10	−.04	−.01	.13	.11		.14	.14	
TCS Z_{co}	.54	.59	.43	.29	.55	.42				−.12	.44	−.06	.12	.12	.28	−.11	.32	−.19	−.20	−.22	−.25	−.34	−.12	−.19	−.25
TCS R_{co}	.62	.63	.52	.14	−.33	.35				−.09	.15	−.11	−.17	−.08	.01	−.13	.05	−.01	−.01	.11	−.08	.25	−.19	−.08	.24
TCS R_{eo}	.60	.60	.60	.15	.39	.33				−.01	.18	−.02	.05	−.01	.16	−.04	.20	.20	.11	−.07	−.12	−.14	−.10	−.07	.05
TCS Q_{eo}	.60	.63		.13	.44	.30				−.01	.16	.14	.00	.00	−.03	−.02	−.01	−.03	−.17	.06	.06		−.01	−.06	
TCS B_{co}	−.32	−.38	−.29	−.01	.09	−.14	−.06	−.13	−.02	.39	.24	.14	.00	.16	−.02	.21	.01	−.05	.06						
TCS I_{ei} or I_{eo}	.30	−.15	.32	.08	.46	.11	.07	−.12	.21	−.46	.24	.33	.40	.47	.22	.32	.26	.49	.50						
TCS S_{ei} or S_{eo}	.44	−.15	.45	.03	.45	.27	−.02	.04	.08	.05	.05	−.44	−.48	.47	−.09	−.46	−.14	−.55	−.14						
TCS V_{ei} or V_{eo}	−.18	.00	−.11	.00	.25	.15	−.05	.09			.21	−.05	.36	.05	.03	.05	.13	.21	−.22						
NTE EExp.					.15																				
NTE CExTot.					.06				.08													−.08		−.05	
NTE ProfInf.					−.04																	−.21		−.10	
NTE EdElSch.					.06	−.10			−.06																
Select. Written Ex.						−.08																			
Select. Oral Ex.																									
Pract. Teach.Mark.						.06																			

* Original criterion items (I_{ei}, S_{ei}, V_{ei}) employed to obtain I, S, and V scores in this sample.

† Elementary 143 Scoring Keys (based on Grades 1–4 women teachers) employed for X_{eo}, Y_{eo}, and Z_{eo} in this sample.

‡ This correlation is the median of correlations yielded by cross-validation samples.

TABLE 64

Summary of Correlations between "Stimulating, Imaginative Teacher Behavior" Schedule Scores, Z_{co}, and Other Indices of Teacher Characteristics

(See accompanying legend for identification of samples 1–21 and of variables listed in Column 1)

Z_{co} Scores correlated with:	ELEM. Elem.(111) 1	2*	3	4	5†	6†	ELEM. All-T.(99) 1	2*	7	SEC. Sec.(100) 8	9*	10	11	12	13*	14	15*	16	17	SEC. All-T.(99) 15*	13*	18	EL&SEC All-T.(99) 19	20*	21
TCS X	.35‡		.41	.54	.10	−.07				.31‡		−.10	.06					.21	.32				.21‡		
TCS Y			.11	.30	.08	.17						−.12	.04					.07	.14						
TCS Z			.39	.61	.22	.16						.16	.29					.06	.21						
TCS P			.29		.05	.04						.20	.19					.02	.13						
TCS X_{co}	.80	.81	.82	.86	.54	.28	.75	.42		.54	.45	.54	.36	.54	.56	.53	.48	.56	.55	.73	.31		.74	.47	
TCS Y_{co}	.48	.51	.43	.29	.55	.42	.31	.07		.12	.44	.06	.19	.12	.28	.11	.32	.19	.20	.28	−.03		.32	.11	
TCS R_{co}	.69	.68	.70	.73	−.24	.27	.69	.41	.58	.38	.44	.36	.29	.36	.42	.37	.32	.37	.37	.62	.70	.66	.67	.56	.64
TCS $R1_{co}$	.62	.65	.62	.65	−.34	.24	.78	.46	.26	.48	.40	.55	.34	.46	.48	.51	.48	.56	.51	.72	.57	.48	.75	.56	.44
TCS O_{co}	.45	.45	.41	.48	.54	.14	.46	.22	.72	−.13	.29	.15	.05	−.11	.13	−.13	.12	.19	.26	.45	.05	.52	.43	.23	.65
TCS B_{co}	−.61	−.63	−.71	−.66	.06	−.18	−.75	−.34	−.59	−.52	−.30	−.52	−.32	−.48	−.53	−.57	−.46	−.57	−.50	−.30	−.24	−.68	−.72	−.31	−.66
TCS I_{ci} or I_{co}	−.45	.21	.54	.45	.68	.25	.45	−.01	.24	−.38	.18	−.38	.20	−.32	.24	.40	.10	.30	.34	.10	−.08	.50	.41	−.04	.32
TCS S_{ci} or S_{co}	.68	.25	.69	.71	.60	.31	.50	−.05	.42	.21	.22	.25	.18	.23	.11	.25	.05	.15	.46	.05	.03	.23	.47	−.04	.36
TCS V_{ci} or V_{co}	−.04	.07	−.06	.07	.25	.09	.04	−.06		.07	.18	.23	.17	.07	−.01	.07	.08	.14	−.18	.09	−.04		−.01	−.02	
NTE EExp					.18																				
NTE CEx Tot					.28				.09													.18			.05
NTE Prof.Inf					.27				.16													.17			.10
NTE EdElSch					.19																				
Select. Written Ex						.09																			
Select. Oral Ex						.04																			
Pract. Teach.Mark					.27																				

* Original criterion items (I_{ci}, S_{ci}, V_{ci}) employed to obtain I, S, and V scores in this sample.

† Elementary 143 Scoring Keys (based on Grades 1–4 women teachers) employed for X_{co}, Y_{co}, and Z_{co} in this sample.

‡ This correlation is the median of correlations yielded by cross-validation samples.

TABLE 65

Summary of Correlations between "Favorable Opinions of Pupils" Schedule Scores, R_{co}, and Other Indices of Teacher Characteristics

(See accompanying legend for identification of samples 1–21 and of variables listed in Column 1)

R_{co} SCORES CORRELATED WITH:	ELEMENTARY TEACHER SAMPLES									SECONDARY TEACHER SAMPLES													EL. & SEC. SAMPLES		
	Elem. (111) Scoring Keys						All-T. (99) Scoring Keys			Secondary (100) Scoring Keys										All-T. (99) Scoring Keys			All-T. (99) Scoring Keys		
	1	2*	3	4	5	6	1	2*	7	8	9*	10	11	12	13*	14	15*	16	17	15*	13*	18	19	20*	21
TCS X........	.79	.79	.20	.28	.14	-.09	.79	.79	.74	.74	.64	.29	.12	.69	.70	.75	.64	.05	.19	.76	.50	.57	.78	.70	.68
TCS Y........	.54	.57	.03	.07	-.18	-.04	.23	.30	.11	-.09	.15	-.10	-.22	-.08	-.17	-.13	.05	-.01	.05	.19	.07	.13	.26	.20	.26
TCS Z........	.69	.68	.16	.32	-.20	-.02	.69	.41	.72	.38	.44	-.17	-.01	.37	.42	.37	.32	.37	.37	.62	.70	.52	.67	.56	.65
TCS P........			.10		-.03	-.06				.79	.71	-.03	-.09	.80	.74	.81	.77	.75	.69	.84	.70	.82	.85	.81	
TCS X_{co}.....	.88	.87	.78	.76	.21	.64	.85	.86		.79	.77	.77	.65	.80	.74	.81	.77	.73	.76	.82	.51	.52	.82	.74	
TCS Y_{co}.....	.87	.76	.52	.14	-.33	.35				.76	.77	-.11	-.17	.72	.74	.81	.79	.75	.73	.84	.70	.70	.85	.81	
TCS Z_{co}.....	.90	.76	.70	.73	-.24	.27						.36	.29	.80	.74	.78	.77	.75	.76						
TCS R_{co}.....	.76	.73	.90	.75	.24	.92	.83	.83		.84	.77	.77	.77				.82	.73	.73	.82	.51	.82	.82		
TCS O_{co}.....	-.69	-.66	.76	.59	-.74	.80	-.66	-.31	-.71	-.72	-.53	.80	.65	-.72	-.68	-.73	-.60	-.62	-.63	-.28	-.43	-.52	-.68	-.34	-.67
TCS B_{co}.....	.49	.13	-.78	-.74	-.08	-.62	.48	.22	.44	-.37	.16	-.69	-.39	.27	.17	.39	.13	.25	.38	.18	.15	.31	.46	.16	.38
TCS I_a or I_{co}.....	.79	.31	.51	.45	.24	.51	.63	.29	.61	.28	.22	.40	.26	.30	.17	.38	.13	.20	.44	.11	.09	.30	.59	.17	.50
TCS S_a or S_{co}.....		-.05	.80	.72	-.59	.76						.31	.19												
TCS V_a or V_{co}.....	-.22		-.28	-.04	-.10	.31	-.26	-.01		-.27	.01	-.27	-.35	-.28	-.11	-.28	-.06	-.28	-.30	.00	-.13		-.23	-.05	.15
NTE EExp........					.10				.14									.05	.19					.05	
NTE CExTot......					.11				.27									-.06	.05			.00		.15	
NTE Prof.Inf.....					.09													-.05	.02			.06			
NTE EdElSch.....																		-.06	.14						
Select. Written Ex...						-.04												-.01							
Select. Oral Ex.....						-.05																			
Pract. Teach.Mark...					.00																				

* Original criterion items (I_{ci}, S_{ci}, V_{ci}) employed to obtain I, S, and V scores in this sample.

TABLE 66

Summary of Correlations between "Favorable Opinions Regarding Democratic Pupil Procedures" Schedule Scores, R_{1co}, and Other Indices of Teacher Characteristics

(See accompanying legend for identification of samples 1–21 and of variables listed in Column 1)

Column groups:
- **ELEMENTARY TEACHER SAMPLES** — Elem. (111) Scoring Keys: 1, 2*, 3, 4, 5, 6 · All-T. (99) Scoring Keys: 1, 2*, 7
- **SECONDARY TEACHER SAMPLES** — Secondary (100) Scoring Keys: 8, 9*, 10, 11, 12, 13*, 14, 15*, 16, 17 · All-T. (99) Scoring Keys: 15*, 13*, 18
- **EL. & SEC. SAMPLES** — All-T. (99) Scoring Keys: 19, 20*, 21

R_{co} Scores correlated with:	1	2*	3	4	5	6	1	2*	7	8	9*	10	11	12	13*	14	15*	16	17	15*	13*	18	19	20*	21
TCS X	.73	.78	.24	.30	.02	-.10	.79	.80		.73	.67	.21	.13	.70	.68	.75	.67	.10	.10	.77	.61		.79	.73	
TCS Y$_{co}$			.04	.08	-.18	.02						-.17	-.16					-.08	-.01						
TCS Z$_{co}$			.21	.28	-.29	.00						-.08	-.07					.02	.00						
TCS P$_{co}$			.16	.72	-.10	-.03						.02	-.08					.02	.08						
TCS X$_{co}$	.62	.63	.72	.15	.06	.59	.19	.30		.01	.18	.74	.64	-.01	.16	-.04	.20	.69	.66	.20	.10		.23	.22	
TCS Y$_{co}$	.62	.65	.60	.65	-.39	.33	.78	.46		.48	.40	-.02	.05	.46	.48	.51	.48	.20	.11	.72	.57		.75	.56	
TCS Z$_{co}$	.88	.87	.62	.65	-.34	.24	.85	.86		.79	.71	.77	.77	.80	.74	.81	.77	.75	.76	.84	.70		.85	.81	
TCS R$_{co}$	.80	.78	.90	.75	.90	.92	.63	.66		.53	.40	.57	.49	.54	.39	.58	.55	.50	.54	.67	.43		.61	.59	
TCS O$_{co}$	-.65	-.66	.83	.52	.10	.85	-.80	-.37		-.89	-.81	-.89	-.43	-.85	-.86	-.36	-.77	-.81	-.82	-.34	-.69		-.81	-.45	
TCS B$_{co}$	.51	.20	-.69	.71	-.61	-.58	-.54	.24		-.57	.22	.59	.52	.41	.23	.57	.19	.42	.52	.20	.19		-.52	.19	
TCS I$_{ci}$ or I$_{co}$	-.78	.30	-.55	-.45	-.17	.50	.61	.28		.06	.03	.11	.05	.17	.08	.23	.07	.06	.38	.06	.10		.55	.15	
TCS S$_{ci}$ or S$_{co}$	-.16	-.02	.78	.69	-.12	.77	-.12	.08		-.07	.02	.00	-.07	-.12	-.01	-.08	.03	.00	-.24	.03	-.10		-.07	.00	
TCS V$_{ci}$ or V$_{co}$			-.19	-.06	-.56	-.31																			
NTE EExp.					.07																				
NTE CExTot.					.17																				
NTE Prof.Inf.					.06																				
NTE EdElSch.					.19																				
Select. Written Ex.						.05																			
Select. Oral Ex.						-.08																			
Pract. Teach.Mark.					-.03																				

* Original criterion items (I_{ci}, S_{ci}, V_{ci}) employed to obtain I, S, and V scores in this sample.

TABLE 67

Summary of Correlations between "Favorable Opinions of School Personnel" Schedule Scores, Q_{co}, and Other Indices of Teacher Characteristics

(See accompanying legend for identification of samples 1–21 and of variables listed in Column 1)

Q_{co} SCORES CORRELATED WITH:	ELEMENTARY TEACHER SAMPLES									SECONDARY TEACHER SAMPLES													EL. & SEC. SAMPLES		
	Elem. (111) Scoring Keys						All-T. (99) Scoring Keys			Secondary (100) Scoring Keys										All-T. (99) Scoring Keys			All-T. (99) Scoring Keys		
	1	2*	3	4	5	6	7	1	2*	8	9*	10	11	12	13*	14	15*	16	17	15*	13*	18	19	20*	21]
TCS X_o	.59	.62	.18	.11	.02	−.09		.59	.59	.41	.31	.19	−.05	.37	.36	.43	.36	−.04	.06	.62	.58		.57	.59	
TCS Y_o	.60	.59	.06	.08	.04	.02		.12	.21	−.01	.16	−.07	−.03	.00	−.03	−.02	−.01	−.01	−.01	.13	.11		.14	.14	
TCS Z_o	.45	.45	.15	.16	.01	−.06		.46	.22	−.13	.29	.11	−.07	.11	.13	.13	.12	−.14	−.13	.45	.05		.43	.23	
TCS P_o	.76	.73	.59	.54	.64	.53		.83	.83	.76	.77	.15	−.05	.75	.72	.78	.79	.19	.26	.82	.51		.82	.73	
TCS X_{co}	.80	.78	.63	.13	.44	.30		.63	.66	.53	.40	.57	.49	.54	.39	.58	.55	.50	.54	.67	.43		.61	.59	
TCS Y_{co}			.41	.48	.54	.14																			
TCS Z_{co}			.76	.59	.24	.80																			
TCS R_{co}			.83	.52	.10	.85																			
TCS R_{oo}			.78																						
TCS B_{oo}	.41	−.46	−.43	−.43	−.27	.36		−.39	−.19	−.34	−.14	−.37	−.16	−.31	−.24	−.38	−.34	−.23	−.26	−.17	−.30		−.38	−.21	
TCS I_{ei} or I_{eo}	.45	.20	.42	.32	.60	.48		.28	.16	.18	.12	.10	.10	.09	.09	.24	.12	.16	.26	−.17	.17		.25	.13	
TCS S_{ei} or S_{eo}	.62	.25	.61	.57	.74	.67		.58	.26	.24	.26	.18	.15	.25	.17	.28	.11	.16	.34	.08	.19		.55	.19	
TCS V_{ei} or V_{eo}	.18	−.05	−.26	.00	−.03	−.31		−.44	−.04	.28	.04	−.32	−.12	−.28	−.11	−.29	−.11	−.25	−.37	−.09	−.09		−.42	−.08	
NTE EExp.					.19																				
NTE CEx.Tot.					.08																				
NTE Prof.Inf.				−.02	.09																				
NTE EdElSch.						−.02																			
Select. Written Ex.						.06																			
Select. Oral Ex.																									
Pract. Teach.Mark					.12																				

* Original criterion items (I_{ei}, S_{ci}, V_{ci}) employed to obtain I, S, and V scores in this sample.

TABLE 68

Summary of Correlations between "Academic-Centered 'Traditional' Educational Viewpoints" Schedule Scores, B_{co}, and Other Indices of Teacher Characteristics

(See accompanying legend for identification of samples 1–21 and of variables listed in Column 1)

B_{co} SCORES CORRELATED WITH:	ELEMENTARY TEACHER SAMPLES									SECONDARY TEACHER SAMPLES														EL. & SEC. SAMPLES		
	Elem. (111) Scoring Keys						All-T. (99) Scoring Keys			Secondary (100) Scoring Keys										All-T. (99) Scoring Keys			All-T. (99) Scoring Keys		
	1	2*	3	4	5	6	1	2*	7	8	9*	10	11	12	13*	14	15*	16	17	15*	13*	18	19	20*	21
TCS X.	−.70	−.70	−.23	−.35	−.36	.01	−.72	−.37	−.72	−.74	−.63	−.14	−.06	−.71	−.70	−.76	−.58	−.13	−.16	−.26	−.64	−.71	−.75	−.41	−.71
TCS Y.	−.32	−.38	.05	−.08	.38	.10	−.06	−.13	−.02	.14	.08	.22	−.02	.16	.02	.21	.01	.16	−.01	−.22	−.25	−.34	−.12	−.19	−.25
TCS Z.	−.61	−.63	−.11	−.41	.20	−.04	−.75	−.34	−.59	−.52	−.31	.03	.02	−.48	−.53	−.57	−.46	.00	−.11	−.30	−.24	−.68	−.72	−.31	−.66
TCS P.			−.09	−.01	−.01	−.02						.01	−.14					−.01	−.15						
TCS X_{co}.	−.69	−.66	−.78	−.72	−.37	−.49	−.66	−.31	−.71	−.72	−.53	−.69	−.39	−.72	−.68	−.73	−.60	−.62	−.63	−.28	−.43	−.52	−.68	−.34	−.67
TCS Y_{co}.	−.65	−.66	−.78	−.74	.06	−.14	−.80	−.37		−.89	−.81	−.89	−.43	−.85	−.86	−.86	−.77	−.81	−.82	−.34	−.69		−.81	−.45	
TCS Z_{co}.	−.41	−.46	−.71	−.71	−.74	−.18	−.39	−.19		−.34	−.14	−.37	−.16	−.31	−.24	−.38	−.34	−.23	−.24	−.17	−.30		−.38	−.21	
TCS R_{co}.	−.36	−.04	−.69	−.61	−.61	−.62	−.59	−.02		−.55	−.16	−.54	−.19	−.39	−.21	−.55	−.12	−.44	−.51	−.02	−.20		−.56	−.04	
TCS Q_{co}.	−.60	−.15	−.43	−.43	−.27	−.58	−.57	−.05	−.56	−.09	.01	−.15	−.07	−.16	−.14	−.28	−.10	−.13	−.31	−.03	−.10	−.55	−.51	−.05	−.50
TCS I_{ci} or I_{co}.			−.47	−.41	−.16	.36			−.58	.10	.08	−.04	.04	.16	.03	.11	.00	−.02	.19	−.04	.06	−.42	−.04	.03	−.49
TCS S_{ci} or S_{co}.			−.69	−.63	−.36	−.38																			
TCS V_{ci} or V_{co}.	.06	.06	.06	.01	.35	−.64	−.01	.04																	
NTE EExp.									−.28													−.10	−.14		
NTE CEx Tot.									−.39													−.11	−.20		
NTE Prof.Inf.					−.18																				
NTE EdElSch.					−.07																				
Select. Written Ex.					−.13	−.06																			
Select. Oral Ex.						.11																			
Pract. Teach.Mark.					.05																				

* Original criterion items (I_{ci}, S_{ci}, V_{ci}) employed to obtain I, S, and V scores in this sample.

TABLE 69

Summary of Correlations between "Verbal Reasoning and Word Recognition" Schedule Scores, I_{ci} or I_{co}, and Other Indices of Teacher Characteristics

(See accompanying legend for identification of samples 1–21 and of variables listed in Column 1)

I_{ci} (or I_{co}) Scores Correlated with:	Elem. (111) Scoring Keys						All-T. (99) Scoring Keys			Secondary (100) Scoring Keys										All-T. (99) Scoring Keys			All-T. (99) Scoring Keys		
	1	2*	3	4	5	6	1	2*	7	8	9*	10	11	12	13*	14	15*	16	17	15*	13*	18	19	20*	21
TCS X_o	.51	.19	.20	.20	.02	.22	.51	.25	.52	.46	.22	.24	.17	.35	.26	.49	.18	−.04	.12	.15	.23	.46	.48	.20	.46
TCS Y_o	.30	.15	.01	.10	−.18	.12	.07	.12	.21	.39	.24	.00	−.06	.47	.22	.32	.26	−.15	.16	.11	.08	.25	.19	.08	.24
TCS Z	.45	.21	.32	.18	−.06	.25	.45	.01	.24	.38	.18	.20	−.09	.32	.24	.40	.10	−.11	.05	.10	.08	.50	.41	.04	.32
TCS P_o	.49	.13	.54	.18	−.02	.12	.48	.22	.44	.37	.16	−.12	−.03	.27	.17	.39	.13	−.02	.32	.18	.15	.31	.46	.16	.38
TCS X_{co}	.51	.20	.51	.41	.63	.52	.54	.24		.57	.22	.42	.37	.41	.23	.57	.19	.33	.41	.20	.19		.52	.19	
TCS I_{co}	.45	.21	.56	.46	.46	.11				.18	.12	.33	.40	.47	.17	.32	.26	.49	.50	.12	.13		.25	.13	
TCS Z_{co}	.51	.20	.54	.45	.68	.25	.59	−.02		.57	.18	.38	.26	.32	.23	.40	.10	.30	.34	.20	.19		.52	.19	
TCS R_{co}	.45	.20	.55	.45	.08	.51	.38	.19	−.56	.18	.16	.40	.20	.41	.24	.57	.12	.25	.38	.12	.17		.56	−.04	−.50
TCS R_{eo}	.54	.24	.60	.32	−.17	.50	.16	.06	.31	.57	.22	.59	.52	.41	.09	.57	.17	.42	.52	.02	.20		.25	.12	.23
TCS Q_o	.28	.16	.32	−.41	.60	.48				.18	.12	.26	.10	.09	.09	.24	.10	.10	.26	.12	.17		.18	.12	
TCS B_{eo}	−.36	−.04	−.47	−.41	−.16	−.38	−.59	−.02		−.55	−.16	−.54	−.19	−.39	−.21	−.55	−.20	−.44	−.51	−.02	−.20	−.55	−.56	−.04	−.50
TCS S_{ci} or S_{co}	.63	.19	.74	.50	.78	.55	.38	.19	.31	−.25	−.07	−.25	−.32	−.23	.09	−.14	.09	−.38	.06	.02	.09	.04	.25	.12	.23
TCS V_{ci} or V_{co}	.08	.06	.10	.06	.22	−.02	.16	.06		.16	.14	.08	.19	.17	.15	.14	.15	.22	−.14	.11	.15	.04	.18	.12	
NTE EExp.					.22																	.48			.47
NTE CEx Tot.					.39				.39													.38			.45
NTE Prof.Inf.					.27				.39																
NTE EdElSch.					.23																				
Select. Written Ex.						.18																			
Select. Oral Ex.						.09																			
Pract. Teach.Mark.					.14																				

* Original criterion items (I_{ci}, S_{ci}, V_{ci}) employed to obtain I, S, and V scores in this sample.

TABLE 70

Summary of Correlations between "Emotional Adjustment" Schedule Scores, S_{ci} or S_{co}, and Other Indices of Teacher Characteristics

(See accompanying legend for identification of samples 1–21 and of variables listed in Column 1)

S_{ci} (or S_{co}) SCORES CORRELATED WITH:	ELEMENTARY TEACHER SAMPLES									SECONDARY TEACHER SAMPLES													EL. & SEC. SAMPLES		
	Elem. (111) Scoring Keys						All-T. (99) Scoring Keys			Secondary (100) Scoring Keys										All-T. (99) Scoring Keys			All-T. (99) Scoring Keys		
	1	2*	3	4	5	6	1	2*	7	8	9*	10	11	12	13*	14	15*	16	17	15*	13*	18	19	20*	21
TCS X_o	.77	.32	.29	.30	.02	-.16	.65	.26	.60	.26	.07	-.13	-.06	.32	.14	.34	.07	.18	.21	.09	.17	.54	.59	.18	.57
TCS V_o	.44	.15	.01	.04	-.12	-.09	-.02	.04	.08	-.46	.05	-.13	-.21	-.47	-.09	-.46	-.14	-.55	-.14	-.07	-.12	-.14	-.10	-.07	.05
TCS Z_o	.68	.25	.24	.36	-.06	-.06	.50	.05	.42	.21	.22	-.04	-.06	.23	.11	.26	.05	.15	.46	.05	.03	.23	.47	.04	.36
TCS P_o	.79	.30	.16	.75	-.14	-.10	.63	.29	.61	.28	.22	.14	-.09	.30	.17	.28	.07	.20	.44	.11	.09	.30	.59	.17	.50
TCS X_{co}	.78	.30	.78	.71	.72	.71	.61	.28		.06	.03	.41	-.10	.17	.08	.23	.07	.06	.34	.06	.10		.55	.15	
TCS V_{co}	.62	.25	.45	.72	.45	.27	.58	.26		.24	.26	-.44	-.48	.25	.17	.38	.07	.16	.44	.08	.19		.55	.19	
TCS Z_{co}			.80	.69	.60	.31						.25	.18	-.17	-.14	.23		.13	.31						
TCS R_{eo}			.72	.57	.24	.76						.31	.19	-.17	-.09	.11		.16	.38						
TCS R_{ieo}			.69		.12	.77						.11	.05	-.14	-.19	.16		.34	.44						
TCS Q_{eo}			.78		.74	.67						.18	.15	-.23		.34		.16	.34						
TCS B_{eo}	-.60	-.15	.61	-.63	-.36	-.64	-.57	-.05	-.58	-.09	.01	-.15	-.07	-.19	-.14	-.31	-.10	-.13	-.31	-.03	-.10	-.42	-.51	-.05	-.49
TCS I_{ci} or I_{co}	.63	.19	-.69	.50	.78	.55	.38	.19	.31	-.25	.07	-.25	-.32	-.06	-.09	-.29	.02	-.39	.06	.02	.09	.04	.25	.12	.23
TCS V_{ci} or V_{eo}	-.09	-.08	.74	-.01	-.04	-.24	-.21	-.08		-.08	-.03	.05	-.02		-.19	-.07	-.12	-.11	-.39	-.12	-.18		-.21	-.12	
NTE EExp.									.12											-.12		-.05	.02		.09
NTE CEx Tot.					.19				.17																
NTE Prof.Inf.					.04																				
NTE EdElSch.					.14																				
Select. Written Ex.						.08																			
Select. Oral Ex.						.07																			
Pract. Teach.Mark					.08																				

* Original Criterion items (I_{ci}; S_{ci}; V_{ci}) employed to obtain I, S, and V scores in this sample.

TABLE 71

Correlations between Validity-of-Response Scores V_{ci} or V_{co} (Estimated from Responses to the Teacher Characteristics Schedule) and Other Indices of Teacher Characteristics

(See accompanying legend for identification of samples 1–21 and of variables listed in Column 1)

V_{ci} (OR V_{co}) SCORES CORRELATED WITH:	ELEMENTARY TEACHER SAMPLES									SECONDARY TEACHER SAMPLES													EL. & SEC. SAMPLES		
	Elem. (111) Scoring Keys						All-T. (99) Scoring Keys			Secondary (100) Scoring Keys										All-T. (99) Scoring Keys			All-T. (99) Scoring Keys		
	1	2*	3	4	5	6	7	1	2*	8	9*	10	11	12	13*	14	15*	16	17	15*	13*	18	19	20*	21
TCS X_{ci}	-.11	.02	.11	.04	-.03	.00			.04			.04	-.06	.00	-.04	-.05	.09	-.09	-.16	.05	-.05		-.10	.01	
TCS Y_{ci}	-.18	.00	.01	.00	-.16	-.02			.09			.01	.21	.05	.03	.05	.13	.21	-.22	.06	-.06		-.01	.06	
TCS Z_{ci}	-.04	-.05	.16	.11	-.03	-.03			-.06			.14	.16	.07	-.01	.07	.08	.14	-.18	.09	-.04		-.01	-.02	
TCS P_{ci}	-.22	-.05	-.09		-.12	-.09			-.01			-.01	.02	-.01			.08	.01	-.11	.00	-.04		-.23	-.05	
TCS X_{co}	-.16	-.02	-.11	-.01	-.02	-.29		-.16	.04	-.02	.02	-.06	-.19	.00	-.04	-.05	.09	.06	-.14	.05	-.09		-.07	.00	
TCS Y_{co}	-.18	-.05	-.11	.00	.25	.15		-.05	.09	.05	.21	.05	.36	.05	.03	.05	.13	.21	-.22	.06	-.01		-.42	.03	
TCS Z_{co}		-.02	-.06	.07	.25	.09		-.04	-.06	.07	.18	.23	.17	.07	-.01	.07	.08	.14	-.18	.09	-.04		-.23	-.05	
TCS R_{ico}	-.06		-.28	-.04	-.59	-.31		-.26	-.01	-.27	.01	-.28	-.36	-.28	-.11	-.28	-.06	-.28	-.30	.03	-.10		-.07	.00	
TCS Q_{co}	.06	.06	-.19	-.06	-.03	.31		-.12	.08	-.07	.02	.00	-.07	-.12	-.11	-.08	.03	.00	-.24	-.09	-.10		-.42	.03	
TCS B_{co}	.08	.08	.06	.00	.35	.16		-.44	.04	-.28	.04	-.32	-.12	-.29	.03	-.29	-.11	-.25	-.37	-.04	.06		-.04	-.08	
TCS I_{ci} or I_{co}	.08	-.05	.06	.01	.22	-.02		-.01	.04	.10	.08	-.04	.04	.16	.15	.11	.00	-.02	.19	-.11	.15		-.18	.12	
TCS S_{ci} or S_{co}	-.09	-.08	-.16	-.01	-.04	-.24		.16	.06	.16	.14	.08	.08	.17	.15	.14	.11	.22	-.14	-.12	-.19		-.21	-.12	
NTE EExp.					.23																				
NTE CExTot.					-.11																				
NTE Prof.Inf.					-.11																				
NTE EdElSch.					.33																				
Select. Written Ex.						.42																			
Select. Oral Ex.						.04																			
Pract. Teach.Mark.					-.38																				

* Original criterion items (I_{ci}, S_{ci}, V_{ci}) employed to obtain I, S, and V scores in this sample.

havior (Z_o), for elementary teachers. With secondary teachers, X_{co}, I_{co}, and possibly R_{co} contribute most to the prediction of Pattern X_o; Y_{co}, $-R_{co}$, and B_{co} aid in the prediction of Y_o; and Z_{co}, I_{co}, and X_{co} all contribute to the prediction of Z_o.

Considering together all of the findings which resulted from correlating Teacher Characteristics Schedule scores with observers' assessments of teacher and pupil classroom behavior, generalizations such as those summarized below seem to be in order.

Elementary Teacher Samples

	OBSERVED BEHAVIOR PATTERNS			
	X_o	Y_o	Z_o	P_o
	X_{co}	Y_{co}	Z_{co}	X_{co}
Most significantly corre-	$-B_{co}$		X_{co}	Y_{co}
lated Teacher Charac-	Z_{co}			Z_{co}
teristics Schedule scores	I_{co}			
	S_{co}			

Secondary Teacher Samples

	OBSERVED BEHAVIOR PATTERNS			
	X_o	Y_o	Z_o	P_o
	X_{co}	Y_{co}	Z_{co}	Z_{co}
Most significantly corre-	Z_{co}			
lated Teacher Charac-	R_{co}			
teristics Schedule scores	S_{co}			
	I_{co}			

From Tables 62–71 it may be observed that among elementary teachers understanding teacher behavior X_o and also stimulating teacher behavior Z_o appear generally to be significantly positively correlated with X_{co}, Z_{co}, R_{co}, R_{1co}, Q_{co}, $-B_{co}$ (permissive viewpoints), I_{co}, and S_{co}. Responsible, businesslike teacher behavior Y_o is also correlated with most of the Schedule scores, but the values are lower than for X_o and Z_o. The intercorrelations among the variables suggest two oblique factors relating to the Schedule scores of elementary teachers, one being contributed to by X_{co}, Z_{co}, and $-B_{co}$ (permissive), and the other being made up of R_{co}, R_{1co}, Q_{co}, and, to a lesser extent, Y_{co}, S_{co}, and I_{co}. Observer assessments of X_o, Y_o, and Z_o are highly intercorrelated and form a third cluster of variables. From matrices of intercorrelations which also include professional teacher examinations, the scores resulting from these variables again appear to be relatively more highly intercorrelated and to suggest a fourth cluster or factor.

The intercorrelations of the variables relating to secondary teachers form patterns generally similar to those of elementary teachers except that the coefficients of correlation are of a lower order. Two principal oblique factors appear among the Schedule scores, one being contributed to by Y_{co} and $-S_{co}$ (below average emotional adjustment) scores, and the second being made up of $-B_{co}$, R_{1co}, R_{co}, Q_{co}, X_{co}, I_{co}, and Z_{co} scores. As was the case with the elementary teacher samples, a third family of intercorrelations is contributed to by the observed teacher behaviors X_o, Y_o, and Z_o.

Bibliography

1. BAKER, P. "Combining Tests of Significance in Cross-Validation," *Educational and Psychological Measurement*, **12**: 300–306, 1952.
2. FLANAGAN, J. C. "The Effectiveness of Short Methods for Calculating Correlation Coefficients," *Psychological Bulletin*, **49**: 342–48, 1952.
3. KELLEY, T. L. "The Selection of Upper and Lower Groups for the Validation of Test Items," *Journal of Educational Psychology*, **30**: 17–24, 1939.
4. RYANS, DAVID G. "Notes on the Criterion Problem in Research, with Special Reference to the Study of Teacher Characteristics," *Journal of Genetic Psychology*, **91**: 33–61, 1957.
5. ———. "Research Designs for the Empirical Validation of Tests and Inventories," *Educational and Psychological Measurement*, **17**: 175–84, 1957.
6. ———. "Some Validity Extension Data Relative to Empirically Derived Predictors of Teacher Behavior," *Educational and Psychological Measurement*, **18**: 355–70, 1958.
7. ———. "The Results of Internal Consistency and External Validation Procedures Applied to the Analysis of Test Items Measuring Professional Information," *Educational and Psychological Measurement*, **11**: 549–60, 1951.

7. Comparisons of the Characteristics of Teachers When Classified with Regard to Various Conditions of Personal Status and Employment

To THIS POINT, the report has been concerned principally with the Study's effort to identify, describe, and quantify (both directly and through the use of correlates data) certain patterns of observable classroom behavior of teachers and the manifestations of related attitudinal, cognitive, and emotional traits.

The present chapter utilizes the findings of the earlier research in providing descriptions, in terms of Teacher Characteristics Schedule scores, of teachers classified according to a number of factors or conditions. The approach is taxonomic. The purpose is to take a look at a cross-section of American teachers during the first half of the decade beginning in 1950 and to compare teacher groups, with respect to their scores on the correlates scales of the Schedule. Comparisons are made, therefore, in light of the means and standard deviations of various teacher classes on the X_{co}, Y_{co}, Z_{co}, R_{co}, R_{1co}, Q_{co}, B_{co}, I_{ci}, I_{co}, S_{ci}, S_{co}, V_{ci}, and V_{co}[1] scales.

Since, as noted earlier, it seemed reasonable to hypothesize that certain subpopulations of teachers might differ systematically from others with regard to teacher characteristics, many of the tables presented will be replicated for different teacher groups or subsamples. Often they will provide not only comparisons of the Schedule scores of teachers in general (elementary and secondary teachers combined), but also comparisons of elementary teachers considered alone, secondary teachers alone, and, for the Basic Analysis Sample, separate comparisons of the major subpopulations of secondary teachers consisting of mathematics-science teachers and English–social studies teachers.

For a number of the comparisons, similar data were available for the Basic Analysis Sample and the Survey Sample and, consequently,

[1] Although the tables which are presented include scores on the V_{co} (or V_{ci}), validity of response, characteristic, introduction of this variable was not intended primarily for purposes of teacher description or as a basis for group comparison. It should be recalled that this V scale originally was developed simply to provide one guide to the usability of the scores obtained for the other nine characteristics measured by the Schedule. The V variable was never thought of as a major dimension of teacher behavior to be used in teacher description or teacher comparison. Some of the comparisons involving V are, nevertheless, interesting to note.

tables are presented for both samples, making possible not only their comparison with each other, but also permitting broader generalization regarding the scores in relation to the bases of classification employed. Replication thus provided adds significantly to the meaningfulness of the results.

For certain comparisons, replication with both Basic Analysis and Survey Samples was not possible. Several control items relating to the state in which teaching was performed, size of community, size of school, etc., which were incorporated in the booklet employed in the nation-wide survey, had not been included in the original form of the Schedule used with teachers participating in the basic analyses. However, similarities of the Basic Analysis and the Survey Samples with respect to other bases of comparison (reported in this chapter and also in chapter 3) suggest the reasonableness of the assumption that replication with respect to such breakdowns in still another sample probably would lead to confirmation of the Survey Sample results.

The Basic Analysis Sample and the Survey Sample Compared

The two major samplings attempted by the Study were described in chapter 3. It will be recalled that the Basic Analysis Sample consisted of teachers in relatively large school systems who were available both for the systematic observation undertaken by the Study and for inventorying with respect to the instruments developed. The Survey Sample, on the other hand, was made up of teachers throughout the United States as a whole who completed the Schedule upon the request of their respective principals, the sampling of principals having been made from national lists with systematic selection to provide probability samples of the available frames.

Before proceeding to the major comparisons and descriptions with which this chapter is concerned, it is appropriate to consider, momentarily, over-all similarities and dissimilarities of the Basic Analysis and Survey Samples relative to the scores yielded by the Schedule.

It is important to note that, in general, the findings based on these two samples confirm one another insofar as direction and statistical significance of differences between teacher groups is concerned, in spite of the differing approaches which were involved in the composition of the two samples. True, the selective factors operating in connection with agreement to participate in the Basic Analysis investigations of the Study[2] resulted, as might be expected, in discernible differences in the

---

[2] Selection also operated in the Survey Sample, in that no pressure was brought to bear upon teachers to complete the Schedule, and it is likely, therefore, that those who did elect

mean scores which were generally favorable to that sample, as shown in Table 72, but the two samples really functioned very much alike in revealing score differences between groups of teachers classified according to various conditions of personal status and employment.

In Table 72, the Basic Analysis Sample and Survey Sample are compared first with regard to scores derived from application of the most general scoring keys—the All-Teacher (99) Keys, and then with respect to the somewhat more sensitive All-Elementary Teacher (111) and All-Secondary Teacher (100) Scoring Keys. The mean scores of both elementary and secondary teachers tend to be higher[3] in the Basic Analysis Sample than in the Survey Sample, although some of the differences between these two samples are less marked among secondary teachers than among elementary teachers.

Teacher Characteristics Schedule Norms Data

The means and standard deviations presented in Table 72, and also those of Tables 96, 97, and 98, may be employed for norms purposes for the characteristics measured by the Schedule. They permit comparison of various teacher groups with the more general data based upon the Basic Analysis and Survey Samples for the scoring keys more likely to be used (Keys 99, 111, and 100).

Standard score norms (providing distributions of the same form as the original raw score distributions, but with common means of 50 and standard deviations of 10) may be prepared readily by obtaining the standard score equivalents of raw scores.

In most of the tables of this chapter, the last line of the table will provide means and standard deviations for the sample (Basic Analysis or Survey) which is the appropriate reference group.

Teacher Characteristics Compared in Light of Personal Status Conditions and Current Activities of Teachers

This section will be concerned with the Schedule scores of teachers when they are classified into subgroups according to such conditions as age, amount of teaching experience, sex, marital status, avocational activities, religious activities, membership in professional organizations,

---

to participate differed as a group from those who did not; but the choice of school systems in which the observations and inventorying were conducted in the Basic Analysis studies and the extent of participation required in them probably resulted in much greater selection in the Basic Analysis Sample as compared with the Survey Sample.

[3] It should be recalled that with respect to the value judgments involved in Characteristic B, lower scores suggest "child-centered," and higher scores, "learning-centered," educational viewpoints.

TABLE 72

Comparison of Teacher Characteristics* Schedule Scores of the Basic Analysis and Survey Samples

ALL-TEACHER SCORING KEYS (99)

CLASSIFICATION	N	99 X_{co} M	σ	99 Y_{co} M	σ	99 Z_{co} M	σ	99 R_{co} M	σ	99 R_{lco} M	σ	99 Q_{co} M	σ	99 B_{co} M	σ	99 I_{co} M	σ	99 S_{co} M	σ	99 V_{co} M	σ
Elementary teachers																					
Basic Analysis Sample	978	38.0	7.3	27.8	3.9	28.6	5.4	36.6	9.4	35.6	6.9	36.5	7.8	16.8	9.2	35.9	7.1	36.6	6.1	22.6	4.7
Survey Sample	670	35.1	7.1	28.0	3.7	27.6	4.7	32.9	8.9	33.0	6.6	33.3	7.2	20.2	8.8	33.3	7.9	33.5	6.3	22.4	5.0
Secondary teachers																					
Basic Analysis Sample	1,065	35.9	7.2	27.0	4.5	27.4	4.8	33.7	9.3	33.2	6.2	35.2	7.5	21.0	9.7	37.6	7.4	33.2	5.9	23.2	4.5
Survey Sample	970	34.1	6.6	26.8	4.4	27.1	4.4	30.7	8.2	31.6	6.2	32.4	7.0	22.8	8.4	36.0	7.9	34.7	6.1	23.8	4.8
Elementary-Secondary teachers																					
Basic Analysis Sample	2,043	36.9	7.3	27.4	4.2	28.0	5.2	35.1	9.5	34.3	7.2	35.8	7.7	19.0	9.7	36.8	7.3	36.4	6.0	22.9	4.6
Survey Sample	1,640	34.5	6.8	27.3	4.2	27.3	4.6	31.6	8.5	32.1	6.4	32.8	7.1	21.8	8.6	34.9	8.0	34.2	6.3	23.2	4.9
Basic Analysis-Survey Samples†	3,683	35.8	7.2	27.4	4.2	27.7	5.0	33.5	9.2	33.3	6.9	34.5	7.6	20.2	9.3	36.0	7.7	35.4	6.2	23.0	4.8

ALL-ELEMENTARY TEACHER SCORING KEYS (111)

CLASSIFICATION	N	111 X_{co} M	σ	111 Y_{co} M	σ	111 Z_{co} M	σ	111 R_{co} M	σ	111 R_{lco} M	σ	111 Q_{co} M	σ	111 B_{co} M	σ	111 I_{co} M	σ	111 S_{co} M	σ	111 V_{co} M	σ
Elementary Basic Analysis Sample	978	51.2	15.6	30.9	9.0	44.4	11.4	40.6	15.2	32.9	11.2	32.6	9.8	22.7	9.4	42.0	7.5	43.0	9.8	24.8	4.7
Elementary Survey Sample	670	44.3	14.4	28.2	8.0	40.3	10.8	34.8	13.5	28.5	10.1	27.9	8.7	25.4	8.5	39.2	9.1	38.1	11.3	23.5	5.3
Elementary Basic Analysis-Survey Samples†	1,648	48.3	15.5	29.8	8.7	42.7	11.3	38.2	14.8	31.1	11.0	30.6	9.7	23.8	9.1	40.8	8.3	41.0	10.7	24.3	5.0

ALL-SECONDARY TEACHER SCORING KEYS (100)

CLASSIFICATION	N	100 X_{co} M	σ	100 Y_{co} M	σ	100 Z_{co} M	σ	100 R_{co} M	σ	100 R_{lco} M	σ	100 Q_{co} M	σ	100 B_{co} M	σ	100 I_{co} M	σ	100 S_{co} M	σ	100 V_{co} M	σ
Secondary Basic Analysis Sample	1,065	36.8	8.5	34.2	7.6	28.0	6.4	40.2	13.0	34.7	12.6	31.4	8.0	51.9	15.4	40.1	9.1	27.3	4.9	22.8	4.9
Secondary Survey Sample	970	34.8	6.9	32.9	6.9	27.5	6.1	36.6	10.8	32.4	10.4	29.0	7.2	53.9	12.5	38.1	10.1	26.7	6.0	23.3	5.8
Secondary Basic Analysis-Survey Samples†	2,035	35.9	7.9	33.6	7.3	27.8	6.3	38.5	12.1	33.6	11.7	30.3	7.7	52.8	14.3	39.2	9.7	27.0	5.5	23.0	5.4

* For a description of the characteristics presumably measured by the Teacher Characteristics Schedule scales, see chapter 6.
† The means and standard deviations for the combined Basic Analysis and Survey Samples provide the most complete normative data available for the Schedule.

and opinions regarding overlap of classroom (teaching) and administrative responsibilities in the school.

RELATION TO AGE

Tables 73, 74, and 75 show the mean scores of teachers on the ten scales of the Schedule when the teachers have been subdivided into age groups. Table 73 is based upon all teachers, elementary and secondary, in the Survey Sample, Table 74 upon elementary and secondary teachers of the Survey Sample, each considered separately, and Table 75 (in three parts) on the Basic Analysis Sample elementary teachers, mathematics-science teachers, and English–social studies teachers.

There appears to be little doubt about the existence of significant differences between teachers comprising different age groups, so far as a number of the teacher characteristics is concerned. (It will be recalled that similar findings were reported in chapter 4 when observers' assessments of teacher-classroom behavior were considered.) Among 60 different F tests computed with the data for these teachers, 45 of the sets of differences between means were found to be significant at or beyond the .05 level. Generally speaking, scores of older teachers (55 years and above) showed this group to be at a disadvantage compared with younger teachers, except in the case of Y_{co}, systematic and businesslike classroom behavior, and B_{co} (indicative of learning-centered, traditional educational viewpoints.) The findings, with respect to age, are summarized below.

Characteristic X_{co} (understanding, friendly classroom behavior): Younger teachers scored relatively higher, and teachers 55 years of age or older, substantially lower.

Characteristic Y_{co} (responsible, systematic, businesslike classroom behavior): There was a pronounced trend here for older secondary teachers to score higher, and younger secondary teachers, lower. The trend also was indicated among elementary teachers, but tests of significance met requirements at the .05 level for elementary teachers only in the Basic Analysis Sample.

Characteristic Z_{co} (stimulating, imaginative classroom behavior): As in the case of X_{co}, statistically significant differences were found in each sample with the older teacher groups showing notably lower scores.

Characteristics R_{co} and R_{1co} (favorable opinions of pupils, and favorable opinions of democratic pupil practices): With the Survey Sample no significant differences between age groups with respect to attitudes toward pupils and attitudes toward democratic classroom procedures were indicated, but with the Basic Analysis Sample, significant differences between groups showed the older teachers to score substantially lower (the mathematics-science sample in the case of R_{1co} being an exception) than others.

TABLE 73

Comparison of Schedule Scores of Teachers (Survey Sample) Classified According to Age

All-Teacher Scoring Keys (99)

Age	N*	X_{co}		Y_{co}		Z_{co}		R_{co}		R_{lco}		Q_{co}		B_{co}		I_{ci}		S_{ci}		V_{ci}	
		M	σ	M	σ	M	σ	M	σ	M	σ	M	σ	M	σ	M	σ	M	σ	M	σ
29 years or under	358	35.3	6.8	26.6	4.3	27.8	4.6	31.4	8.5	32.6	6.5	32.4	6.9	19.6	8.7	27.0	7.3	23.5	8.4	37.6	8.4
30–39 years	409	34.7	6.8	26.6	4.2	27.3	4.5	31.2	8.5	32.0	6.3	32.5	7.3	21.7	8.4	28.2	7.8	22.4	8.2	37.1	8.4
40–44 years	233	35.2	7.1	28.0	4.1	27.7	4.7	32.2	8.9	32.2	6.4	33.0	6.8	21.7	8.7	28.9	7.9	21.8	7.8	38.0	8.1
45–49 years	274	34.9	6.5	27.9	3.7	27.6	4.4	31.7	8.4	32.5	6.1	33.1	7.1	22.0	8.6	28.7	8.0	21.8	7.8	37.5	8.1
50–54 years	173	34.0	6.6	28.1	5.0	26.9	4.5	31.7	8.6	32.0	6.5	32.9	7.5	22.9	8.6	29.7	8.0	20.7	7.6	37.6	8.8
55–59 years	123	31.8	6.5	27.2	4.2	26.3	4.5	31.4	8.2	31.1	6.3	34.0	7.1	24.3	7.8	28.3	8.0	21.1	7.9	35.9	8.8
60 years or over	56	32.2	6.8	27.4	3.9	26.0	4.9	30.5	7.8	30.8	6.7	33.0	7.0	25.6	9.7	29.7	8.2	21.9	7.8	33.8	8.8
Aggregate Survey Sample	1,640	34.5	6.8	27.3	4.2	27.3	4.6	31.6	8.5	32.1	6.4	32.8	7.1	21.8	8.6	28.2	7.9	22.1	8.1	37.2	8.4

* Discrepancy between ΣN and Aggregate N attributable to nonresponse to item.

TABLE 74

Comparison of Schedule Scores of Elementary and Secondary Teachers (Survey Sample) Classified According to Age

Classification	N*	X_{co}		Y_{co}		Z_{co}		R_{co}		R_{lco}		Q_{co}		B_{co}		I_{ci}		S_{ci}		V_{ci}	
		M	σ	M	σ	M	σ	M	σ	M	σ	M	σ	M	σ	M	σ	M	σ	M	σ
Elementary Teachers; All-Elementary Teacher Scoring Keys (111)																					
29 years or under	156	48.1	15.0	27.7	7.7	42.4	11.2	35.3	13.8	29.4	10.6	29.0	9.1	23.7	9.0	25.4	7.1	23.3	8.6	37.8	8.1
30–39 years	155	43.3	15.3	27.4	8.7	39.3	11.4	34.2	13.3	27.4	9.9	26.7	8.1	25.7	8.3	26.8	7.8	21.3	8.0	35.3	8.4
40–54 years	285	44.1	13.2	29.0	7.7	40.4	10.3	35.1	14.5	28.8	10.0	27.9	8.8	25.3	8.2	26.3	7.5	21.1	7.5	36.8	8.1
55 years or over	68	39.4	13.1	28.6	7.5	37.9	9.6	34.3	14.5	28.4	9.4	28.0	8.3	28.1	8.0	26.0	7.3	21.3	7.7	34.3	8.1
Aggregate Elementary Survey Sample	670	44.3	14.4	28.2	8.0	40.3	10.8	34.8	13.5	28.5	10.1	27.9	8.7	25.4	8.5	26.2	7.5	21.7	8.0	36.4	8.3
Secondary Teachers; All-Secondary Teacher Scoring Keys (100)																					
29 years or under	202	35.6	6.3	30.0	6.3	28.0	5.9	35.8	10.4	32.8	10.1	28.3	6.9	52.2	12.1	28.2	7.3	23.7	8.3	37.4	8.6
30–39 years	254	35.7	6.9	30.8	7.1	28.0	6.1	36.3	11.5	31.7	10.4	28.5	7.4	52.9	12.0	29.0	7.7	23.1	8.2	38.2	8.2
40–54 years	395	34.9	6.9	30.6	6.2	27.5	6.1	36.3	10.6	33.1	10.6	29.1	7.1	54.3	12.5	30.5	7.9	21.9	7.9	38.3	8.4
55 years or over	111	31.4	6.7	35.7	6.5	25.3	5.8	35.9	10.1	30.8	10.4	30.8	7.0	58.5	12.9	39.5	8.0	21.4	8.0	35.8	8.6
Aggregate Secondary Survey Sample	970	34.8	6.9	32.9	6.9	27.5	6.1	36.6	10.8	32.4	10.4	29.0	7.2	53.9	12.5	29.7	7.8	22.5	8.1	37.9	8.4

* Discrepancy between ΣN and Aggregate N attributable to nonresponse to item.

TABLE 75

Comparison of Schedule Scores of Elementary and Secondary Teachers (Basic Analysis Sample) Classified According to Age

Age	N*	X_{co} M	X_{co} σ	Y_{co} M	Y_{co} σ	Z_{co} M	Z_{co} σ	R_{co} M	R_{co} σ	R_{1co} M	R_{1co} σ	Q_{co} M	Q_{co} σ	B_{co} M	B_{co} σ	I_{co} M	I_{co} σ	S_{co} M	S_{co} σ	V_{co} M	V_{co} σ
ELEMENTARY TEACHERS; ALL-ELEMENTARY TEACHER SCORING KEYS (111)																					
29 years or under	372	54.4	14.2	29.2	8.7	45.8	10.6	40.0	14.6	32.8	10.9	32.3	9.4	21.2	8.5	42.9	7.0	44.5	9.3	27.0	4.5
30–39 years	220	54.1	14.8	31.5	8.6	45.1	11.3	43.1	14.7	34.2	11.4	32.3	9.7	20.9	10.6	42.9	7.6	44.1	10.1	24.1	4.5
40–54 years	319	48.1	15.7	32.2	9.2	43.3	11.9	40.6	15.6	33.0	11.1	33.3	10.1	24.2	9.1	41.1	7.8	41.6	9.8	23.3	4.2
55 years or over	56	40.0	16.7	31.8	9.5	39.1	11.5	36.5	16.1	29.2	11.8	31.2	10.4	28.2	8.1	39.3	7.4	37.9	9.9	23.3	4.6
Aggregate Elementary Basic Analysis Sample	978	51.2	15.6	30.9	9.0	44.4	11.4	40.6	15.2	32.9	11.2	32.6	9.8	22.7	9.4	42.0	7.5	43.0	9.8	24.8	4.7
MATH-SCIENCE TEACHERS; MATH-SCIENCE SCORING KEYS (97)																					
29 years or under	50	34.1	5.2	32.7	6.3	33.1	5.8	33.6	11.4	28.7	10.2	26.9	6.5	55.3	12.8	36.6	8.2	29.6	4.8	24.4	4.8
30–39 years	101	35.3	5.9	34.1	7.3	33.0	5.8	39.9	13.6	30.1	10.7	30.6	8.5	54.1	13.3	35.6	8.5	30.0	4.4	23.4	5.1
40–54 years	223	32.2	5.9	36.7	7.8	32.7	5.7	38.5	12.5	28.7	11.3	31.4	7.4	59.5	13.7	37.8	8.5	28.4	4.7	22.8	4.6
55 years or over	115	29.2	5.1	37.8	7.8	28.1	6.3	35.9	12.1	27.3	10.5	31.9	7.5	63.6	11.5	36.6	7.9	27.2	4.3	20.8	4.7
Aggregate Math-Science Basic Analysis Sample	497	32.3	6.1	35.7	7.8	31.7	6.3	37.7	12.5	28.5	10.8	31.1	7.7	58.9	13.3	36.5	8.4	28.7	4.7	22.5	4.9
ENGLISH-SOCIAL STUDIES TEACHERS; ENGLISH-SOCIAL STUDIES SCORING KEYS (98)																					
29 years or under	54	40.4	9.1	29.3	6.1	30.1	6.4	41.2	13.5	40.4	10.8	29.0	8.4	40.6	13.2	42.4	7.8	27.3	4.2	24.9	4.8
30–39 years	129	41.6	7.9	30.6	7.1	30.1	6.3	44.8	13.1	42.5	11.6	30.3	8.8	40.3	14.0	42.1	9.6	28.6	4.8	23.4	4.7
40–54 years	258	38.4	8.0	35.7	6.5	29.2	6.1	42.6	12.6	40.0	11.0	32.1	8.0	46.4	13.6	43.2	8.6	25.6	4.3	22.9	5.0
55 years or over	118	34.4	8.6	39.1	6.6	25.4	6.9	39.8	12.9	37.5	12.4	32.6	8.2	41.5	13.3	43.3	8.8	24.0	4.2	21.9	4.2
Aggregate English-Social Studies Basic Analysis Sample	568	38.4	8.6	34.7	7.4	28.7	6.6	42.4	13.0	40.1	11.5	32.0	8.3	45.6	14.1	42.9	8.8	26.1	4.7	23.0	4.8

* Discrepancy between ΣN and Aggregate N attributable to nonresponse to item.

Characteristic Q_{co} (favorable attitude toward administrative and other school personnel): Among secondary teachers only, there appears to be a tendency for younger teachers to attain lower scores than other age groups.

Characteristic B_{co} (learning-centered, traditional *vs.* child-centered, permissive educational viewpoints): There is a consistent tendency here for older teachers to emphasize learning-centered educational viewpoints, and younger teachers more permissive, child-centered viewpoints.

Characteristic I_{co} or I_{ci} (verbal understanding): No clear-cut trend is apparent. F ratios significant at the .05 level were obtained for the Survey Sample with the all-teacher and secondary teacher subsamples (but not the elementary group), older teachers scoring substantially higher with regard to verbal ability. However, in the Basic Analysis Sample, the secondary teachers showed no significant age differences in relation to verbal ability, while among the Basic Analysis elementary teachers, the *younger* groups attained higher mean scores.

Characteristic S_{co} or S_{ci} (emotional adjustment): There is a general tendency here for younger teacher groups to score higher with respect to emotional stability, significant F ratios being obtained for each sample.

Characteristic V_{co} or V_{ci} (validity of response): Interestingly, F ratios significant at the .05 level were obtained for all samples, with the 55 years and older age group scoring significantly lower with respect to "tendency to avoid excessive use of self-enhancing and socially acceptable responses."

Since this is a cross-sectional, rather than longitudinal, approach, the question may be raised (but remains unanswered) as to whether these age differences are dependent primarily on changes in the teacher as he or she grows older, or on cultural influences on teachers, particularly during the time they were in college, which differ substantially for the presently older teacher groups who entered teaching some thirty-five to forty years ago as compared with the younger age groups.

An intriguing sidelight on temperamental differences of teachers, which may be associated with age grouping, is provided by an analysis conducted under the direction of Professor Sydney Pressey, of Ohio State University, employing data made available to him by the Teacher Characteristics Study. In this investigation, the Thurstone Temperament Schedule[4] answer sheets of (a) a group of teachers of 55 years of age and older, and (b) a like-sized group of teachers selected at random from those 30 years of age and younger were forwarded by the Study to Professor Pressey upon his request. His analysis showed distinct differences between the two groups on the scales of the Thurstone Temperament Schedule, with the younger teachers scoring higher on such Thurstone traits as active, vigorous, impulsive, dominant, and sociable,

---

[4] The Thurstone Temperament Schedule was administered to participants in the Basic Analysis study during the first two years of the project.

and the older teachers scoring substantially higher on the Thurstone "reflective" trait.

Pressey's work also included an analysis of the 140 items comprising the Thurstone Schedule, with the goal of identifying individual items which discriminated significantly between older and younger teachers. Thirty-one items were found to distinguish between the age groups studied at the .05 significance level (where some seven might be expected by chance alone).

Some of the more discriminating items favoring *younger* teachers related to the following types of preferences: participation in sports, liking to be where there is something going on all the time, liking work that has lots of excitement, liking work in which one changes often from one task to another, and liking to spend many evenings with friends. Among the more discriminating items which favored *older* teachers were: finding it easy to make up one's mind, usually getting out of bed energetically, preferring to spend an evening alone, preferring to think an important problem through alone, liking to work alone, often being bored with people, and finding books more interesting than people. There seems to be ample support for the common-sense observation that older teachers are likely to be less active and vigorous, but more reflective and dependent upon their own resources, than are younger teachers. The implication for research and practice in the area of teacher personnel probably is that age must be taken into account as a relevant independent variable when teacher characteristics are considered—that personality-wise, teacher variation with age likely interacts with the main effects sometimes described as contributors to teaching performance, and may tend either to make differences in such main effects appear important when they do not exist, or, on the other hand, to obscure main effects.

RELATION TO EXTENT OF TEACHING EXPERIENCE

Table 76 shows the Schedule scores of teachers classified according to extent of teaching experience. The comparisons presented here are based on the Basic Analysis Sample only. As might be expected, the trends are not substantially different from those noted when teachers were classified according to age, there being a general tendency for teachers with extended experience to score lower than less experienced teachers on most of the variables, Y_{co} (responsible, businesslike behavior in the classroom) being a notable exception, with the more experienced teachers scoring significantly higher than the less experienced. Among the elementary teachers, F tests significant at the .05 level were obtained for all scales except R_{co} and Q_{co}. Among secondary teachers,

TABLE 76

Comparison of Schedule Scores of Teachers (Basic Analysis Sample) Classified According to Teaching Experience

EXPERIENCE	N*	Xco M	σ	Yco M	σ	Zco M	σ	Rco M	σ	Rtco M	σ	Qco M	σ	Bco M	σ	Ico M	σ	Sco M	σ	Vco M	σ
ELEMENTARY TEACHERS; ALL-TEACHER SCORING KEYS (99)																				
Less than 1 year	98	39.8	6.5	26.4	3.9	29.2	4.7	36.5	8.9	37.1	6.7	35.5	7.8	13.9	8.3	37.5	6.4	38.2	5.7	23.2	5.1
1-2 years	191	39.3	6.5	26.9	3.9	29.5	5.2	37.4	8.5	36.9	6.3	36.7	7.2	14.3	8.5	36.9	6.8	37.4	5.5	22.6	4.7
3 years	84	39.0	7.4	27.1	4.4	29.0	5.1	36.3	9.3	35.8	6.8	35.7	7.9	15.4	9.2	37.1	7.0	38.0	6.2	23.8	5.1
4 years	55	37.9	7.3	26.8	3.9	28.2	5.7	35.1	9.3	35.1	6.8	35.5	7.6	14.9	8.7	37.1	6.5	37.1	5.9	23.2	4.4
5-9 years	158	38.8	6.9	28.4	3.7	29.3	5.7	37.8	10.0	36.2	7.2	37.0	8.2	16.5	8.5	36.0	7.5	36.6	5.9	22.9	4.3
10-14 years	117	37.1	7.7	28.4	3.4	27.7	5.2	36.7	9.6	34.7	6.7	37.0	7.8	18.8	9.2	34.4	7.6	36.5	5.7	22.2	4.7
15-19 years	105	37.4	7.7	28.4	3.4	28.3	5.7	36.4	9.1	35.0	7.0	36.5	7.0	18.6	10.0	35.3	6.8	35.1	5.7	22.1	4.4
20 or more years	159	35.1	7.8	28.7	3.6	27.4	5.5	36.5	9.9	33.7	7.3	36.7	8.5	20.6	9.1	34.7	7.1	33.9	6.2	21.9	4.5
Aggregate Elementary Basic Analysis Sample	978	38.0	7.3	27.8	3.9	28.6	5.4	36.6	9.4	35.6	6.9	36.5	7.8	16.8	9.2	35.9	7.1	36.6	7.1	22.6	4.7
MATH-SCIENCE TEACHERS; ALL-TEACHER SCORING KEYS (99)																				
Less than 1 year	13	34.9	5.1	24.6	5.8	26.8	2.8	31.4	7.6	31.0	5.1	34.8	5.9	21.1	6.9	35.9	8.9	37.0	5.6	23.5	3.8
1-2 years	22	35.4	6.0	23.8	3.8	27.3	2.8	31.8	9.9	32.4	6.2	32.8	8.1	17.3	6.6	34.8	6.1	39.7	5.7	23.2	5.1
3 years	25	35.9	4.6	24.1	3.9	27.2	5.3	31.8	9.9	32.2	7.7	34.1	6.7	21.9	10.0	33.1	7.6	39.4	7.1	24.6	4.2
4 years	24	36.4	9.2	25.0	4.1	28.4	4.4	30.9	10.7	32.4	7.9	33.3	8.0	19.8	10.0	35.3	6.3	38.0	5.2	23.3	4.6
5-9 years	63	36.7	6.5	25.5	4.4	27.8	4.4	32.9	9.5	32.3	6.5	35.1	7.9	21.0	7.5	36.8	6.8	38.5	5.4	24.0	4.7
10-14 years	59	36.1	6.5	26.3	4.7	27.3	3.8	33.8	8.4	33.1	6.5	34.8	6.9	19.8	8.9	35.8	6.8	36.7	6.4	23.8	4.2
15-19 years	64	34.1	6.9	27.4	4.4	26.9	4.4	33.0	8.4	31.0	6.5	34.5	6.1	24.8	8.5	35.8	8.5	35.0	4.9	23.6	4.2
20 or more years	213	32.8	7.0	26.0	4.9	26.3	4.4	31.7	8.2	30.5	6.4	35.1	6.9	26.4	8.3	34.9	6.7	36.0	5.8	21.9	4.3
Aggregate Math-Science Basic Analysis Sample	497	34.5	7.0	25.8	4.7	26.8	4.3	32.1	8.9	31.4	6.7	34.8	7.0	23.5	9.0	35.4	7.1	36.9	5.8	23.1	4.4
ENGLISH-SOCIAL STUDIES TEACHERS, BASIC GROUP; Xco, Yco, Zco ENGLISH-SOCIAL STUDIES SCORING KEYS (98); Rco, Rtco, Qco, Bco, Ico, Sco, Vco ALL-SECONDARY KEYS (100)																				
Less than 1 year	12	40.0	8.3	30.3	9.1	27.5	6.9	41.2	12.4	41.3	9.2	29.7	7.1	44.3	10.6	43.3	5.2	26.1	5.9	25.2	3.8
1-2 years	32	40.1	8.7	28.2	5.1	28.4	7.7	42.5	13.1	42.0	11.8	31.4	9.6	43.0	13.4	40.4	8.6	28.4	3.7	25.1	4.4
3 years	25	39.9	7.8	28.4	5.3	30.3	6.6	44.8	11.1	41.3	11.4	30.0	8.8	39.6	12.4	42.2	7.8	27.8	5.1	22.8	4.4
4 years	24	42.8	7.9	29.0	7.1	29.5	5.7	45.8	13.9	43.0	12.5	31.6	10.3	36.9	12.8	41.8	11.5	29.3	4.6	23.8	5.5
5-9 years	83	41.7	8.7	31.5	6.4	29.8	5.9	43.2	14.1	41.3	10.6	30.9	8.4	42.1	13.8	42.7	8.6	26.4	3.9	23.6	4.9
10-14 years	75	40.0	7.8	33.3	6.6	29.4	6.3	44.6	11.4	40.9	12.0	32.8	8.8	42.8	14.6	42.7	9.3	26.4	4.8	22.8	4.6
15-19 years	88	37.7	7.7	35.7	6.3	28.8	7.2	43.2	11.4	38.1	10.1	32.9	7.2	46.4	12.7	43.5	8.9	26.2	4.8	22.0	5.3
20 or more years	215	36.1	8.5	33.6	6.3	27.7	6.5	40.3	12.6	38.8	12.0	32.0	8.0	49.6	14.0	43.7	8.6	24.3	4.3	22.7	4.6
Aggregate English-Social Studies Basic Analysis Sample	568	38.4	8.6	34.7	7.4	28.7	6.6	42.4	13.0	40.1	11.5	32.0	8.3	45.6	14.1	42.9	8.8	26.1	4.7	23.0	4.8

* Discrepancy between ΣN and Aggregate N attributable to nonresponse.

294

these same scales, Y_{co} and Q_{co}, and also Z_{co}, R_{co}, R_{1co}, and I_{co} yielded differences between means of experience groups which were insignificant. The results may be summarized as follows:

Characteristic X_{co} (friendly, understanding behavior): The trend here is similar to that found with respect to age, with analyses of variance of experience subgroups showing significant differences in the elementary, mathematics-science, and English–social studies subsamples alike. For each sample the group which was most unlike the others was that made up of teachers with twenty or more years experience, their scores being substantially lower than those of other groups.

Characteristic Y_{co} (responsible, systematic, businesslike classroom behavior): Experience apparently is a significant contributor to this teacher characteristic, significant F ratios being obtained in each sample, with *more experienced* teachers showing higher mean scores.

Characteristic Z_{co} (stimulating, imaginative classroom behavior): There is a slight, but not statistically significant, trend among secondary teachers toward a curvilinear relationship between experience and stimulating classroom behavior, with teachers of little experience and those of extended experience scoring somewhat lower than those of intermediate experience groups. Among elementary teachers, the mean score of the twenty-or-more-years-experience group was significantly below that of the less-than-one-year-experience group.

Characteristics R_{co}, R_{1co}, and Q_{co} (favorable opinions of pupils, favorable opinions of democratic classroom procedures, and favorable attitude toward administrative and other school personnel): There was no significant trend for teachers of different amounts of experience to vary in mean score relative to attitude toward pupils (R_{co}) or attitude toward administrative and other school personnel (Q_{co}). In regard to attitude toward democratic classroom practices (R_{1co}), elementary teachers showed substantial differences in means, with the less experienced groups scoring higher and more experienced groups lower.

Characteristic B_{co} (learning-centered, traditional educational viewpoints): With this characteristic there was a significant trend, found in all three samples, for teachers with less experience to be significantly, and substantially, more inclined toward child-centered, permissive educational viewpoints, and teachers with greater amounts of experience, favoring viewpoints reflecting a learning-centered, traditional emphasis.

Characteristic I_{co} (verbal understanding): Significant differences were found only among the elementary teachers, with the less experienced groups scoring higher than more experienced teachers relative to mean verbal understanding score.

Characteristic S_{co} (emotional adjustment): There was a general trend, most marked among the elementary teachers, for teachers with extended experience to score lower with respect to emotional adjustment. A number of alternative hypotheses might be suggested for this finding.

Characteristic V_{co} (validity of response): There seems to be a very slight trend, barely significant, for groups of teachers with more experience to employ socially acceptable, self-enhancing responses to a greater extent than relatively less experienced groups.

COMPARISON OF MEN AND WOMEN

Table 77 presents comparisons of mean scores yielded by the All-Teacher (99) Scoring Keys on the ten scales of the Schedule for men and women teachers in the Survey and Basic Analysis Samples. Tables 97 and 98, appearing later in this chapter and concerned chiefly with comparisons of teachers' scores according to grade level and subject matter taught, also provide comparisons of men and women teachers.

In Table 77, men and women teachers in the elementary school do not differ significantly with respect to six of the ten characteristics, namely, X_{co}, Z_{co}, R_{co}, Q_{co}, I_{co}, and V_{co}. As a group, however, elementary men teachers scored significantly lower than women with regard to characteristic Y_{co}, suggesting substantially less responsible, systematic, and businesslike classroom behavior.[5] There also is the suggestion (with all-teacher ratios significant at the .05 level in the Basic Analysis Sample, and differences in the same direction although not significant in the Survey Sample) that men teachers in the elementary school may be more favorable in attitude toward democratic pupil practices, more inclined toward permissive, child-centered educational viewpoints, and more emotionally stable than elementary women teachers.

Differences between the sexes, often small in the elementary school as noted above, are fairly pronounced among secondary teachers (particularly in the Survey Sample), with women generally tending to attain significantly higher scores than men on the scales measuring understanding and friendly classroom behavior (X_{co}), responsible and businesslike classroom behavior (Y_{co}), stimulating and imaginative classroom behavior (Z_{co}), favorable attitudes toward pupils (R_{co}), favorable attitudes toward democratic classroom practices (R_{1co}), permissive educational viewpoints (B_{co})—Survey Sample only in this case—and verbal understanding (I_{ci}). Men teachers scored significantly higher with respect to emotional stability (S_{ci}) than did women teachers in the secondary school.

In breaking down the Basic Analysis secondary sample into subject-matter groups, differences between men and women teachers of English–social studies are strikingly like those found among elementary teachers, with only two significant trends to be noted—for women to score higher relative to responsible, systematic classroom behavior (Y_{co}), and men to score higher with regard to emotional adjustment (S_{co}). Among the Basic Analysis mathematics-science teachers, the differences fit,

[5] When the teachers were subclassified as to grade level, and the 111 Scoring Key used (Table 97), the data did not reveal this difference which is so marked in Table 77. The Table 97 data notwithstanding, it seems that women elementary teachers as a group are somewhat more businesslike in their classrooms than are men.

TABLE 77

Comparison of Schedule Scores of Teachers Classified According to Sex

Survey Sample; All-Teacher Scoring Keys (99)

Classification	N	X_{co} M	σ	Y_{co} M	σ	Z_{co} M	σ	R_{co} M	σ	R_{1co} M	σ	Q_{co} M	σ	B_{co} M	σ	I_{ci} M	σ	S_{ei} M	σ	V_{ei} M	σ
Elementary teachers																					
Female	595	35.1	7.1	28.5	3.5	27.6	5.0	32.9	8.9	32.9	6.7	33.2	7.2	20.4	8.8	26.3	7.5	21.5	7.9	36.5	8.3
Male	75	35.2	6.5	24.3	3.1	27.4	4.8	32.8	8.3	33.2	5.9	33.8	7.1	18.6	8.5	25.7	7.7	23.3	8.2	35.7	8.0
Secondary teachers																					
Female	506	35.9	6.4	29.3	4.4	27.6	4.5	31.6	8.3	32.6	6.1	32.4	7.1	22.2	8.5	30.4	7.8	21.1	7.6	37.7	8.4
Male	464	33.2	6.7	24.0	3.6	26.6	4.2	29.7	8.0	30.5	6.1	32.5	6.9	23.5	8.2	28.8	7.8	24.0	8.4	38.0	8.6

Basic Analysis Sample;* All-Teacher Scoring Keys (99)

Classification	N	X_{co} M	σ	Y_{co} M	σ	Z_{co} M	σ	R_{co} M	σ	R_{1co} M	σ	Q_{co} M	σ	B_{co} M	σ	I_{co} M	σ	S_{co} M	σ	V_{co} M	σ
Elementary teachers																					
Female	718	37.9	7.2	28.4	3.5	28.6	5.4	36.8	9.2	35.4	6.9	36.6	7.8	17.3	9.0	35.8	7.1	35.9	5.9	22.6	4.7
Male	116	38.7	7.2	23.3	3.7	28.8	5.3	37.0	9.5	37.0	6.9	36.9	7.4	12.9	8.4	36.3	6.5	41.2	5.9	22.8	4.6
Secondary teachers																					
Mathematics																					
Female	104	34.5	7.9	29.8	3.6	26.8	4.8	32.9	9.3	31.4	6.7	35.2	7.5	25.0	9.3	37.2	7.2	33.8	5.5	23.3	4.3
Male	105	32.3	6.6	22.7	3.8	26.1	4.1	29.4	8.3	29.5	6.6	33.2	6.7	24.5	9.4	32.0	6.2	37.6	5.2	23.3	4.3
Science																					
Female	90	36.6	6.3	29.0	3.2	28.0	4.1	34.7	8.7	33.2	6.8	35.2	6.5	21.2	8.5	38.6	6.9	35.3	5.4	23.3	4.6
Male	148	34.7	6.7	23.3	3.3	26.6	4.2	32.4	8.6	31.7	6.5	35.3	6.9	23.1	8.6	34.5	6.6	39.6	5.2	22.7	4.3
English																					
Female	195	37.5	7.1	30.0	3.3	27.9	5.4	36.1	9.7	35.1	7.5	36.7	8.2	18.9	9.3	40.9	6.6	34.4	5.8	23.3	4.4
Male	86	37.3	7.6	25.1	3.9	27.8	5.1	34.4	10.6	34.9	7.4	35.0	8.4	16.0	9.7	39.4	7.7	38.0	4.9	23.3	4.4
Social Studies																					
Female	121	36.6	7.3	29.1	3.2	27.7	5.1	34.4	9.3	34.5	6.7	34.7	7.3	20.0	10.2	39.8	7.0	33.8	5.8	23.4	4.5
Male	102	36.7	6.3	24.7	3.5	27.8	5.1	34.8	8.3	34.8	7.0	35.2	7.7	19.2	9.1	36.8	7.3	38.7	5.6	22.8	4.8

* Exclusive of members of the hold-out samples.

297

with a few exceptions, the pattern found in the Survey Sample for secondary teachers in general.

Apparently the sex of the teacher was not reflected to any great extent by All-Teacher (99) scores on the scales of the Schedule so far as elementary teachers and English–social studies teachers were concerned, although the findings noted above with respect to Y_{co} and S_{co} must not be overlooked. For mathematics and science teachers, sex differences were more notable.

When the Elementary Teacher (111) Scoring Keys were employed (Table 97), differences favoring elementary men teachers over women were obtained with respect to X_{co}, Z_{co}, R_{co}, R_{1co}, B_{co} (permissive), S_{ci}, and V_{ci}. Use of the Secondary Teacher (100) Keys revealed differences generally favoring secondary women teachers over men relative to X_{co}, Y_{co}, R_{co}, R_{1co}, B_{co} (permissive), I_{co}, and V_{co}, with the men's mean scores significantly exceeding women's only for S_{co}.

RELATION TO MARITAL STATUS OF THE TEACHER

Tables 78, 79, and 80 compare the Schedule scores of teachers when they have been classified according to marital status.

In the Survey Sample, when the marital status classification includes both elementary and secondary teachers, only a few significant differences are in evidence, but others apparently are obscured by the lumping of teachers of different grades and subjects. Significant F ratios (.05 level) were obtained relative to responsible, businesslike classroom behavior (Y_{co}), stimulating classroom behavior (Z_{co}), verbal understanding (I_{ci}), and emotional stability (S_{ci}). Single teachers scored significantly higher on the average than married teachers, with respect to responsible, businesslike classroom behavior and verbal understanding, with the differences in means favoring the married teachers when stimulating classroom behavior and emotional stability were considered. It is interesting to note that the widowed group exceeded both single and married teachers with respect to characteristic Y_{co}, and that they shared high mean scores with the single teachers for characteristic I_{ci}.

Among elementary teachers, F ratios significant at the .05 level were obtained in both the Survey and Basic Analysis Samples for X_{co}, Y_{co}, Z_{co}, and R_{co}. Additional significant F ratios were obtained in the Survey Sample for R_{1co} and B_{co}. Where significant F ratios were obtained, t tests of the differences between means of married and single teachers were significant and favored the married group with respect to understanding, friendly classroom behavior (X_{co}), responsible, businesslike

TABLE 78

Comparison of Schedule Scores of Teachers (Survey Sample) Classified According to Marital Status

ALL-TEACHER SCORING KEYS (99)

MARITAL STATUS	N*	X_{co}		Y_{co}		Z_{co}		R_{co}		R_{1co}		Q_{co}		B_{co}		I_{ci}		S_{ci}		V_{ci}	
		M	σ	M	σ	M	σ	M	σ	M	σ	M	σ	M	σ	M	σ	M	σ	M	σ
Single.............	658	34.2	6.8	28.2	3.9	27.0	4.7	31.5	8.6	32.3	6.5	32.6	7.4	21.5	8.8	28.9	7.8	21.1	7.9	37.0	8.6
Married............	857	34.8	6.8	26.4	4.2	27.5	4.5	31.7	8.5	32.1	6.3	33.1	6.9	21.9	8.6	27.7	7.9	23.1	8.1	37.6	8.3
Separated—divorced....	47	33.6	7.6	26.8	3.3	27.6	5.5	32.0	9.8	32.1	7.2	32.6	7.9	21.7	8.6	27.9	7.4	21.6	7.4	35.9	8.7
Widowed...........	64	35.4	6.1	29.5	3.9	28.3	4.7	31.4	7.4	32.0	5.7	31.2	5.6	21.3	7.4	28.9	8.7	21.2	7.9	36.7	8.5
Aggregate Survey Sample	1,640	34.5	6.8	27.3	4.2	27.3	4.6	31.6	8.5	32.1	6.4	32.8	7.1	21.8	8.6	28.2	7.9	22.1	8.1	37.2	8.4

* Discrepancy between ΣN and Aggregate N attributable to nonresponse.

TABLE 79

Comparison of Schedule Scores of Elementary and Secondary Teachers (Survey Sample) Classified According to Marital Status

MARITAL STATUS	N*	X_{co}		Y_{co}		Z_{co}		R_{co}		R_{1co}		Q_{co}		B_{co}		I_{ci}		S_{ci}		V_{ci}	
		M	σ	M	σ	M	σ	M	σ	M	σ	M	σ	M	σ	M	σ	M	σ	M	σ
ELEMENTARY TEACHERS; ALL-ELEMENTARY TEACHER SCORING KEYS (111)																					
Single.............	288	41.8	14.9	27.3	8.1	37.8	11.0	32.8	13.6	27.1	10.3	27.3	9.0	26.3	8.6	26.7	7.3	21.5	8.0	36.3	8.3
Married............	318	47.0	13.7	29.1	7.8	42.5	10.4	37.0	13.0	30.0	9.5	28.4	8.4	24.2	8.2	25.8	7.5	22.1	8.0	36.8	8.1
Separated—divorced....	27	38.7	13.1	25.9	8.2	36.2	14.6	31.9	14.6	26.0	10.5	28.1	9.6	28.5	9.4	26.0	8.2	20.6	7.6	34.0	8.0
Widowed...........	32	44.9	11.2	30.3	7.9	44.1	8.5	33.3	12.5	29.4	10.3	27.8	7.7	25.8	7.3	27.5	8.5	21.0	7.9	35.6	8.8
Aggregate Elementary Survey Sample...........	670	44.3	14.4	28.2	8.0	40.3	10.8	34.8	13.5	28.5	10.1	27.9	8.7	25.4	8.5	26.2	7.5	21.7	8.0	36.5	8.3
SECONDARY TEACHERS; ALL-SECONDARY TEACHER SCORING KEYS (100)																					
Single.............	370	34.6	6.9	35.7	6.4	27.4	6.4	36.9	10.7	34.9	10.1	29.1	7.7	52.2	12.1	30.7	7.6	20.8	7.9	37.5	8.7
Married............	539	34.9	6.9	30.9	6.5	27.4	4.9	36.3	10.7	30.5	10.5	29.0	6.8	55.4	12.5	28.9	7.9	23.7	8.1	38.0	8.3
Separated—divorced....	20	38.5	6.8	33.5	5.3	28.8	6.5	40.1	12.8	36.6	10.9	28.3	8.0	49.3	11.4	30.4	5.4	23.0	6.9	38.3	9.0
Widowed...........	32	33.8	7.0	34.5	8.9	27.6	6.4	36.3	10.4	33.5	10.1	28.4	6.2	50.5	14.4	30.3	8.6	21.4	7.8	37.8	8.1
Aggregate Secondary Survey Sample...........	970	34.8	6.9	32.9	6.9	27.5	6.1	36.6	10.8	32.4	10.4	29.0	7.2	53.9	12.5	29.7	7.8	22.5	8.1	37.9	8.4

* Discrepancy between ΣN and Aggregate N attributable to nonresponse.

TABLE 80

Comparison of Schedule Scores of Elementary and Secondary Teachers (Basic Analysis Sample) Classified According to Marital Status

Marital Status	N*	X_{co}		Y_{co}		Z_{co}		R_{co}		R_{lco}		Q_{co}		B_{co}		I_{co}		S_{co}		V_{co}	
		M	σ	M	σ	M	σ	M	σ	M	σ	M	σ	M	σ	M	σ	M	σ	M	σ
ELEMENTARY TEACHERS; ALL-ELEMENTARY TEACHER SCORING KEYS (111)																						
Single	283	48.5	16.2	29.7	9.0	41.9	11.8	38.1	14.8	31.4	11.2	31.6	9.4	23.8	10.1	42.3	7.4	41.7	10.3	25.4	5.0
Married	575	52.7	14.9	31.4	8.7	45.5	10.8	41.7	15.0	33.5	10.9	32.8	9.6	22.1	9.1	43.5	7.5	43.5	9.7	24.7	4.6
Separated—divorced	64	52.0	16.0	30.7	10.5	46.1	13.5	42.1	15.6	33.3	12.2	33.3	10.5	22.2	9.0	41.9	7.7	43.5	9.0	24.1	4.0
Widowed	48	47.9	17.8	33.4	8.8	43.3	11.0	41.1	17.1	34.2	12.1	34.9	12.1	23.8	9.4	40.6	8.5	42.2	10.3	23.4	4.4
Aggregate Elementary Basic Analysis Sample	978	51.2	15.6	30.9	9.0	44.4	11.4	40.6	15.2	32.9	11.2	32.6	9.8	22.7	9.4	42.0	7.5	43.0	9.8	24.8	4.7
MATH-SCIENCE TEACHERS; MATH-SCIENCE SCORING KEYS (97)																						
Single	112	32.3	6.3	40.3	8.4	33.4	6.4	38.6	13.3	30.4	10.7	30.7	8.2	57.3	13.6	41.1	8.1	24.8	3.8	22.6	5.0
Married	338	32.6	5.9	34.4	7.0	31.4	5.9	37.3	12.3	27.6	10.9	30.9	7.3	59.7	13.3	35.4	8.0	30.1	4.1	22.7	4.9
Separated—divorced	20	33.2	5.0	36.2	6.4	31.8	7.1	40.2	12.4	33.1	11.0	31.0	8.0	53.9	12.7	37.9	8.1	27.6	4.4	21.4	4.2
Widowed	21	28.0	6.0	40.3	6.5	29.5	7.4	38.6	13.5	32.7	12.6	33.5	8.7	59.3	14.1	39.4	7.8	25.4	4.4	22.4	4.0
Aggregate Math-Science Basic Analysis Sample	497	32.3	6.1	35.7	7.8	31.7	6.3	37.7	12.5	28.5	10.8	31.1	7.7	58.9	13.3	36.5	8.4	28.7	4.7	22.5	4.9
ENGLISH-SOCIAL STUDIES TEACHERS; ENGLISH-SOCIAL STUDIES SCORING KEYS (98)																						
Single	198	36.7	8.7	37.5	6.9	28.2	6.3	40.9	13.8	39.7	11.7	31.5	8.2	46.9	14.7	44.3	8.4	23.0	3.6	23.1	4.6
Married	309	39.9	8.3	32.5	7.4	29.1	6.8	43.8	12.4	40.4	11.7	32.3	8.4	44.4	14.1	41.7	9.0	28.4	4.2	22.9	5.0
Separated—divorced	25	38.2	7.9	35.7	5.6	28.5	5.5	39.7	12.2	40.4	9.0	30.0	8.3	44.7	12.0	45.1	6.9	24.2	3.0	24.2	4.1
Widowed	25	36.8	7.7	37.7	4.7	28.3	6.5	39.0	11.9	38.9	10.9	32.0	8.5	48.6	11.7	43.8	8.8	24.4	3.3	22.2	4.6
Aggregate English-Social Studies Basic Analysis Sample	568	38.4	8.6	34.7	7.4	28.7	6.6	42.4	13.0	40.1	11.5	32.0	8.3	45.6	14.1	42.9	8.8	26.1	4.7	23.0	4.8

* Discrepancy between ΣN and Aggregate N attributable to nonresponse.

classroom behavior (Y_{co}), stimulating classroom behavior (Z_{co}), favorable attitude toward pupils (R_{co}), and child-centered educational viewpoints (B_{co}).

Among secondary teachers in general (Survey Sample), highly significant F ratios (and t ratios between married and single teachers) were obtained, with differences favorable to the single teachers relative to responsible, businesslike behavior (Y_{co}), favorable attitude toward democratic classroom practices (R_{1co}), permissive educational viewpoints (B_{co}), and verbal understanding (I_{ci}), but with married teachers attaining superior scores relative to emotional stability (S_{ci}). Similar differences were found in the Basic Analysis Sample relative to Y_{co}, I_{co}, and S_{co}.

In breaking down the secondary teacher sample into the component subject-matter areas, the conclusions become still more specific to the subject-matter group under consideration. Among mathematics-science teachers, the single teachers scored higher than married teachers on the scales of responsible, businesslike classroom behavior (Y_{co}), stimulating classroom behavior (Z_{co}), favorable attitude toward democratic classroom practices (R_{1co}), and verbal understanding (I_{co}), with married teachers attaining higher scores relative to emotional stability (S_{co}). Among English–social studies teachers, the married group was significantly superior to the single group in average scores on understanding, friendly classroom behavior (X_{co}), favorable attitude toward pupils (R_{co}), and emotional stability (S_{co}), while the single teachers were superior to the married relative to responsible, businesslike classroom behavior (Y_{co}) and verbal understanding (I_{co}).

Quite apart from the actual differences in particular characteristics, it is important to note that the *patterns of differences* are not the same for teachers responsible for different grades and subject matters.

RELATION TO PROFESSED AVOCATIONAL ACTIVITIES

Table 81 is based upon the combined elementary and secondary teachers in the Survey Sample, and compares the scores of teachers who reported recent participation in certain avocational or recreational activities. The differences in mean scores on a particular characteristic for groups of teachers participating in different activities are not great, although there is a tendency for teachers who say they do work in painting and sculpturing to score somewhat higher with respect to understanding, friendly classroom behavior (X_{co}), responsible, businesslike classroom behavior (Y_{co}), stimulating classroom behavior (Z_{co}), favorable attitude toward pupils (R_{co}), favorable attitudes toward democratic

TABLE 81

Comparison of Schedule Scores of Teachers (Survey Sample) Classified According to Reported Recent Participation in Certain Avocational Activities

AVOCATIONAL ACTIVITY	N*	X_{co}		Y_{co}		Z_{co}		R_{co}		R_{tco}		Q_{co}		B_{co}		I_{ci}		S_{ci}		V_{ci}	
		M	σ	M	σ	M	σ	M	σ	M	σ	M	σ	M	σ	M	σ	M	σ	M	σ
Gardening	705	35.3	6.9	27.5	4.3	27.8	4.5	32.5	8.6	32.7	6.6	33.5	7.1	21.2	8.5	28.5	7.8	22.8	8.0	36.7	8.5
Cards, chess, etc.	536	35.7	6.8	28.1	4.2	28.0	4.6	32.9	8.2	33.0	6.5	33.7	7.0	20.2	8.8	28.4	8.0	23.2	8.1	37.3	8.3
Indoor exercise	161	35.1	7.2	26.3	4.9	27.5	4.7	31.8	8.7	32.6	6.7	33.5	7.2	18.9	8.2	27.5	6.8	24.6	8.3	37.0	8.5
Painting, sculpture	148	37.5	7.3	29.0	4.2	29.9	5.1	34.1	9.1	34.8	6.7	33.7	7.0	17.2	8.9	27.2	7.1	22.7	8.0	35.8	8.3
Attending concerts	403	36.0	6.6	28.3	4.1	28.3	4.7	33.5	8.7	33.9	6.6	33.7	7.3	18.6	8.6	29.5	7.9	22.7	7.8	36.2	9.3
No participation in any of above	444	32.9	6.4	26.5	3.9	28.2	4.4	29.7	8.1	30.9	5.8	31.7	6.9	24.2	7.9	29.2	8.0	20.4	7.8	38.0	8.3
Aggregate Survey Sample	1,640	34.5	6.8	27.3	4.2	27.3	4.6	31.6	8.5	32.1	6.4	32.8	7.1	21.8	8.6	28.2	7.9	22.1	8.1	37.2	8.4

ALL-TEACHER SCORING KEYS (99)

* Multiple response possible; a teacher may report participation in several activities listed.

TABLE 82

Comparison of Schedule Scores of Teachers (Survey Sample) Classified According to Reported Participation in Certain Religious Activities

RELIGIOUS ACTIVITY	N*	X_{co}		Y_{co}		Z_{co}		R_{co}		R_{tco}		Q_{co}		B_{co}		I_{ci}		S_{ci}		V_{ci}	
		M	σ	M	σ	M	σ	M	σ	M	σ	M	σ	M	σ	M	σ	M	σ	M	σ
Listened to radio programs	1,212	34.9	6.8	27.6	4.1	27.3	4.6	32.0	8.6	32.5	6.4	33.3	7.2	21.6	8.6	28.3	7.8	22.2	8.0	36.9	8.6
Read articles	1,202	34.9	6.8	27.5	4.1	27.3	4.7	32.0	8.6	32.5	6.5	33.7	7.3	21.6	8.6	28.5	7.8	22.1	8.0	37.0	8.4
Member of church committee	559	35.7	6.5	27.4	4.2	27.7	4.4	32.6	8.2	33.0	6.2	33.7	6.8	20.9	8.3	28.5	7.9	22.6	8.2	36.8	8.7
Taught Sunday school class	356	35.8	6.9	27.3	4.0	27.3	4.5	31.7	8.5	32.5	6.3	32.8	7.2	21.4	8.3	28.8	7.3	22.5	8.1	36.1	9.0
Aggregate Survey Sample	1,640	34.5	6.8	27.3	4.2	27.3	4.6	31.6	8.5	32.1	6.4	32.8	7.1	21.8	8.6	28.2	7.9	22.1	8.1	37.2	8.4

ALL-TEACHER SCORING KEYS (99)

* Multiple response possible. It seems likely a teacher who reported active participation (e.g., committee work; teaching) also participated in the more passive manners exemplified by listening to radio and reading.

classroom practices (R_{1co}), and emphasis upon child-centered educational viewpoints (B_{co}), but somewhat lower than the other avocational activity groups with respect to verbal understanding (I_{ci}) and validity of response (V_{ci}).

Perhaps most interesting is the fact that teachers who report participation in *any* of the avocational activities tend, as a group, to score higher on X_{co}, Y_{co}, Z_{co}, R_{co}, R_{1co}, Q_{co}, B_{co} (child-centered viewpoints), and S_{ci} than teachers who do *not* report participation in any of these activities. Many of the differences between participants and nonparticipants are substantial and significant.

It is of passing interest perhaps that those teachers who do not report participation in any of these activities have somewhat higher validity of response (avoidance of excessive use of self-enhancing and socially acceptable responses) scores than teachers who say they do participate, the differences being most pronounced when teachers reporting participation in painting, sculpture, and "attendance at concerts" are considered.

RELATION TO RELIGIOUS ACTIVITIES

In Table 82 are reported the scores of teachers according to their reported participation in certain religious activities. All of the differences among the different religious participation groups are small. There is a suggestion that teachers who participate *actively* (membership on church committees or teaching of Sunday school class) may score somewhat higher on the understanding, friendly teacher classroom behavior variable (X_{co}) than teachers in general.

It may be significant to note that at least 75 percent of the teachers in the Survey group reported listening to religious programs on the radio or reading religious articles in papers and magazines. Teachers as a group appear to be religiously inclined. This finding has support, also, in the recent survey conducted by the National Education Association (previously noted in chapter 3), which reported some 75 percent of the NEA sample to be active church members.

RELATION TO MEMBERSHIP IN PROFESSIONAL TEACHER ORGANIZATIONS

As may be judged from Table 83, approximately 83 percent of the Survey Sample reported affiliation with some professional teaching organization. (In the recent National Education Association study, only approximately 5 percent of the teachers responding said they were *not* members of professional teaching groups. The discrepancy between 17 percent, as found here, and 5 percent reported by NEA is understand-

TABLE 83

Schedule Scores of Teachers (Survey Sample) Who Profess Affiliation with Some Professional Organization

| | | ALL-TEACHER SCORING KEYS (99) | | | | | | | | | | | | | | | | | | | |
| CLASSIFICATION | N | X_{co} | | Y_{co} | | Z_{co} | | R_{co} | | R_{lco} | | Q_{co} | | B_{co} | | I_{ci} | | S_{ci} | | V_{ci} | |
		M	σ	M	σ	M	σ	M	σ	M	σ	M	σ	M	σ	M	σ	M	σ	M	σ
Professional affiliations	1,352	35.3	6.7	27.4	4.2	27.6	4.6	32.3	8.5	32.7	6.4	33.3	7.1	21.3	8.6	28.4	7.8	22.3	8.1	37.4	8.4
No professional affiliations reported	286	30.7	7.3	26.8	4.2	25.9	4.6	29.3	8.5	29.3	6.4	30.4	7.1	24.2	8.6	27.3	8.4	21.2	8.1	36.3	8.4
Aggregate Survey Sample	1,638	34.5	6.8	27.3	4.2	27.3	4.6	31.6	8.5	32.1	6.4	32.8	7.1	21.8	8.6	28.2	7.9	22.1	8.1	37.2	8.4

TABLE 84

Comparison of Schedule Scores of Teachers (Survey Sample) Classified According to Opinion Regarding Overlapping of Classroom and Administrative Responsibilities

| | | ALL-TEACHER SCORING KEYS (99) | | | | | | | | | | | | | | | | | | | |
| CLASSROOM AND ADMINISTRATIVE RESPONSIBILITIES SHOULD BE: | N* | X_{co} | | Y_{co} | | Z_{co} | | R_{co} | | R_{lco} | | Q_{co} | | B_{co} | | I_{ci} | | S_{ci} | | V_{ci} | |
		M	σ	M	σ	M	σ	M	σ	M	σ	M	σ	M	σ	M	σ	M	σ	M	σ
Separated	549	33.0	6.4	27.2	4.4	25.6	4.4	29.3	8.1	30.6	7.1	32.2	6.2	24.3	8.5	28.6	7.9	22.2	8.0	37.2	8.3
Overlapping	1,078	35.3	6.9	27.3	4.1	28.2	4.5	32.7	8.5	32.9	7.1	33.1	6.3	20.4	8.4	28.1	7.9	22.1	8.1	37.3	8.4
Aggregate Survey Sample	1,638	34.5	6.8	27.3	4.2	27.3	4.6	31.6	8.5	32.1	7.1	32.8	6.4	21.8	8.6	28.2	7.9	22.1	8.1	37.2	8.4

* Discrepancy between ΣN and Aggregate N attributable to nonresponse.

able in light of the sponsorship of the latter study, which favored higher return of the questionnaires by teacher association members.)

Except on the B_{co} scale, respondents in the Survey Sample who reported membership in some professional teaching organization had higher average scores on each dimension of the Schedule than did teachers who reported no professional affiliation. The t ratio was significant at the .05 level for each characteristic. Members of professional organizations had a significantly lower mean on the B_{co} scale, which indicates that they tend to have child-centered educational viewpoints.

RELATION TO TEACHER'S OPINIONS OF SHARING OF CLASSROOM AND ADMINISTRATIVE RESPONSIBILITIES

There is frequent discussion in education circles of whether (*a*) division of responsibility in the school is desirable (with classroom teachers relieved of most of the responsibilities of school administration) or, on the other hand, (*b*) teachers should share administrative responsibilities with the administrative officers through committee activities, special assignments, etc. Table 84 compares the scores of teachers in the Survey Sample according to their opinion of the relative desirability of separation or overlapping of classroom and administrative responsibilities.

These data suggest that teachers who believe administrative and classroom responsibilities should be shared by the classroom teacher and administrator may exhibit more friendly, understanding classroom behavior (X_{co}), stimulating classroom behavior (Z_{co}), favorable attitudes toward pupils (R_{co}), favorable attitudes toward democratic classroom practices (R_{1co}), favorable attitudes toward administrative and other school personnel (Q_{co}), and tendency toward child-centered educational viewpoints (B_{co}). The two groups do not differ with respect to responsible, businesslike classroom behavior (Y_{co}), verbal understanding (I_{ci}), emotional stability (S_{ci}), or validity of response (V_{ci}).

Teacher Characteristics Compared in Light of Conditions of Teacher's Earlier Life History

The comparisons of teacher characteristics reported in this section are concerned primarily with classifications of teachers based upon biographical data involving such considerations as type of college attended by the teacher, source of support while in college, college achievement, influences believed to have affected choice of teaching as a career, activities during childhood and adolescence, and recency of college instruction.

RELATION TO TYPE OF UNDERGRADUATE COLLEGE ATTENDED

Tables 85, 86, 87, and 88 provide comparisons of teachers when they are divided into groups on the basis of type of undergraduate college attended.

Before discussing differences among the scores of the teachers, note should be taken of the differences between the constitution of the Basic Analysis Sample and the Survey Sample (Table 85) with regard to undergraduate education.

Among the elementary teachers in the Basic Analysis Sample, 38 percent marked "teachers college or state college" and 36 percent indicated "large university" as the source of their undergraduate education, followed by a sizable group of 22 percent who reported that they had attended liberal arts colleges. In the Survey Sample, more than half of the elementary teachers had attended teachers colleges or state colleges, while much smaller proportions had attended liberal arts colleges, women's colleges, or large universities.

The distribution of secondary teachers presents a somewhat different picture. Among secondary teachers in the Basic Analysis Sample, 58 percent had taken their undergraduate college work at large universities, as compared with 26 percent at liberal arts colleges. In the Survey Sample the largest percentage of secondary teachers had attended liberal arts colleges (37 percent); somewhat fewer, but equal proportions (28 percent each), marked "teachers college or state college" and "large university"; and about 7 percent signified women's colleges as their undergraduate institutions.

In comparison with the Survey Sample, the Basic Analysis Sample consisted of larger proportions of teachers who had their instruction in

TABLE 85

Composition of Basic Analysis and Survey Samples Relative to Type of Undergraduate College Attended

| KIND OF COLLEGE | PERCENT REPORTING ATTENDANCE | | | |
| | Elementary Teachers | | Secondary Teachers | |
	Survey Sample	Basic Analysis Sample	Survey Sample	Basic Analysis Sample
Teachers college or state college	55 (56)*	38	28 (29)*	13
Liberal arts college............	16	22	37	26
Women's college..............	11	4	7	3
Large university..............	18	36	28	58

* Percent of teachers in NEA survey reporting larger part of college education completed at public or nonpublic teachers college. (Other categories employed by NEA study are not comparable with the classifications employed by the Teacher Characteristics Study.) NEA, *Research Bulletin,* **35:** No. 1, 1957.

TABLE 86

Comparison of Schedule Scores of Teachers (Survey Sample) Classified According to Type of Undergraduate College Attended

KIND OF COLLEGE	N*	ALL-TEACHER SCORING KEYS (99)																			
		X_{co}		Y_{co}		Z_{co}		R_{co}		R_{tco}		Q_{co}		B_{co}		I_{ci}		S_{ci}		V_{ci}	
		M	σ	M	σ	M	σ	M	σ	M	σ	M	σ	M	σ	M	σ	M	σ	M	σ
State or teachers college........	640	34.7	6.8	27.5	4.1	27.5	4.6	31.7	8.5	32.3	6.3	32.9	7.0	21.6	8.2	26.8	7.5	21.5	7.9	37.2	8.4
Liberal arts college........	461	34.2	6.7	26.6	4.2	26.9	4.4	31.0	8.3	31.5	6.2	32.6	6.8	22.7	8.7	29.3	7.8	22.5	8.2	37.3	8.5
Women's college........	146	33.3	7.3	27.9	4.2	26.3	5.2	30.8	9.2	31.7	6.9	32.4	8.1	22.5	8.4	29.3	7.6	21.7	8.1	36.1	8.3
Large university........	370	35.1	6.7	27.5	4.1	27.8	4.6	32.5	8.6	32.8	6.6	33.0	7.1	20.5	9.3	28.9	8.4	23.0	8.2	37.7	8.5
Aggregate Survey Sample........	1,640	34.5	6.8	27.3	4.2	27.3	4.6	31.6	8.5	32.1	6.4	32.8	7.1	21.8	8.6	28.2	7.9	22.1	8.1	37.2	8.4

* Discrepancy between ΣN and Aggregate N attributable to nonresponse.

TABLE 87

Comparison of Schedule Scores of Elementary and Secondary Teachers (Survey Sample) Classified According to Type of Undergraduate College Attended

KIND OF COLLEGE	N*	X_{co}		Y_{co}		Z_{co}		R_{co}		R_{tco}		Q_{co}		B_{co}		I_{ci}		S_{ci}		V_{ci}	
		M	σ	M	σ	M	σ	M	σ	M	σ	M	σ	M	σ	M	σ	M	σ	M	σ
ELEMENTARY TEACHERS; ALL-ELEMENTARY TEACHER SCORING KEYS (111)																					
State or teachers college........	365	44.9	13.4	28.6	7.5	41.0	10.4	35.1	13.1	28.7	9.7	28.0	8.4	25.0	8.1	25.7	7.4	21.1	7.8	36.2	8.5
Liberal arts college........	108	44.8	14.2	27.2	7.4	39.6	10.5	34.5	13.0	28.9	10.0	27.5	8.9	25.9	8.5	27.0	7.5	23.0	7.8	37.2	8.3
Women's college........	74	37.2	15.9	25.8	9.4	35.0	11.2	29.2	12.0	24.8	9.1	26.4	8.7	29.6	6.9	27.1	6.5	22.1	8.1	34.7	8.0
Large university........	112	46.9	15.2	29.8	8.8	42.6	11.0	38.2	15.1	30.1	11.6	29.1	9.1	22.8	9.2	26.6	8.3	22.1	8.3	37.4	7.6
Aggregate Elementary Survey Sample........	670	44.3	14.4	28.2	8.0	40.3	10.8	34.8	13.5	28.5	10.1	27.9	8.7	25.4	8.5	26.2	7.5	21.7	8.0	36.4	8.3
SECONDARY TEACHERS; ALL-SECONDARY TEACHER SCORING KEYS (100)																					
State or teachers college........	275	35.2	7.1	32.1	7.0	26.4	6.1	36.4	11.1	31.8	10.2	29.3	7.4	54.3	12.0	28.5	7.3	22.2	7.9	38.7	7.9
Liberal arts college........	353	34.1	6.8	32.5	6.7	27.5	6.1	36.0	10.9	31.5	10.5	28.8	7.5	54.9	13.6	30.0	7.7	21.3	8.3	37.4	8.5
Women's college........	72	36.3	6.8	36.1	6.5	28.4	6.4	38.4	11.1	37.1	10.5	28.9	7.2	49.8	11.6	31.6	7.9	21.2	8.1	37.5	8.4
Large university........	258	34.9	6.8	33.8	6.7	28.2	5.9	36.8	10.4	33.0	10.3	29.0	6.8	53.4	12.1	29.9	8.3	23.3	8.1	37.8	8.9
Aggregate Secondary Survey Sample........	964	34.8	6.9	32.9	6.9	27.5	6.1	36.6	10.8	32.4	10.4	29.0	7.2	53.9	12.5	29.7	7.8	22.5	8.1	37.9	8.4

* Discrepancy between ΣN and Aggregate N attributable to nonresponse.

TABLE 88

Comparison of Schedule Scores of Elementary and Secondary Teachers (Basic Analysis Sample) Classified According to Type of Undergraduate College Attended

KIND OF COLLEGE	N*	X_{ev}		Y_{co}		Z_{co}		R_{co}		R_{1co}		Q_{co}		B_{co}		I_{co}		S_{co}		V_{co}	
		M	σ	M	σ	M	σ	M	σ	M	σ	M	σ	M	σ	M	σ	M	σ	M	σ
ELEMENTARY TEACHERS; ALL-ELEMENTARY TEACHER SCORING KEYS (111)																					
State or teachers college....	355	49.9	15.3	30.6	8.7	43.3	10.6	39.8	15.1	32.3	11.0	32.0	9.4	23.6	9.7	40.8	7.3	41.6	9.6	24.1	4.7
Liberal arts college.........	213	51.8	15.6	30.6	9.3	44.0	12.2	40.8	14.1	32.7	10.6	32.8	9.9	22.5	9.1	41.9	7.3	42.9	9.9	25.1	4.5
Women's college...........	34	48.6	15.4	28.6	10.0	43.5	10.9	39.5	20.2	32.7	15.0	32.3	12.4	23.6	9.7	41.1	9.7	43.6	12.4	25.0	4.8
Large university...........	327	52.6	15.6	31.7	8.9	45.9	11.6	41.7	15.1	33.9	11.3	33.1	9.8	21.5	9.1	43.7	7.4	44.6	9.5	25.4	4.7
Aggregate Elementary Basic Analysis Sample.......	978	51.2	15.6	30.9	9.0	44.4	11.4	40.6	15.2	32.9	11.2	32.6	9.8	22.7	9.4	42.0	7.5	43.0	9.8	24.8	4.7
MATH-SCIENCE TEACHERS; MATH-SCIENCE SCORING KEYS (97)																					
State or teachers college....	79	33.1	6.2	35.9	7.7	32.5	6.5	40.1	14.0	29.5	13.2	31.5	7.9	56.8	16.2	35.9	8.5	28.7	4.5	22.4	4.6
Liberal arts college.........	132	31.5	5.6	35.1	8.0	30.4	6.3	36.8	11.8	27.8	10.3	31.1	7.9	60.1	12.5	35.4	8.3	29.3	4.4	22.3	4.6
Women's college...........	14	33.7	6.4	40.2	6.6	32.2	9.1	32.6	15.7	25.3	12.3	25.7	8.2	61.5	14.1	37.2	11.5	23.1	4.8	23.8	2.9
Large university...........	271	32.4	6.2	36.4	7.6	32.1	5.8	37.6	12.5	29.0	10.5	30.7	7.5	58.7	13.1	38.0	8.1	28.4	4.7	22.8	5.1
Aggregate Math-Science Basic Analysis Sample......	497	32.3	6.1	35.7	7.8	31.7	6.3	37.7	12.5	28.5	10.8	31.1	7.7	58.9	13.3	36.5	8.4	28.7	4.7	22.5	4.9
ENGLISH-SOCIAL STUDIES TEACHERS; ENGLISH-SOCIAL STUDIES SCORING KEYS (98)																					
State or teachers college....	60	39.3	8.2	34.4	8.0	27.3	6.6	44.7	11.8	40.7	9.9	32.8	9.0	44.8	11.8	42.1	9.0	26.0	4.2	22.8	4.8
Liberal arts college.........	139	38.5	9.1	33.3	7.0	28.8	6.7	42.3	13.5	39.9	12.0	32.1	8.2	45.0	15.1	41.7	8.4	26.8	5.0	22.6	4.8
Women's college...........	16	40.7	8.7	37.7	6.5	29.0	7.8	42.9	13.0	44.5	11.3	29.9	7.4	43.0	13.3	49.1	8.0	23.1	4.6	34.6	4.5
Large university...........	344	38.1	8.4	35.2	7.4	28.9	6.5	41.9	12.9	40.0	11.4	31.8	8.3	45.7	14.2	43.3	8.8	26.0	4.6	23.1	4.8
Aggregate English-Social Studies Basic Analysis Sample.	568	38.4	8.6	34.7	7.4	28.7	6.6	42.4	13.0	40.1	11.5	32.0	8.3	45.6	14.1	42.9	8.8	26.1	4.7	23.0	4.8

* Discrepancy between ΣN and Aggregate N attributable to nonresponse.

large universities, while the Survey Sample had larger proportions coming from the teachers college–state college type of institution. It seems probable that the Survey Sample is more like the population of teachers in the United States from the standpoint of undergraduate college attendance, not only because of the way the sample was accumulated (chapter 3), but also in view of the correspondence between the proportions reporting attendance at teachers colleges in the Survey Sample and those responding similarly to a national questionnaire distributed by the National Education Association and reported in 1957 (see Table 85).

Turning to the Schedule scores of teachers classified according to type of undergraduate college attended (Tables 86, 87, and 88), among the Basic Analysis Sample only ten of thirty F ratios were found to be significant at the .05 level, while for the Survey Sample the total number of significant F ratios was twenty. Thus, more differences were found between type-of-college groups when the Survey Sample was considered. If the suggestion made in the preceding paragraph is appropriate, differences found with regard to the Survey Sample may be somewhat more like those found among teachers in general throughout the United States.

For the Survey and Basic Analysis Samples considered together, no clear picture emerges relative to secondary teachers, and for elementary teachers only with regard to stimulating classroom behavior (Z_{co}) and child-centered educational viewpoints (B_{co}) is there correspondence between the Basic Analysis and Survey Samples (both yielding significant F ratios). In these two cases, teachers from large universities attained scores more indicative of stimulating behavior and permissive viewpoints than did teachers who had attended other types of colleges.

Among the Basic Analysis Sample elementary teachers considered alone, those from large universities obtained higher mean scores, and those from teacher colleges lower, relative to stimulating classroom behavior (Z_{co}), child-centered educational viewpoints (B_{co}), verbal understanding (I_{co}), emotional stability (S_{co}), and validity of response (V_{co}). Analysis of the scores of the English–social studies secondary teachers of the Basic Analysis Sample showed that women's college graduates (a very small sample) obtained higher scores, while graduates of large universities and liberal arts colleges attained lower scores relative to responsible, businesslike classroom behavior (Y_{co}). Among mathematics and science teachers, graduates of large universities scored higher with regard to verbal understanding (I_{co}), with liberal arts college graduates lowest. Women's college graduates were substantially lower than other groups among both English–social studies and mathematics-science teachers with respect to emotional stability (S_{co}) score.

When the Survey Sample is considered alone, the following tendencies may be noted:

Characteristic	Elementary Teachers	Secondary Teachers
X_{co} (friendly, understanding classroom behavior)	Graduates of large universities slightly higher; women's college graduates lower.	Women's college graduates higher.
Y_{co} (responsible, systematic, businesslike classroom behavior)	Graduates of large universities higher; women's college graduates lower.	Women's college graduates higher
Z_{co} (stimulating, imaginative classroom behavior)	Graduates of large universities higher; women's college graduates lower.	Graduates of women's colleges and large universities higher; state or teacher college graduates lower.
R_{co} (favorable opinion of pupils)	Graduates of large universities distinctly higher; women's college graduates lower.	No notable differences.
R_{1co} (favorable opinions of democratic classroom procedures)	Graduates of large universities higher; women's college graduates lower.	Women's college graduates higher.
Q_{co} (favorable attitude toward administrative and other school personnel)	No notable differences.	No notable differences.
B_{co} (learning-centered, traditional vs. permissive, child-centered educational viewpoints)	Graduates of large universities more permissive and child-centered in educational viewpoints; women's college graduates more traditional.	Women's college graduates more permissive and child-centered in educational viewpoints.
I_{ci} (verbal understanding)	Women's college and liberal arts college graduates slightly, but insignificantly, higher than aggregate sample; teachers college graduates lower.	Women's college graduates higher; teachers college graduates lower.
S_{ci} (emotional adjustment)	No notable differences.	No notable differences.
V_{ci} (validity of response)	No notable differences.	No notable differences.

RELATION TO SOURCE OF SUPPORT WHILE IN COLLEGE

Data presented in Table 89, based upon the Basic Analysis Sample of teachers, show the Schedule scores according to principal source of support for the teacher's education.

TABLE 89

Comparison of Schedule Scores of Elementary and Secondary Teachers (Basic Analysis Sample) Classified According to Source of Support While in College

SOURCE	N*	X_{co} M	σ	Y_{co} M	σ	Z_{co} M	σ	R_{co} M	σ	R_{Lco} M	σ	Q_{co} M	σ	B_{co} M	σ	I_{co} M	σ	S_{co} M	σ	V_{co} M	σ
ELEMENTARY TEACHERS; ALL-ELEMENTARY TEACHER SCORING KEYS (111)																					
Self-support............	319	51.2	15.9	31.4	8.5	44.6	11.4	41.9	15.5	34.0	11.0	32.7	9.8	22.4	10.1	41.8	7.8	43.0	10.1	24.5	4.7
Parents or other relatives.....	551	51.1	15.3	30.7	9.2	44.2	11.4	39.7	14.7	32.1	11.3	32.6	9.8	22.9	9.1	42.0	7.4	42.5	9.7	25.1	4.7
Scholarship or fellowship.....	74	54.2	15.5	30.5	9.4	46.5	11.3	44.1	15.9	35.5	10.8	33.5	10.0	21.8	9.4	45.2	7.1	47.1	9.0	24.5	4.5
Aggregate Elementary Basic Analysis Sample...........	978	51.2	15.6	30.9	9.0	44.4	11.4	40.6	15.2	32.9	11.2	32.6	9.8	22.7	9.4	42.0	7.5	43.0	9.8	24.8	4.7
MATH-SCIENCE TEACHERS; MATH-SCIENCE SCORING KEYS (97)																					
Self-support............	229	32.3	6.3	34.4	7.2	31.1	6.2	38.5	13.0	28.2	11.6	31.1	7.6	59.0	13.7	34.3	8.0	29.6	4.3	22.2	5.0
Parents or other relatives.....	208	31.7	5.8	38.2	8.0	32.2	6.3	37.0	12.4	29.1	10.4	31.0	8.2	59.9	13.4	39.5	7.6	27.1	4.7	22.9	4.6
Scholarship or fellowship.....	56	33.7	5.3	35.9	7.2	32.6	5.8	37.7	12.1	29.0	9.3	30.2	6.7	55.4	12.0	38.3	9.5	29.3	4.9	23.7	4.8
Aggregate Math-Science Basic Analysis Sample...........	497	32.3	6.1	35.7	7.8	31.7	6.3	37.7	12.5	28.5	10.8	31.1	7.7	58.9	13.3	36.5	8.4	28.7	4.7	22.5	4.9
ENGLISH-SOCIAL STUDIES TEACHERS; ENGLISH-SOCIAL STUDIES SCORING KEYS (98)																					
Self-support............	198	38.1	8.6	33.0	7.4	28.3	6.6	42.9	13.0	39.0	11.4	32.0	8.6	46.1	14.4	40.0	9.2	26.9	4.6	22.3	4.8
Parents or other relatives.....	289	38.1	8.3	36.0	6.9	28.2	6.3	42.0	13.3	40.5	11.6	32.3	8.3	46.0	13.9	44.4	8.0	25.2	4.5	23.2	4.8
Scholarship or fellowship.....	68	41.0	9.1	34.3	7.9	32.1	6.8	42.4	11.5	41.4	11.5	30.5	7.2	42.1	14.3	44.8	8.7	27.2	4.9	23.9	4.6
Aggregate English-Social Studies Basic Analysis Sample....	568	38.4	8.6	34.7	7.4	28.7	6.6	42.4	13.0	40.1	11.5	32.0	8.3	45.6	14.1	42.9	8.8	26.1	4.7	23.0	4.8

* Discrepancy between ΣN and Aggregate N attributable to nonresponse.

The only general tendency apparent in all samples is for teachers whose support has been dependent upon scholarships or fellowships to score relatively high with regard to verbal understanding (I_{co}), and for teachers dependent upon self-support to obtain substantially lower scores in this area. There is little unexpected about this finding.

Among elementary teachers the scholarship or fellowship group also attained higher mean scores relative to favorable attitude toward pupils (R_{co}), favorable attitude toward democratic school practices (R_{1co}), and emotional stability (S_{co}), in addition to the already-noted superiority with respect to verbal understanding.

Among secondary teachers, those who had been supported in college by parents or relatives scored higher relative to responsible, business-like classroom behavior (Y_{co}), but this same group scored significantly lower than the others with regard to emotional stability (S_{co}). In addition to the superiority of the scholarship-fellowship group with respect to verbal understanding, among the English–social studies teachers this group also scored significantly higher relative to stimulating classroom behavior (Z_{co}).

RELATION TO ACADEMIC SUCCESS

Table 90 shows the mean scores of Survey Sample teachers when they are classified according to their self-reported academic success while in college. It should be noted that these comparisons are made with regard to the teacher's own evaluation of his college achievement, and that this is reflected in the skewedness of the distribution, which is quite typical of self-reported data. (Actually, it might be more appropriate to think of self-reports of "good" academic success as really referring to "average," and self-reports of "average" as really meaning "somewhat below average.") Only 11 of the 1,640 teachers in the Survey Sample thought of themselves as having been poor students.

The picture is a rather clear one, with most of the scales (the exceptions being S_{ci} and V_{ci}) yielding F ratios significant at the .05 level. Generally, the teachers who thought of themselves as having been outstanding students scored higher than the other groups relative to friendly, understanding classroom behavior (X_{co}), responsible, businesslike classroom behavior (Y_{co}), stimulating, imaginative classroom behavior (Z_{co}), favorable attitude toward pupils (R_{co}), favorable attitude toward democratic pupil practices (R_{1co}), permissive, child-centered educational viewpoints (B_{co}), and verbal understanding (I_{ci}). The mean scores decrease in a fairly orderly fashion as the good student, average student, and poor student groups are considered. There were two excep-

TABLE 90

Comparison of Schedule Scores of Teachers (Survey Sample) Classified According to Self-Evaluation of Academic Success in College

EVALUATION	N^*	All-Teacher Scoring Keys (99)																			
		X_{co}		Y_{co}		Z_{co}		R_{co}		R_{1co}		Q_{co}		B_{co}		I_{ci}		S_{ci}		V_{ci}	
		M	σ	M	σ	M	σ	M	σ	M	σ	M	σ	M	σ	M	σ	M	σ	M	σ
Outstanding student	286	36.3	7.0	28.8	4.0	28.9	4.5	32.5	9.0	33.3	6.4	32.8	7.5	20.7	8.9	31.5	7.5	21.6	8.1	37.1	8.6
Good student	811	34.9	6.6	27.2	4.1	27.4	4.5	32.1	8.6	32.6	6.4	33.2	7.2	21.2	8.6	28.9	7.5	22.5	8.0	37.1	8.6
Average student	520	33.1	6.8	26.7	4.3	26.4	4.5	30.4	8.1	30.9	6.2	32.1	6.6	23.3	8.4	25.4	7.7	21.9	8.2	37.7	8.0
Poor student	11	32.5	5.2	26.5	4.1	26.2	5.5	28.9	8.0	29.2	3.6	31.7	6.4	22.6	7.6	30.3	8.1	22.5	8.5	36.2	9.5
Aggregate Survey Sample	1,640	34.5	6.8	27.3	4.2	27.3	4.6	31.6	8.5	32.1	6.4	32.8	7.1	21.8	8.6	28.2	7.9	22.1	8.1	37.2	8.4

* Discrepancy between ΣN and Aggregate N attributable to nonresponse.

tions to this general pattern: on Q_{co} (favorable attitude toward administrative and other school personnel) students who thought of themselves as having been "good" with respect to academic achievement scored slightly higher than those who said they had been outstanding students, and the 11 teachers who admitted to having been poor students scored *second only* to the "outstanding" students with respect to verbal understanding (I_{ci})!

The conclusion seems inescapable that there is a highly significant relationship between academic success in college and such characteristics as those with which the Study was concerned (if self-reports of academic success are to be trusted).

RELATION TO PRACTICE TEACHING

The data presented in Table 91 are based upon the comparison in two teacher education institutions (colleges located in different sections of the United States) of certain Schedule scores of student teachers (teachers engaged in practice teaching while in college) when the students were classified according to mark (or grade) received for their practice teaching performance. The student teachers responded to the Schedule while they were enrolled in college, and their practice teaching marks were obtained following completion of teacher education and college graduation. Although the marking systems differed in the two colleges, the grades of both were converted into a comparable four-point scale, on which Category 4 represented the equivalent of A work, or high-level performance, and Category 1, the equivalent of a D or F mark, or low-level performance.

The average scores of the students at these two teacher training institutions varied little with regard to their practice teaching marks. No F ratios significant at the .05 level were obtained among the means of either sample of elementary teachers. This is not dissimilar to the results reported in Tables 64 and 71, chapter 6, where, in another study, only Z_{co} and V_{co} were found to yield correlations with practice teaching marks which were significantly different from zero.

When secondary teachers are considered in Sample W, significant F ratios were obtained with respect to Z_{co}, B_{co}, and S_{co}. The C (Category 2) group of student teachers received lower mean scores on the scale measuring stimulating classroom behavior (Z_{co}) and emotional stability (S_{co}), and showed significantly less child-centered educational viewpoints (B_{co}), as compared with the other groups. When the groups of elementary and secondary teachers of Sample W were combined, similar results were obtained. There is almost (but not quite) a significant F ratio at the .05 level with regard to understanding, friendly classroom

TABLE 91

Schedule Scores of Student Teachers in Two Colleges Classified According to Judged Quality (Course Marks) of Practice Teaching Performance

Practice Teaching Mark	N	X_{co}		Y_{co}		Z_{co}		R_{co}		B_{co}		I_{co}		S_{co}	
		M	σ	M	σ	M	σ	M	σ	M	σ	M	σ	M	σ
ALL-TEACHER SCORING KEYS (99) ELEMENTARY TEACHERS, SAMPLE M															
(High)4..	19	40.1	6.3	29.5	3.4	30.5	5.0	35.6	11.0	17.6	11.0	37.1	5.4	36.1	4.9
3..	30	36.8	10.5	29.6	13.4	30.2	13.4	35.7	15.1	18.8	9.6	35.4	9.0	34.4	7.8
2..	7	40.3	4.0	28.0	2.0	28.9	3.6	37.9	6.4	16.4	3.0	37.3	5.8	37.0	4.8
(Low) 1..	0														
Total....	56	38.3	8.8	29.4	10.0	30.1	10.3	35.9	13.0	18.0	9.7	36.2	7.7	35.3	6.7
ELEMENTARY TEACHERS, SAMPLE W															
(High)4..	10	39.1	5.7	26.6	3.3	30.7	4.4	39.3	7.6	12.8	8.8	38.7	5.8	42.1	4.3
3..	20	37.3	5.7	25.5	2.8	28.6	4.7	35.0	10.3	14.2	7.9	38.0	7.3	40.2	3.9
2..	8	36.9	4.8	24.5	3.6	28.5	4.6	35.4	10.7	12.5	4.1	38.4	6.8	40.2	4.5
(Low) 1..	8	38.9	5.6	25.7	2.0	29.4	4.0	34.9	6.3	10.2	9.7	41.2	5.2	42.0	4.2
Total....	46	37.9	5.6	25.6	3.0	29.2	4.6	36.0	9.4	12.9	8.1	38.8	6.6	41.2	4.2
SECONDARY TEACHERS, SAMPLE W															
(High)4..	28	37.9	5.8	25.0	3.3	29.1	4.5	33.9	8.2	14.2	6.8	38.2	6.2	39.2	3.9
3..	36	38.2	7.1	25.8	4.0	29.2	4.5	33.6	9.8	11.0	9.0	37.5	6.8	39.6	6.1
2..	36	35.0	5.7	25.2	3.6	26.1	3.6	31.8	7.7	16.7	8.1	36.6	7.8	36.8	4.9
(Low) 1..	9	35.2	6.6	26.1	2.8	28.3	2.5	30.9	6.6	14.8	8.3	36.6	6.0	36.8	6.4
Total....	109	36.8	6.5	25.4	3.6	28.1	4.3	32.8	8.6	14.0	8.4	37.3	7.0	38.3	5.4
ELEMENTARY AND SECONDARY TEACHERS, SAMPLE W															
(High)4..	38	38.2	5.8	25.4	3.3	29.5	4.5	35.3	8.4	13.8	7.4	38.3	6.1	39.9	4.2
3..	56	37.9	6.6	25.7	3.6	29.0	4.6	34.1	10.1	12.1	8.8	37.7	7.0	40.0	5.4
2..	44	35.3	5.6	25.1	3.6	26.5	3.9	32.5	8.5	15.9	7.7	36.9	7.6	37.4	5.0
(Low) 1..	17	36.9	6.4	25.9	2.4	28.8	3.3	32.8	6.8	12.6	9.3	38.8	6.1	39.2	6.1
Total....	155	37.1	6.2	25.5	3.4	28.4	4.1	33.8	9.0	13.7	8.4	37.7	6.9	39.2	5.2

behavior (X_{co}), and there are significant F ratios with respect to stimulating, imaginative classroom behavior (Z_{co}) and emotional stability (S_{co}), with the A student teachers scoring higher and the C students lower on these characteristics. Interestingly, the D–F (Low) group scored fairly respectably on most of the characteristics, and even attained a mean score higher than those of the other groups with respect to verbal understanding (although the difference is not a significant one), suggesting, perhaps, that other variables may influence professors and supervisors responsible for assigning practice teaching marks.

Table 92 compares the scores of student teachers enrolled in the same two colleges referred to in Table 91 with those of in-service teachers comprising the Basic Analysis Sample. There were some differences between the two colleges in their elementary teacher samples—e.g., Sample M scored higher than Sample W with respect to responsible, business-like classroom behavior (Y_{co}), and Sample W scored higher than Sample M with regard to permissive, child-centered viewpoints (B_{co}) and emotional stability (S_{co}). Nevertheless, these student teachers, representing different institutions, curricula, and sections of the United States, do not appear to differ greatly from one another nor from elementary teach-

TABLE 91

Schedule Scores of Student Teachers in Two Colleges Classified
According to Judged Quality (Course Marks) of
Practice Teaching Performance

TABLE 92

Scores of Samples of Student Teachers Obtained in Two Colleges Located in Different Sections of the United States Compared with Scores of In-Service Teachers Comprising the Basic Analysis Sample

	ALL-TEACHER SCORING KEYS (99)																
	Elementary Teachers								Secondary Teachers				Elementary & Secondary Teachers Combined			
	Student Teachers						Basic Analysis Sample (N=978)		Student Teachers		Basic Analysis Sample (N=1,065)		Student Teachers		Basic Analysis Sample (N=2,043)	
	Sample M (N=56)		Sample W (N=46)		Samples M and W Combined (N=102)				Sample W (N=109)				Samples M and W Combined (N=211)			
SCORING KEY	M	σ	M	σ	M	σ	M	σ	M	σ	M	σ	M	σ	M	σ
99 X$_{co}$	38.3	8.8	37.9	5.6	38.1	7.5	38.0	7.3	36.8	6.5	35.9	7.2	37.5	7.0	36.9	7.3
99 Y$_{co}$	29.4	10.0	25.6	3.0	27.7	7.9	27.8	3.9	25.4	3.6	27.0	4.5	26.5	6.2	27.4	4.2
99 Z$_{co}$	30.1	10.3	29.2	4.6	29.7	8.3	28.6	5.4	28.1	4.3	27.4	4.8	28.9	6.6	28.0	5.2
99 R$_{co}$	35.9	13.0	36.0	9.4	35.9	11.5	36.6	9.4	32.8	8.6	33.7	9.3	34.3	10.2	35.1	9.5
99 B$_{co}$	18.0	9.7	12.9	8.1	15.7	9.4	16.8	9.2	14.0	8.4	21.0	9.0	14.8	8.9	19.0	9.7
99 I$_{co}$	36.2	7.7	38.8	6.6	38.8	7.3	35.9	7.1	37.3	7.0	37.6	7.4	37.3	7.1	36.8	7.3
99 S$_{co}$	35.3	6.7	41.2	4.2	37.9	6.4	36.6	6.1	38.3	5.4	36.3	5.9	38.1	5.9	36.4	6.0

behavior (Y$_{co}$) . . . . with respect to stimulating, imaginative teaching (Y$_{co}$) . . . . emotional stability
(S$_{co}$). . . . . and that the Casterle is
lower on this . . . . (two-cru-
. . . several individuals . . . . the extreme . . . . and to . . . . . .
table 92 . . . . those of the College with regard
to values . . . . be . . . . a significant
. . . . reveal a marked score increase . . . .
and superiority . . . . for . . . .

Table 92 . . . . student teachers in the two colleges, the same
two colleges . . . . . referred to in Table 91 . . . with . . . . the teachers
comprising the Basic Analysis Sample. . . . . were some differences between the two colleges in their elementary teacher samples—on Sample
M scored higher than Sample W with respect to reasonable, businesslike classroom behavior (R$_{co}$) and Sample W scored higher than Sample
M with regard to permissive, child-centered viewpoint (B$_{co}$) and emotional stability (S$_{co}$). Nevertheless, these student teachers, representing
different institutions, colleges and sections of the United States, did
not appear to differ greatly from . . . . for . . . . elementary teach-

316

ers in general as represented by the Basic Analysis Sample. This general similarity to the Basic Analysis Sample also is to be noted in the case of the student teachers in Sample W who are preparing to teach in the secondary school, and the combined student-teacher groups from the two colleges, M and W. It is true that some differences between the means of the combined student-teacher samples and those of the total Basic Analysis Sample were significant at the .05 level—favoring the student teachers relative to stimulating, imaginative classroom behavior (Z_{co}), permissive child-centered educational viewpoints (B_{co}), and emotional stability (S_{co}), and favoring the Basic Analysis Sample from the standpoint of responsible, businesslike classroom behavior (Y_{co})—but the actual differences between the means are relatively small. At any rate, it appears that for these two samples at least, student teachers are at no disadvantage in taking the Teacher Characteristics Schedule as compared with teachers in service.

RELATION TO INFLUENCES AFFECTING CHOICE OF TEACHING

It is of considerable interest to review the influences which individuals believe have affected their choice of teaching as a career and to observe certain relationships between such presumed influences and measured teacher characteristics. The comparisons of Table 93 show the scores of teachers according to their indication of certain factors that they believed had influenced their choice of teaching as a life work. In a sense, the tabled data show what might have been expected—that teachers who entered the profession because of its intellectual nature, because they liked school, and because of the public and social service character of teaching generally scored higher on most of the teacher characteristics here considered; and persons who became teachers because they were advised (or perhaps urged) to do so by parents or relatives, or because of attractiveness of teaching from the standpoint of desirable position in the community and favorable prospects for advancement, scored relatively lower.

Among elementary teachers in the Basic Analysis Sample there is a general pattern discernible for teachers who named "satisfying experience in school work," "opportunity for public service," and "desire for intellectual growth" as influences affecting their choice of teaching to attain higher scores relative to understanding, friendly classroom behavior (X_{co}), responsible, businesslike classroom behavior (Y_{co}), stimulating, imaginative classroom behavior (Z_{co}), favorable attitudes toward pupils (R_{co}), favorable attitudes toward administrators and other school personnel (Q_{co}), permissive, child-centered educational viewpoints (B_{co}), verbal understanding (I_{co}), and emotional stability (S_{co}),

TABLE 93

Comparison of Schedule Scores of Elementary and Secondary Teachers (Basic Analysis Sample) Classified According to Factors Believed To Have Influenced Choice of Teaching as a Career

INFLUENCE	N*	X_{co} M	σ	Y_{co} M	σ	Z_{co} M	σ	R_{co} M	σ	R_{1co} M	σ	Q_{co} M	σ	B_{co} M	σ	I_{co} M	σ	S_{co} M	σ	V_{co} M	σ
ELEMENTARY TEACHERS; ALL-ELEMENTARY TEACHER SCORING KEYS (111)																					
Parents or other relatives	60	40.0	15.8	27.4	7.7	35.9	11.2	29.5	14.1	25.0	11.3	27.8	9.7	26.9	9.7	38.8	7.8	36.3	10.1	26.1	3.6
Employer or supervisor	2	61.5	9.5	27.0	5.0	43.9	9.0	54.5	7.5	42.5	4.5	36.5	4.5	13.0	6.0	51.5	3.5	55.5	4.5	25.0	5.0
Educational adviser	48	45.3	15.2	27.5	9.1	39.5	10.3	34.5	16.2	28.7	11.9	37.2	10.4	24.1	9.2	39.4	7.1	39.8	9.1	26.4	4.8
Enjoyment of school environment	106	46.9	15.1	29.7	7.8	40.7	10.6	37.8	14.3	30.7	10.9	30.6	9.5	23.4	8.8	40.2	7.1	40.6	9.9	25.1	4.8
Satisfying experience in school work	680	53.8	14.7	31.8	9.1	46.4	10.9	42.8	14.6	34.5	10.8	34.0	9.5	22.0	9.0	42.8	7.4	44.2	9.5	24.4	4.7
Favorable prospect of advancement	33	37.2	15.1	28.2	9.0	35.5	10.2	28.4	13.5	27.0	10.8	27.0	10.1	28.9	9.0	39.1	8.5	35.5	9.5	27.2	5.1
Desire for satisfying position in community	65	40.2	15.7	30.0	8.3	37.6	12.1	32.0	14.6	27.2	11.1	27.9	9.6	26.8	9.4	38.3	8.3	36.4	10.4	24.9	5.1
Desire to help people	136	49.4	15.2	31.0	9.1	41.5	10.8	38.4	15.1	31.7	11.1	32.4	9.9	24.3	10.6	40.6	7.3	41.8	9.3	26.0	4.7
Opportunity for public service	129	54.8	13.9	32.1	9.1	46.5	11.0	43.8	13.1	35.2	10.4	33.7	9.2	20.4	8.7	42.3	7.1	44.3	9.2	24.4	4.8
Desire for intellectual growth	491	54.5	14.5	31.2	9.2	47.0	10.8	43.8	14.7	34.1	10.8	34.1	9.6	21.4	8.8	44.3	7.3	44.8	9.5	24.3	4.6
Aggregate Elementary Basic Analysis Sample	978	51.2	15.6	30.9	9.0	44.4	11.4	40.6	15.2	32.9	11.2	32.6	9.8	22.7	9.4	42.0	7.5	43.0	9.8	24.8	4.7
MATH-SCIENCE TEACHERS; MATH-SCIENCE SCORING KEYS (97)																					
Parents or other relatives	25	29.2	7.7	35.1	9.2	29.4	9.1	31.8	10.0	24.0	8.3	29.6	6.5	67.7	12.8	33.3	8.2	26.5	3.8	22.6	3.8
Employer or supervisor	10	30.2	8.6	27.4	5.9	31.6	7.0	33.3	11.3	27.4	11.9	27.3	7.0	59.0	14.5	34.6	6.8	31.1	4.2	25.8	2.6
Educational adviser	15	34.9	5.2	33.9	7.0	32.1	4.3	46.3	14.5	34.7	11.9	34.3	8.3	50.4	11.5	36.4	7.5	31.1	5.7	21.7	4.5
Enjoyment of school environment	60	31.0	5.3	33.5	7.5	29.7	5.6	36.8	11.7	25.8	9.4	30.3	7.1	61.0	12.4	33.8	8.7	29.0	4.6	22.4	4.2
Satisfying experience in school work	359	32.8	5.9	33.6	7.5	32.2	6.7	38.6	11.3	29.7	10.1	31.3	7.5	57.9	13.3	38.0	8.2	28.5	4.7	22.3	5.0
Favorable prospect of advancement	33	28.9	6.7	35.4	8.8	28.4	7.6	30.6	12.7	22.4	10.0	29.2	7.7	67.2	11.0	34.6	9.0	26.8	4.8	25.5	3.5
Desire for satisfying position in community	36	29.0	6.2	37.1	8.5	31.4	5.8	34.7	10.5	25.5	10.9	29.5	8.5	64.7	12.0	36.6	8.3	27.3	4.3	25.7	4.0
Desire to help people	73	33.3	5.5	34.5	6.7	31.5	5.8	34.7	11.0	26.5	9.9	30.2	7.4	61.3	12.8	34.1	8.3	29.7	4.3	23.2	4.1
Opportunity for public service	68	33.3	6.3	35.9	7.9	32.3	5.8	38.5	12.0	28.1	9.9	30.7	7.4	58.7	11.8	36.0	7.3	29.5	4.6	22.0	5.0
Desire for intellectual growth	266	32.8	5.8	36.3	7.7	31.7	6.2	39.8	13.1	31.1	11.0	31.7	7.5	55.8	13.6	38.3	7.3	28.5	4.7	21.6	4.9
Aggregate Math-Science Basic Analysis Sample	497	32.3	6.1	35.7	7.8	31.7	6.3	37.7	12.5	28.5	10.8	31.1	7.7	58.9	13.3	36.5	8.4	28.7	4.7	22.5	4.9
ENGLISH-SOCIAL STUDIES TEACHERS; ENGLISH-SOCIAL STUDIES SCORING KEYS (98)																					
Parents or other relatives	321	37.9	8.4	35.9	7.2	27.9	6.8	41.9	13.1	39.7	11.6	31.9	8.3	46.6	14.1	43.6	8.7	25.5	4.5	22.5	4.8
Employer or supervisor	51	39.2	8.4	34.2	6.8	30.3	6.5	43.1	11.6	42.6	9.8	32.6	9.0	40.8	12.8	43.6	9.0	26.9	4.1	22.0	4.6
Educational adviser	157	39.2	8.3	33.6	7.4	29.3	6.4	44.9	12.6	42.0	11.2	32.6	9.0	42.5	12.8	42.5	8.9	27.1	4.5	21.0	4.1
Enjoyment of school environment	412	39.5	8.5	34.5	7.4	28.9	6.4	44.0	12.7	42.0	11.2	32.7	9.3	44.0	14.0	43.4	8.6	26.4	4.4	22.6	4.6
Satisfying experience in school work	418	39.5	8.3	35.0	7.2	28.8	6.7	43.8	12.9	41.0	11.5	32.6	8.4	44.4	14.0	43.4	8.8	26.1	4.7	22.5	4.7
Favorable prospect of advancement	190	38.3	8.2	34.8	7.4	27.7	6.7	42.4	12.9	39.6	11.5	32.6	8.5	45.9	14.2	42.6	8.8	25.9	4.7	22.6	4.4
Desire for satisfying position in community	234	38.7	8.7	34.5	7.3	28.4	6.7	43.4	13.1	40.2	11.7	32.7	7.8	45.2	14.6	43.1	8.5	26.0	4.7	22.1	4.6
Desire to help people	364	40.3	8.0	34.4	7.4	29.4	6.5	45.2	12.4	41.8	11.1	33.5	8.5	45.2	14.6	43.2	9.1	26.6	4.7	21.8	4.4
Opportunity for public service	255	39.7	8.1	34.6	7.4	29.8	6.1	45.2	12.4	41.8	11.1	33.5	8.0	43.3	13.7	43.2	9.1	26.5	4.7	21.2	4.4
Desire for intellectual growth	341	39.6	8.3	34.7	7.5	29.2	6.5	44.4	13.0	42.2	11.2	32.9	8.6	42.9	13.9	44.0	8.7	26.2	4.6	22.2	4.8
Aggregate English–Social Studies Basic Analysis Sample	568	38.4	8.6	34.7	7.4	28.7	6.6	42.4	13.0	40.1	11.5	32.0	8.3	45.6	14.1	42.9	8.8	26.1	4.7	23.0	4.8

* Multiple response possible; a teacher may report more than one influence.

while teachers who named the influence of "parents or other relatives," "favorable prospects of advancement," and "desire for satisfying position in community" tended to score lower. The higher scores on V_{co} (tendency to avoid excessive use of self-enhancing responses) were attained by teachers who frankly named "favorable prospects for advancement" as an influence, and lower scores were achieved by teachers who named socially desirable influences such as "satisfying school experience," "opportunity for public service," and desire for intellectual growth." Such a finding suggests interesting hypotheses.

Among secondary teachers, the differences in average scores among teachers marking different influence categories are much less distinct than among elementary teachers. Differences in mean score between the sources of influence are particularly small for the English–social studies teachers, although such differences as were statistically significant were found to follow the general trend observed with respect to secondary teachers of mathematics and science. And differences in the mathematics-science sample are generally similar (though less extreme), to those obtained for elementary teachers. Generally speaking, teachers who noted as factors in choice of teaching the influence of "educational adviser," "satisfying experience of school work," "desire to help people," "opportunity for public service," and "desire for intellectual growth" tended to score higher on all characteristics except Y_{co} and V_{co} (with "desire for satisfying position in community" also being an influence named by relatively high-scoring persons on Y_{co}). There is also a trend among the secondary teachers, already noted with respect to elementary teachers, for "favorable prospects for advancement" and "desire for satisfying position in community," to be marked by those obtaining higher mean scores on V_{co}.

It may be of interest to note the variation among the three teacher samples (elementary, mathematics-science, and English–social studies) in relative frequency with which each of the "influences" was said to have affected choice of teaching as a career. For the elementary teachers and mathematics-science teachers, the percentages of teachers marking the several possible influences were rather similar with "satisfying experience in school work" and "desire for intellectual growth" noted by half or more of each sample, and with other influences ranging from 1 to 15 percent frequency of mention. The response of the English–social studies teachers presents a rather radically differing picture with "influence of parents and other relatives" being marked by 56 percent of this sample (compared with 6 percent and 5 percent, respectively for the elementary and mathematics-science teachers), "influence of educational adviser" by 28 percent, "enjoyment of school environment" and "satisfying experience in school work" each by 75 percent, "favorable prospects for advancement" by 33 percent, "desire for satisfying position in community" by 41 percent, "desire to help people" by 64 percent, and "opportunity for public service" by 45 percent. Intriguing hypotheses regarding the differences between English–social studies teachers and other groups might be suggested from this sidelight.

RELATION TO ACTIVITIES DURING CHILDHOOD AND ADOLESCENCE

To what extent may certain characteristics of teachers be traceable to behavior patterns which were expressed in related, but different, channels long before the individual entered teaching as a profession? With this question in the minds of the Study staff, participants in the research were queried about their adolescent and childhood participation in certain kinds of activities (hypothesized to be related to the same underlying traits which may predispose one to teaching).

Table 94 shows the mean scores on the Schedule scales of teachers of the Survey Sample (elementary and secondary teachers combined) who professed to have participated in the specified activities during childhood and adolescence.

Of particular interest is the comparison of the scores of those teachers who participated in at least one of the activities named with those of the teachers who participated in *none* of them. Significant t ratios (.05 level) were obtained between nonparticipation and each of the activities listed for understanding, friendly classroom behavior (X_{co}), responsible, businesslike classroom behavior (Y_{co}), stimulating, imaginative classroom behavior (Z_{co}), favorable attitude toward pupils (R_{co}), favorable attitudes toward democratic classroom practices (R_{1co}), favorable attitudes toward administrative and other school personnel (Q_{co}), and permissive *vs.* traditional educational viewpoints (B_{co}). Participation during childhood and adolescence in such activities as those named, it seems, may offer significant clues to the present characteristics of teachers. Among these several activities, teachers who said they had "read to children" and "taken class for teacher" generally tended to score higher (although often the differences did not attain statistical significance) than others, particularly those teachers who said they had "taken care of children in own family" and "played school." Apparently such an activity as "playing school" in childhood is fairly commonplace among persons who now are teachers, since about 61 percent of the sample indicated they had done so.

RELATION TO RECENCY OF COLLEGE TRAINING

Table 95 shows the scores of teachers in the Survey Sample classified according to recency of college enrollment. Significant F ratios (.05

TABLE 94

Comparison of Schedule Scores of Teachers (Survey Sample) Classified According to Professed Participation in Certain Kinds of Activities during Childhood or Adolescence

Activities	N^*	X_{co}		Y_{co}		Z_{co}		R_{co}		R_{lco}		Q_{co}		B_{co}		I_{ci}		S_{ci}		V_{ci}	
		M	σ	M	σ	M	σ	M	σ	M	σ	M	σ	M	σ	M	σ	M	σ	M	σ
										All-Teacher Scoring Keys (99)											
Child care (family)	585	35.1	6.8	27.7	4.0	27.5	4.5	33.4	8.4	32.8	6.3	33.5	6.9	21.3	8.7	28.6	7.8	22.5	8.0	36.9	8.5
Child care (nonfamily)	403	36.2	7.0	28.4	4.0	27.5	4.6	33.6	8.7	33.6	6.4	33.4	7.2	19.8	9.0	28.9	7.4	22.7	8.1	36.6	8.5
Played school	994	35.2	6.8	28.6	3.7	27.5	4.7	32.5	8.5	32.8	6.3	33.2	7.2	21.3	8.6	28.5	7.8	21.8	7.9	37.3	8.4
Read to children	538	36.6	6.8	28.8	3.7	28.1	4.7	34.4	8.6	34.0	6.5	34.2	7.3	19.8	8.7	29.1	7.8	22.7	7.8	36.7	8.5
Took class for teacher	567	36.5	6.4	28.8	3.9	28.1	4.4	33.0	8.4	33.4	6.2	33.7	7.3	20.5	8.3	29.1	7.6	22.6	8.0	36.9	8.3
Participated in none of above activities	244	32.5	6.7	24.4	4.0	26.7	4.5	29.2	8.3	30.9	6.3	31.9	6.6	22.9	8.7	28.4	7.8	23.1	8.3	37.7	8.5
Aggregate Survey Sample	1,640	34.5	6.8	27.3	4.2	27.3	4.6	31.6	8.5	32.1	6.4	32.8	7.1	21.8	8.6	28.2	7.9	22.1	8.1	37.2	8.4

* Multiple response possible; a teacher may report more than one activity.

TABLE 95

Comparison of Schedule Scores of Teachers (Survey Sample) Classified According to Recency of College Enrollment

Recency of College Enrollment	N^*	X_{co}		Y_{co}		Z_{co}		R_{co}		R_{lco}		Q_{co}		B_{co}		I_{ci}		S_{ci}		V_{ci}	
		M	σ	M	σ	M	σ	M	σ	M	σ	M	σ	M	σ	M	σ	M	σ	M	σ
										All-Teacher Scoring Keys (99)											
Now enrolled	310	35.7	7.1	27.2	4.3	27.7	4.9	33.2	8.8	33.4	6.7	33.5	6.9	19.0	8.9	28.0	7.6	23.1	8.4	36.9	8.4
1 year ago	628	34.7	6.7	27.3	4.1	27.2	4.5	31.7	8.4	32.4	6.4	32.9	7.3	21.4	8.4	27.5	7.9	22.4	8.0	37.0	8.7
3 years ago	347	34.1	6.7	26.8	4.0	26.7	4.5	31.0	8.2	31.5	5.9	32.6	6.7	22.6	8.3	28.0	8.0	22.3	7.9	37.6	7.9
5 or more years ago	328	33.6	6.8	27.9	4.3	26.7	4.3	30.5	8.6	31.3	6.4	32.1	7.3	24.0	8.5	30.1	7.9	20.7	7.9	37.7	8.3
Aggregate Survey Sample	1,640	34.5	6.8	27.3	4.2	27.3	4.6	31.6	8.5	32.1	6.4	32.8	7.1	21.8	8.6	28.2	7.9	22.1	8.1	37.2	8.4

* Discrepancy between ΣN and Aggregate N attributable to nonresponse.

level) were obtained with respect to each of the sets of means compared, except for characteristic V_{ci} (validity of response).

Teachers who were currently or recently enrolled in college courses tended to attain higher scores than did teachers who had been away from college for five or more years on the following scales: X_{co} (understanding, friendly classroom behavior); Z_{co} (stimulating, imaginative classroom behavior)—a slight tendency; R_{co} (favorable attitudes toward children); R_{1co} (favorable attitudes toward democratic practices in the classroom); Q_{co} (favorable attitudes toward administrators and other school personnel)—a very small difference; B_{co} (permissive, child-centered educational viewpoints); and S_{ci} (emotional stability). Teachers who had not been enrolled in college courses for five or more years attained higher scores, however, relative to Y_{co} (responsible, businesslike classroom behavior) and I_{ci} (verbal understanding).

Teacher Characteristics Compared in Light of Conditions of Teacher's Current Employment

The third set of comparisons undertaken has to do less directly with the teacher's personal and social status and activities, dealing rather with classifications of teachers according to certain conditions of employment, and thus comparing teacher groups according to grade level and subject taught, size of school in which employed, size of community in which employed, socioeconomic status of community, cultural level of community, auspices of school, methodological emphasis of school, and geographic area in which teaching is performed.

RELATION TO GRADE LEVEL OR SUBJECT TAUGHT

Tables 96, 97, and 98, together with Table 72, serve two purposes: (1) they make possible comparisons of teachers relative to the characteristics measured when teachers have been classified according to grade level or subject matter taught, and (2) they provide grade and subject means and standard deviations which may be employed for norms purposes. Their use as norms needs no discussion beyond the note that means and standard deviations of the scales of the Teacher Characteristics Schedule are provided separately for several scoring keys—e.g., All-Teacher Keys (99), All-Elementary Teacher Keys (111), and All-Secondary Teacher Keys (100) (see chapter 6)—and that evaluation of a teacher's scores, or the scores of a group of teachers, must be made in the light of the scoring key used in arriving at those scores.

Comparisons of the mean scores of the various grade-level and subject-matter groups comprising the Survey and Basic Analysis Samples, although revealing the different patterning of characteristics among dif-

TABLE 96

Schedule Scores of Teachers (Survey Sample) Classified According to Grade (Elementary) or Subject (Secondary) Taught

GRADE OR SUBJECT TAUGHT	N*	ALL-TEACHER SCORING KEYS (99)																		
		X_{co}		Y_{co}		Z_{co}		R_{co}		R_{tco}		Q_{co}		B_{co}		I_{ci}		S_{ci}		V_{oi}	
		M	σ	M	σ	M	σ	M	σ	M	σ	M	σ	M	σ	M	σ	M	σ	M	σ
Elementary																					
Grade 2	187	35.8	7.1	28.5	3.8	28.2	5.1	33.8	8.7	33.4	6.5	33.8	7.5	19.5	8.7	25.7	8.1	22.2	8.1	36.7	8.5
Grades 3–4	250	34.7	6.9	28.2	3.6	27.4	4.6	32.2	9.0	32.7	6.5	32.9	7.2	20.7	7.9	25.9	7.1	21.5	7.7	36.8	8.7
Grades 5–6	188	35.1	7.3	27.4	3.8	27.2	5.1	32.8	8.9	32.8	6.9	33.5	6.7	20.3	9.9	26.6	7.4	21.6	8.3	35.7	7.7
Grades 7–8	45	33.7	6.7	27.9	3.9	27.2	4.6	31.7	9.1	31.9	6.8	32.4	7.4	22.7	7.5	27.0	7.8	20.2	6.7	35.1	6.8
Secondary																					
Art	5	38.8	1.0	30.0	3.9	30.2	2.5	32.2	6.7	34.6	1.0	30.8	5.8	13.2	3.8	32.2	7.1	24.6	8.3	40.2	8.7
Biological science	124	34.7	5.9	25.6	4.3	27.8	4.1	30.7	7.6	31.7	6.2	33.0	6.6	22.5	8.1	28.8	7.5	23.9	8.2	37.0	8.4
Business educ.	30	33.7	6.4	25.4	3.5	27.3	4.5	28.7	6.5	30.2	5.2	30.5	5.5	24.9	7.7	26.7	7.9	22.5	8.1	40.8	6.9
English	280	35.0	6.5	28.9	4.2	27.4	4.6	31.7	8.4	32.6	6.0	32.2	7.7	20.8	8.2	31.6	7.7	20.9	7.9	38.2	8.4
Foreign language	58	34.5	6.6	28.5	4.1	27.8	4.2	30.7	9.4	32.6	6.5	31.8	8.0	20.9	8.5	32.9	8.1	20.4	7.6	36.8	8.2
Handicrafts	9	35.9	5.7	28.0	4.4	29.4	4.6	31.2	6.9	33.3	3.7	29.8	6.5	16.1	5.9	30.6	10.0	22.8	8.5	33.8	11.2
Home economics educ.	9	35.3	7.6	27.2	2.6	25.2	3.3	30.6	8.0	30.0	5.8	33.0	5.2	24.3	8.6	28.4	6.4	26.4	5.2	35.9	8.0
Industrial arts	8	30.4	6.1	24.1	4.6	26.9	5.5	25.6	7.7	27.5	2.6	28.6	5.1	28.0	6.2	21.4	7.9	23.3	8.8	39.5	8.0
Mathematics	279	33.1	6.7	25.8	4.2	26.7	4.2	29.6	7.8	30.4	6.0	32.7	6.5	24.4	8.3	29.2	7.7	24.0	6.9	37.3	8.8
Music	13	30.1	9.9	25.8	8.5	23.2	7.9	25.5	10.0	27.5	8.0	26.8	8.7	22.6	11.1	26.8	7.2	24.0	8.0	36.7	9.2
Physical educ. (boys)	39	31.4	4.8	23.8	2.8	26.7	2.3	26.0	6.1	28.8	4.8	30.1	6.0	23.9	7.4	23.6	6.4	26.1	8.0	36.8	9.0
Physical educ. (girls)	16	34.1	3.9	27.6	3.3	28.3	3.3	29.9	6.1	32.8	4.5	31.3	5.9	21.3	5.9	28.8	8.0	25.1	8.1	35.3	8.5
Physical science	151	34.0	7.1	23.8	3.9	27.0	4.2	31.4	8.3	31.3	6.2	33.9	6.0	23.5	8.6	29.8	7.2	25.0	8.0	36.9	8.7
Social studies	242	34.5	6.7	27.3	4.3	27.0	4.1	30.7	8.8	32.1	6.0	32.1	7.0	22.4	7.8	28.4	7.8	22.4	8.1	38.3	8.7
Vocational educ.	14	35.0	6.2	26.7	3.1	27.0	4.1	29.6	8.2	32.5	6.6	32.1	6.3	21.8	8.3	29.1	6.6	27.6	6.7	34.4	6.9
Aggregate Survey Sample	1,640	34.5	6.8	27.3	4.2	27.3	4.6	31.6	8.5	32.1	6.4	32.1	7.1	21.8	8.6	28.2	7.9	22.1	8.1	37.2	8.4

* Although direction to participants was to indicate "principal" grade or subject taught, a number of secondary teachers believed their principal fields of teaching involved more than one of the categories employed by the Study. Therefore, N exceeds the Aggregate N, particularly for secondary teachers reflecting the overlapping of teaching areas.

TABLE 97

Teacher Characteristics Schedule Scores of Elementary and Secondary Teachers (Survey Sample) Classified According to Grade or Subject Taught and Subgrouped According to Sex

Grade or Subject Taught	N*	X_{co}		Y_{co}		Z_{co}		R_{co}		R_{teo}		Q_{co}		B_{co}		I_{ci}		S_{ci}		V_{ci}	
		M	σ	M	σ	M	σ	M	σ	M	σ	M	σ	M	σ	M	σ	M	σ	M	σ
ELEMENTARY TEACHERS; ALL-ELEMENTARY SCORING KEYS (111)																						
Preschool, Grades 1–2																						
Female	181	45.3	13.9	27.3	8.3	40.6	10.7	39.7	12.6	28.8	10.1	28.9	9.3	23.6	7.9	25.7	8.1	22.2	8.2	36.9	8.5
Male	6	42.0	13.1	29.2	10.5	38.8	9.7	39.1	13.9	31.3	11.4	30.5	13.5	24.8	7.6	24.0	8.4	21.3	7.4	30.2	8.0
Grades 3–4																						
Female	236	43.5	13.8	27.8	7.7	40.5	10.4	33.6	13.5	27.7	9.6	27.7	8.1	26.4	8.1	26.1	7.1	21.4	7.8	37.0	8.6
Male	14	46.3	17.8	29.3	10.8	41.1	9.6	36.1	14.6	28.6	9.5	28.7	11.5	26.3	8.4	23.7	7.7	22.8	7.1	32.0	7.9
Grades 5–6																						
Female	143	43.8	15.5	29.2	7.7	39.8	11.7	34.5	14.1	28.8	10.9	27.2	8.5	26.1	9.2	26.7	7.3	20.8	7.9	35.2	7.7
Male	45	50.2	14.8	30.4	7.2	42.6	11.5	39.0	13.1	31.8	9.5	28.8	7.8	22.3	9.1	26.4	7.5	24.8	8.9	37.1	7.6
Grades 7–8																						
Female	35	41.3	12.1	28.6	7.0	38.1	9.1	33.0	13.4	26.4	9.2	25.9	8.3	28.4	7.6	27.2	7.8	20.4	6.9	34.7	6.6
Male	10	38.4	10.4	25.0	7.9	35.9	7.3	33.0	15.5	26.9	10.4	28.9	8.7	28.1	7.6	26.0	8.1	19.3	5.9	36.6	7.6
Aggregate Elementary Survey Sample	670	44.3	14.4	28.2	8.0	40.3	10.8	34.8	13.5	28.5	10.1	27.9	8.7	25.4	8.5	26.2	7.5	21.7	8.0	36.4	8.3
SECONDARY TEACHERS† ALL-SECONDARY TEACHER SCORING KEYS (100)																						
Biological science																						
Female	51	34.7	6.4	36.2	7.5	29.4	7.2	36.7	10.4	33.6	10.1	27.9	7.0	51.5	14.0	30.2	6.8	22.8	7.9	38.0	8.0
Male	73	34.1	6.2	28.4	6.1	28.0	5.4	35.8	10.2	26.2	9.3	28.6	6.3	57.3	11.3	28.0	7.7	25.0	8.1	36.4	8.6
Business educ.																						
Female	15	33.9	7.6	32.6	6.0	26.3	4.4	33.1	9.2	32.0	9.9	25.4	5.2	57.2	12.6	26.8	8.5	21.9	7.6	40.1	7.4
Male	15	35.1	7.0	25.5	5.0	25.0	3.7	36.6	9.7	27.3	7.7	30.1	6.7	60.0	11.5	26.6	7.4	23.1	8.5	41.5	6.3
English																						
Female	220	35.6	6.4	35.6	6.1	27.5	6.0	38.7	10.5	38.5	9.1	29.2	7.9	47.8	11.0	31.6	7.6	19.9	7.6	37.8	8.2
Male	60	34.9	6.9	29.4	5.9	27.6	6.7	34.9	10.6	34.3	9.3	28.2	7.7	50.3	12.2	31.7	8.4	24.0	8.3	39.7	9.1
Foreign language																						
Female	44	36.8	7.2	35.7	5.7	28.4	5.5	37.5	12.3	38.0	9.2	28.3	8.8	48.8	11.5	33.3	7.0	20.0	7.1	36.1	8.3
Male	14	32.4	7.0	28.9	6.9	26.1	5.7	31.6	13.2	32.9	9.5	28.5	8.1	53.6	13.1	31.8	10.8	21.4	9.0	38.7	7.5
Mathematics																						
Female	121	33.9	7.0	37.7	6.1	26.8	6.4	35.6	10.1	30.7	8.4	28.8	7.0	58.0	11.3	30.1	7.8	21.1	7.8	37.1	8.7
Male	159	32.8	6.6	30.3	5.5	26.6	6.1	34.2	10.6	26.2	9.2	29.3	6.9	59.9	11.6	28.6	7.4	24.1	8.2	37.5	8.8
Music																						
Female	7	37.4	5.3	34.3	5.5	27.7	5.3	33.1	10.2	38.5	10.9	23.3	6.1	46.7	12.4	29.7	7.1	22.4	6.5	39.7	9.9
Male	6	28.4	8.5	31.6	4.5	23.0	4.7	30.0	11.0	23.2	7.9	24.0	5.1	55.4	11.8	23.0	6.2	26.8	7.2	32.2	7.2
Physical educ. (girls)	16	32.9	6.5	30.4	10.0	26.3	6.8	32.5	10.4	34.8	10.7	24.7	8.0	46.3	13.9	29.3	8.4	24.2	7.7	36.0	7.2
Physical educ. (boys)	39	32.6	4.8	25.4	5.6	26.4	4.9	31.3	9.0	27.1	10.1	26.2	6.0	55.3	9.3	24.3	6.1	27.2	7.2	36.0	7.3
Physical science																						
Female	21	35.0	6.9	39.0	4.5	30.4	7.3	41.2	11.2	34.8	9.8	33.7	6.5	55.6	13.5	32.6	8.1	23.1	6.7	37.1	9.0
Male	130	33.8	7.1	29.8	5.6	27.6	5.9	35.3	11.0	25.9	9.0	29.3	6.9	59.7	12.2	29.4	6.9	25.3	8.2	36.9	8.5
Social studies																						
Female	121	36.1	6.0	36.1	5.5	27.7	5.3	39.2	8.5	37.7	8.3	28.9	6.4	48.6	9.9	29.2	7.9	21.4	7.4	37.9	8.6
Male	121	34.5	7.4	28.5	6.5	27.4	6.8	36.4	11.6	32.8	9.9	29.0	7.1	52.3	11.7	27.8	7.5	23.3	8.8	38.7	8.5
Vocational educ.																						
Female	6	31.7	5.6	34.0	4.0	26.7	4.2	31.0	5.8	31.3	4.2	24.5	5.6	52.0	7.6	28.5	7.0	24.3	6.0	35.5	6.8
Male	8	35.6	7.3	26.1	6.0	27.4	8.0	40.1	11.9	33.6	12.1	31.1	6.0	51.0	12.4	29.5	6.2	30.0	6.2	33.5	6.8
Aggregate Secondary Survey Sample	970	34.8	6.9	32.9	6.9	27.5	6.1	36.6	10.8	32.4	10.4	29.0	7.2	53.9	12.5	29.7	7.8	22.5	8.1	37.9	8.5

... of N exceeds the Aggregate N, particularly for secondary teachers, reflecting overlapping of teaching areas.

Schedule Scores of Elementary and Secondary Teachers (Basic Analysis Sample) Classified According to Grade or Subject Taught

Grade or Subject Taught	N	X_{co}		Y_{co}		Z_{cv}		R_{co}		R_{1co}		Q_{co}		B_{co}		I_{co}		S_{co}		V_{co}	
		M	σ	M	σ	M	σ	M	σ	M	σ	M	σ	M	σ	M	σ	M	σ	M	σ
ELEMENTARY TEACHERS; ALL-TEACHER SCORING KEYS (99)																						
Grades 1-2, female*	190	38.2	6.8	28.3	3.2	29.1	4.8	37.0	8.6	35.4	6.0	36.2	7.8	16.6	7.9	35.2	7.0	35.9	5.6	22.8	5.0
Grades 3-4, female*	431	37.6	6.4	28.4	3.5	28.2	5.6	36.3	9.4	35.1	7.2	36.5	7.7	17.7	9.5	35.9	7.2	35.9	5.7	22.6	4.6
Grades 5-6, female*	97	38.5	7.5	28.7	3.3	29.5	5.9	38.4	9.4	36.9	6.6	38.1	8.0	16.8	8.6	36.8	6.4	35.9	5.7	22.1	4.5
Total Grades 1-6, female*	718	37.9	7.2	28.4	3.5	28.6	5.8	36.8	9.2	35.4	6.9	36.6	7.8	17.3	9.0	35.8	7.1	35.8	5.9	22.1	4.7
Grades 3-6, male*	116	38.7	7.2	23.3	3.7	28.8	5.3	37.0	9.5	37.0	6.9	36.9	7.4	12.9	8.4	36.3	6.5	41.2	5.9	22.8	4.6
Hold-out sample*	144	37.9	7.6	28.4	3.5	28.4	5.5	35.7	10.1	35.3	7.3	35.6	8.2	17.6	10.2	36.3	7.8	36.4	5.8	22.7	4.8
Aggregate Elementary Basic Analysis Sample	978	38.0	7.3	27.8	3.9	28.6	5.4	36.6	9.4	35.6	6.3	36.5	7.8	16.8	9.2	35.9	7.1	36.6	6.1	22.6	4.7
SECONDARY TEACHERS OF MATHEMATICS, SCIENCE, ENGLISH, AND SOCIAL STUDIES; ALL-TEACHER SCORING KEYS (99)																						
Mathematics*																						
Female	104	34.5	7.9	29.8	3.6	26.8	4.8	32.2	9.3	31.4	6.7	35.2	7.5	25.0	9.3	37.2	7.2	33.8	5.5	23.3	4.3
Male	105	32.3	6.6	22.7	3.8	26.1	4.1	29.4	8.3	29.5	6.6	33.2	6.7	24.5	9.4	32.0	6.2	37.6	5.2	23.3	4.3
Total	209	33.4	7.4	26.2	5.1	26.5	4.5	30.8	8.9	30.4	6.7	34.2	7.2	24.8	9.3	34.6	7.2	35.7	5.7	23.3	4.3
Science*																						
Female	90	36.6	6.3	29.0	3.2	28.0	4.1	34.7	8.7	33.2	6.8	35.2	6.5	21.2	8.5	38.6	6.9	35.3	5.4	23.3	4.6
Male	148	34.6	6.7	23.3	4.3	26.6	4.2	32.4	8.6	31.7	6.5	35.3	6.9	23.1	8.6	34.5	6.6	39.6	5.7	22.7	4.3
Total	238	35.4	7.0	25.5	4.7	27.1	4.3	33.2	8.7	32.3	6.6	35.3	6.8	22.4	8.6	36.0	7.0	38.0	5.7	22.9	4.4
Total mathematics-science*	447	34.5	7.1	25.8	4.7	26.8	4.4	32.1	8.8	31.4	6.7	34.8	7.0	23.5	9.0	35.4	7.1	36.9	5.8	23.1	4.4
English*																						
Female	195	37.5	7.1	30.0	3.3	27.9	5.4	36.1	9.7	35.1	7.5	36.7	8.2	18.9	9.3	40.9	6.6	34.4	5.8	23.3	4.1
Male	86	37.3	7.6	25.1	3.9	27.8	5.1	34.4	10.6	34.9	7.4	35.0	8.4	16.0	9.7	39.4	6.7	38.0	4.9	23.3	4.4
Total	281	37.4	7.3	28.5	4.2	27.9	5.3	35.6	10.0	35.0	7.4	36.2	8.3	18.0	9.5	40.5	7.0	35.6	5.8	23.3	4.4
Social studies*																						
Female	121	36.6	7.3	29.1	3.5	27.7	5.1	34.4	9.3	34.5	6.7	34.7	7.3	20.0	10.2	39.8	7.0	33.8	5.8	23.4	4.5
Male	102	36.7	6.3	24.7	3.2	27.8	5.1	34.8	8.3	34.8	7.0	35.2	7.7	19.2	9.1	36.8	7.3	38.7	5.6	22.8	4.8
Total	223	36.7	7.1	27.1	4.0	27.8	5.1	34.6	8.5	34.6	6.8	34.9	7.5	19.6	9.7	38.4	7.3	36.0	6.2	23.1	4.6
Total English-social studies*	504	37.1	7.1	27.9	4.2	27.8	4.2	35.1	9.5	34.9	7.2	35.6	8.0	18.7	9.6	39.6	7.2	35.8	6.0	23.2	4.5
Hold-out sample*	114	36.0	7.1	27.2	4.3	27.9	4.8	33.4	9.0	33.0	6.9	35.2	7.6	21.1	9.7	37.4	6.7	36.1	5.7	23.1	4.4
Aggregate Secondary Basic Analysis Sample	1,065	35.9	7.2	27.0	4.5	27.4	4.8	33.7	9.3	33.2	7.2	35.2	7.5	21.0	9.7	37.6	7.4	36.3	5.9	23.2	4.5
MATHEMATICS-SCIENCE TEACHERS; MATH-SCIENCE TEACHER SCORING KEYS 97 X_{co}, 97 Y_{co}, 97 Z_{co}; ALL-SECONDARY TEACHER KEYS (100) FOR REMAINDER OF SCALES																						
Math-science*	447	32.3	6.1	35.7	7.8	31.7	6.3	37.7	12.5	28.5	10.8	31.1	7.7	38.9	13.3	36.5	8.4	28.7	4.7	22.5	4.9
ENGLISH-SOCIAL STUDIES TEACHERS; ENGLISH-SOCIAL STUDIES TEACHER SCORING KEYS 98 X_{co}, 98 Y_{co}, 98 Z_{co}; ALL-SECONDARY TEACHER KEYS (100) FOR REMAINDER OF SCALES																						
English-social studies*	504	38.4	8.6	34.7	7.4	28.7	6.6	42.4	13.0	40.1	11.5	32.0	8.3	45.6	14.1	42.9	8.8	26.1	4.7	23.0	4.8
BUSINESS EDUCATION AND FOREIGN LANGUAGE (SPECIAL STUDY SAMPLES) AND COMBINED MATHEMATICS, SCIENCE, ENGLISH, AND SOCIAL STUDIES TEACHERS; ALL-SECONDARY SCORING KEYS (100)																						
Business education	125	34.7	6.9	33.9	6.6	25.3	5.1	36.6	10.5	30.8	9.8	31.2	7.1	57.4	11.6	34.1	7.9	26.1	4.4	23.0	4.8
Foreign language	116	35.0	7.4	36.0	7.0	27.0	5.9	38.5	11.2	35.1	10.2	31.1	8.0	53.9	12.7	51.3	8.7	24.5	4.8	21.0	8.1
Combined mathematics, science, English, social studies	1,065	36.8	8.5	34.2	7.6	28.0	6.4	40.2	13.0	34.7	12.6	31.4	8.0	51.9	15.4	40.1	9.1	27.3	4.9	22.8	4.9

* Exclusive of hold-out samples.

ferent subsamples of teachers, yield relatively few extreme or startling differences, and they call attention to the extensive overlapping in many respects among different grade-level and subject-matter groups. Some of the general trends which may be inferred from Tables 96, 97, and 98 are, however, worthy of note, as indicated below.

Characteristic X_{co} (understanding, friendly classroom behavior): Elementary teachers in general, and in particular men elementary teachers and women teachers of Grades 1–2 and Grades 5–6, attained somewhat higher scores; teachers of boys physical education and men mathematics teachers, somewhat lower scores. Women teachers of foreign language scored somewhat higher than other secondary groups, and women teachers of Grades 7–8 scored somewhat lower than other elementary groups.

Characteristic Y_{co} (responsible, systematic, businesslike classroom behavior): In general, teachers of English and foreign language scored higher; mathematics teachers, men science teachers, boys physical education teachers, business education teachers, and men social studies teachers scored generally lower. Within the elementary school, Grades 5–6 men teachers scored higher, and Grades 1–2 women teachers scored lower. Within the secondary school, the mathematics and science women teachers showed superiority.

Characteristic Z_{co} (stimulating, imaginative classroom behavior): Grades 1–2 and Grades 5–6 teachers scored higher; mathematics teachers, physical science teachers, and boys physical education teachers scored lower. Within the elementary school Grades 5–6 men were higher scorers, and Grades 7–8 women, lower scorers. In the secondary school, women science teachers scored higher, and business education teachers scored lower, as compared with other secondary groups per se.

Characteristic R_{co} (favorable attitudes toward pupils): Grades 1–2 and Grades 5–6 teachers scored higher; boys physical education teachers, business education teachers, and men mathematics teachers scored lower. Within the elementary school, Grades 5–6 men teachers obtained higher scores, and Grades 7–8 women teachers, lower scores. At the secondary level, physical science teachers and women social studies teachers scored higher and business education and mathematics-science teachers (men and women combined) scored lower.

Characteristic R_{1co} (favorable attitudes towards democratic practices in the classroom): Elementary teachers in general, and particularly Grades 5–6 teachers, attained relatively higher scores; boys physical education teachers and men mathematics teachers attained lower scores in general. Elementary women teachers of Grades 7–8 scored particularly low. Within secondary schools, women English teachers scored relatively higher, and mathematics-science and business education teachers, relatively lower.

Characteristic Q_{co} (favorable attitudes toward administrators and other school personnel): Physical science teachers and women teachers of Grades 5–6 scored higher; physical education teachers scored low. Within the elementary school, men in particular attained higher

scores, and Grades 7–8 women teachers lower scores. Within the secondary school, physical science teachers and men mathematics teachers
scored relatively higher than other secondary groups.

Characteristic B_{co} (traditional, learning-centered *vs.* permissive, child-
centered educational viewpoints): Men teachers in general, and particularly elementary men teachers, tended toward permissive, child-
centered educational viewpoints; mathematics teachers and business
education teachers in particular leaned toward traditional educational
viewpoints. Within the elementary school, there are few differences
between groups except that women teachers of Grades 7–8 scored
relatively lower. Within the secondary school group, English teachers
and foreign language teachers, particularly women, were more permissive in educational viewpoints, with women teachers of mathematics and physical science leaning toward traditional viewpoints in
education.

Characteristic I_{co} or I_{ci} (verbal understanding): Foreign language teachers
and English teachers, particularly women teachers, attained generally
higher scores; business education teachers, teachers of boys physical
education, and men mathematics teachers achieved lower mean scores.
Within the elementary school, Grades 7–8 women teachers scored
higher and Grades 1–2 women teachers lower.

Characteristic S_{co} or S_{ci} (emotional stability): Boys physical education
teachers scored higher, and Grades 7–8 teachers, and women teachers
of foreign language, English, mathematics, and social studies scored
lower. Within the elementary school, men in general attained higher
emotional stability scores, and within the secondary school, women
teachers of English and foreign language scored lower.

Characteristic V_{co} or V_{ci} (tendency to avoid excessive use of self-enhancing
and socially acceptable responses): Social studies, English, and elementary teachers generally tended to score higher; Grades 7–8 teachers and women teachers of foreign language tended to score lower.

RELATION TO SIZE OF SCHOOL

Tables 99 and 100 show the scores of teachers when they are classified
according to size of school in which employed, size of school here referring to the number of teachers constituting a teaching staff. Considering elementary and secondary teachers combined, the means of
teachers classified according to size of school differ significantly at the
.05 level (F ratios) with regard to five of the characteristics studied:
understanding, friendly classroom behavior (X_{co}), stimulating, imaginative classroom behavior (Z_{co}), favorable attitudes toward administrators and other school personnel (Q_{co}), verbal understanding (I_{ci}),
and emotional stability (S_{ci}). The pattern is fairly clear. For these characteristics—as well as for Y_{co}, R_{co}, R_{1co}, and B_{co} (child-centered emphasis), where the mean differences were not statistically significant—
teachers in larger schools (seventeen or more teachers) scored higher,

TABLE 99

Comparison of Schedule Scores of Teachers (Survey Sample) Classified According to Size of School in Which Employed

ALL-TEACHER SCORING KEYS (99)

Size of School	N*	X_{co} M	σ	Y_{co} M	σ	Z_{co} M	σ	R_{co} M	σ	R_{ico} M	σ	Q_{co} M	σ	B_{co} M	σ	I_{ci} M	σ	S_{ci} M	σ	V_{ci} M	σ
1 teacher	39	32.4	5.7	26.7	3.7	26.4	3.8	29.9	8.7	31.3	6.1	30.7	6.2	22.2	8.2	24.8	7.7	20.9	7.8	36.3	8.0
2-5 teachers	71	32.8	5.7	27.8	3.6	26.0	4.0	30.0	7.6	31.1	5.7	31.4	6.5	22.6	6.6	27.4	7.2	20.9	7.7	36.4	8.9
6-16 teachers	448	33.9	7.1	27.4	4.0	27.0	4.8	31.1	8.0	31.8	6.5	32.3	7.3	21.8	8.9	26.8	8.0	21.1	7.9	36.7	8.5
17-50 teachers	786	35.0	6.9	27.4	4.2	27.6	4.6	32.0	8.5	32.4	6.4	33.2	7.0	21.7	8.7	28.7	7.7	22.7	8.1	37.8	8.3
More than 50 teachers	269	34.8	6.5	26.9	4.6	27.5	4.4	31.8	8.6	32.6	6.2	33.0	7.1	21.6	8.6	30.1	7.5	22.6	8.2	36.9	8.6
Aggregate Survey Sample	1,640	34.5	6.8	27.3	4.2	27.3	4.6	31.6	8.5	32.1	6.4	32.8	7.1	21.8	8.6	28.2	7.9	22.1	8.1	37.2	8.4

* Discrepancy between ΣN and Aggregate N attributable to nonresponse.

TABLE 100

Comparison of Schedule Scores of Elementary and Secondary Teachers (Survey Sample) Classified According to Size of School in Which Employed

Size of School	N*	X_{co} M	σ	Y_{co} M	σ	Z_{co} M	σ	R_{co} M	σ	R_{ico} M	σ	Q_{co} M	σ	B_{co} M	σ	I_{ci} M	σ	S_{ci} M	σ	V_{ci} M	σ
ELEMENTARY TEACHERS; ALL-ELEMENTARY TEACHER SCORING KEYS (111)																					
1 teacher	37	42.2	11.2	26.4	6.7	38.9	8.5	30.0	12.1	26.8	8.9	24.3	7.5	27.3	7.8	24.4	7.5	20.0	6.9	36.4	8.0
2-5 teachers	61	39.9	11.8	25.8	7.7	37.7	8.9	32.2	11.2	26.5	8.0	25.8	8.4	27.3	6.5	27.3	7.6	20.8	7.4	35.8	8.1
6-16 teachers	300	42.6	14.8	27.9	8.3	39.1	10.8	33.2	13.4	27.6	10.3	27.8	9.1	26.4	8.7	25.6	7.5	20.9	8.0	36.3	8.3
17-50 teachers	238	47.9	14.0	29.6	7.4	42.4	11.0	37.7	13.4	30.4	10.1	29.0	8.2	23.4	8.4	26.6	7.5	22.8	8.1	37.2	8.1
More than 50 teachers	22	45.5	14.2	28.3	8.6	43.4	11.8	38.6	13.0	29.8	9.4	27.8	7.8	23.7	8.4	28.5	6.8	24.8	7.5	30.9	9.2
Aggregate Elementary Survey Sample	670	44.3	14.4	28.2	8.0	40.3	10.8	34.8	13.5	28.5	10.1	27.9	8.7	25.4	8.5	26.2	7.5	21.7	8.0	36.4	8.3
SECONDARY TEACHERS; ALL-SECONDARY TEACHER SCORING KEYS (100)																					
1 teacher	2	34.5	4.5	33.0	4.0	34.0	2.0	38.5	4.5	42.5	13.5	28.5	7.5	38.0	11.0	38.0	3.0	37.0	3.0	38.0	8.0
2-5 teachers	10	31.0	6.7	26.9	4.6	23.4	6.4	30.5	6.7	28.5	7.7	27.1	3.9	56.9	6.0	27.8	8.4	21.4	9.4	40.2	11.8
6-16 teachers	148	35.2	6.5	31.0	6.3	26.8	5.5	34.7	10.9	30.8	9.8	27.6	7.6	54.4	12.2	28.8	8.4	21.4	7.7	37.5	8.9
17-50 teachers	548	34.9	7.0	32.8	6.5	27.2	6.0	36.6	10.8	32.3	10.5	29.1	7.0	54.5	12.6	29.7	7.7	22.7	8.1	38.1	8.3
More than 50 teachers	247	35.2	7.1	34.7	6.7	28.4	6.7	37.9	10.7	33.6	10.5	29.5	7.2	52.6	12.5	30.3	7.5	22.4	8.2	37.5	8.4
Aggregate Secondary Survey Sample	970	34.8	6.9	32.9	6.9	27.5	6.1	36.6	10.8	32.4	10.4	29.0	7.2	53.9	12.5	29.7	7.8	22.5	8.1	37.9	8.4

* Discrepancy between ΣN and Aggregate N attributable to nonresponse.

and those from small schools (five or fewer teachers) scored lower. The differences were largest with respect to verbal understanding, I_{ci}.

When the Elementary Teacher Scoring Keys were used and elementary teachers considered alone, nine of the ten characteristic comparisons yielded F ratios significant at the .05 level—all characteristics except I_{ci}. Again, teachers from the smaller schools attained lower scores on X_{co}, Z_{co}, R_{co}, R_{1co}, Q_{co}, and S_{ci}, and expressed more traditional, learning-centered viewpoints, B_{co}. Teachers in schools with more than fifty teachers (only twenty-two teachers in this elementary group), however, scored lowest of all groups with regard to V_{ci} (validity of response). Generally, teachers from schools of seventeen to fifty teachers and from those employing more than fifty teachers attained superior scores except on V_{ci}, as noted.

Over one-half of the secondary teachers were employed in schools with seventeen to fifty teachers, and approximately a quarter in schools of more than fifty teachers. With these secondary teachers, and using the Secondary Scoring Keys, only four characteristics yielded significant F ratios, namely, Y_{co}, Z_{co}, R_{co}, and R_{1co}. The trends among the means were similar, both for the characteristics showing significant F ratios and for those which did not, to those already noted for elementary teachers and for elementary and secondary teachers combined. Teachers in the schools employing more than fifty teachers generally attained the higher mean scores on the various characteristics, and expressed more permissive, child-centered educational viewpoints.

RELATION TO SIZE OF COMMUNITY

As might well be expected, the trend with regard to the means of teachers classified according to size of the community in which they teach follows generally that for size of school noted in Tables 99 and 100. Analysis of Table 101 suggests that teachers from smaller communities attained lower mean scores, and those from larger communities, higher mean scores—at least, up to and including communities of 500,000–1,000,000 in population. Interestingly, teachers from the largest cities (1,000,000 and over in population) scored about as low as teachers from the small communities, except with respect to I_{ci}, S_{ci}, and V_{ci}. It seems probable that the selection procedures in operation in large cities (e.g., written and oral examinations) are geared to the selection of teachers high in verbal understanding, but less adapted to the measurement of other characteristics relating to personal and social qualities of the teacher.

Four of the characteristics yielded significant F ratios (.05 level) when the means of elementary and secondary teachers combined were

TABLE 101

Comparison of Schedule Scores of Teachers (Survey Sample) Classified According to Size of Community in Which School Is Located

POPULATION OF COMMUNITY	N*	ALL-TEACHER SCORING KEYS (99)																			
		X_{co}		Y_{co}		Z_{co}		R_{co}		R_{ico}		Q_{co}		B_{co}		I_{ci}		S_{ci}		V_{ci}	
		M	σ	M	σ	M	σ	M	σ	M	σ	M	σ	M	σ	M	σ	M	σ	M	σ
Less than 100	59	33.3	6.3	27.1	4.0	26.7	4.3	30.3	7.9	31.5	5.3	31.6	6.0	22.8	7.1	25.8	7.4	19.6	7.3	36.2	8.5
100–2,500	261	33.5	6.2	26.8	4.4	26.8	4.3	30.1	7.8	31.4	5.7	32.0	6.7	22.7	7.9	27.2	7.8	22.0	8.2	37.1	8.1
2,500–10,000	392	34.5	6.6	27.2	4.6	27.4	4.4	31.1	8.8	31.1	6.6	32.5	7.3	22.3	8.5	27.9	7.9	22.0	8.1	38.1	8.2
10,000–50,000	440	34.7	7.3	27.5	4.0	27.4	4.8	31.9	8.7	32.4	6.3	33.0	7.0	21.5	8.7	28.1	7.8	22.0	7.8	37.3	8.7
50,000–100,000	128	35.0	6.7	27.9	3.8	27.4	4.7	32.4	8.2	32.8	6.6	33.7	7.5	21.5	9.1	28.1	8.0	22.5	8.1	36.3	9.3
100,000–500,000	200	35.0	7.1	27.1	4.4	27.4	4.4	32.7	8.7	32.8	6.7	33.3	7.1	20.6	9.0	29.3	7.5	22.5	8.2	36.9	7.8
500,000–1,000,000	82	36.0	6.7	28.6	3.9	28.3	5.3	34.6	7.7	33.5	6.7	34.0	6.9	20.2	9.3	29.9	8.4	22.5	7.8	36.0	9.0
More than 1,000,000	59	33.9	6.8	26.4	4.2	27.5	4.2	30.4	8.0	32.0	6.5	32.1	7.0	22.0	9.1	29.9	6.9	22.7	9.1	39.1	8.0
Aggregate Survey Sample	1,640	34.5	6.8	27.3	4.2	27.3	4.6	31.6	8.5	32.1	6.4	32.8	7.1	21.8	8.6	28.2	7.9	22.1	8.1	37.2	8.4

* Discrepancy between ΣN and Aggregate N attributable to nonresponse.

TABLE 102

Comparison of Schedule Scores of Elementary and Secondary Teachers (Survey Sample) Classified According to Size of Community in Which School Is Located

POPULATION OF COMMUNITY	N*	X_{co} M	σ	Y_{co} M	σ	Z_{co} M	σ	R_{co} M	σ	R_{lco} M	σ	Q_{co} M	σ	B_{co} M	σ	I_{ci} M	σ	S_{ci} M	σ	V_{ci} M	σ
		ELEMENTARY TEACHERS; ALL-ELEMENTARY TEACHER SCORING KEYS (111)																			
Less than 100	42	41.5	12.1	25.0	7.2	39.0	8.5	31.5	12.0	26.6	8.8	24.9	6.8	27.0	7.6	24.5	7.3	20.1	6.7	35.8	8.7
100–2,500	103	43.4	11.5	28.4	7.2	39.8	8.6	33.9	13.0	28.2	8.5	26.6	6.5	25.7	7.2	26.2	7.1	21.0	7.1	36.0	7.8
2,500–10,000	122	43.6	14.7	28.4	8.9	39.5	10.2	34.4	13.8	27.8	10.6	27.6	9.3	25.8	8.3	25.2	8.0	20.9	7.6	37.3	7.9
10,000–50,000	183	44.1	15.7	28.4	7.9	40.2	11.5	34.1	13.8	28.0	10.7	27.5	8.6	25.3	8.0	25.8	7.5	21.3	8.1	36.3	8.7
50,000–100,000	66	47.2	15.0	29.3	8.4	41.9	11.6	37.8	14.2	30.9	10.7	31.0	9.2	24.4	9.5	26.4	7.3	22.5	8.5	35.9	8.8
100,000–500,000	103	44.6	15.2	28.2	7.4	40.6	12.3	35.0	13.8	29.0	10.3	28.4	8.4	25.3	9.4	28.0	7.1	23.4	8.1	36.6	7.6
500,000–1,000,000	31	45.6	11.0	30.0	6.8	41.8	10.9	39.5	12.8	30.5	8.7	30.5	7.1	24.5	7.1	27.4	7.7	23.5	7.9	34.3	9.0
More than 1,000,000	11	49.2	12.9	27.1	9.5	44.1	11.0	37.5	10.7	31.2	10.3	29.4	5.7	22.3	8.5	30.8	6.1	26.4	8.0	41.5	6.5
Aggregate Elementary Survey Sample	670	44.3	14.4	28.2	8.0	40.3	10.8	34.8	13.5	28.5	10.1	27.9	8.7	25.4	8.5	26.2	7.5	21.7	8.0	36.4	8.3
		SECONDARY TEACHERS; ALL-SECONDARY TEACHER SCORING KEYS (100)																			
Less than 100	17	32.8	6.2	30.4	5.9	26.1	7.0	33.2	7.6	29.1	7.1	27.4	6.5	57.8	7.4	28.9	6.7	18.2	8.3	37.0	7.8
100–2,500	158	33.6	6.1	30.7	6.5	26.4	5.6	34.8	10.3	30.6	10.5	28.6	6.9	54.8	12.7	27.8	8.1	22.7	8.3	37.8	8.2
2,500–10,000	270	34.9	6.7	32.2	7.0	27.5	5.7	31.6	11.3	31.6	10.6	28.7	7.5	55.1	12.3	29.1	7.5	22.8	8.1	38.4	8.3
10,000–50,000	257	35.3	7.1	33.9	6.8	27.6	6.0	37.6	11.2	33.6	10.1	29.6	7.2	52.5	12.3	29.8	7.5	22.5	7.9	38.0	8.6
50,000–100,000	62	34.6	6.5	34.3	7.2	27.4	5.7	36.6	9.4	32.4	9.5	29.0	7.2	54.1	11.6	29.7	8.2	22.6	8.1	36.8	9.8
100,000–500,000	97	34.3	7.9	34.1	7.1	27.4	7.1	36.0	10.3	32.5	10.5	29.4	6.3	54.2	13.2	30.7	7.6	22.4	8.2	37.3	9.1
500,000–1,000,000	51	36.3	8.0	34.3	5.6	29.7	7.2	39.9	10.7	36.9	11.9	29.1	6.6	49.4	13.9	31.2	8.2	22.0	8.0	37.0	9.1
More than 1,000,000	48	34.7	6.4	34.9	6.3	28.8	6.7	35.1	10.7	32.4	10.7	28.0	7.8	55.9	12.3	34.3	7.0	21.9	9.1	38.5	8.2
Aggregate Secondary Survey Sample	970	34.8	6.9	32.9	6.9	27.5	6.1	36.6	10.8	32.4	10.4	29.0	7.2	53.9	12.5	29.7	7.8	22.5	8.1	37.9	8.4

* Discrepancy between ΣN and Aggregate N attributable to nonresponse.

analyzed (characteristics X_{co}, Y_{co}, R_{co}, and I_{ci}), with teachers in communities with populations of up to 2,500 and of 1,000,000 or more scoring lowest, and those from communities of 500,000–1,000,000 population scoring highest, except in the case of verbal understanding, I_{ci}, as noted earlier.

The comparisons for elementary and secondary teachers are presented separately in Table 102. Among elementary teachers considered separately, the same general trend is apparent, although only three F ratios were significant—for the characteristics Q_{co}, I_{ci}, and S_{ci}. Teachers from the smaller communities scored lower and those from large communities attained higher mean scores.

At the secondary teaching level, six F ratios were significant, namely those for the characteristics Y_{co}, Z_{co}, R_{co}, R_{1co}, B_{co}, and I_{ci}. Teachers in smaller communities attained lower scores generally and were more traditional and learning-centered in their educational viewpoints, an exception being the high traditional viewpoints mean score of teachers in very large cities (1,000,000 or more population). Teachers from the cities with 1,000,000 or more population were distinctly higher than teachers from smaller communities relative to verbal understanding, I_{ci}. Teachers in communities of 500,000–1,000,000 population were significantly higher with respect to attitudes toward pupils and attitudes toward democratic classroom procedures, and were significantly more permissive and child-centered in their educational viewpoints than teachers in the largest cities (1,000,000 or over population), and also than teachers in the smaller communities.

RELATION TO SOCIOECONOMIC STATUS OF COMMUNITY IN WHICH SCHOOL IS LOCATED

Tables 103 and 104 show the mean scores of teacher groups classified according to estimates of the socioeconomic level of the community in which the teacher's school is located. Judgment of the socioeconomic status of the communities was made by the teachers themselves.

For the elementary and secondary teacher groups combined (Table 103) F ratios significant at the .05 level were obtained with regard to X_{co}, Z_{co}, R_{1co}, B_{co}, I_{ci}, and S_{ci}. Generally, the *lowest* scores relative to understanding, friendly classroom behavior (X_{co}), stimulating, imaginative classroom behavior (Z_{co}), and favorable attitudes toward democratic classroom practices (R_{1co}), and the most traditional, learning-centered educational viewpoints (B_{co}) scores were attained by teachers in communities judged to be about average in socioeconomic level. The relationship between socioeconomic level and several of the characteristics (e.g., Z_{co}, B_{co}, and I_{ci}) appears to be parabolic, with higher scores

TABLE 103

Comparison of Schedule Scores of Teachers (Survey Sample) Classified According to Teacher's Estimate of Socioeconomic Status of Community Served by School

Socioeconomic Status	N*	All-Teacher Scoring Keys (99)																			
		X_{co}		Y_{co}		Z_{co}		R_{co}		R_{1co}		Q_{co}		B_{co}		I_{ci}		S_{ci}		V_{ci}	
		M	σ	M	σ	M	σ	M	σ	M	σ	M	σ	M	σ	M	σ	M	σ	M	σ
Considerable poverty	35	34.2	6.1	26.1	4.2	27.6	3.9	31.0	7.2	31.9	5.6	32.5	6.3	20.3	8.5	29.1	8.8	20.5	7.2	39.1	7.3
Below average	195	35.1	6.7	27.0	4.7	27.8	4.9	31.8	8.5	32.3	6.5	32.4	7.0	20.5	8.3	27.0	8.3	22.6	8.2	36.9	8.4
Average	844	34.0	6.8	27.4	4.2	26.8	4.6	31.0	8.4	31.6	6.3	32.5	7.0	22.6	8.8	28.7	7.7	21.6	7.9	37.0	8.5
Above average	371	34.9	7.0	27.3	4.1	27.7	4.6	32.3	8.9	31.4	6.4	33.4	7.5	21.4	8.8	28.7	7.7	23.0	8.2	37.7	8.0
Well-off	185	35.6	6.8	27.1	3.7	28.1	4.4	32.5	8.3	33.2	6.7	33.1	7.0	20.2	8.8	29.3	8.2	22.9	8.4	37.6	8.4
Aggregate Survey Sample	1,640	34.5	6.8	27.3	4.2	27.3	4.6	31.6	8.5	32.1	6.4	32.8	7.1	21.8	8.6	28.2	7.9	22.1	8.1	37.2	8.4

* Discrepancy between ΣN and Aggregate N attributable to nonresponse.

TABLE 104

Comparison of Schedule Scores of Elementary and Secondary Teachers (Survey Sample) Classified according to Teacher's Estimate of Socioeconomic Status of Community Served by School

Socioeconomic Status	N*	X_{co}		Y_{co}		Z_{co}		R_{co}		R_{1co}		Q_{co}		B_{co}		I_{ci}		S_{ci}		V_{ci}	
		M	σ	M	σ	M	σ	M	σ	M	σ	M	σ	M	σ	M	σ	M	σ	M	σ
ELEMENTARY TEACHERS; ALL-ELEMENTARY TEACHER SCORING KEYS (111)																					
Considerable poverty	18	42.3	11.9	27.0	7.5	40.0	11.5	35.7	10.6	29.9	10.3	27.7	7.9	24.3	7.5	27.5	7.9	21.6	7.6	38.9	7.0
Below average	88	47.9	11.8	28.2	7.8	41.4	9.5	37.5	13.2	30.1	9.8	28.3	7.9	23.5	8.5	25.4	7.7	21.5	8.2	35.5	7.7
Average	369	42.7	14.7	28.1	8.0	39.1	10.9	33.3	13.3	27.4	9.9	27.3	8.6	26.5	8.3	26.5	7.5	21.7	7.8	37.5	8.5
Above average	141	45.0	15.3	28.6	8.2	41.8	11.1	36.1	14.2	29.7	10.8	28.6	9.7	24.4	8.7	25.8	7.4	22.0	8.5	36.4	8.0
Well-off	47	48.6	12.4	29.7	7.7	43.4	9.6	36.3	12.6	29.8	9.4	29.0	8.0	23.7	8.2	26.1	7.4	23.3	7.3	36.0	8.4
Aggregate Elementary Survey Sample	670	44.3	14.4	28.2	8.0	40.3	10.8	34.8	13.5	28.5	10.1	27.9	8.7	25.4	8.5	26.2	7.5	21.7	8.0	36.4	8.3
SECONDARY TEACHERS; ALL-SECONDARY TEACHER SCORING KEYS (100)																					
Considerable poverty	17	32.5	5.4	32.0	4.7	28.9	6.8	33.7	8.9	29.8	9.3	27.5	5.9	56.3	11.7	30.9	9.3	19.5	6.5	39.4	7.5
Below average	107	34.1	6.4	30.6	7.9	28.2	5.3	35.2	10.9	32.0	10.6	27.5	7.2	53.9	12.0	28.3	8.0	23.4	8.2	38.0	8.7
Average	475	34.6	7.1	32.8	6.8	27.5	8.2	36.2	10.9	31.9	10.0	28.6	7.0	54.6	12.8	29.2	7.8	21.7	8.0	37.5	8.5
Above average	230	35.0	6.7	33.5	6.9	27.5	6.1	37.3	10.8	32.4	10.0	29.8	7.2	54.3	12.0	30.5	7.9	23.6	7.9	38.1	8.4
Well-off	138	36.0	7.2	34.1	6.4	29.1	6.1	37.7	11.1	34.9	10.4	30.0	7.3	51.0	12.0	30.6	8.0	22.9	8.6	38.2	8.3
Aggregate Secondary Survey Sample	970	34.8	6.9	32.9	6.9	27.5	6.1	36.6	10.8	32.4	10.4	29.0	7.2	53.9	12.5	29.7	7.8	22.5	8.1	37.9	8.4

* Discrepancy between ΣN and Aggregate N attributable to nonresponse.

on the characteristics Z_{co} and I_{ci}, and more permissive educational viewpoints scores (B_{co}) being contributed by teachers in the groups representing communities typified by low and high socioeconomic levels. Other relationships also appear to be generally curvilinear, with little or no relationship apparent in moving from "poverty" to "average" levels, but with a positive correlation trend suggested through the upper categories of the socioeconomic classification employed.

Among elementary teachers considered alone, significant F ratios were obtained for X_{co}, Z_{co}, R_{co}, R_{1co}, and B_{co}. Low scores with respect to the first four characteristics named, and more traditional viewpoint scores were found for teachers from schools in average socioeconomic level communities, with teachers from both the categories representing somewhat higher and somewhat lower socioeconomic status attaining higher scores on X_{co}, Z_{co}, R_{co}, and R_{1co}, and seeming to possess more permissive, child-centered educational viewpoints. Change in mean score of the characteristic with socioeconomic level again appeared to be best represented by a parabolic function.

The pattern is somewhat less clear among secondary teachers. The tendency toward curvilinearity is noted in a few cases (e.g., stimulating, imaginative classroom behavior, and emotional stability), but there is somewhat more of a linear trend as the group means are considered, beginning with the "below-average" socioeconomic level and proceeding through the "well-off" category, with respect to such characteristics as Y_{co} (responsible, businesslike classroom behavior), Q_{co} (favorable attitude toward administrators and other school personnel), and I_{ci} (verbal understanding). Significant F ratios (.05 level) were obtained for Y_{co}, Z_{co}, R_{1co}, Q_{co}, I_{ci}, and S_{ci}.

RELATION TO CULTURAL LEVEL OF COMMUNITY

Teachers participating in the Survey Study also were asked to judge the cultural level of the community in which they were employed. Table 105 shows the results for the combined elementary and secondary teachers, and Table 106 presents separately the results for elementary teachers and secondary teachers. The tables are approximately similar in findings, except that I_{ci} and S_{ci} showed significant F ratios for the combined groups (and did not when the separate groups were considered), and Y_{co} showed a significant F ratio for the separate elementary and secondary samples, but not for the combined groups.

The general trend shown in Table 105 is for teachers from communities judged "high" with respect to cultural level to attain higher scores on friendly, understanding classroom behavior (X_{co}), stimulating, imaginative classroom behavior (Z_{co}), favorable attitude toward pupils

TABLE 105

Comparison of Schedule Scores of Teachers (Survey Sample) Classified According to Teacher's Estimate of Cultural Level of Community Served by School

CULTURAL LEVEL	N*	ALL-TEACHER SCORING KEYS (99)																		
		X_{co}		Y_{co}		Z_{co}		R_{co}		R_{lco}		Q_{co}		B_{co}		I_{ci}		S_{ci}		V_{ci}	
		M	σ	M	σ	M	σ	M	σ	M	σ	M	σ	M	σ	M	σ	M	σ	M	σ
High	125	37.3	6.9	27.6	3.9	28.4	5.0	34.3	9.2	34.6	7.0	34.9	7.9	18.8	8.6	30.5	8.3	23.9	8.2	36.7	8.7
Above average	324	34.9	6.5	26.9	3.9	27.5	4.3	32.7	8.1	32.6	6.3	33.8	8.1	21.7	8.5	28.7	7.7	22.9	8.0	37.8	8.2
Average	821	34.0	6.8	27.5	4.2	27.1	4.5	31.2	8.5	31.8	6.2	32.6	7.1	22.4	8.5	27.7	7.8	21.7	8.0	36.8	8.6
Below average	285	34.4	6.7	27.2	4.5	27.2	4.7	30.6	8.4	31.7	6.4	31.7	6.9	21.6	8.5	28.1	7.8	22.0	7.9	37.8	7.9
Low	75	34.4	6.7	26.8	4.6	28.2	5.2	30.4	9.2	31.7	7.1	31.0	7.0	20.1	10.0	28.9	8.4	21.5	8.5	38.9	7.2
Aggregate Survey Sample	1,640	34.5	6.8	27.3	4.2	27.3	4.6	31.6	8.5	32.1	6.4	32.8	7.1	21.8	8.6	28.2	7.9	22.1	8.1	37.2	8.4

* Discrepancy between ΣN and Aggregate N attributable to nonresponse.

TABLE 106

Comparison of Schedule Scores of Elementary and Secondary Teachers (Survey Sample) Classified According to Teacher's Estimate of Cultural Level of Community Served by School

CULTURAL LEVEL	N*	X_{co}		Y_{co}		Z_{co}		R_{co}		R_{lco}		Q_{co}		B_{co}		I_{ci}		S_{ci}		V_{ci}	
		M	σ	M	σ	M	σ	M	σ	M	σ	M	σ	M	σ	M	σ	M	σ	M	σ
ELEMENTARY TEACHERS; ALL-ELEMENTARY TEACHER SCORING KEYS (111)																					
High	31	52.6	13.8	32.4	7.3	45.1	10.8	40.5	14.6	33.6	11.6	31.0	10.5	21.7	9.5	27.5	8.6	23.9	7.7	35.6	8.3
Above average	102	45.9	15.0	29.3	8.2	41.5	10.0	36.3	13.8	29.5	10.5	27.8	9.3	24.6	7.7	25.9	6.8	22.2	7.8	37.4	7.8
Average	382	42.9	13.9	27.5	8.0	39.5	10.7	33.8	13.1	27.6	9.7	27.4	8.5	26.2	8.3	26.2	7.5	21.5	8.0	35.9	8.4
Below average	116	43.5	14.4	28.1	8.0	39.0	10.7	33.7	13.7	28.4	9.6	26.9	8.4	25.3	8.4	26.2	7.6	21.3	7.5	36.8	8.2
Low	33	50.0	14.5	30.0	6.6	45.5	11.9	37.8	13.7	31.7	10.6	29.7	7.0	21.3	10.1	27.6	8.8	21.4	8.8	38.0	8.0
Aggregate Elementary Survey Sample	670	44.3	14.4	28.2	8.0	40.3	10.8	34.8	13.5	28.5	10.1	27.9	8.7	25.4	8.5	26.2	7.5	21.7	8.0	36.4	8.3
SECONDARY TEACHERS; ALL-SECONDARY TEACHER SCORING KEYS (100)																					
High	94	36.9	7.2	34.7	7.2	29.4	6.8	39.0	11.3	35.8	10.4	30.9	7.6	50.2	12.1	31.5	8.0	23.9	8.4	37.0	8.8
Above average	222	35.2	6.3	33.1	6.8	27.8	5.7	38.1	9.9	32.7	9.8	30.6	6.8	54.3	11.8	29.9	7.7	23.2	8.0	37.9	8.3
Average	439	34.3	7.2	32.8	6.7	26.8	6.2	36.2	11.1	32.0	10.5	28.8	7.0	54.5	12.8	29.2	7.8	21.8	8.0	37.6	8.6
Below average	169	34.8	6.6	32.0	7.3	27.7	5.9	35.6	10.4	32.3	10.9	27.3	6.9	53.3	12.6	29.4	7.7	22.6	8.1	38.4	8.4
Low	42	32.3	6.2	33.0	6.6	27.3	6.0	29.6	10.0	28.1	9.6	24.2	6.9	57.8	11.5	29.9	8.0	21.5	8.2	39.5	6.5
Aggregate Secondary Survey Sample	970	34.8	6.9	32.9	6.9	27.5	6.1	36.6	10.8	32.4	10.4	29.0	7.2	53.9	12.5	29.7	7.8	22.5	8.1	37.9	8.4

* Discrepancy between ΣN and Aggregate N attributable to nonresponse.

(R_{co}), favorable attitude toward democratic classroom practices (R_{1co}), favorable attitude toward administrators and other school personnel (Q_{co}), verbal understanding (I_{ci}), and emotional stability (S_{ci}), and to emphasize more permissive, child-centered educational viewpoints (B_{co}), as compared with teachers from communities of other cultural levels. However, teachers from the "low" culture group of communities also achieved relatively high scores with respect to stimulating, imaginative classroom behavior (Z_{co}) and permissive, child-centered viewpoints (B_{co}). From the standpoint of teacher attitudes $(R_{co}, R_{1co}, \text{and } Q_{co})$ the graduation was orderly from the high through the low categories of community cultural level.

Among elementary teachers (Table 106) the relationship between cultural level of community in which the teacher is employed and scores on the Schedule seems to be curvilinear with respect to X_{co}, Y_{co}, Z_{co}, and B_{co}, with teachers from the average cultural communities scoring lower on X_{co}, Y_{co}, and Z_{co}, and expressing more traditional viewpoints on B_{co}, and the extreme categories attaining higher scores with regard to classroom behavior and indicating more permissive educational viewpoints. Generally speaking, the high cultural community teachers were high on all of the characteristics yielding significant F ratios, with teachers from average communities scoring lower.

Among secondary teachers, there is a less pronounced curvilinear trend. Secondary teachers from communities judged to be high relative to cultural level scored higher on $X_{co}, Y_{co}, Z_{co}, R_{co}, R_{1co}$, and Q_{co}, and evinced more permissive educational viewpoints on B_{co}, while teachers from communities which were less privileged culturally attained lower scores and expressed more traditional educational viewpoints.

RELATION TO AUSPICES OF SCHOOL IN WHICH TEACHER IS EMPLOYED

As in the teacher population of the United States as a whole, a large majority of the teachers in the national Survey Sample were employed in public schools. Approximately 9 percent of the Survey Sample were private school teachers, 83 percent were public school teachers, and 8 percent were parochial school teachers. Comparative data indicate that roughly 88 percent of the school enrollment in the United States is in public schools. Percentagewise, the representation of teachers from public, private, and parochial schools in the Survey Sample seems not to be out of line with the national picture based upon school enrollments. The assumption is made, of course, that the proportion of teachers to students is approximately equal in public and independent schools. Whether inferences of far-reaching importance may be made from the samples here reported is a matter that is dependent upon the

TABLE 107

Comparison of Schedule Scores of Teachers (Survey Sample) Classified According to Auspices of School

CLASSIFICATION	N^*	All-Teacher Scoring Keys (99)																		
		X_{co}		Y_{co}		Z_{co}		R_{co}		R_{1co}		Q_{co}		B_{co}		I_{ci}		S_{ci}		V_{ei}	
		M	σ	M	σ	M	σ	M	σ	M	σ	M	σ	M	σ	M	σ	M	σ	M	σ
Private school	146	33.7	6.4	27.2	3.9	27.8	4.4	30.7	8.9	32.3	6.6	31.6	7.8	21.7	8.0	31.2	8.3	22.3	8.3	37.6	8.5
Public school	1,317	35.0	6.8	27.4	4.2	27.5	4.6	32.0	8.5	32.5	6.3	32.5	7.0	21.4	8.7	27.9	7.8	22.3	8.1	37.3	8.1
Parochial school	126	30.4	6.2	26.7	3.9	24.6	4.4	28.1	7.4	28.8	5.9	30.6	6.8	25.1	8.2	27.8	7.3	21.8	8.0	36.4	8.5
No indication	48	33.9	6.9	27.0	4.7	26.9	4.7	30.1	8.0	32.0	6.2	32.1	6.0	23.1	8.2	28.3	7.5	19.7	7.3	37.4	8.6
Aggregate Survey Sample	1,640	34.5	6.8	27.3	4.2	27.3	4.6	31.6	8.5	32.1	6.4	32.8	7.1	21.8	8.6	28.2	7.9	22.1	8.1	37.2	8.4

* Discrepancy between ΣN and Aggregate N attributable to nonresponse.

approximate representativeness of the Survey Sample (as noted in chapter 3).

Table 107 shows the results for the combined elementary and secondary teachers. In the Survey Sample, public school teachers scored significantly higher (.05 level) with regard to understanding, friendly classroom behavior (X_{co}), and parochial teachers scored significantly lower than either private or public school teachers. No significant differences between the groups existed with respect to Y_{co}, systematic, responsible, businesslike teacher classroom behavior. Parochial school teachers scored significantly lower with regard to stimulating, imaginative classroom behavior (Z_{co}), attitudes toward pupils (R_{co}), and attitudes toward democratic pupil practices (R_{1co}). With regard to attitudes toward administrators and other school personnel (Q_{co}) public school teachers attained scores significantly higher than those of either private or parochial school teachers. Considering educational viewpoints (B_{co}) parochial school teachers expressed more traditional, learning-centered viewpoints, and private and public school teachers, more permissive viewpoints. Public and parochial school teachers attained very similar mean scores for characteristic I_{ci} (verbal understanding), with the private school teachers scoring significantly higher than either.

RELATION TO METHODOLOGICAL EMPHASIS OF SCHOOL

Tables 108 and 109 show the scores of teachers classified according to the methodological emphasis that they judged to be typical of their schools. Of the elementary and secondary teachers combined, approximately 44 percent judged their schools to be "progressive" in emphasis, and 56 percent, "traditional."

The obtained differences between means usually were small, but in the light of the substantial sizes of the samples all of the differences relating to the combined elementary and secondary teacher groups, and eight of the differences relating to the elementary teacher sample considered alone, were significant at the .05 level. For teachers in the secondary schools, only four significant differences were found.

So far as teachers in general are concerned, those teachers who taught in school systems they judged to be progressive attained higher mean scores on X_{co}, Y_{co}, Z_{co}, R_{co}, R_{1co}, Q_{co}, and S_{ci}, and also expressed more permissive, child-centered educational viewpoints on B_{co}. With regard to I_{ci} (verbal understanding) and V_{ci} (validity of response), the means of teachers from "traditional" schools were higher than those from "progressive" schools.

Among the elementary teachers, the same trend as that noted in the preceding paragraph was found to obtain, the only differences being

TABLE 108

Comparison of Schedule Scores of Teachers (Survey Sample) Classified According to Teacher's Judgment of Methodological Emphasis of School

ALL-TEACHER SCORING KEYS (99)

METHODOLOGICAL EMPHASIS	N*	X_{co}		Y_{co}		Z_{co}		R_{co}		R_{lco}		Q_{co}		B_{co}		I_{ci}		S_{ci}		V_{ci}	
		M	σ	M	σ	M	σ	M	σ	M	σ	M	σ	M	σ	M	σ	M	σ	M	σ
"Traditional"	916	34.2	6.7	27.1	4.3	27.1	4.5	31.0	8.1	31.7	6.1	32.4	7.0	22.5	8.4	29.3	7.7	21.8	8.1	38.0	8.1
"Progressive"	709	34.9	7.0	27.6	4.0	27.7	4.7	32.3	9.1	32.8	6.7	33.3	7.2	20.8	8.9	26.9	7.9	22.6	8.1	36.4	8.7
Aggregate Survey Sample	1,640	34.5	6.8	27.3	4.2	27.3	4.6	31.6	8.5	32.1	6.4	32.8	7.1	21.8	8.6	28.2	7.9	22.1	8.1	37.2	8.4

* Discrepancy between ΣN and Aggregate N attributable to nonresponse.

TABLE 109

Comparison of Schedule Scores of Elementary and Secondary Teachers (Survey Sample) Classified According to Teacher's Judgment of Methodological Emphasis of School

METHODOLOGICAL EMPHASIS	N*	X_{co}		Y_{co}		Z_{co}		R_{co}		R_{lco}		Q_{co}		B_{co}		I_{ci}		S_{ci}		V_{ci}	
		M	σ	M	σ	M	σ	M	σ	M	σ	M	σ	M	σ	M	σ	M	σ	M	σ
ELEMENTARY TEACHERS; ALL-ELEMENTARY TEACHER SCORING KEYS (111)																					
"Traditional"	304	42.4	13.8	27.7	7.7	38.6	10.5	32.7	12.4	27.4	9.2	27.1	8.1	27.1	7.7	26.7	7.3	21.0	7.7	37.1	7.7
"Progressive"	357	46.1	14.7	28.8	8.2	41.8	10.9	36.6	14.2	29.5	10.7	28.5	9.2	23.7	8.9	25.8	7.7	22.3	8.2	35.8	8.7
Aggregate Elementary Survey Sample	670	44.3	14.4	28.2	8.0	40.3	10.8	34.8	13.5	28.5	10.1	27.9	8.7	25.4	8.5	26.2	7.5	21.7	8.0	36.4	8.3
SECONDARY TEACHERS; ALL-SECONDARY TEACHER SCORING KEYS (100)																					
"Traditional"	612	34.7	6.9	33.0	7.1	27.3	6.2	36.1	10.7	31.8	10.4	28.8	7.1	54.6	12.6	30.5	7.5	22.2	8.2	38.4	8.2
"Progressive"	352	34.9	7.0	32.8	6.5	27.7	6.1	37.4	10.9	33.5	10.4	29.3	7.3	52.8	12.3	28.2	8.0	22.9	7.9	37.0	8.6
Aggregate Secondary Survey Sample	970	34.8	6.9	32.9	6.9	27.5	6.1	36.6	10.8	32.4	10.4	29.0	7.2	53.9	12.5	29.7	7.8	22.5	8.1	37.9	8.4

* Discrepancy between ΣN and Aggregate N attributable to nonresponse.

that characteristics Y_{co} and I_{ci} failed to yield significant t ratios. Approximately 53 percent of the elementary teachers thought their schools were progressive in methodological emphasis.

Apparently, many fewer secondary teachers, compared with elementary teachers, thought their schools espoused progressive education methods, since roughly 64 percent of the secondary teachers judged their schools to be traditional in methodological emphasis. Significant differences between teachers in progressive and traditional schools were few at the secondary level. Teachers in progressive schools scored higher with respect to attitudes toward democratic classroom procedures (R_{1co}) and were more permissive in their educational viewpoints (B_{co}) while teachers affiliated with schools judged to be traditional were higher with regard to verbal understanding (I_{ci}) and tendency to avoid excessive use of self-enhancing and socially desirable responses (V_{ci}).

It should be recalled that the "progressive" or "traditional" character of a school system was simply as judged by the responding teachers. Teachers who judge their school systems to be progressive or traditional may be those who are themselves more progressive or traditional as measured by the Teacher Characteristics Schedule. Thus, one interpretation of these data is that teachers impute to their school the same emphasis that is represented in their educational viewpoints.

RELATION TO GEOGRAPHIC AREA IN WHICH TEACHING IS PERFORMED

Tables 110 and 111 show the mean scores of teachers classified according to the geographic section of the United States in which their teaching is performed.

No significant differences among teachers in different geographic sections of the country were found with regard to understanding, friendly classroom behavior (X_{co}), attitude toward pupils (R_{co}), attitude toward democratic classroom practices (R_{1co}), attitude toward administrators and other school personnel (Q_{co}), or validity of response (V_{ci}). Differences among teachers in various parts of the country (F ratios significant at the .05 level) appeared with respect to I_{ci} (verbal understanding), and S_{ci} (emotional stability) for the elementary and secondary teacher groups combined, and also for the elementary and secondary groups considered separately. Differences also were obtained with regard to stimulating, imaginative classroom behavior (Z_{co}) for the elementary and secondary teacher samples combined and for the secondary sample considered separately. For characteristic Y_{co} (responsible, businesslike classroom behavior) differences were found among geographic regions when elementary teachers were considered sep-

Comparison of Schedule Scores of Teachers (Survey Sample) Classified According to Geographic Area in Which Employed

Geographic Area	N*	ALL-TEACHER SCORING KEYS (99)																			
		X_{co}		Y_{co}		Z_{co}		R_{co}		R_{1co}		Q_{co}		B_{co}		I_{ci}		S_{ci}		V_{ci}	
		M	σ	M	σ	M	σ	M	σ	M	σ	M	σ	M	σ	M	σ	M	σ	M	σ
New England	116	34.2	6.3	26.9	4.7	27.2	4.2	31.2	8.2	31.8	6.1	32.4	6.7	22.1	8.4	29.4	8.2	22.4	8.3	36.8	8.4
Mid-Atlantic	335	35.3	6.8	27.3	4.0	28.1	4.7	31.8	8.7	32.7	6.5	32.9	6.7	20.5	8.9	30.3	7.7	22.4	8.5	37.3	8.6
East-Southern	92	34.3	7.5	27.7	4.2	26.9	4.7	31.3	8.7	31.5	6.1	32.5	6.1	21.9	8.6	26.8	8.1	22.0	8.1	36.1	9.5
Southern	212	34.8	7.1	27.4	4.1	27.1	5.1	31.2	8.7	31.7	6.0	32.5	7.4	22.4	8.5	26.0	7.1	21.1	7.9	37.2	8.6
Central	449	34.1	6.6	27.0	3.9	27.0	4.2	31.4	8.9	32.1	6.4	32.6	6.6	22.4	8.7	27.6	7.7	21.6	7.7	36.9	8.0
Midwestern	83	33.1	6.6	27.2	4.0	26.1	4.4	31.4	8.2	31.4	5.9	33.0	7.6	23.0	8.3	26.9	8.0	21.6	7.8	37.2	9.0
Southwestern	125	33.9	6.7	27.5	4.0	27.4	5.0	31.5	8.1	32.1	6.4	32.5	7.0	21.7	8.5	28.6	8.0	21.9	7.8	38.3	8.0
Mountain	56	34.2	6.8	26.9	3.8	26.9	5.0	31.9	8.0	31.7	6.6	32.3	5.9	21.9	8.3	25.2	8.3	22.3	8.3	37.3	9.1
West Coast	168	35.2	7.0	26.7	3.8	27.8	4.4	32.6	8.6	32.9	6.5	33.4	7.1	20.7	8.6	30.0	7.4	24.3	7.7	38.3	8.0
Aggregate Survey Sample	1,640	34.5	6.8	27.3	4.2	27.3	4.6	31.6	8.5	32.1	6.4	32.8	7.1	21.8	8.6	27.6	7.9	22.1	8.1	37.2	8.4

* Discrepancy between ΣN and Aggregate N attributable to nonresponse.

TABLE III

Comparison of Schedule Scores of Elementary and Secondary Teachers (Survey Sample) Classified According to Geographic Area in Which Employed

Geographic Area	N*	X_{co}		Y_{co}		Z_{co}		R_{co}		R_{1co}		Q_{co}		B_{co}		I_{ci}		S_{ci}		V_{ci}	
		M	σ	M	σ	M	σ	M	σ	M	σ	M	σ	M	σ	M	σ	M	σ	M	σ
ELEMENTARY TEACHERS; ALL-ELEMENTARY TEACHER SCORING KEYS (111)																					
New England and Mid-Atlantic	173	45.4	14.0	28.5	7.5	41.3	10.9	35.0	12.4	29.2	9.4	28.0	7.3	24.4	9.0	28.2	7.8	21.9	8.4	36.1	7.9
East-Southern and Southern	137	42.6	14.2	27.0	8.1	39.4	10.8	32.7	11.8	26.5	9.6	26.8	8.4	25.8	8.2	24.4	6.6	21.1	7.8	35.9	8.4
Central and Midwestern	238	43.5	14.3	29.1	8.2	39.3	10.7	34.8	14.2	28.7	10.3	28.1	9.7	26.1	8.0	25.4	7.4	20.8	7.4	36.1	8.4
Southwestern	39	47.6	14.6	29.9	6.8	43.6	10.3	38.9	13.3	30.4	10.4	28.4	8.8	25.3	9.5	27.9	7.5	22.9	8.7	37.7	7.6
Mountain and West Coast	82	45.4	16.8	26.6	8.4	41.1	11.8	35.9	15.6	28.9	11.1	28.7	8.5	25.7	9.5	27.0	7.5	24.0	7.9	37.7	7.6
Aggregate Elementary Survey Sample	670	44.3	14.4	28.2	8.0	40.3	10.8	34.8	13.5	28.5	10.1	27.9	8.7	25.4	8.5	26.2	7.5	21.7	8.0	36.4	8.3
SECONDARY TEACHERS; ALL-SECONDARY TEACHER SCORING KEYS (100)																					
New England and Mid-Atlantic	278	35.0	6.9	33.4	7.1	28.2	6.1	36.6	11.2	32.9	10.5	28.9	7.0	52.9	12.3	31.2	7.6	22.8	8.5	37.8	8.9
East-Southern and Southern	167	34.7	7.3	33.6	6.9	27.4	6.2	36.6	12.2	32.9	11.0	28.8	7.7	53.3	13.0	27.9	7.8	20.9	8.0	37.6	8.7
Central and Midwestern	294	34.9	6.9	32.7	6.6	26.7	5.8	36.5	10.3	32.0	10.4	28.9	7.7	55.0	12.9	29.3	7.7	22.8	8.4	37.7	7.9
Southwestern	86	33.2	6.2	32.0	7.0	26.3	6.4	34.8	8.8	31.4	9.4	28.5	6.3	55.5	11.7	29.3	7.0	21.4	7.4	38.4	8.2
Mountain and West Coast	142	35.3	6.6	32.4	6.8	28.4	5.7	36.9	10.3	32.4	10.2	29.6	6.9	54.1	11.3	29.8	7.9	23.7	7.5	38.2	8.6
Aggregate Secondary Survey Sample	970	34.8	6.9	32.9	6.9	27.5	6.1	36.6	10.8	32.4	10.4	29.0	7.2	53.9	12.5	29.7	7.8	22.5	8.1	37.9	8.4

* Discrepancy between ΣN and Aggregate N attributable to nonresponse.

arately. Significant differences with regard to educational viewpoints (B_{co}), were obtained for the combined elementary and secondary teacher samples.

Table 110 shows the results for the elementary and secondary teacher groups considered together. Teachers whose schools were located in the Middle Atlantic states and on the West Coast scored higher relative to Z_{co} and I_{ci}, and were more child-centered in their educational viewpoints (B_{co}) than were other section groups. Teachers from the West Coast were highest of all the geographic groups with respect to emotional stability (S_{ci}). With regard to Z_{co} (stimulating, imaginative classroom behavior), the lowest-scoring group was made up of teachers from the Midwestern states; with respect to I_{ci} (verbal understanding), the lowest-scoring groups were from the Mountain states and Southern states; and with regard to S_{ci} (emotional stability), the lowest mean scores were attained by teachers from the East-Southern and Southern states. The Midwestern and East-Southern groups of teachers were most traditional in educational viewpoints as compared with the other groups.

Among elementary teachers considered separately (Table 111), teachers from the Central and Midwestern states, and also the Southwestern states, were the highest-scoring groups, and teachers from the Mountain and West Coast states, the lowest-scoring, with regard to responsible, businesslike classroom behavior (Y_{co}). The New England and Middle Atlantic teachers were highest, and the East-Southern and Southern teachers lowest with regard to verbal understanding (I_{ci}). Mountain and West Coast teachers were highest-scoring, and Central and Midwestern and East-Southern and Southern the lowest-scoring, with respect to emotional stability (S_{ci}).

Considering secondary teachers separately, teachers from the Mountain and West Coast and the New England and Middle Atlantic states scored highest, and those from the Southwest and Central and Midwestern states lowest, with regard to Z_{co} (stimulating, imaginative classroom behavior); teachers from the New England and Middle Atlantic states ranked highest, and from East-Central and Southern states lowest with respect to verbal understanding (I_{ci}); and teachers from the Mountain and West Coast scored highest, and from the East-Southern and Southern states lowest, with regard to emotional stability (S_{ci}).

8. Some Characteristics of Outstanding Teachers

IN EARLIER CHAPTERS, notice was taken of the relative nature of judgments of "effective" and "ineffective" teaching and, consequently, of the dim probability of arriving at universally acceptable definitions and descriptions which might be applied to identifying generally "superior" and "poor" teachers. Instead of approaching the problems of teacher personality in such a fashion, therefore, attention of the Teacher Characteristics Study was directed at the observation and analysis of overt behaviors, or acts of teachers in their classrooms, and at the determination of families or clusters into which such behaviors seemed to fall.

Three such families (major dimensions of teacher classroom behavior) were singled out for study: Pattern X_o (friendly, understanding, sympathetic vs. aloof, egocentric, restricted teacher behavior); Pattern Y_o (responsible, systematic, businesslike vs. unplanned, slipshod teacher behavior); and Pattern Z_o stimulating, imaginative, surgent vs. dull, routine teacher behavior. A considerable portion of the research work undertaken by the Study involved these patterns of classroom behavior in one manner or another. Although it was recognized that these three patterns did not constitute a complete catalogue of dimensions of teacher behavior, it was believed that they represented principal and important clusters of behaviors contributing to teacher-pupil classroom relationships.

An intriguing question arises regarding teachers who receive uniformly high, or low, assessments on all three Teacher Characteristics Study patterns of classroom behavior. Might the teacher whose assessment on *each* of the three Patterns X_o, Y_o, and Z_o, is, say, one standard deviation above the mean (placing him approximately in the top 16 percent of all teachers on each pattern) be considered a "superior" teacher? And might the teacher who is assessed one standard deviation below the mean on each of the three patterns be thought of as a "poor" teacher? The question is a debatable one, and even if agreement on the affirmative reply were reached, its implications for the employing superintendent, or teacher educator, would be limited (particularly in view of the excess of teacher demand over supply) by the fact that regression would probably reduce the number of such individuals (uniformly "high," for example) to 3 or 4 percent of any total teacher group considered.

Regardless of whether or not teachers uniformly rated "high" may be considered superior and those assessed "low" may be considered inferior (or effective and ineffective), such individuals do provide models or prototypes insofar as the several kinds of behavior investigated by the Study are concerned. And the description and analysis of the characteristics of such groups of teachers might reasonably be expected to provide useful clues for the school personnel officer, the teacher educator, and the researcher alike.

In the light of such thinking, the Study staff undertook two investigations, one directed at the identification of characteristics which differentiated between uniformly highly and lowly assessed teachers, and the other designed to assemble case data on a small, highly selected group of elementary teachers. Although independently conducted, the two studies supplemented each other, at least so far as elementary teachers are concerned.

Study No. 1: Some Characteristics Distinguishing Teachers Assessed Uniformly High or Uniformly Low Relative to Classroom Behavior

The first of the research studies on outstanding teachers attempted to segregate criterion groups comprised of teachers receiving uniformly high, average, or low observer assessments on all three major TCS dimensions of teacher classroom behavior and then to isolate characteristics which distinguished between these groups.

THE SELECTION OF CRITERION GROUPS OF TEACHERS

For purposes of determining the distinguishing characteristics of teachers classified according to level of over-all classroom behavior, three groups (high, average, and low) were segregated from (*a*) the Basic Analysis Sample of elementary teachers and (*b*) the Basic Analysis Sample of secondary teachers.

In each teacher sample (elementary and secondary) the high group was so selected that it was comprised of teachers who received a composite observer assessment one standard deviation or more above the mean on *each* of the three Patterns X_o, Y_o, and Z_o.

The average group for each sample consisted of teachers whose composite observer assessment was between two-tenths of a standard deviation below the mean and two-tenths of a standard deviation above the mean on *each* of the three patterns. The low group for each sample was made up of teachers whose assessment placed them one standard deviation or more below the mean of *each* of the classroom behavior patterns.

Within the Basic Analysis Sample of elementary teachers, 4.5 percent met the criterion for the high group, 3.6 percent for the average group, and 2 percent for the low group. For the secondary teachers, the respective percentages were 2.2, 2.5, and 1.6 percents. The substantially smaller intercorrelations among X_o, Y_o, and Z_o for secondary, as compared with elementary teachers (noted in chapter 4), here is evinced in the more extensive regression effect, resulting in smaller proportions of the secondary teacher sample meeting the cutting score on all three patterns. With the higher intercorrelations of dimensions among elementary teachers, the number surviving the selection on all three patterns is somewhat larger.

The means and deviations of composite observer assessments on teacher behavior Patterns X_o, Y_o, and Z_o for the high, average, and low teacher groups are shown in Table 112. Actually, it may be noted that the means of the high and low groups are approximately one and one-half standard deviations above and below the general mean of 50, and that the variability within the selected groups is very restricted compared to the general standard deviation of 10.

TEACHER CHARACTERISTICS SCHEDULE SCORES OF THE HIGH, AVERAGE, AND LOW CRITERION GROUPS

Table 113 shows the means and standard deviations of the scores for teachers making up the over-all high, average, and low groups. Table 114 summarizes the statistical significance of the differences between means shown in Table 113.

As might be expected, the X_{co}, Y_{co}, and Z_{co} scores (Schedule correlates of X_o, Y_o, and Z_o) distinguish, for the most part, between these criterion groups. This is not surprising, since selected upper and lower groups of each pattern, though less extreme than the groupings employed here, provided the standards for the original response analyses. The present high and low groups represent minority portions of the original analysis groups. It is important to note, however, that the small, highly selected secondary "high" and "low" groups in the present study do not yield the anticipated differences (at least not at the .10 level of significance) with respect to Y_{co} scores. In all other instances (X_{co}, Y_{co}, and Z_{co} for elementary teachers, and X_{co} and Z_{co} for secondary teachers) the Schedule scores of the average group are significantly higher than

TABLE 112

Means and Standard Deviations of Composite Observer Assessments on Teacher Behavior Patterns X_o, Y_o, and Z_o, for Teachers Classifiable as Low, Average, or High on All Three Teacher Behavior Patterns

	ELEMENTARY TEACHERS						SECONDARY TEACHERS					
TEACHER BEHAVIOR PATTERN	Low (N=20)		Average (N=35)		High (N=44)		Low (N=17)		Average (N=27)		High (N=23)	
	M	σ	M	σ	M	σ	M	σ	M	σ	M	σ
X_o	35.0	4.7	50.1	1.4	67.2	4.8	36.1	3.6	50.0	1.4	65.9	4.8
Y_o	34.6	4.3	50.2	1.3	66.6	4.8	34.4	4.1	50.1	1.5	64.0	3.5
Z_o	35.3	2.8	50.0	1.4	66.1	1.8	34.3	3.7	49.9	1.5	64.1	3.3

TABLE 113

Means and Standard Deviations of Teacher Characteristics Schedule Scores* for Those Teachers Who Were Classifiable as Low, Average, or High on All Three Teacher Behavior Patterns

	ELEMENTARY TEACHERS						SECONDARY TEACHERS					
TEACHER CHARACTERISTICS SCHEDULE SCORE	Low (N=20)		Average (N=35)		High (N=44)		Low (N=17)		Average (N=27)		High (N=23)	
	M	σ	M	σ	M	σ	M	σ	M	σ	M	σ
X_{co}	40.8	17.2	48.7	15.0	61.8	13.3	30.5	11.1	35.6	8.5	42.0	6.2
Y_{co}	23.1	8.4	29.6	8.4	38.0	7.5	32.7	7.8	33.9	6.8	35.4	6.9
Z_{co}	35.5	11.4	42.1	11.5	52.5	9.7	21.4	5.8	26.3	5.1	31.1	5.4
R_{co}	36.4	15.1	39.7	15.4	46.3	15.4	35.4	13.1	39.8	12.8	45.7	13.3
$R1_{co}$	29.2	12.5	32.4	11.9	37.1	12.1	26.9	14.2	36.7	14.9	38.6	13.2
Q_{co}	30.1	12.1	31.8	8.9	35.1	9.2	30.9	8.7	32.7	10.0	32.9	8.6
B_{co}	22.8	9.9	24.4	8.8	19.6	8.1	58.2	16.4	52.4	16.3	45.3	15.3
I_{co}	38.5	8.9	41.7	7.6	43.9	7.0	36.4	10.5	39.1	8.5	41.6	9.3
S_{co}	38.8	12.1	41.7	11.3	45.9	8.4	25.7	6.2	27.7	4.9	28.8	3.7
V_{co}	25.8	3.7	24.8	4.7	24.2	5.2	22.0	3.9	24.8	4.1	21.6	4.2

* All-Elementary Teacher Scoring Keys (111) employed for elementary teachers; All-Secondary Teacher Scoring Keys (100) employed for secondary teachers.

TABLE 114

Significance Levels for Mean Differences in Schedule Scores between Low and Average, Average and High, and Low and High Groups of Teachers

Teacher Character- istics Sched- ule Score	Elementary Teachers			Scoring Key	Secondary Teachers		
	Low- Average Groups	Average- High Groups	Low- High Groups		Low- Average Groups	Average- High Groups	Low- High Groups
111 X_{co}....	A .10	H .01	H .01	100 X_{co}	A .10	H .01	H .01
111 Y_{co}....	A .01	H .01	H .01	100 Y_{co}			
111 Z_{co}....	A .05	H .01	H .01	100 Z_{co}	A .05	H .01	H .01
111 R_{co}....		H .10	H .05	100 R_{co}			H .05
111 R_{1co}...		H .10	H .01	100 R_{1co}	A .05		H .01
111 Q_{co}....			H .10	100 Q_{co}			
111 B_{co}....		A .05		100 B_{co}			L .01
111 I_{co}....			H .01	100 I_{co}			H .10
111 S_{co}....		H .10	H .01	100 S_{co}			H .05
111 V_{co}....				100 V_{co}	A .10	A .05	

NOTE: In the body of the table the initial H, A, or L indicates which of the two groups compared yielded the highest mean, and the decimal fraction denotes the significance level at which the null hypothesis may be rejected.

those of the low, and the scores of the high group are significantly higher than those of the average group.

On the remaining scales of the Schedule, the high group is rather clearly distinguishable from the low groups, except for Q_{co} (attitude toward school personnel), B_{co} (traditional-permissive educational viewpoints) in the case of elementary teachers, and V_{co} (validity of response).[1]

Special note may be taken of the responses of these selected groups of teachers relative to educational viewpoints (B_{co}). First of all, it should be recalled that on this dimension viewpoints involving academic-centered, teacher-directed learning (traditional educational viewpoints) are represented by *higher* scores, and that *lower scores represent child-centered* (permissive) educational viewpoints. Thus, for secondary teachers, the tables show a difference between the viewpoints of the high and low groups significant at the .01 level of confidence, with teachers in the low group attaining more "traditional" scores. Or, put another way, there is a difference favoring the high rated group over the low when child-centered, permissive viewpoints are considered.

A second point of interest in connection with the B_{co} educational viewpoints scores is that for elementary teachers, who might be expected to be generally more child-oriented as compared with secondary teachers, the high group is somewhat more permissively inclined than the low group, but not sufficiently so to attain statistical significance

---

[1] It should be noted that the V_{co} scale was developed merely as a check, or control, and there was no expectation that it might provide a variable with respect to which specified groups of teachers might differ. It should *not* be considered a comparison variable.

at the levels of significance employed. At the secondary level, it appears that the cleavage between the high and low groups with respect to educational viewpoints is more pronounced and discernible.

CHARACTERISTICS SIGNIFICANTLY MORE FREQUENTLY ASSOCIATED WITH MEMBERSHIP IN THE HIGH OR THE LOW GROUP

The procedure followed in identifying characteristics which distinguished betweeen teachers assessed generally high and low was to: (1) determine for each response of the Schedule the frequency of acceptance by members of the high, average, and low groups separately; (2) convert the frequencies into percentages; (3) compute for each response an approximation of the *point biserial r* between the response and the criterion variable (over-all assessment);[2] (4) test the significance of the differences between proportions of the high and low groups accepting a particular response.

Separate analyses were made of the distinguishing characteristics of the high and low groups of the elementary and secondary teacher samples. In addition, for responses which were commonly available to the elementary and secondary teachers, the high-low distinguishing characteristics for the combined samples were similarly identified following equal weighting to adjust for the disproportionate numbers.

It will be recalled that three separate booklets of the Schedule were employed—one for elementary teachers, one for mathematics-science teachers, and one for English–social studies teachers—each booklet consisting of 300 items involving approximately 1,100 responses. Overlap between the mathematics-science and the English–social studies booklets was to the extent of 194 items, and of the elementary, mathematics-science and English–social studies booklets of 118 items. Therefore, the responses of *secondary teachers in general* could be studied with regard to only approximately 800 responses common to the mathematics-science and English–social studies booklets, and the responses of all teachers could be compared on only approximately 500 responses common to the elementary, mathematics-science, and English–social studies booklets.

The present study actually included consideration of both pictorially and verbally presented situations appearing in the Schedule, and the necessary statistics were computed for both types of items. However, in

---

[2] The approximations employed are not directly comparable with biserial correlations and are indeed to serve only as indices of association. However, subsequent *t* tests of the significance of the difference between proportions, applied to responses where the biserial *r* suggested possible significance, indicated that for such approximations a minimum *r* of .25 appeared to be required for significance at the .05 level for the elementary teacher groups, an *r* of .32 for similar significance with the secondary teacher groups, and an *r* of .20 for significance with the combined elementary and secondary groups.

the light of difficulties of interpretation of the "picture preferences," the data to be reported here will refer to the verbal materials alone.

In all, 89 responses to verbally presented situations were found to distinguish between the high and low elementary groups at or beyond the .05 level of significance. Similarly, 75 responses showed the required discrimination between high and low groups of secondary teachers and 45 responses between the high and low groups of the secondary and elementary teachers combined. Chance expectation would be 50 responses, 36 responses, and 22 responses, respectively, for the three samples of teachers. Employing the formula given in the footnote,[3] the t ratios for obtained/expected responses were 5.7 for the elementary teacher materials, 6.7 for the secondary, and 4.9 for the combined elementary and secondary teacher responses.

Tables 115–120 list separately for elementary teachers, secondary teachers, and combined elementary-secondary teachers the characteristics more frequently associated with membership in (*a*) the high group as compared with the low, and (*b*) the low group as compared with the high.[4] Conditions determining inclusion of a characteristic in a particular list are noted in footnotes to the tables, the conditions varying with the size of the sample under consideration. In addition to the statement of each distinguishing characteristic (response to the Schedule), the tables show the percentage frequency of acceptance of a response in the high group or low group (depending upon the group involved) and the index of association, designated as "biserial *r*" (actually an approximation of that statistic).

In the form represented by Tables 115 through 120, generalization is difficult because of the specificity of the items listed. An attempt was made, therefore, to categorize and summarize the distinguishing characteristics listed in the more detailed tables. Analyses of the contents, and abstraction of teacher qualities which appeared to distinguish between teachers receiving over-all high and low assessments of classroom behavior, suggested the summarization appearing in the lists of personal qualities of high and low group teachers on pages 360 and 361. These lists present the general findings of the present investigation.

[3] $$t = \frac{n(Np) - .5}{\sqrt{Npq}}$$

Where $p = .05$ ($q = .95$),
N = number of possible responses,
n = number of responses significant at the .05 level of confidence.
[4] High-average and average-low comparisons also were made, but are not reported.

(*Text continued on page 358.*)

TABLE 115

Characteristics Significantly* More Frequently Associated with Membership in the Group of Elementary Teachers Receiving Uniformly High Assessments of Observed Classroom Behavior as Compared with the Group Receiving Uniformly Low Assessments†

Elementary Teachers

Characteristic	Percentage Frequency of Response in High Group	Biserial *r*
Would prefer spending a free afternoon working in garden (rather than entertaining friends at home party, attending a recital, or going to a baseball game)	22	.35
Would prefer playing tennis (rather than softball or solitaire)	70‡	.31
Would teach a pet dog tricks to amuse self and friends (rather than teaching it to obey commands or training it as a watchdog)	31	.44
At an amusement park, enjoys the Ferris wheel (more than the roller coaster, merry-go-round, etc.)	20	.33
Would prefer to sell stamps at a post office (rather than sort or collect mail)	90‡	.48
Would prefer to teach school in a tenement district of a large industrial city (rather than in a suburban community or a rural school in a farming or mountainous area)	29	.29
Would prefer to test applicants for a position as typist (rather than compute typing test scores or maintain the typewriters used for typing tests)	70‡	.31
Believes parents should plan for future, so as not to be dependent upon their children (rather than that children are morally obligated to support their parents or that parents should expect to receive help)	47	.57
Would get most satisfaction from making an after-dinner speech (rather than striking a good bargain or making a sale to a difficult customer)	38	.30
Believes there are no high school classes that are almost impossible to control	70‡	.31
Believes very few (5 percent or less) high school classes are disruptive in that students frequently "get off the subject."	54‡	.25
Believes few high school students (about 10 percent) possess irritating nervous mannerisms	47	.30
Believes a minority of people are influenced in their opinions and attitudes toward others by feelings of jealousy	93	.31
Thinks few teachers (not more than 5 percent) suffer from stomach troubles and ulcers brought on by the tensions of teaching	63‡	.34
Thinks very few of parents' visits (10 percent or less) are made to criticize the teacher or the school	86	.28
Thinks a majority of people (60 percent or more) stop to think about the consequences of their acts as they affect their associates	50	.26

* For inclusion in this table it was required that a response:

   a) yield a $\%_H - \%_L$ significant at or beyond the .05 level.

   b) be marked by 10 percent or more of the combined elementary high, middle, and low groups.

   c) yield a biserial *r* of .25 or more.

† TCS Pattern scores X_o, Y_o, and Z_o (to wit: friendly, understanding classroom behavior; responsible, businesslike classroom behavior; and stimulating, surgent classroom behavior) of teachers were derived from replicated observer assessments. Comparison groups for this study were constituted as follows:

High group ($N=44$): Teachers whose composite assessment was equal to, or greater than, the mean plus one standard deviation (based on composite assessments of 978 elementary teachers) on each of the three patterns.

Low group ($N=20$): Teachers whose composite assessment was equal to or below the mean minus one standard deviation (based on composite assessments of 978 elementary teachers) on each of the three patterns.

‡ Indicates the response was a majority response (more than 50 percent) of the high group, and a minority response (less than 50 percent) of the low group.

TABLE 115 (Continued)

Characteristic	*Elementary Teachers* Percentage Frequency of Response in High Group	Biserial *r*
Believes it more important for a teacher to possess "ability to provoke students to think" (as compared with friendliness, versatility and resourcefulness, or enthusiasm).	43	.26
Believes most teachers (at least 80 percent) are willing to assume their full share of extra duties in the school.	52‡	.29
Would prefer being a sales clerk (rather than handling complaints or working in a billing department).	65‡	.31
Would prefer being an actor (as compared with being a judge or a musician).	40	.32
Estimates the typical nine-year-old child can swim approximately twenty-five feet.	24	.37
Believes the proverb "Seeing is believing" contains the *least truth* (as compared with "A new broom sweeps clean," "All that glitters is not gold," "You can't get blood out of a turnip," or "A friend in need is a friend indeed.").	45	.29
Feels most fit during early morning (as compared with late morning, afternoon, or evening).	54‡	.30
Strongly agrees with the statement that "Pupils can behave themselves without constant supervision."	24	.36
Agrees with the statement that "Most pupils are considerate of the teacher's wishes."	84	.30
Agrees with statement "Most teachers are willing to assume their share of the unpleasant tasks associated with teaching."	90	.35
Is between 35 and 49 years of age.	30	.35
Is married.	65‡	.31
Memories of childhood are extremely happy.	31	.31
As a child or adolescent, often read stories to children.	47	.30
Attended a lecture to hear some author, or attended meetings of a writers or literary club or study group during the past year.	65‡	.28
Read one or more books about art, artists, or art history during the past year.	24	.36
Did some painting or other art work during the past year.	47	.30
Visited a science museum or exhibition of scientific inventions during the past year.	56‡	.45
Looked up an answer to some scientific question in encyclopedia or other reference book during the past year.	61‡	.32
Read a new book about science during the past year.	15	.41
Choice of teaching as a career was influenced by relatives, including parents, and/or employer.	81‡	.47
Went hunting, fishing, or camping during the past year.	54‡	.25
Began, or added to, collection (stamps, minerals, etc.) during the past year.	27	.27
Did either painting or sculpture, or attended concerts or exhibits during past three weeks.	42	.25
Engages in either art or dramatics as a hobby.	38	.40
Engages in cooking as a hobby.	59‡	.30
Belonged to a high school or college sorority or fraternity.	68‡	.43
Frequently reads books dealing with travel and adventure during leisure time.	70‡	.26
Spent most of childhood in a town of 5,000 to 25,000 population.	20	.40
Childhood home owned by family.	84	.34
Had a piano in childhood home.	88	.31
Had lessons in dancing, dramatics, art, or music outside of school as a child.	93‡	.57
Had a washing machine in childhood home.	88	.36
Had a telephone in home when a child.	95	.47
Activities in childhood home highly organized.	31	.31

‡ Indicates the response was a majority response (more than 50 percent) of the high group, and a minority response (less than 50 percent) of the low group.

TABLE 116

Characteristics Significantly* More Frequently Associated with Membership in the Group of Elementary Teachers Receiving Uniformly Low Assessments of Observed Classroom Behavior as Compared with the Group Receiving Uniformly High Assessments†

Characteristic	Elementary Teachers Percentage Frequency of Response in Low Group	Biserial *r*
Would prefer to take Christmas baskets to needy families (rather than buy the supplies, canvass for contributions, plan the campaign, or compile statistics relative to campaign)	70‡	.37
Would train a pet dog as a watchdog (rather than teaching it to obey commands or do tricks)	25	.41
At a public beach, would prefer to be manager of the boat service (rather than a lifeguard, ticket-taker, etc.)	25	.41
When in school, was most influenced in dislike for a teacher by excessive preciseness (as compared with lack of sense of humor, impatience, or insistence on too high standards)	35	.37
If working in a post office, would prefer to sort mail or to collect mail from corner mail boxes (rather than to sell stamps)	50	.48
Would prefer to teach school in a consolidated rural school in a prosperous farming area (rather than in a well-to-do suburban community, a rural school in the mountains, or a school in a tenement district of an industrial city)	45	.31
Would prefer to calculate speed and accuracy scores for typing tests (rather than administer typing tests to applicants or make minor repairs on typewriters used for the typing tests)	50	.28
In self, believes "adaptability" a stronger trait than alertness, foresight, or initiative	80	.27
In self, believes "common sense" a stronger trait than enthusiasm, leadership, or refinement	70‡	.28
Believes parents should not deliberately plan to be supported by their children, but should expect and receive help if necessary (rather than that children are morally obligated to support their parents, that children should never have to contribute to support of parents, or that parents should arrange so as not to be dependent on their children)	90‡	.49
Would prefer to teach a class of average children (rather than one of children who were exceptionally bright, slow and retarded, or of widely varying ability)	70	.25
Believes some high school classes (5 percent–15 percent) are almost impossible to control	60‡	.35
Believes a substantial number (25 percent–65 percent) of high school classes are disruptive in that the students frequently "get off the subject."	70‡	.29
Thinks about 80 percent of teachers believe they should have some voice in making administrative decisions	50	.31
Believes 30 percent–50 percent of high school students possess irritating nervous mannerisms.	40	.48
Thinks a majority of persons (60 percent–80 percent) are influenced in their opinions and attitudes toward others by feelings of jealousy	35	.35
Thinks a large number of teachers (40 percent–60 percent) suffer from stomach trouble and ulcers brought on by unusual tensions related to their work	45	.62
Feels a large proportion of people (about 60 percent) are inclined to worry more than they should	50	.31

* See footnote *, Table 115.
† See footnote †, Table 115.
‡ Indicates the response was a majority response (more than 50 percent) of the low group, and a minority response (less than 50 percent) of the high group.

TABLE 116 (Continued)

Elementary Teachers

Characteristic	Percentage Frequency of Response in High Group	Biserial r
Believes a substantial proportion of parents' visits (30 percent–70 percent) to school are made to criticize the teacher or school..........	35	.25
Believes most teachers (about 95 percent) feel they should not have to spend any time on yard duty or similar duties....................	55‡	.33
Thinks about 50 percent of teachers willingly assume their full share of extra duties in the school....................................	50	.28
Would like best a job preparing customers' bills (rather than being a sales clerk or handling complaints).............................	45	.38
Would *least* like to be considered by friends as systematic (as compared with industrious, goodhearted, and cultured)....................	85	.31
In a summer job at a public beach, would *least* like to be a ticket-taker (as compared with lifeguard, manager of bath house, manager of boat service, or head of "lost children's bureau")................................	35	.37
Considers the *least* important failing of a teacher to be a severe and aloof manner (compared with inadequate mastery of subject matter or inability to maintain a systematic and orderly approach)..........	55‡	.27
In self, feels initiative is *weaker* trait than adaptability, alertness, or foresight..	50	.31
In self, feels that resourcefulness is a *weaker* trait than self-confidence, thoroughness, or truthfulness....................................	25	.41
Admires Sarah Bernhardt more than Florence Nightingale, Madame Curie, Margaret Sanger, Queen Victoria...........................	25	.41
Feels more fit during late morning and afternoon (as compared with early morning or evening).......................................	80‡	.44
Prefers to make a personal call on someone who is bereaved (rather than write a letter or send flowers and note).........................	65‡	.29
Is between 50 and 59 years of age....................................	25	.33
Has had one year or less of experience teaching in the elementary grades.	45	.27
Has taught in the district in which now employed less than one year...	45	.31
Is single (rather than married, separated, or widowed)...............	55‡	.33
Remembers childhood as being one of average happiness (rather than more happy than average or unhappy).........................	55‡	.33
Was advised might make a good teacher by a "counselor" (rather than family, a teacher, or friends)...................................	50	.25
Participated in some vocal or instrumental group during past year....	35	.33
Favorable prospect of professional advancement was factor contributing to choice of teaching as a career................................	40	.34

‡ Indicates the response was a majority response (more than 50 percent) of the low group, and a minority response (less than 50 percent) of the high group.

TABLE 117

Characteristics Significantly* More Frequently Associated with Membership in the Group of Secondary Teachers Receiving Uniformly High Assessments of Observed Classroom Behavior as Compared with the Group Receiving Uniformly Low Assessments†

	Secondary Teachers	
Characteristic	Percentage Frequency of Response in High Group	Biserial r
Prefers *Harper's Magazine* (to *American Magazine* or *Popular Mechanics*)	77‡	.36
Would prefer to plan a campaign for helping the needy at Christmas (rather than purchase the food, canvass for contributions, compile data on the progress of the fund, or take Christmas baskets to the needy)	38	.32
If preparing a paper to present to a club, would ask competent criticism, making changes suggested (rather than not asking for criticism, showing the paper only to close friends, etc.)	38	.32
If in disagreement with a friend on politics, usually will explain views and allow friend to explain his, but will not try to change friend's views (rather than trying to persuade friend to accept own views, or refusing to discuss the subject further)	99	.50
Would prefer to develop own course of study for classes (rather than follow a prescribed plan, modify a general plan to suit particular class, or follow no definite course of study)	27	.33
Thinks proverb "One man's meat is another man's poison" contains more truth than "Birds of a feather flock together," "One shouldn't cry over spilt milk," "The early bird catches the worm," or "Better late than never."	33	.33
If among people waiting in a grocery store when a latecomer pushes ahead and gets served, is most likely to call clerk's attention and ask to be waited on as soon as possible (rather than insisting upon being waited on at once or saying nothing about it)	61‡	.34
Considers the most serious failing in a teacher to be a severe and aloof manner (rather than inadequate mastery of subject or inability to maintain orderly approach to the work)	55‡	.37
Believes ambition is stronger trait of own personality (than accuracy, cheerfulness, or decisiveness)	33	.40
Believes thoroughness is stronger trait of own personality (than resourcefulness, self-confidence, or truthfulness)	38	.32
Likes frequently changing activities better than methodical work	88	.38
Believes very few (less than 1 percent) high school students intentionally try to tax the patience of the teacher	88	.32
Believes very few pupils are difficult behavior problems	83	.35

* For inclusion in this table it was required that a response:
  a) yield a $\%_H - \%_L$ significant at or beyond the .05 level.
  b) be marked by 15 percent or more of the combined secondary high, middle, and low groups.
  c) yield a biserial r of .32 or more.

† TCS Pattern scores X_o, Y_o, and Z_o (to wit: friendly, understanding classroom behavior; responsible, businesslike classroom behavior; and stimulating, surgent classroom behavior) of teachers were derived from replicated observer assessments. Comparison groups for this study were constituted as follows:

High group ($N=23$): Teachers whose composite assessment was equal to or greater than the mean plus one standard deviation (based on composite assessments of 1,065 secondary teachers) on each of the three patterns.

Low group ($N=17$): Teachers whose composite assessment was equal to or below the mean minus one standard deviation (based on composite assessments of 1,065 secondary teachers) on each of the three patterns.

‡ Indicates the response was a majority response (more than 50 percent) of the high group, and a minority response (less than 50 percent) of the low group.

TABLE 117 (Continued)

Secondary Teachers

Characteristic	Percentage Frequency of Response in Low Group	Biserial r
Estimates that probably 10 percent of high school students are not respectful toward their teachers	66‡	.39
Believes very few people (10 percent or less) are influenced in their opinions and attitudes toward others by feelings of jealousy	83‡	.44
Believes when teachers send students to principal's office, it is very often (30 percent–60 percent of the time) the fault of the teacher rather than the student	43	.35
Estimates about 50 percent–75 percent of high school teachers (compared with 95 percent estimate of "low" group) feel they should not have to spend time on yard duty and similar tasks	60‡	.41
Thinks listlessness of students is more indicative of a poor class than disorderliness, unsureness, or dependency of students	49	.42
Believes a substantial proportion of grade school pupils (25 percent–50 percent) do some form of art work as a leisure-time activity	65‡	.44
Believes it is possible to develop course content of most high school classes around "real life" situations, i.e., work and leisure activities engaged in by students	88‡	.51
Agrees (or "strongly agrees") with statement that "Pupils usually are quite competent to select their own topics for themes and speeches."	60‡	.33
Agrees with statement that "It is possible to develop most classwork around 'out-of-school' activities."	61‡	.50
Has had from four to nine years experience teaching the secondary grades	44	.36
Has completed either five or six years of college work	66‡	.32
When a student in grade or high school, worked in the school office	22	.50
As a child or adolescent, tutored or coached a student in a subject	38	.45
Was advised would "make a good teacher" by a schoolteacher (rather than by family, counselor, or friends)	61‡	.50
Listened to symphony programs on radio at least once a month during past year	72‡	.32
Attended one or more musical concerts during past year	77‡	.55
Bought phonograph records for home during past year	77‡	.43
Read book reviews in newspapers or magazines at least once a month during past year	88	.32
Listened to religious programs on the radio during past year	83	.37
Volunteered to serve on some church committee or to teach a Sunday school class during past year	54‡	.45
Taught or helped in some direct way a volunteer young people's group, such as Scouts, YWCA, etc.	44	.36
Attended an art lecture or read books about art or artists during past year	60‡	.49
Bought some painting or other art work during past year	38	.67
Attended one or more plays or dramas during past year	77‡	.43
Spent an average of three hours or more per week during the past three weeks at either painting, sculpture, or attending concerts or exhibits.	54‡	.32
Spent an average of three hours or more per week during the past three weeks attending theater, theatricals, movies, etc.	55‡	.46
Frequently listens to Drew Pearson	55‡	.36
Frequently listens to "American Album of Familiar Music."	55‡	.34
Frequently listens to "Truth or Consequences."	33	.41
Frequently listens to Jack Benny	49	.32
Follows cooking as a hobby	27	.34
Belonged to high school or college sorority or fraternity	38	.61
Has belonged to a hobby club	27	.49
Has been a member of an honor society (scholastic, scientific, or professional)	66‡	.32

‡ Indicates the response was a majority response (more than 50 percent) of the high group, and a minority response (less than 50 percent) of the low group.

TABLE 118

Characteristics Significantly* More Frequently Associated with Membership in the Group of Secondary Teachers Receiving Uniformly Low Assessments of Observed Classroom Behavior as Compared with the Group Receiving Uniformly High Assessments†

Characteristic	Percentage Frequency of Response in Low Group	Biserial r
Secondary Teachers		
Prefers to read either *American Magazine* or *Popular Mechanics* (rather than *Harper's Magazine*)	21	.37
If preparing a paper for presentation to a club, would feel own judgment good enough and not ask for criticism or show paper to others	28	.51
If helping a relative give a children's party, would prefer to send out the invitations (rather than prepare or serve refreshments, or direct the games)	35	.52
Would prefer to select and arrange books for a children's room in a library (rather than supervise a summer playground or design children's clothing)	64‡	.38
Considers inability to maintain systematic and orderly approach to work a more serious failing in a teacher than a severe and aloof manner or inadequate mastery of subject matter	57‡	.33
If another teacher said, "Teaching is all right, but it is certainly monotonous!" would be likely to reply, "*Yes, but anything is monotonous at times.*"	42	.32
Believes about half the teachers think they should have some voice in making administrative decisions	35	.47
Thinks very few high school students (less than 1 percent) are not respectful toward their teachers	57‡	.32
Believes a fair proportion of people (40 percent–60 percent) are influenced in their opinions and attitudes toward others by feelings of jealousy	57‡	.44
Believes when teachers send students to principal's office it is seldom (about 10 percent of the time) a fault of the teacher rather than the student	85‡	.43
Believes almost all high school teachers (about 95 percent) feel that they should not have to spend time on yard duty and similar tasks	57‡	.37
Thinks disorderliness and noise are more indicative of a poor class than listless students, dependency of pupils, or hesitancy and unsureness of pupils	50	.32
Estimates that few grade school pupils (5 percent–10 percent) do some form of art work as a leisure-time activity	56‡	.53
Would *least* like to teach a class of children of widely varying ability (compared with classes of average children, slow children, or exceptionally bright children)	57‡	.32
Considers a severe and aloof manner a *less* important failing in a teacher than inadequate mastery of subject matter or inability to maintain an orderly approach	57‡	.37
Feels classroom responsibilities and administrative responsibilities are fairly distinct and should be clearly defined and separated in the most effective school program	28	.41
Strongly disagrees with the statement "Pupils should be allowed to speak with each other before first getting the teacher's permission."	28	.41
Agrees with statement "Parents are usually considerate of the teacher's feelings."	85	.37
Agrees with statement "Parents can usually see the teacher's side of the problem when something happens in school."	71‡	.34

* See footnote *, Table 117.
† See footnote †, Table 117.
‡ Indicates the response was a majority response (more than 50 percent) of the low group, and a minority response (less than 50 percent) of the high group.

TABLE 118 (Continued)

Secondary Teachers

Characteristic	Percentage Frequency of Response in Low Group	Biserial *r*
Agrees with statement "most teachers have a good understanding of child psychology."	78‡	.42
Disagrees with statement "It is possible to develop school classwork around 'out-of-school' activities."	71‡	.55
Strongly disagrees with statement, "At the high school level, planning units of classwork should be a responsibility of the students in the class, who, in turn, make recommendations for the teacher."	35	.48
Is 55 years of age or older	28	.43
Has completed seven or more years of college work (compared with five or six years of "high" group)	35	.33
As a child was assigned home chores either not at all or less than most children	28	.38

‡ Indicates the response was a majority response (more than 50 percent) of the low group, and a minority response (less than 50 percent) of the high group.

TABLE 119

Characteristics Significantly* More Frequently Associated with Membership in the Combined Group of Elementary and Secondary Teachers Receiving Uniformly High Assessments of Observed Classroom Behavior as Compared with the Group Receiving Uniformly Low Assessments†

Combined Elementary and Secondary Teachers, Weighted Equally

Characteristic	Percentage Frequency of Response in High Group	Biserial *r*
Prefers *Harper's Magazine* (to *Popular Mechanics* or *American Magazine*)	67‡	.27
Would prefer to plan a campaign for helping the needy at Christmas (rather than buying supplies, canvassing for contributions, compiling statistics on the campaign, or taking the Christmas baskets to the needy families)	34	.21
Considers a severe and aloof manner a more serious failing in a teacher than inadequate mastery of subject matter or inability to maintain systematic and orderly approach	55‡	.27
Believes ambition a stronger trait in own personality than accuracy, cheerfulness, or decisiveness	27	.26
Believes initiative a stronger trait in own personality than adaptability, alertness, or foresight	20	.30

* For inclusion in this table it was required that a response:
  a) yield a $\%_{OH} - \%_{OL}$ significant at or beyond the .05 level.
  b) be marked by 7 percent or more of the combined elementary high, middle, and low groups, and 10 percent or more of the combined secondary high, middle, and low groups.
  c) show $\%_{OH} - \%_{OL}$ more than 10 percent for the elementary and secondary samples considered separately.
  d) yield a biserial *r* of .20 or more for the *combined* elementary and secondary samples, weighted equally.
† TCS Pattern scores X_o, Y_o, and Z_o (to wit: friendly, understanding classroom behavior; responsible, businesslike classroom behavior; and stimulating, surgent classroom behavior)

(*Footnotes continued on page 358.*)

TABLE 119 (Continued)

Combined Elementary and Secondary Teachers, Weighted Equally

Characteristic	Percentage Frequency of Response in Low Group	Biserial r
Believes very few (less than 1 percent) of high school students intentionally try to tax the patience of the teacher....................	76	.20
Believes no high school classes are "Almost impossible to control."....	79	.27
Believes very few people (not more than about 10 percent) are influenced in their attitudes toward others by feelings of jealousy.......	71	.29
Believes a majority of people (about 60 percent) stop to think about the consequences of their acts as they affect their associates..........	39	.21
Believes about 25 percent of grade school pupils do some form of art work as a leisure-time activity................................	31	.22
Believes the proverb "Seeing is believing" contains *less* truth than others such as "You can't get blood out of a turnip," "A new broom sweeps clean," "A friend in need is a friend indeed," or "All that glitters is not gold.".......................................	50	.20
Agrees with the statement, "Pupils should be allowed to speak with each other without first getting the teacher's permission.".........	46	.19
Is 40 to 49 years of age..	30	.23
As a child or adolescent, frequently read stories to children..........	37	.25
Read book reviews in the newspapers or magazines at least once a month during the past year....................................	75	.22
Attended a lecture to hear some author during the past year.........	53‡	.20
Attended meetings of a writers or literary group or study group during the past year..	24	.32
Frequently listened to religious programs on the radio during the past year..	72‡	.28
Visited an art gallery or museum during the past year...............	79	.21
Read one or more books about art, artists, or art history during past year..	34	.27
Attended an art lecture during the past year......................	19	.31
Spent an average of three or more hours per week during the past three weeks attending concerts, exhibits, etc..........................	34	.26
Spent an average of three or more hours per week during the past three weeks attending theater, theatricals, movies, or debating..........	55‡	.29
Spent an average of three or more hours per week during the past three weeks on hobbies...	55‡	.28
Follows cooking as a hobby......................................	43	.29
Belonged to a high school or college sorority or fraternity...........	53‡	.47
Has been a member of an honor society (scholastic, scientific, or professional)..	60‡	.21
Frequently reads books dealing with travel and adventure during leisure time...	74	.22
As a child, family owned an automobile...........................	83	.20
Had a bathtub in the family home when a child....................	95	.23
When a child, had more home chores or duties than other children.....	26	.27

of teachers, were derived from replicated observer assessments. Comparison groups for this study were constituted as follows:

High group ($N=67$): Teachers whose composite assessment was equal to or greater than the mean plus one standard deviation (based on composite assessments of 2,043 elementary and secondary teachers) on each of the three patterns.

Low group ($N=37$): Teachers whose composite assessment was equal to or below the mean minus one standard deviation (based on composite assessments of 2,043 elementary and secondary teachers) on each of the three patterns.

‡ Indicates the response was a majority response (more than 50 percent) of the high group, and a minority response (less than 50 percent) of the low group.

(*Text continued from page 349.*)

It is important to note in connection with Tables 119 and 120 that the Schedule forms used were *not* identical for elementary and secondary teachers (approximately one-third of the possible responses were the

TABLE 120

.Characteristics Significantly* More Frequently Associated with Membership
in the Combined Group of Elementary and Secondary Teachers Receiving
Uniformly Low Assessments of Observed Classroom Behavior
as Compared with the Group Receiving Uniformly
High Assessments†

	Combined Elementary and Secondary Teachers, Weighted Equally	
Characteristic	Percentage Frequency of Response in Low Group	Biserial *r*
Would prefer to take Christmas baskets to needy families (rather than plan a Christmas campaign for needy, buy food and supplies, canvass for contributions, or compile statistics on the campaign)...........	56‡	.24
Would train a pet dog as a watchdog (rather than teach it to obey commands or to do tricks).....................................	27	.33
Believes inability to maintain systematic and orderly approach is more serious failing of a teacher than a severe and aloof manner, or inadequate mastery of subject matter...............................	59‡	.28
Believes accuracy is stronger trait of own personality than ambition, cheerfulness, or decisiveness................................	30	.21
Believes common sense is stronger trait in own make-up than enthusiasm, leadership, or refinement..................................	70	.20
Likes methodical work better than frequently changing activities.....	34	.23
Believes about 15 percent of high school students intentionally try to tax the patience of teacher (compared with high group discriminating responses of "less than 1 percent").............................	37	.24
Believes 5 percent–15 percent of high school classes are almost impossible to control (compared to high group's response of 0 percent)....	44	.27
Believes a substantial number of people (about 40 percent) are influenced in their opinions and attitudes toward others by feelings of jealousy...	30	.31
Believes very few people (about 10 percent) stop to think about the consequences of their acts as they affect their associates..............	33	.22
Believes most teachers (95 percent) feel they should not have to spend any time on yard duty and similar tasks.........................	56‡	.30
Is 55 years of age or older...	24	.41
Favorable prospect of professional advancement was contributing factor toward choice of teaching as a career.......................	52‡	.26

* See footnote *, Table 119.
† See footnote †, Table 119.
‡ Indicates the response was a majority response (more than 50 percent) of the low group, and a minority response (less than 50 percent) of the high group.

same for all teachers). It is probable that many of the distinguishing
characteristics noted in the separate elementary and secondary tables
also would have distinguished between the high and low combined
samples had the responses been commonly accessible to all teachers.

The abstract models of teachers represented by the qualities noted in
the lists on pages 360 and 361 appear to have several rather marked
characteristics, notably the general tendency for high teachers to: be
extremely generous in appraisals of the behavior and motives of others;
possess strong interests in reading and in literary affairs; be interested
in music, painting, and the arts in general; participate in social groups;
enjoy pupil relationships; prefer nondirective classroom procedures;

PERSONAL QUALITIES WHICH APPEAR TO DISTINGUISH TEACHERS SELECTED TO BE "HIGH" AND "LOW" WITH RESPECT
TO OVER-ALL CLASSROOM BEHAVIOR: CHARACTERISTICS OF "HIGH" GROUP TEACHERS

Elementary Teachers	Secondary Teachers	Elementary-Secondary Teachers Combined
A. "High" group members more frequently (than "low"):	A. "High" group members more frequently (than "low"):	A. "High" group members more frequently (than "low"):
1. Manifest extreme generosity in appraisals of the behavior and motives of other persons; express friendly feelings for others.	1. Manifest extreme generosity in appraisals of the behavior and motives of other persons; express friendly feelings for others.	1. Manifest extreme generosity in appraisals of the behavior and motives of other persons; express friendly feelings for others.
2. Indicate strong interest in reading and in literary matters.	2. Indicate strong interest in reading and in literary matters.	2. Indicate strong interest in reading and in literary matters.
3. Indicate interest in music, painting, and the arts in general.	3. Indicate interest in music, painting, and the arts in general.	3. Indicate interest in music, painting, and the arts in general.
4. Report participation in high school and college social groups.	4. Report participation in high school and college social groups.	4. Report participation in high school and college social groups.
5. Manifest prominent social service ideals.	5. Judge selves high in ambition and initiative.	5. Judge selves high in ambition and initiative.
6. Indicate preferences for activities which involve contacts with people.	6. Report teaching experience of 4–9 years.	
7. Indicate interest in science and scientific matters.	7. Report teaching-type activities during childhood and adolescence.	
8. Report liking for outdoor activities.	8. Indicate preference for student-centered learning situations.	
9. Are young, or middle-aged.	9. Manifest independence, though not aggressiveness.	
10. Are married.		
11. Report that parental homes provided above-average cultural advantages.		
B. "High" group (compared with "low" group):	B. "High" group (compared with "low" group):	B. "High" group (compared with "low" group):
1. Indicates greater enjoyment of pupil relationships (i.e., more favorable pupil opinions).	1. Indicates greater enjoyment of pupil relationships (i.e., more favorable pupil opinions).	1. Indicates greater enjoyment of pupil relationships (i.e., more favorable pupil opinions).
2. Indicates greater preference for non-directive classroom procedures.	2. Indicates greater preference for non-directive classroom procedures.	2. Indicates greater preference for non-directive classroom procedures.
3. Is superior in verbal intelligence (I_{co} scores).	3. Is superior in verbal intelligence (I_{co} scores).	3. Is superior in verbal intelligence (I_{co} scores).
4. Is more satisfactory with regard to emotional adjustment (S_{eo} scores).	4. Is more satisfactory with regard to emotional adjustment (S_{eo} scores).	4. Is more satisfactory with regard to emotional adjustment (S_{eo} scores).

PERSONAL QUALITIES WHICH APPEAR TO DISTINGUISH TEACHERS SELECTED TO BE "HIGH" AND "LOW" WITH RESPECT TO OVER-ALL CLASSROOM BEHAVIOR: CHARACTERISTICS OF "LOW" GROUP TEACHERS

Elementary Teachers

A. "Low" group members more frequently (than "high"):
   1. Are from older age groups.
   2. Are restricted and critical in appraisals of the behavior and motives of other persons.
   3. Are unmarried.
   4. Indicate preferences for activities which do *not* involve close contacts with people.

B. "Low" group (compared with "High" group):
   1. Is less favorable in expressed opinions of pupils.
   2. Is less high with regard to verbal intelligence (I_{eo} scores).
   3. Is less satisfactory with regard to emotional adjustment (S_{eo} scores).

Secondary Teachers

A. "Low" group members more frequently (than "high"):
   1. Are from older age groups.
   2. Are restricted and critical in appraisals of the behavior and motives of other persons.
   3. Indicate preference for teacher-directed learning situations.
   4. Value exactness, orderliness, and "practical" things.
   5. Indicate preferences for activities which do *not* involve close contacts with people.

B. "Low" group (compared with "high" group):
   1. Is less favorable in expressed opinions of pupils.
   2. Is less high with regard to verbal intelligence (I_{eo} scores).
   3. Is less satisfactory with regard to emotional adjustment (S_{eo} scores).

Elementary-Secondary Teachers Combined

A. "Low" group members more frequently (than "high"):
   1. Are from older age groups.
   2. Are restricted and critical in appraisals of the behavior and motives of other persons.
   3. Value exactness, orderliness, and "practical" things.
   4. Indicate preferences for activities which do *not* involve close contacts with people.

B. "Low" group (compared with "high" group):
   1. Is less favorable in expressed opinions of pupils.
   2. Is less high with regard to verbal intelligence (I_{eo} scores).
   3. Is less satisfactory with regard to emotional adjustment (S_{eo} scores).

361

manifest superior verbal intelligence; and be above average in emotional adjustment. Turning to the other side of the coin, low teachers tend generally to: be restricted and critical in their appraisals of other persons; prefer activities which do not involve close personal contacts; express less favorable opinions of pupils; manifest less high verbal intelligence; show less satisfactory emotional adjustment; and represent older age groups.

Study No. 2: Case Analyses of Highly Selected Women Elementary Teachers

The second approach employed in seeking clues to the characteristics of teachers who appeared to be outstanding with regard to over-all classroom behavior was through individual analyses (case studies) of a number of selected women elementary teachers. It seemed reasonable to believe that such study might throw additional light on the model of the generally superior teacher. Dr. J. C. Gowan, a member of the staff of the Study, undertook, therefore, to interview a number of highly assessed elementary women teachers and to obtain additional information about them through the administration of certain personality inventories [5].

A group of 60 women teachers in an area surrounding the central offices of the Study was originally selected. These teachers had participated in earlier phases of the Study and appeared, in the light of the observation records, to comprise a highly selected group in the sense that they exhibited classroom behavior that placed them in the highest 5 percent of the teachers observed. Of the 60 teachers originally selected, 25 agreed to participate. The composite observer assessments of these teachers (in standard scores with a general mean of fifty and a standard deviation of ten for each observer) showed means and standard deviations respectively of 65.6 and 1.56 for X_o, 63.7 and 1.37 for Y_o, and 63.7 and 1.37 for Z_o. They thus comprised a very highly rated and homogeneous group relative to the observed behavior patterns.

Each teacher was interviewed for one and one-half hours, the materials employed being of a modified Adorno type. They were biographical in nature and involved especially relationships with parents, siblings, and community. Questions relating to religious and philosophical viewpoints held by the teachers also were introduced. Finally, the interviewees were given four personality inventories to complete at their convenience: the Guilford-Zimmerman Temperament Survey, the California Psychological Inventory, the Allport-Vernon Study of Values, and the Kuder Preference Record—Vocational.

Of the 25 teachers who originally agreed to participate, five failed to return the inventory materials. The findings summarized in the following paragraphs are based on the 20 women elementary teachers for whom both interview and inventory data were available.

All ages were represented in this criterion group of highly assessed teachers, the youngest teacher being 22 years of age and the oldest 56 (with a median age of 39). Thirteen of the teachers had their training in the western portion of the United States and seven in the Midwest. Eastern and southern sections of the country were not represented, a condition which may not be surprising in view of the locale of the investigation—southern California. Fifteen of the teachers had been married at some time, and 13 were married at the time of interview.

There appeared to be strong teaching traditions in the families of these highly selected elementary teachers. In 11 cases, either the father, mother, or both parents had been teachers. Teaching also was frequently mentioned as the occupation of other relatives.

School records indicated superior attainment on the part of 12 teachers. For five teachers, school attainment was approximately average, and for three, below average. Thirteen of the group admitted to feelings of having been more scholarly than their classmates when in high school. Parental stress on "doing well in school" frequently was mentioned during the interviews.

There were instances of early teaching experiences on the part of all 20 of the teachers, and, in some cases, the experience appeared to have been surprisingly extensive. One girl taught elementary school when she was seventeen, and another had considerable experience as a substitute teacher while still in high school. A third founded and conducted her own nursery school while still in high school. "Taking charge of a class in the absence of the regular teacher" while in high school, extensive participation in, and enjoyment of, playing school with peers as children, and similar experiences were reported very frequently.

Responses of the interviewees relative to questions about various aspects of teaching as a vocation suggested that the work-libido of these teachers was high. To the question, "What are the main satisfactions and appeals of teaching?" 35 responses which were judged to involve genuine work sublimations were obtained, the responses including: "being with children," "watching change and growth of children," "observing changing attitudes," "dealing with individual differences," "dealing with leaders of tomorrow," "encouraging progress of children," "stimulating pupil reactions," "observation of happy accomplishment," "fun of meeting children," "personal contact with children and people," "creative opportunities offered," "opportunity to enlarge the security areas of a child," "improving emotional atmosphere for children," and "joy in putting across ideas."

When the teachers were asked, "What would be your choice if you could do anything you wanted vocationally?" 14 of the 20 teachers said they would still be teachers. Two said they would write professionally, and one teacher *each* said she would travel, maintain a home, be a clothes buyer, or be a professional dancer.

It appeared to be almost impossible for the teachers in this selected group to project blame or to think ill of other persons. Such questions as "Do any of your associates have it in for you?" "Do children misbehave on purpose?" and similar ones all drew answers which seemed to indicate lack of suspicion of others and lack of any sort of blame-projection.

The family backgrounds of these teachers seemed to reveal a closely knit structure in which family solidarity, loyalty, and conformance were pronounced. Family vacations and other group family activities were the rule. The parental home was considered to be a happy one in most instances, with relatively few crises reported. There was the suggestion of strong needs on the part of teachers when they were children to conform to parental standards, and it seemed possible that this tendency may have resulted in some idealization of the standards and perhaps lack of insight into the actual dynamics within the home. Parents frequently were reported as being "just wonderful," although some fear of parental punishment or discipline was expressed.

Both with respect to their family groups and their social groups, most of the teachers expressed the opinion that they had possessed a strong sense of "belonging" during childhood and adolescence. There also seemed to have been early development of participative responsibilities in the family group and their extension to other social groups. There was little recall of worry as a child.

This group of teachers appeared to exhibit a somewhat stronger-than-average interest in religious activities. All of them agreed that religious values played an important part in their teaching, although few made definite statements of how such values actually were utilized in the classroom.

The teachers appeared to be friendly, cooperative, and social, but not gregarious in the ebullient sense. They expressed enjoyment of quiet activities with friends, small parties, and generally few, rather than many, acquaintances and social associates. They objected to noisy social activities and boorish behavior. They frequently were active members and officers in clubs and other organizations.

These teachers appeared particularly to enjoy reading and writing and other literary experiences, and, generally, to be more scholarly than their peers.

With regard to the personality inventory data, members of this group, as compared with norms data, gave responses which indicated them to be somewhat more restrained, objective, friendly, emotionally stable, cooperative and agreeable, tolerant, and interested in social service. Interestingly enough, they tended to give exaggeratedly good impressions of themselves. This may well have had some basis in the fact they were generous in their impressions of everyone, with virtually no expression of skepticism or criticism.

The list which follows summarizes the personal qualities, abstracted from the interview and inventory data, which appear to characterize the group of highly selected elementary women teachers.

Personal Qualities Which Appear To Characterize a Group of Elementary Women Teachers Highly Selected with Respect to Over-All Classroom Behavior

Frequently give as reason for teaching, liking for children and interest in their development.

Express admiration of such qualities as friendliness, permissiveness, definiteness, and fairness in teachers.

Dislike in teachers such qualities as arrogance, intolerance, sarcasm, and partiality.

Typically appear to be "accepting," and generous in appraisals, of other persons. See good points of a person rather than bad.

Express satisfaction with teaching (and also with teacher salaries); intend to continue teaching indefinitely.

Frequently engaged in teaching activity as child (e.g., taking charge of class in absence of teacher).

Decision to become teacher frequently was made prior to college enrollment; had planned to be a teacher from relatively early age.

Enjoyed school when they were students themselves.

Showed superior accomplishment when in school.

Report large number of teachers among parents and relatives.

Report participation in religious activities.

Enjoy activities with friends, but prefer small groups.

Frequently are members and officers of clubs.

Are married (85 percent of group).

Interested and active in literary affairs (e.g., write poetry, have published books, etc.).

More emotionally stable than average adult (Guilford-Zimmerman).

More friendly than average adult (Guilford-Zimmerman).

More cooperative and agreeable than average adult (Guilford-Zimmerman).

More restrained than average adult (Guilford-Zimmerman).

More objective than average adult (Guilford-Zimmerman).

More tolerant than average adult (California Psychological Inventory).

More inclined to "try to give a good impression" than average adult (California Psychological Inventory).

More interested in social service than average adult (Kuder Preference Record).

Less interest than average adult in computational and clerical activities (Kuder Preference Record).

Some Generalizations Regarding Outstanding Teachers

A growing body of evidence is accumulating that indicates certain characteristics which may contribute to the model of the teacher. Certain generalizations are suggested, based not only on the results of investigations conducted by the Teacher Characteristics Study, but also on data growing out of various other researches, employing quite different approaches and criteria.

Superior intellectual abilities, above-average school achievement, good emotional adjustment, attitudes favorable to pupils, enjoyment of pupil relationships, generosity in the appraisal of the behavior and motives of other persons, strong interests in reading and literary matters, interest in music and painting, participation in social and community affairs, early experiences in caring for children and teaching (such as reading to children and taking a class for the teacher), history of teaching in family, family support of teaching as a vocation, strong social service interests, and descriptions similar to those noted in this chapter appear to apply very generally to teachers judged by various kinds and sets of criteria to be outstanding. (See Bibliography for summarizations and lists of references relating to studies of teacher competence.)

While extreme caution should be taken in guarding against an overgeneralized picture of the good or effective teacher, or the opposite exemplified by the inferior, or ineffective, teacher, the results of a variety of investigations do point to certain recurring descriptions which may have some validity insofar as contemporary culture in the United States is concerned. Certainly, the evidence suggests leads and clues which provide starting points for thinking about teaching competencies and for more intensive investigations and which open the way for more adequate conceptualizing about teacher performance.

Bibliography

1. BARR, A. S. "The Measurement and Prediction of Teaching Efficiency," *Review of Educational Research*, 1949; **10**: 182–84, 1940; **13**: 218–23, 1943; **16**: 203–8, 1946; **19**: 185–90, 1949; **22**: 169–74, 1952; **25**: 261–70, 1955.
2. ———. "The Measurement and Prediction of Teaching Efficiency: A Summary of Investigations," *Journal of Experimental Education*, **16**: 203–83, 1948
3. CASTETTER, D. D.; STANDLEE, L. S., and FATTU, N. A. "Teacher Effectiveness: An Annotated Bibliography," *Bulletin of the Institute of Educational Research*, Vol. 1., No. 1. Bloomington, Ind., Indiana University School of Education, 1954.
4. DOMAS, S. J., and TIEDEMAN, D. V. "Teacher Competence: An Annotated Bibliography," *Journal of Experimental Education*, **19**: 101–218, 1950.
5. GOWAN, JOHN C. "A Summary of the Intensive Study of Twenty Highly Selected Elementary Women Teachers," *Journal of Experimental Education*, **26**: 115–24, 1957.
6. McCALL, W. A. *Measurement of Teacher Merit*. Raleigh, N.C.: North Carolina Department of Public Instruction, 1952.
7. MORSH, J. E. *Systematic Observation of Instructor Behavior*. Lackland Air Force Base, Texas: Personnel Research Laboratory, Air Force Personnel and Training Research Center, 1956.
8. RYANS, D. G. "Some Correlates of Teacher Behavior," *Educational and Psychological Measurement*, **19**: 3–12, 1959.
9. TOMLINSON, L. R. "Pioneer Studies in the Evaluation of Teaching," *Educational Research Bulletin*, **34**: 63–71, 1955.
10. ———. "Recent Studies in the Evaluation of Teaching," *Educational Research Bulletin*, **34**: 172–86, 196, 1955.
11. WATERS, W. A. "Annotated Bibliography of Publications Related to Teacher Evaluation," *Journal of Experimental Education*, **22**: 351–67, 1954.

9. Summary

THE TEACHER CHARACTERISTICS STUDY was a research project sponsored by the American Council on Education and supported by subventions from The Grant Foundation. During the period over which the Study was conducted approximately one hundred separate researches were carried out, and over six thousand teachers in seventeen hundred schools and four hundred and fifty school systems participated in various phases of the investigations. Some of the basic studies undertaken involved extensive classroom observation of teachers by trained observers with the purpose of discovering significant patterns of teacher classroom behavior. Other activities of the project had to do with the development of paper-and-pencil tests and inventories for the identification of teacher differences relative to selected patterns of classroom behavior, attitudes, and educational viewpoints; verbal intelligence; and emotional stability. Still other investigations were concerned with the comparison of defined groups of teachers (elementary teachers and secondary teachers, married teachers and unmarried teachers, etc.), from the standpoint of specified personal and social characteristics.

The Study was in part an outgrowth of the program of the National Committee on Teacher Examinations—a service program to school systems originated in 1939 by the American Council on Education. The important role of personal and social behavior patterns of teachers was recognized from the first in planning the National Teacher Examinations, but lack of reliable research data in these areas discouraged inclusion of measures in these domains in the test battery which evolved. Consequently, the National Teacher Examinations were limited to the measurement of verbal and nonverbal abilities, basic English skills, general cultural knowledge, professional educational information, and understanding of subject matter to be taught.

In 1946 discussions of the desirability of measuring nonintellectual characteristics of teachers were renewed, and preliminary studies were conducted in conjunction with the National Teacher Examination program to appraise the practicality of undertaking a major research project aimed at the identification and assessment of teacher behaviors in the personal-social domains. The results of these pilot studies were promising. The Grant Foundation expressed interest in research in this area, and the American Council on Education's Committee on Measurement and Guidance agreed to consider sponsorship. Plans for a project involving systematic study of teacher behavior were prepared, approved by the Council, and forwarded as a formal proposal to The Grant Foundation. In May 1948 the trustees of The Grant Foundation allocated funds to be used by a project staff in starting the research. The Grant Foundation continued support of the Study through preparation and publication of the present report.

The advisory committee for the Study was appointed in the summer of 1948, consisting of Dr. L. L. Thurstone, Dr. G. Frederic Kuder, Dr. Willard B. Spalding, Dr. Lester Nelson, Dr. Roscoe West, and Dr. Robert C. Challman. Dr. Herold C. Hunt was appointed chairman of the committee in 1950. Seventy-five individuals served on the staff of the Teacher Characteristics Study at various stages of the research. In addition, a number of other persons were employed as test administrators or as assistants in minor projects. Project offices were established at the University of California, Los Angeles, in October 1948, with the author as director, and preliminary work on the Study was begun during the same month.

Objectives of the Study

The major purpose of the Study was to compile information on significant teacher characteristics and to develop objective measures that might be used in evaluating and predicting teacher behavior. More specifically, the objectives were: (1) To identify, analyze, and describe some of the patterns of teachers' classroom behavior and teachers' attitudes, viewpoints, and intellectual and emotional qualities. (2) To isolate and combine into scales significant correlates (provided by responses to self-report inventories concerned with teachers' preferences, experiences, self-appraisals, judgments, and the like) of some of the major dimensions of teacher behavior—scales which might be used in evaluating and predicting important teacher characteristics. (3) To compare the characteristics of various groups of teachers when they had been classified according to such conditions as age, experience, sex, size of school, cultural climate of the community, and the like.

Pursuance of these objectives involved the development of techniques for the reliable assessment of classroom behavior, determination (largely through factor analysis) of some of the more prominent patterns of teacher behavior, development of inventories made up of materials hypothetically related to teacher-classroom behavior dimensions and other personal and social characteristics of teachers, empirical derivation of scoring keys for such instruments in the light of response-criterion correlations, and finally comparison of defined groups of teachers.

Teacher Effectiveness and the Teacher Characteristics Study

Few would deny that good teaching is the focal point of our educational system. If an ample supply of effective teachers could be attracted to our schools, the likelihood of attaining desirable educational objectives is substantial. On the other hand, if teachers are incompetent or are misfits, excellent material resources in the form of buildings, equipment, and textbooks are likely to be ineffective, if not wasted.

Yet, in spite of universal recognition of the importance of the teacher, relatively little progress has been made in defining "good teaching" or in specifying the distinguishing characteristics of competent teachers. Personnel decisions are constantly being made by teacher education institutions in admitting students and by school boards and administrators in selecting and promoting teachers, but there is little agreement about the relative importance of qualifications such as intelligence, formal education, pedagogical training, interests, and various personal and social characteristics.

If one were pressed, he might say that teaching is effective to the extent that the teacher acts in ways that are favorable to the development of basic skills, understandings, work habits, desirable attitudes, value judgments, and adequate personal adjustment of pupils. But this sort of definition is very general and abstract and is not easily translatable into terms relating to specific teacher behaviors. For educators and laymen, alike, disagree widely on aspects of learning that should be emphasized and on the role the teacher should play in a learning situation. Furthermore, it seems reasonable to suspect that learning emphases and teacher roles vary in relation to the characteristics of the pupils taught, to grade level, and to field of learning (subject matter). An aloof, rigorously academic teacher might be well suited to teach bright, academically minded, well-adjusted high school students, but he might be entirely unsuited to teach certain younger children vitally in need of sympathy and understanding above all else.

Considerations such as the above are extremely important in approaching the study of teacher behavior. Disagreement and ambiguity with respect to the description of teacher effectiveness are to be expected and cannot be entirely avoided because competent teaching undoubtedly is a relative matter. A person's concept of a good teacher seems to depend on (*a*) his acculturation, his past experience, and the value attitudes he has come to accept, (*b*) the aspects of teaching which may be foremost in his consideration at a given time, and (c) characteristics of the pupils taught. A description of competent or effective teaching must, therefore, be considered to be relative—relative to perhaps three major sets of conditions: (1) the social or cultural group in which the teacher operates, involving social values which frequently differ from person to person, community to community, culture to culture, and time to time; (2) the grade level and subject matter taught; and perhaps (3) intellectual and personal characteristics of the pupils taught.

It is not surprising, then, to note the difficulties that have confronted those seeking to establish criteria of teacher effectiveness, the dearth of testable hypotheses produced in research which has been undertaken, and the general lack of understanding of the problem of the characteristics of effective teachers. Two very important reasons why effective and ineffective teachers cannot be described with any assurance are the wide variation in the value concepts underlying descriptions of desirable teaching objectives and the differences in teacher role at different educational levels, in different subjects, and with different pupils.

But in addition to these considerations, and important in its own right as a deterrent to the study of teacher effectiveness, is the fact that there is a lack of any clear knowledge of the *patterns of behaviors* that typify individuals who are employed as teachers. It seems probable that, without losing sight of the importance of developing means of recognizing "good" teachers, attention of the researcher might first more properly and profitably be directed at the identification and estimation of some of the major patterns of personal and social characteristics of teachers.

This represents the point of departure for the research conducted by the Teacher Characteristics Study. It was felt that a major first task was to learn more about teacher behavior and its components, patterns, variations, and relationships. In the Teacher Characteristics Study, considerations of the effectiveness, or value, of particular teacher behaviors were to a large extent disregarded. Instead, attention was focused on the study of possible teacher behavior dimensions, such dimensions being hypothesized to represent generalized trait continua. From this point of view teacher behavior variables are assumed to consist of clusters of relatively homogeneous (positively intercorrelated) behaviors, such component behaviors being of the nature of simple predicates, capable of operational definition. Implied in this approach is the assumption that a teacher may be described in terms of positions on specified behavior dimensions, such descriptions being essentially factual and relating to observable manifestations of overt behavior or else to responses known to be correlated with some behavior pattern to a degree that may permit indirect estimation of that behavior.

Some Basic Issues in the Study of Teacher Behavior

The basic concerns of research on teacher behavior are, as implied in the statement of the objectives of the Teacher Characteristics Study, description and prediction. The goals of the researcher become (1) the identification and description of specific teacher behaviors and the major dimensions they comprise, and (2) the determination of how and to what extent various data descriptive of teachers (verbal responses, overt acts, biographical information, kind of training, etc., all of which may be subsumed under *teacher characteristics*) are either (*a*) antecedents or (*b*) concomitants of some behavior agreed to be a component of some criterion of teacher behavior.

The extent to which such descriptions and relationships can be uncovered depends on (1) how unambiguously and operationally *agreed-upon* behaviors or criterion dimensions can be defined, and how validly and reliably estimates of the criterion behaviors can be obtained, (2) how successfully hypotheses can be generated relative to individual characteristics which will correlate significantly with criterion estimates, and what specific objectives and predictor-criterion research designs are employed, and (3) the over-all research design, taking into account sampling, control, and replication.

A word should be added here regarding another basic issue in the study of teacher behavior—the desirability of research being carried out within a framework of theory. Few attempts have been made to organize and formulate principles of teacher behavior, and the study of teachers has been largely of a blunderbuss sort. Evidence has tended to accumulate slowly in the form of isolated bits of information, with little consideration for basic assumptions, postulates, and hypotheses, or for systematic relationships among findings. It seems probable that as more attention is directed to theorizing about teacher behavior, to organizing known information about teacher characteristics, and to testing hypotheses derived from the growing body of generalizations, understanding of teacher behavior and conditions which contribute to it (and perhaps light on teacher effectiveness) will make notable progress.

DESIGNATION AND MEASUREMENT OF CRITERION DIMENSIONS

Conceptually and chronologically the first problem in the study of teacher behavior has to do with the identification of major dimensions of the criterion—definition of specific behaviors which are relevant to teaching, investigation of their interrelationships and their patterning into homogeneous clusters or dimensions, and the development of means for measuring individual differences with respect to the various dimensions of criterion behavior.

Thus, a first major activity of research on teacher characteristics has to do with the derivation of a working model of teacher behavior (i.e., designation of the criterion dimensions to be studied and the components of each). Ideally, this is a function of the interaction of both *rationally* and *empirically* obtained evidence. The final decisions in which the process culminates must necessarily be a set of judgments, closely related to the value systems embraced by the culture in which the teaching is accomplished. The problem set for the researcher has to do with (*a*) the determination of the dimensions of the over-all behavior and what kinds of acts or performances go to make up these dimensions, (*b*) how different teacher behavior dimensions are interrelated, (*c*) how they may be adequately sampled, and (*d*) perhaps above all, the determination of how generalizable (or, on the other hand, how specific) designated criterion dimensions may be with respect to different teaching situations.

Proceeding concurrently with consideration of the criterion dimensions of teacher behavior and their composition must be the development and selection of measures suitable for obtaining working criterion data (e.g., measurements of individual differences with respect to the specified dimension of teacher behavior). It is immediately apparent that if decisions regarding important areas of teacher behavior are to have the advantage of empirical evidence as well as rational support, data must be obtained through criterion *measures* which cannot themselves be chosen until after decisions relative to the nature of the criterion have been reached; and some of the judgments relative to the criterion must remain tentative until reliable estimates of the hypothesized dimensions have been obtained through the application of suitable measures. Criterion definition (designation of relevant teacher behaviors) and criterion assessment (measurement of teacher behavior dimensions) therefore interact, and conclusions concerning criterion behavior always are relative to the measurement or observation approach employed.

Various methods of criterion measurement have been employed or suggested. The major categories into which these fall include: (*a*) direct measurement based on observation of *ongoing* teacher behavior (e.g., time sampling involving replicated systematic observation); (*b*) indirect measurement based on preserved records of ongoing teacher behavior (e.g., tape recordings); (c) indirect measurement by nontrained observers, based on recall of teacher behavior and assessment thereof (ratings by students, administrators, peers, etc.); (d) measurement of a product (student behavior) of teacher behavior; and (e) measurement of concomitants (secondary criterion data) of a criterion of teacher behavior.

These different approaches to criterion measurement vary in nature of rationale employed to support them, in reliability of the criterion data produced, and in the order of obtained relationships between criterion estimates, thus differently derived, and specified predictors— this last observation, of course, merely bearing testimony to the fact that most criteria are very complex and any one set of estimates is likely to be incomplete with respect to the over-all criterion.

Broadly speaking, approaches to criterion measurement in the study of teacher behavior thus involve the evaluation of (1) teacher behavior *in process*, (2) a *product* of teacher behavior, or (3) concomitants of teacher behavior. Measurement of ongoing behavior of the teacher is the most direct approach; measurement of products and of concomitants are less direct and more subject to the effects of confounding conditions.

Concomitants (which, in a sense, may be thought of as secondary criterion data) usually are not acceptable for criterion measurement when direct measurement of behavior in process or the measurement of isolable products of teacher behavior can conveniently be used. However, in investigations involving extensive sampling and where other measurement approaches are impractical, the use of known correlates as substitutes for process or product data frequently is defensible.

Of the measurement approaches employing observation and assessment of ongoing teacher behavior (i.e., teacher behavior in process) only *time sampling involving replicated systematic observation by trained observers* produces sufficiently reliable data to recommend its use in fundamental research, although less well controlled variations (e.g., ratings by students) may be employed when only coarse discrimination (e.g., "highest" and "lowest" teachers with respect to some criterion component) is required, and when the larger expected error is recognized and accepted. Various assessment techniques have been developed among which the more reliable and promising appear to be (1) graphic scales with operationally, or behaviorally, defined poles and/or units, (2) observation check lists, and (3) forced-choice scales. The chief shortcoming of observation and assessment techniques has been lack of reliability, a shortcoming which research has indicated can fairly readily be overcome with care to definition and to scale development, and with adequate training of the observers or judges.

Product measurements (estimates of the behavior or achievement of the pupils of teachers) have been widely acclaimed as desirable criterion data, but have been infrequently used in the study of teacher behavior. Actually, the seeming relevance and appropriateness of the measurement of pupil behaviors and their products as indicators of teacher performance may be more apparent than real, for the producers of (or contributors to) pupil behavior or pupil achievement are numerous, and it is difficult to designate and parcel out the contribution to a particular "product" made by a specified aspect of the producing situation, such as the teacher. It also must be noted that the different facets of a product (various understandings, skills, and attitudes, etc., of pupils in various content fields and areas of personal behavior) are numerous, and each must be capable of valid measurement of at least partial isolation for study when the product approach to criterion measurement is employed. The comparability of estimates of various components or aspects of a product (different pupil achievements, for example) also becomes a special problem when measurements of student behavior or achievement are employed as estimates of teacher behavior. And when measurement of the product is accomplished by obtaining estimates of student change (i.e., pre-test–post-test data), the problem of variable potential gain (students who score high on the initial measurement being closer to their "ceilings" than students who originally score low are to theirs) is particularly plaguing to the researcher. However, if the rationale of the product (student performance) criterion is accepted and if the complex control problem presented by a multiplicity of producers and the multidimensionality of the criterion can be satisfactorily coped with, student change becomes an intriguing approach to the measurement of teacher behavior.

In dealing with any of the several approaches to measuring the criterion, the researcher must be thoroughly familiar with, and guard against, the various sources of criterion measurement bias, particularly those which have to do with (*a*) incompleteness and (*b*) contamination by nonrelevant factors—conditions leading to invalid estimates of criterion dimensions.

DETERMINATION OF PREDICTORS OF A CRITERION

After a criterion dimension has been identified and described and an appropriate method of criterion measurement chosen, prediction of the criterion (determination of conditions which correlate significantly with the criterion data) usually becomes a problem of major concern. This involves, *first*, the development of materials and procedures for obtaining data which the researcher hypothesizes may be predictive of, or correlated with, the obtained criterion measurements, and, *next*, determination of the extent to which such hypothesized predictors are valid for estimating the criterion behavior.

The effectiveness of a predictor is dependent upon a number of conditions, some having to do with the criterion data, some with the hypothesized predictor itself, and still others with the specific approach to the predictor-criterion relationship which is incorporated in the research design. Questions like those noted below, therefore, represented basic concerns of the Teacher Characteristics Study as the derivation of correlates of dimensions of teacher behavior was planned and carried out.

Is prediction to be attempted from single bits of information (e.g., answers to single questionnaire, test, or inventory items) or from scores based on combinations of such bits of information forming sets of homogeneous items, or scales? And, if the latter, does the combination of bits involve equal or differential weighting?

Is the derivation of correlates (original selection of items or combinations of items, as predictors of the criterion) to be based upon experience with a single sample, or has replication been employed involving multiple samples of teachers?

Is validation of the predictors, and their ultimate use, to be with (*a*) additional random samples of the same population as the samples employed in deriving the predictors (e.g., cross-validation) or (*b*) samples of populations other than that from which the predictors were derived either (1) employing the same criterion measure (validity generalization) or (2) a different criterion measure (validity extension)?

Is prediction to be attempted for predictor data and criterion data which have been collected at approximately the same time, or under conditions where obtaining of criterion data is delayed and carried out with a considerable time interval separating the collection of the predictor and the criterion estimates?

Is prediction to be attempted for situations where the predictor data are obtained under incentive conditions (e.g., in connection with selection for employment) or under nonincentive conditions (e.g., as in basic research)?

Is prediction to be attempted for selected criterion dimensions singly (e.g., classroom discipline) or for a composite criterion made up of a number of heterogeneous components or dimensions (e.g., over-all teaching behavior)?

PREDICTABILITY OF TEACHER BEHAVIOR

What are the possibilities of predicting teacher behavior? What are some of the limiting conditions? From what sorts of generalizations may the investigation of correlates of a criterion of teacher behavior proceed?

It seems probable the summary statements which follow provide a reasonable starting point. Some of these are derived from rational analysis of the problems involved, but many also have substantial support from empirical data.

1. The predictability of teacher behavior undoubtedly is affected by the *multidimensionality of the over-all criterion.* There is accumulating evidence that prediction can be accomplished with better than chance results for specified criterion dimensions. On the other hand, the prediction of over-all teacher behavior would seem problematical. Certainly it is possible only to the extent that some general agreement can be reached regarding the dimensions comprising such behavior (involving, of course, acceptance of a common set of educational values) and how they should be combined to form a composite; and such a criterion by its very complexity limits the likelihood of discovering significant predictors.

2. The predictability of teacher behavior varies, depending on the *degree of control* it is possible to exert in dealing with the multiplicity of predictors and the multidimensionality of the criterion.

3. The predictability of a criterion behavior varies with the *kind of measure* employed in obtaining the criterion data.

4. The predictability of a criterion varies with the *adequacy* (reliability and validity) *of measures* of (*a*) the criterion and (*b*) the predictor variables.

5. The predictability of a criterion is so limited by conditions associated with measurement of the criterion, measurement of predictors, and practical conditions, that relationships representing common variance of perhaps one-fifth or one-fourth of the total variance probably approach the maximum to be expected except in chance instances.

6. The predictability of a teacher behavior dimension from a specified predictor probably varies depending upon the cultural milieu which provides the setting for an investigation, particularly the values and objectives prominent in the teacher-training curriculum at the time the teachers studied were in college.

7. Predictability of a criterion behavior varies directly with the degree of similarity between the sample with respect to which predictors are derived and the sample to which the predictors are applied in attempting to determine predictor-criterion relationships.

8. Predictability of a criterion dimension varies with the *particular teacher population* (e.g., Grades 1–2 women teachers, men science teachers), and *student population* studied.

9. Predictability of a teacher behavior varies inversely with the *time interval* separating the obtaining of predictor measurements and criterion measurements.

10. Predictability of a criterion behavior probably varies depending upon the association of *incentive or nonincentive conditions* with the obtaining of predictor data.

11. The regression of predictor measurements on criterion measurements frequently is *curvilinear* (e.g., positive correlation between amount of teaching experience and certain criterion measures of teacher behavior of secondary school teachers during first five years or so, followed by leveling off and decline in criterion estimates with extensive experience).

12. Prediction of teacher behavior must be considered largely in the *actuarial* sense; individual prediction, as generally is the case in attempting to predict human behavior, is much more limited and is accomplished with a lesser degree of confidence.

DEALING WITH THE BASIC PROBLEMS

The activities of the Teacher Characteristics Study in working toward its major objectives were guided to a large extent by consideration of the aforementioned problems having to do with determination of the criteria of teacher behavior (the major dimensions of teacher behavior) and with the validity of their prediction. The Study's research thus includes (1) *designation of certain major dimensions of teacher classroom behavior*, involving (*a*) development of appropriate observation and assessment procedures, (*b*) conduct of systematic observations of teachers in their classrooms, and (*c*) carrying out of factorial analyses of observers' assessments relative to a number of aspects of teacher behavior; (2) following determination of major dimensions of teacher classroom behavior and the components of such dimensions, *conduct of systematic observation and assessment* of relatively large samples of teachers of different grades and subjects to obtain criterion data; (3) development of inventory materials requiring responses which it was hypothesized might be correlated with major dimensions of teacher classroom behavior and other teacher traits, and determination of significant predictor-criterion relationships by (a) administering such materials to teachers for whom criterion data were available, (b) analyzing the responses to determine the value of each possible response as a predictor of a specified teacher behavior, and (c) casting the selected items into scoring keys which, in light of the analysis, might be expected to be reliably related to the major teacher behavior dimensions and traits; and (4) carrying out researches involving cross-validation, validity generalization study, and validity extension study to obtain evidence relative to the probable usefulness of the scoring keys.

Samples Employed in the Research

Generalizability of the results of any research is, of course, dependent upon the sampling procedure followed. And ideally either a representative or random sample would be desired to provide maximum information about the generalizability of research data resulting from the Teacher Characteristics Study to the population of teachers of the United States.

Obviously, it was not possible under the existing educational system in this country to adopt either a random sampling or representative sampling design. Cooperation of school systems, schools, or teachers in a research project must remain voluntary in any decentralized system of education. Furthermore, adequate population control data necessary for making possible adjustments for systematic errors in sampling are for the most part not available.

In the light of the sampling difficulties encountered by the Study, it is impossible to conclude that the samples employed were either representative or known random samples of the totality of teachers in the United States. It is appropriate therefore that the teacher characteristics investigated be described strictly operationally in such standard terms as "TCS understanding, friendly behavior," "TCS attitude toward pupils," "TCS emotional stability," etc. This is the same as saying that the research findings apply most exactly to the hypothetical population of which the teachers who voluntarily cooperated in the Study comprise a random sample. The extent to which the results of the Study may be generalized to teachers in general, or to any particular group of teachers, is a function of the similarity between the teachers studied and the group in question at any particular time.

Within the limits of sampling described above, activities of the Teacher Characteristics Study fell into three classes: (1) those involving the observation of teacher classroom behavior and the selection of inventory responses for the prediction of classroom behavior dimensions and other sets of teacher characteristics; (2) those involving a national survey of teacher characteristics, estimated from the Teacher Characteristics Schedule; and (3) special studies growing out of the investigations of teacher behaviors and their prediction. The first group of activities have been referred to as the *Basic Analysis Study*, and the teachers involved as the Basic Analysis Sample, and the second as the *Survey Study*, and the teachers as the Survey Sample, and the third as *Special Studies*, and the teachers as various Special Studies Samples.

The Basic Analysis Sample consisted of teachers in relatively large cities who were available for the systematic observations undertaken by the Study and for inventorying with respect to the predictor instrument developed (e.g., the Teacher Characteristics Schedule). The Survey Sample, on the other hand, was made up of teachers from the United States as a whole, teachers who had completed the Teacher Characteristics Schedule upon request of their respective principals— the sampling of principals having been made from national lists with systematic selection to provide probability samples of the available sampling frames.

Since it seemed reasonable to hypothesize that certain subpopulations might differ systematically from others with regard to teacher characteristics, investigations and comparisons were conducted not only with different groups of teachers in general (combined elementary and secondary school teachers), but also with the elementary teacher sample considered alone, the secondary teacher sample alone, and with major subsamples of secondary teachers consisting of mathematics-science teachers and English–social studies teachers.

Some Patterns of Teacher Classroom Behavior

As already has been noted, one of the major undertakings of the Teacher Characteristics Study was the designation of some of the prominent traits of personal-social teacher behavior, the obtaining of data relative to teacher manifestations of such traits or behaviors, and the determination of the major patterns into which such observed teacher behaviors fall.

In attempting the identification of major dimensions of teacher classroom behavior, the interplay of the rational and empirical approaches to criterion designation was prominent. Intensive study was made of the literature covering the function of the teacher as seen from various viewpoints and of previous research undertaken in the areas of human personality. Reports of critical incidents of teacher behavior are accumulated and analyzed. Assessments of teacher behavior relative to a number of dimensions (tentatively adopted in light of teacher traits suggested by the literature and reported critical incidents) then were obtained, intercorrelated, and factor-analyzed.

The first step in this phase of the research was the development of preliminary lists of (a) teacher behaviors frequently referred to in the literature and (b) significant behaviors of teachers generalized from reports of critical classroom incidents. The immediate task was to devise an observation and assessment record and even more important, an appropriate "glossary" describing behaviorally and operationally the behaviors to be assessed. The assessment procedure which was adopted assumed that many personal-social traits of teachers could be hypothesized to constitute dimensions, the opposite poles of which might be described operationally with considerable precision. In selecting behavior dimensions to be assessed, each potential trait was reviewed in the light of criteria which required that the behavior be within the personal-social domain, be one for which there was considerable evidence, preferably both logical and empirical, of its relation to teaching, and be capable of identification in terms of observable teacher acts. The resulting observation and assessment blank was known as the Classroom Observation Record. Specific teacher acts exemplifying the poles of each behavior dimension were described in the Glossary.

In its final form the Classroom Observation Record related to four dimensions of pupil classroom behavior (alert-apathetic, responsible-obstructive, confident-uncertain, initiating-dependent) and eighteen teacher behaviors (fair-partial, democratic-autocratic, responsive-aloof, understanding-restricted, kindly-harsh, stimulating-dull, original-stereotyped, alert-apathetic, attractive-unimpressive, responsible-evading, steady-erratic, poised-excitable, confident-uncertain, systematic-disorganized, adaptable-inflexible, optimistic-pessimistic, integrated-immature, broad-narrow).

Effective employment of direct observation of teacher behavior and assessment with the Classroom Observation Record required the thorough training of observers. Such training was accomplished by conducting a series of practice sessions, each followed by critical evaluation and comparison of the resulting assessments. Training was continued until the assessments of an observer-trainee and those of a senior observer (trainer) correlated approximately .80.

In using the Classroom Observation Record an observer noted the specific behaviors of a teacher in relation to those behaviors listed in the Glossary, then summarized the observed acts relative to a particular dimension by estimating the extent to which one or the other pole of the dimension was approximated by the behavior of the teacher in question. On the seven-point scale, marked occurrence of the behaviors described by one or the other of the poles of the dimension were assigned assessments of one or seven, an assessment of four representing an average, or neutral, assessment with respect to the teacher behavior dimension under consideration.

The standardized procedure adopted by the Teacher Characteristics Study called for two observations of each teacher, the observations being made at different times by different observers. The two independent assessments of a teacher's classroom behavior became the complete record for the teacher, provided the two assessments did not show substantial discrepancy. If the assessments were found to differ significantly with respect to a teacher behavior pattern, a third observation and assessment, made by a third independent observer, was carried out.

As a result of the direct observation and assessment of teacher classroom behavior and subsequent statistical analyses of the measurement data, several interdependent patterns of teacher behavior were suggested. Three in particular appeared to stand out in separate factor analyses of elementary and secondary teacher data:

TCS Pattern X_o—warm, understanding, friendly *vs.* aloof, egocentric, restricted teacher behavior.

TCS Pattern Y_o—responsible, businesslike, systematic *vs.* evading, unplanned, slipshod teacher behavior.

TCS Pattern Z_o—stimulating, imaginative, surgent *vs.* dull, routine teacher behavior.

It is of interest to observe that these behavior syndromes, TCS Patterns X_o, Y_o, and Z_o, are not entirely unique to the Teacher Characteristics Study. They are supported not only by rational analysis of the teaching process but also by reports of other factor analyses of teacher behavior data which have appeared in the literature during recent months.

X_o, Y_o, and Z_o scores derived from observers' estimates of teacher behaviors in the classroom appeared to possess sufficient reliability to permit comparisons of teacher groups with respect to such patterns and, also, to justify their use for criterion purposes in attempting to identify inventory responses which might be used to predict teacher classroom behavior.

Among elementary school teachers, the Patterns X_o, Y_o, and Z_o were highly intercorrelated, and each also seemed to be highly correlated with pupil behavior in teachers' classes. Among secondary school teachers the intercorrelations of the patterns were less high, that between patterns X_o (friendly) and Y_o (organized) being of a very low order. The three teacher classroom behavior patterns were much less highly correlated with pupil behavior in regard to secondary teachers as compared with elementary teachers.

Elementary and secondary teachers, as major groups, differed little with respect to mean assessments on Patterns X_o, Y_o, and Z_o. However, Grades 5–6 women teachers, represented by a relatively small sample, were assessed somewhat higher on the several classroom behavior patterns (particularly on Y_o) than teachers of other elementary grades. Among secondary school groups, social studies teachers and women English teachers received the highest mean assessments on Pattern X_o (friendly behavior). Women mathematics teachers (with women social studies teachers not far behind) scored highest on pattern Y_o (businesslike behavior). Women social studies and science teachers surpassed other groups on Pattern Z_o.

Teachers over 55 years of age received distinctly lower mean assessments on Pattern X_o (friendly), and also slightly lower with regard to Pattern Z_o (stimulating), than younger teacher groups. Teachers over 40 years of age generally tended to receive higher mean assessments on Pattern Y_o, this being particularly true of English–social studies teachers.

Among elementary teachers the mean assessments on the classroom behavior Patterns X_o, Y_o, and Z_o were slightly but insignificantly higher for married as compared with single teachers. Among secondary mathematics-science teachers, single teachers received higher mean assessments on all three patterns than did those who were married. With respect to English–social studies teachers, single teachers were assessed higher than married teachers on Pattern Y_o, but somewhat lower on Patterns X_o and Z_o.

Mean assessments of teacher classroom behavior did not vary significantly when teachers were classified according to scores on the several scales of the Minnesota Multiphasic Personality Inventory and the Allport-Vernon Study of Values. However, the "dominant" and "sociable" scales of the Thurstone Temperament Schedule did distinguish between teachers with respect to Pattern X_o (warm, friendly) and Pattern Z_o (stimulating), the more highly assessed teachers tending to attain higher scores on the Thurstone Temperament Schedule scales.

In general, differences between teacher groups compared on the observed classroom behavior Patterns X_o, Y_o, and Z_o were not pronounced, and it is of interest to note that scores yielded by the Teacher Characteristics Schedule scales which were derived to predict classroom behavior Patterns X, Y, and Z, frequently distinguished different teacher groups more sharply and with greater assurance than did the X_o, Y_o, and Z_o criterion data.

Patterns of Values, Verbal Ability, and Emotional Stability

Inevitably the Teacher Characteristics Study sought other evidences of teacher behavior in addition to those provided by assessments of overt classroom performance. In order to extend the understanding of conative and cognitive aspects of teacher behavior and to permit the more complete investigation of relationships between teacher characteristics and specified conditions of teaching, the Study undertook a number of researches directed at analyses of teachers' attitudes, their educational viewpoints, their verbal intelligence, and their emotional adjustment, and attempted to develop direct-inquiry instruments for estimating from a teacher's responses his status relative to such behavior domains.

In one set of studies a number of opinionnaires relating to teachers' attitudes toward groups of persons contacted in the school were developed and the organization of teacher attitudes was studied through factor analysis. In keeping with the results of the factor analyses, the Study centered its attention chiefly on the attitudes of teachers toward pupils, their attitudes toward administrators, and their attitudes toward fellow teachers and nonadministrative personnel.

The educational viewpoints of teachers with respect to curricular organization and scope, pupil participation and class planning, academic achievement standards, etc., also were investigated (separately for elementary and secondary teachers) through the employment of direct-inquiry items and factor analysis of the intercorrelations among responses. The patterns of viewpoints which emerged were not clear-cut from the standpoint of ready interpretation, and there seemed to be justification for considering teachers' educational beliefs from the standpoint of a single continuum, oversimplified perhaps by its designation as a "traditional-permissive" dimension.

To obtain estimates of the verbal understanding of teachers, vocabulary and verbal-analogy items were constructed, experimentally administered, and the responses analyzed, the procedure culminating in the selection of a small number of highly discriminating items comprising a verbal ability scale. In a similar way forced-choice, self-descriptive materials were prepared and analyzed to obtain items for providing estimates of the emotional stability of teachers. And to aid in the detection of "tendency to make a good impression" when dealing with responses to direct-question materials, a set of items intended to measure probable validity of response of teachers also was assembled.

Various studies and comparisons of the attitudes, educational viewpoints, verbal understanding, and emotional adjustment of teachers were undertaken in the course of the development of such measuring devices as those noted above. Some of the trends which were observed included the following:

1. The attitudes of elementary teachers toward pupils, toward administrators, and also toward fellow teachers and nonadministrative personnel in the schools were markedly more favorable than were similar attitudes of secondary teachers.

2. The attitudes of teachers who were judged by their principals to be superior in teaching performance were significantly and distinctly more favorable toward pupils, and also toward administrators, than the attitudes of teachers who were judged by their principals to be unsatisfactory or poor.

3. Neither amount of teaching experience nor age appeared to be very highly associated with teacher attitudes, although there was a slight tendency for the attitudes of secondary teachers of greater experience to be slightly more favorable toward administrators and somewhat less favorable toward pupils than other experience groups.

4. More favorable attitudes toward pupils were expressed by women teachers in the secondary school, but among elementary teachers there was a tendency for men to possess more favorable pupil attitudes than did women.

5. Teachers whose observed classroom behavior was judged to be more characteristically warm and understanding (TCS Pattern X_o) and more stimulating (TCS Pattern Z_o) possessed more favorable attitudes toward pupils and also more favorable attitudes toward administrators.

6. Actual pupil behavior in the classroom (based upon observers' assessments) did not appear to be related to the attitudes held by teachers.

7. The educational viewpoints expressed by secondary teachers were of a more traditional or learning-centered nature, while those of elementary teachers leaned more in the direction of permissiveness; within the secondary school, science and mathematics teachers appeared more traditional in their viewpoints and English and social studies teachers more permissive in theirs.

8. Teachers judged to be more warm and understanding in their classroom behavior, and to a somewhat lesser extent, those judged to be more stimulating, expressed more permissive educational viewpoints.

Teachers judged to be more businesslike and systematic showed a slight tendency toward more traditional viewpoints.

9. The verbal understanding scores obtained by secondary teachers were significantly higher than those of elementary teachers, English and foreign language teachers excelling other subject-matter groups within the secondary school.

10. Men teachers at both the elementary and secondary levels appeared to be markedly more emotionally stable than women teachers.

11. There was a tendency for elementary teachers who were judged to be warm and understanding in classroom behavior, and also those judged to be stimulating in their classes, to manifest superior emotional adjustment.

12. There seemed to be no observable relationship between scores on the validity-of-response scale and the classification of teachers by amount of teaching experience, age, sex, grade or subject taught, or observed classroom behavior.

Indirect Estimation of Teacher Classroom Behaviors and Other Teacher Characteristics

The actual sampling of the teachers' classroom behaviors usually is inconvenient and frequently is impossible in practice. And the employment of direct-question inventory methods to obtain a sample of responses in a particular trait domain may result in distorted estimates if an incentive situation conducive to either intentional or unintentional falsification to responses is involved.

To circumvent some of these difficulties, an alternative approach to the estimation of teacher classroom behaviors and certain teaching-related personal and social traits of teachers was undertaken—that of attempting to predict teacher traits and behaviors from *correlates*, or symptoms, of those behaviors and traits. Such a procedure is somewhat less satisfying than that which is based upon actual samples of the behavior in question, but it is useful and is widely employed in science and the applications of science.

Usually, indirect estimation through the use of correlates would not be undertaken if direct estimation were feasible. The chief, and very obvious, disadvantage of estimation from correlates lies in the fact that it is a step removed from direct estimation. The amount of variance common to an estimate of behavior obtained by direct methods and any single correlate seldom exceeds 25 percent and often is 5 percent or less, even though the relationship may be a highly reliable one. This situation demands the accumulation of a reasonably large number of such correlates to permit useful indirect estimation. The advantages of the use of correlates for measurement and prediction are, however, substantial. The employment of correlates makes measurement possible in areas of behavior which otherwise would be inaccessible in many practical situations. It also often provides far more economical estimation than does direct measurement. Furthermore, it helps to avoid distortion in the measurement of personal characteristics, which frequently occurs when there is a tendency to give socially acceptable responses. And the use of correlates may enable the tapping of subtle aspects of a criterion behavior which ordinarily elude description and are not immediately apparent from direct estimates.

Much of the research conducted by the Teacher Characteristics Study was devoted to problems concerned with the determination of correlates (signs, symptoms, or indicators) of teacher classroom behaviors, and also estimates of teacher attitudes, educational viewpoints, verbal ability, and emotional stability. To this end some twenty-five different instruments were invented by the project staff, each consisting of stimulus materials hypothesized to evoke responses which might be correlated with various teacher characteristics. The original instruments employed a wide range of approaches involving self-judgment, interpretation of pictorially presented situations, estimation of unknown conditions, report of biographical data, indication of preferences, report of activities, and other data-providing techniques.

Following a series of preliminary response selection and validation studies, materials were selected from the original instruments and assembled into a single booklet known as the Teacher Characteristics Schedule. The Schedule, thus, was an omnibus self-report type of inventory, made up of items culled from the originally separate instruments. In its final form it consisted of 300 multiple-choice and checklist items relating to personal preferences, self-judgments, frequently engaged-in activities, biographical data, and the like.

Employing as criteria (a) observers' assessments of teacher classroom behaviors X_o, Y_o, and Z_o and (b) scores on the direct-response scales relative to teacher attitudes, viewpoints, verbal intelligence, and emotional stability (R_{ci}, R_{1ci}, and Q_{ci}, B_{ci}, I_{ci}, and S_{ci}), hundreds of response analyses were carried out. Criterion groups of teachers were selected with respect to each trait or behavior under study and response-criterion correlations were obtained for each response to each item of the Teacher Characteristics Schedule. This procedure was followed for a variety of conditions, and correlate scoring keys, employing responses associated with the criterion behaviors as signs or indicators of behavior, thus were derived for a large number of teacher groups.

The most generally applicable sets of scoring keys, and those most frequently used in other phases of the Study's research, were the All-Elementary Teacher Scoring Keys, the All-Secondary Teacher Scoring Keys, and the All-Teacher Scoring Keys (based on elementary and secondary teachers combined). Teacher Characteristics Schedule scores became obtainable relating to the following teacher characteristics:

Teacher Characteristic X_{co}—warm, understanding, friendly *vs.* aloof, egocentric, restricted classroom behavior.
Teacher Characteristic Y_{co}—responsible, businesslike, systematic *vs.* evading, unplanned, slipshod classroom behavior.
Teacher Characteristic Z_{co}—stimulating, imaginative *vs.* dull, routine classroom behavior.
Teacher Characteristic R_{co}—favorable *vs.* unfavorable opinions of pupils.
Teacher Characteristic R_{1co}—favorable *vs.* unfavorable opinions of democratic classroom procedures.
Teacher Characteristic Q_{co}—favorable *vs.* unfavorable opinions of administrative and other school personnel.
Teacher Characteristic B_{co}—learning-centered ("traditional") *vs.* child-centered ("permissive") educational viewpoints.
Teacher Characteristic I_{co}—superior verbal understanding (comprehension) *vs.* poor verbal understanding.
Teacher Characteristic S_{co}—emotional stability (adjustment) *vs.* instability.

Reliability data for the correlates scoring keys and various kinds of validity data relating to the several teacher characteristics were obtained. Generally, the reliability coefficients fell between approximately .70 and .80. The validity coefficients were of varying magnitude depending upon the kind of validity investigated (cross-validity, validity generalization, validity extension, concurrent validity, predictive validity), the particular teacher behavior or characteristic estimated, and the teacher group from which the key was derived and to which it might be applied. Concurrent validity coefficients from correlate scores on classroom behavior Patterns X_o, Y_o, and Z_o, for example, were typically between .20 and .50; predictive validity coefficients were similarly positive but generally low, seldom exceeding .20 or thereabouts. Cross-validation was the approach employed to validity study in the case of teacher attitudes, viewpoints, verbal ability, and emotional stability. Such coefficients typically were between .40 and .60.

Intercorrelations among scores resulting from the application of the several correlate scoring keys estimating classroom behaviors, attitudes, educational viewpoints, verbal intelligence, and emotional stability were positive and often substantial. There appeared to be a notable tendency for characteristics X_{co} (warm, understanding), Z_{co} (stimulating), and $-B_{co}$ (permissive) to be highly correlated among elementary teachers, suggesting a factor contributed to by friendly and stimulating teacher behavior combined with permissive, child-centered educational viewpoints. There also was a tendency for Y_{co}, R_{co}, R_{1co}, and Q_{co} to be interrelated, suggesting a factor made up of organized teacher behavior and favorable opinions on the part of teachers regarding other persons. These trends were somewhat less evident among secondary teachers, but the X_{co} and $-B_{co}$ combination (friendly, warm behavior and permissive educational viewpoints) seemed again to be very much in evidence in one factor, and Y_{co} (businesslike, well-organized teacher behavior) appeared also to be prominent in a second major pattern.

Looking at the various findings which resulted from correlating Teacher Characteristics Schedule scores with observers' assessments of teacher classroom behavior, it appears that:

Among elementary teachers, X_o (warm, friendly classroom behavior) is best predicted by X_{co}, $-B_{co}$, Z_{co}, I_{co}, and S_{co}; Y_o (businesslike, systematic classroom behavior) is best predicted by Y_{co}; and Z_o (stimulating classroom behavior) is best predicted by Z_{co} and X_{co}.

Among secondary teachers, X_o (warm, friendly classroom behavior) is best predicted by X_{co}, Z_{co}, R_{co}, S_{co}, and I_{co}; Y_o (businesslike, systematic classroom behavior) is best predicted by Y_{co}; and Z_o (stimulating classroom behavior) is best predicted by Z_{co}.

Some Comparisons of Teachers in the Light of Estimated Characteristics

The third of the major objectives of the Teacher Characteristics Study was to compare the characteristics of teachers who had been classified with regard to various conditions. The comparisons summarized here are made in light of the several personal-social traits measured by the Teacher Characteristics Schedule. The approach is strictly taxonomic, and its purpose is to take a look at a cross-section of American teachers during the first half of the decade beginning in 1950.

Comparisons of teachers with respect to their Schedule scores were, for the most part, replicated with the two samples, the Basic Analysis Sample and the Survey Sample, previously described. For some comparisons, however, such replication was not possible: certain control items relating to geographic area in which teaching was performed, size of community in which school was located, etc., were incorporated in the

Teacher Characteristics Schedule booklet employed in the nation-wide survey, but were not a part of the original form of the Schedule used with teachers participating in the basic analyses.

The inferences reported in the following paragraphs are based on the *mean* scores of the groups of variously classified teachers.

TEACHER CHARACTERISTICS IN RELATION TO AGE

There appears to be little doubt about the existence of significant differences between teachers comprising different age groups with respect to a number of teacher characteristics. Among 60 different F tests computed with the data for these teachers, 45 of the sets of differences between means were found to be significant at or beyond the .05 level. Generally, scores of older teachers (55 years and above) showed this group to be at a disadvantage compared with younger teachers, except from the standpoint of Y_{co} (systematic and businesslike classroom behavior) and B_{co} (indicative of learning-centered, traditional educational viewpoints). Younger teachers generally attained higher scores relative to the other scales.

Since the approach was cross-sectional rather than longitudinal, the question may be raised, but remains unanswered, as to whether these age differences are dependent primarily on changes in the teacher's characteristics as he or she grows older and becomes more experienced, or on cultural influences, particularly those associated with emphases impressed on teachers during their training, which have some common effect upon a given generation of teachers. Influences of this latter sort may differ substantially for the presently older age teacher groups who entered teaching some thirty-five to forty years ago as compared with the younger age groups who have been subjected to a substantially different educational philosophy.

The implication for research and practice in the area of teacher personnel probably is that age must be taken into account as a relevant independent variable whenever teacher characteristics are considered; that concerning personality, teacher variation with age interacts with the main effects sometimes described as contributors to teaching performance, and may either make differences in such main effects appear important when they do not exist or obscure them when they really are present.

TEACHER CHARACTERISTICS IN RELATION TO EXTENT OF TEACHING EXPERIENCES

As might be expected, trends with regard to extent of teaching experience are not substantially different from those noted when teachers were classified according to age. There was a general tendency for teachers with extended experience to score lower than less experienced teachers on most of the variables. Y_{co} (responsible, businesslike behavior in the classroom), however, was a notable exception; in this case the more experienced teachers scoring significantly higher than the less experienced.

COMPARISON OF THE TEACHER CHARACTERISTICS OF MEN AND WOMEN

Men and women teachers in the elementary school appear to differ with respect to only four of the personal-social characteristics studied. Women score significantly higher than men with regard to Characteristic Y_{co}, a finding that leads to the inference of less responsible, systematic, and businesslike classroom behavior on the part of the male teachers of elementary grades.

On the other hand, there is the suggestion (t ratios significant at the .05 level in the Basic Analysis Sample, and differences in the same direction although not significant in the Survey Sample) that men elementary teachers may be more favorable in attitude toward democratic classroom practices, more inclined toward permissive, child-centered educational viewpoints, and more emotionally stable than women elementary teachers.

Differences between the sexes, often insignificant in the elementary school as noted above, were fairly general and pronounced among secondary teachers with women generally tending to attain significantly higher scores than men on the scales measuring understanding and friendly classroom behavior (X_{co}), responsible and businesslike classroom behavior (Y_{co}), stimulating and imaginative classroom behavior (Z_{co}), favorable attitudes toward pupils (R_{co}), favorable attitudes toward democratic classroom practice (R_{1co}), "permissive" educational viewpoints ($-B_{co}$) and verbal understanding (I_{co}). Men teachers scored significantly higher with respect to emotional stability (S_{co}) than did women teachers in the secondary school.

Breaking down the Basic Analysis Sample for secondary teachers into subject-matter groups, differences between men and women among the English–social studies teachers are strikingly like those found among elementary teachers, with only two significant trends to be noted—for women to score higher relative to responsible, systematic classroom behavior (Y_{co}), and for men to score higher with regard to emotional adjustment (S_{co}). Among the Basic Analysis mathematics-science teachers, the differences fit, with a few exceptions, the pattern found in the Survey Sample for secondary teachers in general.

TEACHER CHARACTERISTICS IN RELATION TO
MARITAL STATUS

In the Survey Sample when marital status classification is considered relative to elementary and secondary teachers combined, only a few significant differences are in evidence. Others apparently are obscured by the lumping together of teachers of different grades and subjects. Significant F ratios (.05 level) were obtained relative to responsible, businesslike classroom behavior (Y_{co}), stimulating classroom behavior (Z_{co}), verbal understanding (I_{ci}), and emotional stability (S_{ci}). Teachers who were not, and had not been, married scored significantly higher on the average than married teachers, with respect to responsible, businesslike classroom behavior (Y_{co}) and verbal understanding (I_{ci}), but the differences in means favored married teachers when stimulating classroom behavior (Z_{co}) and emotional stability (S_{ci}) were considered.

Among elementary teachers, F ratios significant at the .05 level were obtained in both the Survey and Basic Analysis Samples for X_{co}, Y_{co}, Z_{co}, and R_{co}. Additional significant F ratios were obtained in the Survey Sample for R_{1co} and R_{co}. Where significant F ratios were obtained, t tests of the differences between means of married and single (never married) teachers were significant and favored the married group with respect to understanding, friendly classroom behavior (X_{co}), responsible, businesslike classroom behavior (Y_{co}), stimulating classroom behavior (Z_{co}), favorable attitude toward pupils (R_{co}), and child-centered educational viewpoints $(-B_{co})$.

Among secondary teachers in general (Survey Sample), highly significant F ratios (and t ratios between married and single teachers) were obtained, with differences favorable to the single teachers relative to responsible, businesslike behavior (Y_{co}), favorable attitude toward democratic classroom practices (R_{1co}), permissive educational viewpoints $(-B_{co})$, and verbal understanding (I_{ci}), but with married teachers attaining superior scores relative to emotional stability (S_{ci}). Similar differences were found in the Basic Analysis Sample relative to Y_{co}, I_{co}, and S_{co}.

In breaking down the Basic Analysis Sample of secondary teachers into the component subject-matter areas, the conclusions become still more specific to the subject-matter group under consideration. Among mathematics-science teachers, the single teachers scored higher than married teachers relative to responsible, businesslike classroom behavior (Y_{co}), stimulating classroom behavior (Z_{co}), favorable attitude toward democratic classroom practices (R_{1co}), and verbal understanding

(I_{co}), with married teachers attaining higher scores relative to emotional stability (S_{co}). Among English–social studies teachers, the married group was significantly superior to the single group relative to understanding, friendly classroom behavior (X_{co}), favorable attitude toward pupils (R_{co}), and emotional stability (S_{co}), while the single teachers were superior to the married teachers relative to responsible, businesslike classroom behavior (Y_{co}) and verbal understanding (I_{co}).

Quite apart from the actual differences relative to particular characteristics, it is important to note that the *patterns of differences* are not the same for the teachers responsible for different grades and subject matters, and although general trends are apparent, it probably is more important to recognize the interaction of marital status with grade or subject taught when considering many of the teacher characteristics which have been studied.

TEACHER CHARACTERISTICS IN RELATION TO PROFESSED AVOCATIONAL ACTIVITIES

Teachers who report frequent participation in *any* of a number of avocational activities (gardening, chess or cards, painting, sculpting, music, etc.) tend, as a group, to score higher on X_{co}, Y_{co}, Z_{co}, R_{co}, R_{1co}, Q_{co}, $-B_{co}$ (child-centered viewpoints), and S_{ci} than teachers who do *not* report participation in any of these activities. Many of the differences between participants and nonparticipants are substantial and significant. Teachers who actively engage in outside-teaching interests appear generally to score relatively high on the characteristics measured.

TEACHER CHARACTERISTICS IN RELATION TO RELIGIOUS ACTIVITIES

Differences in mean characteristics scores between teachers professing various kinds of religious participation are small. There is a suggestion, however, that teachers who participate *actively* (membership on church committees, or teaching of Sunday school class) may score somewhat higher on the understanding, friendly teacher classroom behavior variable (X_{co}) than teachers in general.

It may be significant to note that at least 75 percent of the teachers in the Survey Sample reported listening to religious programs on the radio or reading religious articles in papers and magazines. Teachers as a group would appear to be religiously inclined. This finding has support, also, in the recent survey conducted by the National Education Association which reported some 75 percent of the NEA sample to be active church members.

TEACHER CHARACTERISTICS IN RELATION TO TYPE
OF UNDERGRADUATE COLLEGE ATTENDED

No clear picture is indicated relative to score differences among secondary teachers when considered from the standpoint of kind of college in which teacher training was attained. For elementary teachers the scales measuring stimulating classroom behavior (Z_{co}) and child-centered educational viewpoints ($-B_{co}$) yielded significant F ratios. In these cases teachers from large universities scored higher than those attending other types of colleges.

TEACHER CHARACTERISTICS IN RELATION TO ACADEMIC SUCCESS

Considering teacher characteristics in relation to academic achievement, the picture is a rather clear one with most of the scales (the exception being that having to do with emotional stability) yielding F ratios significant at the .05 level. Generally, the teachers who reported themselves as having been outstanding students scored higher than the other groups relative to friendly, understanding classroom behavior (X_{co}), responsible, businesslike classroom behavior (Y_{co}), stimulating, imaginative classroom behavior (Z_{co}), favorable attitude toward pupils (R_{co}), favorable attitude toward democratic school practices (R_{1co}), favorable attitude toward administrative and other school personnel (Q_{co}), permissive, child-centered educational viewpoints ($-B_{co}$), and verbal understanding (I_{ci}). The mean scores decrease in a fairly orderly fashion as the "good" student, "average" student, and "poor" student groups are considered.

TEACHER CHARACTERISTICS IN RELATION TO INFLUENCES
AFFECTING CHOICE OF TEACHING

It is of interest to review the influences which individuals believe have affected their choice of teaching as a career and certain relationships between such presumed influences and measured teacher characteristics. In a sense, the data show what might have been expected—that teachers who say they entered the profession because of its intellectual nature, because they had liked school, and because of the public and social service character of teaching, generally scored higher on most of the teacher characteristics here considered; and persons who became teachers because they were advised (or perhaps urged) to do so by parents or relatives, or because of attractiveness of teaching from the standpoint of desirable position in the community and favorable prospects for advancement, scored relatively lower.

TEACHER CHARACTERISTICS IN RELATION TO ACTIVITIES DURING CHILDHOOD AND ADOLESCENCE

To what extent may certain characteristics of teachers be traceable to behavior patterns which were expressed in related, but different, channels, long before the individual entered teaching as a profession? In this regard, such childhood and adolescent activities as "playing school," "reading to children," etc., were considered.

Of particular interest is the comparison of the scores of those teachers who participated in *any* of the activities inventoried with teachers who participated in *none* of them. Significant t ratios (.05 level) were obtained between nonparticipation and participation in each of the activities studied with respect to understanding, friendly classroom behavior (X_{co}), responsible, businesslike classroom behavior (Y_{co}), stimulating, imaginative classroom behavior (Z_{co}), favorable attitude toward pupils (R_{co}), favorable attitudes toward democratic classroom practices (R_{1co}), favorable attitudes toward administrative and other school personnel (Q_{co}), and permissive *vs.* traditional educational viewpoints (B_{co}). Participation in school-like activities during childhood and adolescence may offer significant clues to the present characteristics of teachers. Teachers who said they had "read to children" and "taken class for teacher" generally tended to score higher than others.

TEACHER CHARACTERISTICS IN RELATION TO SIZE OF SCHOOL

Considering elementary and secondary teachers combined, the means of teachers classified according to "size of school in which employed" differed significantly at the .05 level (F ratios) with regard to five of the characteristics studied: understanding, friendly classroom behavior (X_{co}), stimulating imaginative classroom behavior (Z_{co}), favorable attitudes toward administrators and other school personnel (Q_{co}), verbal understanding (I_{ci}), and emotional stability (S_{ci}). The pattern is fairly clear. For these characteristics (as well as for Y_{co}, R_{co}, R_{1co}, and $-B_{co}$ where mean differences existed, but did not attain statistical significance) teachers in larger schools (seventeen to fifty or more teachers) scored higher, and those from small schools (one-teacher schools, and three- to five-teacher schools) scored lower. The differences were most extreme with respect to verbal understanding (I_{ci}).

TEACHER CHARACTERISTICS IN RELATION TO SIZE OF COMMUNITY

As might well be expected, the trend with regard to the means of teachers classified according to size of the community in which they teach follows generally that for size of school just noted. Analysis of the data suggests that teachers from smaller communities attain lower mean scores and those from larger communities, higher mean scores—at least, up to and including communities of 500,000 to 1,000,000 population. Interestingly, teachers from the *largest* cities (1,000,000 and over population) scored relatively *low* (about as *low* as teachers from the very small communities) on most characteristics, verbal understanding (I_{ci}) being a notable exception. It seems probable that the teacher selection procedures in operation in large cities (e.g., written and oral examinations) are geared to the selection of teachers high in verbal understanding, but less adapted to the identification of other characteristics relating to personal and social qualities of the teacher.

TEACHER CHARACTERISTICS IN RELATION TO SOCIOECONOMIC STATUS OF COMMUNITY IN WHICH SCHOOL IS LOCATED

When the teacher characteristics were studied in relation to the socioeconomic level of the community in which the teachers' schools were located, F ratios significant at the .05 level were obtained with regard to X_{co}, Z_{co}, R_{1co}, B_{co}, I_{ci}, and S_{ci}. Generally, the *lowest* scores relative to understanding, friendly classroom behavior (X_{co}), stimulating, imaginative classroom behavior (Z_{co}), favorable attitudes toward democratic classroom practices (R_{1co}), verbal understanding (I_{ci}), and emotional stability (S_{ci}), and the most *traditional*, learning-centered educational viewpoints scores (B_{co}) were attained by teachers in communities judged to be about *average* in socioeconomic level. The relationship between socioeconomic level and several of the characteristics (e.g., Z_{co}, B_{co}, and I_{ci}) appears to be parabolic, with higher scores on the characteristics Z_{co} and I_{ci}, and more permissive educational viewpoints scores being contributed by teachers in the groups representing communities typified by both low socioeconomic and high socioeconomic levels. Other relationships also appear to be generally curvilinear with little or no relationship apparent in moving from "poverty" to "average" levels, but with a positive correlation trend suggested through the upper categories of the socioeconomic classification employed.

TEACHER CHARACTERISTICS IN RELATION TO GEOGRAPHIC AREA IN WHICH TEACHING IS PERFORMED

Teachers whose schools were located in the Middle Atlantic states and on the West Coast scored higher relative to Z_{co} and I_{ci}, and were more child-centered and permissive in their educational viewpoints ($-B_{co}$) than other sectional groups. Teachers from the West Coast were highest of all the geographic groups with respect to emotional stability (S_{ci}). With regard to Z_{co} (stimulating, imaginative classroom behavior), the lowest scoring group was made up of teachers from the Midwestern states; with respect to I_{ci} (verbal understanding), the lowest scoring groups were from the Mountain states and Southern states; and with regard to emotional stability (S_{ci}) the lowest mean scores were attained by teachers in the East-Southern and Southern states. The Midwestern and East-Southern groups of teachers were more traditional in educational viewpoints as compared with other groups, and Middle Atlantic and West Coast teachers were more permissive.

No significant differences between teachers in different geographic sections of the country were found with regard to understanding, friendly classroom behavior (X_{co}), attitude toward pupils (R_{co}), attitude toward democratic classroom practices (R_{1co}), and attitude toward administrators and other school personnel (Q_{co}).

A Comparison of Teachers Assessed as Generally High and Generally Low

One investigation conducted by the Teacher Characteristics Study was concerned with identifying, and then comparing, teachers who fell into different groups with regard to general classroom behavior. One group was comprised of teachers, each of whom had received observer assessments one standard deviation or more above the mean on each of the three classroom behavior patterns X_o, Y_o, and Z_o; a second group consisted of teachers who were all between .2 of a standard deviation on either side of the mean on the three different teacher classroom behavior dimensions; and a third group was made up of teachers, all of whom received observers' assessments one standard deviation or more below the mean on each of the three classroom behavior dimension patterns.

After having identified teachers who qualified for membership in each group, an attempt was made to determine some of the distinguishing characteristics of the high, middle, and low groups, as revealed by Teacher Characteristics Schedule responses. Of particular interest were responses of teachers generally assessed high which distinguished them from those generally assessed low.

For elementary and secondary teachers combined, some of the more notable characteristics which distinguished the high group from the low and the low group from the high are those which follow.

There was a general tendency for high teachers to: be extremely generous in appraisals of the behavior and motives of other persons;

possess strong interest in reading and literary affairs; be interested in music, painting, and the arts in general; participate in social groups; enjoy pupil relationships; prefer nondirective (permissive) classroom procedures; manifest superior verbal intelligence; and be superior with respect to emotional adjustment. On the other hand, low teachers tended generally to: be restrictive and critical in their appraisals of other persons; prefer activities which did not involve close personal contacts; express less favorable opinions of pupils; manifest less high verbal intelligence; show less satisfactory emotional adjustment; and represent older age groups.

Limitations of the Findings of the Study

In considering the results growing out of the research conducted by the Teacher Characteristics Study, it is important and proper to recall that one is dealing with inferences from empirical data and therefore, that: (1) generalization is appropriate only when made to populations which it seems reasonable to believe are not significantly dissimilar to the populations employed in the Teacher Characteristics Study; (2) any obtained relationships are limited by, and may be expected to vary with, conditions such as those noted in the introductory chapters to this volume and in the first sections of this summary chapter; (3) all "conclusions" or inferences to be drawn necessarily are approximate, as are all inferences based on empirical data, which are by their very nature characterized by some degree of unreliability, and are probability estimates rather than statements of invariable relationships; (4) relationships, differences, and predictions which have been noted are in terms of averages for groups of teachers, and, as is true of all such findings pertaining to human behavior, greater confidence can be placed in the conclusions when they are applied to groups of teachers (i.e., actuarial applications) and less when applied to the individual case.

It is also important to recall that the data, for the most part, relate to response-response relationships derived from cross-sectional studies rather than antecedent-consequent types of relationships provided by longitudinal experimentation.

The usefulness of these research findings for the prediction of teacher behavior will be greatest when the results are considered in an actuarial context, rather than in attempting highly accurate predictions for given individuals, and when there are taken into account variations in relationships found (a) among different classifications of teachers and (b) with the use of different approaches to the predictor-criterion relationship.

Needed Research Relative to Teacher Characteristics

THE RESEARCH reported in this volume has been of an essentially exploratory nature. It is believed that the possibility of measurement in a very complex area, that of teacher behavior, has been demonstrated and that the importance of a number of relevant variables which must be considered in investigations in this area has been pointed out.

One of the most important values of such a study might be expected to be the encouragement of further research and analysis of problems of teacher behavior. It is believed that the availability of the Teacher Characteristics Schedule represents a significant step toward the provision of "secondary" criterion data having known relationships to operationally defined teacher behaviors and personal characteristics of teachers. Use of the Schedule, employing correlates scales as more practical substitutes for criterion estimates based upon direct observation and pupil change, makes possible the investigation of many problems not easily approachable. These include appraisal of the effectiveness of professional education factors, such as course content, curriculum, recruitment and advisement procedures, etc., and analyses of in-service conditions that influence teacher characteristics.

The unknown answers to questions concerning teacher behavior, answers which could do much to improve both teacher education and teaching practice, are legion, and the possible lines of further research into teacher characteristics are many—both of a (1) taxonomic or appraisal sort, dependent upon data yielded by survey samples relative to teacher characteristics, (2) the experimental type, concerned with the determination of the effects of the introduction of a hypothesized "influence" upon criterion data relative to teacher characteristics. The number of possible investigations of teacher behavior is limited only by the insight and creative imagination of research workers in the area. Those noted below represent only a few of many studies which should be conducted to advance the frontiers of knowledge regarding the teacher and the conditions which affect teacher behavior. The projects listed are merely some of those that loom more prominently in the minds of the Study staff because they are direct outgrowths of steps already taken by the research reported in this volume.

1. Extension of the Survey Study, aimed at a sample of perhaps 10,000 teachers.
2. Periodic cross-sectional appraisal studies, similar to the Survey Study, at intervals of perhaps five years, and extending over a twenty-five-to-fifty-year span, to determine possible changing trends in the characteristics of American teachers.
3. Studies of the influence of different kinds of teacher education pro-

grams, education courses, course content, practice teaching, and educational experiences on developing patterns of teacher characteristics, particularly teacher behaviors X (understanding, friendly classroom behavior), Y (responsible, businesslike classroom behavior), and Z (stimulating, imaginative classroom behavior).

4. Studies of the influence of different in-service experiences of teachers, both organized and informal, upon patterns of teacher characteristics.

5. Longitudinal studies of teacher characteristics, and changes in characteristics, based upon readministration of the Schedule each five years to the same teachers, over a span of perhaps twenty-five years of the teacher's life.

6. Comparative studies of teacher characteristics, based upon administration of the Schedule, and translations thereof, to teachers of different national, political, and cultural backgrounds.

7. Comparisons of the Schedule scores of education students and students enrolled in other college departments and professional schools.

8. Comparisons of Schedule scores of teachers with those of other occupational and professional groups (lawyers, physicians, ministers, executives, sales personnel, etc.).

9. Follow-up studies of classroom behaviors of teachers for whom Schedule scores had been obtained when they were college students.

10. Readministration of the Schedule to teachers in service who had completed the Schedule originally when they were students in college.

11. Additional studies of "pupil change" and its relation to Schedule scores.

12. Analysis of Schedule scores of teachers selected by various organizations and groups as particularly outstanding (e.g., "teacher-of-the-year").

13. Analysis of opinions of superintendents of schools (subclassified by geographic area, size of school, auspices of school, etc.) with regard to their conception of characteristics contributing most prominently to "teaching effectiveness."

14. Analyses of relationships between Schedule scores and scores on various commercially available tests and personality inventories.

15. Factor analyses of Schedule scores of elementary and secondary teachers.

16. Research into the refinement of observing and assessing techniques, leading perhaps to the development of behavior check lists and forced-choice scales, to the end of providing more valid behavior-in-process criterion data.

17. Development and refinement of predictor (correlate) materials such as those comprising the Schedule (e.g., development of large reservoirs of comparable test items, development of "suppressor" scoring keys, pattern analyses of responses, etc.).

APPENDIX B

Staff of Teacher Characteristics Study*

Director: Dr. DAVID G. RYANS, Chairman, Department of Educational Psychology, University of Texas; formerly Professor of Educational Psychology, University of California, Los Angeles

Central Office Staff

Miss Joan Aubuchon, Secretary (1956–58)
Mr. Hilton Barry, Statistical Clerk (1949–50)
Miss Beverly Bennett, Statistical Clerk (1949–51)
Miss Renee Chudnoff, Statistical Clerk (1951–52)
Mrs. Dorothy Cloutier, Secretary (1951–52)
Mr. Louis Cohen, Statistical Clerk (1949–51)
Miss Helen Curcio, Statistical Clerk (1951–53)
Mrs. Claire Danneskiold, Statistical Clerk (1950–52)
Mr. Rex Danneskiold, Statistical Clerk (1950–52)
Dr. James Degan, Consultant (1950–51)
Mrs. Joyce Dickey, Statistical Clerk (1954–55)
Mr. Albert du Aime, Art Assistant (1950–52)
Miss Opal Goodrich, Statistical Clerk (1949–50)
Miss Joanna Hart, Statistical Clerk (1952–53)
Mr. George Holloway, Statistical Clerk (1949–50)
Miss Floy Hopkins, Statistical Clerk (1949–50)
Mr. Alfred Jackson, Statistical Clerk (1950–51)
Mrs. Doris Jackson, Statistical Clerk (1951–52)
Mr. Eugene Jacobs, Statistical Clerk (1950–51)
Mr. Kenneth King, Statistical Clerk (1949–51)
Miss Audrey Kopp, Statistical Clerk (1952–53)
Miss Shirley Krause, Secretary (1948–50)
Miss Margaret Lampher, Statistical Clerk (1951–52)
Mrs. Benita Leavitt, Statistical Clerk (1951–54)
Miss Mary Marks, Statistical Clerk (1951–52)
Mrs. Jane Mattocks, Secretary (1950–51)
Miss Jean McCulloch, Secretary (1951)
Miss Alice Meyers, Statistical Clerk (1949–50)
Miss Kenee Miller, Secretary (1954–56)
Miss Eda Mae Parris, Statistical Clerk (1952–53)
Miss Dorothy Pierce, Statistical Clerk (1951–52)
Miss Cathy Pritchird, Statistical Clerk (1953–54)
Miss Marilyn Ripka, Statistical Clerk (1949–50)
Miss Irene B. Robbins, Secretary (1952–54)
Dr. David G. Ryans, Director (1948–58)
Miss Marjory Sadoff, Statistical Clerk (1949–50)

* A list of the members of the Committee on Teacher Characteristics Study appears on page ii.

Dr. May Seagoe, Associate Director (1948–50)
Mr. Carleton Shay, Statistical Clerk (1949–51)
Mrs. Hanna Shay, Statistical Clerk (1949–50)
Dr. M. Stephen Sheldon, Statistical Aide (1956–57)
Mrs. Winifred Smith, Statistical Clerk (1950–51)
Miss Elizabeth Stern, Statistical Clerk (1951–52)
Mrs. Minchen Strang, Statistical Clerk (1948–49)
Mrs. Louise Urista, Statistical Clerk (1952–54)
Dr. Robert Voas, Statistical Clerk (1949–51)
Dr. Edwin Wandt, Research Associate and Statistician (1948–51)
Mr. Howard Webster, Art Assistant (1952–53)
Miss Elizabeth Winkler, Statistical Clerk (1949–50)
Dr. Theodore Yuhas, Statistical Clerk (1949–50)
Mr. James R. Ziegler, Research Associate and Statistician (1951–56)
Miss Seville Zipser, Statistical Clerk (1953–54)

Field Staff

Dr. Melvin Anderson, Observer (1952–53)
Dr. Richard Axen, Observer (1951–52)
Dr. Adolph Brugger, Observer (1952–53)
Mr. Francis Diaz, Observer (1952–53)
Mrs. Eleanor Ehmann, Observer (1948–49)
Miss Verna Ellis, Observer (1949–50)
Dr. Glen Fulkerson, Senior Observer (1951–54)
Dr. John Gowan, Observer (1950–53)
Dr. Terrance Hatch, Observer (1952–53)
Mr. Elly Heckscher, Observer (1952–53)
Mr. Virgil Howes, Observer (1951–52)
Mrs. Mildred Hughes, Observer (1953–54)
Dr. Alfred C. Jensen, Senior Observer (1949–51)
Mrs. Elaine McGee, Observer (1952–53)
Dr. Henry McGee, Observer (1952–53)
Mr. Francis Miller, Observer (1951–52)
Dr. Arthur Phelan, Observer (1949–50)
Mrs. Enid Reiser, Observer (1951–52)
Mr. Lawrence Reiser, Observer (1951–52)
Mrs. Barbara Sebastian, Observer (1952–53)
Mrs. Helen Sheats, Observer (1948–50)
Dr. Dennis Smith, Observer (1952–53)
Mrs. Ruth Stanley, Observer (1950–51)
Mr. Harry Woods, Observer (1952–53)

Research Projects Completed by the Teacher Characteristics Study, 1948–55

1. Development of Classroom Observation Record and Accompanying Glossary:
   A. Elementary Teacher Form, 1948–49
   B. Secondary Teacher Form 1949–50
   C. All-Teacher Form 1951–52
2. Observer Reliability Studies:
   A. No. 1, Elementary Teachers, 1948–49
   B. No. 2, Secondary Teachers, 1949–50
   C. No. 3, Secondary Teachers, 1951–52
3. Development of Educational Viewpoints Inquiry:
   A. Elementary Teacher Form, 1948–49
   B. Elementary Principal Form, 1948–49
   C. Secondary Teacher Form, 1949–50
   D. Secondary Principal Form, 1949–50
4. Relationships between Teachers' Scores on the Rosenzweig Picture Frustration Study and Observed Classroom Behaviors, 1948–49
5. Development of an Equal-Appearing Intervals Scale Measuring Attitude Toward Teachers and Teaching, 1948–49
6. Development of an Equal-Appearing Intervals Scale Measuring Attitude Toward Pupils, 1948–49
7. Development of an Incomplete Statements Test and Study of Teachers' Responses in Relation to Observed Classroom Behaviors, 1948–49
8. Development of a Picture Situation Test and Study of Teachers' Responses in Relation to Observed Classroom Behaviors, 1948–49
9. Development of Homonyms Test and Study of Teachers' Responses in Relation to Observed Classroom Behaviors, 1948–49
10. Development of Synonym-Antonym Association Tests and Study of Teachers' Responses in Relation to Observed Classroom Behaviors, 1948–49:
    A. Form CA 1—Free Response
    B. Form CA 2—Free Response
11. Development of Estimating Tests and Study of Teachers' Responses in Relation to Observed Classroom Behaviors, 1948–49:
    A. Form J-1
    B. Form J-2
12. Development of an Individually Administered Picture Preference Test (Form Y) and Study of Teachers' Responses in Relation to Observed Classroom Behaviors, 1948–49

13. Development of an Expressive Movement Test and Study of Teachers' Responses in Relation to Observed Classroom Behaviors, 1948–49

14. Development of a Free Association (Fluency) Test and Study of Teachers' Responses in Relation to Observed Classroom Behaviors, 1948–49

15. Development of Controlled Word Association Test and Study of Teachers' Responses in Relation to Observed Classroom Behaviors, 1948–49:
    A. Form CA 1—Multiple Choice
    B. Form CA 2—Multiple Choice

16. Development of a Picture Title Test and Study of Teachers' Responses in Relation to Observed Classroom Behaviors, 1948–49

17. Development of a Case History Questionnaire and Study of Teachers' Responses in Relation to Observed Classroom Behaviors, 1948–49

18. Study of a Case History Check List and Study of Teachers' Responses in Relation to Observed Classroom Behaviors, 1948–49

19. Development of an Activity Log and Study of Teachers' Responses in Relation to Observed Classroom Behaviors, 1948–49

20. Development of a Desirable-Undesirable Trait Check List and Study of Teachers' Responses in Relation to Observed Classroom Behaviors, 1948–49

21. Responses of Teachers to the Educational Viewpoints Inquiry in Relation to Their Observed Classroom Behaviors, 1949–50

22. Relationships between Scores Yielded by Scales of the Minnesota Multiphasic Personality Inventory and Observed Teacher Behaviors, 1949–50

23. Relationships between Scores Yielded by Scales of the Thurstone Temperament Schedule and Observed Teacher Behaviors, 1949–50

24. Relationships between Scores Yielded by the Allport-Vernon Study of Values and Observed Teacher Behaviors, 1949–50

25. Development of a Teacher Preference Inventory (PI 49a) and Study of Relationships between Inventory Responses and Observed Teacher Behaviors, 1949–50

26. Development of Likert-Type Scales Measuring Teachers' Attitudes Toward Groups Contacted in the Schools, 1949–50:
    A. Attitude Toward Administrators
    B. Attitude Toward Supervisors
    C. Attitude Toward Pupils
    D. Attitude Toward Parents
    E. Attitude Toward Teachers
    F. Attitude Toward Nonteaching Employees of the Schools
    G. Attitude Toward Democratic Classroom Procedures
    H. Attitude Toward Democratic Administrative Procedures

27. Development of a Structured Picture Preference Test (Form Z) and

Study of Teachers' Responses in Relation to Observed Classroom Behaviors, 1949–50

28. Development of Verbal Preference Inventories and Study of Teachers' Responses in Relation to Observed Classroom Behaviors, 1949–50:
   A. Form B
   B. Form N

29. Development of a Biographical and Activity Check List and Study of Teachers' Responses in Relation to Observed Classroom Behaviors, 1949–50

30. Criterion Studies: Factor Analysis of Observed Classroom Behaviors of Elementary Teachers, 1949–50

31. Preliminary Study of Relationships between Observed Teacher Behaviors and Selected Personal Data and Conditions of Teaching, 1949–50:
   A. Observed Behaviors of Teachers Classified According to School System in Which Employed
   B. Observed Behaviors of Teachers Classified According to Socioeconomic Status of Neighborhood in Which School Served by Teacher Is Located
   C. Observed Behaviors of Teachers Classified According to Amount of College Training
   D. Observed Behaviors of Teachers Classified According to Amount of Teaching Experience
   E. Observed Behaviors of Teachers Classified According to Marital Status
   F. Observed Behaviors of Teachers Classified According to the Extent of Teacher's Agreement With School Principal in Response to the Educational Viewpoints Inquiry

32. Study of Teacher Empathy Based on the Comparison of Picture Preferences of Teachers and Their Pupils, 1949–50

33. Analysis of Biographical and Activity Data Reported by Teachers, Classified According to Grade or Subject Taught, 1949–50

34. Comparison of Patterns of Teacher Behavior in Different Communities, 1949–50

35. Sex Differences in Teachers' Responses to Preference Inventory and Biographical and Activity Check List Items, 1949–50

36. Studies of Critical Incidents in Teaching, 1949–50:
   A. Critical Incidents in Secondary Teaching
   B. Critical Incidents in Elementary Teaching

37. Validation Studies of Selected Preference Inventory and Biographical and Activity Check List Materials, 1949–50

38. Relation of Responses to (1) A Structured Picture Preference Test and (2) Certain Personality Traits Revealed by Verbal Inventory Materials, 1949–50

39. Factor Analyses of Teachers' Attitudes, 1950–51
40. Assembly of Preliminary Form of a Single-Booklet Teacher Characteristics Schedule (Form X), 1950–51
41. Criterion Studies: Factor Analysis of Observed Classroom Behaviors of Secondary Teachers, 1950–51
42. Preliminary Study at Secondary School Level of Certain Conditions Frequently Believed To Be Associated with Teaching, 1950–51
43. Interim Validation Studies of Teacher Characteristics Schedule (Form X) Items, 1950–51
44. Study of Teacher Characteristics Schedule Responses of Teachers in Relation to Ratings Assigned by School Principals: Study No. 1, 1950–51
45. Preliminary Studies of the Relation between Responses to the Teacher Characteristics Schedule and Form Q and L Scores of the American Council on Education Psychological Examination, 1950–51
46. Comparison of Item-Test Correlations with Item-Criterion (Principals' Ratings) Correlations for Test Items Measuring Professional Educational Information, 1950–51
47. Study of the Relationship between Pupil Behavior and Teacher Behavior, 1950–51; 1954–55
48. Comparison of Attitudes of Contrasting Groups of Teachers, 1951–52
49. Revision of Teacher Characteristics Schedule, 1951–52:
    A. Elementary Teacher Form
    B. Mathematics-Science Teacher Form
    C. English–Social Studies Teacher Form
50. Some Clues Relative to the Bases of Principals' Ratings of Teacher Effectiveness, 1951–52
51. Relation between Scores of Teachers on the Teacher Characteristics Schedule and the National Teacher Examinations, 1951–52; 1953–54
52. Follow-up Observations of Teachers Employed in a Public School System: Teachers Who Completed the Teacher Characteristics Schedule as College Students Prior to Teaching Experience, 1951–54
53. Study of Teacher Characteristics Schedule Responses of Teachers in Relation to Ratings Assigned by School Principals: Study No. 2, 1952–53:
    A. Elementary Teachers
    B. Mathematics-Science Teachers
    C. English–Social Studies Teachers
54. Observer Reliability Studies: Variation in Assessed Teacher Behaviors over a Period of One Year, 1952–54
55. Criterion Studies: Comparison of Methods of Weighting Criterion Data, 1952–53
56. Studies of Reliability of Scoring Keys of the Teacher Characteristics

Schedule: The Stability of Response of Test-Retest over Periods of Two–Three Years, One Year, and Three Weeks, 1953–54

57. Follow-up Observations of Teachers Employed in a Public School System: Teachers Who Completed the Teacher Characteristics Schedule as Part of the School System's Teacher Selection Program, 1953–54

58. Résumé of Teacher Personnel Research in Progress in the United States in 1953, 1953–54

59. Extension of Teacher Characteristics Schedule, 1953–54:
   A. Elementary Teacher Form
   B. Mathematics-Science Teacher Form
   C. English–Social Studies Teacher Form

60. Item Analysis Studies: Determining the Division Points for Criterion Groups Based on Observation Data, 1953–54

61. Development of an Omnibus Pupil Inquiry for the Estimation of Pupil Status and Change in Grade 4, 1953–54

62. Observer Reliability Studies: 1952–53 Observations, 1953–54

63. Development of a Short Inventory for Estimating Verbal Ability, Emotional Adjustment, and Validity of Response, 1953–54

64. Comparison of Women Graduates of a University Elementary Teacher Education Curriculum with Teachers Holding Emergency Credentials, 1953–54

65. Study of Teacher Characteristics Schedule Responses of Teachers Who Left the Teaching Profession (*not completed*), 1953–54

66. The Use of a High-Speed Electronic Computer in Carrying Out Item Analyses, 1953–54

67. Comparison of Older and Younger Teachers' Responses to the Thurstone Temperament Schedule (Pressey), 1953–54

68. Item Analysis Studies: Comparison of Cross-Validation Data Obtained from Different Procedures of Item Selection Employed in the Development of a Predictor, Study No. 1, 1953–54

69. Observer Reliability Studies: Reliability of the Basic Dimensions Listed on the Classroom Observation Record, 1953–54:
   A. Reliability of Observations for Elementary Teachers
   B. Reliability of Observations for Secondary Teachers

70. Observer Reliability Studies: Differences between Observers in Number of Confirming Observations Required, 1953–54

71. Development of Correlates Keys Based on Self-Reports of Typical Behavior for the Prediction of Verbal Ability, Emotional Adjustment, and Validity of Response, 1953–54

72. Studies of the Reliability of Scoring Keys of the Teacher Characteristics Schedule: Plus Key and Minus Key Correlations, 1954–55

73. Item Analyses of the Teacher Characteristics Schedule and Development of Factor X, Factor Y, and Factor Z Scoring Keys for Various Samples of Teachers, 1954–55:

Key 71 (Grades 1–2 Women Teachers)
Key 72 (Grades 3–4 Women Teachers)
Key 73 (Grades 5–6 Women Teachers)
Key 74 (Grades 3–6 Women Teachers)
Key 75 (Grades 1–6 Women Teachers)
Key 76 (Grades 5–6 Men Teachers)
Key 77 (Grades 3–6 Men Teachers)
Key 78 (Grades 5–6 Men and Women Teachers)
Key 79 (Grades 3–6 Men and Women Teachers)
Key 143 (Grades 1–4 Women Teachers)
Key 150 (Grades 3–6 Men Teachers and Grades 5–6 Women Teachers)
Key 111 (All-Elementary Teachers)
Key 81 (Mathematics—Men Teachers, Secondary School)
Key 82 (Mathematics—Women Teachers, Secondary School)
Key 83 (Science—Men Teachers, Secondary School)
Key 84 (Science—Women Teachers, Secondary School)
Key 85 (English—Men Teachers, Secondary School)
Key 86 (English—Women Teachers, Secondary School)
Key 87 (Social Studies—Men Teachers, Secondary School)
Key 88 (Social Studies—Women Teachers, Secondary School)
Key 89 (Mathematics-Science—Men Teachers, Secondary School)
Key 90 (Mathematics-Science—Women Teachers, Secondary School)
Key 91 (English–Social Studies—Men Teachers, Secondary School)
Key 92 (English–Social Studies—Women Teachers, Secondary School)
Key 93 (Mathematics Teachers, Men and Women, Secondary School)
Key 94 (Science Teachers, Men and Women, Secondary School)
Key 95 (English Teachers, Men and Women, Secondary School)
Key 96 (Social Studies Teachers, Men and Women, Secondary School)
Key 97 (Mathematics-Science Teachers, Men and Women, Secondary School)
Key 98 (English–Social Studies Teachers, Men and Women, Secondary School)
Key 100 (Mathematics, Science, English, Social Studies Teachers, Men and Women, Secondary School)
Key 99 (Men and Women, Elementary and Secondary Teachers)

74. Criterion Studies: Refinement of Dimensions of Observed Teacher Behavior, 1954–55
75. Case Study of Twenty Highly Selected Elementary Women Teachers, 1954–55
76. Interrelationships among Criteria of Teacher Behavior Derived from Observation Data, 1954–55
77. A Study of Pupil Change in Relation to Observed Teacher Behavior, 1954–55 (*not completed*)
78. Theory Development and the Study of Teacher Behavior, 1954–55

79. Teacher Characteristics Schedule Scores of College Students in Teacher-Training Curricula, 1954–55

80. Item Analysis Studies: Comparison of Cross-Validation Data Obtained from Different Procedures of Item Selection Employed in the Development of a Predictor, Study No. 2, 1954–55

81. Comparison of the Predictive Power of Scoring Keys Derived from Different Samples When Used To Predict an External Criterion, 1954–55

82. Cross-Validation of Factor X, Factor Y, and Factor Z Keys of the Teacher Characteristics Schedule, 1954–55:
    A. Key 99
    B. Key 100
    C. Key 111

83. Item Analysis Studies: Considerations in the Determination of Criterion Groups for Item Analysis, 1954–55

84. Some Characteristics of Teachers Judged To Be Generally Superior in Classroom Behaviors, 1954–55:
    A. Characteristics of Superior Elementary Teachers
    B. Characteristics of Superior Secondary Teachers

85. Some Characteristics of Teachers Judged To Be Generally Inferior with Respect to Classroom Behaviors, 1954–55:
    A. Characteristics of Inferior Elementary Teachers
    B. Characteristics of Inferior Secondary Teachers

86. Comparisons of the Teacher Characteristics Study (1) Mail Survey Sample and (2) Basic Observed Sample, 1954–55

87. Observer Reliability Studies: Comparison of Differences between Teacher Behavior Assessments Assigned by the Same Two Observers with Varying Intervals of Time Lapsing between Observations, 1954–55

88. Criterion Scores for Verbal Ability, Emotional Adjustment, and Validity of Response in Relation to "Correlates" Scores Derived from the Teacher Characteristics Schedule, 1954–55

89. Teacher Characteristics Schedule Scores of Teachers Compared with Assessments of Observed Behavior of Their Pupils, 1954–55

90. Relation of Teacher Characteristics Schedule Scores and Practice Teaching Marks of Teachers in Training, 1954–55

91. Effects of Adjusting Teacher Characteristics Schedule Keys for "Faking" or "Tendency To Make a Good Impression," 1954–55

92. Intercorrelations among Ten Scores Yielded by the Teacher Characteristics Schedule, 1954–55:
    A. Intercorrelations among Scores Yielded by All-Teacher Keys (Key 99)
    B. Intercorrelations among Scores Yielded by Secondary Keys (Key 100)

Index

Academic-centered educational viewpoints, 150–51

Academic success of teachers, comparisons of Schedule scores with, 312–14, 394

Activity items, 181

Administrative responsibilities, opinions about teachers sharing, 304–5

Advisory committee, Teacher Characteristics Study, 8, 369

Age of teacher: comparisons of observer assessments with, 129–30; comparisons of Schedule scores with, 289–93, 390; sample distribution, 69

All-Elementary Teacher Scoring Keys (X_{co}, Y_{co}, Z_{co}), 198, 201, 203–5; comparisons of teachers' scores, 285–342

All-Secondary Teacher Scoring Keys (X_{co}, Y_{co}, Z_{co}), 199, 202–6; comparisons of teachers' scores, 285–342

All-Teacher Scoring Keys, 199; comparisons of teachers' scores, 285–342

Allport-Vernon Study of Values, 134, 362

American Council on Education, 6–8, 368–69

American Educational Research Association, 14, 40, 56

Assessment

Of classroom behavior, 73–76, 83–92; comparisons of Schedule scores with, 270–84; comparisons of teacher groups with, 126–35; reliability of, 107, 115–22

Immediate, 40–42

Procedure: development of, 83–92; in practice, 94–95; reliability of, 107, 115–22

Association items, 179

Assumptions of teacher behavior theory, 16–23; interaction of teacher characteristics and situational factors, 16–21; observability of teacher behavior, 21–23

Attitude items, 141, 166–67, 172, 180, 208–9; disguised-structured, 144

Attitudes: comparisons of Schedule scores with, 285–342; comparisons of teacher groups, 145–47; teachers' toward school groups, 139–48, 385–86

Auspices of school, comparisons of Schedule scores with, 336–38

Avocational activities of teachers, comparisons of Schedule scores with, 301–3, 393

Background of Study, 7–9

Baker, P., 284

Barr, A. S., 135, 367

Basic Analysis Sample, 66–70

Basic Analysis Study, described, 60, 62–70

Basic issues in teacher study, 372

Basic postulates of teacher behavior theory: relative behavior, 16, 21–23; social behavior, 16, 19–21

Baxter, B., 135

Bayroff, A. G., 135

Behavior, teacher. *See* Teacher behavior

Behavior items, typical, 172–73, 179

Bellows, R. M., 56

Bias: in the criterion, 32; in the criterion measurement, 37–38

Biographical and Activity Check List, 173

Biographical items, 170, 173, 181

Brogden, H. E., 27–29, 31–32, 37–38, 56

Brouha, L., 136

Businesslike teacher behavior, 97–135, 196–206, 285–342

California Psychological Inventory, 362–66

Campbell, D. T., 160, 243

Case analyses of highly selected teachers, 362–66

Castetter, D. D., 367

Cattell, R. B., 78, 110, 135

Characteristics, Teacher Characteristics Study: *B*—conservative *vs.* liberal educational viewpoints, 146–53, 206–18; *I*—verbal understanding, 153–58, 218–26; *Q*—favorable *vs.* unfavorable opinions of school personnel, 142–47, 206–18; *R*—favorable *vs.* unfavorable pupil opinions, 142–47, 206–18; R_1—favorable *vs.* unfavorable opinions of democratic classroom procedure, 142–47, 206–18; *S*—emotional stability, 153–58, 218–26; *V*—validity of response (control), 153–58, 218–26; *X*—warm, understanding *vs.* aloof, egocentric, 97–135, 196–206; *Y*—responsible, businesslike *vs.* evading, slipshod, 97–135, 196–206; *Z*—stimulating, imaginative *vs.* dull, routine, 97–135, 196–206

Characteristics of groups of teachers assessed generally "high" and "low," 259–66, 343–67

Characteristics of outstanding teachers summarized, 360–61

Charters, W. W., 56, 135

332–34, 396; source of support when student, 310–12; teaching experience, 293–95, 390–91; teaching level, 288, 322–27; teaching-related activities of teachers during youth, 320–21, 395; type of undergraduate college attended, 306–10, 394

Scoring keys:
  Derivation of correlates: of teacher attitudes and educational viewpoints, 206–18; of teacher classroom behaviors, 183–206
  Reliability, 234–38; validity, 238–67; verbal understanding and emotional adjustment, 218–26

Sears, R. R., 17, 19–20, 57

Self-judgment items, 179

Seltzer, C. C., 136

Sex of teacher: comparisons of observer assessments with, 127–29; comparisons of Schedule scores with, 296–98, 322–27, 391; sample distribution, 68–69

Sheldon, M. S., 268–69

Shen, E., 126

Size of community: comparisons of Schedule scores with, 329–32, 395–96; sample distribution, 67–68

Size of school, comparisons of Schedule scores with, 327–29, 395

Smalzried, N. T., 110, 136

Social nature of teacher behavior, 16

Socially acceptable response, 153–58; direct-inquiry items to detect, 155

Socioeconomic status of teaching community, comparisons of, 133, 332–34, 396

Staff of Study, 8–9, 401–2

Standlee, L. S., 367

Stimulating teacher behavior, 97–135, 196–206, 285–342

Subject taught: comparisons of observer assessments by, 127–219; comparisons of Schedule scores by, 322–27

Support of Study, 8

Survey Sample, 66–70

Survey Study, described, 60, 65–70

SWAC, 183

Symonds, P. M., 136

Systematic observation: in criterion measurement, 40–42; of teacher classroom behavior, 71–76, 83–95

Taft, R., 136

Taylor, E. K., 27–29, 31–32, 37–38, 56

Teacher adjustment: comparison of Schedule scores with, 285–342; direct-inquiry items, 154–58; relationships with other traits, 157

Teacher attitudes: comparisons of Schedule scores with, 285–342; comparisons of teacher groups with, 145–47; construc-

tion of measures of, 140–41, 144–45; disguised-structured items, 144; Factors R, A, N, 142–46; Inventory of Teacher Opinion, 141; relationships with other traits, 143; toward groups contacted in school, 139–48

Teacher behavior: criterion problems, 26; defined, 15; dyadic unit of, 17, 19, 21; integration of, 18; needed research on, 399–400; observation of, 71–136; prediction problems, 51–56, 377–78; relativity of, 16; social nature of, 16; some basic issues, 372

Teacher behaviors: critical, 79–83; glossary of, 87–92; identifying correlates of, 164–65; mentioned in literature, 78–79; original selection, 77–83

Teacher characteristics: comparisons of, 285–342; description necessary for definition of teacher competency, 5, 370; identifying correlates of, 164–65, 196–229; interaction with situational conditions, 16, 20; lack of understanding of, 4; needed research on, 399–400; outstanding teachers, 259–66, 343–67; and teacher behavior, 16–19

Teacher Characteristics Schedule: 159, 165, 177–84; All-Elementary Teacher keys (X_{co}, Y_{co}, Z_{co}), 198, 201, 203–5, 228; All-Secondary Teacher keys (X_{co}, Y_{co}, Z_{co}), 199, 202–6, 228; All-Teacher keys (X_{co}, Y_{co}, Z_{co}), 199, 228; comparisons of scores, 285–342, 389–97; derivation of scoring keys, 183–284; examples of items, 178–83; falsification of scores, 267–70; norms data, 287–88, 323–25; reliability of scores, 234–38; samples employed in studies of, 272, 286–88; scores of outstanding teachers, 259–66, 345–48; validity of scores, 238–67

  Responses: B_{co} examples, 217–18; I_{co} examples, 222–23; Q_{co} examples, 215–16; R_{co} examples, 212–13; R_{1co} examples, 214–15; S_{co} examples, 223–24; V_{co} examples, 225–26; X_{co} examples, 201–2; Y_{co} examples, 203–4; Z_{co} examples, 204–5

  Patterns X_o, Y_o, Z_o: 77, 97–111, 382–84; comparison of teacher groups relative to, 126–35; comparisons of teacher groups based on Schedule scores, 285–342; composite assessments of, 122–24; correlation with pupil behavior, 125; derivation of inventory correlates, 196–206; generality of, 109–11; interrelationships among, 124–26; reliability of assessment, 115–22

  Scoring keys: All-Elementary Teacher, 198, 201, 203–5; All-Secondary Teacher, 199, 202–6; All-Teacher, 199; English–Social Studies, 199; falsification, 267–70; Grades 1–4 keys, 199; I_{co}, S_{co}, V_{co}, 218–

AMERICAN COUNCIL ON EDUCATION

Arthur S. Adams, *President*

The American Council on Education is a *council* of national associations; organizations having related interests; approved universities, colleges, teachers colleges, junior colleges, technological schools, and selected private secondary schools; state departments of education; city school systems and private school systems; selected educational departments of business and industrial companies; voluntary associations of higher education in the states; and large public libraries. It is a center of cooperation and coordination whose influence has been apparent in the shaping of American educational policies and the formation of educational practices during the past forty-two years.